THE PREOEDIPAL ORIGIN AND PSYCHOANALYTIC THERAPY OF SEXUAL PERVERSIONS

THE PREOEDIPAL ORIGIN AND PSYCHOANALYTIC THERAPY OF SEXUAL PERVERSIONS

Charles W. Socarides, M.D.

INTERNATIONAL UNIVERSITIES PRESS, INC.

Madison

Connecticut

Library of Congress Cataloging-in-Publication Data

Socarides, Charles W., Date:
  The preoedipal origin and psychoanalytic therapy of sexual perversions.

  Bibliography: p.
  Includes index.
  1. Sexual deviation—Case studies.   2. Sexual deviation—Treatment.   3. Psychoanalysis.   I. Title.
  [DNLM: 1. Paraphilias—therapy.   2. Psychoanalytic Theory.   3. Psychoanalytic Therapy.   WM 610 S678p]
  RC556.S67   1987   616.85′83   88-2956
  ISBN 0-8236-4287-9

Manufactured in the United States of America.

To my patients

CONTENTS

PREFACE

This book undoubtedly had its origins over thirty years ago, shortly after the completion of my psychoanalytic training at the Columbia University Psychoanalytic Center for Training and Research, when I first undertook the treatment of what were often referred to then as "impossible," "difficult," or "refractory" patients; namely, those with sexual perversions. Those who initially came to see me were homosexuals whose favorable response to treatment was both surprising and encouraging. With the passage of years, I published the first psychoanalytic textbook on homosexuality under single authorship, *The Overt Homosexual* (1968b). My widening clinical experience and increasing knowledge of this condition led to clarifications and distinctions, refinements, and explanations of my earlier theories and culminated in a new, expanded work, *Homosexuality* (1978a).

Throughout the years, those suffering from pedophilia, voyeurism, sadomasochism, fetishism, transvestitism, transsexualism, and many other forms of sexual deviation, sought my psychoanalytic help. A record of these experiences is found within these pages. I repeatedly discovered that those with well-structured perversions were invariably suffering from a basic nuclear conflict: the wish/dread of maternal reengulfment due to a failure to successfully traverse separation–individuation phases, a disturbance in gender-defined self identity, and varying degrees of pathology of internalized object relations dependent upon the level of fixation. Although *structural* conflicts, between major structures of ego, id, and superego (i.e., between the subject's aggressive, sexual, and other wishes, prohibitions, and ideals), could be discerned in many cases, these conflicts were a later accretion to a more important and crucial preoedipal conflict: an object-relations class of conflict (Dorpat, 1976), anxiety and guilt associated with the failure of development in the phase of self–object differentiation. Advances in our knowledge of the pathology of internal object relations, ego-developmental psychology (including self psychology), ongoing psychoanalytic infant-observational studies, new concepts of narcissism, and new knowledge of primary psychic development provided theoretical foundations for my clinical observations made well in advance of their theoretical explanation.

Defining and redefining of both my clinical findings and theoretical hypotheses were stimulated by presentation of my work before numerous scientific groups; for example, the American Psychoanalytic Association and various local psychoanalytic societies. New ways of looking at psychic phenomena were prompted by the informal and challenging exchange with psychiatric residents during my seminars at the Albert Einstein College of Medicine/Montefiore Medical Center, Department of Psychiatry, New York City since the mid-1960s. Comments of friends and colleagues and the intellectual exchange with members of the Discussion Group devoted to "The Sexual Deviations: Theory and Therapy," under the auspices of the American Psychoanalytic Association, which I cochaired with Dr. Vamik D. Volkan, Professor of Psychiatry of the University of Virginia, were especially valuable during the last three years.

I believe that the theories and detailed clinical findings in this book can find ready application to all cases of sexual perversion and improve our understanding of each condition. I have seen and treated hundreds of perverse patients in a psychoanalytic setting and I believe I have overcome a difficulty noted by Greenacre (1968) which faces any investigator in the area of perversions, namely, that there is a "multiplicity of forms and varying intensities of the perversions from the slightly deviant to the extreme or even bizarre [which] confuse us in our understanding of its essential character." One must have "sufficient experience on which to base broad generalizations. . ." (pp. 300–301).

Until the present time, there has been no systematic or unifying textbook under single authorship devoted entirely to the integration of the multiple facets of these disorders, as exists for the transference neuroses, psychoses, borderline conditions, and narcissistic personality disorders. This book attempts to remedy this condition. It is a matter of psycho-analytic history that few psychoanalysts have had the opportunity to treat or report upon more than one or two patients with perversions during their psychoanalytic careers. Confounded by the ego-syntonic nature of perverse symptoms, by the need for such patients to engage in perverse acts whenever they experience anxiety, and to "act out," dismayed by the seemingly unyielding nature of a condition which brought instant pleasure instead of painful suffering to those afflicted, many psychoanalysts and psychoanalytic institutes have limited their goals to the alleviation of associated symptomatology, or pronounced such cases unsuitable for psychoanalytic treatment and certainly "too difficult" for the neophyte psychoanalytic candidate. I owe to those who persevered in their efforts to remove perverse symptoms and establish normal sexual functioning a profound debt of gratitude. This book would not have been possible without their earlier theoretical, clinical, and therapeutic observations. I am especially indebted to a number of psychoanalysts whose papers on sexual perversion proved invaluable in the development of my own theories; for example, Sandor Lorand, William Gillespie, Gustav Bychowski, Robert Bak, Masud Khan, Edward Glover, Robert Dickes, Renato Almansi, Otto Fenichel, Anna Freud, Ralph Greenson, Hanns Sachs, George Wiedemann, Melitta Sperling, Phyllis Greenacre, and, of course, Freud. My indebtedness extends to Margaret Mahler and her associates for their psychoanalytic infant-observational studies and theories of separation–individuation, a pillar for my theoretical explanations; to Rene Spitz for his theory of synchronicity of maturation and psychological development, an absolutely essential feature of normal development; to Hanns Sachs (1923), for his discovery of the mechanism of the repressive compromise in perversion; to Otto Kernberg for his groundbreaking discoveries in the field of narcissistic personality disorders and the pathology of internalized object relations; to Heinz Kohut for fresh insights supplied by self psychology into the function of erotic acts in perversions; to Sandor Rado, for his brilliant "Adaptational View of Sexual Behavior" (1949), which to my mind has helped restore the study of sexual arousal patterns from the realm of metaphysical theorizing to that of scientific inquiry; to Freud for his monumental achievement, the "Three Essays On Sexuality" (1905b); and to many others whose penetration into preoedipal pathology has helped widen the therapeutic scope of psychoanalysis.

Several panels of the American Psychoanalytic Association served to elucidate various theoretical, clinical, and therapeutic problems (AP sa A, Panels 1952, 1954, 1960b, 1962, 1977). Important new questions as regards etiology and mechanisms were raised by the Ostow Report on Sexual Deviations sponsored by the Psychoanalytic Research and Development Fund (Ostow, Blos, Furst, Gero, Kanzer, Silverman, Sterba, Valenstein, Arlow, Loomis, & Rappaport, 1974). Bak (1953), Greenacre (1953, 1960, 1968), and van der Leeuw (1958) were among the first to put forth the idea that in perversions, conflicts of the preoedipal phase might well prove to be as important as those of the oedipal period. Bak's (1956) shift of investigative interest from the vicissitudes of libidinal development and their relation to perversion to that of aggression brought theoretical explanations closer to clinical findings. Distinctions made by Bak (1971) between perversions in schizophrenics and nonpsychotic individuals helped crystallize my conceptualization of a psychoanalytic classification of perversion. All in all, however, despite brilliant contributions by individual analysts on particular perversions, the tendency to explain observable clinical findings as regression from oedipal-phase conflict (i.e., due to structural conflict), to which psychoanalytic technique should adapt itself, brought, in my opinion, the treatment of sexual perversions to a virtual standstill.

It is my intention in this book to lead the reader into a sharing of my clinical experience and the evolution of my theoretical formulations in the area of sexual perversions, applying them to old and new cases. My theories were first grounded simply in all that Fenichel cited in his important work, *The Psychoanalytic Theory of Neurosis* (1945). I suggest a preoedipal nuclear core origin for all perversions, delineate a unitary theory (Socarides, 1979a), provide a *psychoanalytic* classification (Socarides, 1978a) into which specific perversions and their various forms may be placed, explore the crucial importance of aggression, anxiety, and depression in perversion, describe the meaning and content of perverse dreams, provide clinical illustrations and an explanation of the meaning and function of each perversion, as well as define therapeutic methods employed for their alleviation. My unitary theory of preoedipal causation expands our understanding and knowledge, integrates earlier clinical and theoretical concepts with new information, promotes further research, and, I trust, will lead to improvements in treatment. Finally, the preparation of this book, a product of a never consciously intended (at the outset) lifetime psychoanalytic clinical research project, has been well worth the effort and dedication required. In the course of its writing, my belief in the validity of the intellectual foundations of psychoanalysis has only been strengthened, and the psychoanalytic method has once again revealed itself as an endless source of new discoveries and of refinements of earlier theories and explanations for the wide range of human behavior.

I am deeply grateful to the late Marna Walsh for her endless patience and devotion in the typing and revision of the early drafts of this book.

Part I
THEORETICAL

Chapter 1
GENERAL CONSIDERATIONS IN THE PSYCHOANALYTIC TREATMENT OF SEXUAL PERVERSIONS

During the early years of psychoanalysis, the view that perversion was the "negative of the neurosis" as Freud put it, that the pervert accepted sexual impulses which the neurotic tried to repress, led to the general belief that patients with perversions could not be treated in analysis because they gratify their infantile wishes consciously, without interference from the ego or the superego. A successful analysis was possible only if the patient suffered from his symptoms, desired to eliminate them, and wished to cooperate in searching for the unconscious elements causing them. Since interpretation did not result in therapeutic change (i.e., the cessation of the perverse act), the material elicited from the analysis of a pervert was considered by many to be of little or no value. If the patient repressed nothing, he had nothing for the analyst to uncover and decipher. As a result, many analysts were disinclined to treat perversions or treated only their associated symptoms.

Over time, these obstacles were gradually overcome so that today they no longer pose serious problems. It became increasingly apparent that the pervert had indeed repressed something: a part of infantile sexuality. The part that was admitted to consciousness and was allowed gratification was connected to a very strong pregenital fixation, and helped eliminate the danger of castration. What was approved of in the perverted action was *not* identical with a component instinct, and did not amount to a simple gratification of it. The component instinct had undergone extensive change and masking in order to be gratified by the perverted action. This masking was conditioned by the defenses of the pervert's ego. Thus, the perverted action, like the neurotic symptom, resulted from a conflict between the superego, ego, and id. It represented a compromise and contained elements of both instinctual gratification and frustration, all the while satisfying the demands of the superego. Similar to a symptom, the instinctual gratification could then be seen as taking place in a masked form, its real content remaining unconscious.

Comprehension of the psychopathology of the perversion has been dependent upon the status of our theoretical and clinical knowledge of psychiatric disorders in general. Theoretical propositions have often preceded their clinical validations and, conversely, clear-cut and accurate distinctions have been made decades in advance of a theoretical understanding of the structure of the phenomena described. For example, Freud's (1905b) observation that in homosexuals there is an early intense fixation to the mother was to be thoroughly documented over fifty years later. The discovery of infantile sexuality and the view that the perversion was the negative of the neurosis was of compelling significance in our approach to these patients during the earliest years of psychoanalysis, later giving way to new information gained from advances in the formulation of ego psychology, and improvements in analytic technique based on our understanding of both the transference relationship and, more recently, research findings derived from the psychoanalytic observational studies of the mother–infant relationship.

The work of Mahler (1967, 1968) and her associates (Mahler, Pine, and Bergman, 1975) among others, delineating symbiotic and separation–individuation phases of human development, when applied to clinical data already gathered through the psychoanalysis of adult perverts, helped to explain that the fixation of the pervert lay, in all probability, in the various phases of the separation-individuation process, producing a disturbance in self identity as well as in gender identity; a persistence of the primary feminine identification with the mother; separation anxiety; fears of engulfment (restoring the mother-child unity); and disturbance in object relations and associated ego functions. By combining both clinical data and theoretical explanations, I believe major advances into the question have been made. Most recently, new problems have become more accurately conceptualized and their solutions suggested by advances in our knowledge of the pathology of internal object relations, ego developmental psychology (including self psychology), new concepts of narcissism, and new knowledge of primary psychic development.

I have psychoanalytically investigated and treated a wide variety of cases of sexual deviation. My patients have suffered from voyeurism, fetishism, sadomasochism, pedophilia, transvestitism, transsexualism, spanking perversion, multiple perversions, homosexuality, and other forms of perverse activity, detailed accounts of which will be found in this book. Some case reports, spanning nearly a quarter-century of analytic work, were originally published elsewhere, but have been updated from their original form as my theoretical and clinical experience and understanding of these conditions widened and deepened. The largest number of patients were those who underwent psychoanalysis for obligatory homosexuality.

General Problems

In contrast to the current vast public interest in the homosexual, one discerns a relative neglect in scientific circles of the homosexual and others with sexual perversion, when compared to the theoretical and clinical investigations of the transference neuroses, psychoses, borderline conditions, and the narcissistic personality disorders. The reason for this neglect, in my opinion, may lie in the following:

Psychoanalysts have found that patients who experience pain and suffering from their conditions are motivated to

change, while patients who do not are very often not motivated in this way. The homosexual symptom itself, as well as
other perverse symptomatology, is ego-syntonic in well-
structured cases; these patients are intolerant of anxiety,
and the relief from anxiety through acting out promotes
therapeutic nihilism and countertransference reactions.
Furthermore, the neutralization of conflict allows for the
growth of certain ego-adaptive elements of the personality,
so that some perverts, especially those with milder forms of
narcissistic pathology, appear upon superficial examination
to have no other symptoms of emotional disorder.

Perversion remains high on the list of symptoms of emotional origin which serve as defenses. The perverse act, when
successful, provides for limited intervals a neutralization of
profound psychic conflicts and succeeds in producing a
pseudoadequate equilibrium, together with a high pleasure
reward (orgasm). Until recently, the consensus was that
homosexuals could be treated like phobics. However, urging
the patient to eliminate his phobic avoidance of women and
to cease his homosexual activities leads to the production of
excessive anxiety and premature termination of treatment.
A major difficulty in treating homosexuality arises, of
course, from the misconception that this disorder is of hereditary origin, the patient commonly believing that he was
born that way, or, that he is simply engaging in an alternative life-style.

The basic issues were clearly perceived by Fenichel
(1945). He noted that the treatment of the perversion is complicated by one factor not present in the neurosis: that the
very symptom itself brings pleasure in perversion, and that
treatment not only threatens to remove it but also to rekindle
the very conflicts the patient has evaded by means of his
symptom. Treatment also threatens to destroy the only sexual pleasure the patient knows. The possibility of normal
sexual pleasure may seem most remote. The prognosis depends on the patient's determination to change, or to what
extent this determination can be awakened in analysis. A
trial analysis, therefore, will have as its main task the evaluation of the will to recover.

Which perverts seek therapy? Many homosexuals seek

our help because of a long-hidden wish or hope that they might somehow become heterosexual after a long period of being homosexual; others out of a declared "curiosity" that something much deeper may be troubling them, while others desperately desire help to overcome what they perceive to be a serious difficulty. The most promising cases, I have found, are those in which the patient feels worse, not only from the point of view that his perversion may be accompanied by neurotic symptoms, but that he can no longer tolerate his perverse adaptation. Some of my patients with a sexual perversion are prompted to enter therapy because of disturbing symptoms that have invaded their lives: episodes of depersonalization, regressive desires to isolate themselves from others, fears of self dissolution, splitting phenomena, sudden breakthrough of feelings of femininity, episodes of sadistic and/or masochistic behavior in their sexual encounters, and tendencies to severe mood swings or depressions or bursts of rage or anxiety. Some begin to perceive that the perverse act itself serves to save them from a mysterious fragmentation, and that a magical restoration occurs whenever they engage in perverse activities. In others, the perverse needs have become increasingly insistent and imperative, intruding into everyday functioning and thus interfering with every aspect of the patient's life.

Some perverts are aware that they are not simply responding to an instinctual need but are dominated by a tension which they can neither understand nor control. Many seek therapy because they are severely distressed about having a perversion, not only because of socially induced guilt or shame, but because they find their lives meaningless and alien to the biological and social realities of life around them.

Khan (1965) has accurately described the "inconsolability of the pervert" who uses the "technique of intimacy" as a therapeutic device in an attempt to achieve ego satisfaction, but only succeeds in "the idealization of instinctual discharge processes" (p. 403). The ultimate failure of this technique leads to a sense of depletion, exhaustion, a reduction in expectations, and despair. At this point, those with perversions frequently enter therapy.

Soon after beginning therapy, associated neurotic symptoms may disappear and the patient feels much better due to the protection of the analytic setting. Paradoxically, it is at this point that we as analysts may face our first crisis: if the patient is entirely relieved of his accessory symptoms before any insightful connections are made between them and his perverse activities, a strong resistance consisting of an intensification of his continued need to feel omnipotent and magically restored by the perversion may appear. Some patients may begin therapy with the proviso that no attempt be made to alter their perverse acts. In these instances, while a concerted effort may be made to deal with other problems besetting the patient such as anxiety, depression, passivity, masochism, or narcissism, and while these problems may be relieved, the perversion will usually be found to have invaded and influenced every aspect of the patient's life. In this connection, Anna Freud (1954) reported three cases in which the homosexual symptom was completely removed as a result of psychoanalytic treatment, despite the wish of the patients at the beginning of therapy that it not be altered. The loss of the homosexual symptom or any other perverse activity may also be unconsciously feared since sexual enactment provides narcissistic restoration of the self representation and is experienced by the patient as vital to his sense of "well-being" for long periods of time. Consequently, premature therapeutic incursions in this direction may be met with hostility, castration anxiety, a sense of personal dissolution, and rage against the analyst in anticipation of an impending crisis.

The technique of psychoanalysis precludes a focal attack on the symptom itself. Effective interpretation of resistance guides the analyst. Assurances must be made that we do not attempt a forcible removal of the symptom. A general policy is not to interdict perverse acts; alleviation comes about through a gradual resolution of the unconscious anxieties and motivations that produce them. We attempt to discover the root disturbance responsible for the symptom and the psychic purpose it serves. The patient must be shown that his nuclear conflict consists of anxiety and guilt associated with the failure of development in the phase of self-object differentiation (in preoedipal perversion), and anxiety and guilt arising from the patient's aggressive, sexual, and other wishes and his own prohibitions and ideals (in oedipal perversions). The preoedipal pervert's inability to adequately separate from the preoedipal mother produces an unconscious wish and/or dread of merging with her. Perversion is an ego-survival measure in these more serious cases.

If the perverse symptom is to disappear, it will do so through the healing of the patient's underlying gender-defined self identity disturbance and inability to separate from the preoedipal mother. As he begins to overcome some of his difficulties, the patient will begin to have heterosexual impulses. Such impulses and acts represent a developmental achievement and when they occur are encouraged. (It is difficult to satisfactorily treat a perverse patient when he is left without any sexual pleasure as a result of a progressive decrease in interest in perverse sexual aims and objects.) The symptom diminishes in intensity through the filling-in of ego deficiencies and the gradual achievement of a sense of self. The homosexual no longer needs to engage in short-circuiting attempts to find masculine identity through incorporation of and identification with another man's body and penis (A. Freud, 1954).

To emphasize: premature attempts at the removal of the symptom, either by the patient or analyst, are theoretically unsound. The factor tiding the patient over some of the crises is the degree to which he is capable of forming a working alliance with the analyst.

The Working Alliance

From the outset, it is vital that in treating the pervert the working alliance (Greenson, 1967; Dickes, 1975) be established and maintained. The patient forms this relatively nonneurotic, rational rapport with the analyst because of his motivation to understand and overcome his perversion, his sense of helplessness and ego depletion. This therapeutic rapport has been referred to by Greenacre (1971) as "the basic transference" and connotes a capacity for sufficient emotional engagement between therapist and patient so that real communication takes place. The therapeutic or working alliance should be distinguished from the reactions of the transference neurosis, the former being determined by the earliest relationship between mother and infant, a complex and ambivalent relation with remnants of trust and enough positive feelings which can be exploited therapeutically, so that a durable rapport can be established with another individual. This implies that the patient is willing and able to follow the lead of the analyst in the mutual endeavor at tracing the genesis of the patient's condition. It is imperative that the working alliance be maintained, especially in view of strong resistances derived from the pleasure reward of orgasm, the equilibrium-producing nature of the symptom, and the imperativeness of impulse.

The therapist's attitude should be one of empathic understanding. Although he is continually faced with a symptom that is ego-syntonic and affords orgastic release, creating a temporary equilibrium, the therapist must not be seen to be a threat but an ally to the patient's goals; and thus the working alliance is preserved. Alleviation of the patient's distress in all its protean manifestations must be continually conceived of as a dual effort. Any prolonged disruption of the working alliance can have a devastating effect, leading to a termination of therapy. Despite correct interpretations, the patient may remain unaffected, engage in prolonged periods of perverse activity without apparent conflict, and produce an endless, obsessive recitation of perverse activities. These therapeutic stalemates are to be interpreted as soon as they are formed, and traced to the patient's underlying anxieties (especially manifest in his dream life), his fear of change, his fear of loss of pleasure, and his projective anxieties of being hurt and misunderstood.

A sign that a patient has begun to be engaged in his therapy is his commitment to discovering the motivational context of each individual perverse act; at first, after its enactment, and, later, even before its expression. For example, homosexual patients often are not aware that intrapsychic conflict is causing the imperative need for homosexual contact. A patient may not be aware that he is anxious or depressed or experiencing paranoidal anxieties preceding his need for homosexual relief. The "fix" provided by perverse acts helps him to artificially restore his sense of self, to alleviate anxieties, and lend him a feeling of omnipotence.

Transference

Vital to the analyzability of perverse patients is neither the presenting symptomatology (even apparent extreme femininity) nor the life history of the pervert, but the nature of the spontaneously developing transference (Greenson, 1967). Do transferences develop in the treatment of perverts and, if so, what is their particular nature?

Transferences in the oedipal pervert are ideal, similar to those seen in neurotics. In preoedipal type I perverts* they are good, as there is sufficient self–object differentiation and internalization of object representations. In preoedipal type II, a more severe form of perversion, the transference relationship is fair to poor, depending upon the severity of pathology of object relations, the construction of a grandiose self, the presence of splitting mechanisms, and the primitivism of the transference. The preoedipal type II pervert (except for borderline cases) has for the most part an organizing, differentiating self and has not completely lost internal object representations. In the schizopervert transference is poor, as he lacks an adequate separation of self and object.

It is in the preoedipal pervert that we find the well-structured perversion. The preoedipal pervert has the capacity to differentiate between the self and the object world, and has maintained the ability to displace reactions from a past object representation to an object in the present. He has, therefore, an organized, differentiated self (although it has suffered impairment), an entity separate and distinct from the environment with the capacity to remain the same (not be destroyed) in the midst of change. This is the hallmark of his capacity to form a transference neurosis, in contrast to psychotics, who have lost their internal object representations and strive to fill up the feeling of a terrible void by creating new objects (Kernberg, 1970). For example, in homosexuality the homosexual object stands for the self: it is narcissistic but still an object relationship—that between

*Refer to chapter 4 for *classification* of perversions.

mother and child. In contrast to oedipal homosexuals (those in whom object relationships consist of a relation between the infantile submissive self and a domineering, prohibitive father (self to object), the object relationship in the preoedipal homosexual is between object and self, or, in the severest degree of narcissism, from a pathological grandiose self to self (Kernberg, 1975).

The preoedipal pervert meets the criteria for analyzability (Greenson, 1967). When he misunderstands the present in terms of the past, his misunderstanding is only partial and temporary. When he suffers regressions in ego functions, they are circumscribed and largely limited to certain aspects of his relationship with the transference figure. While he may allow himself to regress in his object relations and ego functions and may renounce certain reality testing functions, he is able, however, to work with and understand his reactions with his observing ego.

Psychoanalytic investigation of preoedipal narcissistic perverts (type II) reveals that, similar to those with narcissistic grandiose character disorder pathology, they are not seriously threatened by the possibility of an irreversible disintegration of the archaic self or object (Kohut, 1971). The activation of these stable *narcissistic transferences* and their archaic structures is the central work of much of the early and middle phases of the analysis, until sufficient structuralization of the mental apparatus is attained (see chapter 10). The spontaneous establishment of a *stable* narcissistic transference in perverse patients is one of the most reliable signs differentiating these patients from psychotic or borderline cases on the one hand, and from those with ordinary transference neuroses on the other. Therefore, trial analysis is of greater diagnostic and prognostic value than overt perverse behavior even of the most extreme and bizarre kind. The analyst must provide the perverse patient with opportunities to admit to the transference figure the extent of his desolation. This is impossible if the therapist is impatient, condemnatory, or belittling of the patient's activities or his inability to modify his sexual practices. In some patients a somewhat lengthy interval will be required before the patient's unconscious material reveals aspects of the self which he abhors and wishes to change. Symptomatic cures, usually transient in nature, in which the patient who previously engaged exclusively in perverse acts is able to participate in heterosexual intercourse, may be due to his overcoming his phobic avoidance of the female genitals because of a reduction in his incestuous (oedipal) fear of the mother. The therapeutic alliance and the positive transference relationship facilitates the patient's feeling of strength and ability to face oedipal dangers. Many patients may be able to engage in successful sexual approaches to females within a relatively short period of time (weeks to months) because the analyst assumes the role of protecting the patient against his own dangerous, destructive impulses and fears of merging with the mother. Furthermore, when the analyst fills this role in the patient's mind, he still remains perversely motivated, and it is misleading to regard this change as anything more than partial and temporary. Our aim is not simply heterosexual functioning, but opening a path to true object love.

Problems Secondary to Deficiencies in the Structure of the Ego

Fixation does considerable psychic damage to the ego functions of the pervert. Reality testing, for example, is often intact but consciously or unconsciously ignored to serve the pleasure principle in preoedipal type I perverts; whereas in preoedipal type II cases the boundary between fantasy and reality can be indistinct and severe anxiety results in a flight from reality. Impulse control in type I may be incomplete, leading to acting out impulses and pursuit of instantaneous gratification. In the more severe type, impulses are grossly acted out, suggesting a complete loss of ego and superego controls. In the milder preoedipal type I, thinking may be clear but dominated by the pleasure principle. Self-concept frequently fluctuates between feelings of self-depreciation and an elevated sense of self-esteem bordering on omnipotence. Ego boundaries may be fragile but there is a strong need for narcissistic supplies. There may be an unconscious and severe sense of worthlessness and emptiness with extreme disturbance of self-concept. Under stress, ego boundaries may show severe impairment with the removal of the narcissistic facade. Affect and affect control in both types of preoedipal perverts are poor, and these patients may frequently respond with anxiety, depression, and bursts of anger. The most severe cases lack the capacity to neutralize aggression. Foremost among these vicissitudes is that self and object representations are insufficiently structured, resulting in a lack of self cohesion and fears of fragmentation. Primitive representational configurations and confusions between self and object produce a striking vulnerability to stress and a clinical picture similar to that found in other patients suffering from preoedipal developmental arrest.

With developmentally arrested patients, as with preoedipal perverts, one must adopt a therapeutic stance which gradually promotes the structuralization of the precarious self and object representations. The analyst allows himself to increase his capacity for self observation until a proper transference of the neurotic type is ultimately achieved. The treatment of the preoedipal narcissistic pervert type II is essentially, at this point in therapy, that of a severe narcissistic character disorder proper.

Specific transference problems arise from the patient's pathological narcissism. While he may idealize the analyst, he also externalizes the pathological grandiose self, including the pathological grandiose self, onto the analyst, and therefore loves, fears, blames, and hates him. The full-blown narcissistic transference must be allowed to develop for a time with its mirroring function (Kohut, 1971), but is ultimately replaced by the transference neurosis. These patients are dominated in their self-esteem regulation by the aim of attaining a perfect self-image, a perfect experience both in their narcissistic behavior and especially in their perverse activities.

In dealing with structural conflicts (oedipal perversion), our aim is to reactivate infantile experiences which have been repressed and defended against, and to analyze them in the transference relationship. In contrast, the patient with ego developmental arrest has missed or prematurely lost experiences legitimately needed, which must be understood and repaired within the transference in order to assist the patient's ego in its belated development before interpretations of a structural nature can be made. It is necessary to deal first with what the arrested ego needs to achieve, and interpret only later what the ego needs to ward off (Stolorow and Lachmann, 1978).

Discoveries in the fields of the psychology of the self, the pathology of internalized object relations, and newer concepts of narcissism make it imperative that we employ special techniques to promote the growth and maturation of our perverse patients who show arrested ego functions. Through permitting structuralization of ego functions we allow for a later exploration of the defensive aspects of the patient's psychopathology in terms of the instinctual conflicts they serve to ward off (oedipal conflicts). Maturational failures as well as advances can be reconstructed from the patient's dreams and the transference, and can be placed correctly in the specific developmental stage in which they belong. For example, for my patient Sumner [reported in detail in Socarides (1978a)], self and object representations were vulnerable to regressions in which the patient yearned for self-object dissolution and mystical oneness with the saints (Jesus, St. Sebastian, Hindu mystics, and so on). These fantasies were an important part of a self-restitutive attempt during a desolate childhood. Vulnerability to these regressions blocked or vitiated his progress. He needed archaic selfobjects for self-esteem regulation, and, as a result, a long period of symbioticlike idealizing and mirroring transference had to be promoted. This ultimately helped him to regain a feeling of an individual, idealized self (a real self), first based on identification with the analyst.

The Imperativeness of the Perverse Impulse and the Problem of Acting Out

The pervert's inability to postpone the enactment of perverse impulses, and his pursuit of instantaneous gratification with its capacity to allay anxiety, had led many analysts to lay down their therapeutic arms, and many patients to concede defeat of their therapeutic aims. While this intolerance of anxiety and its erotization has neurotic determinants, a fuller comprehension of this phenomenon requires that we also view it as a manifestation of early preoedipal damage to the structure of the ego.

The patient suffers from an impairment of ego boundaries and self-concept. Sexual orgasm has the capacity to restore this sense of self (Eissler, 1958a; Stolorow, 1975; Lichtenstein, 1977). The effect is transitory, leading to an insistent need for multiple and frequent sexual contact. In those requiring multiple and frequent encounters, boundaries between self–object representations may be quite fragile. The greater the capacity of the orgasm to restore the patient's sense of self, the more difficult it becomes to remove the perverse need. Conversely, the less the orgasm functions in this way, in a better structured ego, the greater will be the success of early removal of perverse symptoms. The analyst must consider this factor in any attempt at cessation of perverse activity, because the patient, especially preoedipal type II, may suffer greatly and withdraw from treatment due to the eruption of intolerable anxiety.

The need to engage in perverse activity should be treated as a manifestation of an arrested developmental phase: in a sense, as a developmental necessity, at least for the time being, and not as a resistance. In preoedipal narcissistic patients, even the slightest comment on their sexual encounters is extremely hazardous, as it is regarded as a narcissistic injury in addition to other threats such a remark poses.

Neurotic determinants for homosexual behavior often represent a defense against aggression and an identification with the phallic qualities of other men. In the latter instance, to ask a patient to desist from or restrict his homosexual activities may urge him to commit self-castration. What then ensues is an immense resistance and hostility to the analyst if he insists on imposing the restrictive edict. Interpretation of the multiple neurotic determinants for homosexual behavior must come first in order for the patient to assume his own phallic properties and no longer be dependent on the homosexual partner for his masculine identity.

The homosexual encounter is intimately related to the patient's pathological narcissism. It represents a search for both the narcissistic and the grandiose self representations. In uniting with another man there is a fusion of the self with various images of both mother and father, without facing the imminent danger of the loss of self through merger with the mother. Suffering from a loss of normal self-esteem (healthy narcissism) and filled with pathologically disturbed relations to internalized objects, these patients, as well as those with other perversions, remedy their sense of emptiness and inertia by giving pleasure to external objects and the self simultaneously. In all perverse sexual acts they induce dependence in the partner and compel the external object into instinctual surrender (Khan, 1965). This augments a sense of power, reduces the sense of isolation, and captures a pseudoempathy for the external world through a primitive mode of communication. What is lacking in these encounters, however, is the ability to trust and to surrender the self to emotional experiences. Thus the encounter, while averting an intrapsychic trauma and constructing a pseudorelationship, always fails to achieve true gratification and true object relations. The perverse act promotes alleviation of feelings of emptiness and loss of self, but it is only transitory and evanescent and must be continually repeated with fresh partners who provide a sense of temporary intactness (Khan, 1965).

During psychoanalysis, the patient becomes increasingly aware that many of his fears, whether they have to do with work or social engagements, have been libidinized into perverse activity (erotization of anxiety). Threats to the self, fears of engulfment by the woman or loss of the mother, and feelings of inadequacy are defended against by erotization and by union with another masculine figure through incorporation and identification in homosexuality, or by dressing as a woman in transvestism. What is strikingly apparent is that it is not the erotic infantile experience per se which is sought in the perverse act; it is the reassuring and reaffirming function of the erotic experience which is reanimated and pursued (Stolorow and Lachmann, 1978; Socarides, 1978a).

The perverse sexual life is an important source of internal regulation of self-esteem. Through these sexual escapades the patient attempts to secure narcissistic balance, to over-come an overriding aggression, and to consolidate a sense of self. In those with severe narcissistic character pathology, the act is a substitute for the sought-for inner ideal, an exter-nalization of the wish to be powerful. Only later in therapy can we demonstrate to the patient that his escapades con-tinue to rob him of his own external ideal through its sexualization.

Extrinsic Problems

I wish to comment briefly on some external problems in the therapeutic relationship: (1) the secondary neurotic gratifi-cations that accrue to certain patients who have immersed themselves in the homosexual world; and (2) the misunder-standing even among behavioral scientists as to what con-stitutes a "perversion" and as to need for therapy, clinical research, and prophylaxis of these disorders. In the face of ever-increasing propaganda over the past decade attempt-ing to promote deviant sexual practices as nothing but an alternative life-style and those who oppose this view as "undemocratic," the analysis may have to deal with these issues as they become a source of resistance and misunder-standing, threatening to disrupt the therapy.[1]

Person (Panel, 1977) described some of these issues:

There are "special problems in the treatment of sociosexual homosexuals . . . related to the way in which the homosexual world lends itself to easy gratification of neurotic and nar-cissistic wishes, gratifications which tend to consolidate a patient's identity as homosexual and tip the balance toward homosexuality in patients who are already functionally marginal or bisexual" [pp. 189–190].

Parenthetically, the medical counterpart to this is the tendency of some sex therapy clinics to treat homosexual

---

[1]That such impediments to a scientific understanding of homosexuality are not strictly a modern phenomenon is indicated by Freud's (1910a) comment: "It must be stated with regret that those who speak for the homosexuals in the field of science have been incapable of learning any-thing from the established findings of psychoanalysis" (p. 99).

dysfunctions on a par with heterosexual sexual dysfunction, as if there were no psychopathology producing the homosexuality and thereby raising the anus to the level of a vagina. Person states:

> In the homosexual a [homosexual man] may reap the benefits characteristically open to a woman. There he may be rewarded for his youth, charm, and good looks by advancement, money, or adulation. Fantasies of being kept are common. The homosexual world is potentially more glamorous than the attainable world of most marrieds. The homosexual is also able to avoid the demands of financial responsibility and assertiveness made of the head of a household. In addition, the homosexual world's focus on nurturance, the ease of access of sexual partners and easy introductions abroad provide external antidotes to depression, and may serve as a kind of collective hypomanic defense as well as providing dependent gratification. The treatment of socio-sexual homosexuals requires a long and intense analysis of the ways of immersion in the homosexual world, [which] with the risks and thrills of the double life, facilitates the avoidance of depression, narcissistic gratification, and acting out in place of remembering [p. 190].

Summary

The perverse patient has posed serious difficulties to the psychoanalyst attempting alleviation of his psychosexual disorder and promotion of healthy adult functioning in all areas of life. Historically, Freud was the first to note the difficulties attendant in the treatment of these conditions in his apt phrase, "the perversion is the negative of the neurosis" (1905b). With an increased understanding of the nature, meaning, and content of the perversion, many obstacles are being gradually overcome so that the perverted action, like the neurotic symptom, can be seen to be a result of conflict, a compromise formation allowing instinctual gratification, a substitute for deeper anxieties whose real content remains unconscious.

Research and psychoanalytic investigations over the past three decades have revealed that those with perversions, especially of the preoedipal types, are fixated at various phases of the separation–individuation phase (mostly at rapprochement) and thus are developmentally arrested and structurally deficient. Theoretical advances in our comprehension of object-relations conflict of this early period have greatly aided our understanding and ability to deal not only with the problems of homosexual patients in many aspects of their behavior, but with all individuals suffering from sexual deviations.

It is my intention in this book to lead the reader into a sharing of my clinical experience and theoretical framework in the area of sexual deviation which was, at first, grounded in all that Fenichel cited in his monumental work, *The Psychoanalytic Theory of Neurosis* (1945), and to document the assertion that the psychoanalytic method is an endless source of new discoveries and refinements of earlier theories and explanations for the wide variety of human behavior.

Chapter 2

DEFINING PERVERSION

From the outset, the field of sexual disorders has tended to be clouded by confusion and mystery. Poets, historians, philosophers, sociologists, anthropologists, and psychiatrists have all played a part in making this one of the murkiest areas of science. Freud himself deplored the word *perversion*, as it carried a moralistic connotation. But he continued to use it free from its pejorative meaning and in a scientific sense. He used it to denote sexual arousal patterns that are unconsciously motivated, stereotyped, and derived from early psychic conflict. Perversions were "the negative of the neurosis" and, unlike neurotic symptoms, brought pleasure not pain. In 1905 Freud coined the term *inversion* for homosexuality and Ferenczi followed with his term, *paraphilia*, to encompass all the perversions (1909). The term *sexual variation*, introduced many years later, eliminated any moral or social disapproval but obscured the nature of these conditions as true disorders. The term *sexual deviation* is more acceptable to many, as it neither moralizes nor normalizes. Some behavioral scientists insist that there are no sexual perversions or deviations, only alternative or different lifestyles, and that these conditions are merely a matter of social definition, some made permissible by society and others socially condemned.[1]

---

[1]Arlow (1986) succinctly deals with this approach as follows:

As scientists, our interest is in understanding the psychodynamics and the genesis of those patterns of sexual activity that deviate in a considerable degree from the more usual forms of gratification.

Many of our values could use change, but scientific findings cannot be altered to meet the demands of social change. Some statisticians, beginning with Kinsey, and behavioral psychologists and psychiatrists (in contrast to psychoanalysts) supply incidence rates of certain phenomena as if behavior had no connection with motivation. Since neither conscious nor unconscious motivation is even acknowledged, these studies arrive at a disastrous conclusion: that the resultant composite of sexual behavior is the *norm* of sexual behavior. Their next step is to demand that the public, the law, medicine, psychiatry, religion, and other social institutions accept this proposition.

With remarkable prescience, Lionel Trilling, the social and literary critic, predicted as early as 1948 in commenting on the statistical findings of the Kinsey Report that in the future

> [T]hose who most explicitly assert and wish to practice the democratic virtues [will have taken] as their assumption that all social facts—with the exception of exclusion and economic hardship—must be *accepted* not merely in the scientific sense but also in the social sense, in the sense, that is, that no judgment must be passed on them, that any conclusion drawn from them which perceives values and consequences will turn out to be "undemocratic" (1948, p. 242).

In general, there is no reason to dispute Kinsey's data as to the *incidence*. The value of the exhaustive and informative study was that it enumerated the manifold forms taken by a force so powerful it cannot be denied expression. The enormous public curiosity in Kinsey's figures blinded most people to some of the erroneous interpretations to which some of the figures gave rise, especially in the area of homo-

---

While it is true that the term "perversion" in current usage carries the connotation of adverse judgment, the essential meaning is a turning away from the ordinary course. As such, the term "perverse" is an accurate one . . . the origin and meaning of unusual sexual behavior is the subject matter of our scientific concern. The phenomenology of perversion should be approached from a natural science point of view, divorced from any judgmental implications [p. 249].

sexuality. These conclusions and interpretations have become the banner under which have rallied political and social activists, psychiatrists, special advocates, and even some of those who have been entrusted with the task of formulating and modifying recent psychiatric classification systems.

Psychoanalysts comprehend the meaning of a particular act of human behavior by delving into the motivational state from which it issues. In their investigative and healing aims, psychoanalysts and psychodynamically oriented clinicians continually ask three questions: "What is the meaning of an event or piece of behavior or symptom?" (cause searching); "Where did it come from?" (end-relating, means to ends); and "What can be done to correct things?" (healing function). By studying individuals with similar behavior we arrive at objective conclusions as to the meaning and significance of a particular phenomenon for that individual under investigation. Thus is insight achieved. To form conclusions as to the specific meaning of an event simply because of its frequency of occurrence is to the psychoanalyst scientific folly. Only in the consultation room, using the techniques of introspective reporting and free association, protected by professional ethics, will an individual, pressed by his suffering and pain, reveal the hidden (even from himself) meaning and reasons behind his acts. Using these techniques, it can be ascertained that the sexual perversions are roundabout methods of achieving orgastic release in the face of overwhelming fears. It becomes apparent that the differences in sexual behavior are the different arousal patterns aimed at releasing the orgastic reflex. The study of perverse or deviant sexual practices itself can be reduced to a simple proposition: the study of the arousal patterns by which the reflex is released.

In an effort to put disordered sexual behavior on a scientific footing and to remove all trace of pejorative terminology, intended or not, Rado (1949) divided sexual activities into those occurring in the *standard* coital pattern and those occurring in the *modified* coital pattern. Disturbances of the standard coital pattern (sexual relations occurring between adult male and female pairs in which penetration is desired and possible) include those of frigidity, vaginismus, premature ejaculation, retarded ejaculation, and disturbances of sexual desire, for example. Modified sexual patterns may be considered disturbances in themselves as they do not fulfill the requirements for standard sexual performance (e.g., sexual variations, deviations, perversions). Modified sexual patterns that are a result of unconscious fears and the inhibiting action of those fears may be considered *reparative* patterns, in which the sexual pattern is inflexible and stereotyped. *The person has no choice.* Similarly, McDougall (1972), from her extensive clinical studies maintains:

> [O]ne factor [that] would appear to characterize a pervert....
> is that he has no choice: his sexuality is fundamentally
> compulsive. He does not choose to be perverse and cannot be
> said to choose the form of his perversion any more than the
> obsessional could be said to choose his obsessions or the
> hysteric his headache and phobias [p. 371].

If forced to participate in male–female sexual relations, he experiences the act with little or no pleasure. Deviant or modified sexual patterns are roundabout methods of achieving arousal and orgastic release as the usual channels for sexual behavior in the standard male–female pattern are blocked by massive fears. They are characterized by exclusivity, unconscious determinants, and stereotypy of object choice. Rado further noted that modified sexual patterns may arise from *situational* and *variational* motivations and are consciously motivated, not fear induced, and that the person is able to function with a partner of the opposite sex.

My definition of perversion corresponds to that of Freud. At various points in the "Three Essays" (1905b), Freud made it abundantly clear what he meant by perversion: "Perversions are sexual activities which either (a) extend, in an anatomical sense, beyond the reaches of the body that are designed for sexual union, or (b) linger over the immediate relations to the sexual object which should normally be traversed rapidly on the path towards the final sexual aim" (p. 150). Regarding fetishism:

> [T]he situation only becomes pathological when the longing
> for the fetish passes beyond the point of being merely a

necessary condition attached to the sexual object and actually *takes the place* of the normal aim, and, further, where the fetish becomes detached from a particular individual and becomes the *sole* sexual object. These are, indeed, the general conditions under which mere variations of the sexual instinct pass over into pathological aberrations [p. 154].

In connection with voyeurism he stated: "this pleasure in looking [scopophilia] becomes a perversion (a) if it is restricted exclusively to the genitals, or (b) if it is connected with the overriding of disgust (as in the case of *voyeurs* or people who look on at an excretory function), or (c) if, instead of being *preparatory* to the normal sexual aim, it supplants it" (p. 157). Regarding sexual sadism, he stated that:

[S]adism oscillates between, on the one hand, cases merely characterized by an active or violent attitudes to the sexual object, and, on the other hand, cases in which satisfaction is entirely conditional on the humiliation and maltreatment of the object. Strictly speaking, it is only this last extreme instance which deserves to be described as a perversion [p. 158].

In his summation of the issue, Freud removed all doubt:

In the majority of instances the pathological character in a perversion is found to lie not in the *content* of the new sexual aim but in its relation to the normal. If a perversion, instead of appearing merely *alongside* the normal sexual aim and object, and only when circumstances are unfavourable to *them* and favourable to *it*—if, instead of this, it ousts them completely and takes their place in *all* circumstances—if, in short, a perversion has the characteristics of exclusiveness and fixation—then we shall usually be justified in regarding it as a pathological symptom [1905b, p. 161].

A carefully taken in-depth case history (not survey questionnaire) reveals that the developmental history of individuals (whether male or female) suffering from well-structured sexual perversions show disturbances in the preoedipal phase of development. Object-relations conflicts involving anxiety and guilt associated with self–object differentiation are present. This type of conflict leaves unmistakable signs in the developing personality and its future maturation.[2] There is anxiety in sexually approaching a person of the opposite sex, pronounced gender-defined self identity confusion (either hidden or overt), and a predominance of archaic, primitive mental mechanisms. Clinically, there are signs or symptoms of a continued, undue fixation to the mother. Thus, an in-depth life history is a central task to be undertaken before the diagnosis of true sexual perversion can be made. The sexual perversion itself neutralizes warring intrapsychic forces so that these individuals may often attain a high degree of personal development. With the exception of the sexual perversion, they may appear upon superficial examination to be without psychopathology. Only when subjected to penetrating investigation of their defensive system does the underlying psychopathology appear.

The theoretical chasm separating these views from those who would declare perversions alternative life-styles is striking. This is exemplified in the statements of a recent chairman of the Nomenclature Committee of the American Psychiatric Association who asserted: "If . . . [homosexuality] is in conflict with the individual's own value system, then it is best to regard it as a mental disorder, since it then is likely to *lead* [emphasis added] to distress at the inability to function heterosexually" (Spitzer, 1974, pp. 11-12). Such a nonsensical argument turns back the clock on scientific research in these conditions, confuses the individual suffering from the condition, and misinforms the public and the healing professions. Psychoanalysis, on the other hand, utilizes concepts of variational and reparative motivations to categorize varieties of sexual behavior to arrive at the

---

[2]In this connection, McDougall (1972) has noted that:
     [T]he individual whose sex life is expressed mainly through manifest and organized perversion usually displays a singularly impoverished fantasy life. This may mean that his inner object world allows him to imagine sexual relations solely from a limited perspective. . . . *The erotic expression of the sexual deviant is an essential feature of a psychic stability and much of his life revolves around it* [p. 371].

answer to the question of whether certain sexual activities can be considered to be perversions. The basic principle was supplied by Freud in 1916: "Let us once more reach an agreement upon what is to be understood by the 'sense' of a psychical process. We mean nothing other by it than the intention it serves in its position in a psychical continuity" (1916, p. 40). Thus, whether or not sexual practices can be termed *perversions* can be determined by a study of the conscious and/or unconscious motivations from which they issue.

Frank A. Beach (1942, 1947), the eminent ethologist, made comparative studies of sexual development during the evolution of the vertebrates and made a stunning discovery. He found that in lower vertebrates sex is an almost automatic activity, a self-regulatory sequence of events. In the course of development, this stereotyped pattern breaks down during encephalization; that is, the machinery of copulation becomes less and less automatic and depends more and more on the individual animal's personal experience. At the level of the chimpanzee, he found only three automatic mechanisms remaining—erection, pelvic thrust, and orgasm. With these three items man builds his sexual pattern with his own cerebral cortex. What follows from this discovery is (1) that there is no innate (inherited) desire for the same or opposite sex partner; (2) that the answer to the question of modified sexual arousal patterns (i.e., perversions) is a question of man's ontogenetic development; (3) that in the training of children we could undoubtedly teach them to respond orgastically to any kind of stimulus, but for obvious reasons this is not feasible; and (4) that wish fulfillment and fantasy play a large role in the formation of sexual patterns in man. In man, therefore, the development of the cerebral cortex and the lessening of the role played by spinal reflexes and automatic mechanisms leaves motivation at center stage of the development of both standard sexual patterns and their disturbances and of modified sexual patterns.

In man, heterosexual object choice is neither innate nor instinctual, nor is homosexual object choice or any other perverse behavior—all are learned. The choice of sexual object is not predetermined by chromosomal tagging. How-

ever, most significantly, heterosexual object choice is outlined from birth by anatomy and then reinforced by cultural
and environmental indoctrination. It is supported by universal human concepts of mating and the tradition of the
family unit, together with the complementariness and contrast between the two sexes (Rado, 1949). The term *anatomically outlined* does not mean that it is instinctual to choose a
person of the opposite sex. The human being, however, is a
biological emergent entity derived from evolution, favoring
survival.

In considering the differences between normality and
abnormality, Kubie's (1978) comments are succinct and invaluable. He concluded that stereotypy and automatic repetitiveness are signposts of the neurotic process. Therefore,
when we term perversions not simply alternative life-styles
or normal acts, we are not issuing a judgment of value but
rather a clinical description of attributes of behavior common to neurotic actions and absent from normal ones. The
essence of normality is flexibility, in contrast to the:

> [F]reezing of behavior into patterns of unalterability that
> characterizes every manifestation of the neurotic process,
> whether in impulses, purposes, acts, thoughts, or feelings.
> Whether or not a behavioral event is free to change depends
> not upon the quality of the act itself, but upon the nature of
> the constellation of forces that has produced it. No moment
> of behavior can be looked upon as neurotic unless the pro-
> cesses that have set it in motion predetermined its auto-
> matic repetition irrespective of the situation, the utility, or
> the consequences of the act. This may be the most basic
> lesson about human conduct that has been learned from
> psychoanalysis. Let me repeat: no single psychological act
> can be looked upon as neurotic unless it is the product of
> processes that predetermine a tendency to its automatic
> repetition [Kubie, 1978, p. 142].

Since the predominant forces in perverse patients are unconscious, they will not respond to experiences of pleasure or
pain, to rewards, punishments, or logical argument, ". . .
neither to the logic of events nor to any appeals to mind or
heart. The behavior that results from a dominance of the
unconscious system has the insatiability, the automaticity,

and the endless repetitiveness that are the stamp of the neurotic process" (Kubie, 1978, p. 143). These patients are unable to learn from experience, to change, and to adapt to changing external circumstances. In the course of this book, the processes predetermining these tendencies will be explored in detail.

In his textbook on sexual perversions, Ismond Rosen (1979) chose to use the word *perversion* in the title to his introductory chapter (pp. 29-64). He noted the emotional response of some people to the use of the terms *perversion* and *sexual deviation* because they are often considered "unnecessarily pejorative, degrading in self-esteem, and better replaced by less specific phraseology, if referred to at all" (p. 29). In rebuttal, he notes that we should remember "that acceptance of sexuality in all its forms received its main impetus this century from Sigmund Freud" and that "psychoanalysts still follow his tradition and treat patients, teach and [do] research into sexual problems with tolerance and respect" (p. 29). He argues for the retention of the term *perversion* because historically and theoretically it "denotes a group of clinical and psychopathological entities in which common features can be elucidated. . . . Perversions can thereby be distinguished from neuroses, psychoses and character disorders, although aspects of these latter conditions may coincide with established perversions, or interact dynamically with them" (pp. 29-30). Rosen recalls Freud's clarification in the "Three Essays" (1905b). Perversion denotes a sexual preference which departs from accepted norms of heterosexual coitus with orgasm. The preferred sexual mode derives from any of the basic drives or objects: part-objects, transitional objects, and whole objects. Actual genital behavior in intercourse becomes either impossible, unsatisfying, or facilitated only by the perverse act. He urged that perversions must now be investigated from various points of view: drives, ego functions, gender-identity, superego, object relations, internal representations of self and object, the inner and outer effect of the personality on the whole, and from the point of view of narcissism. He commented that, as of 1979, "no succinct, generally accepted theory has emerged" (pp. 29-30).

The proponents of the "normality" of sexual perversions insistently remind us that in perversion there is no suffering, no guilt, no psychopathology. My clinical findings indicate that perverse patients endure great suffering, massive unconscious guilt masked by defenses, profound psychopathology, and severe overall impairment in functioning. These findings are not readily available to those investigators who do not deal with in-depth psychoanalytic research. Of all the clinical conditions of emotional origin that serve simultaneously as defenses, perversions are unique in their capacity to use profound psychic conflicts and struggles to attain, for limited intervals, a pseudoadequate equilibrium and pleasure reward (orgasm), often permitting the individual to function, however marginally or erratically. This neutralization of conflict allows for the growth of certain ego-adaptive elements of the personality, and the pervert may therefore appear to others not to be ill at all except for a masquerade in his sexual life.

With regard to the question of guilt, Le Coultre (1956) clearly distinguishes between real guilt feelings attached to repressed conflicts of perverse acts which are *eliminated* by the perversion, and social guilt feelings on the surface that are often interpreted as real guilt feelings. The former have the quality of being easily removed by fairly simple measures. He was able to observe the absence of "real guilt feelings" (p. 42) and showed how a transformation had actually taken place; that is, the removal of guilt feelings through the construction and enactment of a perversion. These transformations make a perversion ego-syntonic and wipe out all traces of conscious guilt derived from unconscious conflict. Le Coultre showed how perversion eliminates guilt; societal guilt or societal fears are not the same as unconscious guilt.

> In the actual perverse act, the patient plays the role of the partner in the central conflict but vicariously experiences the feeling of the real object. The satisfying element is the climax which in truth is impaired. Furthermore, orgasm is impaired as was once pointed out by Freud. . . . The ego is definitely impaired because the most important feelings are denied and repressed, and there is an absence of attachment to the object [pp. 53–54].

In perversions, genital sexuality has been replaced by one component of infantile sexuality. The pervert has only one way of gaining sexual pleasure and his energies are concentrated in this direction. Obstacles blocking his capacity for other sexual pleasures are overcome, wholly or in part, by the perverse act. The gratification of the perverse instinctual drive constitutes the end-product of a defensive compromise in which elements of inhibition as well as gratification are present. The component instinct itself undergoes excessive transformation and disguise in order for it to be gratified in the perverse act (Hanns Sachs mechanism).

The term *ego-syntonic* has long been used in psychoanalysis to denote behavior compatible with the integrity of the self. This concept requires further explanation and refinement. In 1923, Freud described "in the roughest outline" the neurosis as:

> [T]he expression of conflicts between the ego and such of the sexual impulses as seem to the ego incompatible with its integrity or with its sexual standards. Since these impulses are not ego-syntonic, the ego has repressed them; that is to say, it has withdrawn its interest from them and has shut them off from becoming conscious as well as from obtaining satisfaction by motor discharge [p. 246].

Such a patient is considered to be suffering from ego-alien formations or neurotic symptoms, for the dammed-up libido "finds other ways out from the unconscious" (p. 246). For example, it regresses to earlier, weaker phases of development and earlier attitudes toward objects (points of fixation) and breaks through into consciousness, obtaining discharge in the form of symptoms. "Consequently, symptoms are in the form of compromises between the repressed sexual instincts and the repressing ego instincts; they represent a wish-fulfillment for both partners to the conflicts simultaneously, but one which is incomplete for each of them" (p. 242).

A number of ego-syntonic phenomena can be successfully analyzed at the present state of our knowledge. These include neurotic character traits, addiction, psychopathy, borderline conditions, psychotic characterology, and perversions. Some analysts believe that the choice between a

symptom neurosis and a neurotic character trait or other
ego-syntonic formation depends upon the libidinal type to
which the patient belongs: for example, narcissistic types
usually employ ego-syntonic rather than ego-alien defenses.
On the other hand, unconscious defenses will produce symptoms in patients who belong to the obsessional type.

When one speaks of the ego-syntonicity of homosexuality
or any other perverse act, it is evident that we are dealing
with two components: conscious acceptance and unconscious acceptance. The degree of conscious acceptance of a
perverse act varies with the person's reactions to societal
pressure and consciously desired goals and aspirations. The
conscious part of ego-syntonicity can be more readily modified than its unconscious component. Analysis of perverse
patients reveals that ego-syntonic formations accepted by
the patients are already the end-result of unconscious defense mechanisms in which the ego plays a decisive part. In
contrast, where superego or id plays the decisive role, the
end-result is often an ego-alien symptom. The splitting of the
superego promotes ego-syntonicity. The superego is especially tolerant of this form of sexuality as it may represent
the unconscious acceptable aspect of sexuality derived from the
parental superego. The split in the ego and the split in the
object lead to an idealized object relatively free of anxiety
and guilt. The split in the ego leads also to an ego relatively
free of anxiety, which is available for purposes of an incestuous relationship at the cost of the renunciation of a normal
one.

The perverted act, like the neurotic symptom, results from
conflict. It represents a compromise formation which at the
same time must be acceptable to the demands of the superego. As in the case of neurotic symptoms, instinctual gratification takes place in disguised form while its real content
remains unconscious. However, a perversion differs from a
neurotic symptom, first by the form of gratification of the
impulse (i.e., orgasm), and second, by the fact that the ego's
wishes for omnipotence are satisfied by the arbitrary ego-
syntonic action. We can conclude that a perversion differs
from a neurosis in that the symptom is desexualized in the
latter; discharge is painful in the neurosis, while it brings
genital orgasm in the perversion.

The low incidence of perversions such as voyeurism, fetishism, and transvestism in women (with the exception of female homosexuality which may approximate the incidence of male homosexuality) invites psychoanalytic scrutiny, which yields considerable information as to the original disturbances producing these conditions. In this connection, I noted as early as 1968 and again in 1980 that it was my belief that the significant incidence of homosexuality in the general population was due to the necessity for all human beings to successfully traverse the separation–individuation phase of early childhood, which is decisive for gender-defined self-identity. A substantial number of children fail to complete this developmental process and are therefore unable to form a healthy sexual identity in accordance with their anatomical and biological capacities—the core difficulty from which all perversions arise. The likelihood of the correctness of this view was reinforced by Greenson (1968), who had studied transsexual children, transvestites, and homosexuals for five years as part of a University of California, Los Angeles (UCLA) Gender Identity Research Project. In the course of this study, he sharply emphasized the vicissitudes in the psychological development of the preoedipal boy as differentiated from that of the preoedipal girl. His major conclusion was that the male has a double task: he must first undo the primary feminine identification with the mother and make a counteridentification with the father. In contrast, the female does not have to cancel out her feminine identification with the mother, but must make her own unique feminine identification in contrast to that of the mother. His far-reaching observations and conclusions, which tend to explain the low incidence of perversions in women, may be summarized as follows:

1. The male child, in order to attain a healthy sense of maleness, must replace the primary object of his identification, the mother, in order to identify with the father.

2. This "additional step of development" is in fact a difficulty from which girls are exempt. Failures in this task "are responsible for certain special problems of the man's gender-identity, a sense of belonging to the male sex" (p. 308).

3. The girl must also disidentify with the mother in order to develop her own unique female identity, but her "identifi-

cation with mother *helps* her establish her femininity." In this connection, I am in full agreement with Greenson when he comments that "men are far more uncertain about their sense of maleness than women are of their femininity" (p. 308). One may conclude that women's certainty about their gender-identity and men's uncertainty about theirs seems to be rooted in this early identification with the mother.

4. The male child's inability to disidentify from the mother will determine the success or failure of his later identification with his father. The two, "disidentifying from mother and counteridentifying with father, are interdependent and form a complementary series." It goes without saying that "the personality and behavior of mother and father play an important and circular role in the outcome of these developments." Either father or mother may encourage or discourage disidentifying" (p. 306).

5. The girl may acquire feminine characteristics by means of her identification with the mother, and her femaleness is assured if she is raised by a female mothering person. It is important for her to find her own individual feminine identity, unique and separate from that of the mother. She is not burdened, however, with the task of disidentifying from the mother and forming a counteridentification with the father. An exception to this may be found in very masculine women who have engaged in a disavowal of their femininity. From this group come a limited number of female voyeurs, transsexuals, transvestites, and fetishists, as well as the large number of female homosexuals.

The process of identification underscored by Greenson is only one of three major factors playing roles in the achievement of normal gender-defined self identity. The other are (1) the awareness of the anatomical and physiological structures in one's self which make for masculinity or femininity—the genitals; and (2) the assignment to a specific gender defined self identity promoted by the parents and other important social figures.

Ostow, Blos, Furst, Gero, Kanzer, Silverman, Sterba, Valenstein, Arlow, Loomis and Rappaport (1974) had the opportunity to study a large number of cases of perversion (eight cases in detail and 35 vignettes of case histories of perverse patients over a four-year period in a research study group composed of eminent psychoanalytic clinicians). Their report concluded that there was no better definition of perverse sexuality than that provided by Freud (1905b), who used the term *inversion* to denote deviant behavior with respect to the *object* of the sexual instinct, and the term *perversion* to denote behavior in which there was deviation with respect to the *aim* of the sexual instinct. This distinction between inversion and perversion is no longer generally used, and Ostow's group decided to use the term *perversion* for both. It noted that sexual behavior should be considered pathological only when the perversion is "fixed and predominant," imperative and insistent, and inappropriate "when judged by any reality-based criteria" (p. 7); and concluded that perversion and homosexuality were two aspects of the same disorder for the following reasons: (1) the developmental arrest required for one appeared to favor the other; (2) both phenomena represented infantile fixations with respect to the object in homosexuality and to the aim in other perversions; (3) narcissism, infantilism, and acting out were common in both perversion and homosexuality; (4) homosexuality was sometimes used as a defense against other forms of sexual perversion which would predominate in heterosexual relations if permitted to do so.

The crucial importance of the Ostow psychoanalytic clinical research group lies in the fact that it represents the status of our knowledge of these disorders circa 1975. The report is filled with brilliant clinical observations, theoretical considerations, and speculations on the definition of perversion, the role of early experiences, the dynamics of perversion, the question of guilt in perversion, and treatment possibilities. It adumbrated future developments in our psychoanalytic understanding by noting that there appeared to be gender disturbances,[3] object-relations conflicts, and

---

[3]This forecast was to be expressed with conviction reinforced by further clinical experience ten years later by one of the group; that is, Arlow (1986) in his assertion: "No matter what other factors pertain, perversions constitute problems of gender identity, of male–female differentiation" (p. 248).

severe disturbances in early ego development in these individuals. The report did not suggest a comprehensive and
integrated systematized theory of perverse development, as
theoretical constructs had not yet been made in the areas of
the pathology of internalized object relations, concepts of
narcissism, and knowledge of the earliest primary psychic
development derived from infant observational studies.

Chapter 3
A UNITARY THEORY OF SEXUAL PERVERSION

The delineation of perverse practices and fantasies remains a milestone in the evolution of psychoanalytic thought. Freud's (1905b) earliest discoveries of infantile sexuality led him to assert that in perversion sexuality is replaced by one component of infantile sexuality, that perverse tendencies or occasional perverse acts or fantasies are present in the life of every individual, whether normal or neurotic, and that, in the latter case, during analysis, symptoms are often revealed to be disguised as perverse acts. Perverse sexuality was deemed to be identical with infantile sexuality, and therefore we were all capable of manifesting perverse acts or experiencing perverse fantasies by the very fact that once we were all children.

Perversions could result from arrested (sexual) development or, "secondary to repression," sexual disappointment. Fenichel's (1945) "simple formula" that "persons who react to sexual frustrations with a regression to infantile sexuality are perverts; while persons who react with other defenses or employ other defenses after the regression are neurotics" (p. 325) reflected psychoanalysts' thinking on this issue during the first five decades of psychoanalytic history. This formulation placed the perversions firmly in a position of singular importance alongside the neuroses and affirmed that, in understanding the secret of the cause of perversions, one would be casting light on the etiology, dynamics, and course of the neuroses.

Clinical observations during psychoanalytic treatment of perverse patients have led me to prepare a unifying system in which sexual perversions may be placed and understood. I am suggesting that all perversions have a common core disturbance. This theory has been especially stimulated and reinforced by new theoretical and clinical knowledge of the earliest years of life, secured by the technique of direct psychoanalytic observation of infants and children, as well as by further refinements in our knowledge of ego psychology.

This unifying system initially grew out of my intensive work with homosexual patients in which a preoedipal nuclear conflict emerged dramatically and repetitively in individuals showing no evidence of overt psychosis; and who, except for their perversion and its attendant difficulties in their external lives, were apparently functioning relatively well. I have observed the same phenomena in cases of fetishism, transvestism, pedophilia, exhibitionism, sexual masochism, sexual sadism, voyeurism, and transsexualism.

My provisional theory is restricted to perversions of the obligatory type, where nonengagement in perverse practices would induce severe anxiety. It is distinguished by two central areas of emphasis: the stress of preoedipal causation, and my view that object relations pathology is more important for the development of perversions than the vicissitudes of the drives. In other words, the central conflict of the pervert is an object relations one rather than a structural one involving the three agencies of the mind. What I have to say, therefore, applies to relatively pronounced cases in which perverse development is clear and definite. Because the perverse acts are usually the only avenue for the attainment of sexual gratification, and are obligatory for the alleviation of intense anxieties, and because the intensity of the need for such gratification is relatively pronounced, I refer to such cases as "well-structured perversions." It may be that there are other cases of sexual perversion that do not originate within the etiological framework described. And it goes without saying that preoedipal conflict may also be responsible for clinical states other than perversion.

Previous Theoretical Contributions

In 1955 Gillespie presented a paper on "The General Theory of Sexual Perversion," a landmark in our understanding of these conditions (Gillespie, 1956a). He remarked that the subject of perversion, although not neglected by psychoanalysts, had received surprisingly little attention, especially since it occupied a place of such central importance in Freud's theories, both of sexuality and neurosis. The explanation was simple: Freud (1905b) had written a masterpiece on the subject in the pioneer years of psychoanalysis. The "Three Essays on the Theory of Sexuality" was an outstanding example of his genius, and in this work he clearly perceived that the manifestations of earlier sexuality were of profound relevance for, and had intimate connections with, the later development of adult sexual perversion and of neuroses and psychoses.

Gillespie's formulation represented the psychoanalytic theory and understanding of sexual perversions of twenty-nine years ago. His paper is remarkably comprehensive, taking infantile sexuality into account and affirming that the problem of perversion lies in the defense against oedipal difficulties. He underscores the concept that in perversion there is a regression of libido and aggression to preoedipal levels rather than a primary fixation at those levels. While I am in major agreement with Gillespie's formulations and have found them to be immensely valuable theoretically and therapeutically in dealing with all cases of perversion, my hypothesis proposes an alternative theory of causation, placing it earlier.

Four years before Gillespie's comprehensive paper was published a panel (1952) was held by the American Psychoanalytic Association on the "Psychodynamics and Treatment of Perversions." The opening statement by Lorand highlighted the consideration that the perversions constitute a

[W]ide and varied set of clinical phenomena for which no clear-cut specific concept of classification, etiology or psychodynamics has been established. An organized summing-up of our knowledge in this field is therefore in order. Is fixation at a pregenital sexual level of primary significance in the etiology of perversions, and if so, how does it influence the psychodynamic understanding of therapeutic achievement? On the other hand, if frustration and regression to previous levels of fixation are more significant causally, is it possible in the course of therapeutic technique to bypass the systematic sexual development in infancy and concentrate mainly on the cause and effects of such frustrations? [Panel, 1952, pp. 316–317].

While the panel members noted that an increasing number of clinical studies had begun to emphasize the role of separation anxiety in the formation of perversion, most of the participants maintained that the derivation of perversions was still to be found in oedipal-phase conflict and that castration anxiety was of central importance. Supporting the view of an earlier causative process, Bak, illustrating from the analysis of two fetishists, suggested that the "utilization of fetishism as a defense against castration anxiety ... must be determined by early experiences, experiences from the prephallic stage. . . . the untoward results of disturbed early mother-child relationships" (Panel, 1952, p. 317). It was Bak's opinion that in the potential fetishist, "the threat of separation from the mother is experienced as an equal if not greater danger than the loss of the penis" (p. 318).

My clinical research during the ensuing decades gave further substance to my growing conviction in both a preoedipal theory of causation and a common origin for all the perversions. In 1968 Greenacre (personal communication) conveyed to me her feeling that there may well be a "unifying structural relationship between the perversions ... [and] that all the perversions [are] derived from a similar base of disturbance in the early ego (especially in the sense of identity). . . ." The type of perversion itself was in all likelihood dependent on the degree of increase in early aggression, both primary and secondary; the degree and nature of involvement of the body–ego (in contributing to the defective ego development); specific traumata at particularly vulnerable times in the libidinal progression (the organizing trauma); the special nature of the superego development and ego-ideal, which is dependent on the extent of invasion of the Oedipus complex by the narcissism and the actual character of the parents (Greenacre, 1968).

Preoedipal Theory of Causation

My preoedipal theory of causation was first introduced in Socarides (1968b). It has undergone considerable elaboration during the second decade of this research, especially with regard to the inclusion of new and valuable information derived from our advances in object relations theory, differentiating criteria that exist between perversions and perversions in psychotics, and an increased understanding of the differences that exist between preoedipal and oedipal forms of the same perversion. A considerable number of these findings arrived at from the analysis of adults have been in many instances confirmed by infant and child observational studies, especially those in the area of the development of sexual identity. The proposition set forth here, that the genesis of perversions may well be the result of disturbances that occur earlier than has been generally assumed and accepted, namely, in the preoedipal phase of development, is grounded in the following tenets:

1. The nuclear conflicts of all sexual deviants derive from the preoedipal period of development, forcing these individuals into sexual behavior that not only affords orgastic release but also ensures ego survival.

2. The preoedipal period, especially the years between one-and-a-half and three, is crucial to the genesis of a sexual perversion. In this period, a preoedipal fixation occurs and is primary; a regression may occur to this early fixation point under conditions of stress.

3. The sexual deviant has been unable to pass successfully through the symbiotic and separation–individuation phase of early childhood, and this failure creates the original anxiety from which sexual perversions arise. This develop-

mental failure results in severe ego deficits and faulty gender-defined self identity.

4. Sexual perversion serves the repression of a pivotal nuclear conflict: the urge to regress to a preoedipal fixation in which there is a desire for and dread of merging with the mother in order to reinstate the primitive mother–child unity, and in the most severe cases, those fixated at practicing and differentiating phases, a threat of fragmentation to self cohesion.

The preoedipal theory of the origin of the perversion rests on three pillars: the first is the presence of a fixation in the first three years of life during the separation–individuation phase; the second is the early disturbance in gender-role formation (sexual identity) found in all these patients; and the third is the Spitz (1959) theory of synchronicity.

The Separation-Individuation Phase and Preoedipal Nuclear Conflict

The formulation of my unitary theory relies heavily on the separation–individuation theory of Mahler and her co-workers (Mahler and Furer, 1966; Mahler, 1968; Mahler, Pine, and Bergman, 1975). The term *separation–individuation* refers to an intrapsychic, developmental, gradual process of separation of the self from the mother and the beginnings of the establishment of individual identity. This process is an intrapsychic event, independent of the physical separation, and infers an intrapsychic conflict existing around both a wish for and a fear of "re-engulfment by the object" (Mahler, 1966a). Mahler uses the term *symbiotic* to define an archaic state serving a restitutive function by insuring survival through the infant's delusion of oneness with the mother. Opposite needs in the infant lead him to separateness and differentiation and to regaining the primitive state of his original unity with the mother. These needs leave their imprint on the developing modes of drive manifestations and ego formation. They exercise a determining influence on the structuring of the introjects and their subsequent projective dramatization in the external world.

In previous writings (Socarides, 1968a,b, 1969b), I noted

that the fixation to the mother so prominent in homosexual patients, and their characteristically narcissistic object choice (Freud, 1905b) may be traced back to the separation-individuation phase of development. Although it was my original impression that the fixation was to the earlier subphases of the separation–individuation process—even to the symbiotic period, because of the revival of intense archaic ego states in which there was a threat to ego cohesion and a threat of loss of object relations during analytic therapy—it is now my belief that the fixation has occurred at later periods; that is, at the rapprochement subphase or differentiating-practicing subphases (see chapters 9 and 10). I was led to this conclusion by the observation that although some patients reenact and relive fears and wishes derived from the earliest months of life (even at the oral phase), these patients do not suffer a complete loss of object relations and other ego functions. Furthermore, even in the depths of regression, they maintain the transference relationship to the analyst and, despite florid transference reactions of even a transitory psychoticlike character and the vivid reenactment of oral fantasies, they do not become psychotic. In agreement with Arlow (1963), I think it important to realize that we are not dealing with an actual regression to an oral fantasy that originated during the oral phase, but to one that originated during the phallic-oedipal period, but derived from pre-oedipal-phase difficulties.

To the sexual deviant, the mother has, in his infancy, been dangerous and frightening, threatening the infant with loss of love and care. On the other hand, the mother's conscious and unconscious impulses were felt as working against separation. The infant's anxiety and frustration press for withdrawal of libidinal cathexis from the mother and result in a shift of libido toward increased aggression. This image of the introjected mother leads to a rupture (split) of the ego. In his narcissistic object choice, the homosexual, for example, not only loves his partner as he himself wished to be loved by the mother, but reacts to him with sadistic aggression as once experienced toward the hostile mother for forcing separation.

The inability to make the progression from the symbiotic

phase of earliest infancy to separation–individuation results in a fixation, with the concomitant tendency to regression to the symbiotic phase. This is manifested in the threat of personal annihilation, loss of ego boundaries, and sense of fragmentation.

Homosexuals, for instance, and other types of sexual deviants, repeatedly demonstrate that they were unable to make these advances. In a child so unsuccessful:

> [T]he fear of re-engulfment threatens a recently and barely started individual differentiation. . . . Beyond the fifteen- to eighteenth-month mark, the primary stage of unity and identity with mother ceases to be constructive for the evolution of an ego and an object world. By this age, the father has become an important object. This relationship ordinarily has the advantage that the inner image of the father has never drawn to itself so much of the unneutralized drive cathexis as has the mother's, and therefore there is less discrepancy between the image of the father and the real father. . . . From the very beginning, the infant creates a world in his own image, wherein the symbiotic partner is the indispensable catalyst and beacon of orientation [Mahler and Gosliner, 1955, p. 200].

During the separation–individuation phase (eighteen to thirty-six months), the infant is attempting to evolve and jealously guard his developing self-image "from infringement by mother and other important figures. . . . A quasi-normal negativistic phase . . ." can be observed along with "the process of disengagement from the mother–child symbiosis." The more parasitic the symbiotic phase, "the more prominent and exaggerated will be this negativistic reaction." If there is severe negativism there is severe fear of reengulfment.

> Inasmuch as all happenings in the symbiotic phase are dominated by orality, the infant furthermore loses the necessary and normal delusional experience of incorporating and thus having the good mother in himself, restoring the blissful state of omnipotent fusion with the mother. Instead, he struggles in impotent rage and panic, with the catastrophic fear of annihilation by introjected bad objects,

without being able successfully to invoke the good part object, the soothing breast of the ministering mother [Mahler and Gosliner, 1955, pp. 200–201].

Sometimes the "symbiotic parasitic mother cannot endure the loss of her hitherto vegetative appendage. . . ." (Mahler and Gosliner, 1955, p. 201). This type of mother-child relationship I have found in the study of homosexuals and other sexually deviant patients. The father could constitute an important support against the threat of maternal engulfment, but this resource is totally absent. In actuality there is a complete lack of the necessary support from either parent. Under such conditions, "a re-engulfment of the ego into the whirlpool of the primary undifferentiated symbiotic stage becomes a true threat" (Mahler and Gosliner, 1955, p. 210). (The contribution of the father to this fixation and to future development is explored in chapter 11.)

Several clinical indicators may be cited as pathognomic of preoedipal fixation. Foremost among these is the observation that in all sexual deviants there exists a primary identification with the mother, with concomitant sexual (gender) confusion. This identification with the all-powerful, the almighty preoedipal mother permeates every aspect of the patient's life: he feels he cannot survive without her. Efforts to separate from the mother result in his experiencing intense anxiety, which is well evident before the age of three and persists unabatedly throughout life. In this connection it is important to recall that, following the birth of the child, the biological oneness with the mother is replaced by a primitive identification with her. The male child must proceed from the security of identification and oneness with the mother to active competent separateness and male (phallic) striving. If this task proves too difficult, pathological defenses, especially an increase in primary identification and archaic aggressiveness, may result. (The consequences of an increase in primary and secondary aggression and their relevance for the development of sadomasochistic perversions are explored in chapter 5.) These developments are of the greatest importance for the solution of conflicts appearing in the oedipal phase and in later life. In the oedipal phase, under the pressure of castration fear, an additional type of identification with the mother in the form of passive feminine wishes for the father is likely to take place. However, beneath this feminine position in relation to the father, one may often uncover the original passive relation with the mother; that is, an active feminine preoedipal identification.

Second, I have noted that the general behavior of these patients is markedly pregenital, characterized by acting out, poor affect control with occasional aggressive outbursts, and a predeliction for fantasy over reality. Preoedipal material is, furthermore, closely linked with particular traits characteristic of the psychosexual phases of that period of development (e.g., oral and anal fantasies and practices predominate).

Third, there is a severe disturbance in the sense of ego boundaries and body image.

Finally, oral-aggressive and incorporative tendencies, along with tendencies toward paranoidal anxiety, largely dominate the patient's life and may result in oral (transitory) delusional formation, dreams of internal persecuting objects, fears of poisoning, and fears of being swallowed.

The pervert therefore struggles with preoedipal fantasies, but these may serve as a defense against the emergence of oedipal material and vice versa. Hoffer (1954) has aptly described these phenomena under the heading of defense organization. Thus, castration anxiety, the direct result of the superimposed oedipal conflict, may also be utilized as a defense against anxieties of the preoedipal phase. Similarly, preoedipal drives may have a defensive importance in warding off oedipal wishes and fears. There is always an interplay between the two.

Sexual perversions, therefore, constitute early developmental fixations or developmental arrests. In some the fixation is less than in others. Upon meeting vicissitudes of later development, patients regress to those conflicts which have left a weak point or scar formation. The greater the oedipal weakness, the stronger the tendency to regression to the preoedipal period with the danger of severe psychoticlike manifestations threatening loss of ego functions and other regressive symptomatology, together with reenactment of the earliest traumata. The tendency toward regression is dependent not only upon the preoedipal fixation, but also on the strength of the ego and on superego formation. Some sexual deviants may therefore vacillate in the enactment of their perversions and not vividly portray the merging phenomenon, the threat of dissolution, and the striking elaborations of anxiety. Some patients, unable to construct a stabilizing perversion experience multiple fantasies (see chapter 21) and the merging phenomena may be seen in its derivative forms; for example, the fears, dreams, and fantasies of being surrounded by snakes, being swept into whirlpools, being enclosed in a cage, being propelled in an elevator whose walls are disintegrating, and so on. Some patients with well-established perverse practices may never approach the merging phenomena with its danger of regression to the earlier phases of development, especially if they do not seriously attempt to interrupt their perverse practices. Others, deeply afraid of facing this overwhelming anxiety, may prematurely terminate psychoanalytic therapy in a period of resistance, and with many rationalizations for a premature interruption. Some of these will return to therapy for shorter or longer periods of time to relieve their suffering, only again to escape facing the deepest conflicts. The failure to successfully understand and resolve these conflicts and overcome these fixations is largely responsible for the inevitable later continuance of perverse practices.

Disturbances of Gender-Defined Self Identity

Central to the concept of etiology in the preoedipal perversion is the disturbance of gender-defined self identity in all of these patients. This observation, while more apparent in some individuals than in others, emerged as a central finding in all my psychoanalyzed cases of sexual perversion, despite structures and personality traits which attempt to compensate for this inadequacy. Even a masculine-appearing homosexual, for example, reveals deep feminine unconscious identification during analysis. I use the term *gender-defined self identity*[1] to indicate an individual's awareness of being masculine or feminine in accordance with anatomy. Although its foundation is laid by the ages of three to four, gender-defined self identity is not a fixed entity, but is subject to fluctuations and variations even into adulthood in later life.

In their most recent publication, Mahler and her co-workers (1975) note that in the course of understanding the attainment of enduring individuality they discovered that this consists of the attainment of two levels of the sense of identity: the first being the awareness of being a separate and individual entity, and the second a beginning awareness of a *gender-defined self identity*. They noted that gender identity in the male develops with less conflict if the mother "respects and enjoys the boy's phallicity ... especially in the second half of the third year." The early beginning of the male's gender identity is facilitated by an identification with the father or possibly with an older brother. The mother must be able to relinquish her son's body and "ownership of his penis to him." Crushing activity or forcing passivity is extremely damaging to the development of gender-defined self identity. The rapprochement struggle unfortunately may take on the character of a more or less desperate biphasic struggle on the part of the boy to ward off the dangerous mother after separation. Mahler et al. (1975) contend that "fear of engulfment by the dangerous mother after the separation, fear of merging that we sometimes see as a central resistance in our adult male patients, has its inception at this very early period of life" (p. 215).

While Mahler and her associates' major interest was to achieve an understanding of the development of the human infant and child in the course of normal separation and individuation processes, leading to the establishment of object constancy, self constancy, and enduring individuality (the attainment of a separate and individual self), Galenson and Roiphe (1973), in their psychoanalytic observational study of infants and young children over a ten-year period,

---

[1] I have found this phrase useful as it helps eradicate the terminological confusion raised by use of phrases such as *sexual identity, gender identity, sexual role,* and so on.

directed their attention to illuminating the factors in the preoedipal phase that lead to the awareness of a *gender-defined self identity* (sexual identity).

I would like to briefly highlight their results, for they provide further theoretical validation to my clinical findings which were made in advance of their hypothesis. In 1968 Roiphe made a definitive connection between the fear of object loss and early castration anxiety, noting that the major thrust of development during the period between eighteen and twenty-four months of age was a concern with the differentiation of the self from the object and the internalization and solidification of the object representation. This early period of genital interest and activity takes place entirely during the preoedipal period and is concomitant with the consolidation of object representation and self representation. During these early phases of genital arousal, a primary genital schematization is taking place which gives shape to an emerging sexual current and a later primary genital schematization. Roiphe concluded that early experiences that tend to challenge the child unduly with a threat of object loss or body dissolution result in a faulty and vacillating genital outline of the body at the time when a genital schematization normally undergoes a primary consolidation (1968).

Galenson and her associates concluded from their work with healthy and disturbed children that there exists an early castration anxiety (a "nursery castration," if you will) which is later compounded by the castration anxiety of the phallic phase. In such children not only are there faulty, blurred, or vacillating body–ego outlines, but in addition one can clearly discern the beginnings of perversion formation (Galenson, Vogel, Blau, and Roiphe, 1975). Somewhat earlier, in 1972, Roiphe and Galenson had firmly established that there is a normal period of genital interest occurring somewhere between fifteen and nineteen months of age, involved with the consolidation of object representations in the body-self schematization, and free from oedipal resonance.

Roiphe and Galenson's findings suggested to me an additional explanation for a common clinical finding in patients with perversions, usually attributed to oedipal-phase conflict and castration fear, namely, the presence of the "ubiquitous fantasy" (Bak, 1968) of the phallic woman. This fantasy helps deny that castration of the oedipal period can take place and, even more importantly, it lessens the body dissolution anxieties of the preoedipal period. For example, the belief in "completeness," absence of differences between the sexes, would tend to reaffirm and reinforce in those patients so traumatized a vacillating body–genital outline and early genital schematization which has been imperilled by experiences constituting object loss and threats to body integrity.

Important as the role of the mother is in allowing the child to separate and individuate, the father also serves a vital function. Abelin (1971) notes that it "might be *impossible for either* the mother or child *to master* [intrapsychic separation] *without their having the father to turn to*" (p. 248). The absent, domineering, hostile, detached father will not allow the male child to make an identification with him and thus become a bridge in achieving both an individual sense of self and a gender-defined self identity. This is later dramatized in the continuation of a lifelong poor relationship between father and son (see chapter 11). Similar clinical phenomena are observed in the adult analysis of female patients, although perversions of the female are not common, except in those with a strong masculinity complex. In this connection, Greenson (1964) noted the importance of substituting a normal identification with the father in place of the mother—in his phrase, "dis-identifying with the mother." Stoller's important work during the past two decades underscores the crucial importance of a father with whom a boy can identify (1968b).

Lastly, Edgcumbe and Burgner (1975) of the Hampstead Child Therapy Clinic have examined the development of object-relatedness and drive development in the "preoedipal phallic phases" (a precursor of the oedipal phase) and the oedipal phase proper, tracing the development of the body representation as an integral part of the developing self representation and the processes of identification affecting these representations. They state: "This development of self- and body representations and of identifications makes a crucial contribution to the establishment of differentiated sexual identity..." (p. 163). They concluded: "The process of acquiring a differentiated sexual identity rests largely on the child's capacity to identify with the parent of the same sex" (p. 165). They verify that the acquiring of a sense of gender-defined self identity begins during the child's second year, continues through the anal phase, and reaches its peak during the phallic phase. Although in agreement with Mahler's concept, they differ from Mahler with respect to timing (she holds that the sense of sexual identity is formed somewhat later, beginning in the earliest period of the phallic phase) and "attach great importance to the phallic-narcissistic (preoedipal) phase as the time in which the child may be expected to acquire and to shape his own sexual identity; having done this, the child is then better able to enter the oedipal phase of development" (p. 166).

I have cited the work of these investigators in some detail because it constitutes considerable verification of the second pillar of my theory, namely, that in all perverts there is a pronounced disturbance in gender-defined self identity which began in the separation–individuation phase and was not a secondary development resulting from a negative oedipal reaction. My clinical findings in this regard are to be found in my several writings (1968a, 1968b, 1969b, 1970a, 1973, 1974b, 1979a, 1982b) on various perversions and in Socarides (1978a).

Synchronicity of Maturation and Psychological Development (Spitz)

Spitz (1959) has shown that:

> [W]hen a psychological development, which is age-adequate for a given critical period, cannot take place, it will be difficult, if not impossible, for the individual to acquire it at a later stage [because] at the appropriate critical period a given item of psychological development will find all the maturational conditions favorable for its establishment [p. 76].

He called this *maturational compliance* and its counterpart *developmental* (psychological) *compliance*: "synchronicity of maturation and development is an absolutely essential feature of normal development" (pp. 76-77). Spitz showed that, if a child does not have the wish to walk when the maturation of the innervation of the lower part of the body enables it to walk, the child may later be unable to stand or walk without support. Later:

> [A]s a consequence of a traumatic affect deprivation, he regress[es] to the stage when he could neither walk nor stand nor sit. . . . If, during the critical period, the appropriate [psychological] developmental item is not forthcoming, then the maturational factors will seize on other [psychological] developmental items available. These developmental items will be modified and distorted until they comply with maturational needs. An integration will be established which deviates from the norm. . . . As a result, when the bypassed (psychological) developmental item finally does become available at a later stage, it will find the maturational positions occupied by a *compensating, though deviant, structure and unavailable for normal integration* [pp. 77-78; emphasis added].

Spitz's observations can be applied to the problem of the early development of the sexual deviant. He has failed to make the separation from mother at the proper stage of development, and as a result a chronic intrapsychic stimulation, a fixation point remains to which he stays fixed, despite other developmental-maturational phases he may have in part successfully passed. In these maturational positions, compensating and deviant structures have been formed because of the infantile deficiency. These structures are intimately concerned with identity, disturbance in object relationships, faulty ego boundaries, introjective and projective anxieties, and fears of invasion and of engulfment.

More specifically, the patients with sexual perversions were unable to pass through the developmental phase in which they would have established a separate identity. This deficit in development led to profound difficulties; for example, faulty identification, disturbances in both the sense of self and in the development of an appropriate sexual identity, a fluidity of ego boundaries, impairment of body–ego, introjective and projective anxieties, and fluctuating states of object relationships. Out of the inability to separate and the wish for continuing the primary identification with the mother, which have continued in the unconscious through the years, emerge a threat of identifying and a threat of merging, a threat of being annihilated and a threat of the consequences should the patient retreat inside the mother's body. The fear that crystallizes is then compounded by castration fears of the oedipal period.

These male patients enter late childhood with an inhibition of self-assertion and profound conscious and/or unconscious female identification. The strong inhibition of male sexuality insures the avoidance of the female and of the merging phenomenon. These patients attempt to attain masculinity or forfeit it or try to cling to the illusion of femininity. For example, the male homosexual transiently obtains masculinity through incorporation of the partner's body and penis and thereby avoids the dangers connected with the mother, all the while remaining close to her. He substitutes the male for the female, the penis for the dreaded breast and the genitalia of the maternal body. The mechanism by which this occurs was first described by Sachs (1923), and I have suggested (1968b) that these intricate intrapsychic events be called the Sachs mechanism of perversion formation. The Sachs mechanism, which can be observed in the formation of all perversions, giving to each perversion its surface manifestations, all the while excludes from consciousness the deeper, more destructive anxieties. It is a solution by division, whereby one piece of infantile sexuality enters the service of repression (i.e., is helpful in promoting repression through displacement, substitution, reaction formation, and other defense mechanisms) and so carries over pregenital pleasure into the ego, while the rest undergoes repression. This repressive compromise mechanism allows a conscious suitable portion to be supported and endowed with a high pleasure reward so that it competes successfully with genital pleasure. It is acceptable to both the ego and to the superego: a split-off part of the superego derived from the parents may sanction the perversion, and the manifest perversion gives expression to preoedipal drives in a masked form. On the other hand, a repressed portion may still remain strong enough so that in the course of life it may threaten a breakthrough, and the pervert may at any time develop neurotic symptoms. Thus, the instinctual gratification takes place in a disguised form while its real content remains unconscious. Viewed in this light, the manifest perversion can be likened to the relationship which exists between the manifest dream and latent dream content, and the true meaning of the perversion can be ascertained only through the analysis of the unconscious meaning of the perverse action.

In perversions, the patient attempts to rid himself of the damaging, destructive union with the mother, ward off incorporative–introjective needs, and seeks to maintain an optimal distance from and/or closeness to her. When the pressures of adaptation to the masculine role become too intense, regression to the earliest phases of ego development occurs. The great dangers inherent in this regression promote further perverse behavior in a frantic attempt to seek relief.

Perversions and Schizophrenia

Elaboration and refinement of my theory has required an explanation for those perversions which exist in schizophrenic individuals. While psychotics may also suffer from perversion, most individuals with a perversion are not psychotic and, in my experience, do not become so during psychoanalytic therapy, or indeed during long follow-up periods. The frequent coexistence of schizophrenic symptoms with perversions has been explained in various ways. Gillespie suggested that this affinity existed because strong castration anxiety leads these patients to a partial regression to pregenital levels. "A successful perversion evades psychosis by means of a split in the ego, which leaves a relatively normal part capable of coping with external reality while allowing the regressed part to behave in a limited sexual sphere in a psychotic manner" (Gillespie, 1956b, pp.

36–37). In Gillespie's view, therefore, the pervert is saved from psychosis largely by the mechanism of splitting. While splitting mechanisms of both ego and object are ubiquitous in perversions, they cannot, in my opinion, be assigned a prophylactic function as their major achievement. A more modest function can be directly observed through the analysis of the patient's unconscious fantasy system (the unconscious significance of the perverse act) and the multiple substitutions, displacements, and splitting mechanisms inherent in it. Through these mechanisms of disguise, the perverse act becomes possible, yielding pleasure and simultaneously avoiding more serious intrapsychic dangers, those related to both drives and object relations. A second objection, that which arises from Gillespie's belief in "regression from oedipal conflict" theory, is diametrically opposed to my own and has been discussed in earlier parts of this chapter. My disagreement with Gillespie and others as to the etiology of well-structured perversion lying in the oedipal period does not in any way detract from my appreciation of the accuracy of his conceptualizations (including those of others) with regard to many of the mechanisms involved in the formation of perversions. I would reserve much of the etiological explanation provided by Gillespie for a different form of perversion, the oedipal form of these disorders.

Before turning to the differentiation on the oedipal from preoedipal forms of perversion, it is important to discuss what I consider to be essential differences between well-structured perversions and those which appear in the psychoses, and to explain why I think that these schizoperversions should not be included in the unitary system I have described. For example, *schizohomosexuality* (the coexistence of homosexuality with schizophrenia), a term coined by this author (1978b), is due neither to a fixation to the preoedipal phase of development nor to a failure of resolution of the Oedipus complex and a flight from castration fears leading to a regression in part to anal and oral conflicts. One may postulate a similar designation for other perversions which coexist with schizophrenia (e.g., schizopedophilia, schizotransvestitism, schizoexhibitionism, and so on). Although unconsciously motivated and arising from anxiety, the perverse act in the schizophrenic does not serve the magical restorative function of the preoedipal form of perversion. Severe gender-identity disturbances, when present, are part and parcel of an underlying schizophrenic process which has led to profound identity disturbances and a confusion with the object. The schizopervert shows a failure to invest the object successfully, and thus the object cannot be retained or cathected, even though there are fused body images and fused genital representations. This is in direct contrast to the nonpsychotic preoedipal perversion in which objects are retained, protected, and invested successfully despite some degree of fused body-image or fused genital representation.

Bak's contributions on this topic are close to my own. He suggested that "the frequent coexistence of schizophrenic symptoms with perversions indicates a common fixation point in the undifferentiated phase and in defenses against unneutralized aggression; the perverse symptoms represent an attempt at restitution of the narcissistic object relationship. . ." (1956, p. 240). Indeed, the severity of the regressive experiences of my patients, the pronounced use of primitive and archaic psychical mechanisms, and the transference reactions bordering on psychoticlike manifestations initially led me to believe that perversions may be explained by their relationship to autistic and symbiotic modes of adaptation [this was strongly suggested in Socarides (1968b)]. This assumption would connote a fixation at the autistic phase in order to ward off the fear of a dissolution of the self representation. The absence of true psychotic reactions, despite intense regressive experiences and the capacity of these patients to recover from them, indicated, however, both a capacity to synthesize new structures from these experiences and a capacity to maintain object relations and analyzable transferences.

When perversions coexist or alternate with overt psychosis, it may be due to "alterations of the ego" (Bak, 1971, p. 242). For example, the "ego may resort to temporary *abandonment* of object-representations [during the psychotic phase] . . . but not to the abolition of representations as in schizophrenia." I am in agreement with Bak's opinion that

"there is *a basic qualitative difference* between the schizophrenic process and the neuroses and other incidental
psychoses, and there can be no possibility of a continuum
between them" (p. 242).

Although the schizopervert has a preponderance of insistent and intractable anxieties and an abundance of incorporative and projective anxieties similar to the preoedipal
type, together with fears of engulfment, ego dissolution, and
loss of self, the perverse act in the schizopervert does not
insure ego survival but only fleetingly decreases anxiety
over the impending loss of self. The perverse symptom in
these cases is ego-syntonic as in the preoedipal type, but the
aim of the perverse act is not the reconstitution of a sense of
gender-defined self identity: it is a frantic attempt to *create*
object relations.

Bak (1971) brilliantly defined the differences between
perversion in the nonpsychotic individual and the schizophrenic. His conclusions can be listed as follows: perverse
impulses are a frantic attempt to maintain object relations.
These impulses, so often seen in paranoid schizophrenia, are
not "etiological" but represent conflicts and their delusional
elaborations, which are "consequences of a schizophrenic
process rather than its cause" (p. 239). Bak warned against
concluding that there is a neurotic structure in those individuals with paranoid delusions operating within a "relatively benign schizophrenic process" (p. 239), even though a
perverse conflict may be discovered behind these delusions.
Perverse acts in schizophrenics with self–object differentiation difficulties show significant differences from the well-
organized perversion. The latter show better object relations
and considerably more intact ego functions. There is a basic
qualitative difference between perversions in schizophrenics and those in nonpsychotic individuals. In the true well-
structured preoedipal perversion, object relations are maintained despite a diffuse body image and confusion in genital
representation, in contrast to perverse activities in the
schizophrenic. In some instances, paranoid delusions with
perverse content do occur. In those cases the object relationship may still be highly pathological, but is nevertheless
preserved. Perverse symptoms in the psychotic are an

attempt to create object relations in the face of severe regression, threatened or actual destruction of object relations in an individual severely damaged by a primary defect or deficiency in the autonomous functions of the ego, and an inability to maintain a protective stimulus barrier (see chapter 4 for the rationale for classifying perversion into oedipal, preoedipal, and schizo terms).

Preoedipal and Oedipal Forms of Perversion: Differentiating Criteria

To distinguish preoedipal perversion from oedipal forms of these disorders is of equal importance to differentiating them from perversions coexisting with schizophrenia. It is clinically verifiable that perverse symptoms can also arise from the oedipal phase of development. In those instances the pathological behavior is usually slightly deviant, transitory, and not well structured. Failure to engage in the perverse act does not induce severe or intolerable anxiety. The oedipal form of perversion does not constitute a *well-structured perversion*.[2] These forms must be differentiated from preoedipal perversions, which arise from preoedipal levels of development with which we associate narcissistic neuroses and impulse disorders. We may find pedophiliac, voyeuristic, transvestite, homosexual, fetishistic, and so on, behavior in which the clinical picture is largely one of oedipal-phase conflicts, and regression does not involve severe impairment in object relations or other ego functions.

Several differentiating criteria are briefly noted here:

1. In oedipal forms, object relations are unimpaired and consist of a relation of self to object, in contrast to preoedipal forms in which object relations are mildly to moderately impaired and consist of object to self.

2. In the oedipal forms, the prognosis for the removal of

---

[2]These are the relatively well-pronounced cases in which the perverse development is clear and definite. For these patients, nonengagement in perverse practices produces severe anxiety. The perverse acts are usually the only avenue for the attainment of sexual satisfaction, are obligatory for the alleviation of intense anxiety, and the intensity of the patient's need for such satisfaction is relatively pronounced.

the perverse symptom and the attainment of object love is more favorable than in the preoedipal forms.

3. In the oedipal forms, the perverse symptom is due to the failure of the resolution of the Oedipus complex and castration fears which lead to a negative oedipal position. In preoedipal forms, oedipal conflicts may be present or apparently absent, but preoedipal conflicts predominate.

4. In the oedipal forms, there is no fixation at preoedipal levels but often a partial regression to the preoedipal phase. In preoedipal forms, fixations may be mild to moderate and are located in the later phases of the separation–individuation process, in the rapprochement subphase. In the more severe perversions, those in which primitive aggressive impulses predominate, in association with a high degree of narcissistic pathology, fixation may be considerably more intense and may lie in very early phases of separation–individuation (differentiating and practicing subphases), bordering on the symbiotic phase.

5. In the oedipal forms, the conflict is *structural*—one between ego, id, and superego. A regression to preoedipal levels may produce an object relations conflict existing alongside that of the oedipal period. In the preoedipal forms, an *object relations* conflict predominates. This consists of anxiety and guilt associated with the failure of development of self–object differentiation.

6. Clinical observations reveal that the Sachs mechanism may play a minor role in the oedipal forms in which regression takes place and is partially effective; therefore, the symptom remains ego-alien. In preoedipal forms, the intense attachment, fear, and guilt in the boy's relationship with his mother brings about certain major psychic transformations, which are effective through the mechanism of the repressive compromise.

7. In the oedipal forms, the tendency to regressive states is mild, and when it occurs it is similar to that which appears in neurotics. The threats of the oedipal period have disrupted the already formed identity; a regression occurs to an earlier period in an escape from the dangers of the oedipal period. This is a partial preoedipal regression to anal and even oral conflicts. In the preoedipal forms, the tendency to regressive

states is moderate to severe, although there is an adequate capacity in most instances to circumscribe these regressions and to recover from them.

8. In the oedipal forms, transference manifestations are similar to those which appear in the transference neuroses, and therefore the degree of potential analyzable transferences is ideal. In the preoedipal forms, a transference neurosis may also take place because there is sufficient self–object differentiation and internalization of object representations (Panel, 1977).

9. In the oedipal forms of perversions, reality testing and impulse control are intact. Thinking is unimpaired, and self-concept and ego boundaries are essentially unimpaired. Conflict is internalized, affect is appropriate, and aggression is essentially well defended against. In the preoedipal forms, reality testing is often intact but unconsciously or consciously ignored. The boundary between fantasy and reality can be indistinct. Impulse control may be incomplete, or only partial control may be present, which leads to acting out of impulses and pursuit of instantaneous gratification. Preoedipal patients frequently reveal an elevated sense of self-esteem bordering on omnipotence, which alternates with feelings of extreme self-depreciation. Ego boundaries may be fluctuating. There may be a disturbance in affect and affect control in the preoedipal type.

As I have suggested elsewhere (Panel, 1977), further refinement in our understanding of the types of perversions may well lead us to conclude that indeed the true perversions are preoedipal disorders and do not arise from oedipal conflict with a regression to earlier phases. Oedipal perverse symptoms constitute a different form of perversion, which may be treated similarly to the neuroses and may be called *perverse behavior*. Perverse behavior occurs secondarily to a temporary regression and does not represent a primary fixation and developmental failure with gender-defined self identity disturbance; nor are the manifestations by which we know these disorders a result of the repressive compromise, as in the true perversions. (Detailed clinical illustrations of each perversion are to be found in Part II.)

Common Psychical Origins and Distinguishing Features of Nine Perversions

A schematic representation of nine major sexual perversions in the male is given in Table 3.1. This table briefly summarizes the major origin, function, motivation, and sexual object choice or aim of the perversions. It depicts the stratification, from a root preoedipal nuclear conflict, of subsequent superimposed oedipal conflict and the resultant perversion. This schema depicts the common psychical events and differences in the production of the various perversions and the crucial differences in their formation and meaning. It should be noted that the oedipal conflicts are superimposed on the preoedipal and that a continuum exists between the two. Were preoedipal conflict not present (the root of our schematic design), no well-structured perversion would be formed. It can be seen that the various forms of perversion all reflect different compromises between the simultaneous identifications with the mother who is seen as possessing a penis and, at the same time, castrated (Bak, 1968).

In all nine perversions the individuals have failed to successfully pass through the separation–individuation phase of childhood development. Common to all of them is a fear of fusion and merging with the mother, a tendency to lose ego boundaries, and a fear of loss of self or ego dissolution.

They all suffer from a primary identification with the mother, conscious and/or unconscious faulty gender-defined self identity, and disturbances in object relations. Faulty gender-role identity plays an important role in propelling them in various directions in search of psychic equilibrium: the homosexual toward men; the transvestite toward accepting his feminine identification contrary to anatomy; the fetishist toward alternately being man and woman (consciously not accepting his feminine identity but unconsciously desiring it); the homosexual pedophile to becoming a child and/or mother alternative with an attempt to maintain his masculinity; the exhibitionist toward visual reassurance of masculinity; the sexual masochist toward a passive–submissive reenactment of the dreaded destruction and reengulfment at the hands of the "cruel" mother, with a built-in assurance of survival; the sexual sadist toward an angry, defiant reenactment of the dreaded destructive reengulfment at the hands of the "cruel" mother, with a built-in guarantee of victory; the transsexual toward the "achievement" of femininity through radical surgical procedures; and the voyeur toward reinforcing masculinity through visual reassurance and warding off severe engulfment.

The choice of a specific perversion is a multifactorial one, depending on variables under current investigation. For reasons not yet completely established, one person finds it much easier to accept one particular aspect of infantile polymorphous sexuality than another. This may be due to specific organizing experiences[3] and traumata occurring at vulnerable periods of libidinal-phase progression in the context of a defective early ego development. The ego's acceptance of this aspect of infantile sexuality into consciousness serves to keep it in repression and also alleviates the deeper anxieties.

There may be fluctuations in the balance of psychic economy that force the individual to manifest now one, then the other perverse practice. On these occasions the defensive value of one type of perversion appears insufficient to maintain the mental equilibrium, and multiple perversions may appear. The alternation between or combination of perversions, or the inability to form a well-structured perversion in the face of intense primitive anxieties (see chapter 21) may in some instances indicate that we may be dealing with an underlying schizophrenic process or that there has been an unsuccessful splitting of the ego and object, a precondition for the formation of a sexual perversion (Gillespie, 1956b); or, on the other hand, the perverse activity is unacceptable to the superego.

---

[3] "Organizing experiences" are those early sexual activities (often of a traumatic nature) recovered in the analysis which played a crucial role in the later design of the perversion. They not only provided genital excitement but, by virtue of the accompanying affective release, supplied an initial sense of self cohesion, a means of relating to the internal world and external objects. As such experiences help create the "end-product" (Freud, 1919), they may be considered to play an essential role in the "choice" of the perversion.

Table 3.1

A Unitary Theory of Sexual Perversion in the Male (A Schematic Representation)

Basic Preoedipal Nuclear Conflict
↓ (6 months — 3 years)

Failure in Traversing the Separation-Individuation Phase of Development
(Failure to make intrapsychic separation from mother)
1. Merging and fusion phenomena
2. Predominance of primitive and archaic mental mechanisms
3. Defective early ego development
4. Increase in early aggression, both primary and secondary
5. Disturbance in body-self schematization, particularly of the genital area
6. Disturbance in the attainment of object constancy

↓ *Persistence of Primary Feminine Identification*

↓ *Faulty Gender-Defined Self Identity*

↓ *Specific Organizing Experiences and Traumata Leading to Choice of the Later Perversion*

↓ *Passage Through the Oedipal Phase*
(3-5 years)
(increased castration anxiety, negative oedipal position; specific ego and superego problems superimposed on preoedipal fixation)

↓ *Perversion*
All perversions reflect:
1. Different compromises between simultaneous identifications with the "phallic and penisless" mother

(Continued)

Table 3.1 (*Continued*)

---

2. Wish to maintain optimal distance from and/or closeness to the mother without fear of engulfment
3. Faulty development of object representations
4. Lack of adequate separation of self and object
5. A reassuring and reaffirming function
6. A warding off (of dangers) function
7. Need–tension gratification through the sensori-perceptive apparatus

---

Upon entering the oedipal phase, patients with perversions often experience a negative oedipal complex superimposed on earlier development. A split in the ego and/or object is more evident in fetishism and a split in both ego and object is commonly found in pedophilia. Common to all forms of perversion is a varying degree of body-disintegration anxiety and a fluctuation of body-ego boundaries, most pronouncedly seen in pedophilia and fetishism. At the center of all of these conditions lies the basic nuclear fear; that is, the fear of merging with and inability to separate from the mother.

The Perversions

Transvestitism

Function: Achieves "femininity" through cross-dressing while retaining penis; reassures against and lessens castration fear; diminishes separation anxiety.

Psychosexual Motivation: Orgastic desire; yearns for femininity: (1) envies mother and sisters; (2) wants to be powerful like mother; (3) wants to have babies; (4) in wearing feminine apparel, experiences a heightening of the pleasure of vicarious feminine identification while retaining the phallus.

Sexual Object Choice or Aim: Person of same or opposite sex. Occasionally no sex object, but sexual aim important (blissful reunion with mother).

Transsexualism

Function: Achieves "femininity" through radical surgical and endocrinological preparations designed to remove all traces of true anatomical gender and to promote enactment of synthetic and assumed feminine role in the environment and in the sexual act; escapes from homosexuality; undergoes the dreaded castration ("riddance phenomenon"); vicariously identifies with the powerful mother, neutralizes fear of her, and consciously enjoys infantile wish for intercourse with the father (the negative Oedipus complex realized); escapes paranoidlike fear of aggression from hostile, stronger men who could damage him in homosexual relations; neutralizes aggression, diminishes separation anxiety.

Psychosexual Motivation: Orgastic desire; consciously yearns for femininity and enacts it with full anatomical reassurance; wishes to displace mother with father.

Sexual Object Choice or Aim: Person of sex prior to elective recasting.

Homosexuality

Function: Male achieves "masculinity" through identification with and incorporation of the male sexual partner; reassures against and lessens castration fear; diminishes separation anxiety.

Psychosexual Motivation: Orgastic desire, yearns and searches for masculinity; narcissistic object choice; tie to mother through breast–penis equation.

Sexual Object Choice or Aim: Person of the same sex.

Pedophilia

Function: Achieves the status of being the "loved" child and also of being the "loving" mother without giving up his penis; discharges and relieves disintegrative aggression;

reassures against and lessens castration fear; diminishes separation anxiety.

Psychosexual Motivation: Orgastic desire; yearns for and desires to become the loved object, the loved child, through incorporation of the "good" love object (the child a substitute for the mother) within the self (splitting of the object), thereby maintaining a relationship to objects and preserving the self through a fused relationship. Also wants to be the child, envies other children.

Sexual Object Choice or Aim: A prepubertal child; if a boy, the ideal representation of the self (homosexual pedophilia); if a girl, the fear and dread of engulfment by the genitalia of the mother is still present, although alleviated by the lack of pubic hair (heterosexual pedophilia).

Exhibitionism

Function: Achieves "masculinity" through the visual reassurance to himself and the emotional reaction of others: "If I show myself to a woman and she reacts, then I am a man and I do not need men (avoids homosexuality) and I am not a female" (defense against feminine identification); reassures against and lessens castration fear; diminishes separation anxiety.

Psychosexual Motivation: Orgastic desire; yearns for masculinity and dramatizes it, simultaneously denies his strong feminine identification.

Sexual Object Choice or Aim: Mode of sexual release (sexual aim) rather than sexual object choice of importance.

Sexual Masochism

Function: Achieves masculine sexual functioning through the playacting of the dreaded event and achieves a "victory" over the hating but seemingly loving mother; reassures against engulfment and destruction, and provokes love responses from the object; vicariously identifies with the cruel, aggressive mother; controls aggression through projective identification; reassures against and lessens castration fear; painful sensory stimulation enhances consolidation of a threatened self representation; diminishes separation anxiety.

Sexual Object Choice or Aim: Person of same or opposite sex.

Sexual Sadism

Function: Forces and extracts love; destroys the threatening body of the mother rather than be destroyed by her; discharges aggressive impulses that threaten annihilation of the self even to the point of sexual murder; achieves temporary freedom from fear of the engulfing mother until next episode of resurgence of fear of the female body; reassures against and lessens castration fear; cancels out separation anxiety.

Psychosexual Motivation: Orgastic desire; to force love from the depriving mother; to overcome body-disintegration anxiety by inflicting rather than by passively enduring pain and destruction (sexual-lust murders often include disembowelment, ripping out of external genitalia and internal generative organs in order to diminish anxiety over engulfment).

Sexual Object Choice or Aim: Person of same or opposite sex, more often adult woman; less commonly a female child or old woman.

Voyeurism

Function: Reinforces masculinity through visual reassurance of the female body and/or heterosexual intercourse (sexual intercourse is taking place outside of himself and he is not being swallowed up through the female's orifices; frequently accompanied by masturbation [exhibitionistic component]); avoids homosexuality and is relieved of castration fear; diminishes separation anxiety.

Psychosexual Motivation: Orgastic desire; dramatizes masculine strength and "control." In some instances voyeurism proceeds from looking to touching to seizing to assaulting and destroying (sexual sadism).

Sexual Object Choice or Aim: Person of the opposite sex.

Fetishism

Function: Achieves "femininity" with the capacity "to have babies"; can be alternately male and female and often does not seek homosexual or heterosexual orgastic release because he can use his fetish; reassures against body-ego dissolution and lessens castration fear; cancels out separation anxiety.

Psychosexual Motivation: Orgastic desire; unconsciously yearns for and search for femininity: (1) wishes to be like mother; (2) wishes to have babies, with resultant body-disintegration anxiety arising from wish for and dread of pregnancy; (3) remains masculine in appearance and attempts to enact the role of the male.

Sexual Object Choice or Aim: The fetish is a durable, inanimate, immobile object or nonsexual part of the body which (1) defends against body-disintegration anxiety and merging phenomena; (2) substitutes for the penis; (3) is a split representation (e.g., can serve either male or female identity—female covering over the body); splitting of the object, hence sexual release (sexual aim) rather than sexual object choice of importance.

Chapter 4

PSYCHOANALYTIC CLASSIFICATION OF SEXUAL PERVERSION

A psychoanalytic classification of any disorder cannot derive from a single frame of reference, such as the symptom alone, whether it be a phobia, a conversion reaction, or a perversion (Rangell, 1965, and Panel, 1960a). Neither can we fully comprehend a condition by a knowledge of the processes of symptom formation, for example, defenses. Rather, as suggested by a panel on nosology (Panel, 1960a), we must adhere to a multidimensional approach. This should include data derived from a number of sources including (1) the level of libidinal fixation or regression (instinctual framework); (2) the stage of maturation, fixation, or regression of the ego (developmental framework); (3) the symptom itself as an "end-product"; (4) the processes of symptom formation; and (5) an inventory of ego functions, including object relations.

The challenge confronting us is to understand not only the different perversions, but clinical forms of the same perversion, from the mildest to the well-structured perversion, to that occurring in an individual with a florid psychosis. Greenacre (1968), in the context of describing genetic and dynamic aspects of perversions, succinctly stated the difficulties facing any investigator. She noted that (1) the multiplicity of forms and varying intensities of the perversion, from the slightly deviant to the extreme or even bizarre, confuse us in understanding its essential character; (2) the analyst usually treats the relatively pronounced cases in which "perverse development is clear and definite" (p. 47); and (3) while careful psychoanalytic investigation of a small number of well-structured cases is very important, "it is nonetheless difficult to accumulate sufficient experience on which to base broader generalizations" (pp. 47–48).

Specific forms of perversion must be seen in relation to other forms. A comprehensive classification system must correlate, integrate, and group many factors in a logical fashion.

Three contributions aimed at describing the origins of sexual perversion set the stage for attempting a comprehensive psychoanalytic classification of perversion: the first by Gillespie (1956a), the second by Greenacre (1968), and the third by this writer (1974a, 1978a). Gillespie's general theory of causation relied heavily on infantile sexuality and affirmed that the problem of perversion lies in the defense against oedipal difficulties (see chapter 3, pp. 39–40). It underscored the concept that in perversion there is a regression of libido and aggression to preoedipal levels rather than a primary fixation at those levels. This theory provided all-important insights into ego defenses, the Sachs mechanism, the role of the superego in perversion formation, splitting processes, and the relation of perversion to psychosis.

In a comprehensive summing up of her extensive clinical research in 1968, Greenacre suggested that:

> [O]ur more recent studies of early ego development would indicate that the fundamental disturbance is . . . that the defectively developed ego uses the pressure of the maturing libidinal phases for its own purposes in characteristic ways because of the extreme and persistent narcissistic needs. . . . Probably in most perversions there is a prolongation of the introjective–projective stage in which there is an incomplete separation of the "I" from the "Other" and an oscillation between the two. This is associated with a more than usually strong capacity for primary identification [Greenacre, 1968, p. 302].

In a 1967 presentation (Socarides, 1978a), I first suggested that the genesis of well-structured perversions, including homosexuality, may well be the result of disturbances which occur earlier than had been generally assumed, namely in the preoedipal phase. In a 1974 article on homosexuality, I divided the homosexualities into oedipal and preoedipal forms, and described the characteristics of each (Socarides, 1974a). In Socarides (1978a) I divided the homosexualities into oedipal form, preoedipal type I and preoedipal type II, and schizohomosexuality. These were considered by me to be the clinical forms of homosexuality, and "situational" and "variational" homosexuality (Rado, 1949) were considered to be nonclinical forms. It appeared increasingly evident that the classification system which I suggested for "the homosexualities" (1978a) could well be applied to the various forms of other perversions. Pedophilia, for example, could be classified in the following way: oedipal pedophilia, preoedipal pedophilia, and schizopedophilia. My classification demonstrated that the same phenomenology may have different structures in different individuals.

The essential ingredient of any perverse act is the unconscious and imperative need to pursue and experience sexual pleasure and orgastic release in a particular manner (sexual aim) or with a specific, particular object. This act expresses, in a distorted way, repressed, forbidden impulses and usually brings temporary relief, either partial or complete, from warring intrapsychic forces. The perverse mechanism for the relief of unconscious conflict exists at any level of libidinal fixation and ego development, from the most primitive to the more highly developed levels of organization. The underlying unconscious motivational drives are distinctly different, depending upon the level from which they arise. Oedipal perverse activity arises from a phallic organization of development and must be differentiated from preoedipal perverse behavior, which arises from preoedipal levels of development. We associate narcissistic neuroses and impulse disorders with the latter. The perverse symptom can operate at an anal level, especially when it represents a regression from genital oedipal-phase conflict.

In the schizophrenic the symptom may represent an archaic and primitive level of functioning, a frantic and chaotic attempt to construct object relations.

There is a wide range of clinical forms of perverse behavior, from those that derive from very archaic, primitive levels to those that are a product of more highly differentiated ones. Each individual case is hierarchically layered with dynamic mechanisms stemming from multiple points of fixation and regression. We can conclude that the clinical picture of the perverse activity itself does not necessarily correctly describe the origin of the particular mechanism responsible for it. This requires a study of the developmental stages through which the individual has passed, the level of fixation, the state of his object relations, and the status of his ego functions.

The General Criteria for Each Form

The classification system presented here derives from the psychoanalytic clinical research study of perverse patients over a thirty-year period. Implicit in its presentation is the author's indebtedness to earlier contributions in this direction. The classification itself has at its core the following concepts: (1) the concept of conscious and/or unconscious motivation; (2) the developmental stage from which the nuclear conflict arose; and (3) the degree of pathology of internalized object relations in the perverse patient.

There are three major forms of clinical overt perverse activity derived from unconscious conflict and not due to situational or variational motivations (leaving aside the latent forms for the moment). They are: (1) preoedipal perversion; (2) oedipal perversion; and (3) schizoperversion (the coexistence of perversion and schizophrenia). In the milder preoedipal type (type I) the surface clinical picture of oedipal conflicts may obscure the deeper and more important preoedipal ones, and regression does not involve severe impairment in object relations and other ego functions. In the more severe preoedipal type (type II), preoedipal fixations are of prime importance, and constantly dominate the psychic life of the individual in his search for identity and a cohesive self. Oedipal conflict and castration fear may defend against deeper fears, and preoedipal fantasies may defend against the emergence of oedipal material. There is always an interplay between the two.

Further refinements in our understanding of the forms of perversion may lead one to conclude that the true perversion is a preoedipal disorder and does not arise from an oedipal conflict with a regression to earlier phases. Oedipal perversion is a different form of deviant sexual behavior which occurs secondary to a temporary regression, does not represent a developmental arrest, and can be treated in similar fashion to a neurosis (Panel, 1976).

The detailed characteristics of each form (in outline) requires some repetition of material presented in chapter 3.

The Preoedipal Forms

1. The preoedipal form is due to a fixation to the preoedipal phase of development from age six months to three years.

2. It is unconsciously motivated and arises from anxiety. Because nonengagement in perverse practices results in anxiety, and because the partner or act is a stereotyped one, it may be termed obligatory perversion. The sexual pattern is inflexible and stereotyped.

3. Severe gender-defined self identity disturbance is present: for example, in a homosexual male there is a faulty and weak masculine identity; in the female homosexual there is a faulty, distorted, and unacceptable feminine identity derived from the mother, who is felt to be hateful and hating. This disturbance in gender-defined self identity is never absent from any well-structured perversion, but may only become apparent when the patient's unconscious material is subjected to close analytic scrutiny.

The persistence of the primary feminine identification is a consequence of the inability to traverse the separation–individuation phase and develop a separate and independent identity from the mother.

4. Perverts of the preoedipal type are beset by anxieties of an insistent and intractable nature, leading to an overrid-

ing, almost continual search for sexually perverse actions.

5. Persistence of primitive and archaic mental mechanisms leads to an abundance of incorporation and projection anxieties.

6. The anxiety which develops is due to fears of engulfment, ego dissolution, and a loss of self and ego boundaries, dissolution of the self, self fragmentation and/or separation anxiety, "identity diffusion" (Erikson, 1950). These patients need the perverse act in order to insure ego survival and transiently stabilize the sense of self. Consequently, they must repeat the act frequently, out of an inner necessity to ward off intense anxiety. (The rare exceptions in this type who cannot consciously accept the perverse acts struggle mightily against it and, therefore, the symptom remains latent, as explained in the section on latent forms of perversion.)

7. The perverse symptom is ego-syntonic, as the nuclear conflicts, including fear of engulfment, loss of ego boundaries, disturbance of self cohesion, have undergone a transformation through the mechanism of the repressive compromise, allowing the more acceptable part of infantile sexuality to remain in consciousness (Sachs mechanism).

8. There is a predominance of pregenital characteristics of the ego: remembering is often replaced by acting out, and so on.

9. The aim of the perverse act is ego survival. In addition, in the male homosexual there is a reconstitution of a sense of sexual identity in accordance with anatomy. The male achieves "masculinity" through identification with the male sexual partner; this lessens castration fear. The female achieves "resonance identification" with the woman partner; this lessens castration fear. She also creates the "good" mother–child relationship. Other perverse activities have well-delineated functions in addition to those of ego survival.

10. The subtypes of preoedipal perversions (preoedipal type I, preoedipal type II) can be defined and differentiated by the degree of pathology of internalized object relations. The solution to this complex problem of separating the various types of preoedipal perversion has been facilitated by

Kernberg's important work (1975) defining criteria for understanding borderline conditions and pathological narcissism. In utilizing this approach the meaning of oedipal perversion is increasingly clarified as well.

In the milder preoedipal form type I, while the preoedipal fixation is etiological, the clinical picture may be largely one of oedipal-phase conflict and regression, and does not involve severe impairment in object relations or other ego functions. In the more severe preoedipal form type II, an earlier preoedipal fixation is of prime importance both etiologically and clinically, constantly dominating the psychic life of the individual in his search for identity and a cohesive self (see chapter 9 for a description of preoedipal form type II in a homosexual man with associated narcissistic personality disorder proper). Oedipal conflict and castration fears may defend against deeper fears, and preoedipal fantasies may defend against the emergence of oedipal material (Hoffer, 1954). In preoedipal type II perverse patients there is usually an associated narcissistic personality disorder of various degrees of severity. The analysis of such patients leads me to conclude that the fixation of these patients lies in the practicing and differentiating subphase of the separation–individuation process (see chapter 9). I owe to Kernberg (1980a) a scientific debt of gratitude for his division of the spectrum of narcissistic pathology into "most severe or lowest level, middle range, highest level of functioning" (p. 29). These ranges appear to be at least in part related to the "extent to which aggression has been integrated into the pathological grandiose self or, to the contrary, remains restricted to the underlying dissociated and/or repressed primitive object relations against which the pathological grandiose self represents the main defensive structure" (Kernberg, 1980a, p. 29).

At the highest level of functioning, the patient with specific narcissistic pathology (my preoedipal type I pervert) may show (1) no neurotic symptoms; (2) good surface adaptation; (3) little awareness of any emotional illness except a chronic sense of emptiness and boredom; (4) may appear quite creative in his field (and highly intellectual), but is superficial and flighty in his relationships. He may come to treatment in middle or advanced age, secondary to the development of chronic depressive reactions, and almost never for his homosexuality. In addition to emptiness and boredom, other symptoms include an immediate need for approval from others. His predominant defenses may be denial, devaluation, and hypomanic episodes as a defense against depression.

The middle range of pathology (and the middle range of functioning) are those individuals diagnosed as narcissistic personality disorder proper. They correspond to my preoedipal type II homosexual patients with associated narcissistic personality disorder. Their surface function shows very little disturbance except with diagnostic exploration. Their symptoms are: (1) excessive degree of self-reference in interaction with others; (2) excessive need to be loved and admired; (3) a curious contradiction between the inflated concept of self and occasional feelings of inferiority; (4) inordinate need for tribute from others; (5) a shallow emotional life; (6) "remarkable absence of the capacity for an integrated conception of others" (Kernberg, 1980a, p. 26)—while they usually present an integration of a sort of their own conscious self-experience which differentiates them from borderline personality organization patients (Kernberg, 1980a), in a sense they feel little empathy for others; (7) their relationship to others is characterized by inordinate envy; (8) they idealize those from whom they expect narcissistic supplies, and treat with contempt those from whom they don't expect anything (often, former idols); (9) their relationship to others is exploitative and parasitic, charmingly engaging, but beneath this facade they are cold and ruthless. As regards their affective life, they are restless and bored when there are no sources to feed their self-regard. They may appear dependent because of their need for adoration and tribute, but in reality they are unable to depend on anyone due to their own feelings of (a) underlying distrust, and (b) a devaluation unconsciously spoiling what they receive due to conflicts around unconscious envy.

The defenses in the middle range of narcissistic pathology are a predominance of the same primitive defensive operations that characterize borderline personality organization (e.g., splitting, development of pathological grandiose self, and so on).

Perverse patients who have the severest degree of narcissistic pathology may be considered the lowest level in the spectrum of narcissistic pathology. Pathological grandiosity is very prominent, but there is some continuity in social interactions in the presence of overt borderline features. Overt borderline features are (1) generalized impulsivity; (2) lack of anxiety tolerance; (3) disposition to explosive or dissociative rage reactions; and (4) severely paranoid distortions of their interpersonal field. This individual may engage in "joyful types of cruelty" (Kernberg, 1980a), self-mutilation, express a combination of paranoid and explosive personality traits, rage, attacks, and blaming others. If aggression has been integrated into some existing superego functions, they show a capacity for depression and/or self-directed aggression. They also function as "as-if" personalities, in which case the as-if personality is a secondary defense against the pathological grandiose self. In this, the worst type of pervert with narcissistic pathology, we see "dissociative, aggressively invested part-object relations directly manifest" (Kernberg, 1980a, p. 30). This is accompanied by condensation of partial sexual drives, so that sadistically infiltrated polymorphous perverse fantasies and activities are strongly manifest. Furthermore, "when such primitive aggression directly infiltrates the pathological grandiose self, a particularly ominous development occurs, characterological sadism" (Kernberg, 1980a, p. 30). It is in this instance where we find perversions practiced in which direct sadistic pleasure and aggression are linked with sexual drive derivatives. Kernberg refers to these patients as suffering from a "malignant perversion" (Kernberg, 1984b). It is important to differentiate the borderline (the most severe range of narcissistic pathology) from the narcissistic personality disorder structure proper, for in the former an unwelcome and uncontrolled aggression emerges in the transference which unfortunately may militate against the patient's intrapsychic change (Kernberg, 1980a, p. 31). In less severe narcissistic pathology, however:

[T]he grandiose self is remarkably free from direct expressed aggression, and repressive mechanisms protect the
patient against the underlying primitive object relations
that condense sexual and aggressive drive derivatives. In
these cases "narcissistic rage" or paranoid reactions develop in later stages of the treatment, as part of the therapeutic process, and have much less ominous implications
[Kernberg, 1980a, p. 31].

Furthermore, as regards treatment, in cases "where
aggression has been integrated into some existing superego
structures" [Kernberg, 1980a, p. 31], we have a clinically
more favorable type of therapeutic situation. In addition, in
some of the higher-level functioning narcissistic personalities, the high and middle range may have arrived at some
capacity for sublimation and integration of aggression into
adaptive ego functions, so that therapeutic goals may be
appropriately pursued. Kernberg notes, as regards therapy,
that in those cases in which an as-if personality predominates, we may find beneath this defensive constellation
"very severe paranoid fears, less frequently from unconscious guilt" [Kernberg, 1980a, p. 32].

In the preceding material I have not attempted an explanation for the *development* of the narcissistic personality
disorder nor the development of the grandiose self. There are
several views on this subject, including those of Kohut,
Kernberg, Volkan, and others. This may be due to a disturbance in an independent line of development from autoerotism via narcissism to a mature self (Kohut's theory, 1971,
1977) or due to a pathological development as outlined by
Kernberg (1970, 1975). Both Kernberg and Kohut agree that
there is a cohesiveness of the self in narcissistic personality
disorders which differentiates them from borderline organization, although in both primitive splitting dominates as a
defense. Volkan has noted that primitive splitting refers to
keeping apart contradictory ego states that include self
representations, object representations, and their affects
(Volkan, 1976). He asserts that the pathology lies in the fact
that:

[T]he early ego has a developmental defect in integrating early "good" and "bad" self- and object-images that reflect the child's pleasurable and unpleasurable interactions with the mothering person and are thus contaminated respectively with libidinal and aggressive drive derivatives. If "bad" units are excessively loaded with aggression, the simple defect in integration becomes a defensive organization that keeps "good" self-images apart from "bad" in order to keep them intact. The unacceptable aspects of the real self, disparaged external objects and their representations, and sadistic superego forerunners are primitively split in a narcissistic personality [Volkan, 1976, p. 134].

Volkan also feels that these patients, effectively use repression with primitive splitting.

The Oedipal Form

1. The oedipal form is due to a failure to resolve the Oedipus complex and to castration fears, leading to the adoption of a negative oedipal position and a partial regression to anal and oral conflicts (a partial preoedipal regression). In homosexuality, the male assumes the role of the female with the father (other man); the female assumes the role of the male with the mother (other woman). In oedipal transvestitism, the male assumes the role of the female with the father (other men), recasting himself (without change of genital) into a woman (the mother).

2. In this oedipal form perverse wishes are unconsciously motivated and dreaded; engagement in perverse practices is not obligatory. The sexual pattern is flexible in that heterosexuality is usually the conscious choice, but for intrapsychic reasons cannot be practiced at the time.

3. Gender-defined self identity disturbances in the male (or deficient feminine sexual identity in the female) is due to a secondary identification with the person (parent) of the opposite sex. This is simply a reversal of normal sexual identification in the direction of the same-sex parent.

4. The male develops anxiety due to fears of penetration by the more powerful male (father); the female fears rejection by the more powerful female (mother). Common to both are conscious and unconscious shame and guilt arising from the superego and conflicts when such practices are engaged in or occur in dreams (since there has been no splitting of the superego or ego). Perverse acts of the oedipal form are attempts to insure dependency, to attain power through the seduction of the more powerful partner in homosexuality. The motivations in other oedipal perverse acts can be similarly delineated.

5. Primitive and archaic pyschic mechanisms may appear due to regression. They are intermittent and do not indicate pregenital character of the individual, as they do in preoedipal form.

6. The perverse symptom is ego-alien. Although unconsciously determined, the anxieties which are held in repression through the Sachs mechanism are not those concerned with primitive archaic conflicts and fixations or arise from a persistence of the primary feminine identification. When the symptom threatens to break into awareness, anxiety develops. However, under certain conditions—for example, defiant rage overriding the restraining mechanisms of conscience, or periods of intense depression secondary to loss with resultant needs for love, admiration, and strength from a person of the same sex—deviant acts may take place. Such acts, however, do not achieve the magical symbolic restitution of the preoedipal form. They may exacerbate the situation through loss of pride and self-esteem.

Perverse acts of the oedipal form may occur, especially in group situations, where the superego of the patient has been projected onto a leader of a group who acts as a collective superego. This promotes sexual acting out (Sperling, 1956).

7. The aim of the perverse act is to gratify dependency needs, to acquire security from "powerful" figures of the same sex (in homosexuality). In pedophilia, the function is to achieve the status of being both the "loved" child and the "loving mother" without giving up one's penis; in male transsexualism the motivation is a yearning for femininity

and its enactment with a full anatomical reassurance that one "is" of the opposite sex, together with a wish to displace mother with the father.

The sexual pattern of the negative oedipal form is not as inflexible or stereotyped as in the preoedipal form. There are remissions in the sense of masculine identity in the male, and in the sense of pride and achievement in feminine identity in the female, secondary to successful performance in other (nonsexual) areas of life. An increase in self-esteem, success, and power may diminish any fantasied or actual enjoyment in perverse sexual practices in these patients.

The Latent Form

1. The latent form has the underlying psychic structure of either the preoedipal or oedipal form, without perverse practices.

2. The latent perverse individual may or may not have any conscious knowledge of his preference for orgastic fulfillment of a perverse nature. On the other hand, there may be a high level of elaboration of unconscious perverse fantasies and perverse dream material, with or without conscious denial of its significance. These individuals may live an entire lifetime without actualizing their perverse propensities.

3. Another pattern is that of the individual who, fully aware of his perverse preference, abstains from all perverse acts. Others, as a result of severe stress, infrequently and transiently do engage in overt perverse acts, living the major portion of their lives, however, as latent perverse individuals. In the latent phase, they may maintain a limited heterosexual functioning, albeit unrewarding, meager, and usually based on perverse fantasies. They may utilize perverse fantasies for masturbatory practices, or may abstain from sexual activity altogether. These individuals are suffering from a perversion at all times; the shift between latent and overt, and the reverse, constitutes an alternating form of sexual perversion.

Schizoperversions

Schizoperverse individuals are those perverse individuals whose fixation point is in the symbiotic phase. Accordingly, their symptom is part and parcel of a psychotic condition. Of overriding importance is the treatment of the schizophrenic decompensation with its associated delusions, hallucinations, ideas of reference, and other secondary symptoms of schizophrenia. With a return to a compensated state of schizophrenic adaptation, their perverse symptoms may remain unaltered alongside their primary symptoms of schizophrenia. Paranoia and paranoid symptomatology are striking features in such cases.

The history of schizoperverse individuals, the emergence of their symptoms, and the enactment of their perversion on superficial examination bear striking similarities to preoedipal perverse individuals, type II. For example, in similar fashion to preoedipal type II patients, there is an early intense fixation to the mother; severe separation and fragmentation anxiety; early pronounced feminine identification; severe difficulties in relating to the opposite sex from earliest years; perverse sexual interests beginning in childhood. Such manifestations should, however, be viewed against the backdrop of the degree of ego pathology present, which is strikingly dissimilar from that found in preoedipal type II perverse individuals, especially of the higher or middle range (Kernberg, 1975). The presence of overt psychotic symptoms obviously militates against confusing the two. The differences between schizoperversion and preoedipal perversion, briefly noted in chapter 3, require fuller explanation here. They were brilliantly defined by Bak (1971) in his paper "Object Relationships in Schizophrenia and Perversion." He noted:

1. Perverse conflicts and their delusional elaborations are "consequences of a schizophrenic process rather than its cause" (p. 239).

2. In true perversions (preoedipal forms), object relations are maintained despite a "fused body image or fused genital representation," in contrast to perverse activity in the schizophrenic where they are not maintained (p. 242).

3. Perverse impulses, as well as other sexual impulses, are a frantic attempt to *create* object relations in schizophrenia.

4. Perverse impulses so often seen in paranoid schizophrenics are not "etiological"; these conflicts and their delusional elaboration are "consequences of the schizophrenic process rather than causative of it" (p. 242).

5. *Paranoid delusions with perverse content* often occur in schizophrenics. In those instances, however, an object relationship may be highly pathological and yet nevertheless be preserved. The delusions are an attempt to maintain object relations in the face of (a) severe regression; (b) attempted destruction of object relations; (c) the presence of primary defect or deficiency in the autonomous functions of the ego; and (d) the inability to maintain a protective stimulus barrier. If the regression is severe, the delusional content contains a less experiential basis, and a systematized delusion similar to that found in paranoia cannot be formed or maintained.

6. There is a basic qualitative difference between the schizophrenic process, and perversions and the neuroses and the incidental psychoses. In the "incidental psychosis" (Bak, 1971), there is only a temporary abandonment of object representation.

Schizoperversion may be explained by its relationship to autistic and symbiotic modes of adaptation. This connotes a fixation at the autistic and/or symbiotic phase in order to ward off the fear of dissolution of the self representation through reengulfment by the mother and somatopsychic fusion. This is in striking contrast to the fixation in preoedipal form type I which has taken place during the later phases of the separation–individuation process, and preoedipal type II, whose fixation may now be seen to occur in earlier subphases; for example, practicing and differentiating.

Object Relations and the Degree of Pathology in Perversions

The object relations of the preoedipal type I patient are mildly impaired and are from object to self; for example, in homosexuality the homosexual object stands for the self, in pedophilia the child also stands for the self. Such a patient has a conflictual identification (due to lack of separation) with the preoedipal mother, and in homosexuality he "loves" his partner as he himself wished to be loved by the mother, but reacts to him with sadistic aggression as once felt toward the hostile mother for forcing separation. (A similar relationship exists in other perversions.) This relationship is also a "narcissistic" one, and is especially evident in homosexuality, as originally suggested by Freud (1914). Preoedipal type I homosexuality, for example, connotes a more complete form of object relationship in contradistinction to that found in preoedipal type II homosexuals in whom the object relation is from pathological grandiose self to self; that is, from the self to "self" (Kernberg, 1975). In the latter, the homosexual partner is loved as an extension of the patient's own pathological grandiose self, and is most commonly found in association with narcissistic personality disorder structure proper. For these reasons I have suggested that these patients be designated preoedipal type II narcissistic homosexuals. Similarly, such pedophile patients may be designated as preoedipal type II narcissistic pedophiles, and so on.

The relationship to the object in all forms of perversion may be described as "narcissistic," whether they are of the oedipal or the preoedipal type I or II variety, since the object is a narcissistic one, that is, it represents the self. This may be obvious in cases of homosexuality, but less so in fetishism, pedophilia, voyeurism, transsexualism, transvestism, and other perversions. The fetish, for example, represents the self free from disintegration and fragmentation, it embodies a feminine identification with the mother (with or without the phallus) (Socarides, 1960); the unwilling object in voyeurism represents the feminine phallic self (Socarides, 1974b); the young prepubertal boy, the object of such importunate desire, is the idealized self of childhood (Socarides, 1959); transvestitism, a merger and fusion with the preoedipal phallic mother–self (Socarides, 1980b).

Let us examine how this hypothesis (of "narcissistic" relationship) applies to homosexuality. For example, in *oedipal* homosexuality, a patient regresses to a narcissistic object choice in a negative oedipal situation in which there is a partial projection of the self onto an "object similar to the self" (Kernberg, 1975). This goes hand in hand with object-libidinal ties to such an object, a "relation between self and object both intrapsychically and in external interaction" (p. 324). In preoedipal type I patients, there is a regression or fixation to an infantile—in contrast to a more mature—libidinal investment of self and object. This is carried out "under the condition of an identification of the self with an object, while the self is projected onto an external object it is loved because it stands for the self" (p. 324). This is in conformity with Freud's (1914) earlier equation that such an individual loves according to his narcissistic type: "(a) what he himself is (himself), (b) what he himself was, (c) what he himself would like to be, (d) someone who was once part of his self" (Freud, 1914, p. 90). In preoedipal type II patients, "the investment of objects representing the projected grandiose self is usually transitory and superficial with a lack of awareness in depth or empathy for the object" (Kernberg, 1975, p. 330). The object and its individual and autonomous characteristics are completely hidden by "a temporary projection of the grandiose self onto it" (Kernberg, 1975, p. 325); in essence a narcissistic relationship has *replaced* the object relationship. I have found that similar object relationships exist in oedipal and preoedipal forms of sadomasochism, fetishism, transsexualism, transvestism, voyeurism, and so on. When a "narcissistic relationship" replaces a true object relationship, we are faced with serious transference problems and a poorer prognosis until object relatedness can be established at a later point in therapy. Unlike schizoperverts, preoedipal type II narcissistic perverts have not, however, suffered a complete loss of internal object representations, nor are they striving to fill up the feeling of a terrible void by creating new objects through their perversion (Bak, 1971; Kernberg, 1975; Socarides, 1978b).

Preoedipal Type II Perverse Patients

Pathological Grandiosity

At this point I would like to acknowledge my indebtedness to Kernberg's theoretical formulation that the spectrum of pathology in individuals with preoedipal disorders can best be understood when examined from the vantage point of the *degree* of self–object differentiation achieved. Each stage of self–object fixation/differentiation, whether symbiotic, differentiating or practicing, or rapprochement, produces its unique clinical features, although overlapping of features may occur (Kernberg, 1980c). In preoedipal type II perverts, I have found, self–object differentiation is severely impaired, and the self is only just emerging as autonomous and its cohesiveness greatly damaged by resultant "identity diffusion" (Erikson, 1950; Kernberg, 1975). The predominant anxiety in these patients is of fragmentation related to an imperilled self representation, in contrast to that of separation anxiety seen in preoedipal type I patients. Fragmentation anxiety all but obscures the separation anxiety and "separation guilt" (Modell, 1965) arising from the unresolved mother–infant tie. A vitally important clinical finding is that fixation in the practicing and differentiating phases produces deficiencies in the self representation with a tendency to develop grandiosity. Pathological grandiosity produces a clinical picture in which the perverse patient may appear more integrated, less conflicted, more at ease with himself, and less distressed, especially when he is in narcissistic balance and not challenged by external reality. Beneath this facade of normality, it is apparent that the patient is unable to discriminate between the realistic and the fantasied aspects of the self, is incapable of participating in activities that do not protect his grandiosity, and avoids those that threaten it. He tends to withdraw from others and continually overvalues or devalues both himself and the social reality surrounding him. All activities which are not in the service of enhancing his grandiosity are avoided, postponed, delayed, not responded to, and aborted.

These individuals often seek psychoanalytic help when

they are in a state of narcissistic decompensation (i.e., are experiencing threats of regressive fragmentation), or when grandiose fantasies of success have failed to produce expected rewards. When they view their perverse sexuality as a distinctly severe social disadvantage (i.e., an affront to their concept of perfection and ideal behavior), or when the intensity of the need for perverse enactment is so severe that they are continually occupied with its performance, and increasingly depressed and discouraged by being unable to form lasting relationships to anyone including sexual partners, they may seek our help (see chapter 10). Others may be sent for consultation under threats of legal punishment (e.g., in pedophilia, exhibitionism, voyeurism, and sexual sadism).

Disturbance in Superego Formation and Freedom from Internal Conflict

Since sufficient structuralization of the psychic apparatus has not taken place, these patients show a marked absence of internal conflict. Their behavior is not regulated by a superego identified with the moral power of the parents (moral self-regulation), since the patients have not developed beyond the "first stage of superego formation" (Sandler, 1960). Instead, they "evoke and employ object representations to comfort, punish, control or guide their activities in a manner similar to [but less reliable than] superego formation" (Dorpat, 1976, p. 871). The severe deficits in ego and superego formation create a crisis in their overall functioning, for they are unable to carry out the acts of comforting, controlling, guiding, approving, and so on, which "individuals with a structured superego and ego are able to do for themselves" (p. 871). This dilemma is temporarily resolved by using external objects (selfobjects), including *sexual selfobjects*, whose function is to substitute for missing structures and the functions they perform. The narcissistic (selfobject) transferences (mirroring and merging) encountered in psychoanalytic therapy are manifestations of this underlying developmental defect. Furthermore, the absence/presence of a defective superego (an automatic self-regulatory conscience mechanism) may create serious therapeutic obstacles as these patients may remain unaffected as regards alleviation/removal of their perverse practices, at least temporarily, through the transference relationship.

Defenses in a Primitive Stage of Development with Splitting Predominating over Repression

The defenses of preoedipal type II patients are in the prestages of development (Stolorow and Lachmann, 1978), and splitting predominates over repression. In preoedipal type I patients, in contrast, repression predominates with some splitting phenomena, but the major defense mechanisms are introjection, projection, and identification. The pathological use of splitting is due to a fixation to or defect in the developmental process, interfering with the sense of identity and development of object constancy. While splitting may be found in the rapprochement subphase of the separation–individuation process (Mahler, 1971), there is more primitive splitting occurring in the practicing and differentiating subphases. Kohut (1971) describes two types of splitting: (1) "vertical splitting," which produces a side-by-side "dissociation of mental contents" that keeps primitive, archaic, grandiose, exhibitionistic impulses dissociated from reality functioning; and (2) a "horizontal" form of splitting which separates the "reality ego from unfulfilled narcissistic desires by virtue of repression" (p. 240). Differing from Kohut, Kernberg believes that the motive force behind splitting seems to be due to separate negative and positive charged self and object representations in order to protect the ego core from destructive aggression (Kernberg, 1975).

The controversy over the meaning of the splitting phenomenon highlights the apparently insoluble debate arising from alternative views of pathogenesis of preoedipal disturbances; for example, developmental deficit versus conflict-induced distortions. I do not intend at this point to describe the crucial theoretical differences between the two major camps except to note three of them: (1) whether these individuals remain fixated on an archaic grandiose self and archaically, narcissistically cathected objects unrelated to any vicissitudes of aggression; (2) whether the *grandiose self* (a term coined by Kohut in a different theoretical framework than Kernberg's) is a compensation for early experience of severe oral deprivation, rage, and envy, or is simply a fixation on an "archaic, normal primitive self" (Panel 1973); and (3) whether the shifts between idealization and devaluation (including self devaluation) are defenses against rage, envy, paranoidal ideation, and guilt over aggression directed against frustrating parental images, or are partly manifestations of absence *and/or* a deficiency in the psychological structure that maintains a self representation and the functional use of objects for sustaining an object relationship and the response to its loss. Both theoretical points of view have yielded significant insights into the structures of the ego of the perverse individual.

Self-Object Differentiation

Equal in importance to comprehending the degree of pathology of internalized object relations and the severity of narcissistic pathology and its relation to the formation of a pathological grandiose self, is ascertaining the degree of self-object differentiation that has been achieved by a particular perverse patient. I shall contrast the characteristics of self-object differentiation of a preoedipal type I and a preoedipal type II patient. Careful attention to these differences leads to greater understanding of the symptomatology, transferences, resistances, stages of defense, and the therapeutic outcome. In the following material I apply Kernberg's object relations theory and its correlation to Mahler's separation–individuation phases (Kernberg, 1980c, pp. 105–117) to the structure of types of perversions.

The following are characteristic of the status of self-object differentiation in preoedipal type I patients: (1) the self is nearly separated from the object; (2) there is some splitting-off of aspects of the self and object representations; (3) the focus of treatment concerns itself with the integration of split-off *aspects* of self and object representations (Kernberg, 1980c). The key characteristics of this type of patient as regards the clinical manifestations of the degree of his self-object differentiation are: (1) gradually emerging autonomous self must be protected from engulfment by the mother; (2) further integration of the split-off aspects of the self and object representations has taken place; (3) the issue, both from the point of view of the nuclear pathology and treatment, is that of the nonintegrated self versus the integrated self; (4) reality testing is nearly established in a quite firm manner. Defenses are not predominantly centered around splitting, but around repression, introjection, and projection. The transference is from object to self; the "self" is narcissistically chosen with a minimal degree of grandiosity and without a well-structured, pathological grandiose self. Regressive fragmentation is not as severe or as deep as in those patients who are fixated in the phase of differentiation and/or practicing. Primitive defenses are not usually called into play, nor are there frequent dramatic crises in the analytic sessions, except on rare occasions involving bodily dissolution, regressive fragmentation, and regressive reenactment of rapprochement phase struggles.

In preoedipal type II perverts, fixation is in the early separation subphases of the separation–individuation process (e.g., differentiation and practicing phases); the earlier the fixation, the closer to borderline personality organization and the presence of severe ego weakness or defects. (These are present to a minimal degree in preoedipal type I patients.) What are the clinical manifestations and characteristics found with this degree of self–object differentiation? (1) there is a gradually emerging autonomous self; (2) there is a splitting of "good" and "bad" objects; (3) the focus of treatment is to promote a "holding" environment (Winnicott, 1965)—promoting an empathic context while permitting the patient to retain autonomy vis-á-vis the therapist. In treatment, temporal continuity is often lost, a distorted perception of others occurs, and very little empathy is shown; in short, relations are often chaotic and shallow. The key characteristics of preoedipal type II patients are: (1) regression and/or fixation to the subphase of differentiation; (2) splitting of "good" and "bad" self and object representations; (3) the issue both pathologically and therapeutically is between the true versus the false self; (4) the major and characteristic anxiety of this type is the tendency to "identity diffusion" (Erikson, 1950; Kernberg, 1980b). The term *identity diffusion* may be equated with Kohut's term *impairment in self cohesion* or threats of fragmentation. Characteristically, such patients with severely imperilled self cohesion have a poorly integrated concept of self and significant others; chronic subjective feelings of emptiness; contradictory self perceptions; contradictory behavior that the patient cannot intregrate; shallow, flat, or impoverished perception of others (Kernberg, 1975, p. 8); a pathological grandiose self which obscures the underlying identity diffusion; that is, the inadequate cohesion. In effect, the pathological grandiose self + splitting mechanisms = the diagnosis of narcissistic personality disorder.

The type of transference and the degree of regression are typical of the differentiation subphase; that is, mirroring and merging transferences (in Kohut's terminology, *selfobject transferences*, or *primitive narcissistic transferences* in Kernberg's terminology). The patient uses the therapist as a transference object, a selfobject. He is unable to achieve object constancy; that is, he is unable to maintain a representation of the "good" object, especially under the impact of being frustrated by it, or where he is not mirrored, reflected, or admired by the analyst.

These primitive transferences (Kernberg, 1980b, p. 155) reflect the internalized object relations of these patients, a defensive constellation of self and object representations directed against an *opposite* and dreaded, repressed self and object constellation.

As regards regression, there is a tendency in preoedipal type II patients to regressive fragmentation of the self cohesion. The patient usually is able, however, to maintain reality testing with the analyst despite transference regressions, and the analysis of these regressions may ultimately facilitate the restoration of reality. In some instances such regressive transferences involve prolonged periods of psychosislike transference manifestations with the analyst representing the split-off part of the bad self with a pronounced degree of aggression aimed at the analyst.

In such patients defenses are primitive and centered

around splitting. They are, in a sense, a prestage of defense (Stolorow and Lachmann, 1978). During this phase of treatment, two major mechanisms dominating the psychoanalytic sessions are coercion and splitting of the object world.

From the foregoing it should follow that fixations in subphases antecedent to the rapprochement have certain particular consequences of a severe nature. For example, a preoedipal type II pervert (1) engages in splitting rather than repression as a major defense mechanism; (2) does not suffer from guilt but may develop shame; (3) is subject to powerful regressions in contrast to preoedipal type I patients; (4) searches for idealized selfobjects to represent his grandiose self, and responds with bouts of aggression and periods of regression if these needs are not met; (5) has part-object relations rather than whole-object relations; (6) suffers from a fragmented body image and is subject to feelings of dissolving and disappearing, in contrast to a much more stable body image in preoedipal type I patients; (7) experiences grandiosity, omnipotence, and demands for flawlessness due to the infiltration of the ego-ideal with these characteristics. He may be surrounded by what has been termed a "narcissistic state of consciousness" (Bach, 1977) (see chapter 9). Preoedipal type II patients appear to have a seriously defective or absent superego, and their activities at best are held together by certain idealizations. When the idealizations fail or the idealized object fails him, the patient is capable of engaging in behavior bordering on sociopathy and intense if not murderous hostility in many instances.

Perverse Sexual Activity

In preoedipal type II narcissistic perverts, the patient attempts to find a tranquil integrity of being through perverse acts; in a sense, to settle a crisis of diffusion of the self through soothing experiences which he insistently and imperatively pursues without any concerns for the demands of reality (a good example is provided in chapter 9). The often insatiable and voracious sexual acts function as a substitute for action in the external world, helping him to fill a void created by the inability to take part in life.

The sexual acts do not function as a prophylactic device in response to a fear of object loss or fear of losing the object's love, nor are they due to sensitivity to approval or disapproval by the parents or parental surrogates so typical of rapprochement phase conflict seen in preoedipal type I patients. Instead, these acts serve to diminish the defect in the self and supply the self with stimulation. For example, Willard, a fifty-year-old preoedipal type II narcissistic homosexual (see chapter 9), states: "There are specific ways in which I am intrinsically incomplete and need to be completed in sexual action. I need to find an idealized person in the partner. I care about being accepted by these men and being one of them, but they are used by me to do certain functions that I cannot perform." It is not the individual himself he desires, because the partner is insignificant or interchangeable.

> I am trying to accomplish something that I can't do by myself, despite the intensity and hotness of my passion. The only thing I want is that I set the time and I set the place, and they relate to me as much as I want them to, and I don't have to relate to them any more than I wish to. That seems to be the significant and governing factor.

The sexual object is in effect similar to a transitional object in that it must show a readiness to comply, lend itself to be manipulated, used, abused, discarded, cherished, symbolically identified with, but must not intrude upon him. Unlike the sexual object in preoedipal type I cases who is "loved" according to the model of "narcissistic love" (Freud, 1914), it must surrender itself to his omnipotent control, must wish to provide him with something, do something to show its vitality and reality, and must supply warmth and comfort to him.

In all such perverts, through acting out and mobilizing interest on the part of the partner with imaginative sharing and playacting activities, the "deadness" of the internal world is ameliorated and the fragmented self is temporarily healed (Khan, 1965). Preliminary to sexual relations these patients may experience overexcitement, depletion, and depression, archaic defenses against sadism and aggression. They attempt to resolve this internal despair through restitution and restoration by giving pleasure to a real external object and to the self simultaneously (Khan, 1965). In this connection Willard explains: "I'm trying to put something right in myself, something that I didn't get as a child. I'm trying to get back my relationship with my mother and my father, also with other people, even as a child." He desires to produce a "big involvement" in order to find a "place to put emotions which I don't know where to place." The lack of emotional sustenance and depth present in these patients, making for a deep maladjustment throughout their lives, is remedied by producing pleasurable excitement and thrills in the partner so that the patient finds himself in the reflection of the partner's responses. At that moment he may feel emotion. Willard states:

> I will spoil him with my financial ability and he will spoil me with his beauty, charm, sweetness, easiness to relate, and his desire to compensate me for what I give him. . . . Seeing the situation in that light, I'm looking forward to it with pure joy, with delight, and with great reassurance. It means that the quest that I make through homosexuality will have temporarily resolved itself and it will no longer be necessary. . . . For some little while this quest will be temporarily satisfied within me.

However, such "cures" are short-lived. The pleasure experienced soon wears off, and such patients compare themselves to the Flying Dutchman, doomed never to find a place where they can rest, left homeless when the responsiveness of the partner or his availability ceases. This leads to an endless pursuit of partners and repetitious perverse sexual acts. When the pervert loses his sexual object, it is not the loss of the object nor the loss of the object's love which the pervert grieves for. He feels the anguish of the child, undernourished to the point of starvation, who has lost a self–object response that keeps him whole and complete and free of fragmentation. For example, Willard, in narrating such an event to the analyst, was again immediately reduced to tears and sobbing in response to the analyst's empathic comment. "I believe it is some sort of ideal representation of myself in him, and that all the things he does for me are ways for me to complete myself and to feel alive and in reality."

Preoedipal type II narcissistic patients with perversion develop anxiety and the need to engage in their perversion when their self cohesion, rendered fragile by developmental interferences, reinforced by the internal image of an omnipotent and flawless archaic, grandiose self, encounters situations which make them acutely and painfully aware of the discrepancy between the actual self and the wishful grandiose self (an external conflict). This is experienced as a *traumatic exposure* with intense feelings of inferiority leading to feelings of rebuff, humiliation, self fragmentation, and threats to self cohesion. As one of the attempted solutions to this crisis, the patient attempts to restore self cohesion by engaging in primitive perverse acts. In contrast, preoedipal type I patients experience anxiety and guilt associated with separation due to the fear of the loss of the maternal object's love or separation from it (internalized conflict). The fear of engulfment by the mother leads them to perverse acts.

All preoedipal type II narcissistic patients show: (1) a profound damage to the nascent emergence of the self, and (2) associated severe disruption of the process of self–object differentiation. These patients are prone to regressive fragmentation, in contrast to preoedipal type I patients who are well on the road to object constancy.

Transference and Therapeutic Considerations

In the transference, preoedipal type II narcissistic patients are unable to maintain a representation of the "good object," especially under the impact of being frustrated by it, or when they are not mirrored, admired, or reflected by the analyst. These are "primitive transferences" (Kernberg, 1975) reflecting the state of the patient's internalized object relations. For example, my homosexual patient, Willard, often viewed himself as a submissive, impotent person vis-à-vis a powerful and protective maternal object image; or, at other times, his self representation consisted of a rebellious, repressed self vis-à-vis a sadistic and controlling parental imago. These self representational units are dyads of split objects and split self.

While there is a strong tendency for these patients to fragmentation of their self cohesion, they are able to maintain reality testing despite psychoticlike transference regressions. In contrast, preoedipal type I patients form transferences from object to self, the self representing an ideal self-image in the person of the object. The patient is eventually able to maintain a representation of the good object, even when frustrated by it, does not require constant mirroring or merging, and does not easily regress.

In the therapy of these patients we must treat the severe narcissistic character disorder proper as well as the perversion. Specific transference problems arise because of the patient's pathological grandiosity. Mirroring and merging transferences and attacks of full-blown narcissistic rage occur toward the analyst. In time, the full-blown narcissistic transference ultimately must be replaced by a transference neurosis. In these patients who suffer from severe ego developmental arrest, in addition to dealing with the perverse activities in all their associated meanings, we are dealing with persons who have suffered, missed, or prematurely lost experiences, legitimately needed, which must be understood and repaired within the transference in order to assist the patient's ego in its belated development. This must be done before interpretations of a structural nature can be made. It is necessary to deal first with what the arrested ego needs to achieve, and interpret only later what the ego needs to ward off (Stolorow and Lachmann, 1980). These patients need selfobjects for self-esteem regulation and, as a result, a long period of symbioticlike idealizing or mirroring transferences is promoted. This ultimately helps these patients to regain a feeling of an individual, idealized self (a real self) first based on identification with the analyst. This promotes a gradual eradication of the primitive, grandiose, pathological self, and the acquisition of new realistic goals in accordance with their real abilities.

In contrast, the transference relationship in preoedipal type I patients allows for a new identification with the analyst as a substitute for the attachment to the object or person in the perversion to take place. The patient has to integrate relatively mild splits between self and object representations, in contrast to the severe splits in those with narcissistic personality disorder with perversion. The gradually emerging autonomous self is more easily helped in its efforts to achieve true integration (all the while being protected from engulfment by the mother) through the transference relationship in the milder cases.

Criteria Among Perverse Patients: Preoedipal Type I, Preoedipal Type II, Oedipal Perversion, and Schizoperversion

In what follows I shall summarize and make differentiating criteria between preoedipal type I and type II patients, in schizoperverts and the oedipal type of perversion, with the aim of further demonstrating and clarifying both their similarities and their differences as regards: (1) status of object relations; (2) prognosis for recovery; (3) the meaning of the perverse act; (4) the degree and level of fixation; (5) the class of conflict; (6) the Sachs mechanism and ego-syntonicity; (7) the tendency to severe regressive states; (8) the degree of potential analyzable transferences; (9) the capacity of the orgasm to restore the sense of having a bounded and cohesive self; (10) the status of ego functions other than object relations; and (11) defenses. In making these differentiations I am suggesting what may be legitimately expected during the course of a well-conducted psychoanalysis of this type of patient. Some comments will be made on schizoperversion for the purpose of clearly separating it from preoedipal perversion type II.

Status of Object Relations

In oedipal perversion, object relations are unimpaired and consist of a relation of self to object, in a sense, from "infantile submissive oedipal self" to the "domineering prohibiting oedipal father" (Kernberg, 1975). In preoedipal form type I, object relations are mildly impaired and consist of an object relation which fits the formula of object to self. In preoedipal form type II, object relations are moderately to severely impaired and consist of object to self. In both types I and II the object stands for the self, it is a narcissistic one but "still an object relation, i.e., that between mother and child" (Kernberg, 1975, p. 329). Preoedipal form type II is often complicated by a severe degree of narcissism in which case the object relation is from a pathological grandiose self to self. In schizoperversion the psychotic has lost his internal object representations and strives to fill up the feeling of a terrible void by creating new objects. There is a lack of adequate separation of self and object.

Prognosis for Recovery

In the oedipal form the prognosis for the removal of the perverse symptom and the attainment of object love is often excellent. In the preoedipal form the prognosis varies from good to more reserved. Similar to the oedipal form, preoedipal form type I patients usually do not require specific modifications in psychoanalytic technique. In the more severe cases (preoedipal type II), modified techniques may be required on occasion, as in the borderline conditions. Those with a "narcissistic personality structure proper" (Kernberg, 1975) may pose special problems in that the attempted removal of the narcissistic character neurosis produces severe depressive attacks, feelings of emptiness and worthlessness, and attacks of narcissistic rage.

In the schizoperversion, the prognosis is poor as there is a qualitative difference in the perverse symptom in these individuals. It should be kept in mind that these perverse symptoms are *consequences* of a psychotic process and not causative of it (Bak, 1971). The schizophrenic process itself has undone repression, destroyed object relations, and laid bare the pregenital phase and primitive ego states. Even with the disappearance of the secondary symptoms of schizophrenia, it is not unusual for the perverse symptom to remain during compensated phases of the psychosis. The advisability of the attempted removal of perverse symptoms during compensated phases of schizophrenia must be carefully weighed against the possibility of exacerbation of the psychosis. An exception to this observation may be found in those who experience "incidental psychoses" (Bak, 1971), as they have retained their capacity to restore object relations.

Meaning of the Perverse Act

In the oedipal form, the perverse symptom is due to the failure of the resolution of the Oedipus complex and castration fears which lead to a negative oedipal position. There is a sexual submission to the parent of the same sex. Genital oedipal conflicts predominate.

In preoedipal form type I, oedipal conflicts are prominent and superimposed on more basic preoedipal anxiety. In type II, preoedipal conflicts predominate over genital ones. The pursued partners in both types of the preoedipal form are representatives of the patient's own self (narcissistic) in relation to an active, phallic mother. Essential to both types I and II in homosexual patients is an identification with and incorporation of the partner's masculinity in the sexual act. This major mechanism of preoedipal homosexuality was first introduced by Anna Freud (1954). In addition, there is an unconscious enactment of the mother–child role (penis–breast equation). In type II, the homosexual partner is "loved" as an extension of the patient's own "pathological grandiose self" (Kernberg, 1975). Splitting processes of the ego, object, and superego are especially prominent.

In schizoperversion the patient attempts to make relationships to external objects through the perverse act, defending himself against imminent disruptive incorporation by the mother.

Degree of Level of Fixation

In the oedipal form, there is no fixation at preoedipal levels, but often a partial regression to the preoedipal phase. In preoedipal form type I, a fixation may be mild to moderate and is probably located in the later phases of the separation-individuation process, in the rapprochement subphase. In preoedipal type II, the severity of fixation is earlier and more damaging in its effect.

In schizoperversion the fixation is in earlier phases of the separation-individuation process, in the symbiotic phase. Symbiotic relationships are based on degrees of fusion.

The basic nuclear conflict that is affectively revived during therapy in the preoedial type II patient does not represent an actual return to practicing and differentiating phases, despite the appearance of symptoms of fears of merging with the mother, threatened loss of ego boundaries, feelings of fragmentation, and fears of annihilation. I am in agreement with Arlow (1963) that such primitive and regressive experiences and fantasies derive apparently from phallic or late prephallic phase fantasies and do not originate in the oral phase. My own clinical experience supports this view, as preoedipal type II patients do not become psychotic despite these frightening experiences.

Class of Conflict

Although there was no satisfactory set of concepts before 1973 proposed for the study of the psyche before its differentiation into id–ego–superego (Gedo and Goldberg, 1973), Dorpat (1976) noted that the *foundations* had already been laid for a systematic theory of such early conflicts by Fairbairn (1954), Jacobson (1964), Modell (1968), Gedo and Goldberg (1973), among others. He notes: "At a higher developmental level, the hierarchical model includes the tri-partite model, and at a lower level it includes on object-relations model. . . . The object-relations class of psychic conflict covers the phase of psychic development prior to id-ego-superego differentiation" (Dorpat, 1976, p. 873).

In the oedipal perversion, a *structural conflict* exists which involves the major psychic structures of ego, id, and superego; that is, between the subject's aggressive, sexual, and other wishes and his own prohibitions and ideals. The nuclear conflict in homosexuality, for example, may consist of the renunciation of oedipal love for the mother in the male and a corresponding conflict in the female.

In both types of the preoedipal form an *object-relations conflict* predominates. This consists of anxiety and guilt "associated with the failure of development in the phase of self-object differentiation" (Modell, 1968, p. 328). As a consequence, the nuclear conflict in this form is a preoedipal fixation in which there is a desire for and dread of merging with the mother in order to reinstate the primitive mother-child unity (Socarides, 1968a,b).

The Sachs Mechanism and Ego-Syntonicity

In preoedipal perversions, the intense attachment, fear, and guilt in the boy's relationship with his mother brings about certain major psychic transformation which are affected through the mechanism of the repressive compromise. It is a solution by division whereby one piece of infantile sexuality enters the service of repression; that is, is helpful in promoting repression through displacement, substitution, and other defense mechanisms. Pregenital pleasure is thereby carried over into the ego while the rest is repressed. This major mechanism in the development of perversion was first described by Sachs in 1923. It is the basic mechanism in the production of preoedipal perversions of both types (Socarides, 1968a) and promotes ego-syntonicity.

The Sachs mechanism plays a *minor* role in oedipal forms of perversion in which regression takes place. It is only partially effective in schizohomosexuality. It is most often not utilized successfully in the oedipal form and the homosexual symptom remains ego-alien. Although unconsciously determined in oedipal forms, the symptom is not the outcome of the repressive compromise. The symptom may remain at the level of unconscious thoughts, dreams, and fantasies, and is not a disguised, acceptable representation of a deeper conflict. When perverse desires threaten to break into awareness, anxiety develops. Under certain conditions of stress or seduction and feelings of helplessness, homosexual acts may take place.[1] Such acts, however, do not achieve the magic symbolic restitution of the preoedipal types. This may, in fact, exacerbate the situation.

It should be noted that the absence of a successfully functioning Sachs mechanism in the oedipal form makes the task of the removal of the homosexual symptom a much easier one once the unconscious motivations; for example,

---

[1]Otto Sperling (1956) has described a special form of homosexuality which he terms *induced perversion*, in which there is a splitting of the superego in which a leader in group perverse activities replaces the patient's superego. This is a reactivation of a split in childhood which had remained latent. "Induced" homosexuality, or other perversions, can be either oedipal or preoedipal.

retreat from active, phallic strivings and dependency needs for the homosexual desire are analyzed, since the magical restorative and equilibrium-producing functions of this mechanism are ineffective.

Tendency to Severe Regressive States

In the oedipal form, the tendency to regressive states is mild, and when it occurs it is similar to that which appears in neurotics. The threats of the oedipal period have disrupted the already-formed identity so that a regression occurs to an earlier period in order to escape the dangers of the oedipal period. This is a partial preoedipal regression to anal and even oral conflicts.

In the milder preoedipal form, the tendency to regression is moderate and temporary, while in type II it is moderate to severe, although there is an adequate capacity in most instances to circumscribe these regressions. In the more severe cases, these regressions are often chronic and not easily removed. They may temporarily disrupt the analytic relationship, and reintegration may be difficult (Panel, 1977).

The severity of the preoedipal developmental fixation may be crucial to the outcome and also to the forward movement of the therapy as regards the formation of a working alliance, transference, resistance, analyzability, and the capacity to undergo analysis without succumbing to severe regressive episodes which border on near-psychotic manifestations. A detailed study of regressive phenomena with clinical examples can be found in Socarides (1978a, chapter 25).

In schizoperversion deficiencies of the ego in forming, maintaining, and investing object representations have led to a "paucity of object representations" and a "predominance of fused self-object representations" (Bak, 1971, p. 241). This "defective capacity is [later experienced] as a danger to the self" and there are frequent "regressive adaptations with a further destruction of object representations" (p. 241). Thus, the tendency to severe regressive states in schizoperversion is extreme and occurs concomitantly with manifest secondary symptoms of schizophrenia.

Degree of Potential Analyzable Transference

I noted in an earlier work (1978a, chapter 24) that crucial to the analyzability of homosexual patients is not the presenting symptomatology (even apparently extreme femininity), nor even the life history of the homosexual, but the nature of the spontaneously developing transference. This holds true in the analysis of all perversions.

In the oedipal form, transference manifestations are similar to those which appear in the transference neuroses, and therefore the degree of potential analyzable transferences is ideal. In preoedipal type I it is good because of sufficient self-object differentiation and internalization of object representations. Preoedipal form type II reveals that analyzable transferences are present to a fair degree, but the outcome depends upon the tendency to externalize parts of the self, as well as the presence of severely repressive episodes.

Fortunately, however, we have sufficient clinical experience to conclude that the preoedipal pervert has a capacity to form neurotic transferences. The relationships that exist between transference, object relations, and ego functions, so well described by Greenson (1967) as regards neurotics, apply as well to the preoedipal pervert's psychic functioning. For example, the homosexual differentiates between the self and object "and has the ability to displace reactions from a past object representation to an object in the present" (p. 173). Therefore, he has for the most part "an organizing differentiated self, an entity separate and distinct from his environment, which has a capacity to remain the same in the midst of change" (p. 173). These are hallmarks of his capacity to form a transference neurosis in contrast to psychotics, "who have lost their internal object representation" (p. 173).

Therefore, if the preoedipal homosexual "misunderstands the present in terms of the past, this misunderstanding is only partial and temporary" (p. 174). When he "suffers regressions in ego functions" they are "circumscribed" and largely "limited to certain aspects of his relationship to the transference figure" (p. 174). He may allow himself to "regress in terms of his object relations and ego functions" and he "renounces certain of his reality testing functions partially and temporarily"; but he is able to work with these reactions and to understand them with his "observing ego" (Greenson, 1967, pp. 173-175).

Capacity of the Orgasm to Restore the Sense of Having a Bounded and Cohesive Self

In the oedipal form the sense of self and ego boundaries are essentially unimpaired, and therefore the orgasm does not function as it does in the preoedipal form. Although the orgasm has the capacity to reinforce and consolidate self cohesion in all individuals to some extent, whether normal or neurotic, the disturbances in ego formation in sexual perverts renders them specifically in need of such reinforcement. In preoedipal types I and II there is a strong capacity for the restoration of self, but in the more severe form the effect may be transitory, leading to an insistent and imperative need for multiple and frequent sexual contacts. In the latter instances, boundaries between self-object representations may be very fragile.

The greater the capacity of the orgasm to restore a sense of having a bounded and cohesive self (Eissler, 1958a; Stolorow, 1975; Lichtenstein, 1977), the more difficult it becomes to remove the perverse symptom. Conversely, the less the orgasm functions in this manner (in those with a less structurally deficient ego), the greater will be the success in early removal of the perverse symptom. This factor must be considered in any attempted cessation of perverse activity during therapy, as the patient (especially preoedipal type II) may suffer greatly or withdraw from treatment due to the eruption of intolerable anxiety.

Status of Ego Functions Other Than Object Relations

In the oedipal form of perversion, reality testing and impulse control are intact. Thinking is unimpaired and is dominated by the reality principle. Self concept and ego boundaries are essentially unimpaired, and conflict is internalized. Affect is appropriate, and responses of anxiety and depression are frequently encounters. Aggression is essentially well defended against. These findings are similar to those which prevail in the transference neuroses.

In the preoedipal form type I, reality testing is often intact, but "consciously or unconsciously ignored to serve the pleasure principle" (Kolansky and Eisner, 1974). In type II, the boundary between fantasy and reality can be indistinct. Severe anxiety results in a flight from reality in these instances.

As regards impulse control, there may be incomplete or partial control leading to "acting out of impulses and pursuit of instantaneous gratifications" (Kolansky and Eisner, 1974) in preoedipal type I. In the more severe type, impulses are grossly acted out in an instantaneous manner suggesting the complete loss of ego and superego controls. In the milder preoedipal type, *thinking* may be clear and dominated by the pleasure principle. Such thinking, combined with poor impulse control, leads to actions which involve a denial of reality. In less severe cases, thinking may be of a type which reflects the patient's own projective anxieties. In the more severe cases, serious impairment of thinking may occur with occasional and fleeting semidelusional convictions.

As regards self concept, preoedipal type I patients frequently reveal an elevated sense of self-esteem bordering on omnipotence which alternates with feelings of extreme self-depreciation. Ego boundaries are in the main intact, and there is a strong need for narcissistic supplies. Occasional feelings of grandiosity may appear without the formation of a well-organized, split-off pathological grandiose self. In preoedipal type II there is an unconscious and severe sense of worthlessness and emptiness with an extreme disturbance in self concept. Under stress, ego boundaries show severe impairment in these cases with the removal of the narcissistic facade.

In connection with affect and affect control, there is an inability to bear "external frustration" (Kolansky and Eisner, 1974) in both types of preoedipal perversion. In type I the patient responds to anxiety and depression with aggressive reaction. In type II bursts of rage are frequent as the capacity to neutralize aggression has been lost. The invasion of a well-organized split-off pathological grandiose self by aggression leads these individuals (in the most severe degree of narcissistic pathology) into perverse acts marked by cruelty.

Defenses

The defenses of oedipal perverts are similar to those found in neurotics (e.g., repression, displacement, identification with the aggressor, and so on). The defenses of preoedipal type II patients are in their prestages of development and splitting predominates over repression. In preoedipal type I patients, repression predominates with some splitting phenomena, but the major defense mechanisms are introjection, projection, and identification.

In the above I have limited myself to eleven differentiating categories which separate, contrast, and clarify the three major forms of clinical perversion. It is hoped that grouping in an integrated fashion, as I have commented earlier in this section, has revealed what can be expected during the psychoanalysis of each type of patient; has provided information as to the ultimate outcome as regards the removal of perverse impulse, establishment of heterosexual functioning, and capacity of the individual to cathect a heterosexual love object; has noted resistances; has described transference manifestations; has noted the depth and frequency of regressive experiences and the capacity of the individual patients to use them therapeutically and recover from them; has informed us as to the basic nuclear conflict that will be affectively revived during therapy, and the capacity of the individual ego to deal with it; has specified the class of conflict to be met with (structural versus object relations); and has indirectly provided information as to the presence of areas of healthy object relatedness which will serve as our therapeutic allies during the course of psychoanalysis. Ongoing clinical observations and data collecting will undoubtedly lead to further clarification and refinement of the distinctly different forms of the same perversion, and thereby increase the efficacy of psychoanalytic treatment.

Chapter 5
AGGRESSION IN PERVERSION

Introduction

In 1956, Bak, a leading theoretician in the area of sexual perversion, observed that the psychoanalytic understanding of perversion in midcentury rested almost entirely on the dominance of pregenitality in sexual functioning, the traumata of the phallic phase, and a gradually emerging interest in the traumatic influences of the prephallic era. These concepts, however, had been investigated mostly in connection with the role of the development of the libido and its vicissitudes. The concept of fixation had been explained almost entirely in relation to libidinal development with no attention to aggression. From his wide clinical experience Bak began an integration of aggression into sexual pathology as an "equal partner" of libido. He suggested that "we can assume in perversions an increased quantity of aggression, either constitutionally . . . or as a consequence of those very early environmental stresses that sometimes increase the impetus of the aggressive drives" (Bak, 1956, p. 232). Environmental factors influence the course of aggression, and he predicted (what was later to be documented not only clinically but by infant observational studies) that these reactions will depend upon a "temporal factor"; that is, the stage of structural development and the established rate of object relationship. He opined that the earliest periods of life, the preoedipal phases of development, and the stages of object relations of that period are of particular importance, and suggested that the group of perversions that are "the most ego-syntonic," and so for the most part "escape our investigation [due to their not coming for analysis]—contain highly developed object relationships and originate from a phase near the Oedipus constellation" (pp. 232-233). While Bak was correct in that extremely well-structured perversions are ego-syntonic, I have found that the degree of ego-syntonicity is not as dependent on fixation on the phallic-oedipal phase as Bak noted. Most well-structured perversions are fixated in the rapprochement phase of the separation-individuation process, and thus are definitely preoedipal in origin. Bak put forth a proposition that traumatic overstimulation occurred in the undifferentiated phase of development, affecting both libidinal and aggressive drives in their early nascent state simultaneously, with resultant tendencies to the development of various forms of perversions. From his clinical experience he noted that physiological dysfunctions threatening survival (e.g., operations, illnesses, etc.), or a disequilibrium of the mother-child relationship at an early phase (citing the work of Greenacre) not only seemed to produce an increase of primary and secondary aggression, but appeared to be causative factors in the most severe cases of perversion. This substratum of aggression, together with a "confused sexual identity and a vagueness of body periphery and the boundaries of the body-self," he considered as playing an important role in perversions, and especially in fetishism. The disturbances of body-ego boundaries, disturbance in sexual identity, and overproduction of aggression were cited as a substratum of all perversions, and beyond that they "play a much greater role in sado-masochism than has hitherto been emphasized" (Bak, 1956, p. 233).

From his clinical research he concluded:

1. Overstimulation of an undifferentiated libido and aggression is a determinant for heightened sadistic disposition with its character of "unusual inner pressure and drivenness for gratification" (p. 233).

2. "Large quantities of excitation" during early phases of

ego development tend to lead to "uncontrolled libidinal and aggressive discharge without interference from the ego" (p. 233). Such discharges are important since the defenses at this stage of development are "autoplastic, and largely based on a magic omnipotence which consists of denial of the outside world" (p. 233). In this connection, he observed that there is an "overflowing" between self and object as the ego is in a process of development. This may well lead to a continuation of a feminine identification and a predominance of the introjection-projection mechanisms. The type of perversion produced under such circumstances he believed was closely allied to schizophrenia.

3. Perversions in schizophrenics seem to represent "different forms of defenses against the unneutralized aggression threatening the object" (p. 234). He was later to develop this line of thinking in a major paper late in his career entitled "Object Relationships in Schizophrenia and Perversion" (1971).

4. While Bak considered aggression as equal to libido in the causation of perversions, he continued to emphasize the crucial importance of castration anxiety and the oedipal conflict. Common to all perversion, in Bak's opinion, was the dramatized denial of castration. Such denial is augmented by a projection of heightened aggression, and "marked by sexual identification which was established as a defense against destruction of the object, in whole or in part" (p. 239). It should be noted that Bak's views differ considerably from my own, for it is my belief that castration anxiety and oedipal fears are a secondary overlay to what is basically a preoedipal nuclear conflict in perversion, and that castration anxiety plays a more modest secondary role than was believed by Bak in 1956.

5. Bak felt that the increased impetus of the aggressive drive was a consequence of overstimulation in the undifferentiated phase. Such overstimulation causes damage to the neutralizing function of the ego and to the establishment of "discharge patterns prior to ego development" (Bak, 1956, p. 240).

Bak believed that it was "the task of the ego to differentiate between the two drives as to their aim and object."

Neutralization tends toward change of the aim, whereas the differentiation as to the object of the drive fails in perversions: "the love object remains the object of aggression" (p. 240). In effect, Bak made neutralization or the lack of it, and the overstimulation in the undifferentiated phase central to his pathogenesis of perversions. This is in marked contrast to my own belief that it is the nuclear conflicts occurring in the rapprochement subphase, and in practicing and differentiating subphases, which are crucial to the genesis of perversions, although aggression and its vicissitudes play an important role. If the major disturbances were primarily in the undifferentiated phase the individual would tend to develop psychotic states rather than perversion. Bak concluded: "Perverse symptoms are regressive adaptations of the ego to secure gratification without destroying the object and endangering the self which is identified with the object" (Bak, 1956, p. 240).

Bak then applied his theories of aggression in perversion to various clinical states. As regards the exhibitionist, Bak confirmed that the first task of the exhibitionist was to reassure himself against castration. The acting out of his aggression in the exhibitionistic act itself serves as a means to deny his deeper passive, feminine identification. The male exhibitionist identifies with the female child, and expresses awe and ambivalence toward the paternal phallus. Due to the greater degree of "ego syntonicity of aggression" in men (Bak, 1956), the passive feminine self was then externalized onto the object. The fetishist, on the other hand, uses the fetish and reveres it as a means to denying and protecting himself against the destructive wishes directed at the object, especially the breast. A transvestite defends himself against the loss of the object by taking on its external appearance and, in so doing, denies castration and destruction. In homosexuality there is (1) a shift from aggressive rivalry to love, making the object of aggression into the object of sexual desire; (2) an "intense attachment to the mother [which] leads to identification with her but contains an intermediate phase of aggression motivated by disappointment" (Bak, 1956, p. 238); (3) destructive impulses against the mother which are resolved, and at the same time in their resolution pave the way for a libidinization of aggression against the rival. The homosexual thus succeeds in defending himself against retaliation from both sexes.

Bak's profound clinical observations and theoretical formulations as to the role of aggression in perversions were a giant step forward in a poorly understood area of etiology and psychopathology of perversions. His concepts were both daring and innovative, and I have found them to be valuable and challenging, and for the most part easily assimilated within the unitary theory of sexual perversions which I have proposed. They constituted theoretical and clinical advances and set the stage for a further understanding of the role of aggression in perversion. Before I proceed with the task of defining this role, it is essential that I put forth my theoretical views of the nature of aggression itself and the developmental factors present in those individuals who later develop perversions.

Theoretical Considerations

Aggressive Drive Theory

In the early history of psychoanalysis, the ontogeny of aggression was modeled on that of libido. In the "Three Essays" (1905b), Freud viewed manifestations of destructiveness and cruelty as components of sexuality, as an "admixture to it, a propensity to subdue, the biological significance of which lies in the necessity of overcoming the resistance of the sexual object by acts other than courting" (pp. 157–158). Aggressive impulses were seen to be derivatives of the drive for sexual mastery whose vicissitudes were to be formulated in terms of oral, anal, and phallic phases of psychosexual development. Aggressiveness and destructiveness were part of libidinal development and were to be considered at their core erotic or sexual. The early psychoanalytic literature is dotted with landmark clinical discoveries which emerge from this theoretical frame of reference. Notable among them are papers by Starcke (1920) and Van Ophuijsen (1920). Freud's belief that there exist nonerotic forms of aggression was to be underscored in "Instincts and Their Vicissitudes"

(1915), a few years later, when he asked how it could be that for so long we had overlooked the existence of nonerotic aggression.

Freud's first correction that destructiveness was part of sexuality appeared in his first instinctual drive theory prior to 1915. Aggression (sadism) was to be considered part of the ego (self-preservative instinct) and was juxtaposed to the sexual instincts (libido). The second drive theory, formulated in 1920, proposed that there was a tendency within the organism to return to its original inorganic state, a tendency to destroy the self (death instinct). This death instinct theory "was juxtaposed to the life instinct" (1920a). The life instincts were represented by the libido and subsumed the sexual and formerly separate self-preservative instincts. The death instinct was now represented in the id and the psyche by the destructive drive. Freud was not clear as to whether a distinction was to be made between the destructive drive and the aggressive drive, and he used the terms at times interchangeably and at other times side by side, implying a difference between them, although he never stated nor implied the nature of that difference (Parens, 1973). Destructive drives were mitigated in the course of development in order to protect the self and external object, especially those cathected with libido. This lessening of aggression was achieved by fusion of libido with destructiveness. Later theoretical advances, especially those made by Hartmann, Kris, and Loewenstein (1946), postulated that destructive energy undergoes neutralization, and therefore is available for psychic development. All in all, destructiveness could now be seen to contribute not only to the development of psychopathology, give patterning to discharge and gratification of sexual and aggressive drives, decide the character of the superego to a large extent, but also play a part as to the nature of psychic development itself (Parens, 1973).

However, this did not answer the question as to whether there was a destructive trend in the aggressive drive which is of primary origin, and also whether there is a trend in aggression which seems inherently nondestructive.

Perversion and Aggression

In keeping with the views of Anna Freud (1949a), and Parens (1973, 1977, 1979), it is my belief that the aggressive drive has two equally important currents: a destructive and a nondestructive one, both essentially ego-syntonic. Since the determining factors in the genesis of perversion lie both in the expression of libidinal needs and the retention of primary aggression or an increase in secondary aggression by frustration (Greenacre, 1968), these observations on the inherent character of aggression are of vital theoretical importance in understanding sexual perversions. Perversion, libidinal and aggressive (nondestructive), and aggressive destructive drives are in constant interplay with one another. The resultant perversion is a consequence of a complex series of negations, displacements, substitutions, reaction formations, changing into the opposite, and other defensive maneuvers which characterize the Hanns Sachs mechanism (Sachs, 1923). The manifest perverse behavior and its relationships to its unconscious hidden meaning, with both libido and aggression prominently represented, can only be likened to that which exists between the manifest content of the dream in relation to latent dream thoughts (Joseph, 1965; Socarides, 1980b). Despite surface manifestations to the contrary, all perversions have been found by me to include overt and/or covert sadistic or sadomasochistic impulses or behavior.

While much is known of the aims of the libidinal drive in perversions, what of the aims of the destructive current of the aggressive drive and the nondestructive current? In its most severe form of expression, the destructive current of the aggressive drive seems to be directly concerned with the total destruction of an object, animate or inanimate. Hartmann, Kris, and Loewenstein (1946) agree that the question as to the specific aims of the aggressive drive can be classified according to the degree of discharge they allow for, and according to the means utilized in discharge. Destructive aggressive impulses threaten the existence of the object, while the investment of the object with libido acts as its protection. As a consequence, destructive aims invariably undergo some degree of modification because of the fusion of instinctual drives with libido prevailing over aggression. Destructive aggression (as well as nondestructive aggression) may be modified by (1) displacement; (2) restriction of the aims; (3) sublimation; (4) fusion, the result of comingling of instinctual drives; and (5) neutralization (an activity of the ego).

Such neutralization is due to deaggressivization and delibidinization of the primitive drives. We can therefore assume that neutralization develops under the influence of secondary process activity and object constancy, and is closely related to instinctual fusion and sublimation (Kris, 1955). Indeed, the hallmark of ego strength may be the individual's capacity to neutralize large quantities of aggression. Similarly, the presence of unneutralized aggressive energy in the ego constitutes a weak or eventually masochistic ego. Damming up of aggression within the self, when it exceeds a certain limit, may provide the matrix for the subsequent development of introjected bad objects; conversely, the cathexis of external sources of libido and their incorporation become associated with the formation of good internalized objects (Kris, 1955).

The two clarifications cited above (the existence of both erotic and nonerotic aggression), and the belief that there exists within the aggressive drive two equally important currents—a destructive and a nondestructive one—leads me to emphasize what has already been stated, namely, that aggressive behavior directed at objects in which there is pleasure derived from mastery and other nonsexual motivations should be distinguished from that which is directed against objects in which a specific kind of pleasure is obtained; that is, sexual pleasure at the infliction of pain and suffering. Aggressive, violent, destructive impulses (various forms of destructive aggression against the self), for example, nonsexual (nonerotic), violent aggression (self-inflicted wounds, suicide), moral masochism, and so on, should be separated from sexual violent aggression (sexual sadism and sexual masochism). In both the latter—sexual sadism and sexual masochism—the new aims of the impulses receive their particular coloration and configuration from an inherent comingling of both aggression and libido, as will be described in this chapter. Since pleasure may be a regular complement to aggressive destructive acts, it is therefore justifiable to restrict the meaning of the term *sadism* to only those destructive, aggressive activities whose conscious or unconscious aim is the production of sexual excitation and orgasm. Sadism connotes *sexual sadism*; both terms can be used interchangeably, the word *sexual* adding emphasis. Freud himself used the terms *sadism* and *sexual sadism* interchangeably at various points in his career, often without differentiating between nonsexual aggressiveness (e.g., "sadistic superego") and sexual violent destructiveness. One is aided in making this definition by Freud's own statement:

> Let us once more reach an agreement upon what is to be understood by the "sense" of a psychical process. We mean nothing other by it than the intention it serves and its position in a psychical continuity. In most of our researches we can replace "sense" by "intention" or "purpose" [Freud, 1916, p. 40].

Clearly, the meaning of an act or piece of behavior is its place in a motivational context.

Developmental Factors

The early history of individuals prone to sadomasochistic behavior is replete with childhood instances of inability to bear frustration and profound difficulties in forming permanent object relationships. The severely diminished capacity to form such object relationships is a fertile matrix for the later expression of sadistic impulses. Furthermore, such individuals show proneness to acting out.

The most violent and primitive manifestations of self directed and object directed aggression occur precisely in those individuals who are the most narcissistically vulnerable; that is, those who have the most fragile and precarious self representation. The experience of infliction of pain is utilized in the service of restoring self boundaries and recovering narcissistic integrity, especially when self preservation has been threatened. In such patients, even relatively minor frustrations are experienced as narcissistic insults with concomitant threats to the self representation. The desperate need for narcissistic restoration revives primitive aggression which in turn threatens both self and object. Through libidinization, impulses of hostility and aggression may be suspended or sidetracked with greater or lesser success.

A severe degree of narcissistic rage is an essential component for the expression of sadistic acts of the most primitive type. Kohut (1971) has noted that a child or a narcissistically fixated adult possesses archaic narcissistic structures which remain unmodified, because they become "isolated from the rest of the growing psyche after the phase-appropriate narcissistic demands of childhood have been traumatically frustrated" (p. 386). Rage arises when the self and object fail to live up to the high expectations directed at their functions.

> The most intense experiences of pain under the most violent forms of narcissistic rage arise in those individuals for whom the sense of absolute *control* over an archaic environment is indispensable because the maintenance of self-esteem—indeed of the self—depends on the unconditional availability of the approving-mirroring function of the admiring self-object, or the ever-present opportunity for a merging with an idealized one [Kohut, 1971, p. 386; emphasis added].

This "archaic mode of experience" explains how sadistic individuals in the grip of narcissistic rage are able to show total lack of empathy toward their victims. There is an:

> [U]nmodifiable wish to blot out the offense which is perpetrated against the grandiose self, resulting in unforgiving fury. . . . As regards metapsychology, it is the disorganized mixture of massive discharge (tension decrease) and blocking (tension increase) in the area of unneutralized aggression, arising after the non-compliance of the archaic self-object, which is the metapsychological substratum of the manifestation of the experience of narcissistic rage [Kohut, 1971, p. 396].

Clinical observations of sadomasochistic patients repeatedly affirm that the ego "does not acknowledge the inherent limitations of the power of the self, but attributes its failures and weaknesses to the malevolence and corruption of the uncooperative object" (Kohut, 1971, p. 396). The "uncooperative archaic object" in cases of sadism is almost always the malevolent mother or her scapegoat which has undergone disguise and substitution.

The severity of sadistic and/or of sadomasochistic impulses is directly dependent on another developmental factor of central importance: the quality of the introjects. Child observation studies (Mahler, Pine, and Bergman, 1975) reveal that "during the period of normal symbiosis, the narcissistically fused object was felt to be 'good,' that is, in harmony with the symbiotic self—so that primary identification took place under a positive valence of love" (p. 117). The more suddenly intrapsychic separation occurs or the more damaging and unpredictable the parents are, "the less does the modulating, negotiating function of the ego gain ascendancy" (p. 117). The less reliable the love-object's emotional attitude to the outside world has been, "the greater the extent to which the object remains or becomes an unassimilated foreign body—a 'bad' introject in the intrapsychic emotional economy" (p. 117). These children "develop an increased proclivity to identify the self-representation with the 'bad' introject or at least to confuse the two" (p. 117). During the rapprochement subphase, aggression may then "be unleashed in such a way as to inundate or sweep away the 'good object,' and with it the good self-representation" (p. 117). This would be indicated by early severe temper tantrums, and by increased attempts to "coerce mother and father" in various ways. Severe ambivalence "mars smooth development toward emotional object constancy and sound secondary narcissism" (p. 117). They develop all too suddenly and all too intensely a realization of their helplessness with a:

> [T]oo sudden deflation of their previous sense of omnipotence, i.e., without "emotional buffering" and with a tendency to split the object world into good and bad. The "mother in the flesh" and the "mother after separation" is

always disappointing and the child's self-esteem regulation
is most precarious [Mahler et al., 1975, p. 118].

In a summing-up of genetic and dynamic factors which
promote an increase in primary and secondary aggression,
Greenacre (1968) cites: (1) disturbances in the first years of
life which impede the orderly progression of separation-
individuation; (2) failures of maternal care leading to a negative depressive affective response. Consequent separation
and grief reactions, temper tantrums leading to despair,
impotent resignation, and surrender create an overproduction of rage and depression which is then neutralized by
perversion formation (see chapter 5); (3) disturbances in self-
object differentiation with resultant impairment and/or
slowing of the formation of object relationships; (4) discovery of the anatomical sexual differences against a backdrop
of the above-mentioned difficulties; (5) severe physical childhood trauma in which "aggression becomes bound or frozen
in a way that suggests a physiological grounding of it with
an accompanying alteration in the quality of conscious perceptions" (Greenacre, 1968, p. 306). The large component of
primitive aggression during the first months of life is often
associated with earlier histories of abandonment; later
exploitative overwhelming produces severe rages. Under
such conditions aggressive outbursts are utilized for discharge purposes of lessening anxiety. Furthermore, intense
aggression may be aroused without the child's having the
ability for immediate discharge. These two conditions—the
use of aggression to lessen anxiety and the inability for
effective discharge—favor sadomasochistic tendencies (Greenacre, 1968).

A destructive family life provides little chance for healing
and it is especially devastating when it occurs in the context
of the wider social environment, community, society, or
family, which tends to stimulate and perpetuate the dominance of sadomasochistic development. While the primordial aggressive life-force is "prenatally in the service of body
differentiation and enormous growth . . . postnatally there is
a severe degree of interference with the contact with the
mother (in the autistic and early individuation periods)"

(Greenacre, 1968, p. 313). This leads to what Greenacre has termed *phase-hunger*, through clinging, touching, oral activities, and a resultant biological aggressive pressure.

The nucleus of the most severe cases, those characterized by enactment of violent and criminal tendencies (Nacht, Diatkine, and Favreau, 1956; Williams, 1964, 1965; de M'Uzan, 1973; Socarides, 1974b), shows in their historical reconstruction and in their dynamic structure the major elements enumerated by Greenacre. True or full genital pleasure does not occur and genitality is "abandoned altogether in favor of narcissistically driven aggressive orgies" (Greenacre, 1968, p. 60). Occasionally there is a "wavering" period in which other perversions such as homosexuality and/or fetishism constitute a "perverse pathwork" of sexual (genital) satisfaction which then gives way to the use of violence. Such severely ill individuals experience strong oral drives of a devouring quality and demonstrate a grandiose desire to control and conquer others. Of central importance is the observation that whenever pain and distress are experienced, aggression is aroused but remains unrelieved by relating with the maternal object or her representative.

Although there is a normal pressure of aggression in the first months of life, this cannot be considered hostile or truly sadistic until there is at least some small margin of object relatedness. If, however, that margin of object relatedness is very much diminished or interfered with so that it almost seems lacking, then the primary masochism or primary sadism of the child may gain the ascendancy.

Clinical Manifestations
of Aggression in Perversions

It is well known that libido can act as a counter or neutralizing agent to violent destructiveness. By the option of perversion, a pervert may be able to protect his reality sense from gross interference which might otherwise give rise to violent destructiveness, psychotic or nonpsychotic manifestations. In this connection, during the analysis of psychotic crises, it can often be observed (especially in depressive individuals and schizoids) that patients develop transitory perverse formations of a standard type, with the temporary relief of depression and corresponding recovery of reality sense (Glover, 1933, 1964). The opposite of this situation may also be true: the inability to form a perversion and thereby neutralize violent destructiveness may result in the loss of an important prophylactic device.

Beneath surface perverse symptoms of all types lie deeper layers of sadistic fantasies. Perversions represent attempts to protect the individual from the anxiety and guilt associated with primitive aggressive drives by a process of excessive libidinization. Even in those homosexuals who treat their sexual objects with apparent love and tenderness, the strength of sadistic components has undergone transformation. The presence or absence of *manifest* sadism may well be due to the *strength* of aggression, for severe aggression can cancel out libidinal drives and "aggression can inhibit sublimation giving rise either to inadequate sublimation or to a tendency to reversal of sublimation, a reregression" (Glover, 1964, p. 147).

In fact, the breakdown of partially effective fusion and neutralization processes may lead to an abrupt awareness of a separation between libido and destructive aggression. This can be observed during the psychoanalytic treatment of perverse individuals. When regression occurs, deneutralization follows with resultant reinstinctualization. This leads to a striking phenomenon: intense aggressive, destructive feelings alternating with equally intense libidinal impulses. The rapid alternation of these "pure cultures" of libido and destructive aggression produces alternating impulses to hurt and/or love the object. The patient responds to these crises with severe anxiety and confusion.

For example, during the psychoanalysis of a patient with multiple perverse fantasies and acts (see chapter 21), ideas of violence appeared intermittently and threatened to overwhelm him. His destructiveness was a defense against his unconscious feminine wishes: "These ideas may start with loving feelings like I would incorporate you, like you are becoming part of my hands. I'll hold you so tight that there is no room for you except within me." The patient reported the impulse to suddenly embrace the analyst and almost simultaneously its opposite, an overriding desire to attack and hurt him. "Almost like it's the same thing. There is no clue to which is which, and I can't tell them apart."

In another instance, a twenty-six-year-old homosexual college student (see chapter 10), during his fifteenth and sixteenth months of analysis, reported that homosexual feelings came on whenever he was afraid of his mother "turning around and engulfing me." He experienced a weird excitement whenever his mother approached him suddenly: if he were half-asleep, if she suddenly sat on his bed, or walked into the bathroom when he was there. This "excitement" had, in several instances, proceeded to a strong conscious sexual feeling of which he was "terribly afraid." Simultaneously, the erotic sensation was mixed with violence and murderous aggression, obliterating the former libidinal urges. "I don't know what I would do to her, have sex with her or murder her."

The ego's readiness to acknowledge and accept the sexual nature of impulses and their efficacy in producing conscious sexual arousal is the decisive factor as to whether we are presented with any of three clinical phenomena that are sadistic in nature: (1) cruel acts and/or fantasies with concomitant pleasure. These are not appreciated either at the time or later as being sexual in nature, as their aim remains unconscious;[1] (2) cruel acts and/or fantasies without ejaculation but with conscious slight or full sexual satisfaction, sometimes accompanied by erection; (3) acts of cruelty accompanied by full sexual satisfaction, preceded by erection and concomitant with ejaculation. While acts of sexual sadism may vary from the minor acts of spanking, pinching, punching, and so on, to actual murder, they all contain elements in common: pleasure derived from the infliction of pain; the visual observation of suffering and humiliation; the forcible control of the object and enjoyment of its de-

---

[1]This category may include enigmatic slayings of various kinds; for example, assassination of loved, hated, or envied figures (Socarides, 1982c); or the unprovoked single or massive random killings of individuals whom the murderer did not know personally and against whom he had no grudge.

fenselessness; and vicarious enjoyment of suffering through identification with the object. It is not the pain itself but the accompanying sexual excitation that is sought. Although hate may be present, this is likely to be derived from the additional conviction that the object is also a threat and source of continual pain, despite its powerlessness.

A classification of sadistic phenomena may be made according to the degree of actualization or enactment required to produce sexual excitement leading to orgasm:

Class I: Sadistic and/or sadomasochistic fantasies while alone or in an illusory twosome leading to orgasm, with or without masturbation.

Class II: Sadistic or sadomasochistic fantasies during sexual relations, with same or opposite sex partners, without enactment of sadistic or sadomasochistic fantasies.

Class III: Sadistic or sadomasochistic acts leading to sexual satisfaction. Such enactment can be further categorized according to the degree of actual harm inflicted on the object or subject. The degree of destructiveness is also determined both by the strength of the sadistic impulse as well as the efficacy of fusion processes, and also by the strength or healthiness of the ego's defenses (e.g., sublimation, substitution, displacement, and so on).

Since violent destructiveness may lie at the core of perversions, how is it discharged and how does it seek expression? Moreover, why do not all perversions include a manifest sadistic component? Provisional answers to these questions are supplied by clinical material under several headings.

Destructive Aggression Discharged in Sadistic/Masochistic Perversion

Psychoanalytic investigation of a large number of sexual perverts over a period of thirty years leads me to certain conclusions as to the function of sadistic/masochistic impulses and acts. In brief, the function of sexual sadism is to force and extract love; attack the threatening body of the mother rather than be harmed by it; discharge aggressive impulses which threaten annihilation of the self; achieve temporary freedom from the fear of the engulfing mother (Socarides, 1973); restore the self representation; reassure against and lessen castration fear; and overcome body disintegration anxiety by inflicting rather than by passively enduring pain and destruction. In contrast, the function of sexual masochism is to achieve "victory" over the hating but seemingly loving mother through passive submission; reassure against engulfment and destruction by provoking love responses from the object; vicariously identify with the cruel, aggressive mother; control aggression through projective identification (injecting one's own aggression into another and thereby being relieved of it), and also reassure against and lessen castration fear. The masochist extracts love from "cruel" women and individuals, and undergoes dreaded cruelties (being enclosed, beaten, held down, painfully "drowned" and so on) in order to overcome body disintegration anxiety while simultaneously restoring self representation and closeness (Socarides, 1978b).

In severe cases of sadomasochism, the subject vicariously enjoys the total abasement of the personality of the victim through identification. "To abolish all will in one's self is to renounce possession of a phallus, anal and narcissistic and is therefore to renounce power of any kind" (de M'Uzan, 1973, p. 460). Such abasement serves, however, as a cover for affirmation of feelings of omnipotence and inviolable power of megalomania. The apparently bizarre behavior of a forty-year-old masochist becomes understandable. In the absence of his female companion, who he feels has cruelly abandoned him as his mother once did, he masturbates to orgasm with fantasies of being beaten, demeaned, and humiliated, utilizing amylnitrate to heighten his sense of self cohesion. He falls upon his bed and attempts to strangle himself, exclaiming (in triumph), "Ah, now I have everything!"

The pain inflicted upon an object sets in motion a violent and mounting sexual excitement both in the sadist and in the masochist. It then becomes an instrument in the process of individuation in addition to becoming a source of discharge of sexual tension. The patient's aim is "to feel and recognize himself, in a sense to recover narcissistic integrity" (de M'Uzan, 1973, p. 460). Similarly, Stolorow (1975) concluded that "pain which leads to orgasm helps restore the structurally deficient individual's sense of conviction about the truth and reality of his having a bounded and cohesive self" (p. 350). In both sadist and masochist there is a desperate need for narcissistic restoration that makes the primitive destructive aggression necessary.

Sadist and victim are often one and the same person; that is, different aspects of the self-image in the unconscious of the aggressor. The masochist attracts and solicits sadism as though to complete himself in this way. Many sadists show how consistently they have been driven to danger and self-destruction, their real aim being death or isolation from life by prolonged incarceration. The Marquis de Sade, who spent nearly two-thirds of his life in prison, is a case in point.

The marked tendency in all sexual sadists to become sexual masochists is illustrated by the following clinical example. Martin, a voyeur and rapist whose case history is described at length in chapter 17, had an imperative need to view, touch, and sexually attack young women. He needed to be able to control a female, have her in his power, touch her, and have sexual relations with her. On most occasions, he was the violent, controlling, sadistic rapist, the wielder of weapons in order to intimidate and frighten women into sexual relations. At other times, however, he became the victim of destructive attacks through identification with a victim and experienced sexual excitement and orgasm. Martin reported:

> Tonight I was watching Hitchcock's *The Birds*. There was a scene where the female lead goes up to the attic of a house and is attacked by birds. She gradually succumbs, slipping to the floor after having been bitten repeatedly. Her face is all bloody. The hero saves her. I believed I was she. I got very excited sexually and had an orgasm spontaneously.

Several factors play an important role in pushing those with sadistic fantasies or minor sadistic practices into a full-scale destructive sadistic attack. They are: (1) The failure of the Hanns Sachs mechanism to disguise and neutralize the intrapsychic conflict. (2) Situations which increase aggression such as imprisonment, abandonment by parental figures or their surrogates, either real or imagined slights inflicted by one's associates. These all tend to revive the anachronistic cruelties of childhood. Increased aggressive impulses then cancel out libidinal ones and inhibit sublimatory processes. (3) A decrease in the ego's capacity for displacement, substitution, or sublimation; (4) severe regressive episodes. Such regression destroys neutralization processes and promotes reinstinctualization.

Destructive Aggression in Perverse Fantasy or Expressed in Disguised (Nonsexual) Perverse Acts

In contrast to cases of criminal sadism, milder cases may engage in sadistic fantasies without enactment, the sexual activity having undergone disguise. Such a patient often demonstrates greater ego strength and a greater capacity for fusion of instinctual drives and neutralization. For example, a twenty-five-year-old business executive had utilized homosexual sadistic fantasies exclusively to achieve orgasm since the age of fourteen. During analysis, he became aware of his violent destructiveness and aggression directed against the preoedipal mother. From ages two to three he suffered intensely from a chronic middle-ear infection and mastoiditis. In his adult fantasy life, he forced men to perform rigorous physical tasks and duties against their will which demeaned and debased them. Orgasm was achieved through masturbation at the height of their humiliation, defeat, abasement, and their being reduced to the status of "helpless children," often in diapers. Through the Hanns Sachs mechanism, he was both child and dominant male. The man in the fantasy was a disguised representation of his (phallic) mother. A weak, effeminate homosexual male was substituted for the female. Instead of the patient being submissive as he was forced to be in childhood, he became dominant. In place of his interest in the breast, there was a desire to view the man's penis. The fantasy was thus ego-syntonic and escaped superego prohibition. In later phases of the analysis, these fantasies changed in content and became direct sadistic attacks against the genitalia of both mother and father.

Sadistic acts may undergo strong displacement and substitution in an effort to wipe out all connections with important individuals and even eliminate one's own involvement with a sexual partner. A vivid example of such a sadistic perversion is provided by Stolorow and Grand (1973), Stolorow (1975). His twenty-five-year-old male patient, who suffered from marked ego weakness and masochistic trends:

> [W]ould stroll about outside until he found a woman standing alone, would walk up to her and, when she was not looking, would place a bug upon her shoulder. He would then tell her there was a bug on her. If the woman brushed the bug off and squashed it with her foot, the patient would experience intense sexual excitement. He would then go home and masturbate to the image of the woman squashing the bug [Stolorow and Grand, 1973, p. 349].

Although masochistic elements are striking in this perversion, the sadistic impulse and act are of paramount importance.

Obscene, painful, or frightening telephone calls made to unknown individuals ordinarily escape detection as sadistic perversions. One of their major aims is to cause pain, inflict anxiety, and thereby control the object. Thus sets the stage for sexual excitation, masturbation, and orgasm. Elements of substitution and disguise are compounded by the *distancing* between the subject and object. (The many facets of the telephone perversion are extensively dealt with in chapter 13.)

Severe Violent Destructiveness as the Essential and Manifest Element in the Perverse Act

Few criminal sadists are seen or reported by analysts due to their fear and distrust of the analyst. Valuable information is gained, however, from the analyses of milder cases in this category. Fortunately, much can be deduced by studying the literature of nonanalytic writers devoted to the biography of mass murderers and criminal sadists such as Jack Olsen's book, *The Man With the Candy: The Story of the Houston Mass Murders* (1974) and Gerrold Frank's *The Boston Strangler* (1966); or, in the writings of sadists themselves, notably de Sade (1791). When such individuals are incarcerated, they are almost always seen by nonpsychoanalysts and then only for a short period of time. Happily, we no longer must concede that no criminal sexual sadist has undergone psychoanalysis as was stated in Fenichel's *The Psychoanalytic Theory of Neurosis* (1945), for remarkable psychoanalytic studies of sexual murderers have been reported by A. Hyatt Williams (1964, 1965). Williams (1964) describes the subject's impasse between sexual and destructive feelings toward a person who arouses libidinal or erotic feelings. This type of murderer, who is also a sexual pervert, has much in common with other nonmurderous perverts. He "is imprisoned by the restrictions of the perversion which limit his relationship with a sexually stimulating person to that of destruction in the idiom of and within the narrow boundaries of his perversion. . ." (p. 357). He develops relationships with people that arouse sexual excitement, and as long as the perversion exists, the situation remains "dangerous."[2] "The inexorable and sombre outlook determined by the internal situation and the attempts to escape from it to a less destructive and happier relationship with other people sometimes lifts the tortured and torturing life of the sexual murderer to real tragedy" (p. 357). Compassionate elements, when present in these individuals, are handled by negation. The sadistic killer may attempt in vain to still his murderous impulses by trying to turn exclusively to reparative activities. His destructive criminal actions are not only highly symbolic but are also "part of a coherent and dominating internal situation which from time to time explodes into compulsive action with a strictly limited and fully-defined pattern" (p. 357). In most of Williams's cases, there is an attempt to neutralize aggression through the acceptance of

---

[2]The destruction of the object by stabbing, and so on, may be synchronous with orgasm or may provide the necessary release for a mounting sexual excitement leading to orgasm after the sexual act.

femininity, masculinity being equated with violence and aggression. When this fails, the "masculine component" comes to the surface and powerful aggressive drives are worked out against the object. Being "refused" or "abandoned" by an important person sets in motion the powerful unconscious compulsion to reenact revenge upon a scapegoat with every repetition of the original rejection and deprivation. With a splitting of the subject's ego (many such killers lead double lives), there is a simultaneous splitting of the image of the mother into a good, idealized one and a bad, demonified one. Internalized painful objects are subsequently gotten rid of by being projected onto others and such objects are then destroyed in order to afford relief (Williams, 1965).

Sadistic murders may prevent a psychotic delusional regression through projective identification of an internalized bad object. By exteriorization onto the outside world, the individual is relieved of intense disorganizing and disintegrating anxiety through the enactment of violent inner destructiveness. Sadism may therefore prevent an overt psychosis or may temporarily relieve it.

Destructive Aggression Neutralized by Perversion

We are most familiar with those patients in whom the libidinal element has achieved sufficient superiority and control over violent destructiveness, so that the latter seems to play little or no part. This is most commonly found in the well-structured perversion of homosexuality, for in these instances the homosexual finds the narcissistic selfobject in the partner, thereby avoiding or nullifying the need to harm the object while simultaneously libidinizing it and thus gaining relief. Under various conditions, however, even this equilibrium may be rudely shaken. A frequently encountered example is that of a late middle-aged, successful homosexual man, previously given only to tender expressions of "love" and affection for his sexual partners, who seeks psychoanalytic help when he is frightened and overwhelmed by the emergence of increasingly severe and violent sadistic and masochistic impulses. He feels exploited financially and socially by his much younger partners and can now only achieve orgasm by beating them, being beaten, and urinated upon.

The successful handling of more manifest violence and aggression through a complex web of interlocking psychic mechanisms may be seen in the formation of a fully developed fetishistic perversion. See the case of Calvin, a male underwear fetishist whose case history is fully described in chapter 12. In this patient, violent destructiveness did not have to be acted out upon the object, for the fetish substituted for the object. In the case of pedophilia described in chapter 18, the prepubertal child serves a similar function. The fetish becomes libidinized. Successful sublimatory activities such as the creation of puppets and his own choice of career, which involved creative pursuits, lend a measure of integration to the total personality. Depressive anxiety and mild persecutory thoughts could be alleviated through a masochistic defense and through the utilization of the fetish. In addition, narcissistic overestimation, grandiosity, and omnipotence were not as striking in this patient as in many others. He could be classified as a preoedipal type I fetishist. His childhood was devoid of harsh, cruel parental figures and a degree of object relations had been maintained throughout his life. The perversion functioned as an effective device for his salvation from violent, destructive, and sadistic impulses. As a result of a five-year analysis, he was completely delivered from the prophylactic device (the perversion), was enabled to tolerate separation from his mother, successfully engaged in heterosexual relations, and was able to fully cathect a heterosexual love object.

Other well-structured perversions may function in a similar manner. For example, in the analysis of an exhibitionist, Rosen (1964) clearly revealed the violent destructiveness beneath the libidinal and aggressive impulse to expose the penis. The impulse not only safeguarded against castration, but against a greater danger: having stopped exhibiting his penis as a result of analysis, Rosen's patient later lost his job and his wife and returned desperate for help as he was afraid that he would "murder someone." Rosen concluded:

The exhibitionist regresses to the sadistic phase of childhood when any loss of object, self-esteem or threat of rejection results in a withdrawal of libido from the object or
external reality, and [there is] a subsequent investment of
this libido as secondary narcissism in the infant's body via
a specific organ, his penis [Rosen, 1964, p. 304].

Clinical Illustrations of Sadomasochistic
Perversions from the Psychoanalytic Literature

The rich and variegated symptomatology and protean clinical forms that sadomasochistic perversions take are well
illustrated in fascinating accounts by several analyst/
authors over the past three decades. (The contribution of the
Kris Study Group report (1957) on "Beating Fantasies:
Regressive Ego Phenomena" is noted in chapter 16.)

Ruffler's Contribution (1956)

"The Analysis of a Sadomasochist" by Ruffler (1956) is one
of the few detailed case reports other than my own (see
chapter 16) of an overt beating perversion. Significantly, as
early as 1956, this little-known paper emphasized the pregenital themes in which beating was connected as a punishment inflicted on his mother for an action:

> [I]ncompatible with [her] lofty moral attitude. . . . He also
> felt that the beating symbolized coitus as a process in which
> his father made his otherwise prudish mother submit to
> him. On the one hand, his mother's humiliation gave him
> deep satisfaction and, on the other it filled him with
> jealousy of his father. . . . He saw his difficulties in relation
> to his father as being based on secret guilt at his inability to
> step out of the feminine sphere, by an identification with his
> mother [p. 226].

Ruffler's case differed from Freud (1919) in some essential
points. (Freud's findings as to the meaning of beating fantasies are delineated in chapter 16.) (1) Instead of being feminine and masochistic, the conscious fantasies of the patient
were sadistic. (2) He experienced himself in his dreams in a
feminine sexual position. It is not a boy who is being beaten

in his fantasies, but a girl, and the beating person is either he himself or a female person in authority. This case then is similar in many ways to my patient's case. While Freud derived the beating fantasy from the incestuous tie to the father, the incestuous link of Ruffler's patient was directed toward the mother, not because of a predominant Oedipus complex (i.e., the regressive identification with the mother in order to escape the castration threat from the father), but because of a "pregenital fixation upon the mother." "The patient entered the oedipal stage in tense dependence [on] the maternal world. This dependence was strengthened by the fact that the father failed to a large extent to stand for a positive formative figure, and that the female element was predominant in the patient's environment" (p. 228). This early clinical material was reported long before theoretical explanation in terms of separation–individuation and the status of self–object differentiation, and the understanding of the primary feminine identification that all boys have and which must then be removed through a counteridentification with the father. Furthermore, the sadistic beating was based on the personality structure of his parents, and beating for him had a complex meaning. He was not only sadistic, but masochistic, inasmuch as he saw himself as the beaten child. The fantasy was not projected onto a boy because of his still-feminine identification, as reported in my patient. Here again the preoedipal factor was essential in that the primary separation from the mother was "not yet achieved" (p. 229).

Niederland's Contributions (1958a,b)

Further rich unconscious meanings of various aspects of beating perversion were discovered by Niederland (1958a) and described in his article entitled "Early Auditory Experiences, Beating Fantasies, and Primal Scene." Niederland's patient was a thirty-year-old male, an overt homosexual and masochist who would induce older, athletically built men "to insult and threaten him verbally, to make him kneel before them, suck their genitals, and finally have them perform anal intercourse on him" (p. 472). The patient was brought up in a household full of females, mother and four older sisters. He felt like a girl during most of his childhood. In one of the sessions he reported a particularly satisfactory experience of anal intercourse with an older man in these words: "I liked the way he did it. It was a *good beat.*" The associations to the words "good beat" then led to a beating experience at the age of four when his father beat him in the parental bedroom with a belt, after having locked the bedroom door. The patient's mother stood outside the locked door screaming and begging to be let in, and was prevented from doing so by the enraged father. The patient was trying to "recreate the passion my father was in during this beating. This is what I want, this kind of athletic man grabbing me, holding me. . . . It really was breathtaking, father holding me with his strong arms tightly and I cringing" (p. 472).

Throughout this case history there were oedipal components: primal scene elements, the father's "passion," the mother's screaming, and his taking the mother's place in a breathtaking passionate experience—being beaten—one which he repeated in a never-ending succession of encounters.

His choice of partner is derived from this scene, seeking elderly, strongly built males; also dirty, greasy-looking like the father, who was a plumber. This type of man must make certain angry, violent-sounding noises. These sounds excited the patient and were a prerequisite for sexual gratification. The sounds were usually short verbal insults, obscene words, angry growls. The sounds were similar to those enjoyed by my patient (see chapter 16); for example, the provocative words that "Linda" kept repeating, and the "enraged" passionate upheaval in the prostitute who then spanked him.

The impact of sound meant a lot to this masochistic patient. He revealed that the sound kept him from undergoing a chaotic feeling, a shrinking feeling, as if he were shrinking to a one-year-old baby, perhaps less, without body, without anything (fear of ego dissolution). Therefore, sounds were both disturbing to him and, in the perversion, reassuring. Sounds were a powerful direct threat to which the "archaic mental apparatus" reacted reflexively with anxiety. The threat of castration was heightened, according to Niederland, through the admixture of a primitive archaic precursor; that is, the threat of bodily disruption or annihilation, or what may perhaps be called impending "auditory extinction." This phenomenon may be similar to Greenacre's 1953 concept of primitive, disintegration anxiety, or my own concept of fear of ego dissolution (Socarides, 1968b, 1978a). Niederland felt that the patient mastered this danger by *organizing* the auditory experience.

What this patient did sexually was as follows: Under the impact of an *auditory threat*—after he had left the shelter of his home or office—he looked for a man, a prospective sex partner, who had some of the father's external attributes, and then instructed this man to emit angry, quick, violent sounds and words. Sometimes he paid for this complicity. The verbal, often idiomatic and obscene, but organized sounds spoken in an angry tone of voice were much less threatening than the primitive, unorganized ones of the original experience. Moreover, they were emitted at the patient's request and were in the patient's control and under his influence. He "structured the situation" and transformed the

> [T]hreatening unorganized noise into organized, meaningful sounds emitted at his behest. . . . He transformed the passively endured and dreaded situation into an "actively willed" one, terminating the whole experience (whenever possible) with an act of instinctual gratification, i.e., anal intercourse, with himself as the passively enjoying succubus (return of the repressed)—an experience he characteristically calls the "good beat" [p. 475].

This patient was not actually beaten but his being humiliated, berated, and screamed at was essentially a beating scene: being beaten by the paternal phallus (voice). He revealed, "The only time my father came close to me was on the occasion of that beating." He also equated the father's belt with the paternal phallus, "because the belt was so close to the genitals."

Niederland noted that Freud in a later paper (1925b) made a connection between beating fantasies and sound perception. Freud stated: "The child which is being beaten (or caressed) may at bottom be nothing more nor less than the clitoris itself, so that at its very lowest level [it] will contain a confession of masturbation. . ." (Freud, 1925b, p. 193). Thus, we see in women that there may be an outright transformation of clitoridal sensations into auditory perceptions. It should be further noted that there is a close anatomical relationship between the acoustic sphere with the vestibular apparatus. The latter can be stimulated by rocking, rotating, and other rhythmical excitation. Furthermore, sensations of equilibrium play an essential part as a source of sexual excitation (Fenichel, 1945). It has been suggested by Knapp (1953) that there are profound reflex interactions between acoustic sense and its anatomic neighbor, the vestibula.

It can be said that the state of being beaten "also represents a group of too indirect, intermittent, rhythmical, auditory and affective contact"—a truly "breathtaking and passionate" experience, according to Niederland's patient. Niederland states the hand is appreciated and used as the *tool* of aggression. It is also one of the earliest body organs employed in the service of object relations, reality testing. He hypothesizes that "auditory and possibly also equilibratory stimuli, archaically perceived or elaborated, constituted significant elements in at least some types of such fantasies" (p. 472). Niederland refers to his 1958a paper which discusses the archaic meaning of the hand as (1) procreative; (2) health- and life-giving; and (3) closely related to semen and other phallic elements (Niederland, 1958a). The hand "administering the beating may be unconsciously perceived as a phallic, procreative organ which magically inseminates, fertilizes, imparts power and health" (p. 478).

De M'Uzan's Patient (1973)

In describing the most severe form of a sexual masochistic perverse pathology, Michel de M'Uzan (1973) observes that the psychoanalyst in his normal psychoanalytic practice rarely sees a perverse masochist who actively experiences with pleasure physical punishment of a destructive and life-endangering quality.

In the case he describes, the practices are so extreme and dramatic that he "at first did not know what to say" (p. 455). His patient showed outwardly great friendliness, all the while maintaining a mocking and provocative attitude toward him. De M'Uzan attributed his reluctance to publish the case or to study it further to (1) the fact that the patient was not seen in psychoanalysis but in consultation, and (2) the "monstrosity" of the masochistic practices. He had been sent to him by a radiologist whom the patient had consulted for hemoptysis. During the consultation he told him of his perverse practices. The patient also narcissistically thought that the meeting with the analyst might prove of value one day for others who had the same perversion. The patient found in the consultation "a situation in which he would be humiliated as well as perhaps being able to understand his strange condition more fully" (p. 455).

Characteristically, the patient "had both the appearance and habits of a man who seemed at peace with himself and the world." He wanted no one to have the slightest knowledge of his perversion. He himself could not be in a supervisory position or one of exercising authority; such positions were found repugnant. "Both to give orders and to receive them was to take away his freedom. . . . In short, he appeared to lead a life singularly unmarked by moral masochism" (p. 456).

The patient engaged in the following tortures: (1) Tattooing over practically his entire body except for the face, tattooing of obscene phrases on his buttocks, stating:

> I'm a dirty whore, I am fucked, long live masochism, I am a living shit, I have people shit and piss in my mouth and I swallow it with pleasure. My body loves to be hit, hit me hard. I am a whore, fuck me. I am a prostitute. Help yourself to me like a she-animal. You'll really enjoy it. I'm the kind of arse holes. My mouth and my arse are waiting for pricks [p. 456].

There were many scars and traces of masochistic practices. (2) The right breast had virtually disappeared as it had been burned with a red-hot iron and had been torn away. (3) The naval had been transformed into a kind of crater as molten lead had been poured into it. (4) Strips of skin had been cut into the patient's back "to receive hooks so that he could be suspended while being penetrated by a man" (p. 456). (5) The little toe of his right foot was missing; he had amputated it himself with a hacksaw. (6) "Needles had been introduced into almost everywhere, even into his thorax" (p. 456). (7) "His rectum had been enlarged to be more like a vagina. Some photographs had been taken during this operation." (8) The genitals had not escaped the practices described above. "Gramophone needles were injected into his testicles, and the penis was entirely blue, perhaps as the result of injection of ink into a blood vessel. The end of his penis had been cut open with a razor blade to make the orifice larger" (p. 456). (9) He "had been able to withstand perfectly the daily ingestion of urine and excrement over a period of many years" (p. 456). Many other horrors were present on his body.

The patient had married a cousin at age twenty-five. The cousin was not destined to play the well-known role of the authoritarian and cruel woman (as depicted in my own patient, Dr. X.), for she was a masochist herself, and it was precisely their common perversion that brought them together. They had the opportunity of maltreating each other "out of mutual affection." Both husband and wife were then mutually sadistically treated and tortured by men whom they engaged for this purpose.

The patient's history revealed that he was the only son of relatively elderly parents whom he described as always being kind and attentive. He saw his mother as very affectionate, his father as too rigid. He told the analyst he had been very attached to his father who had been interested in the patient's studies without being excessively severe, and that the patient had grown progressively closer to him. At the age of four the patient apparently underwent (what I consider) an "organizing experience." He saw a small neighbor girl, whose name he still remembered, eating her excrement. His comment about the incident was, "I was disgusted, and afterwards I had second thoughts" (p. 458). At school he searched for corporal punishment, and had an attraction for urine. He experienced sodomy from a dormitory master, became the object of various acts of brutality from his comrades, acts in which the sexual element was perfectly clear. He occasionally had homosexual adventures, but following these all perverse practices disappeared for a while. However, during the perverse practices themselves there were homosexual cruel acts inflicted on him. Since before puberty the perversion seemed to have been practically his only sexual activity, although at times he was able to engage in regular sexual relations with his wife.

The patient stated that on the whole it was the pain that released his ejaculation. He willingly spoke of the process of "escalation." At the crucial moment he did not fear anything and it was the sadist who hesitated before the extreme demand could be carried out. It would seem that the pain assumed a double function. It catalyzed the sexual excitement, and it amplified the excitement and carried it to climax while at the same time the pain lost its specificity. He stated that the whole surface of his body was excitable, with pain being the intermediary. The pain in itself did not constitute the final pleasure. It was only the means to an end. The place where the torture was being applied hurt. Then the erection came, then the pleasure began to emerge. The ejaculation followed at the moment when the pain was the strongest. Only after ejaculation did he experience the physical suffering brought on by his tortures.

While humiliation was searched for in this patient, this was not the end aim. What he desired after all, he stated, was "abasement of his personality." Homosexuality itself was essentially a degradation, as witness the phrases he had written in his flesh to manifest this disgrace. "I gave the impression of being an invert, but I wasn't one for pleasure, but for humiliation. I got no physical satisfaction from it; it was moral satisfaction" (p. 460). He depicted himself as motivated by a powerful need to be humiliated. Homosexuality was an instrument for its attainment.

The "removal of his will" or "total annihilation of his will" hid other elements. In actuality, he did not feel degraded. Beneath servility and humility were the opposite feelings. He had a profound scorn for others, and there was derision in his attitude. The annihilation of his own con-

scious volition was nothing but a mask. "To abolish all will
in one's self is to renounce possession of the phallus, anal
and narcissistic, and is therefore to renounce power of any
kind" (p. 460). "His renunciation of the phallic symbol was
no more than a cover for an affirmation of omnipotence. Or
to put it more precisely, he did not renounce anything" (p.
460). Beneath his omnipotence, so well camouflaged, was an:

> [I]mmense pride which came through on these occasions
> when the patient alluded to the terrible tortures he had
> endured. . . . In actuality, pride established itself simultane-
> ously in anal satisfaction and phallic affirmation, the suf-
> fering endured representation, in fact, a potent phallus with
> the help of which he would seek the relief of the primordial
> narcissistic wound with which his being had been afflicted
> [p. 461].

De M'Uzan comments: "He fears nothing, not even castration. He desires everything, including castration, which
is within his grasp. . ." (p. 426). "The primacy of the phallus
and his orgastic power assure him of the inviolable position
of a megalomaniac. The other person is negated as someone
susceptible to desire, is relegated to a purely instrumental
function" (p. 462).

This patient would be classified as preoedipal type II,
masochistic pervert, at the most extreme degree of narcissistic pathology (i.e., borderline). He suffered from a severe,
grandiose split-off pathological self whose core consisted
of malignant omnipotent wishes to be superior, inviolate,
and capable of exercising a primordial sense of power in
the sense of destroying himself in one final act of defiance
against paternal imagos and his environment.

I agree with Greenacre (1968) when she suggests that the
masochist wishes to complete himself by enlisting others to
torture him. In fact, the patient identified completely with
his tormentor who, in the doctor's opinion, can well be
nothing more than the original part of the ego and the "nonego," the part onto which is projected a powerful destructive
tendency through splitting. This theory provides a plausible
explanation for de M'Uzan's patient's self-destructive be-

havior. It also complements Freud's 1924a hypothesis, "that another portion (of the destructive instinct) does not share in this transposition outwards: it remains inside the organism and with the help of the accompanying sexual excitation . . . becomes libidinally bound there. . ." (pp. 163–164).

In such patients there has been a failure to integrate tensions and conflicts at the psychic level. There is a tendency toward the total discharge of excitation. The same process may be noted in certain psychosomatic diseases where there is actual destruction of tissue.

De M'Uzan notes that the masochist:

> [T]hreatens his identity in a regressive fashion and mobilizes his destructive tendencies, aimed at making a new effort to establish the boundaries of the ego to provide the economically necessary orgastic experience. We can thus see that the factor of excessive quantity is the agent, at one and the same time, of the demand for orgastic enjoyment and of the retention of the destructive tendencies [p. 465].

The effort to rediscover ego boundaries (in those with deficient body–ego) fails, in part at least, because of the archaic character of the destructiveness (in the functional sense described above). De M'Uzan speculates that in these patients the separation of the ego from the nonego starts in a primitive, brutal, and predatory manner comparable to a "tearing apart" rather than gradual individuation. Lastly, de M'Uzan emphasizes that this form of masochism does have a "constructive function" in that it promotes the recovery of narcissistic integrity despite the gross damage done to the organism.

Ferber's Patient (1975)

Ferber (1975) described a thirty-year-old male with a masochistic perversion and beating fantasy (apparently without overt participation in the perverse act) which led to ejaculation. Unlike my patient, Dr. X., the fantasy of Ferber's patient consisted of being excited by a sadistic young *man* who was sometimes a criminal wearing tight-fitting blue

jeans and black leather boots. The buttocks outlined in tight
pants overwhelmed the patient with a desire to fondle them
and put his face between them and smell the anal area. Thus
the homosexual element of the perversion was readily and
consciously acceptable. The sadistic young man chosen as a
partner in the perverse act would become very angry over
some minor thing that the patient had done to displease him,
and the patient would then be ordered to grovel at his feet
and lick his boots. He was also threatened with severe beatings, whereupon the patient would cringe and, in a humble
voice, beg forgiveness, pleading to be spared. He was spared
from the beating by allowing himself in his fantasy to be
placed in a humiliating way in the tough young fellow's lap
and whipped. A long masturbation accompanied this
fantasy.

Ferber's patient was a middle child, an irritable baby, a
chronic nail-biter up to the age of seven. He had a four to five
year's older, active brother who behaved sadistically toward
him, alternately hugging, squeezing, pinching him, throw-
ing him down, and riding on him. (This may have constituted an organizing experience for his later perversion.)
When he was two-and-a-half, both he and his brother became
ill. The brother died of pneumonia, and the patient developed
deep throat abcesses with mastoid infections that required
surgery. (Such traumatic surgical activities in the preoedipal
period frequently set the stage for a later masochistic
perversion.)

The meaning of Ferber's patient's beating fantasy was
an unconscious wish for reunion with the brother, represented by the tough young guy and a denial of the brother's
death and a need for punishment for unconscious aggressive
wishes. What was crucial was that after the patient's illness
at this tender age, the mother became increasingly overpro-
tective and encouraged a symbiotic tie to herself, impeding a
successful traversing of the rapprochement phase. The boy
was "infantilized" and this infantilization fostered "an
already existing wish for a union with the powerful mother
who would protect him from injury, death, and a sadistic,
threatening world" (p. 216). His patient, in my opinion,
showed a severe anxiety at separation, a battle for control

between the mother and son during the anal period, including control of eating functions. He was also given enemas at which times he would attempt to run away from the mother. He was caught by the father, placed in the mother's lap (similar to the requirements of the perversion itself), and an enema tube forcibly inserted in his rectum. This stimulated not only his anus but also his penis. Withholding, resisting, and being forced to submit became parts of the beating fantasy, as well as parts of his own character.

Ferber deduced that (1) the buttocks that excite him so much symbolize the mother's breast that he wished to fondle, bite, and completely devour; (2) he projected his cruel sadistic impulses and turned them against himself; pushing himself into the mother's breast was a way of pushing his brother away, and pushing his face into her buttocks was a wish to push himself inside the mother, explore the contents of her body, force out the fetus that was inside, but yet escape engulfment. "To smell and lick the buttocks is incorporation of the mother through inhalation, a breathing her in in the form of swallowing her, and an attempt to merge with her" (p. 217). This incorporation and fusion with the mother protected against the feeling of being abandoned. It also defended against the wish to destroy her. Ferber further determined that the person who did the beating not only stood for the brother, but for the mother and the patient himself. The black boots were a fetish indicating the patient's struggle with intense castration anxiety and a need to deny that any object was without a penis. Mastoid surgery stimulated castration fears, increased the wish to fuse and identify with the mother, to become like her. The sadistic man stood for the phallic sadistic father. It indicated a passive sexual relationship with him. The perverse fantasies occurred whenever he felt disappointed or rejected. Frustration of intense oral needs led to intense rage and fears of loss of control, and the perverse fantasies served the purpose of "erotizing the aggressive drive he feared would destroy both himself and the object" (p. 219). Frustration also meant a deep narcissistic wound. Through the use of the beating fantasy "he established a kind of narcissistic equilibrium by attempts at fusion with the exclusive possession of the omnipotent narcissistic object" (p. 219). Through the perverse fantasy he would become "the greatest, the best, the first, and this could temporarily compensate the loss of esteem and damaged self-representation" (p. 220). In essence, by fusing with an omnipotent powerful object, he would become admired.

It was Ferber's belief that the fantasy had a preoedipal origin as its most important and central feature. While Freud emphasized the importance of the relationship to the father as being one of a passive sexual attitude (i.e., a negative Oedipus complex), Ferber suggested that the "relation to the preoedipal mother was of equal significance," for desires for fusion in some form or other, and a sado-masochistic attachment to her was conspicuous (p. 221).

Robinson's Contribution (1979)

Robinson's (1979) article, "A Screen Memory in a Child Analysis," describes the psychoanalysis of an eight-year-old boy with a beating fantasy who began treatment at the age of seven because of aggressive behavior, uncontrollable rage, sadistic attacks upon animals, placing himself in dangerous situations such as walking in front of moving cars, refusal to eat at the family table, frequent nightmares, "passionate relationships with boys," often embracing and kissing in public, little contact with and fear of father, clumsiness and lack of coordination, inability to play games, slowness, and inability to learn at school. The boy was described an "an odd child" by most adults because of a marked preoccupation with horror, sadism, and violence.

Until the age of two he seemed to be a content, thriving baby. Difficulties in the mother–child relationship developed when her concern about a close relative caused her withdrawal from him. A long separation followed, and David refused to recognize her when she returned. He then became "difficult, demanding, irritating, clung to her, wept." Sleep disturbances occurred and toilet training, introduced at two years, had to be abandoned because he screamed and ran away at the sight of the toilet. At the same time, he engaged in highly stimulating sexual play with a five-year-old sister. David bathed with his father and was allowed to play with his father's penis.

A screen memory consists of his falling into a lake as he had not been discouraged from going near it. The lake signified succumbing to passive wishes in relation to the father.

> Following more work on David's masturbation conflicts, we began to see that his wish to be "father's lover" also implied that to be loved by the father meant to be beaten by him. The masochistic nature of his fantasies became apparent when David first hinted at his torturing himself mentally. He would either place himself in or fantasize about dangerous situations which would culminate in a fantasy of rising anxiety usually about being beaten. He would go over and over these scenes in his mind. For example, he tore a boy's coat and lived in fear that this boy would come and beat him; for weeks he was "on the lookout," all the while frequenting places in which this boy regularly appeared. He was never actually beaten, but he wished that something dramatic would happen [pp. 318–319].

At age seven or eight he became sexually aroused by sex magazines with pictures of women being beaten on the buttocks by men. At first the fantasy person beating him was his mother. He remembered masturbating and becoming excited by women on television beating up men. He even thought of mother doing this to him. Analysis revealed his wish to be castrated and to become the father's "lover." The identification with the beaten women was a further link to these wishes. "Thus, to be loved by the father ultimately meant to be beaten by him" (p. 319).

In "Perverse Symptoms and the Manifest Dream of Perversion" (Socarides, 1980b), I described a homosexual patient who did not ordinarily have sadomasochistic homosexual fantasies or sadomasochistic aspects to his homosexual life, except on certain occasions when his psychic economy was in severe imbalance. Sadomasochistic perverse practices helped to ward off threats of ego dissolution. In that paper (see chapter 7), I described the sequential appearance of a bondage, sadomasochistic homosexual fantasy, leading to a sadistic homosexual dream and, upon awakening, to a homosexual sadistic fantasy and then to enactment of a perverse act. This symptomatology was part and parcel of a rapprochement crisis. Significantly, he developed overwhelming and florid fantasies of sadomasochistic perversions involving torture, being bound, gagged, humiliated, hung, genitals injured. All but the most severe of these were actually practiced. He often bound himself and performed sadistic acts upon various parts of his body. The efflorescence of these sadomasochistic fantasies and practices was in part an attempt to ward off threats to the integrity of the self against disintegration, and were compensatory in that they would help him restore the boundaries of his body-ego. His sadomasochistic preoccupations could temporarily relieve his anxieties and avoid his suicidal ruminations.

Kligerman's Patient (1981)

In a panel presentation on "Masochism: Current Concepts" (Panel, 1981), Kligerman described the case history of a man with a classic spanking perversion. The beating or spanking was done by a "strong, dominating woman—a 'dominatrix.'" Like my patient, Dr. X. (see chapter 16), his patient was a highly successful individual, able to make decisions, self-disciplined, well educated, whose father was prone to dogmatic pronouncements, brooked no "counterlogic," and threw his son into an adversary position in which he could not win. He chronically withdrew in frustration, loneliness, disappointment, and humiliation. In addition, he had high ideals, had an air of bravado, and displayed grandiosity and precocity that "covered an internal sense of deficit" (p. 681). The spanking perversion provided him with a feeling of strength and potency in his sexual life. It provided feelings of separateness and a painful sense of "autonomy" when threatened by attacks on self-esteem. As in other instances of this perversion, the unconscious meaning of the perverse fantasy was anal penetration by the powerful father. The dominatrix who would administer his beatings was a substitute for the father (Hanns Sachs mechanism). In contrast to

Dr. X., Kligerman's patient only fantasied his beatings without actual participation in the overt perverse act. He needed the fantasy for sexual performance with a woman, but later on detached the sexual act from the fantasy, using it to relieve narcissistic tension in general, apparently without sexual arousal. Kligerman chose to explain this perversion in part as follows: his patient "failed to make an adequate internalization of a consistent external authority that could then form an automatic self-disciplining function and provide him with a secure sense of conviction" of having a bounded and cohesive self (p. 681). His infantile grandiosity was reinforced in the perversion. Kligerman applied Kohut's systematic conceptual model of the psychology of the self to explain the connection between the patient's masochism (his beating fantasies) and his narcissism: "By means of a fantasy a merger with an omnipotent self-object, or simply by reminding one's self of the existence of the body–self in a very painful way" he counteracted a "feeling of deadness" (p. 681). Kligerman noted quite correctly that such masochistic, self-harming fantasies may be interwoven with "very well-organized structure formation stemming from much higher levels of psychic development" (p. 681). As in the case of Dr. X., although oedipal issues may be present, they were not predominant. They were secondary accretions to the basic preoedipal core of the perversion. Utilizing my terminology, Kligerman's patient would be classified as preoedipal type II narcissistic masochist (spanking) pervert.

Concluding Comments

In sexual sadomasochism the attainment of orgastic release is achieved through the infliction of and/or experiencing painful stimulation on a partner, whether of the same or opposite sex, directly to the body or to the mind alone (humiliating experiences or experiences of helplessness), whether in fantasy or reality. If one receives the punishment or painful stimuli, one vicariously identifies with the sadistic partner so that roles are interchangeable and both provide relief. In many perversions the aggressive component is not manifestly expressed, as libidinal activity has functioned successfully, neutralizing both fears and aggression. "Pure" sadistic perversions (Glover, 1964) are relatively rare compared to other perversions, as the "guilt engendered by highly charged aggressive or sadistic reactions is [mostly] dealt with partly by repression and partly by displacement to a non-sadistic component" (Glover, 1964, p. 155).

Glover also pointed out that:

> [E]xtensive infantile anxiety and guilt predispose to perversion formation. . . . The exaggeration of infantile components of sexuality characteristic of regressions of sexual deviation help to "contain" the aggressive impulses at the cost of an infantile canalization of sexual impulse and a reduction or suspension of normal heterosexual impulse [p. 153].

In most instances we can determine in the perversions to what extent the libidinal activity, the erotization, functions successfully as a counter to aggression. This appears to be dependent on the developmental level from which the aggression derives its strength.

In those perverts with sadomasochistic perversions or in the more severe sadistic perversions, the perverse act mixed with aggression aims at immediate gratification and alleviation of urgent destructive feelings, threatening extinction of the self. In these cases the sexual partners are the instruments through which the perverts can seek expression and release from oppressive and importunate anxiety, guilt, incestuous feelings, and above all, aggression. It seems likely that the greater the degree of aggression and depression the more importunate the need for enactment of sadomasochistic perversions. The production of pain in one's self or in others leads to orgasm, thus helping to restore a structurally deficient individual's sense of conviction of his having a bounded and cohesive self (Eissler, 1958a; Socarides, 1978a; Stolorow and Lachmann, 1980). There is a desperate need in such cases for narcissistic restoration that makes the primitive destructive aggression necessary in the first place, and which is relieved through the sadomasochistic act. A further determinant is the status of object relations; the more severe the impairment in object relations, the greater the need for enactment of perverse activity and the production of orgasm with its capacity for restoring the sense of having a bounded and cohesive self. (Despite the urgency of the need and its enactment, many of these individuals often cannot obtain orgasm and are driven to wild, frenzied "sexual murders.") These patients react to anxiety and depression with object directed or self directed aggression (sadism and masochism), and with an imperative need to alleviate this destructive aggression through libidinization. Immersed in the pain of these crises, the ego of the pervert is unable to sustain itself. He has few choices: to undergo disintegrative anxiety; to engage in nonsexual aggressive episodes with primarily defensive reactions in the face of danger, thus temporarily releasing his contact with reality in a symbolic reenactment of the mother-child unity (e.g., killing of a mother surrogate), or to engage in the perverse act. The wish-fulfilling function and the discharge function in these acts may be insufficient for the alleviation of importunate anxiety drives and for maintenance of the structure of the cohesion of the ego. This must be supplemented through further play action ("raising the stakes" through increasing the pain of torture), the social acting out of infantile conflicts in the "strange and often bizarre sado-masochistic acts" (Glover, 1964). Thus the ego may be freed for the moment, and an independent and coherent organization, and even a sense of identity may be temporarily enjoyed. While an object relationship may be achieved, it is a pseudo one, subjectively created by the pervert.

It should be emphasized that masochism is not only a method for neutralizing aggression, but also for keeping the tie to the mother. The masochist wishes to escape the all-powerful, retaliative mother, but he dares not cease being her masochistic, thinly disguised slave. In the masochistic state, guilt over the incestuous feelings toward the mother is continually warded off through self-punitive activities. However, the pain and masochism which are self controlled and self induced, give rise to a false sense of victory, elation, and omnipotence, a state of masochistic invulnerability.

We are reminded that in all sexual perversion repressive efforts are directed against both libidinal and aggressive drives. The result of the repressive compromise (Sachs mechanism) produces a remarkable transformation of aggression, hate, hostility, envy, and jealousy into their opposites, and provides a high pleasure reward: orgastic satisfaction and relief from severe conflicts. For example, the homosexual's deepest conflicts may arise from an intense desire to eat, suck, and bite the breast of the mother with a simultaneous reaction formation against the breast, repressing interest in it and turning toward the phallus of the male. Aggression itself (destructive aggressive impulses) threaten the existence of the object, and the investment of the object with libido acts as its protection.

In similar fashion the erotization of anxiety produces a remarkable transformation of fear and apprehension belonging to a deeper level of conflicts, into their opposites: libidinal pleasure and orgastic satisfaction. This is made possible by the multiple defense mechanisms, including substitution and displacement. Much is to be learned as to the exact mechanism involved in the erotization of anxiety or aggression. A fundamental observation is that when a pervert's insufficient self and object representations are threatened, he develops anxiety and/or aggression, and is faced with the necessity to shore up a precarious and imperilled self representation (Stolorow and Lachmann, 1980) He utilizes his early psychosexual experiences for this purpose. It is crucial to note that it is not the fixated erotic experiences per se (i.e., the instinctual drive), that is then aggressively reanimated in the perversion, but rather it is the *early function* of the erotic experience peculiar to that particular individual that is retained and regressively relied upon. In this way, erotization both of aggression and anxiety allows the pervert to maintain the structural cohesion and stability of a threatened and/or disintegrating self and object representation (Stolorow and Lachmann, 1980). Ego survival is thereby insured.

Major psychic transformations are effected through the mechanism of the repressive compromise (Hanns Sachs mechanism). For example, a homosexual having developed infantile libidinal strivings of an intense nature toward his mother, which result in guilt, anxiety, and savage hostility, attempts to repress these strivings. This is accomplished through perverse acting out. As repression is only partially successful in obtaining relief, he must occasionally resort to sadomasochistic expression of his unconscious drives. Sadistic aggression may escape repression and disguise. I believe that in such instances we are dealing with a partial failure of the Sachs mechanism to achieve its desired result, and quantities of primary and secondary aggression erupt into consciousness and are expressed directly in the perversion itself.

Of special significance are those individuals who engage in sadomasochistic perversions and who show overt borderline features. They are classified as preoedipal type II narcissistic perverts, at the extreme range of narcissistic pathology (Kernberg, 1980a, 1984a,b, 1986). They are characterized by generalized impulsivity, lack of anxiety tolerance, a disposition to explosive and chronic rage reactions, and tendency to severe paranoid reactions (Kernberg, 1980a, 1984b). Some of them engage in "joyful" types of cruelty fantasies. They are self-mutilative, and the combination of paranoid and explosive personality leads them to severe aggressive attacks upon themselves or others in order to secure orgastic relief. Since their aggression is not integrated into a superego structure, they are capable of engaging in sadomasochistic acts with willing partners to the point of potential or actual damage to themselves or others. During the course of psychoanalytic therapy an unrelieved and continuous incursion of reality into their narcissistic grandiose structures may produce an alarmingly intense disintegration of the self-concept with threats of fragmentation, regressive experiences, paranoidal psychoticlike transferences, and an intensification of perverse activities.

Chapter 6
DEPRESSION IN
PERVERSION

Introduction

The depressive affect holds a position of central importance alongside that of anxiety in the formation, meaning, content, and expression of sexual perversion. While frequently alluded to in clinical studies of perversion, the depressive affect has not been systematically studied or elucidated in relation to perversion. My aim in this chapter is to attempt an integration of this affect into the unitary theory of perversion (see chapter 3).

The affect of anxiety has primacy over all other affects (Freud, 1926) in the causation of psychiatric disorders, and the task of the scientific observer was at first to delineate and describe the function and content of various forms of anxiety; that is, separation anxiety, engulfment anxiety, fragmentation anxiety, castration anxiety. These have received considerable attention by psychoanalysts during the past two to three decades. These anxieties have been associatively connected with deficits in the body–ego, fears of bodily disintegration, unusual sensitivity to threats of bodily damage, the increase in primary and secondary aggression (see chapter 5) leading to threats to the object and the self, threats to the loss of the object as well as loss of the object's love.

Our understanding of the role of depression in perversion had to await theoretical contributions and infant observational studies which were never as far advanced as those in the area of the affect of anxiety. One reason for this lack of knowledge was the difficulty in defining the precise nature of depression in infants and children.

I shall briefly review the work of several analysts who have investigated the infantile genetic matrix of the depressive affect. Analytic reconstruction has been enriched by our knowledge of primary psychic development as it pertains to separation-individuation phases and has expanded our current knowledge of the effect of earlier traumatic experiences. I suggest that the matrix out of which perversions arise is one in which there is a negative affective predisposition characterized by the sense of helplessness, hopelessness, narcissistic deflation, and a consequent disturbance in gender-defined self identity. This occurs concomitantly with, and is intimately interwoven with, the affect of anxiety.

Perverse acts function to reduce suffering due to both anxiety and the painful affect of depression. The relief of the depressive affect through perverse acts helps restore the self against threats of fragmentation, diminished separation anxiety, and compensates for narcissistic injury. It constitutes an erotized flight from despair and helplessness, perceived in the unconscious as a threat of starvation, a finding common in depressed patients. Furthermore, I hope to show that it is not the fixated erotic experience per se (i.e., the instinct derivative that is regressively reanimated in the perversion), but rather that it is the *early function* of the erotic experience that is retained and regressively relied upon (Socarides, 1978a; Stolorow and Lachmann, 1980). In this way, through erotization, the pervert attempts to diminish and/or erase anxiety and depression [both "basic ego responses" (Bibring, 1953)] and maintain "the structural cohesion and stability of crumbling, fragmenting, and disintegrating self and object representations" (Stolorow and Lachmann, 1980, p. 149).

I shall illustrate these findings by clinical examples of depressive moods and depression in transvestism, pedophilia, and homosexuality.

Theoretical Contributions on Depression in Infancy and Childhood

In 1953 Bibring made an outstanding contribution to our understanding of depression in children by applying our then expanding knowledge of primary psychic development. He introduced the concept of "basic depressive affect" and proposed that anxiety and depression are *both basic ego reactions*. They represented opposing basic ego responses: anxiety, a reaction to external or internal danger which indicates the ego's desire to survive, the ego responding with signals of anxiety, while in depression the ego becomes paralyzed, finds itself incapable of meeting the danger, and in extreme situations "the wish to live is replaced by the wish to die" (Bibring, 1953, p. 35).[1] His theoretical concepts provided a bridge to the understanding of relationships between adult clinical depressions and their ontogenesis in earliest infancy and adulthood.[2] They laid the groundwork for later infant observational studies, especially those made by Mahler (1961, 1966b; Mahler, Pine, and Bergman, 1975).

Bibring contended that frequent frustrations of the infant's oral needs at first may mobilize anxiety and then anger, which then leads to exhaustion, helplessness, and depression. This is an "early self-experience of the infantile ego's helplessness, of its lack of power to provide the vital supplies," and is "probably the most frequent factor predisposing to depression" (p. 37). He noted that it is not the oral frustration and fixation per se, but the "infant's or little child's shock-like experience of and fixation to the feelings of

---

[1] Rene Spitz (1946) had already described a potentially lethal form of depression in infants, "anaclitic depression," a product of severe maternal deprivation and neglect in the first twelve months of life.

[2] It should be noted that, as early as 1946, Jacobson predicted the impact of early disappointments in parental omnipotence and the subsequent devaluation of parental images on the little child's ego formation; that is, a devaluation and destruction of the infantile self, and a "primary childhood depression" which, if repeated in later years, produced a similar "disillusionment" (Bibring, 1953, p. 19).

helplessness" (p. 37) that is pathogenic. Bibring wrote not only of the child's need for affection and need to be loved, but of the opposite defensive need "to be independent and self-supporting." In this way he antedated Mahler's concept of separation-individuation phases leading to object constancy. He noted furthermore that certain of the child's strivings and cherished sources of gratification fight against interferences by the object (the rapprochement struggle of Mahler). In a different context he describes the helplessness of the anal phase.

> The child struggles to independent ego strength, to control his body through defiance and mobilization of forms of aggression, and he may attempt separation from the mother. Intense aggression may lead to remorse and guilt, fear of punishment, and corresponding aspirations . . . to be good, not to be resentful, hostile, defiant [p. 38].

Mahler's Infant Observational Studies

The major contributions of Mahler and her co-workers in the area of sadness, grief, and depression in infancy and early childhood spans two decades of research. They are to be found in three articles: "On Sadness and Grief in Infancy and Childhood: Loss and Restoration of the Symbiotic Love Object" (1961); "Notes on the Development of Basic Mood: The Depressive Affect" (1966b); and "The Epigenesis of Separation Anxiety, Basic Mood and Primitive Identity" (1975c). In her first paper Mahler agrees with Bibring that anxiety and depression are indeed basic affective reactions, and that such "depressions" at this early age, since sufficient structuralization of the mental apparatus has not occurred, express a state of helplessness and not a clinical depression as we know it in adults. Such frustrations lead to anxiety and anger, and if they continue are replaced by feelings of exhaustion, helplessness, and larval states of depression.

Synchronous with the advances of the rapprochement phase; for example, acquisition of primitive skills, cognitive faculties, clearer differentiation, and the formation of intrapsychic representation of the love object, is the realization of a large number of obstacles in the way of magic omnipotent wishes and fantasies. The world is no longer the "child's oyster," and he has to cope on his own as a relatively helpless, small, and lonesome individual. He begins to find that his parents withhold omnipotence, no longer permit him to share in everything, deny emotional needs and supplies. Disturbances in separation due to faulty mother–child interaction in the context of an "abdicating father" (Socarides, 1982b; see chapter 11) lead not only to sadness, grief, and helplessness, but to increased ambivalence, loss of self-esteem, an increase in unneutralized aggression, a disturbance in the child's progress toward object constancy.

In the rapprochement phase one can clearly discern a basic depressive mood in those whose self representation is imperilled (Mahler, 1966b). Unneutralized aggression may be handled by splitting and projection, and potentially pathological combinations of defenses are employed to ward off the child's hostility and his fear of annihilating the love object. He may begin to feel an acute deflation of his omnipotence which was formerly used to ward off injuries to the self-esteem. The resultant critical "negative depressive affective response" (Mahler, 1966b) may take the following forms: (1) separation and grief reactions following dramatic struggles with the love object, marked by temper tantrums and giving up in despair; (2) impotent resignation and surrender; (3) masochistic reactions; (4) discontented anger; (5) increased clinging to the mother. These are formidable obstacles to the attainment of object constancy.

In 1975 Mahler and her associates included the disturbance in "gender-defined self-identity" (a central finding in all sexual perverts I have analyzed) as one of the developmental issues which is seriously affected by the "negative depressive affective state." She commented: "Our data indicate that the boy's active aggressive strivings, his gender-determined motor-mindedness seems to help him maintain (with many ups and downs, to be sure) the buoyancy of his body ego feelings, his belief in his body strength, and his pleasure in functioning" (p. 13). Under normal conditions the momentum of the body's motor functions counteracts too-abrupt deflation of the practicing grandeur and omnipotence and helps him overcome increasing hypersensitivity about separation from the mother during the rapprochement phase.

Appropriate gender-defined self identity occurs under the following conditions, ones which I find are never met by mothers of boys who later develop perversions: (1) the mother respects and enjoys the boy's masculinity and phallicity, especially in the second half of the third year; (2) she encourages an identification with the father, or possibly with an older brother, thereby facilitating the boy's gender-defined self identity; and (3) she happily and willingly relinquishes the son's body and ownership of his penis to him (Mahler, 1973).

In contrast to those mothers who set the stage for perverse formation in their male children, favorable mothering leads the boy to (1) cope with the anxiety feelings of helplessness, loss of sources of infantile gratification associated with symbiosis and separation; and (2) disidentify with the mother and make a counteridentification with the father (Greenson, 1968). Mother must not be intrusive and interfere with the boy's phallic strivings, and the boy must not give in with passive surrender. This is particularly harmful if the father does not lend himself to idealization and identification so that his son may find comfort and joy in his sense of masculinity.

Clinical Illustrations

A Transvestite Patient

Alfred (see also chapter 15), a thirty-nine-year-old, highly successful professional man, had practiced a transvestite perversion since the age of thirteen. Transvestite acts made up for maternal coldness, neglect, and deprivation of childhood, and provided him with a sense of power and control, dissipating his sense of emptiness, making him feel "alive" emotionally, and reducing feelings of sadness and melancholy.

He frequently searched the trash baskets at his apartment house in order to find discarded women's pantyhose which he then put on and masturbated.

The boredom and depression I feel then leaves me. I want to be filled up. I feel I could get an erection if I could fill myself up with a fountain syringe . . . if I had a bra on my thighs my emptiness would be overcome. My hunger is so great and my loneliness for other people so overwhelming. I want women to cry for me, feed me, fill me up. I want them to cry even after I leave them.

He sought revenge and restitution for the suffering he experienced during his early years: a tonsillectomy at age two; frequent enemas administered by a "kooky," chronically depressed mother who never touched him except when she bottle-fed him (he was told); a weak, passive, and compliant father who abdicated his responsibility as a father in protecting him from his mother; feelings of personal physical ugliness ("big lips, short stature, too much hair").

She couldn't handle me, forced me to eat, then gave me enemas, and I remember my screaming. She couldn't get me to move my bowels, and she caused me to cry. I picture myself at maybe two years of age not being in control of my own destiny. And then I was sent away. I would argue with her, talk back. And she never held or hugged me.

Alfred's temper tantrums made him unmanageable in his mother's eyes, and resulted in his being sent away to a home for "difficult boys" at the age of four-and-a-half years for six months.

I recall saying goodbye to my parents. It is so upsetting now. I didn't want to leave them. I always felt embarrassed by mother. I wonder why she was so mean to me. My cries were filled with loneliness and rage. I could not bear to be separated from her, and I could not bear to go to school. I would just cry and cry, and my mother just wouldn't listen to me.

He recalls recurrent dreams in late childhood of being in a war, coming out of a trench, and as he lifted his head he gets shot in the heart and is dying or dead—a "toddler over the top."

Homosexual Preoedipal Type II Patient with Associated Narcissistic Personality Disorder

Willard was a fifty-year-old, attractive, highly articulate and intelligent man who suffered from both a homosexual perversion and narcissistic personality disorder proper. (Willard's case history is extensively described in chapter 9.)

When the "bombardment of reality" interfered with his "tranquil integrity," grandiose exhibitionistic demands came out of repression and collided with reality, leading to regressive fragmentation and a depletion depression. In this state of decompensation he often retreated to his bed, depressed, lethargic, unable to move, often defecated on the floor, would not clean it up for days, and put clamps on his nipples during masturbation or in homosexual relations to heighten his sense of self by direct erotic stimulation. These actions made him feel alive, restored him from his former self, and tended to decrease the strong depressive affect and his inability to act, which permeated these regressive periods.

When such a patient loses his sexual partner it is not the loss of the object nor the loss of the object's love for which he grieves. He feels the anguish of the undernourished child (Tolpin and Kohut, 1979). Narrating such an event for the analyst one day, Willard was immediately reduced to tears and sobbing in response to the analyst's empathic comment.

> When I came back to my room following my session, I got to thinking about P. and I started to cry. I wept disconsolately for about an hour and a half, and I kept saying, "my baby, my baby." I was in a lamentation. I really don't know what this great profundity of emotion was apropos of. I'm not sure I would have had it at all if you hadn't said this morning that it was a pity he was going. ... Whether you were sympathizing with me for losing my friend for a time, or whether you meant that he was a constructive or beneficent influence upon me, something that I *needed*, I can't tell. I have a feeling that it was the latter, that I was somehow bereft because his good presence for me was gone, and you noticed. My sexual feelings for him have not been so urgent lately, but my tears were absolutely unstoppable. I was shouting with *grief*, shouting with grief. And it went on for at least half an hour, and I couldn't believe it

was some sort of ideal representation of myself in him, and that all the things he does for me are ways for me to complete myself and to feel alive and in reality.

Willard's homosexuality was a consequence of disturbance belonging to the early infancy-childhood developmental stage in which self and body-ego boundaries are in the process of being established through maternal care and management. He tries to remedy the result of a disturbance in object differentiation and integration through perverse activity, through the use of self-objects. The homosexual contact allowed him to participate in a sense of maternal calmness and composure, and to overcome feelings of grief and helplessness. Through acting out and mobilizing interest on the part of the partner with imaginative sharing and playacting activities (Khan, 1979), the deadness of Willard's internal world is ameliorated and his fragmented self is temporarily healed. Conversely, the loss of the homosexual object leaves him bereft, in inconsolable grief, with a resurgence of helplessness, apathy, weakness, and empty depression.

Discussion

In this chapter, I have noted the significance of the depressive affect for the success and/or failure in traversing separation-individuation phases of development, and described how a developmentally arrested ego seeks out perverse activities in an erotized flight from feelings of helplessness, deadness, and grief.

Through acting out (1) an intrapsychic crisis is averted: passivity, guilt, and anxiety are reversed by an erotized flight to reality and toward an external object; (2) there is a denial of sensations of depression, heaviness, and sadness by specifically opposite sensations (Sachs, 1923). Winnicott (1935), in a different theoretical frame of reference, has correctly defined this function of perverse acting out as a "sexual variant of manic defense" in which there is a "reassurance against death, chaos and mystery . . . a flight to external reality from internal reality" (p. 132). Superego strictures are sidestepped, depression and psychic pain are eliminated through the exploitation of every possible aspect of sexuality, bodily sensations, in order to deny stillness, slowness, seriousness, discord, failure, and boredom.[4]

Denial of certain aspects of depression is facilitated through symbols. The "need to view phallic erections" and "inflatable bodies," or to hear flatus are contradepressive and displace objects. Bright clothing or articles such as diaphragms (see case of transvestism), douche accompaniments, and so on, have both depressive and contradepressive significance. A young, cherubic, prepubertal youth, or a youthful adolescent of a particular type may function as a contradepressant equivalent to a pedophile or to an aging homosexual, respectively. The use of colorful clothing, a humorous mood, "dance versus inanimacy," "rising rather than sinking," "lightness rather than heaviness," "luminousness versus darkness," movement in contrast to stillness, form rather than formlessness, may perpetuate a defensive position against the depressive affect. All these are seen in the predilections, interest, and preoccupation of perverse individuals (Winnicott, 1935, pp. 133–134). The inhibitions and/or lack of feelings which perverse individuals complain of in analysis, the complaint that they have "lost their ego," a common feature in all depressions, is magically remedied.

Affects require passage through certain developmental stages before their maturation and integration. The formidable task of delineating under what circumstances the depressive affect is tolerated and can be integrated in childhood and throughout development has been recently explored by D. Socarides and Stolorow (1985). They conclude: All depressive disorders have their origin in "early self–object failure, leading to an inability to integrate depressive feelings."

---

[4] It is tempting to note here that the word *gay*, commonly and currently used to refer to homosexuals and homosexuality, with its connotation of liveliness, gladness, joy, and merriment, represents a wholesale flight from the opposite sensations: sadness, misery, and despair. These emotions are a defensive position against the depressive affects in order to escape the deadness of an internal world, the futility and ego depletion secondary to the inability to establish sustained and permanent object relations.

> Depressive affect is integrated into the structure of the self
> through consistent, reliable, empathic self-object attune-
> ment.... The capacity to identify and withstand depressive
> feelings without a corresponding loss of self, fear of self-
> dissolution, or tendency to somatize the affect has its ori-
> gins in the early affect-relatedness between the child and
> primary care-giver [p. 113].

This "lends definition to the child's experience of himself,
solidifying self boundaries." What is crucial to the child's

> [G]rowing capacity to integrate his sadness and his painful
> disappointments in himself and others is the reliable pres-
> ence of a calming, containing, empathic self–object, irre-
> spective of the "amount" or intensity of the affects involved.
> When the caregiver is able to tolerate, absorb, and contain
> the child's depressive affect states, which presupposes that
> they do not threaten the organization of *her* sense of self,
> she then functions to "hold the situation" (Winnicott, 1965)
> so that it can be integrated [p. 114].

If this condition is present, "the care-giver's self-object functions gradually become internalized in the form of a capacity
for self-modulation of depressive affect and an ability to
assume a comforting, soothing attitude toward one's self"
(p. 114). When this does not occur, the child is unable to effect
the task of affect integration (D. Socarides and Stolorow,
1985, p. 114). This explanation in terms of self psychology is
readily applicable to my analyzed cases of sexual perversion, both as regards the family pathology and the inability
of the family to respond in a manner which assists the child
in affect integration.

The depressive pattern in a sexual pervert who has
reached the oedipal phase with full structuralization of the
mental apparatus, is clinically different from that found in
those fixated in the practicing and differentiating phases of
the separation–individuation process; for example, the preoedipal type II pervert with associated narcissistic personality disorder (Socarides, 1982a). The former is characterized
by classical symptoms of a cyclothymia: (1) dislocation of
mood downward; (2) vegetative imbalance; (3) psychomotor

retardation; (4) associated feelings of guilt and sense of unworthiness; (5) resentment that life has not given one a "fair deal." In the latter, there is a pronounced absence of guilt, and mood regulation is exceedingly dependent on external circumstances, with many ups and downs. The mood swings of the narcissist differ from those of the classical cyclothymic in that they follow a narcissistic loss or defeat, have a primary quality of apathy, and show a predominance of shame over guilt. However, the patient fears he may overshoot the mark and become "too excited," lose contact, and be unable to stop, be consumed and die. This hyperarousal is associated with physical transcendency, grandiosity, and megalomania (Bach, 1977, p. 224).

In those perverts who are also schizophrenic, rare psychotic forms of depression may occur with total adaptive incompetence rather than adaptive impairment, with the presence of self-accusatory delusions and hypochondriacal convictions that their gastrointestinal system has been destroyed, that they are being turned into a woman, or that they are being poisoned. In those perverts who are borderline, narcissistic schizoid, the absence of neutralization leads to a lack of fusion between libidinal and aggressive drives, producing intense affective states. When rage is felt, it is profound and shattering. Such depressions in the pervert are marked by regressive, psychoticlike transferences, loss of executive functioning, hollowness, inferiority, and other profound incapacities (Socarides, 1978a, pp. 307–341).

The pervert attempts to regain his capacity for pleasure and for the enjoyment of life, by spurious means, bringing about the illusion of control through the magical powers of seduction and sensuality. His triumph lifts him to a state of intoxication, euphoria, and even elation. Elsewhere I have termed the homosexual's reintegration through incorporation of another man's body and phallus as the "optimal fix" (Socarides, 1968b), resembling the experience following the intake of opium derivatives, restoring body–ego boundaries, and producing a sense of well-being and temporary integration. In other circumstances, the pervert may forestall depression by a spell of preventive sexual enactment with associated euphoria; though a short-lived euphoria because it reinforces dependence and insures future reenactments.

Chapter 7

PERVERSE SYMPTOMS AND THE MANIFEST DREAM OF PERVERSION

During the psychoanalytic treatment of perverse patients, I have been confronted with a singular and regularly occurring phenomenon, namely, that among these patient's dreams are some that depict the same perverse acts for which they seek therapy. Upon awakening, the dreamer often pursues the apparent hallucinatory wish-fulfillment of the dream, first in fantasy and then in real life, external reality becoming a setting for gratification. In the pure form of manifest perverse dream content, the perversion is pictured without interfering factors, anxieties, or frustrations; in contrast, there are the more common, impure forms in which elements of frustration and additional conflicts of various kinds are commingled. In both, the perverse content is explicit and conforms to the actual perversion in real life. In pure forms, the patient experiences little or no anxiety in the dream, and sexual pleasure is an accompanying affect. The patient often awakens considerably relieved of the overwhelming anxiety preceding sleep. Often, when these dreams are analyzed, no new information is gathered by free association with regard to their unconscious meaning; what is encountered is the diffuse anxiety that precipitated them.

In *The Interpretation of Dreams* (1900), Freud observed that a psychological theory should not be based on a single category of mental phenomena, even that of dreams, but that dreams themselves should be related to other products of mental life, especially neurotic symptoms. Psychoanalytic theory should cast light on what dreams have in common with symptoms, as well as define the ways in which they differ from them. He repeatedly compared dreams to symptoms and noted (1909) that both often said the same thing and were in part the results of identical processes— condensation, reversal, multiple identifications, and so on— and that symptoms undergo distortion of the censorship analogous to the hallucinatory ones of dreams. Although Freud firmly asserted that "the most trustworthy method of investigating deep mental processes" was through the study of dreams (1920a, p. 13), there have been few subsequent investigations in the direction of understanding specific symptoms in their relation to dreams. Several notable exceptions have included Lewin (1950, 1952, 1955, 1958), Noble (1951), Katan (1960), Richardson and Moore (1963), and Frosch (Panel, 1969). The relative scarcity of such reports well may be due to Freud's early shift in attention from investigating the connection between dream and symptom to the more urgent problem of explaining the relation between symptom and anxiety.

In this chapter several examples of this phenomenon are presented as occurring in well-structured perversions, the psychological events precipitating it are described, as are the psychic mechanisms responsible for its formation, and its relationship to perverse acts themselves is examined. I am suggesting that the manifest dream of perversion, similar to the symptom, plays an integral part in maintaining the pervert's psychological equilibrium and efforts at adaptation. Understanding the manifest perverse dream enhances our knowledge of the earliest shadowy and indistinct psychic mechanisms responsible for perversion. I am further suggesting that dreams of perverse acts may well belong to Freud's (1920a) *second group* of dreams, which he considered to be exceptions to the proposition that dreams are fulfillments of wishes.

From the outset, it should be noted that the hallucinatory (visual) reenactment in a manifest dream with very little or no distortion of the sexual practices carried out in waking life is not, of course, the only kind of dream reported by those with perversions. More common are manifest dreams of being surrounded by snakes, swept into whirlpools, enclosed in caves, and so on, representing merging and fusion. Fears of the dissolution of the self representation (body–ego disturbances) are often depicted in the manifest dream as fears of shooting out into space, being in an elevator whose sides are collapsing, being lost in space, becoming progressively smaller against a backdrop of darkness, or afloat in a vast sea. Castration anxiety is commonly pictured by open wounds, bloody scenes of mutilation, similar to those seen in neurotics. Dreams representing negative oedipal situations are common: for example, passive sexual surrender to an overpowering masculine figure, often seen with severe anxiety or in disguise. Dreams representing severe regression embody regressive reenactment of preoedipal and oedipal fantasies, such as becoming a small infant or losing one's teeth. Dreams representing simultaneous identification with the phallic mother may be depicted by images of females with breasts appearing as elongated penises, penises growing above the vagina or on various parts of the body. Manifest content, of course, may include perverse activity in symbolic form. In general, these themes are found in all perversion, and the latent dream content can then be decoded through the technique of dream analysis and free association, as with other patients. In these dreams, the latent dream content has undergone disguise in an attempt to alleviate anxiety, even though the patient may often awaken in fright, even of nightmarish proportions. In contrast, the manifest dream of perverse activity diminishes anxiety, is easy to recall, remains in consciousness upon awakening, and commonly is followed by perverse fantasies and actions. Fantasy and act may precede as well as follow the appearance of the manifest perverse dream.

Theoretical Background

Historically, the explanation that symbolism disguises manifest sexual and sexually perverse content put into bold relief the fact that there was no satisfactory explanation for a dream of explicit perverse or nonperverse sexual content. In these dreams, sexual wishes and thoughts had evaded the unconscious middle operations (the dreamwork), had not been barred from consciousness or from direct gratification by the ego's defenses, and invaded the manifest dream itself.

Freud commented on this vexing problem in 1925. He asked:

> How can it happen . . . that this censorship, which makes difficulties over more trivial things, breaks down so completely over these manifestly immoral dreams?

> The answer is not easy to come by and may perhaps not seem completely gratifying. If, in the first place one submits these dreams to interpretation, one finds that some of them have given no offence to the censorship because *au fond* they have no bad meaning. They are innocent boastings of identifications that put on a mask of pretence; *they have not been censored because they do not tell the truth* [emphasis added]. But others of them—and, it must be admitted, the majority—really mean what they say and have undergone no distortion from the censorship. They are an expression of immoral, incestuous and perverse impulses or of murderous and sadistic lust. The dreamer reacts to many of the dreams by waking up in fright, in which case the situation is no longer obscure for us. The censorship has neglected its task, this has been noticed too late, and the generation of anxiety is a substitute for the distortion that has been omitted. In still other instances of such dreams, even that expression of affect is absent. The objectionable matter is carried along by the height of the sexual excitement that has been reached during sleep, or it is viewed with the same tolerance with which even a waking person can regard a fit of rage, an angry mood, or the indulgence in cruel phantasies [1925a, pp. 131-132].

Freud provided two explanations: These dreams either "truly mean what they say," in which case the dreamer may awaken in fright, the current anxiety a substitute for the distortion that has been omitted; or they have not had to undergo distortion because they have no "bad meaning." Advances in our theoretical and clinical understanding of perversions have proven that Freud's second explanation was correct on both counts. These dreams "have no bad meaning" for in the pervert's unconscious, it is ordinary sexual congress that is filled with guilt, anxiety, and destructive aggression.

Glover (1960) succinctly dealt with this issue, noting that:

[I]n the unconscious of the sexual pervert, there is a renunciation of adult sexuality as a moral act. His regression to infantile sexuality, though by no means guilt-free, is the lesser of two evils. . . . In the sense of primitive unconscious morality, both the neurotic and the sexual pervert are more "moral minded" than the normal heterosexual adult [pp. 183–184].

These dreams "do not tell the truth" because perverse acts themselves are products of a repressive compromise (Sachs, 1923). It is a solution by division whereby one piece of infantile sexuality enters the service of repression; that is, it helps to promote repression through displacement, substitution, and other defense mechanisms. Pregenital pleasure is thereby carried over into the ego while the rest is repressed. The unrepressed part is the perverse act, which is analogous to the manifest dream in that it is disguising a more threatening latent content. Indeed, perverse symptoms (the perverse facade) might even be considered roughly analogous to manifest dreams (Joseph, 1965; Socarides, 1978a), so that perverse acts or symptoms may be referred to as the "manifest perversion" and their true meaning as the "latent content of the perversion." That perverse dreams of symptoms do not mean what they say is especially evident in those perversions with unusual or bizarre content. A vivid example is the "bug perversion" reported by Stolorow and Grand (1973); see p. 124.

In *Beyond the Pleasure Principle*, Freud (1920a) noted that some patients repeat in their manifest dreams what they had experienced in real life. These were dreams in which "enough is left unexplained to justify the hypothesis of a compulsion to repeat—something that seems more primitive, more elementary, more instinctual than the pleasure principle which it overrides" (p. 23). Such dreams are similar to the dreams of children, to the hallucinatory dreams occurring in toxic states of high fever, or to the dreams of traumatic neurotics, and "are exception[s] to the proposition that dreams are fulfillments of wishes." They include "dreams during psychoanalysis which bring to memory the psychical traumas of childhood [and] arise . . . in obedience to the compulsion to repeat . . . what has been forgotten and repressed" (p. 32). Freud explained:

> Thus it would seem that the function of dreams, which consists in setting aside any motives that might interrupt sleep, by fulfilling the wishes of the disturbing impulse, is not their *original* function. It would not be possible for them to perform that function until the whole of mental life had accepted the dominance of the pleasure principle. If there is a "beyond the pleasure principle," it is only consistent to grant that there was also a time before the purpose of dreams was the fulfillment of wishes. This would imply no denial of their later functions. But if once this rule has been broken, a further question arises. May not dreams which, with a view to the psychical binding of traumatic impressions, obey the compulsion to repeat—may not such dreams occur *outside* analysis as well? And the reply can only be a decided affirmative [pp. 32–33].

It should be noted that Freud did not mention in this group of recurrent dreams those with manifest perverse content, perhaps because he did not conceive of them as representing situations from which the patient wished to escape, that is, traumatic states, but as derivatives of infantile sexuality.

In 1967 Stewart noted the occurrence in borderline cases of "overtly sexual, incestuous, sadistic or perverse dreams" and suggested that they could be better understood if we conceived of them as modeled along the lines of the traumatic dream in the sense that they serve the original function of mastery. Because of the early points of fixation and the arrest in development, the conflicts in severely ill patients are less completely internalized than in neurotic patients and are represented in terms of the relation of self to object. Stewart cited several factors responsible for the production of these dreams: (1) the existence of an ego defect affecting the operation of the synthetic function, with the failure of free associations to cluster around the significant material; (2) the inability to master primitive fears and outbreaks of uncontrollable primitive aggression; and (3) the fear of the loss of a sense of identity. In this connection, Pulver (1978), in reviewing studies on the manifest content of dreams, commented that if the particular kind of dream reported by Stewart occurs at all frequently, it is of "real clinical importance" and "deserves further recognition" (p. 682).

My clinical material suggests that recurrent manifest perverse dreams in patients with well-structured perversions should also be included in Freud's second group of dreams, whose original purpose is "the psychical binding of traumatic impressions." These dreams are precipitated by an increasing threat to a precarious and marginal equilibrium in patients with ego deficiencies that produce uncontrollable anxiety and rage—in effect, a traumatic state. The manifest perverse dream represents a regression to a primitive mode of mastery. It brings discharge of tensions provoked by the patient's emotional crisis and ensures sleep in the face of overwhelming tension which it would otherwise be impossible to master. In analyzing such dreams, one comes up against the precipitating situation itself, a predicament from which the patient wishes to escape. It is one in which the patient's psyche is reacting with overwhelming anxiety to a disturbing change in the condition of the self, a serious depressive loss of self-esteem, or impending self dissolution.

Homosexual Sadomasochistic Dreams

Patient A[1]

The sequential appearance of a bondage sadomasochistic homosexual fantasy, leading to a sadistic homosexual dream and, upon awakening, to a homosexual sadistic fantasy, and then to the enactment of a perverse act, was described by a thirty-year-old sadomasochistic homosexual actor/writer.

---

[1]The significance of this patient's sadomasochistic practices was discussed in chapter 5. A portion of that material is repeated in this chapter.

The patient dreamed:

> I was just fucking X., putting in one finger, then two, three, then four, and then my whole hand was in his anus with vaseline on it. I could see him wanting more. He was an absolute helpless mass in front of me. This aroused me.

Upon awakening, the patient masturbated to the dream images, first of X. with the patient's hand in his anus, then of himself playing the passive role. After ejaculation, he went to the home of X. and engaged in the sadomasochistic homosexual acts as both passive and active partner in anal intercourse.

Patient B

The following dream of a twenty-three-year-old homosexual musician shows explicit perverse activities with very little distortion, activities which he pursued in his fantasy life every day. It expresses additional unconscious motivations such as the desire to be a female, to engage in sadomasochistic acts as a woman, to acquire the partner's penis and masculinity through incorporation, and the intensity of his overwhelming aggression. His dreams and fantasies served the function of narcissistically restoring his self representation. Here is one of his dreams:

> In some home, and this man is there with a very long penis. He's very muscular. There's something uncouth about him. He's dark, manly, and rough. And we're in bed and I want him to fuck me and he won't. However, he has me by the penis, there's a rush of excitement. Then I think other people are coming into the room, interrupting us. Then later he's still lying in bed eating a salad. The salad is on his chest but I dump it all over his head because he wouldn't fuck me. I'm so angry. The salad turns into a jellylike substance, like sperm, I guess. Then we start kissing each other.

The patient presented the following associations: He had awakened frequently during the dream, and it appeared to take a long time; it was pleasurable on the whole except for the anger and frustration, but it culminated in a relief through kissing. He noted that Y. had stayed over at his house the night of the dream. He had been very attracted to Y., but he was unable to get him into bed. He became severely anxious, depressed, and had to go out "cruising" in an attempt to find another person who would fill him up, reducing his feeling of emptiness and tension—and his dread that he might somehow "go out of control."

A Masochistic Dream of Spanking

Patient C[2]

The patient was a dignified fifty-year-old academician of considerable professional achievement and social position who, since his childhood, had suffered from a beating fantasy and since adolescence had practiced his perversion (spanking perversion) which had undergone very little change over the past thirty years.

The spanking perversion appeared frequently and explicitly in his manifest dream content. He dreamed:

> I was with a woman in a red sweater [the color of his buttocks]. A little boy was there, and the little boy said, "Mommy, may I have a spanking?" "Yes, if you like. Get the hairbrush." She got the hairbrush, pulled his pants down over him, and spanked him. "Have you had enough?" "Yes." Then he went off to play. I asked her if the little boy had this before as she put her hairbrush away, and the next moment I was on top of her, excited sexually, kissing her. Watching the spanking aroused me.

Associations: The patient could say little about the meaning of his dream. The "spanking part" was part of his daily fantasy life. Almost every day it functioned to make him feel better. The dream occurred on the night he stayed at a hotel in a distant city where he was to deliver a lecture. He felt overwhelmingly sad and unhappy at being away from his wife. Performing the perverse act with her had been a source of restoration. He experienced severe separation anxiety and panicky feelings which seemed almost to drag him

---

[2]The patient's psychoanalysis is reported in detail in chapter 16.

from his bed toward a window from which he might be forced to leap. Intense anxiety led him to lock himself in the bathroom, writhing in agony on the floor. He sensed that he was about to "fall apart."

In most of his dream, the patient appeared as an adolescent girl, but because of the split in his ego he also dreamed of himself as a young boy. The female figure was a substitute for the male, and through his unconscious homosexual wish, heavily disguised, he could incorporate the male partner's body and his penis. What usually preceded the manifest perverse dream were severe anxiety, feelings of emptiness, threats to his self cohesion, and separation anxiety. Beneath the surface (manifest) perversion lay deeper conflicts (fear of engulfment, loss of self) representing the wish for and dread of merging with the mother in the primitive mother–child unity.

Transvestite Dreams

Patient D[3]

A thirty-nine-year-old professional man had practiced a transvestite perversion since the age of thirteen, when he first began to wear women's clothes.

In the following series of dreams, perverse practices appeared in undisguised form and were enacted in real life:

Dream 1:

> I am in some sort of legitimate setting where wearing women's clothes is a part of a test project [superego sanction]. I'm trying on a woman's nightgown. A lot of people there. It is too small for me and won't fit. I think that there should be some regulation about the impossibility of getting a fit. It seems I want to legitimize this fully: there ought to be some change in the rules.

---

[3]The detailed case history of this patient is presented in chapter 16. The role depression played in its origin and in the enactment of the perversion is presented in chapter 15.

Associations:

Last night I was in another city and met a woman to whom I became attracted, but I couldn't have her. Before we went to dinner, I went up to her fifteen-year-old daughter's room, looked in her drawers, found a nightgown that was too small. It was a child's nightgown like the one in my dream. It fit only over my head. I was frustrated.

Upon returning home later that evening, he was compelled to practice his transvestite perversion despite his wish to control its enactment.

Dream 2:

I am wearing women's clothing and someone is coming down the hall who might see me, a woman. I wonder how to get the clothing off without being seen.

Associations:

The associations concerned his fear of discovery and a memory that when he told his ex-wife early in their marriage about his perversion, she had not responded; in fact, she disapproved of his perversion. On another occasion he dreamed the following:

Dream 3:

I'm supposed to be baby-sitting for somebody but I'm not there. I'm somewhere else talking, perhaps I've gone to get some women's clothes.

Associations:

Why am I choking up now? This is the dilemma: I'm there in order to be baby-sitting the way I wanted someone to be baby-sitting with me and not to feel abandoned. On the other hand, if I'm not there, someone will call and find out that I'm not doing my job of baby-sitting.

Dream 3 was precipitated by an incident in which a new girl friend told him that she would "let him know" when she was willing to have sex with him. This greatly frustrated him, stimulating his overwhelming aggression:

> But I still want to have sex with her, the feeling of being on and off. I can't see her until Saturday night. She's being cold and cynical. It's like a punishment being with her, being without her. That's not a relationship, no sex! I think of everything, about the trash basket, the garbage basket, wondering what's in there—maybe underwear. I want to go down the hall and look in there and find something. Also that night I felt I needed to call a girl in Los Angeles I was terribly lonely. I am choking up with emotion now. I am thinking about being left as a child in that home—being frightened, being torn apart, like I'm losing myself. Like I might vanish like a wisp of smoke.

Manifest dreams of perversion were regularly followed by fantasies and their enactment in real life. Following one of these dreams he revealed:

> It is being alone with myself that is so terrifying; and when I'm traveling alone I get very upset. It is then that I have to take women's clothing along with me. When I get anxious I feel like I'm losing myself, and also I have a déjà-vu feeling and I experience fear. I am looking out the window, I see her face for an instant, waiting for mother to come to the institution—being hungry, waiting for her, standing next to the window, screaming, trying to get out. Mommy had put me there and I'm angry. I want to get out. Angry at the crib, angry at mother. Thinking of my girl friend now and the silence she gives me. All of my feelings of loneliness refer to previous loneliness. I'm concerned that I'll never be happy as long as I live, that I have no connection with anyone, that everyone's life is connected and normal except for mine. I want to belong to someone, like I want to belong to you.... I want everything from women, I want women and all the things they can give me. And every time I try to have a good time, I'm conscious of the transient nature of everything—something that is going to spoil it if I do something to foul it up. Whatever I do well is going to end up badly. What is it that I want: mother love, sense of self, sense of identity?

The "worst" dreams were not those dealing with the manifest dream of perversion, dreams bringing relief and self restoration, but those concerned with body disintegration anxiety, feelings of annihilation and imminent destruction, expressed in dreams of rocket ships about to be launched with their sides missing, or finding himself hanging on the side of a building by his fingertips and fearing that he will be forced to let go. Particularly distressing were infrequent dreams of homosexuality, which the patient interpreted as a complete loss of his masculine identity and therefore a loss of the ability to secure supplies from women.

In transvestitism, he enacted the role of the phallic mother, thereby overcoming loneliness, depression, and enjoying narcissistic and oral supplies in identification with women by becoming one of them. Similarly, he enacted the role of the woman in sexual intercourse on some occasions, being penetrated with a dildo while dressed as a woman. His perversion was an enactment of his dream; the gratification experienced tended to keep in repression deeper conflicts involving separation, threat of loss of object relations, and fears of annihilation. Both dream and symptom are the end product of the same intense conflict handled in a particular manner by a deficient ego.

Primitive Roots of Perversion Dreams

From the case material cited, it appears that the pervert has manifest dreams of perversion when he is threatened with a further disturbance in his object relations or is confronted with a threat to his narcissistic self-image. Early impairment in ego structure has produced a defective capacity in dealing with both internal and external worlds, and his equilibrium is tenuously maintained. These patients experience severe tension, overstimulation, and threats of disintegration similar to those seen in other traumatic states in which there is a threat of disintegration of the self. The source of tension is the fear of dissolution of the self representation, threat of imminent destructive incorporation by the mother, increasing stress on ego boundaries already severely impaired, onslaughts against a narcissistic defensive position, and threats of eruption of severe aggression endangering both self and object in the face of the ego's inability to sufficiently neutralize aggression. Manifest perverse dreams occur when the ego is in urgent need of reinforcement. The hallucinatory visualization of the dream of the perversion protects and buttresses the endangered self and object representations during sleep, as well as protecting sleep itself. The ego does its work in sleep by discharging panic-creating experiences which the repressive barrier has difficulty excluding from consciousness. Otherwise, the ego might well be inundated by unbearable archaic affective perceptual experiences and feel threatened with disintegration. Such states of severe regression are experienced as threats of engulfment, loss of self, and fears of disintegration, and are not unusual during the psychoanalytic treatment of perversions (Socarides, 1968b, 1973, 1978a; also chapter 21 in this book). In these psychosislike regressive episodes, both the manifest dreams and perverse acts have been unable to defend against primitive early mental contents invading the waking life, with a resultant regressive evocation of the symbiotic phase or a fantasied elaboration of it (Arlow, 1963).

Manifest perverse dreams are similar to the "self-state" dreams described by Kohut (1977) in severely narcissistic patients undergoing decompensation. In these dreams, the patient is pictured explicitly engaged in acts of extreme grandiosity or archaic exhibitionism.[4] Kohut notes that "the very act of portraying these vicissitudes in the dream constitutes an attempt to deal with the psychological danger by covering frightening nameless processes with nameable visual imagery" (p. 109). The dream does not express in visual imagery the content of drives or wishes in an attempted solution to a conflict represented by the manifest content, but helps the narcissist to reintegrate himself by pressing into service primitive modes of adaptation which

---

[4] "Self-state" dreams and perverse dreams may well be different expressions of the same phenomenon, especially if we accept Kohut's view that it is "specific circumscribed disturbances in the narcissistic realm which are usually the nucleus of these widespread disorders" (1971, p. 69). However, not all perversions are accompanied by the severe degree of narcissistic pathology described by Kohut.

have proven useful and necessary in the earliest years of life. Sexualization has played and continues to play a major role to this end. A sexualization of narcissistic needs promotes a discharge of narcissistic tension: seeking a penis, incorporating the body of the male partner in homosexuality, wearing the clothes of the opposite sex in transvestism (see chapter 15), the libidinization of aggression in a spanking perversion (see chapter 16), are all attempts at achieving internalization and structure formation.

Denial in Perversion Dreams

A prominent mechanism involved in both manifest perverse dream and perverse symptom is denial. It occurs in response to the ego's requirement of reconciling reality with instinctual strivings and superego demands. The denying fantasy expressed in the perverse act—for example, the choice of a male partner instead of a female, dressing in female clothes contrary to anatomy, beating fantasies with multiple substitutions, displacements, changing of roles—serves the function of the ego by attempting to preserve intact the function of reality testing (Glover, 1933). The patient's hallucinatory wish fulfillment in the manifest dream is one of the early expressions of the denying fantasy serving to protect the ego from overwhelming tension. Denial helps protect "the object against aggression as well as protect the ego against narcissistic mortification," and it operates "in the service of the synthetic function of the ego to resolve disturbances in the body image and sense of identity" (Moore and Rubinfine, 1969, p. 33). Denial avoids painful affects around anxiety relating to threats encountered by the developing ego, involving loss of body–ego boundaries, self concept, loss of object, loss of love, and superego disapproval. The need-satisfying object is provided by the self in transvestism, by the willing participation of the female in the beating fantasy, by the body of the male in homosexuality, by the fetish protecting against body-disintegration anxiety in fetishism (Socarides, 1960; Greenacre, 1968, 1969; also see chapter 12). All relieve castration anxiety and diminish fear of loss of the mother. Gratifying experiences with a substitute object are invented in order to postpone pain, loneliness, disturbances in the sense of self, fears of separation, and the painful awareness of the loss of the object.

In repetition–compulsion, both asleep and awake, the pervert dramatizes the repeatedly unsuccessful attempt by the ego, both in the past and in the present, to achieve mastery of libidinal and aggressive impulses and of their archaically cathected objects. Such an ego, when faced with the task of object cathexis in the absence of suitable substitute objects and satisfactions, and in the context of threats of further impoverishment, resorts to manifest dream formation of perverse content.

Perverse Symptoms and Perverse Dreams

In 1968 (Socarides, 1968b), I suggested that the greatest threat to the pervert is the threat of ego dissolution or ego destruction. Salvation is achieved through the perversion, which diminishes or cancels out such threats. It should be noted that it is not the fixated erotic experience per se, the instinctual drive derivatives, that are regressively reanimated in the perversion, but rather it is the early function of the early experiences in "shoring up a precarious and imperilled representational world" (Stolorow, Atwood, and Ross, 1978) that is retained and regressively relied upon in the perversion in later life (Socarides, 1978a). To discover what is sexualized and why—that is, the specific experiences involving not only the mother and father, but other psychological factors as well—to produce a particular form of perversion, is the ongoing task of clinical investigators in the field.

It is well known that some perverts do not enact their perversion, and therefore the perversion remains latent; or they engage in alternating forms of perverse activity, undergoing both overt and latent stages of the perversion (Socarides, 1968b). An ego with fewer deficiencies or subject to less stress well may resist threats to its integrity, and engagement in perverse acts does not occur, despite the appearance in the dream life of a prolific and obviously perverse content. It may well be that, in these cases, dreaming of this type may constitute a prophylactic device against the enactment of a perversion: perhaps the dream diminished overwhelming states faced by an archaic ego during sleep. Commonly, however, when the patient struggles against his perversion and its enactment, he experiences emotional flooding in the form of fits of despair, crying, anxiety, often leading to suicidal preoccupation—even acts—and the fear that he is "going crazy."

Through acting out, the pervert further stabilizes his sense of self, reinforces his object relations, overcomes destructive aggression and feelings of vulnerability, and brings pleasure to an internalized self object (Kohut, 1971). The symptom represents an overcoming of his severe intrapsychic crisis by displacing and projecting the inner need and tension onto another person or object by concocting what Khan has termed "active ego-directed experimental play-action object-relations" (Khan, 1965, p. 409) in which the "technique of intimacy" plays a major role. Affective release into the external world diminishes internal threats provoked by destructive aggression. Pathological internalized object relations which have led to despair and hopelessness are mitigated. The perversion is experienced as a creative and reparative act. Similarly, the absence of healthy self-esteem in relation to internal parental figures is lessened through "creating a pseudo-object relationship and mutual pleasure" (Khan). It furthermore establishes a "rudimentary mode of communication with the external object" (p. 408). The pervert, despite his attachment to the preoedipal mother, does not experience meaningful communication with either parent, and his perverse act helps break down isolation and reduces despair by contact with a real object. Because no true object relatedness is achieved through the perverse act, and no internalization of the object takes place, there is no true ego enhancement, and the perversion must be incessantly repeated. Such acting out is facilitated by: (1) deficiencies in the ego, due in part to the lack of neutralized energy which has impaired the ability to control immediate responses and instinctual discharge and aggression; (2) lack of internalization of superego functions and a splitting of the superego, so that the perversion is sanctioned by the split-off part repre-

senting parental attitudes. In a primitive manner, acting out
helps maintain the cohesiveness of the ego and supplies it
with the opportunity to initiate reparative moves toward a
real object.

The manifest perverse dream is an example of the "primitive adaptive function" (primitive goal-seeking behavior) as
described by Palombo (1978). The pervert is under the control
of an archaic ego whose needs must be met both in dreaming
and in waking life. The adaptive function of these dreams is
as important as the performance of the perverse act; both
alleviate overwhelming anxiety and stabilize the sense of
self. It is an attempt at mastery. The mechanisms involved—
sexualization, denial, and so on—belong to an "archaic portion of the adaptive ego . . . [and are] automatisms, in the
sense that they do not make use of reflective conscious
thought that Freud associated with the secondary process"
(Palombo, 1978, p. 449).

Clinical Applications

Connections made between the daytime threats to the maintenance of his psychic equilibrium, largely maintained
through the practice of perversion, and their occurrence in
dream life help make the patient aware of the psychic mechanisms with which he must deal and the function of his
perverse activities, in the same way that analysis of the
conscious and unconscious motivating factors in daily life
illuminate the need for perverse acts and their function.
While dreams portray aspects of his archaic ego and the
class of conflict with which we have to deal, that is, an object
relations conflict consisting of anxiety and guilt associated
with the failure of development in the phase of self–object
differentiation, a careful examination of their contents
reveals healthy sectors of the patient's ego with which we
can work, including elements that result from structural
conflict.

Perverse symptoms are the consequence of disguise
through the use of primitive mechanisms. The transformation of an ego-syntonic symptom, through the analysis of its
heavy disguise and encrustations and pleasure-fulfilling
functions, into ego-alien elements leads to discomfort and

anxiety. This is a necessary therapeutic measure in our goal of converting the syndrome into neurotic conflict, which can then be analyzed.

Developmental deficits must be corrected in patients with perversions before we can deal therapeutically with the defensive aspects of their psychopathology in terms of the instinctual conflicts it serves to ward off. Once sufficient structuralization has taken place, one can proceed with the analysis of transference manifestations and of libidinal and aggressive conflicts. The perverse patient must be helped to develop a more stable and cohesive self differentiation, aided in the formation of external object relations, and in the overcoming of separation anxiety and pathological early feminine identifications. While the task of therapy is to awaken the dreamer from his dream and thereby bring him to reality, a complete elimination of perverse symptoms must await the strengthening of the pervert's ego by supplying experiences that he legitimately needed but missed, before this can be successfully accomplished.

Chapter 8
THEORETICAL CONSIDERATIONS ON FEMALE HOMOSEXUALITY

In 1923, Georg Groddeck in succinct simplicity posed a question, the answer to which would greatly increase our comprehension of female homosexuality. It is natural that the boy should retain the mother as a love object, "but how is it that the little girl becomes attached to the opposite sex?" (Groddeck, 1923). In his last work, *An Outline of Psycho-Analysis* (1938a), Freud inferentially emphasized the importance of this issue in his famous statement:

> If we ask an analyst what his experience has shown to be the mental structures least accessible to influence in his patients, the answer will be: in a woman, her desire for a penis, and in man, his feminine attitude toward his own sex, a precondition of which would necessarily be the loss of his penis [p. 194].

Psychoanalysis has dealt extensively with one derivative of this problem (i.e., male homosexuality). Its counterpart, female homosexuality, is relatively neglected. Its literature is meager in comparison, both quantitatively and in the thoroughness and depth of scientific investigation, with some notable exceptions. Perhaps the inattention to this aspect is derived from the phallocentric culture in which we live (Horney, 1925), but in all probability the answer may lie

183

in the "unconscious moralities that dwell in the more archaic layers of the unconscious mind" (Glover, 1960). In addition, few analysts, even of long experience have had the opportunity to treat more than a very small number of overtly homosexual women.

Since the early 1960s there has been no comprehensive study of female homosexuality reported in the psychoanalytic literature with the exception of a panel report of the American Psychoanalytic Association (1962) and a lengthy review of the "Historical Development of Theoretical and Clinical Aspects of Female Homosexuality" (Socarides, 1963). In Socarides (1968b), I included developmental and clinical material on the subject which I then further expanded in a later work (1978a).

Historical Development of Theoretical and Clinical Aspects of Female Homosexuality

The existing significant work on female homosexuality (prior to 1962) may best be comprehended under seven headings: constitutional versus acquired factors; the concept of bisexuality; Freud's contributions; developmental factors; contributions from ego psychology; the relationship of female homosexuality to other perversions and psychoses, including nosological considerations; and therapy.

Constitutional and Acquired Factors in Female Homosexuality

When considerable significance is attached to the constitutional factor in mental disorders, including sexual perversion, this does not indicate a repudiation in any way of those psychological factors which are responsible for a predisposition to female homosexuality. In actuality, we are thereby emphasizing precisely these developmental factors which remain. An extreme view in the opposite direction is that homosexuality is due wholly to psychological causes and that the assumption of a constitutional or hereditary factor is unnecessary if not unwarranted. The ultimate choice of sexual object is psychologically determined. However, this does not apply either to the infantile component that determines the sexual aim or to the degree of activity or passivity of sexual impulse in general. The latter may be accentuated or diminished in the course of development, but the original force is undeniably *constitutionally* determined (Glover, 1960). From the point of view of therapy, an overemphasis on the constitutional factor often might well produce a tendency toward defeatism in therapy.

Freud (1905b) concluded that the nature of inversion is explained neither by the hypothesis that it is innate nor by the alternative hypothesis that it is acquired. This discovery was a radical departure from the existent theory that all inversion was considered an innate indication of nervous degeneracy. Freud based his view on the following: (1) even in absolute inverts it is possible to show that very early in their lives a sexual impression occurred which left permanent aftereffects in the shape of a tendency toward homosexuality; (2) in others it is possible to point to external influences which led sooner or later to a fixation of their inversion; such influences are exclusive relations with persons of their own sex, comradeship in war, dangers of heterosexual intercourse, and so on; (3) inversion can be removed by hypnotic suggestions. "Psychical hermaphroditism would gain substance if the inversion of the sexual object were at least accompanied by a parallel changeover of the subject's other mental qualities, instincts and character traits into those marking the opposite sex. But, it is only in inverted women that character-inversion of this kind can be looked for with any regularity. In men the most complete mental masculinity can be combined with inversion" (p. 142). On the other hand, female homosexual patients were found to show considerably greater constitutional deviations from the general average than those heterosexually adjusted (Henry, 1934). In contradiction have been the observations of other investigators that homosexuality even in hermaphrodites is not primarily caused by direct hormonal or rather physiological factors, but by environmental ones (Ellis, 1945). T. Benedek in 1952 concluded that correlation of psychodynamic constellations with bodily and hormonal indicators of the sexual aberrations are lacking. Any variations of endocrine imbalance (androgen–estrogen ratio), physical appearance of masculinity, are also present in so-called normal individuals without homosexuality.

The Concept of Bisexuality

Bisexuality does not imply a discounting of psychological factors responsible for the production of a homosexual perversion. The existent controversy is largely a nosological one, based on a restrictive view of the nature of infantile sexuality. "The essence of infantile sexuality is its polymorphous (component) nature, and there can be no doubt that these components are constitutionally determined and consequently vary in strength" (Glover, 1960, p. 207). On the other hand, the essence of homosexuality lies in the choice of an object of the same sex, and that object choice develops along exclusively psychological lines starting with early identifications. The argument has been proposed that the term *bisexuality* is misleading, that the "combination of manifest homosexuality with manifest heterosexuality forms a continuum from faintly heterosexual and predominantly homosexual to predominantly heterosexual and faintly homosexual" (p. 207). However, this does not apply either to the infantile components that determine the homosexual aim or to the degree of activity or passivity of sexual impulse in general. The original force of these is constitutionally determined. The statement that bisexuality is *not* constitutionally determined is in any case incapable of conclusive proof.

E. Gley (1884) was the first to suggest bisexuality as an explanation of inversion. Herman (1903) was convinced that masculine elements and characteristics are present in every woman and feminine ones in every man. Krafft-Ebing (1893) stated that every individual's bisexual disposition endows him with masculine and feminine brain centers as well as with somatic organs of sex. According to Freud (1905, p. 143), W. Fliess subsequently claimed as his own the idea of bisexuality in the sense of duality of sexes. Freud's correspondence with Fliess on bisexuality had at its onset a salutary effect on their relationship (see Kris's introduction to *The Origins of Psychoanalysis, 1887-1902*). Freud responded to

Fliess's "attractive theory" (setting forth the existence of both male and female "periods") with the hypothesis that the "dominant sex of the person, that which is more strongly developed, has repressed the mental representation of the subordinated sex into the unconscious. Therefore the nucleus of the unconscious [that is to say, the repressed] is in each human being that side of him which belongs to the opposite sex" (Freud, 1919, pp. 200-201). Ernest Jones (1912) approached the issue of inborn bisexuality with hesitancy and doubt that it could be taken for granted.

Understanding bisexuality lends much to our understanding of human behavior. For example:

> But without feminine wishes and feminine sublimation could the man understand a woman, identify with her and love her? By projecting his own femininity upon her, he can love her free from guilt and fear. Vice versa, by projecting her own masculinity upon the man, the woman can accept him and love him without fear, guilt or shame. It appears that bisexuality is a necessary prerequisite for the understanding and tolerance so important in sexual and social adjustments between sexes [Kestenberg, 1956b, p. 475].

Bisexuality is intimately tied up with the choice of sexual object. Freud (1905b) felt that ordinarily the sexual object is not someone of the same sex but someone who combines the characters of both sexes; there is, as it were, a compromise between an impulse that seeks for a man and one that seeks for a woman; or, as regards the female, a compromise between the one that seeks for a woman and one that seeks for a man, while it remains a paramount condition that the object's body (i.e., the genitals), be of the opposite sex. Thus the sexual object is a kind of reflection of the subject's own bisexual nature. He added that the position in the case of women is less ambiguous for among them the active inverts exhibit masculine characteristics, often both physical and mental, and look for femininity in their sexual object; but here again a closer knowledge of the facts might reveal greater variety. A person's final sexual attitude is not decided until after puberty and as a result of a number of factors not all of which are yet known. Some are of a constitutional nature, but others are accidental; no doubt, a few of these factors may happen to carry so much weight that they may influence the result in a sense, but in general there is a multiplicity of determining factors. At this time, Freud was of the opinion that in "inverted types the predominance of archaic constitutions and primitive psychical mechanisms are regularly to be found" (p. 145). He emphasized the operation of narcissistic object choice and a retention of the significance of the anal zone in inverts, especially males.

E. Weiss (Panel, 1962) locates topographically the constitutional bisexuality in the biological id, where the "sexual drives are neither ego- nor object-invested. [Therefore] the normal bisexuality in the id cannot be conceived in the same way as an ego-invested bisexuality" (p. 585). Weiss felt that in normal heterosexual development the masculine needs of the male become to a great extent "ego-invested"; that is, the ego feels the need to discharge personally and directly this masculine tension. The feminine need becomes "object-invested," which means that the ego feels the need for a feminine sexual partner whose feminine urges it cares to satisfy. "By so doing the ego can obtain vicarious gratification, as it were, of its own feminine needs" (p. 588). In Weiss's opinion, the more an ego "egotizes the urges of its own sex and externalizes into a proper object representation the urges of the opposite sex, the more does such an ego feel complete.... On the other hand, the more an ego egotizes the biological urges of the opposite sex, for the satisfaction of which it is not anatomically and physiologically equipped, and externalizes instead the urges of its own sex into an object representation, the more it feels mutilated" (p. 585). This condition constitutes inversion. Rado (1949) was severely critical of the theory of bisexuality.

In both lines of experimental study, the available evidence points to the same conclusion: the human male and female do not inherit an organized neurohormonal machinery of courtship and mating. Nor do they inherit any organized component mechanisms that would—or could—direct them to such goals as mating or choice of mate. In the light of this evidence, the psychoanalytic theory of sexual instincts evolved in the first decades of this century has become an historical expedient that has outlived its scientific usefulness. Each of the sexes has an innate capacity for learning, and is equipped with a specific power plant and tools. But in sharp contrast to the lower vertebrates, and as a consequence of the encephalization of certain functions first organized at lower evolutionary levels of the central nervous system, they inherit no organized information [Rado, 1955, p. 314].

In Rado's opinion (with which I am in agreement), the theory of constitutional bisexuality first evolved by von Krafft-Ebing assumes there exists, besides an *innate* desire for the opposite sex, an *innate* desire for same-sex partners in human beings; this concept should now be relegated to the realm of psychoanalytic mythology, once perhaps useful for conceptualization but now scientifically erroneous (see chapters 2 and 3).

Freud's Contributions

Freud's work on the sexual perversion in general has been summarized notably by Gillespie (1956a) and Wiedemann (1962) in his historical survey of male homosexuality. These remarks will not be repeated here except for comparison to those observations concerning female homosexuality as they appeared throughout Freud's writings.

Beginning with the "Three Essays" (1905b), Freud felt that in the female, in contrast to the male, there are more severe early inhibitions or reaction formations against sexuality, such as shame, disgust, pity, and so on, and there is greater passivity of the instinct components. Among women, as occurs in men, the sexual aims of the inverts are varied with a special preference for contact with the mucous membrane of the mouth.

The focal point of Freud's discussion of both male and female inversion became the Oedipus complex and castration fear. These were frequently alluded to in the *Collected Papers* (1893–1938) as the motivational force for potential or actual inversion.

Fifteen years later, Freud published his first clinical study on female homosexuality, "Psychogenesis of a Case of

Homosexuality in a Woman" (1920c). His patient was a beautiful and clever young woman of eighteen, belonging to a family of good standing, who adored a society woman about ten years older than herself. She adopted the characteristic type of masculine love, for example, humility, tender lack of pretension, blissfulness, and so on, toward her love object. The precipitating event leading her toward her love object was a new pregnancy of her mother and also the birth of a third brother when she was about sixteen. The object choice corresponded not only with her feminine but also with her masculine ideal (a combined gratification of the homosexual tendency with that of the heterosexual one). Freud's patient wished to bear the father's child (unconsciously) and "it was not she who bore the child but the unconsciously hated rival [the mother]." This led to resentment, embitterment, and turning away from men and father altogether. She repudiated her wish for a child and the love of a man. The patient "changed into a man" and took her mother in place of the father as a love object. Freud carefully considered the implications inherent in the choice of object on the one hand, and of the sexual characteristics and sexual attitude of the subject on the other. The answer to the former necessarily does not involve the answers to the latter (choice of object versus sexual characteristics and sexual attitude of the subject). Experience proves that a man with predominantly male characteristics and also masculine in his love life may still be inverted in respect to his object, loving only men instead of women. Freud added that the same is true of women, but here mental sexual characteristics and object choice *do not necessarily coincide*. Therefore, the problem of female homosexuality is by no means so simple as it is commonly depicted in popular expositions of male homosexuality (e.g., a female personality attached to a male's body) which must have a man.

Freud (1917) acknowledged the theme that all sexual perverts including female homosexuals alter their sexual object. A female may dispense with the mutual union of the genital organs and substitute for the genitals in one of the two partners another organ or part of the body, mouth or anus, in place of the vagina. He felt, in short, that perverted sexuality is nothing else but infantile sexuality, magnified into its component parts.

Freud (1923a, 1924b) underscored certain crucial questions. There was a lack of insight into the corresponding processes in the little girl regarding incest wishes, the effect of the threat of castration, the internalization of the object, and the formation of the superego to be distinguished from the ego and the id. By 1924 he contrasted the girl to a certain degree with her brother, describing her as (1) accepting castration as an accomplished fact rather than fearing it as a threat; (2) consequently lacking a powerful motive for the erection of a superego and breaking up of her infantile female sexuality; (3) therefore relinquishing the Oedipus complex more gradually than the boy, however, while retaining a strong conscious wish for a penis and child from the father.

By 1925 Freud published the first of his studies on female sexuality (Freud, 1925b). He described more fully the castration complex of the girl and its effect upon infantile masturbation and the Oedipus complex. The second period of infantile masturbation is disturbed by the inferiority of the clitoris. The girl is forced to rebel against phallic masturbation that agrees less well with her than with the boy and develops penis envy with its reaction formation in order to finally accept fully her castration. In addition, this acceptance introduces her to the Oedipus complex with its wish for the penis (equaling the wish for a child) and superseding a previous attachment to the mother, who is the original love object of the infant of either sex. [See R. Fliess (1950) also for a complete, authoritative critique of Freud's changing concepts on female sexuality.

Even more important is the fact that a comparison between the relation of the castration complex and the Oedipus complex in the sexes shows that the castration complex *terminates* the Oedipus complex for the boy and *initiates* it in the girl. Since the Oedipus complex is never completely relinquished by the girl, its heir, the superego, is in the normal female never as inexorable as in the male.

Six years later Freud (1931) traced the lines of development that accrue from the acknowledgment of the fact of castration: the superiority of the male, and the inferiority of the girl and her rebellion. The first developmental line leads to her turning her back on sexuality altogether. "The little girl, frightened by the comparison with boys grows dissatisfied with her clitoris, and gives up her phallic activity and with it her sexuality in general as well as a good part of her masculinity in other fields" (1931, p. 229). However, a second line is that she clings in obstinate self-assertion to her masculinity; the hope of acquiring a penis is sometimes cherished to an incredibly late age and becomes the aim of one's life, while the fantasy of really being a man in spite of everything often dominates long periods of a girl's life. This "masculinity complex" may also result in a *manifestly homosexual object choice.* The third circuitous path is one which arrives ultimately at a normal feminine attitude in which the girl takes her father as love object; and thus arises the Oedipus complex in its feminine form. This Oedipus complex in the woman represents the final result of a lengthy process of development whose motive force has been castration fear. The Oedipus complex in women therefore escapes the strong, hostile influences which in men tend to its destruction. Freud postulated that women with strong father fixations show a long period prior to the establishment of the positive Oedipus attitude, a period which he called "preoedipal" (1931, p. 232). In this phase the mother is the love object, though the relation to her is highly ambivalent in character. Hostility increases with each fresh experience of frustration until the recognition of the absence of a penis, interpreted as punishment by the mother for masturbation, brings the girl's fear to such an intensity that she throws over the mother in favor of the father. In other words, it is still the phallic frustration which is really decisive for femininity, and the core of the complaint against the mother was the fact of being born a girl rather than the oedipal rivalry. A strong father fixation implies a strong mother fixation, and the hostility to the mother is complemented by oedipal rivalry but *not* initiated by it. The solutions are, therefore: (1) a general retreat from sexuality; (2) a retention of masculinity which may result in *manifest homosexual object choice;* or (3) a transference to the father ushering in the positive oedipal attitude and subsequent feminine development. In other words, the girl must choose between sacrificing her erotic attachment to the father and sacrificing her femininity. Either the father or the vagina, including the pregenital vagina, must be renounced. The bond with the father is often retained, but the object relationship is converted to *identification* (i.e., a penis complex is developed).

In 1932, Freud summarized his thoughts on the matter of female sexuality and homosexuality. He reiterated his belief in the presence of an exclusive mother attachment preceding the Oedipus complex. This is of greater intensity and duration than in the male. The preoedipal phase in girls extends into the fourth or even fifth year of life and includes most of the phallic period. During the phallic period, a girl's sexual aim toward the mother is at first passive, then active and corresponds to the partial libidinal stages through which she has journeyed from infancy (i.e., oral, anal, sadistic, and phallic). The girl's giving up of the mother and her acknowledgment of castration, that is, change of object and change of zone, occur in a complementary fashion. Castration, conceived of as a denial of the male genital *by the mother*, forms the nucleus of her reproach and hostility toward the mother. What follows is a transition from the mother to the father. Analytic experience shows that female homosexuality is seldom if ever a direct continuation of infantile masculinity. It seems to be characteristic of female homosexuals that they, like male homosexuals, take the father as love object for a while and thus become implicated in the oedipal situation. However, they are then driven by the inevitable disappointments which they experience from the father into a regression to their early masculinity complex. These disappointments, however, should not be overestimated. Girls who eventually achieve femininity also experience them without the same results. The preponderance of the constitutional factors seems undeniable: the two phases in the development of female homosexuality are admirably reflected in the behavior of homosexuals who just as often and just as obviously play the parts of mother and child toward each other as those of man and wife.

Finally, Freud (1938) stated that if the girl persists in and adheres to her first wish to grow into a boy, in extreme cases she will end as a manifest homosexual or in any event will show markedly masculine traits in the conduct of her later life.

Developmental Factors

It is generally accepted that in all sexual perversion the manifest activity represents the peak of a broadly based unconscious construction. There is a scattering of fixation points varying in depth or developmental level of the ego. This is, of course, of crucial significance for prognosis in therapy. Psychic localization is difficult, unconscious content variable, and the etiology of female homosexuality is beset with severe difficulties. (One might compare this with obsessional or hysterical neuroses where the symptomatic processes are often localized and sometimes encapsulated in an ego that may otherwise show no crude disturbances.)

Proceeding *chronologically*, I can only allude to the main significant developmental factors which have been set forth by a number of investigators.

Deutsch (1923) saw that at the beginning of every new sexual function (at, for example, puberty, sexual intercourse, pregnancy, and childbirth), the phallic-phase conflict is reanimated and has to be overcome every time before a feminine attitude can be attained once more. This complicates the development toward adult female sexual functioning and sets up a condition wherein female homosexuality may be activated at any of these periods.

Horney (1925) emphasized that the oedipal fantasies and the ensuing dread of the internal vaginal injury, as well as the clitoris, play an important part in the infantile genital organization of women. She thought it of causative importance that the little boy can inspect his genital to see whether any consequences of masturbation are taking place, whereas the little girl is literally in the dark on this point. An inner uncertainty so often met in women is due to this circumstance. Under the pressure of anxiety, the guilt may then take refuge in the production of a fictitious male role. The wish to be a man subserves the repression of feminine wishes and secures the subject against libidinal wishes in connection with the father, the female role having been burdened with guilt and anxiety.

In 1925, Jones had the good fortune of analyzing simultaneously five cases of overt female homosexuality. He expressed his views at the Innsbruck Congress (1927). In the main, Jones felt that female homosexuality could be traced back to two crucial factors: (1) an intense oral erotism, and (2) an unusually strong sadism. Together with Deutsch's (1932) and Freud's (1920c, 1932) clinical studies, Jones's paper constituted the most incisive penetration from the theoretical and clinical points of view into this disorder at the time. I will briefly list his contributions:

In homosexual women, the unconscious attitude toward both parents is always strongly ambivalent: there is evidence of an unusually strong infantile fixation in regard to the mother, definitely connected with the oral stage; and it is always succeeded by a strong father fixation whether temporary or permanent in consciousness. He postulated that castration anxiety is only a partial threat and coined the term *aphanisis* (Jones, 1927, p. 461) as the total threat; that is, threat of total extinction which includes sexual capacity and enjoyment as a whole. The privation experienced by the girl in not being allowed to share the penis in coitus with the father or thereby to obtain a baby, is an unendurable situation, the reason being that it is tantamount to the fundamental dread of aphanesis. Jones slightly preceded Freud as to the correspondence of their views on the future outcome. There are only two ways in which the libido can flow for self-expression: the girl must choose, broadly speaking, between sacrificing her erotic attachment to her father and sacrificing her femininity; that is, either the object must be exchanged for another or the wish must be denied. It is impossible to retain both: either the father or the vagina, including the pregenital vagina, must be renounced. A result of this is that the father may be retained but the object relationship is converted into identification (i.e., a penis complex is developed). Faced with aphanisis as a result of an inevitable privation, she must renounce either her sex or her incest wishes. What cannot be retained is an incestuous object relationship. A girl may frequently choose the solution of inversion and homosexuality because it is bound up with this dread aphanisis. In essence, she can surrender the position of her object libido (father) or can surrender the position of her subject libido (sex) which is then followed into the field of homosexuality itself.

Jones furthermore distinguished three types of homosexual women (1927). In one group are homosexual women who retain their interest in men but who set their hearts on being accepted by men as one of themselves. To this group belongs the familiar type of women who ceaselessly complain of the unfairness of woman's lot and their unjust, ill-treatment by men; (2) Another group consists of homosexual women who have little or no interest in men but whose libido centers on women. Analysis shows that this interest in women is a vicarious way of enjoying femininity they merely employ other women to exhibit it for them; [cf. Panel (1960b) for a corresponding view on overt male homosexuality, i.e., male homosexuals identify with the maleness of their partners]; (3) A third group is found in homosexual women who obtain gratification of feminine desires providing two conditions are met: that the penis is replaced by a surrogate, such as the tongue or finger, and that the partner using this organ is a woman instead of a man. Though clinically they may appear in the guise of completely homosexual women, such cases are nearest to the normal than either of the two described before.

Jones was of the opinion that identification with the father is thus common to all forms of female homosexuality, although it proceeds to a more complete degree in the first group than in the second, where in a vicarious way some femininity is, after all, retained. There is little doubt that identification serves the function of keeping feminine wishes in repression. It proclaims: "I cannot possibly desire a man's penis for my gratification, since I already possess one of my own, or at all events I want nothing else than one of my own" (1927, p. 468). This is surely the most complete defense against the aphanistic danger of privation from the non-gratification of the incest wishes. Jones remarks that this identification may be regarded as universal among young girls, "and so we have to seek for motives which heighten this to an extraordinary extent" (p. 469). Those inborn factors which appear decisive are at an unusual intensity of oral erotism and sadism which converge in an *"intensification of the oral-sadistic stage"* which Jones regards as the "central characteristic" of homosexual development in women (p. 469).

De Saussure's work, "Homosexual Fixations Among Neurotic Women" (1929) is a noteworthy contribution to the psychoanalytic literature and is the only monograph on the subject. De Saussure's conclusions are that at the bottom of homosexual fixations there is always a warped bisexuality which comes from the fact that the woman has not been able to accept her femininity. This refusal is conditioned by the idea of castration and penis envy. In his case material, the identification with the woman becomes impossible and the girl identifies herself with her father in order to give a child to the mother. Homosexual fixations correspond to the patient's projections. More often she *projects her femininity onto the mother* and then onto other women who continue to represent the mother. Almost as often the patient, thwarted at not being able to satisfy her own masculine tendencies, *exaggerates her feminine qualities*, becomes excessively narcissistic, and sees herself mirrored in some way in other women who have a high degree of feminine narcissism. In these cases, the woman projects her femininity onto others and enjoys an identification with herself. Finally, in homosexual fixations, we frequently find certain women refusing themselves to men, giving themselves to other women who have known how to make men suffer. It is their identification with their ideal of aggressiveness, with their superego (after C. Odier). De Saussure had never seen homosexual fixations in which women attach themselves to other women who represent the male because they themselves wish to be male (1929).

With puberty, the final decision as to choice of object and readiness for the passive attitude takes place. Developmentally, girls show much stronger dependence upon the mother during the latency period than do boys, although the cornerstone for later inversion has already been laid in the first infantile period (Deutsch, 1933). In her article on female homosexuality, Deutsch's analysis revealed an aggressive murderous hate against the mother. Childhood memories (four to six years) which turned out to be the nucleus of some of her patients' inversions included the inhibition of masturbation by the mother and the inability of the father to aid the daughter in her distress. Homosexual tendencies always included a reproach against the father and a very strong reaction to the castration complex.

Brierley (1932) laid stress on the masochistic thoughts that prevail concerning intercourse which have proved to be a repetition of injury already experienced at mother's hands. These masochistic ideas have to do with disembowelment according to the internal life injuries of the Kleinian type. "It is these masochistic ideas which make the heterosexual position untenable. In these cases, however, homosexuality is not a way out too often because it is too sadistic" (p. 440). She firmly believes that there is nothing in most of these situations which is peculiar to women in the sense that there is no counterpart in male sexuality; for example, men have difficulties due to oral conflicts, failures in coordination of hetero- and homosexual interests, and archaic superego formation. What would seem to be specific in women is not any psychic drive as such but the balance which has to be achieved or maintained in order to produce an integrated feminine personality. A distribution of cathexis which might be normal in women would be abnormal in men (p. 446). "The only differences which we can register clinically seem to be differences in integration of drives common to both sexes. . . . If we ever achieve a psychological definition of femininity it looks as if it might have to be a definition in terms of types of integration" (Brierley, 1932, p. 447).

By 1933 the preoedipal relation and its significance for the girl's later life began to assume more importance. Deutsch emphasized the identification with the active mother (after Freud) which as yet has no relation to the Oedipus complex. In such play the child makes others suffer or enjoy what she has suffered or enjoyed at the hands of the mother. If the libido remains attached to the original active and passive roles of the mother–child relationship, this play will be continued into later life under the guise of homosexuality. In the analysis of homosexual women, Deutsch found that the preoedipal libidinal components appear repeatedly. "The situation is independent of the man; and in libidinal relationships only the roles of mother and child are taken into account without reference to men" (1933, pp. 478-479).

Brierley (1935) suggested that there is some evidence that *female genital impulses* do appear even in the suckling period and, if they do, those impulses must be repeated as *primary* because they arise in the genital system itself. If they are (indeed) primary, they do constitute a *specific* instinctual determinant in feminine development and from that fact Brierley developed her own theory of the development of female homosexuality. She felt that the occurrence of true vaginal activity in early infancy is *associated* with oral impulses. The relative weak cathectic investment of the urovaginal system matters less than its establishment under pleasurable or painful conditions; that is, the degree of sadism with which it is invested. While endorsing Jones's view (1927) concerning the role of oral sadism in the genesis of female homosexuality, what is significant is not the purely oral sadism but a strong blend of oral and urethral sadism. "Where the primitive oro-urethral system is highly charged relatively to the other ego-nuclei, it tends to retain its dominance in later life, and to produce overt homosexuality or a life of sublimated activity without direct gratification" (Brierley, 1935, p. 169). To her mind, the accomplished fact is not frustration, as Freud stated, but separation from the nipple. From this point of view, the girl's discovery of the lack of a penis is a painful rediscovery of the desolating fact that the vitally essential nipple is not her own. She feels that what is common in homosexual women is not so much that they feel castrated as they are convinced that they are the possessor of a bad penis and not a good one.

The recognition grew that the psychic situation of female homosexuals is indeed more complex than in males as originally suggested by Freud (1905b). Homosexual attachment, which may be due to early sister rivalry, is extremely common. In all cases there are two complicating factors to be taken into account: (1) the female passes through a negative mother attachment *before* reaching a positive father Oedipus complex, not after, as in the case of the boy; (2) the castration anxiety links up with deeper fantasies of bodily mutilation than in the case of the male. The little girl believes that she has already suffered castration and that she is bound to suffer still further injury. In addition, penis dread is reinforced by earlier breast dread which in its turn was provoked by oral hate of the breast. Furthermore, the girl has had stronger sadistic reactions against the mother's insides, babies, and reproductive organs (Glover, 1939).

Lampl-de Groot (1933) was among the first to describe the girl's fantasies of phallic coitus with the mother. This is a blow aimed at the mother which gratifies the girl's own narcissistic conceit and vindictiveness but which does not gratify her sensual love. Only later, in some women, after puberty, is this fantasy given a sensual meaning and serves them as a byasis on which to erect a homosexual attitude.

Rado (1933) traced female homosexuality to what he felt was its masochistic core, that is, masochism derived from castration fear. The central source of danger for the masochistic woman is the man. The line of defense in her neurosis will be toward him. There are three types of defensive means at her disposal: (1) flight; (2) combat; and (3) choice of the lesser evil. It is the mechanisms of flight which, if extreme, will lead to female homosexuality. However, the neurotic disturbance peculiar to female homosexuality is a sense of guilt, the avowed source of which is the perversion itself with its attendant exclusion from the group. This sense of guilt has at its roots a tormenting sense of inferiority, an uneasiness that one will be found inadequate, a fear of being exposed as ridiculous. The fear of exposure is a derivative of and an expression of the fear of castration.

According to the Kleinian school, homosexuality is intricately involved with the primary phases of libidinal development; that is, the primary oral and anal anxieties. These constitute the chief factors in the homosexual fixation. The anxieties stimulated by cannibalistic fantasies are the most potent factor in oral fixation.

[T]he dread of the internal object (devoured and therefore inside) can only be allayed by continued oral pleasure.... It is this insatiable need which binds the libido to oral and anal forms. We know that such fixations of the oral phase with all its fantasies and anxiety lead to profound disturbance in the genital function [p. 179].

Furthermore:

[E]arlier stages have definite and positive contributions to make to the genital phase, contributions from the oral phase strengthen genital impulses. Similarly, the woman's genital impulses and fantasies take over her happy experiences at the breast. With regard to these positive contributions to the oral phase, it is not enough to say that they are displacements of certain elements from the oral phase to the genital; this is true but it is an incomplete statement [Klein, Heimann, Isaacs, and Riviere, 1952, p. 180].

Fenichel (1930b, 1934) returned to the importance of the castration complex in the formation of female homosexuality, stating that (1) the repulsion from heterosexuality originates in the castration complex, and (2) the attraction through early fixation on the mother is of vital importance. These factors supplement each other. The fixation on the mother may have a protective and reassuring function balanced against the force of the castration complex (1934).

Bacon (1956) enlarged upon the thesis that homosexuality and bisexuality are developmental and not constitutional in origin.

Homosexuality and masculine identification may serve as a protection against anxiety. The mechanism by which homosexuality accomplishes so much is inherent in its tendency to restore triangular relationships to two-way relationships. In giving up the father attachment, the girl goes back to a two-way relationship with the mother (sister) figure in which, in fantasy, all real love comes from the partner and all real giving goes to the partner. In spite of her disappointment [in her father] the patient is unable to go to another man because of fear of retaliation on the *father's part* [pp. 158–159].

Bergler (1951) considered the genetic basis of female homosexuality to be due to the many pathological aberrations of the unsolved masochistic attachment to the preoedipal mother. Its origin is to be found in the unresolved oral masochistic conflict of the preoedipal child with the mother. It is not libidinous but of aggressive content. Beneath female homosexuality lies a savage hatred for the mother which is warded off by the libidinous, "I don't hate her, I love her, sexually." This defense is unconscious and is then shifted secondarily to other women. The following unconscious psychic constellation produces female homosexuality: (1) an aggressive, dominating mother is the sole educator of the child or the father has a "weak personality"; (2) the child hates the mother and is incapable of splitting off the preoedipal ambivalent attitude toward her; (3) the Oedipus complex therefore never reaches the normal height; (4) self-damaging tendencies predominate under a pseudo-aggressive facade. The decisive point is often that a female may have to handle an overwhelming compensatory hatred of her mother covering deep masochistic attachment and may choose the way of homosexuality.

Contributions from Ego Psychology

Freud's early theory (1905b) that perversions were a breakthrough of impulses unopposed by the ego or superego has now undergone considerable modification. The introduction of the structural approach into psychoanalysis made it possible to clarify the fact that not only the instinctual drives but also the defenses against them are unconscious. As a result, the gratification of a perverse instinctual drive actually constitutes the end product of a defensive compromise in which elements of inhibition as well as gratification are present. In homosexuality, the component instinct which seems to be approved had undergone extensive transformation and disguise in order to be gratified in the perverse action. We see, therefore, that the perverted action, like the neurotic symptom, results from the conflict between the ego and the id and represents a compromise formation which at the same time must be acceptable to the demands of the superego. In female homosexuality, as in the case of neurotic symptoms, the instinctual gratification takes place in disguised form while its real content remains unconscious. For this reason, a perversion differs from the neurotic symptoms, first by the form of gratification of the impulse (i.e., that achieved by the orgasm), and second in the fact that the ego's wishes for omnipotence are satisfied by the arbitrary ego-synthetic action. Certain broader dynamics of female sexuality must always be considered; for example, the defensive aspects of female homosexuality and warding off of guilt-laden fantasies are crucial for the role of object relations; family constellations and the specific opportunities to make adequate identifications, and so on. The importance of Freud's dual-instinct theory (1920a) was therefore indispensable in analyzing female homosexuality. The fusion of aggressive and libidinal impulses, the presence of guilt and hostile aggressive drives, the need for punishment, played important roles. In female homosexuality as well as in male homosexuality and perversions in general, the earliest experiences of life may play a decisive role; that is, the preoedipal period and its subsequent influence on psychic structure and ego functioning. The importance of early identifications and the later development of female homosexuality or prostitution was clearly understood by Lichtenstein (1961).

Female homosexuality may to a large extent be analogous to male homosexuality except for one factor which complicates the picture: with women the exclusion of heterosexual genitals can be achieved by regression. The first object of every human being is the mother. All women, in contra-distinction to men, according to Deutsch, have a primary homosexual attachment which may later be revived if normal heterosexuality is blocked. A man in this situation has only the possibility of regression from object relationship to mother to "identification" with mother; a woman can regress from object relationship to father to object relationship to mother (Deutsch, 1932a).

Often a young girl will respond to disappointment over her oedipal wishes with an identification with the father and consequently assume an active relation to women who represent mother substitutes. The attitude of these active masculine homosexual women toward their mother-equivalent objects is often combined with all the features of a wish-fulfillment type of female castration complex.

One sees that the goal of masculine women is in opposition to the pregenital aim of incorporation found in the feminine goal in men. In cases where frustration of the wishes for incorporation has led to a sadistic attack of taking by force what was not given, this force, originally thought of as a penetration of the mother's body, may be remobilized into later masculinity (Klein, 1954).

Masculinity in women is not necessarily connected with homosexuality. This would depend upon two circumstances: the intensity of the early fixation to the mother, and a special configuration of the castration complex. Some active homosexual women, after having identified themselves with their father, choose young girls as love objects to serve as ideal representatives of their own person. They then behave toward these girls as they wished to have been treated by their fathers (Fenichel, 1935).

Another configuration may be present, for example, an antagonism between sisters becomes overcompensated and a mild homosexual love interwoven with a great deal of identification may develop. Beneath the latter lies the original hatred. In addition, the turning away from heterosexuality is a regression, reviving memory traces of the earlier relationship to one's mother. Female homosexuality, therefore, has a more archaic imprint than male homosexuality. It brings back the behavior patterns, aims, pleasures, and also the fears and conflicts belonging to the earliest years of life. The usual activities of homosexual women consist mainly of the mutual playing of mother and child. Oral erotism is in the foreground as compared to anal erotism in the male (Fenichel, 1935).

Homosexuality has proved to be the product of specific mechanisms of defense which facilitate the persistence of the repression of both the oedipal and the castration complexes. At the same time, the aim of the homosexual in object choice is the avoidance of the emotions around the castration complex which otherwise would disturb the sexual pleasure or at least the attainment of reassurances against them (Freud, 1911; Sachs, 1923).

Other writers (Jones, 1927; Glover, 1939; Bergler, 1951) have stressed the observation that the hatred of the mother may lead to an intense sense of guilt which may then lead to transformation of the hate into a masochistic libidinal attitude. Often the fundamental attitude, "I do not hate you, I love you," originally held toward the mother, is reflected in not only the form of a direct oral satisfaction in homosexual intercourse with a young girl but also in the submissive–passive attitude toward an older love partner. The homosexual woman may transform the hate toward her mother into love while she is giving the mother's breast to her partner. At the same time, she can be the active suckling mother and thereby transform the aggression into activity.

Deutsch (1932b) has also observed the results of direct prohibitions of masturbation and forceful interference with masturbatory activity which may arouse hostility against the disciplining mother to a high pitch. If, at the same time, the discovery of the anatomic defect is made known, the girl blames the mother for her deprivation. The sadistic impulses of the phallic phase are directed against the mother and become the impetus for the change of object. The change in the direction of a sadistic attitude toward the mother facilitates the passive–masochistic attitude toward the father; Deutsch calls this "the thrust into passivity" (p. 503). Aggression is not entirely conducted, however, into this passive attitude. Much of the aggressive impulse is turned against the disappointing father and much remains attached to the mother who is now regarded as a rival. The intensity in any case is dependent upon the strength of the phallic activity. However, the passive attitude is, as regards the development of masochism, full of danger, and the patient has bloodthirsty and murderous revenge wishes toward the mother, especially the pregnant mother or one who already has another child. This aggression leads to guilt, and the new turning to the mother lies in the release from the feeling of guilt together with the protection from the threatened loss of object: "If my father won't have me and my self-respect is undermined, who will love me if not my mother?"

In homosexual activity free rein is given to masturbation. These are motives held in common by all forms of female homosexuality. This is a new edition of the mother–child relationship bringing along with it the compensation and satisfaction derived from these activities.

In all female homosexuals there is an element of *identification* with the object. If we apply this to Jones's (1927) classification, we find that members of his first group, those interested in men, exchange their own sex but retain their first love object. The object relationship, however, becomes replaced by identification and the aim of the libido is to procure recognition of this identification. Members of the second group, those interested in women, also identify themselves with the love object but then lose further interest in her; the external object relationship to another woman is very imperfect for she merely represents the patient's own femininity through identification, and the aim is vicariously to enjoy the gratification of this at the hand of the unseen man (the father incorporated in herself). The identification with the father requires emphasis as it is common to all forms of female homosexuality, though it proceeds to a more complete degree in Jones's first group than in the second, wherein in a vicarious way some femininity is after all retained (cf. male homosexuals who also identify with their own sex). Identification serves the function of keeping feminine wishes in repression and constitutes the most complete denial imaginable of harboring guilty feminine wishes, for it asserts: "I cannot possibly desire a man's penis for my gratification, since I already possess one of my own, or at all events I want nothing else than one of my own."

Certain factors lend their imprint to female homosexuality. For example, to protect herself against aphanisis the girl in late childhood and adolescence erects various barriers, notably *penis identification*, against her femininity. Prominent among these is a strong sense of guilt and condemnation concerning feminine wishes, most often unconscious. As an aid to this barrier of guilt she develops the idea that her father and other men are strongly opposed to feminine wishes. To ease her own self-condemnation she is forced to believe that all men in their hearts disapprove of femininity (Jones, 1927).

Bonaparte (1953) made some correlations between types of homosexual women and prognosis in therapy. For example, there are some women who refuse to abandon their masculinity and will neither give up their first love object nor the phallic predominating erotogenic zone. Others again, though they succeed in passing from the mother to the father as the love object, and though they cannot conceive of a love object so contemptible as to lack a phallus, nonetheless cling tenaciously to the predominating phallic erotogenic zone and with that organ, essentially male and inappropriate to the feminine function, will love and desire love objects that are themselves malelike. Every analyst knows the difficulties that generally attend the cure of this last kind of woman. On the other hand, psychoanalysis may claim a number of successes to its credit, as we see from the number of newly sexually active women enabled by the help of analysis to pass from a solely clitoridal sensitivity to one essentially vaginal. In such cases it is difficult to distinguish between what the analyst has accomplished and what life alone might have done. We know that, contrary to the male, a certain period is almost always needed to allow the woman to adapt to her sexual function and, given that, she may often succeed. Far more striking are those cases of *clitoridal* women whose retarded adaptation to the vaginal function psychoanalysis sometimes enables us to observe. In these clitoridals of long date, successful analytic treatment remains difficult since the patient manifests a surprisingly tenacious fixation to the phallic zone that will survive even analysis of the primary mother fixations. Such partial frigidity, though often limited to vaginal anesthesia, frequently has a poorer prognosis than that of total frigidity, that is, both vaginal and clitoral anesthesia (Panel, 1960d). Totally frigid women, even of long standing, generally show more improvement than purely clitoridal women as a result of analysis or even sometimes with the passage of time. This is perhaps due to the essentially hysterical nature of their inhibition. These clitoridal women, whether manifestly homosexual or having passed from the mother to the father, succeed in developing the object relation proper to the female but may always unconsciously remain mostly passively fixated, cloacally and phallically, on the mother they knew when a child. If manifest homosexuals, they continually reenact the primary scene of active-passive alternations of the mother's ministering to the baby. The most active among them, superimposing her identification with the father on the primary identification with the active mother, will become the more specifically active type of homosexual female and even occasionally dress like a man (Bonaparte, 1953).

The Relationship to Neurosis, Psychosis, and Other Perversions: Nosological Considerations

Manifest homosexuality occurring from midadolescence onward is due to a disturbance of the normal unconscious balance of instinct and inhibition. Some writers, notably Glover (1933), have felt that it is quite impermissible to refer to manifest homosexuality as a neurosis. Very often it does not have the structure of a neurosis and can be described only as an "equivalent of a neurosis"; but even this may be erroneous. For example, some manifest cases of homosexuality serve to preserve the individual from a psychosis or may appear only during a psychosis, or, on the other hand, disappear during a psychosis. Often the psychosis and homosexuality show no relationship as regards onset of either (see Panel, 1962).

Some female homosexuals show fetishistic and transvestite symptomatology, as reported by Barahal (1953). In his patient, transvestism was considered to represent a partial drive for masculinity rather than a manifestation of homosexuality. Transvestism may be particularly common in active masculine types of female homosexuals. According to Fenichel (1935), the meaning of transvestism in females is problematical. Not all are overtly homosexual, and female transvestites covet the penis, desire to possess it, and identify themselves with men (Bonaparte, 1953). Fetishism in the female and female homosexual is not as frequent as in men due to the ability of the female to disguise her lack of sexual orgastic response and thereby escape narcissistic mortification (Greenacre, 1953, 1955; Socarides, 1960).

Most of the literature on homosexuality and psychosis has been devoted to overt male homosexuality [e.g., "Homosexuality, Magic and Aggression" by Nunberg (1938); "Some Neurotic Mechanisms of Jealousy, Paranoia and Homosexuality" by Freud (1922b); "Homoeroticism and Paranoia" by Brill (1934); in this connection, see also Freud's paper on the Schreber case (1911)]. The theory that homosexuality is a defense against paranoia has not been proven conclusively in woman; statistical studies support the view that homosexual material was not of causally significant importance in the productions of schizophrenic paranoid women (Klein and Horowitz, 1949; Klaif and Davis, 1960).

Therapeutic Considerations

In his 1920 investigation, Freud remarked that the evidence of successes in the treatment of female homosexuality was not very striking. The homosexual who wants or is asked to give up her pleasure cannot be guaranteed a satisfactory substitute for the pleasure she has renounced. Therefore, if she comes to be treated at all, it is mostly through the pressure of external motives such as social disadvantages, other neurotic symptoms, and dangers attached to her choice of objects. She often has in the back of her mind a secret plan, namely, to obtain from the failure of her attempt the feeling of satisfaction that she had done everything possible against her abnormality to which she can then resign herself with an easy conscience. Where there is a considerable rudiment or vestige of heterosexual choice of object, that is, "in a still oscillating or in a definitely bisexual organization . . . one may make a more favourable prognosis for psycho-analytic treatment" (1920c, p. 151). A more formidable resistance, as in Freud's case (1920c), proved to be defiance of the male therapist and wishes for revenge against her father. Freud detected this attitude and suggested ultimately that it would be worthwhile for the work to be continued by a woman, if at all. Positive transference toward the male was only slightly present in Freud's case. He remarked, "It is not for psychoanalysis to solve the problem of homosexuality. It must rest content with disclosing the psychical mechanisms that resulted in determining of the object-choice, and with tracing the paths from them to the instinctual dispositions" (1920c, p. 171).

Deutsch (1932b) warned against a specific form of the analytic transference wherein the patient with a female therapist detaches her affection from the person of the analyst and transfers it to other women and has her wishes and gratifications realized with a new object. This often produces a therapeutic stalemate.

Bergler (1944, 1951) felt that pessimism on the part of analysts in the treatment of both male and female homosexuality was not entirely warranted if the case material is chosen suitably (Panel, 1960b). Optimal prerequisites are: (1) a feeling of guilt on the part of the patient for the unconscious wishes experienced under the guise of homosexuality; (2) a voluntary acceptance of treatment by the patient, not for the sake of others in the environment; (3) that the degree of self-damaging measures such as law-breaking, prostitution, and so on, be slight; (4) that the secret plan to misuse analysis to live out the perversion be analyzed and the oral hate and constant projection of being maltreated by the analyst be dealt with intensely; (5) the fortunate absence of a complete psychic dependence on a woman to whom the patient can run; (6) that the use of homosexuality as an aggressive weapon against the father be of mild intensity; (7) that no authoritative assertions of incurability by other analysts have been made; and (8) that the decisive *oral* material be brought to consciousness.

In a panel on perversion in general (Panel, 1962), therapeutic effectiveness was often seen to be dependent upon the solution of the following issue: "The patient will discuss the attractiveness of pregenital experience in order to avoid admitting that [she] is aware of [her] desire for normal heterosexual gratification. The essential therapeutic task is the removal of the obstacles which stand in the way of heterosexual gratification" (p. 325). Other specific technical modifications in treatment depend upon the underlying structure of the case.

If we assume from our investigations that female homosexuality has an etiology similar to that of the neuroses, we can thereby make the application of psychoanalytic treatment a rational endeavor. Sachs (1923) and Waelder (1960) have emphasized this point; namely, that homosexuals *do* advance along the road to heterosexuality but, like neurotics, run into conflicts around the Oedipus complex and withdraw to other activities which serve somewhat in the manner of reaction formations to protect them against the dangers of heterosexuality.

Waelder (1960) states:

> If this is so, the function of psychoanalysis becomes clear. If the sense of danger can be revived in all that it implied, it can now be viewed with the knowledge and resources of an adult; and in this reappraisal, anxiety may be sufficiently mitigated to allow a resumption of the road toward heterosexuality. The reintegrating therapy of psychoanalysis is clearly applicable if the condition is based on anachronistic anxiety; it would be a different story if the condition were based on something akin to so-called habit formation in addiction [pp. 219–220].

The psychoanalyst [searches] for the neurotic elements in homosexuality. "It therefore seems that homosexuality offers a good prognosis to psychoanalytic treatment if, and to the degree that, it is built like a neurosis" (p. 222).

Female Homosexuality: Current Conceptualizations

Despite the penetrating and brilliant contributions cited above, there has been no comprehensive, systematized, and integrated psychoanalytic work on female homosexuality covering the entire range of the disorder: etiology, theoretical considerations, psychoanalytic case studies, and therapy. In Socarides (1968b, 1978a), I described basic concepts found in female homosexuality, specific mechanisms, theoretical features, and presented three detailed case histories and several shorter vignettes of female homosexual patients. As regards psychoanalytic therapy, the selection of patients, modifications of technique, transference considerations, analysis of regressive phenomena, and classification of patients, have corresponding applications in the female (see chapters 3 and 4).

Etiological Considerations

The nuclear conflicts of female homosexuals originate in the earliest periods of life, as they do in male homosexuals, forcing them into choosing partners of the same sex for ego survival. The obligatory female homosexual has been unable to pass successfully through the later stages of the separation-individuation phases of early childhood, the rapprochement subphase, as well as earlier phases, practicing and differentiating. Severe ego deficits and insufficient self-object differentiation are a consequence of this maturational (psychological) developmental failure. Homosexuality serves the repression of a pivotal fixation in which there is a desire for and dread of merging with the hateful/hated mother in order to reinstate the primitive mother-child unity.

Fast's (1984) exhaustive study of the vicissitudes in the development of female gender identity appears to corroborate my position as to etiological factors.

> To boys a recognition of their gender difference from their mothers may seem another and powerful dimension of difference to be added to those required of them in separation-individuation processes. Now any regressive wishes to merge with the mother stimulate a new anxiety: to merge with the mother means the loss of masculinity. Such fears appear to be represented in perversions. . . . For girls the problem is different. Merging with the mother does not threaten their femininity. It does, however, threaten their *independent* femininity. Girls, like boys, develop their gender-defined relationship to their mother in the context of [the] earlier separation-individuation process. . . . In the separation-individuation processes girls have normally made major progress in establishing themselves as individuals distinct from their mothers. Now they must perceive themselves as both like their mothers in gender and distinct from them as individuals. They must establish secondary identifications with their mothers as feminine, in which attributes, previously shared with their mothers in a two-person unity now become depersonified aspects of their individual feminine selves distinct from but related to the mother whose way of being feminine is her own. Each of the secondary identifications represents a separation. The devel-

opmental danger is of a regressive return to the more primitive identification and relationship of a two-person feminine unity with the mother. One reaction, to avoid the dangers of both fusion with the mother and separation from her, is the repudiation of the mother and turning to the father [pp. 105–106].

In the mother–child unity one can discern: (1) a wish for and dread of incorporation; (2) the threatened loss of personal identity and personal dissolution; (3) guilt feelings because of a desire to invade the body of the mother; (4) an intense desire to cling to the mother which later develops, in the oedipal period, into a wish for and fear of incestuous relations with her; and (5) an intense aggression of a primitive nature toward her.

On a conscious level, the patient attempts to compensate for her primary nuclear conflict by certain activities designed to enclose, ward off, and encyst the isolated affective state of the mother–child unity. She does not approach any man sexually, as this will activate fears of narcissistic rebuff, oedipal fears, preoedipal fears of castration, separation, and/or fragmentation anxiety. She is tied to the mother and does not attempt to leave her, both because of her primary feminine identification with the hateful object and her fears of provoking engulfing incorporative tendencies by the mother. Any attempt to separate from the mother produces an exacerbation of her unconscious ties. All sexual satisfactions are carried out through substitution, displacement, and other defense mechanisms. Her secondary identification as a male leaves her prone to invent a fictive penis with which she attempts to approach other women (the good mother) and simultaneously find her lost femininity. Another alternative to her primary feminine identification (a hateful one) is to restore strength and reaffirm her sense of self through a transitory feminine identification with the (good) female partner. In so doing she unconsciously enjoys sexual closeness with the good mother and avoids oedipal rebuff by the father.

The female homosexual is prone to regression to earlier stages of development. She experiences a threat of loss of her (constructed) self representation, loss of the object (separation anxiety related to the mother). In sexual union with a man, an event to be avoided at all costs, she fears narcissistic mortification in her lack of a penis. The female homosexual's life and development are designed to forestall and prevent the realization of this powerful affective state. Homosexual behavior is a solution to the anxiety connected with the pull to return to this earlier, less differentiated phase of ego development, when she attempted to disturb the optimal distance/closeness to the mother by separating from her during the course of attempting heterosexual relations. The homosexual object choice, achieved through the Sachs mechanism, is crucial to the repression of the basic conflict: the fear and dread of the mother–child unity.

From her analysis of a number of homosexual women, McDougall (1970) arrives at conclusions which are similar to my own as regards the meaning of female homosexuality, although she does not conceptualize her findings in terms of separation–individuation theory. She states:

> When a woman builds her life around homosexual object relations she is unconsciously seeking to maintain an intimate relation with a paternal imago but symbolically possessed through identification. At the same time she achieves an apparent detachment from the maternal imago represented in the unconscious as dangerous, invading and all-forbidding. The idealized aspects of the maternal imago are now sought in the female partner. . . . With the creation of a pathological identification with the father the young girl need no longer fear a return to the fusional relation with the mother which spells psychic death [In my terms, the fear of engulfment, fear of fusion with the engulfing mother].

> We might sum up the psychic economy of female homosexuality as follows: an attempt to maintain a narcissistic equilibrium in the face of a constant need to escape the dangerous symbiotic relationship claimed by the mother-imago [an attempt to find her unique, individual identity separate from the primary feminine identification with the mother] . . . through conserving an unconscious identification with the father, [this being] an essential element in a fragile structure. Costly though it may be, this identifica-

tion helps to protect the individual from depression or from psychotic states of dissociation, and thus contributes to maintaining the cohesion of the ego. . . . [One may conclude that she] can now believe that she still contains all that is essential to *complete* her mother. Unconsciously she assumes the role of the mother's phallus—but it is a phallus with an anal quality which only the mother may control or manipulate. A devouring love for the mother and a phobic clinging to her in childhood is paralleled by unconscious wishes for her death in order to acquire the right to separate from her. In that decisive moment, when the girl decides to leave her mother for the woman who will become her lover, she symbolically castrates the mother of her phallus-child. It is a moment of intense triumph. It is to the other woman that she will now offer herself as the incarnation of all that she has symbolically taken away and what she believes is needed to complete or repair her partner. . . . [McDougall, 1970, pp. 209–212].

One may conclude that in female homosexuals there is an attempt to regain "essential femininity with an idealized female partner" while in male homosexuality there is a need to find (idealized) masculinity in an identification with a male partner and his penis.

Contrasting Features to Male Homosexuality

It is useful to compare some dynamic features found in the female homosexual with those in the male homosexual. In the study of family patterns of female homosexuals, one uncovers a fear and dread of the mother and a fixation to her similar to that found in the male. The female, however, directs a more intense aggression toward the mother. In their early histories one commonly finds a dread of being hurt, devoured, or destroyed by a mother perceived in her unconscious to be malevolent. This dread is aggravated by the girl's secret wish to be loved exclusively by the father—a wish which she renounces almost completely because of her conviction that her father not only refuses to love her but also rejects and hates her—especially for a phallic deficiency. If, in late childhood, the father does offer care and affection, she turns away "in revulsion," seeking the company, admiration, and love of other females. With the onset of homosexual behavior, she displays to the mother her guiltlessness regarding unconscious sexual wishes toward her father. Through this apparent lack of interest in the male organ, she thereby hopes to insure maternal love and care.

As regards oral-sadistic feelings, as in the male, the potentially homosexual female always presents a history of oral deprivation and intense sadistic feelings toward her mother. Such patients, some breast-fed, complain that they did not receive enough milk, lost weight, and screamed continuously as infants. They fear that the mother wished them dead, often had fantasies of poisoning, and fears that the mother would punish them to the point of killing them. Analysis reveals that these semidelusional convictions are usually projections of the little girl's sadism toward her mother.

Primitive psychical mechanisms in female homosexuality are even more pronounced than in the male. They often take the form of outright denial of the anatomical differences between the sexes. For example, the girl often hallucinates the fictive penis, identifies her entire body with the male organ, or may substitute some characterological feature, such as intellectuality, for the penis. She may then continue to a protracted age to deny feelings of having been castrated, and to cling to the idea of somehow acquiring a penis of her own.

She engages in wholesale projection of her own fear and hatred onto the mother, who, she is convinced, has denied her the male organ as a punishment, often for masturbatory practices in early childhood. The mother, and subsequently all women are unconsciously perceived as malevolent or potentially malevolent beings who must be placated through a show of affectionate behavior. They thereby become good, safe, and loving. If this belief collapses as a result of personal slight or threat of infidelity, the homosexual woman may develop temporary or permanent delusional fears of being poisoned or future mistreatment, at least from her homosexual partner. With the patching up of differences what may remain is a chronic distress and suspicion of the partner.

Psychodynamic Features

The homosexual woman is in flight from men. The source of this flight is her childhood feelings of rage, hate, and guilt toward the mother and a fear of merging with her. Accompanying this primary conflict are deep anxieties and aggression secondary to disappointments and rejections, both real and imagined, at the hands of the male (father). Any expectations of the father fulfilling her infantile sexual wishes poses further masochistic dangers at an oedipal level. On the other hand, her conscious and unconscious conviction that her father would refuse her love, acceptance, and comfort produces a state of constant impending narcissistic injury and mortification. This refusal she bases on her lack of a penis and a sense of narcissistic defeat. Such narcissistic injuries commonly occur at the birth of a brother at a specifically vulnerable phase (i.e., that of rapprochement). Some homosexual women complain that this event was the most fateful and harmful day of their lives, especially if it involved the mother's almost complete turning from the daughter to the little boy, producing threats of object loss, which is experienced as preoedipal castration anxiety (Roiphe and Galenson, 1981) and a subsequent intensification of penis envy (see chapter 3).

The conviction that one is not appreciated, admired, and loved by the father leads the female child to turn to the earliest love object, the mother, with increasing ardor despite her fear of her. What prevents a complete regression to this primitive unity is an unconscious fear of merging with and being engulfed by the mother. In this connection, Deutsch (1923b) noted that the advantage of this attachment to the homosexual partner (a substitute for the mother) decreases guilt feelings and protects against threats of her loss.

The genital pressures of adolescence in the female are less distinctly expressed than in the boy. At adolescence, the girl is forced to make a change of genitals which the boy never has to make. The girl feels at the same time that she must shift from clitoris to vagina, feels a lack of interest from her father and hostility from the mother, and is likely to repudiate vaginal erotism and attempt to create a male role for herself. If she believes that nobody wants her in this "castrated, mutilated state"—not even her father—a prolonged and pathological extension of tomboy behavior into middle adolescence ensues. Such a renunciation of feminine strivings may create a temporary equilibrium. During this period she may engage in mutual masturbation or sexual investigation with girl friends, but this is accompanied by considerable anxiety and guilt and is soon relinquished. The shift between ego, id, and superego drives instituted by physiological sexual pressures does not usually produce in the female a multiplicity of overt sexual practices or disturbances, although some masochistic, masturbatory, heterosexual or homosexual fantasies may be entertained for brief periods. It is only upon reaching late adolescence and early adulthood, when she is confronted with society's and her own demands for appropriate role-fulfillment, and is forced to consider sexual intercourse, marriage, and children, that her previous conflict, apparently laid to rest in early adolescence, is reactivated in all its intensity.

Preoedipal fears of being poisoned and devoured by the mother lead to giving up in utter failure when confronted by the later conflicts of the oedipal period (Klein, 1954). The homosexual woman resorts to flight to the mother in an attempt to gain her love and protection; to alleviate fears of murderous aggression toward her; and to protect herself against the assumed murderous impulses of the mother. These fears of poisoning and being devoured relate to the earliest anxiety of the infant. Therefore, this type of homosexual patient, beset by primitive anxieties, demands the utmost effort and concentrated attention on the part of the analyst.

In homosexual women there are intense desires for revenge and incontrollable aggressive feelings. The impulse to attack is associated with revenge ideas for betrayal by the father, especially, as noted above, in instances where another sibling has been born, replacing the patient during the preoedipal years. Strong penis envy components are mixed with intense oral wishes. The oedipal revenge ideas may exist in nonhomosexual women whose behavior stops short of the complete avoidance of men. These women get along fairly easily with less virile, presumably impotent men. This is due not simply to these men being less dangerous; they offer less temptation to the woman's sadism. Although oedipal revenge ideas may exist in nonhomosexual women, these revenge impulses reinforce violation anxiety, and the two together produce a strong tendency to complete detachment from the father. It is a truism, however, that hate as well as love can bind, and the homosexual can find herself neurotically bound to the father, his life, and his activities.

Beneath the more obvious oedipal determinants of violation and revenge ideas is a wealth of tangled fantasies of the primal scene leading back through all the pregenital phases, apparently to the womb, as noted by Brierley (1932, 1935). At deeper levels, analysis reveals certain guiding threads. One set of masochistic thoughts expresses the fear that intercourse would prove a repetition of injury already experienced at the mother's hands. This injury has a vivid phallic version, but equally definite fecal and nipple connotations. It harks back to the deprivation of weaning and castration and is in the latter phases a punishment for masturbation. Another set of masochistic ideas revolve around internal life injuries of a Kleinian type (Klein, 1954): disembowelment and feminine impotence. It is these masochistic ideas that make the heterosexual position further untenable. Homosexuality, however, is no complete solution because even sexual acts with a female partner arouse severe sadistic impulses at times.

Interwoven with masochistic fantasies are highly aggressive fantasies connected with the primal scene father, the penis, and the mother's body. One often

finds self-sufficient fantasies [which] are genital, fantasies of hermaphroditism, and dreams of self-violation, dreams of babies and lovers ... appearing as fecal characters. These are definitely archaic oral fantasies. There are fantasies also of oral intercourse and oral parturition. . . . Genital ideas are not lacking ... but the impression gains ground that in spite of evidence of regression we are here up against an *original pregenital core* [emphasis added] which has a

vital connection with the later genital failure and especially
with the accentuation of aggression which bulks so largely
in it. These fantasies center around introjected nipple–penis
objects; there is a sense of oscillation between external and
internal dangers [Brierley, 1932, p. 440].

This primal oral sadism does not always lead to homosexuality, but sometimes results in a flight from homosexuality
and indeed all sexuality, according to Brierley (1932).

All homosexual women markedly identify with the father,
since they must renounce any approach to femininity. A
striking feature of these identifications was suggested by
Jones (1927), when he termed them *maimed*. The ego is
always a castrated father or a barren, shattered mother, and
the ego's conduct in life is correspondingly crippled. This
nevertheless provides an economic advantage as it protects
the homosexual woman from the dangers of gratification of
her intense sadism, although at great expense to her ego.

Some prepubescent or adolescent girls may identify with
the sexuality of an older female who they know participates
in sexual intercourse with men. I have referred to this form of
identification, following de Saussure's (1929) suggestion, as
"resonance identification" (Socarides, 1968b). In so doing,
they attempt to bolster up a burgeoning femininity. By sharing the guilt in sexual encounters with these females, they
increase their own capacity for erotic feelings.

Those women who openly identify with males are, in
effect, saying to the mother that she has nothing to fear from
their sexual wishes toward the father, that they themselves
wish only to be male. In such instances, the oedipal conflict
is superimposed upon a deeper preoedipal nuclear conflict;
that is, the fear of engulfment and merging with the preoedipal hateful mother. They thereby escape the fantasied retal-
iatory aggression of the mother toward them.

Other homosexual women, after identifying themselves
with the father, choose young adolescent girls as love objects
who are representatives of themselves (narcissistic object
choice). They then love these girls as they wish their father
had loved them. In those homosexuals who assume a very
masculine manner toward men, there is an open wish to
acquire traits of virility of their own. They believe they can

be loved by the father only if they have a penis, convinced that the father once denigrated and demeaned them for this lack. In extreme cases of such male identification, homosexual women may adopt transvestism as an ancillary perversion (see chapter 16).

Certain women manifest their homosexuality only after marriage. There are common features in their reaction to marriage in that they suffer from excessive guilt due not only to the incest and oedipal meaning which intercourse has for them, but even more from the rude awakening of their sexual sadism when engaged in the sexual act. Violation–revenge impulses are frequently found. These patients are demanding revenge for childhood injuries but they often express disappointment if they are not hurt enough in heterosexual relations. This apparent contradiction is resolved when one realizes that actual sexual intercourse satisfies neither their primal scene expectations nor their need for punishment. Continuing to feel guilt-ridden, their superego threatens them with severe bodily punishment after marriage. The husband may symbolize the safe and tender father without sexuality and therefore without sexual satisfaction or danger (Brierley, 1932). Deutsch (1933) described a similar type of homosexual woman, in whom sexual sensation depends entirely upon the fulfillment of masochistic conditions. These women are accordingly faced with the necessity of choosing between finding happiness in pain or respite in renunciation.

Being married provokes already-present masculine trends: penis envy takes the form of rivalry with the husband. The unconscious conviction that the penis ought to have been the wife's, based on the fantasy that the mother had deliberately given the infant's breast/penis to the father, is further augmented. The failure of the marriage transforms unconscious (latent) homosexual attitudes into overt homosexuality.

Homosexual women are exceedingly sensitive to being financially dependent because they regard this as a mark of inferiority. Beneath this resentment are deep feelings of guilt for their inordinate wishes to be completely sustained by the husband. These demands derive from their insatiable need for oral supplies from the mother. Prior to marriage they may "enjoy all the advantages of a man's life plus certain prerequisites belonging to womanhood without the disadvantages of either" (Brierley, 1932, p. 444). If such woman are obliged to give up a career for marriage, this loss of outlet may play an important part in precipitating severe neurotic symptoms with or without overt homosexuality.

Meaning of the Homosexual Symptom

The female homosexual usually does not seek psychoanalytic treatment in order to change her homosexuality. She may enter therapy because of family pressure, or due to a depression secondary to the loss of a love partner, or accompanying symptoms more often neurotic than psychotic. It is usually feelings of loss, loneliness, and severe anxiety arising out of rejection by another woman which impels her to seek help.

Although many overt homosexuals experience little conscious guilt over their deviant sexual practices, many suffer intensely from a deep sense of inferiority, often masked by the outward appearance of self-confidence and superiority. Indeed, inferiority feelings have been largely responsible for their covert homosexual activities, enabling them to lead double lives among their peers and associates. Some homosexual women engage only in a companionate relationship, having little orgastic desire, while others intensely seek orgastic and erotic pleasure. Homosexual women may suffer from vaginismus or vaginal anesthesia. Recently it has been noted that many homosexual women do not feel that they have a vagina (do not, in effect, possess a genital) but have an "empty hole" at a position where the vagina would be (E. Siegel, 1988). In some, orgastic desire for persons of the same sex may be so strongly repressed that there may be complete or almost total unawareness of homosexual desires and wishes.

The homosexual libidinal relationship is basically masochistic: it temporarily wards off severe anxiety and hostility, only to give way at times to florid neurotic symptoms. The mother-substitute (homosexual partner) temporarily neutralizes infantile grievances by providing sexual satisfaction. Many overtly homosexual women acknowledge the mother–child relationship implicit in their choice of love object. Sexual satisfaction is usually obtained by a close embrace; mutual sucking of the nipples and genitals; anal practices; mutual cunnilingus; and vaginal penetration by the use of artificial devices. There is quadruple role-casting for both partners: one now playing the male and the other the female; one the mother and the other the child. Female homosexuals are particularly engrossed in and satisfied by the sameness of their sexual responses.

In analysis it readily becomes apparent that in sexual experiences occurring between homosexual females, the homosexual is able to transform the hate of the mother into love. At the same time, she is being given the mother's (partner's) breast, and thus obtains what she once felt deprived and frightened of as a child. Invariably present is an intense conflict over masturbation which began in early childhood. In the homosexual act, "mother" sanctions masturbation through sharing the guilt mechanism.

Many homosexual women suffer from a double disappointment: that they are in a primary feminine identification with a hateful, malevolent, and hated mother whom they believe wishes to destroy them, and a feeling of rebuff and lack of acceptance of their femininity by the father. They are attempting, therefore, to find their lost femininity (compared to men who are attempting to find their lost masculinity) in the body and personality of their female partner. The object relationship, therefore, is a narcissistic one, similar to that described by Freud (1914).

If she can overcome her reticence to confide in a man, the female homosexual may display intense envy of the penis and hostility toward a male analyst from the very beginning of therapy. Often she suffers from suicidal ideas and murderous fantasies toward her mother (and partner), both arising from preoedipal unconscious wishes and dreads. The aggressive, murderous hatred occurs simultaneously with the desire to merge with the mother and fears of such merging. As in the male, this is the nuclear conflict.

Sexual excitement in most homosexual women is bound up with maternal prohibition. On a conscious level, there are extremely intense aggressive impulses toward the mother. These aggressive impulses are resisted and, in reaction to them, unconscious guilt toward the mother is generated. Hate impulses are then transformed into a masochistic libidinal attitude that disguises these feelings, diminishes guilt, and punishes through suffering. By punishing the mother, these patients are unconsciously dramatizing their self-defeat and reproaches against the mother.

Deprived of their love object, homosexual women very often become suicidal. They interpret this loss as a threat to survival and a total abandonment: they fear total extinction, that is, aphanisis (Jones, 1927). Similarly, the male homosexual has a marked proclivity to become suicidal whenever he is rejected by a man who represents his ideal narcissistic image.

Phenomenological View of Homosexual Women

The clinician treating homosexual women encounters varied and at times even bewildering forms of this disorder. The behavior and appearance of the patient depend on the strength of repression, the capacity for sublimation, the defensive techniques of the ego and superego, the ego-adaptive capacity of the individual, and a complex series of multiple identifications. Thus, homosexual women show *great variation* regarding their external appearance, general behavior, and their choice of an attitude toward their sexual partner. The following groupings are useful in illustrating this complexity by describing the content and degree of their identifications.

Group I: The women in this group have an intense identification with the father. Their aim is to procure acknowledgment of this "masculinity" from their female partners. They have exchanged their gender identity but retain their first love object, the mother.

Group II: In the second group, some femininity is retained, but external object relationships to other women is very imperfect; they merely represent the patient's own femininity through identification. Women in this group wish to enjoy vicariously gratification at the hand of the unseen man (the father incorporated in themselves). An identification with the father is present in all forms of female homosexuality, but is more intense in the first group (according to Jones [1927]). This identification with the father serves the function of keeping feminine wishes in repression and constitutes a complete denial of harboring guilty feminine wishes, for it asserts that one could not possibly desire a man's penis for gratification since she possesses one of her own.

Group III: These women are reared in an environment in which their father's disapproval of their femininity engenders a strong sense of guilt, self condemnation, and inferiority. In response, they create a masculine identification superimposed upon their maimed feminine one, and may equate their bodies with a phallus and often fantasy a fictive penis on their own body.

Group IV: This type derives from a "warped bisexuality" (Jones, 1927) conditioned by the ideas of castration and penis envy. In these cases, homosexual fixations correspond to the patients' projections. A woman may therefore project and thereby relinquish her femininity to the mother and displace it into other women who continue to represent the mother. She then sees herself mirrored in other women who must have a high degree of feminine narcissism.

Group V: This group identifies with the active mother and plays out a mother–child relationship in the conscious and unconscious context of excluding the intruding father.

Group VI: The younger member of this group plays a passive role with an older, maternal, protective partner. The clitoris is their executive organ of pleasure and they abhor the presence of a penis or a penislike substitute.

Group VII: This group has a double identification: with the primary active mother who cares for the child, and with the father. In these women the double identification is superimposed one upon the other, with clitoral fantasies. They wear masculine clothing and many find it extremely difficult to admit to any passive wishes to be caressed, fondled, genitally stimulated, or penetrated.

Group VIII: This group cannot appreciate any love object that lacks a phallus. Although basically homosexual in their search for a loving female (the mother), they seek the father as their love object. Psychoanalysis reveals that unconsciously they cling tenaciously to the idea that they possess a phallus that they can put on or take off at will. Although they may engage in heterosexual relationships, these are extremely ambivalent, and their greatest pleasure is to be admired and sought after by women with whom actual sexual relations are infrequent and transitory. They are the most difficult of all homosexual women to treat psychoanalytically as they have established what they consider to be fulfilling adjustments to both sexes.

Group IX: In this group there is the appearance of extreme femininity, due to the special configuration of the castration complex: having identified herself with the father, she then chooses young girls as love objects to serve as ideal representatives of her own person. She thereby preserves her femininity. Feminine-appearing homosexual women then behave toward masculine-appearing homosexual women as they wish they had been treated by their fathers (Jones, 1927; Bonaparte, 1953; Socarides, 1963).

Classification of Female Homosexuals

In Socarides (1978a) I presented three detailed, lengthy psychoanalytic studies of female homosexuals, placing them in my new classification system. The reader is referred to this material (pp. 349–401) for a complete illustration of preoedipal type I, preoedipal type II, and oedipal forms of homosexuality as they occur in the female. I shall cite here the major clinical findings reported and the rationale for the position of each patient in my classification system.

The Case of Anna (Preoedipal Type I Female Homosexual): Anna, an aspiring twenty-four-year-old actress, had been unable to successfully traverse the separation–individuation phase of development, the rapprochement subphase. In addition, she utterly lacked the support, reassurance, protection, and strength of her father. The mother, upon whom she depended for all gratification, denied and deprived her. This intensified her oral craving and produced a desire to be close and never separated from her mother. She experienced any attempt to move away from the dependency on her mother with grave anxiety because of a fear of retaliation and the fear of her own aggression toward the mother. She had a deep need to have substitute teachers, older girl friends, and other females for love and affection. Her father reacted to her during her childhood with severe aggression, kicking her in the head, deploring her femininity, openly wishing for a boy, becoming depressed and severely rejecting, and shaming her for her sexual interest in him during the early oedipal phase. She could only regress to the previous fixation to her mother, but her image of her mother was filled with malevolence, inadequacy, and martyrdom. As a result, she searched for other women (good mothers). She greeted all signs of femininity, including the wearing of feminine clothing, the development of breasts, and menstruation with antagonism. She felt that these would lead to further devaluation and demeanment. While unconsciously desiring femininity, she equated it with worthlessness.

Anna was representative of those patients who suffer from preoedipal type I homosexuality. The deep unconscious tie with the malevolent mother (revealed in the analysis) represented a wish for and dread of merging with the mother. She expressed this as a fear of loss of self, being swallowed, becoming a fecal mass and so on. Her salvation lay in finding the good mother in the form of a loving and caring female in homosexual relations. Superimposed on her preoedipal conflict was an oedipal conflict of severe proportions that could be discerned only during the course of analytic therapy. Her denial of tender, affectionate, loving feelings for men arose from traumatic incidents suffered at the hands of a rejecting father whose love she urgently desired, attempted to acquire, and finally despaired of finding. Successful working through of the oedipal material was of paramount importance to the ultimate solution of her problem.

As in other preoedipal type I cases, the degree of ego deficits was mild. A transference relationship was possible once she had worked through her feelings that she would be demeaned by the analyst for her lack of a penis. Her object relations were from object to self, and the self was equated with the good loving female sexual object.

The Case of Sarah (Preoedipal Type II Female Homosexual): Sarah, a thirty-five-year-old accountant, was representative of those cases of female homosexuality in which the basic disorder and fixation occur in the earliest period of infancy. Compared to milder preoedipal forms of homosexuality (type I), in which the fixation is likely to have occurred in the rapprochement phase (just prior to the formation of object constancy), the fixation in this instance occurred in the practicing and differentiating subphases. Such fixation indicated a greater tendency to psychosis. Sarah's conflicts revolved around the most primitive, aggressive, destructive, and incorporative urges of the infant toward the mother, and defenses against them. Her defenses were those of projection and splitting, and the anxieties associated with them resembled those seen in borderline cases. This type of homosexuality is frequently seen in patients entering therapy for concomitant symptomatology (e.g., paranoid anxieties), rather than because of a desire for heterosexuality. Attempts to challenge or change their homosexual state should proceed with great caution, as there is marked possibility of severe decompensation to psychotic symptomatology. Sarah's fear of destruction by the female was clearly evident in her fear of being poisoned by her partner. The fear of merging was represented as a fear of contamination and death at the hands of a woman. Because of her projective sadism there was a compensatory death wish for the destruction of the homosexual love object.

Preoedipal type II female homosexuality carries with it a guarded prognosis as to therapeutic reversal, because there is a severe degree of pathology of internalized object relations, object relations are severely impaired, sometimes bizarre and distorted. The preoedipal type II female homosexual loves the partner in order to achieve narcissistic restoration. There is a failure in the development of sufficient self–object differentiation, and when regressive states appear, they may completely disrupt the analytic relationship. Projection, introjection, and splitting are common defense mechanisms, and impulses of aggression are poorly bound.

The Case of Joanna (Oedipal Female Homosexual): Joanna was a nineteen-year-old, attractive college student whose college career was abruptly terminated by a dramatic, attention-getting suicide attempt when rejected by a potential female sexual partner. In Joanna's case, genital oedipal conflicts dominated the clinical picture with a renunciation of her oedipal love for her father and a turning toward a woman. She experienced a structural conflict (in contrast to the other two patients mentioned, who suffered from an object relations class of conflict) between aggressive and libidinal wishes on the one hand, and her own inner prohibitions on the other. There was no fixation at a preoedipal level, but there was at times a partial regression to that earlier period. Her homosexuality represented a failure to resolve the Oedipus complex and castration fears leading to a negative oedipal position. This involved a sexual submission to a parent of the same sex. This form of homosexuality is the only type in which it can be accurately stated that the flight from the opposite sex partner is a major etiological factor. The tendency to regress was mild, although there was some regression as in neurotics. In these cases, although the homosexual symptom appeared to be ego-syntonic, it was upon careful analysis revealed to be ego-alien, that is, quite unacceptable.

Since the self was bound and cohesive and there was no impairment in ego boundaries, the orgasm in Joanna's case did not fulfill the unconscious purpose of buttressing a failing self representation, as in preoedipal female homosexuals. The patient could therefore much more easily terminate her homosexual activity when the underlying neurotic symptomatology was analyzed. Joanna, like other oedipal female homosexuals, developed analyzable transferences similar to those found in neurotics, which can be dealt with effectively. Reactivation and reenactment in the transference of oedipal wishes led to their resolution. Her object relations, as well as other ego functions, were unimpaired.

Part II
CLINICAL

Chapter 9
PREOEDIPAL TYPE II HOMOSEXUAL WITH NARCISSISTIC PERSONALITY DISORDER PROPER: THE CASE OF WILLARD

Introduction

In preoedipal type I patients, there is a regression or fixation to an infantile, in contrast to a more mature libidinal investment of self and object. This is carried out "under the condition of an identification of the self with an object, while the self is projected onto an external object that is loved because it stands for the self" (Kernberg, 1975, p. 329). This view is in conformity with Freud's (1914) earlier equation that such an individual loves "according to the narcissistic type, i.e., (a) what he himself is, i.e., himself, (b) what he himself was, (c) what he himself would like to be, (d) someone who was once part of himself" (p. 90). In preoedipal type II patients, "the investment of objects representing the projected grandiose self is usually transitory and superficial with a lack of awareness in depth or empathy for the object" (Kernberg, 1975, p. 329). The object and its individual and autonomous characteristics are completely hidden by a

233

"temporary projection of the grandiose self onto it" (p. 329); in essence, a narcissistic relationship has replaced the object relation.[1]

Pathological grandiosity in these patients produces a clinical picture in which the patient may appear more integrated, less conflicted, more at ease with himself, and less distressed when he is in narcissistic balance and not challenged by external reality. Beneath this facade of normality, however, he is unable to discriminate between the realistic and fantasied aspects of himself; is incapable of participating in activities that do not protect his grandiosity, and avoids those that threaten it; tends to withdraw from others; and continually overestimates or devalues both himself and his social reality.

The behavior of these patients is not regulated by a superego identified with the moral power of the parents (moral self regulation), since they have not developed beyond the "first stage of superego formation" (Sandler, 1960, p. 154).[2] Instead, "they evoke and employ object representations [introjects] to comfort, punish, control, or guide their activities in a manner similar to [but less reliable than] superego functioning" (Dorpat, 1976, p. 871). The defects in ego and superego formation create a crisis in their overall functioning, for they are unable to carry out the acts which individuals with structured superegos and egos are able to do for themselves. This crucial dilemma is temporarily resolved by using external objects (selfobjects), including *sexual* self-objects, whose function is to substitute for missing structures and the functions they perform (Dorpat, 1976). The narcissistic (selfobject) transferences encountered in psychoanalytic therapy are manifestations of their underlying developmental defect.

---

[1]Unlike schizohomosexuals (Socarides, 1978a), preoedipal type II narcissistic homosexuals have not suffered a complete loss of internal object representations, nor are they striving to fill up the feeling of a terrible void by creating new objects through homosexuality (Bak, 1971).

[2]In contrast, the disturbance of superego function, according to Kernberg, is a pathological development of *earlier* structures interfering in later normal development (Kernberg, 1975).

Clinical Study[3]

Willard was a fifty-year-old, attractive, highly articulate and intelligent man suffering from both a homosexual perversion and narcissistic personality disorder proper (the middle range of narcissistic pathology). When first seen, he was living with his severely ill father upon whom he had always been financially dependent. He entered treatment because he did not want to endanger a sizable inheritance at his father's death. Only later in treatment did it become apparent that this rather unusual aspect of his motivation for analysis was an expression of his basic core disturbance: a need for selfobjects to guide and control his behavior. He was also experiencing periods of depression, lethargy, feelings of exhaustion, and was engaged in intense homosexual activity. One of his worst symptoms was that he had been unable to complete actions which he felt were normal for adult human beings, and attempts to do so left him exhausted and depleted. He capsulized his position by stating that "there is a terrible negative force of energy in me which puts me in thrall. I'm continually putting reality on hold, keeping reality not so far away but just far enough so that I cannot be touched by it. I am a cipher with an incapacity to act at all."

The patient grew up in a wealthy household where the mother, a severely critical woman, withdrew from the father, "had a terrible sex life," and chronically expressed superiority and disdain for worldly pursuits. The father was a hard-working merchant who could not tolerate his wife's coldness and drank at night, arguing constantly with her. The most significant early memory of childhood was one which produced inordinate envy and rage: "The birth of my brother at three-and-a-half literally put my life in tatters. I remember being horrible, angry, belligerent, and hostile to my brother, and my father feeling this was ignoble, unworthy, and inap-

---

[3]The *narcissistic pathology* depicted by this patient was explainable from two theoretical frames of reference: self psychology (developmental deficiency hypothesie—Kohut) or conflict-induced pathology (Kernberg). Although the latter was increasingly important in later phases of the analysis, the former was strikingly evident and explanatory of the symptoms from the outset.

propriate. I can remember his rejecting me for this. Oh, how I hated my brother!" Throughout his early life, Willard felt effeminate, terrified of his peers, and unattractive. He engaged in secret fantasies of being "beautiful, superbly intelligent, and endlessly rich." He felt that he might become "impure through growth and aging," and in midadolescence engaged in what he felt was "ideal behavior, ideal values, ideal virtues." He feared that by making adjustments to the external world, he would "compromise the very sacred essence, the integrity of my being." Homosexual desires were present ever since he could remember, and he had several homosexual "romances" with idealized older men since the age of nineteen. He was now engaged in an active homosexual life with a series of casual partners, including male prostitutes.

The rich and variegated symptomatology of Willard's narcissistic personality disorder cannot be related within the limits of this chapter. Briefly stated, the guiding principles of his behavior revolved around the status of his self cohesion: to protect it when it was threatened, to minister to it when it was damaged, and to recapture it when it was lost. In narcissistic compensation, Willard was comfortable in his environment of fine hotels, servants, and restaurants: they helped create a "perfect" world in which he felt safe, provided him with emotional supplies, and all but removed his sense of inadequacy. When the "bombardment of reality" interfered with his "tranquil integrity," grandiose exhibitionistic demands came out of repression and collided with reality. He then suffered from regressive fragmentation and depletion depression. In this state of decompensation, he retreated to his bed, often defecated on the floor, and put clamps on his nipples during masturbation or in homosexual relations to heighten his sense of self by direct stimulation of the erogenous zones. These actions made him feel alive and restored him to his former self.

In periods of narcissistic compensation he frequently had self-state dreams (Kohut, 1971) of Italian palazzi, riding a huge horse on water, and so on. In states of decompensation, his palace was in disrepair and decay, his effects were scattered, and his once "glamorous" mother was now in great dishevelment. In one such dream he begged his mother to bequeath to him some lamps, to which she replied in refusal, "But you'll never have a place for them, you have no place. It would be ridiculous to give them to you!" His recollection of this dream was accompanied by overwhelming pain. Such dreams reflected all "good" and all "bad" split self and object images as well as pathological archaic grandiosity and deep sense of unworthiness.

Regressive loss of self cohesion and splitting were interchangeable emotional states for Willard. In both, perverse sexual practices became pronounced and punctuated by attacks of rage if he felt rejected.

Perverse Homosexual Activity

Willard's insatiable and voracious homosexuality functioned as a substitute for action in the external world, helping him to fill a void created by his inability to take part in life. He did everything possible to create emotional surrender and joy in his partners, but the pleasure he experienced soon wore off, and he compared himself to the Flying Dutchman, left homeless when the responsiveness of his partner ceased.

His sexual acts did not function as a prophylactic device in response to a fear of object loss or fear of losing the object's love, nor were they due to sensitivity to approval or disapproval by parents or parental surrogates so typical of rapprochement-phase crises. Instead, these acts served to diminish the defect in his self and supply it with stimulation. He noted that there were "specific ways in which I am intrinsically incomplete and need to be completed in sexual action. I care about being accepted by these men and being one of them," but it is not the individual himself he desired, as the partner was insignificant or interchangeable. "I am trying to accomplish something that I can't do by myself, despite the intensity and hotness of my passion. The only thing I want is that I set the time and I set the place, and they relate to me as much as I want them to and *I don't have to relate to them any more than I wish to.*" The sexual object is, in effect, a transitional object in that it must show a readiness to comply, lend itself to be manipulated, used, abused, discarded, cherished, symbolically identified with, but must not intrude upon him. Unlike the sexual object in preoedipal type I cases, which is loved according to the model of narcissistic love (Freud, 1914), it must surrender itself to his omnipotent control and must supply warmth and comfort to him.

Preliminary to sexual relations, he experienced over-excitement or depression, the former representing archaic defenses against unconscious sadism and aggression, and the latter the threat of loss of self cohesion. He attempted to resolve his internal despair through restitution by giving pleasure to a real external object and to himself simultaneously (Khan, 1965). He desired to produce a "big involvement" in order to find a "place to put emotions which I don't know where to place." The homosexual act served to temporarily correct the split between self and object by putting together the self representation with the appropriate charge. He achieved this by evoking pleasurable excitement in the partner so that he found himself in the reflection of the partner's responses. At this moment, he felt emotions.

When he lost his sexual partner, he did not grieve for the object nor the loss of the object's love. He felt the anguish of the undernourished child (Tolpin, 1979) who has lost a self-object response that keeps him whole and complete and free of fragmentation.

Discussion

Willard's homosexuality was a consequence of a disturbance belonging to the early infancy-childhood developmental stage in which self and body-ego boundaries are in the process of being established through maternal care and management (Khan, 1965). This produced interferences with self-object differentiation and integration, and with internalizations crucial to development and maturation. He attempted to remedy these defects through perverse activity. The homosexual contact allowed him to participate in a maternal calmness and composure. To be truly effective, such an empathic merger with the selfobject must be followed by need-satisfying *actions* performed by the selfobject (Ornstein, 1978). The partner is needed not only for sensory stimulation of a sexual nature, but as an object to complete tasks which he is incapable of doing for himself.

> I want him to read about how a Cadillac runs so I will know how, so that he can show me; and I want him to read the book about how the IBM typewriter works so he can tell me. And I want him to do practical things like that: drive me, take care of my mail. And I really want him to do things for me, not because I want him to serve, but because I'm not complete yet myself, and so I really want him to perform actions which would complete me and which will bring me into reality; that is, complete my reality activities which otherwise I could sort of not be.

While there is considerable disagreement as to the meaning of various phenomena (i.e., development-deficiency theory versus conflict-induced pathology) portrayed by my patient and found in narcissistic personality disorders (Panel, 1973), there is general agreement that early interferences with development and maturation are etiological factors for the later emergence of either healthy or pathological narcissism. Mahler and Kaplan (1977) conclude: (1) the absence of mirroring by admiring adults, especially during the differentiating subphase and even during the symbiotic phase, produces imbalances in fueling, which result in distortion of healthy narcissism; (2) disturbances in the practicing subphase, when the triad of self-love, primitive valuation of accomplishments and omnipotence is at its height, deprive the infant of both the internal source of narcissism derived from the autonomous ego sphere and the narcissistic enhancement afforded by the normal, active, aggressive spurt of practicing (p. 199); (3) by the end of the practicing subphase, splitting is commonly encountered along with confusion between paternal images and a lack of internalization of erotic and aggressive impulses. Too sudden a deflation of omnipotent grandeur during these stages leads to profound mood changes and production of ambivalently loved and hated objects, "split off and externalized in favor of internally contained, undifferentiated, negative, recathected self-representations" (p. 207). This leads to the production of an "omnipotent, grandiose ego ideal . . . not adjusted to reality" (p. 207) and the search for substitutes in the external world who will meet the needs of highly overcathected self-representational units;[4] (4) during the rapprochement subphase, narcissism is, of course, specifically phase-vulnerable.

From the analysis of Willard and several other preoedipal type II narcissistic homosexual patients (in this middle range of narcissistic pathology), I wish to briefly highlight differentiating criteria and their therapeutic implications.

Meaning of the Homosexual Symptom

The homosexual encounter in preoedipal narcissistic type II patients is related to their pathological narcissism, representing a search for both the narcissistic and the grandiose self representation. In uniting with another man there is a fusion of the self with various images of both mother and father with their associated emotions. Suffering from a severe loss of normal narcissistic self-esteem and filled with pathologically disturbed object relations, these patients remedy their sense of emptiness and inertia by giving pleasure to an external object and the self simultaneously. In the homosexual act, they induce dependence in the partner, compel an external object into instinctual surrender, augment a sense of power, and reduce a sense of isolation. What is lacking in all preoedipal type II homosexual encounters is the ability to trust, to surrender one's self to emotional experience, and to construct a true object relation. The aim of the act is to shore up a failing self representation and ward off regressive fragmentation. The homosexual encounter provides a "place to put emotions" in an integrated fashion so that the patient is made to feel alive and whole, at least for the moment. The homosexual object can be seen to function as a transitional object.

In contrast to preoedipal type II patients, in preoedipal type I homosexuals the pursued partner is a representation of the patient's own self (narcissistic) in relation to an active

---

[4]To Kernberg, the *"grandiose self,"* a term coined by Kohut (1971) is a compensation for early expression of the real parental object (Kernberg, 1975). It is not, therefore, a fixation on an "archaic, normal, primitive self" (Panel, 1973, p. 621).

phallic mother. The patient identifies with and incorporates the partner's masculinity through the sexual act. An unconscious reenactment of the mother-child role via the breast-penis equation tends to undo separation. The preoedipal type I homosexual seeks salvation from engulfment by the mother by fleeing to other men.

Nuclear Conflict

Preoedipal type II narcissistic homosexual patients develop anxiety and symptoms when they encounter situations that make them acutely and painfully aware of the discrepancy between the actual self and the wishful grandiose self (an external conflict) (Kohut, 1971). In contrast, preoedipal type I patients experience anxiety and guilt associated with separation due to fear of loss of the maternal object's love or separation from it (internalized conflict).

Defenses

The defenses of preoedipal type II patients are in their pre-stages of development (Stolorow and Lachmann, 1980), and splitting predominates over repression. In preoedipal type I patients, repression predominates with some splitting phenomena, but the major defense mechanisms are introjection, projection, and identification.

Transference

The transference in preoedipal type II homosexual patients is typical of the differentiation and practicing subphases: that is, mirroring and merging transference or selfobject (narcissistic) transference. The patient uses the therapist as a transference object, a selfobject. He is unable to maintain a representation of the "good" object, especially when frustrated by it (when the analyst does not mirror or admire him). Transference in preoedipal type II homosexuals may also be termed *primitive transferences* (Kernberg, 1980b), reflecting the state of the patient's internalized object relations; namely, a defensive constellation of self and object representations directed against an opposite and dreaded repressed self and object constellation. For example, Willard often viewed himself as a submissive, impotent person vis-à-vis a powerful and protective maternal object image; or, at other times, his self representation consisted of a rebellious, repressed self vis-à-vis a sadistic and controlling parental object. It should be noted that these patients are able to maintain reality testing despite a moderate tendency to psychosislike transference regressions. Preoedipal type I patients, in contrast, are able to maintain a representation of the "good" object, even when frustrated by it, do not require constant mirroring or merging, and do not easily regress.

Implications for Therapy

With preoedipal type II narcissistic patients, the analyst allows himself to function as a selfobject and the patient is encouraged to increase his capacity for self-observation until a proper transference of the neurotic type is achieved (Socarides, 1979b). The treatment of preoedipal type II narcissistic homosexual patients is essentially that of a severe narcissistic character disorder proper. The full-blown narcissistic transference must be allowed to develop for a time with its mirroring function, but is ultimately replaced by a transference neurosis.

In these patients who suffer from severe ego developmental arrest, we are dealing with persons who have suffered missed or prematurely lost experiences, legitimately needed,[5] which must be understood and repaired within the

---

[5] An alternative hypothesis is that these patients suffer from a lack of normal emotional caring and warmth in the second or third year of life. with a resultant easily activated *destructiveness* (Kernberg, 1975). They deny dependency on the analyst as it is a defense against narcissistic rage, envy, fear, and guilt, and they have a longing for a loving relationship that will not be destroyed by hatred (p. 621). Their idealization defends against the dangers and too-early emergence of intense envy and destruction, and their tendency both to idealize and devalue are "defenses against earlier oral rage, envy, and paranoid fears related to projection of sadistic trends, terrifying feelings of loneliness, guilt, and aggression" (Kernberg, 1975, p. 75).

transference in order to assist the patient's ego in its belated development before interpretations of a structural nature can be made. It is necessary to deal first with what the arrested ego needs to achieve, and interpret only later what the ego needs to ward off (Stolorow and Lachmann, 1980). This ultimately helps these patients to regain a feeling of an individual, idealized self (a real self), first based on identification with the analyst, and promotes a gradual eradication of the primitive grandiose pathological self and the assumption of new, realistic goals in accordance with their real abilities.

In contrast, the transference relationship in preoedipal type I patients allows for a new identification with the analyst as a substitute for the homosexual attachment. The gradually emerging autonomous self must be helped in its efforts to achieve true integration, all the while being protected from engulfment by the mother, through the transference relationship.

Summary

In this chapter I have presented theoretical, clinical, and therapeutic aspects of preoedipal type II narcissistic homosexual patients by describing their clinical picture, the content and meaning of their perverse acts, their defenses, their transference, and implications for treatment. Differentiating criteria between preoedipal type I and type II homosexuals are noted. Explanations of the various phenomena these patients present are now possible because of advances in our theoretical knowledge provided by new concepts of narcissism and self psychology, especially when correlated and integrated with our expanding knowledge of primary psychic development as it pertains to the practicing, differentiating, and rapprochement subphases of the separation-individuation process.

My clinical research with these patients leads me to suggest that the causative process involved in the formation of this particular form of homosexuality is dependent upon vicissitudes that have their genesis in the differentiating and practicing subphases of the separation-individuation process.

Chapter 10
THE RAPPROCHEMENT SUBPHASE CRISIS IN A PREOEDIPAL TYPE II NARCISSISTIC HOMOSEXUAL: THE CASE OF CAMPBELL

Introduction

I shall here attempt to further elucidate the psychopathology of the homosexual through the application of theoretical concepts of primary psychic development, especially that of the rapprochement subphase of the separation–individuation process.

Mahler (1972a) described the "dramatic fights with the mother" (p. 495) as characteristic of the rapprochement subphase, conflicts between the child's individual interests as opposed to his love for the object, and the painful and precipitous deflation of the delusion of his own grandeur. She concluded that the failure to traverse successfully the rapprochement phase produced a centrum or nidus of intrapsychic conflict which may later lead either to neurosis or to faulty or incomplete structural development, setting the stage for later narcissistic or borderline disorders (Mahler, 1972a, pp. 492-504). Although not mentioned by Mahler, I believed then, as I do now, that there is overwhelming evidence to add perversions to this list of conditions which arise from the second group of disorders, those associated with arrested or deficient structural development.

245

In treating cases of homosexuality (as in all perversion), my aim is to discover the location of the fixation point and to make it possible for the patient to retrace his steps to that part of his development which was distorted by infantile and childhood deficiencies. Following the lessening of compensatory reparative moves in the adaptive processes that had distorted and inhibited his functioning, and the analysis of self-perpetuating defenses, I have repeatedly encountered head-on what seemed to be reenactments of rapprochement subphase conflicts and vicissitudes, complicated by oedipal and other subsequent experiences. In almost all instances, anxieties relating to separation from the mother were revived and relived. Maturational achievement, the successful taking of career examinations in a patient previously unable to do so, activity undertaken without the mother's approval, for example, produced anxiety and guilt of varying degrees as they were unconsciously equated with *intrapsychic* separation.

Some Theoretical Comments on
Preoedipal Reconstruction

In an important paper, Settlage (1977) utilized expanding theories of early psychic development to cast light on the psychopathology of narcissistic and borderline personality disorders in adults and children. He suggested that if we are to define the pathogenesis, the "pathological formations," and the means of treatment of narcissistic and borderline personality disorders, we must attempt to make a "precise correlation of traumatic experience during the first years of life" (p. 806) with the phases of early psychic development. He stressed that, while theoretical formulations of early psychic development "are based primarily upon the process of reconstruction" (p. 803), a much closer view of the "beginnings of formation of psychic structure and function" can be obtained by direct observational studies. Both reconstructive and direct observational approaches have merits and limitations; they are "complementary to rather than in conflict with each other and . . . both of them are valuable and essential to a full psychoanalytic understanding" (p. 807).

Blum (1977) comprehensively reviewed the reservations psychoanalysts must have with regard to preoedipal reconstruction. He noted Mahler's cautionary comment that we should not be led into the belief that "preverbal . . . phenomena . . . are isomorphic with the verbalizable clinical material" (Mahler, Pine, and Bergman, 1975, p. 14), and Anna Freud's early warning (1971, p. 24) that more highly developed functions are always superimposed on more archaic layers and "the original simplicity of the primitive picture cannot but be distorted." Blum observed that:

> [T]here is no reason to expect that any of the later normal developmental phases of life or pathological states will exactly replicate point by point any of the subphases of separation–individuation or psychosexual development. The early phases of development are not literally recapitulated; various consequences are inferred in terms of residue and influences, or forerunners which undergo further developmental vicissitudes, and . . . are subject to regressive transformations [p. 781].

We may conclude, with Blum that "the integration of psychoanalytic reconstruction and direct child observation promises a deeper understanding of ego development and disturbance, character formation, and preoedipal determinants of oedipal conflict and the infantile neurosis" (1977, p. 783).

Thus, we may speak of the potential for defining the psychopathology (Settlage, 1977, p. 806) in severe borderline and narcissistic disorders and say that analytic reconstruction profits by its articulation with our current knowledge of development. In this connection it should be noted that as early as 1937 Freud perceived the uncertainties attendant on preoedipal reconstruction when he said that an infantile psychological reaction and pattern dating from a time when the child could barely speak may force "its way into consciousness, probably distorted and displaced owing to the operating of forces that are opposed to this return" (1937, p. 267).

Clinical Study

In the case to be presented, the precipitating factor was a premature attempt to effect separation from an engulfing mother. The precipitating event itself was merely a small act of self-assertion. The patient, in what seemed to be an effort to comply with the father–analyst's wishes, was thinking of establishing himself in an apartment of his own—certainly something his mother would view with disfavor.

The extensive case history of this patient and an account of his psychoanalysis may be found in Socarides (1978a, pp. 245–277). My major emphasis here will be on the derivatives of the rapprochement crises as they occurred during analytic therapy of this homosexual patient with narcissistic pathology (highest level of functioning).

The patient was a thirty-six-year-old, highly intelligent, attractive, and cultured man who experienced periods of confusion, depression, and anxiety that could be alleviated only by having a homosexual experience.

Campbell was an only child. His mother was highly cultivated, his father a rugged explorer, an alcoholic, contemptuous of what he deemed his wife's ultrarefined tastes. She treated him with a condescension born from her conviction of her social, aesthetic, and moral superiority. After years of dissension, the mother instigated a separation when Campbell was fourteen, after which the father resided nearby, contributing intermittently to the support of his wife and son. In effect, the mother's depreciation of the father forced his withdrawal from the family.

Campbell had been born within ten months of the marriage. It was a difficult birth requiring extensive surgery for the mother in order to repair a severe perineal tear. Because of the mother's long convalescence and a series of secondary physical complications, the child was placed in the care of a nurse. Periodically during the first year-and-a-half postpartum, the mother went on several long trips lasting one to two months. The child was not breast-fed; early on he developed a mild to moderate degree of feeding difficulty. He suffered repeated ear infections around age two. From age one-and-a-half to four he had protracted "screaming fits" when he was separated from the mother—for instance, if the nurse or anyone else attempted to supplant the mother in wheeling the carriage.

In early childhood, when his mother went on one of her

frequent vacations, she left him with a Scottish maid who was a strict disciplinarian. Upset by the boy's masturbation, she continually punished him for it.

Campbell had numerous childhood fears. One was that if he left his hands outside the covers when he went to sleep, someone would cut them off. Another was that there was someone, especially his father, at the foot of the bed who had come to murder him. Often, upon going to sleep, he would suddenly be awakened with a terrifying sensation that his legs were going to drop off.

Memories of his early childhood included recollections of having liked dolls—he had a family of teddy bears with which he played until he was nine—of dressing up in his mother's clothes, of his marked interest in clothes. He could recall over many years a particular costume either his mother or her friends had worn. He always felt that his mother wanted to "keep me home." Her attitude toward her husband led Campbell to view his father as insubstantial and weak. The father habitually demeaned his son for his lack of athletic abilities, openly referring to him as a "sissy."

As a small boy, he hated sports and felt awkward. His mother pushed him into going to dances, told him where to stand and with whom to dance. He did everything possible to stay away from girls, but became increasingly close to his mother, who undressed in front of him, sharing with him discussion of her social and personal life, her clothes, and so on. As an adolescent, he gradually became her escort to social events.

Ever since he was about eight years old, Campbell had daydreams in which he planned to "eradicate" his father. Alongside his aggression against the father was a great need to be loved by him.

In adolescence, Campbell always felt depressed after his weekly outings with his father. The father sent him home punctually in a taxi, but Campbell felt he was curtailing their time together. During adolescence, he was terrified of his mother's touch, for it stimulated sexual feelings. At age thirteen he began asking her not to kiss him goodnight. When he was fourteen or fifteen, she invited him to sleep in the same bed with her the night before he left for boarding school to insure his remaining faithful to her. "Mother was very stupid about coming into the bathroom when I was in there. I was rather offended that I didn't seem to have any sex at all to her."

When Campbell went off to boarding school, he fell in love with the first in a series of beautiful blond boys a few years older than himself, realized he was homosexual, and was seized by an intense need to dye his own hair blond. Later, in college, he was seized by another "compulsion"—he shaved off all his body hair, except for that in the pubic area. The enactments of his "compulsions," that represented both his identification with the all-powerful (blond) mother and the defeat of his masculinity, and which protected him against the anxiety of not being loved by men, were often followed by a "kind of hysterics" in which Campbell sobbed, felt intensely confused, and occasionally wished for death.

In college, he was increasingly unable to adapt adequately to environmental demands, feeling that he was "not enough of a man." Frightened and weakened by these reality stresses, homosexual urges became more conscious and terrifying. He resisted their enactment until, unable to study, he failed the academic requirements of graduate school and was drafted into the Navy. He then engaged in a "calculated career of homosexuality" that continued away from home. He commented, "Homosexuality saved my sanity. Before, at college, I had reached the end of the world, an awful fear. Then I suddenly failed my exams." In the Navy, homosexuality quieted his general distrust and relieved his projective anxieties that bordered on paranoidal symptomatology, although no psychotic symptoms developed. It furthermore defended against extreme outbursts of aggression.

Early in therapy, Campbell felt that his homosexual problem must somehow be tied up with his mother and his feelings toward her. "There's a big 'voltage' toward my mother . . . a strong resentment against her and a tremendous dependency." His homosexuality was also a way of controlling men so that they did not attack him, especially when he felt vulnerable—following the loss of a job, for example. Furthermore, he felt that the homosexual act sometimes saved him from a strange sort of chaotic, mysterious frag-

mentation of himself: "I will fall apart if I don't have it."
Magically, after homosexual intercourse, he felt relieved,
whole and strong. He sometimes experienced a split in himself, "like two selves existing," and that he did not know who
he was. He noticed that homosexual feelings came on whenever he was afraid of his mother "turning around and
engulfing me." By late adolescence, he frequently experienced a weird excitement when his mother approached him
suddenly, particularly if he was half-asleep and she unex-
pectedly walked into his bedroom. This excitement proceeded on several occasions to overt sexual feeling toward
her of which he was "terribly frightened." At the same time,
this had an admixture of aggression: he didn't quite know
what he would do to her, "either have intercourse with her, or
perhaps murder her."

The onset of homosexual desire was often ushered in with
severe shudders and chills. "I have to run to the Turkish bath
for sex and then I suddenly feel better. I have a feeling that
I'm acting like a girl. I'm like my mother. The anal business
is the only thing that satisfies me. Before I go I feel, somehow, I'm going to be engulfed, or that I may lose my mind.
This reestablishes me."

Intermittently and frequently during the first three years
of the analysis, when weak and defenseless, the patient
underwent regressive experiences with sensations of being
engulfed and losing himself in the mother. He had experienced these on numerous occasions for seven or eight years
previous to his beginning therapy—agonizing episodes of
overwhelming anxiety, rolling on the floor, various psychosomatic complaints (stomach pain, short stabbing pains in
his low spine), fears of being physically attacked, fears of
loss of parts of his body. These attacks of "confusion" began
with extremely severe tension headaches, occasionally one-
sided and migrainous in nature. At these times, he felt he
might "crack up" or fragment into a "million pieces." He felt
a loss of direction and orientation. Lights became exceedingly bright. The room sometimes appeared to shift somewhat and he became frightened. "It's a sort of terrible fright,
then a compulsion to homosexual activity."

In these dramatic regressive episodes, he experienced

severe autonomic reactions: a feeling of generalized collapse, pervasive panic, loss of identity, and fears of engulfment.

These feelings disorganized every thought I have, and homosexuality is my only outlet. They go all over my body and seem to sweep through my nerve centers. I feel it everywhere. It can be compared to water rushing through the rooms of a house. It activates certain things first, like certain centers, first my stomach, then my head, and I don't feel two things simultaneously. Within an hour or two my hands are trembling. There's tension in the pit of my stomach, I have a diarrhea feeling, a terrible feeling at the base of my spine, a pain. Also, strangely enough, a feeling of intense genital excitement. My headaches then begin and are very intense, and I'm almost in a state of hysteria. I feel aches and pains, and I feel mad and disgusted with myself, but I can't calm my mind. I am completely dead, too, completely automatic, a robot.

The relationship between the regressive phenomenon, its precipitants, and the homosexual solution to the dangers of regression could be readily discerned. The regression was activated by any attempt to seek closer contact with the mother. The danger of an intensification of his closeness to her was that he would be forced into the affective state of his preoedipal fixation. Any desire to get closer to her than the guarded optimal distance that allowed partial satisfaction produced a cataclysmic and catastrophic fear of merging with her.

To illustrate: In the third year of his analysis, I received a call from Campbell on a Sunday, asking for an immediate appointment. When he arrived at my office, he was distraught, flushed, severely agitated, and complained of an excruciating headache. He was nearly screaming, and alternated between crying and a bitter, childlike half-laughter. Tears streamed down his face. He was unkempt, complained that he felt "paralyzed," and did indeed fall from the couch to the floor. He had, in effect, lost a characteristic behavioral concomitant of the rapprochement phase: the mastery of upright locomotion. Regressive material appeared when the patient, aided by the positive transference, attempted a premature separation from his mother, openly defying her.

He had spent Friday and Saturday with his mother, but when on Saturday he told her he was planning to leave earlier than usual on Sunday, she was enraged, especially as she was thereby losing her escort to a cocktail party on Sunday night. "I felt as if mother was saying that if I left her she'd leave me to daddy. She compared me to him, how thoughtless I was. Last night, I had dreams in which my teeth were all knocked out and were rotten and falling." Campbell frequently had dreams of losing his teeth. Not only did this signify his fear of castration and his wish to become an infant, it also indicated that his self representation was being severely threatened. It was a harbinger of an oncoming severe and imminent regressive reaction.

He felt apprehensive on his drive back to the city. His mother had misplaced her automobile license and, just before he left, had angrily asked him to look for it in her bureau drawers. Upon entering the bedroom of their city home, he opened the drawers only to find lingerie and underwear mixed up as if they had been thrown in there. He compared it to a garbage can fantasy he used to have up to adolescence. In this fantasy (a childhood correlate to fears of engulfment), he was immersed in garbage up to his mouth. This always aroused disgust and extreme fright. "This is the garbage can, the underwear thrown into the drawers; this is like being inside her. I begin breathing very hard as if I were inside her, and I felt sick at my stomach and as if I would be compressed and choke and die. I think I'm going to faint now, like I'm going under an anesthetic." Campbell began to scream and cry uncontrollably, his hands clenched, his body rocking back and forth. He felt better crying, as if somehow that restored him to himself. He recalled that he had felt like this numerous times before. He suddenly began to roll on the floor. When I helped him to rise, he slumped and collapsed on the couch. "I'm a child, I'm a child. Mommy is coming back to the room. She's got to come back. I think I'm yelling; it's a funny yell, like a child's yell. I think it's rage."

The patient could quite easily be brought back to reality in the midst of such episodes. "I have a terrible ear abcess and the pain, it's terrible, and I'm yelling now, a terrible abcess and the pain won't go away. This happened when I was two, I was told. It is mommy, if only she would come back to me." Campbell's voice was now that of a baby. "If she'd only understand me, protect me." He was pleading, whimpering, crying, face contorted, eyes glaring and wild-looking.

> She must protect me. She said this morning she'd leave me to daddy. Yes, this is what I've been afraid of, that daddy would kill me and that she would leave me. I was never allowed to chew the blanket. My mother saying, "Don't chew the blanket"— something to do with losing my teeth. Last night I felt some of this, some of her disapproval. I must be under an anesthetic. It's as if I was under ether. The picture I have is of a wish to lie in mother's arms and her loving and enfolding me, but it scares me. The conflict is I want to love her terribly, but we can't because of the sex business. When I went into her drawers, a childish impulse . . . I see the drawers, and I feel a terrible impulse to get inside her, not intercourselike. I thought of totally entering her. I remember I would never open her pocket-book or any of her drawers. I actually was rejoining her and I couldn't do it. Before I came here, I tried to stop it all. I bought some peroxide for my hair and then I realized I shouldn't do this any more, and I washed it out. Then I felt terribly depressed, and I can't change my sex. I thought I'd then go back to lie on her bed and I'd die there, die there like in her arms . . . and I looked at myself in the mirror and was shaking, and I thought, "Oh, you bitch."

The reenactment of this strong affective state led to a gradual cessation of the patient's overwhelming anxiety, and he became restored to his former self. While a running commentary on the meaning of his experience was given during the experience, what was vitally important was the presence of the analyst so that object relations were reinforced and were ultimately restored. In support of this, he telephoned me the next day as an attack began, and, as he talked, the threat of personal dissolution vanished.

Discussion

Campbell was unable to pass through the developmental phase in which he could separate his identity from that of the mother and achieve object constancy. Out of the inability to separate and the need to identify with the mother came a threat of merging with her. The preoedipal fear that crystallized was then augmented by the later castration fears of the oedipal period.

Campbell entered later childhood with an inhibition of self-assertion and a pronounced feminine (maternal) identification. He had a strong inhibition of all male sexuality to avoid his fear of merging. He achieved a spurious masculinity, acquiring a penis and affection from men, thereby avoiding the dangers connected with his mother, but he still wished to maintain a close tie with her. In his homosexuality, he tried to rid himself of his damaging, destructive urge toward union with her and attempted to ward off his incorporative needs. When the pressures of adaptation and appropriate masculine-role functioning became too strong in adulthood, he regressed to a less demanding state of maternal closeness fraught with more primitive unconscious fears, which led to urgent needs for homosexual experiences. They reassured him against ego dissolution, were a substitute for a reunion with the mother, and allowed the expression, alleviation, and discharge of severe aggression aroused by the imperative need to merge with her. It was a lesser danger compared to merging with the mother. He established masculine identity by uniting with a male and his penis in homosexual intercourse, thereby reconstituting his ego. If he was unable to have homosexual relations, he felt "somehow I'm going to be destroyed, that I'm in terrible danger." For example, his mind suddenly "felt fatigued"; his body reactions became uncontrolled. "The idea of something jumping all through my body as if my heart suddenly hits a bit harder, as if I'm terribly hungry, and suddenly I'm conscious of all the blood in my stomach." This was quickly followed by impulses to act irrationally "like I might want to kill you. I know you're not going to attack me, but I somehow fear this, and I'm frightened also of myself." An explanation for these bursts of aggression may well be that the breakdown of formerly partially effective fusion and neutralization processes led to an abrupt awareness of a defusion of libido and destructive aggression. When regression occurred, deneutralization followed, with resultant reinstinctualization. This led to a striking phenomenon: the experiencing of intense aggressive destructive feelings alternating with equally intense libidinal impulses, reminiscent of the splitting and ambivalency of rapprochement. The patient exclaimed: "I want to hug you and kiss you and then, just as suddenly, I want to hurt you and crush you."

He had strange feelings that he would swallow parts of his body, such as his hand or foot (primitive incorporative anxiety); felt he would lose part of his face or be separated from his face, or that in "separating" from his face, another face would be found to exist beneath it. Splitting of the ego was also evident in less dramatic forms during his daily life on numerous occasions.

The patient felt that he actually became a baby. He revived memories of the pain and screaming due to a chronic mastoid infection. He enacted fear of abandonment, loss of his mother, and his inability to separate from her. Concomitantly, he had a desire to merge with her, but this was mixed with fears of personal dissolution and self-destruction. His mother's threat to give him back to "daddy" with the implicit threat of loss of mother and castration by the father, caused an intensification of his wish to be close to her, with an ultimate joining and merging with her. This gave rise to severe anxiety. The wish to merge became a fear of merging, a fear of exploding, a fear of dying, a fear of personal dissolution.

The attacks occurred in the general setting of insecurity, feelings of weakness, loss of power, threats of loss of mother, her anger or disapproval of him, and her "coming at me," and anything perceived as a threat from the external world. This inordinate sensitivity to parental disapproval and threats resembled a manifestation of a rapprochement crisis. When these crises occurred, he at first was unwilling and then afraid to move. His affective life underwent a progressive decline in terms of his control over it; extreme anxiety, with its psychosomatic accompaniments, depression, feelings of loss of self, and emptiness made their appearance. Similar to the rapprochement child of fifteen to twenty-two months, he was attempting to effect increasing psychical separation from his mother, induced by the analysis. Increased separation anxiety, however, began to appear with the fear of object loss. Increasing independence from mother was changed suddenly into a constant concern, and he was both afraid of and resented the attempt at separation from her.

Attributing the patient's homosexuality to preoedipal factors does not minimize the importance of the oedipal period and its castration fear. Campbell suffered severe castration anxiety. Upon entering the oedipal period, he was assailed by many fears related to his "cruel" father, in part a consequence of allegiance to his mother and murderous wishes and guilt feelings toward his father. Campbell expressed this fear of his father in his negative oedipal attitude, in which he unconsciously offered himself sexually to the father in place of the mother. At the same time, he could be more like his mother, exaggerating and emphasizing his feminine identification, with the hope of gaining safety and narcissistic supplies. Unconsciously, he was not only castrated by the father, but also attained sexual pleasure from him masochistically through substituting male partners. This led in part to a desire for and a dread of anal rape. He successfully fought off conscious awareness of this dread of anal rape by attacking other men anally and by transforming them from threatening figures into "love figures." But above all, his homosexuality served the repression of a pivotal nuclear conflict: the drive to regress to a preoedipal fixation in which there is a desire for and dread of merging with the mother in order to reinstate the primitive mother–child unity; the homosexual object choice was crucial to the repression of this basic conflict between the wish for and dread of the mother–child unity.

Campbell suffered ego defects, deficiencies in reality testing, and a disturbance in body–ego boundaries. Although his thinking was clear, his behavior was dominated by the pleasure principle. This, combined with poor impulse control, led to actions which seemingly denied reality. His thinking also reflected his projective anxieties. Alternating with an elevated sense of self-esteem were feelings of self-depreciation, need for narcissistic supplies and for narcissistic restoration. Ego boundaries were impaired but remained mainly intact, except under conditions of severe stress. He was intolerant of external frustrations which aroused anxiety, and action was substituted for normal anxiety or depression. These ego deficits, though severe, suggested that the mother–infant relationship was not hopelessly destroyed during the first half-year of life, that is, during the symbiotic phase. His tendency to respond to anxiety and depression with object directed or self-directed aggression connoted a disturbance and exacerbation of both primary and secondary aggression due to frustration. Despite these ego deficits, Campbell's object relations both inside and outside of the analysis were of self to object and not of grandiose self to self as is present in those homosexuals and other perverts with associated narcissistic personality disorder proper (see Chapter 9, the case of Willard). His nuclear conflict derived from fears of engulfment although fears of fragmentation commonly found in the more severe preoedipal type II cases was present. Although splitting mechanisms were present they did not predominate over mechanisms of repression. Furthermore, he did not suffer from pathological grandiosity although a narcissistic wish for restoration ran through his life history. Libidinal availability and absence of helpfulness on the part of the mother during the rapprochement subphase, due to her frequent absences, posed a threat of intrapsychic loss. This alternated with an overweaning closeness, dependency, and mutual clinging. His partners for sexual relations were representatives of his self (narcissistic) in relation to an active phallic mother. Furthermore, he identified with and incorporated the partner's masculinity in the sexual act. What he was unconsciously enacting was a mother–child role via the breast-penis equation. Splitting processes of ego, superego, and object were present.

The patient's failure to achieve age-adequate ego autonomy, gender-defined self identity, a separation of self from object, body–ego delineation, and a structuralization of psychic functions played vital roles in the pathogenesis of his homosexuality. From the soil of his preoedipal disorder the well-structured perversion arose; its mechanism was erotization. A fundamental observation is that, when a homosexual's insufficient self and object representations are threatened, he develops anxiety and is faced with the necessity to shore up his precarious or "imperiled representational world" (Stolorow & Lachmann, 1980). Early psychosexual experiences are utilized to this end. It is not the fixated erotic experiences per se, that is, the instinct derivatives, that have been regressively reanimated in the perversion: it is the *early function* of the erotic experiences that is retained and regressively relied upon. In this way, through erotization, the homosexual, like other perverts, attempts to maintain structural cohesion and stability in the face of a disruptive or disintegrating self and object representation. Ego survival is thereby assured.

A reconstruction of the childhood experiences could be achieved through their revival in the transference. The disruption in the successful traversing of the rapprochement subphase produced difficulties in the transference and therapeutic alliance. Since self and object representations were merged, he could not tell the source of his feelings and frequently accused the analyst of not believing him when a serious or incisive comment was made; he thought that the analyst might laugh at him behind his back after he left the consultation room. The analyst was viewed as fluctuating between being all good and all bad. The splitting was due to a developmental deficiency in his self–object boundary maintenance, with a confusion between self and object. He wished to see his narcissistic self mirrored in the approval of the analyst and distrusted the latter's observations. A positive working alliance would be maintained only intermittently, and the patient frequently missed sessions during the first two years of therapy, before sufficient structuralization of his ego had taken place. The absence of the analyst during periods of vacation led to severe separation anxiety. Similarly, the mother's absence produced separation anxiety.

At the other pole of the dyadic relationship, his mother reacted to his attempted acts of independence with a lack of empathy, with rage, threats of castration, threats of abandoning him to the father, threats of loss of the object (mother), and a disruption of the symbiotic unity which still remained in the archaic layers of his mind. What ensued was a further regressive impairment of object relations, an exacerbation of splitting processes, separation anxiety, and dangers of annihilation together with fears of reengulfment. In several such instances, he experienced and regressively reenacted (1) the early trauma of the mastoid infection at age two, at the height of the rapprochement subphase; (2) severe separation anxiety upon attempting to leave the mother; (3) overwhelming fears of father; (4) (partial) fears of fragmentation of the self due to an underlying failure to fully and satisfactorily traverse the practicing subphase of separation-individuation with the resultant partial instability; (5) the fear of losing ego differentiation (the threat of further ego regression into an amorphous phase, with further loss of ego functions). His homosexuality was a prophylactic device, preventing defensive regression of the ego and helping him to maintain the optimal distance from and closeness to the mother through substitution (male in place of female, penis in place of breast).

During therapy, the patient's mother demonstrated a complete lack of receptivity to his nascent individuality or an understanding of his need to be independent. To emphasize what I have already stated: upon attempting intrapsychic separation, severe castration anxiety was experienced at both the mother's and father's hands, together with deeper preoedipal anxieties, fears of maternal reengulfment, and a severe deflation of his own feelings of self-esteem. In essence, he reproduced a rapprochement crisis in which he was once again unsuccessful. The mother did not wish him to separate either in childhood or adulthood, and used him as an object for her own needs, endlessly manipulating, controlling, and keeping him a part of her. The regression produced a further impairment of object relations, a threatened dissolution of his self representation, and the fear of merging into the symbiotic mother–child unity. It stimulated aggressive responses of an intense severity and castration fears of an overwhelming nature, in part derived from superimposed oedipal fears and in part due to object loss which was associated with an earlier faulty genital schematization (Roiphe, 1968). The father was absent, cold, and showed a lack of empathy and understanding. He was devalued and diminished by both mother and son. The end result was a power-less and impotent male figure with whom the patient could not identify. An identification with a powerful, strong, and loving male figure could only be provided later in the analy-sis through the transference.

As a result of the transference and working alliance induced by the therapeutic relationship, Campbell attempt-ed prematurely to effect separation from his pathological attachment to his mother and was catapulted into a crisis that had all the characteristics of a rapprochement crisis. He experienced incorporation anxieties, projective anxieties, fears of loss of self and loss of the object. In effect, what resulted was a threatened dedifferentiation of psychic struc-ture and of object relations.[1]

While there is no direct line (Mahler, 1973) between the patient's adult psychopathology and his developmental fix-ation, it is my belief that the revival of primitive ego states and their essentially hallucinatory reenactment found so frequently in homosexual patients of the preoedipal type are a confirmation of the enormously valuable developmental data of the earliest phases of human existence, thoroughly documented by Mahler. These episodes have enormous rele-vance for the ultimate solution to the etiology and problem of homosexuality and other sexual perversions. It is my further belief that the significant incidence of homosexuality in the general population is due to the necessity for all human beings to traverse the separation–individuation phase of early childhood, which is decisive for gender-defined self identity: a substantial number of children fail to successfully complete this developmental process and therefore are un-

---

[1] Campbell was in analysis for nine-and-a-half years, at which time he procured highly desirable employment in Europe. His overall psycholog-ical functioning was vastly improved and rapprochement crises com-pletely disappeared by the third year of analysis. He was able to function heterosexually but continued to depend (when under severe stress) on homosexual activity. Several follow-up interviews during the ensuing five years revealed that he has maintained the progress achieved, but that under severe emotional strain he engaged in infrequent and isolated homosexual encounters. All in all, he has profited greatly by increasing his performance and functioning in the major areas of life and he has felt increasing confidence and pleasure in living.

able to form a healthy sexual identity in accordance with their anatomical and biological capacities.

Summary

I have attempted to cast light on the psychopathology of well-structured cases of homosexuality of preoedipal type II by utilizing our expanding knowledge of primary psychic development as it pertains to the rapprochement subphase of the separation–individuation process. Analytic reconstruction is enriched by its articulation with current knowledge of development, especially when correlated as precisely as possible with earlier traumatic experiences which have caused developmental interferences.

I have focused mainly on the rapprochement subphase origin of clinical phenomena observed and on the three great anxieties of the rapprochement subphase: fear of object loss, fear of losing the object's love, and the undue sensitivity to approval/disapproval by the parent. Reenactments of rapprochement crises in the transference were depicted.

Chapter 11
ABDICATING FATHERS, HOMOSEXUAL SONS: TWO CLINICAL EXAMPLES

Introduction

A disturbed father–son relationship has long been alluded to as contributing to adult male homosexuality. Freud, in several instances, commented on the importance of the father in the psychogenesis of homosexuality. As early as 1905 he predicted with remarkable prescience the family constellation so commonly noted in subsequent decades (Bieber, Dain, Dince, Drellich, Grand, Gundlach, Kremer, Rifkin, Wilbur, and Bieber, 1962; Socarides, 1968b) in the psychoanalysis of homosexual patients: a domineering, psychologically crushing mother and an absent, weak, hostile, or rejecting father. In "Leonardo da Vinci" (1910a) Freud observed:

> In all our male homosexual cases the subjects had had a very intense erotic attachment to a female person, as a rule their mother, during the first period of childhood, which is afterwards forgotten; this attachment was evoked or encouraged by too much tenderness on the part of the mother herself, and further reinforced by the small part played by the father during their childhood [p. 99].

He stated that the mothers of homosexual men were frequently masculine women "who were able to push the father out of his proper place" (p. 99). He was strongly impressed by cases in which the father was absent from the beginning or left the scene at an early date, so that the boy found himself left entirely under feminine influence. "Indeed, it almost seems as though the presence of a strong father would ensure that the son made the correct decision in his choice of object, namely someone of the opposite sex" (p. 99). Again, in a 1915 footnote to the "Three Essays" (1905b), he reflected that the presence of both parents played an important part in normal development and that "the absence of a strong father in childhood not infrequently favours the occurrence of inversion" (p. 146). Freud concluded that homosexual men show a lack of regard for the father or a fear of him. Their motivation in turning toward other men was in all likelihood a result of their need to diminish castration anxiety secondary to oedipal conflict. They sought reassurance by the presence of the penis in the sexual partner, avoided the mutilated female, and denied all rivalry with the father (Freud, 1920c).

In subsequent decades, numerous analysts, though corroborating Freud's impressions, increasingly noted the homosexual's inability to make an identification with the father. This inability was apparent not only in his lifelong poor relationship with the father, but also in his pervasive conscious and unconscious feelings of femininity or deficient sense of masculinity, or both, reported during psychoanalytic treatment. A fuller comprehension of the significance of many of these clinical observations was contingent on advances in our theoretical knowledge of psychic events that antedated the oedipal phase (Mahler and Furer, 1968; Abelin, 1971, 1973; Galenson, Vogel, Blau, and Roiphe, 1975; Mahler et al., 1975).

In this chapter I describe what is specifically *homosexogenic* in the families of male prehomosexual children as reconstructed from their analyses, and depict the resulting nuclear conflict of these patients. Though my intention is to focus on the impact of paternal forces on maturation, it is readily apparent that I must take into account the larger context in which they occur, especially the mother–child interaction [Socarides (1968b, 1978a); see chapter 3]; thus, frequent references to the interlocking effect of both maternal and paternal attitudes will be made.

It should be noted that I have found striking resemblances in the early family environment of *all* sexual deviants. The theme of excessive closeness, a lack of respect for the father, and his consequent hostility and/or abdication from the son runs like a fine thread through the histories of all children who later develop perversions.

Homosexogenic Families

My psychoanalytic studies reveal that each of the families of the male preoedipal homosexual patients I observed was markedly deficient in carrying out many of the functions necessary for the development of an integrated heterosexual child. Despite the varied environments of each family, specific distorting influences could be isolated, influences that led to emotional and cognitive difficulties characteristic of preoedipal homosexuality. I invariably found in my homosexual patients an interlocking family pathology dating back to the patient's early years of life, and affecting the child's separation–individuation process, profoundly interfering with his capacity to resolve his primary feminine identification, and producing severe ego deficiencies. The specific homosexogenic factors in the great majority of these families was the *dominant mother* in the area of child rearing and influence.

Indeed, the father's resignation of power, authority, and rightfully held influence may well be termed an *abdication.* Paternal abdication, when it occurred in the context of a psychologically crushing mother, had especially severe consequences, for it made the task of separation from the mother extremely difficult, and left the child structurally deficient and developmentally arrested.

Two specific consequences emerge from this family matrix:

1. The boundary between self and object, the self and mother, is blurred or incomplete, with a resultant persistence of primary feminine identification with her and a disturbance in gender-defined self identity.

2. This developmental deficiency produces an *object*

relations class of conflict (Dorpat, 1976), one in which the patient experiences anxiety and guilt associated with the failure of development in the phase of self–object differentiation. The nuclear conflict of preoedipal type I homosexuals consists of a desire for and dread of merging with the mother in order to reinstate the primitive mother–child unity, with its associated separation anxiety. In preoedipal type II homosexuals, the class of conflict is similar but with an earlier level of fixation: in the differentiating subphases of the separation–individuation process, with severe disturbances in self cohesion marked by fragmentation anxiety.

The father's libidinal and aggressive availability is a major requirement for the development of gender identity in his children, but for almost all prehomosexual children the father is unavailable as a love object for the child. Nor is he available to the mother as a source of emotional support. If physically present, he rarely limits or prohibits, but is often exquisitely passive (Panel, 1978).

Although most homosexual men portray their fathers as weak, passive, or unable to stand up against the mother, it should not be assumed that all abdicating fathers give the appearance of submission and defeat. Some adopt an affective stance of arrogance, hostility, and superiority, compensatory defensive reactions to what they consciously and/or unconsciously may perceive as the insurmountable challenge of fatherhood. As one patient noted, "My father never can say, 'I do not want this' against my mother's wishes. So he rationalizes not doing it, but I've seen through that. I'm angry at what he doesn't allow himself to be. He is weak in front of my mother. Weak means he's afraid of her. The facade he may present is that he is master of his house, but mother is the boss."

Some homosexuals complain that their fathers actively disliked or disapproved of them, resented them, or thought of them as "sissies." If the father attempted to introduce masculine activities into their lives, he did so in an abrasive manner, with little empathy and often with open derision. In order to avoid, lessen, or eliminate disagreements and confrontations often bordering on violence with their wives, many fathers willingly relinquished the entire supervision of their sons to the mother. In effect, the fathers sacrificed their sons in order to escape their wives.

In some instances, the elder of two male children raised in such an atmosphere does not become homosexual if during the middle to late preoedipal phase another male child is born. The control over the older child is then loosened, and his male identification with an inhibited but partially available father is reinforced, while the newborn becomes the recipient of the mother's endless domination and manipulation and ultimately becomes homosexual. In all homosexogenic family settings there appears to be a disturbed, unsatisfactory heterosexual relationship between the parents.

Many mothers of homosexuals suffer from a sense of low self-esteem and from castration anxiety and penis envy. These attitudes and fears profoundly influence their approach to their young male children. They may regard their sons' bodies as penis substitutes or symbols of their own masculinity, "attaching to [them] either positive or emotional valence" (Mahler, 1975a, p. 245). They commonly treat their sons' bodies as if they were part of themselves, or put obstacles in the way of the child's individuation and self-expression, especially during the quasi-negativistic phase beginning at the age of two years. Behaving contemptuously toward the phallic masculinity of their sons, they interfere with the formation of self identity as well as that of sexual identity by crippling phallic self-assertion and self-esteem. The abdicating fathers do not interfere with the crushing attitudes of these mothers.

Unless the father shows his readiness to be identified with, and the mother respects the father's masculinity and permits him to act as a role model, the little boy is unable to disidentify (Greenson, 1968) with the mother and establish an identification with the father. This shift requires the mutual cooperation of mother, father, and child; and, in Abelin's words (1971), may well be "impossible for either [the mother or child] to master without their having the father to turn to" (p. 248). These findings confirm Greenacre's earlier (1960) impression that the life history of perverse patients is one in which the father has indeed suffered a severe and chronic, often unremitting devaluation by the mother, especially during the earliest years of the child's life.

In the rapprochement subphase of separation–individuation, the child uses the mother to fulfill regressive fantasies, but she simultaneously arouses intense feelings of resentment and frustration. In contrast, the father, although taken for granted, may represent "a stable island of external reality, carrying over his role from the lost practicing subphase" (Abelin, 1971, p. 243). This is because there is less discrepancy between the child's image of the father and the real father at this age. During this period, toddlers, when they are disappointed by their mothers, begin to evoke their fathers in their play through drawings, calling them on the telephone, playing games with them, and other methods of spontaneous father play.

Such play is almost completely lacking in the histories of prehomosexual boys, as reconstructed during their adult psychoanalyses or elicited from histories obtained from their families. Furthermore, it is strikingly apparent that prehomosexual children have great difficulty in attaching themselves to "father substitutes," as compared with normal children, who easily substitute older brothers, grandfathers, and older males for the father.

Dramatic reenactments of rapprochement crises secondary to attempts at intrapsychic separation from the mother are a frequent occurrence during psychoanalytic treatment of homosexual men (see chapter 10). The patients feel threatened as they regress, with maternal reengulfment. Regressive experiences of this type are also a reflection of the father's earlier failure to function as one of a wide range of nonmaternal objects helping the child to establish and hold onto reality. They are ameliorated and ultimately mastered through the new object relationship created in the transference with the analyst–father. For it is the father's love that helps diminish the child's fear of loss of the mother's love and the loss of the object, a fear that can become so intense that the child's developmental spurt is completely blocked or frustrated and his reality functioning disturbed. If the child does not have the father to turn to, he experiences a severe deflation of his developing sense of self-esteem, caused by overwhelming feelings of weakness and the painful realization of his own helplessness. A self that has been rendered helpless and fragile by such developmental interferences is likely to develop extreme narcissistic vulnerability. A spurious sense of self cohesion and self-esteem is then maintained by the construction of a pathological grandiose self (Kohut, 1971). Narcissistic personality disorders are commonly found in association with preoedipal homosexuality.

To recapitulate what has been stated in chapter 3, a normal boy must find his own identity as a prerequisite to the onset of both true object relations and partial identifications with his parents. To the male homosexual, the mother has, in infancy, been on the one hand dangerous and frightening, forcing separation and threatening the infant with loss of love; on the other hand, the mother's conscious and unconscious tendencies are felt as working against separation. Anxiety and frustration press for withdrawal of libido from the mother and increased aggression. The resulting introjected "bad" mother image leads to a split in the ego in order to maintain the image of the "good" mother. In his narcissistic object choice, the homosexual not only loves his partner as he himself wishes to be loved by the mother, but also reacts to him with the sadistic aggression he once experienced toward the hostile mother for forcing separation, and often forces separation from his many "lovers."

The unconscious hostility reinforces denial of any of the mother's loving and giving aspects. The homosexual seeks to rediscover in his object choice—in the most distorted ways—his narcissistic relationship with the different images of the mother (and later of the father) as they were first experienced.

Homosexuality can be seen, therefore, as an attempt to separate from the mother by running away from all women. The homosexual is trying to undo whatever separation he has achieved and remain close to his mother in a substitutive way by utilizing the male. Of central significance is that the male sexual partner represents the father, to whom the son is looking for salvation from engulfment. He is seeking a reduplication of himself as an object through the sexual partner.

Case Material

Clinical Study 1

Roger, a twenty-five-year-old preoedipal type II homosexual,[1] described the severe devaluation of his father by his mother, the father's ultimate abandonment of him, and its consequences. He was an only child, conceived during the father's military leave during World War II. Because the father was in combat overseas, Roger did not see him during the first year of his life. During that time he lived with his mother, who was intermittently employed in an administrative capacity in an industrial plant. When his father returned, there were frequent arguments leading to severe violence between his parents. His most significant memory was of witnessing, at age four or five, a physical fight between his parents. By this time his father, after many arguments with his wife, no longer lived with them and on this occasion was visiting them.

After this incident, the parents eventually divorced, and the patient saw his father again on only two occasions. The first was at the age of eight, when he and his mother accidentally encountered his father on the street: "Mother abruptly turned me around and we ran for the subway." At the age of eleven:

> Father called her and told her he wanted to see me, and then she tells me, of course, he never really wanted to see me. She always tells me that, that he never cared for me. That my father was an alcoholic, a sick man ... I feel so sorry for him. She said that she married him only out of sympathy. He said that he really wanted to see me, and she said she just wanted to protect me and that he was a bad influence; he was a drunkard, and so she got rid of him.

---

[1] Roger's symptomatology was complicated by a severe degree of narcissism in which his object relations were from pathological grandiose self to self. His level of fixation was at practicing and differentiating subphases. He suffered regressive episodes and experienced severe body–ego disturbances and pathological perceptions; for example, being inside the mother's womb.

Roger yearned and wept for his absent father. One of his earliest dreams or memories, he could not tell which, was of being with his father in the bathroom. The father was urinating and the boy was looking at his father's penis. The father had a pleasant smile on his face. This represented the boy's desire to be loved by the father, and to be endowed with masculinity through identification with the father and his penis, which he accomplished later in the homosexual act. During analysis, Roger became aware that he was angry with the father and that in his homosexual relations was trying to find and love him. His homosexual partner represented a fusion of maternal and paternal images. In sucking a man's penis (father's penis), he was not only possessing the good and giving maternal breast through substitution, but also relieving aggression by seizing the penis and becoming whole again through identification with a male partner.

Roger was unable to give up the security of closeness and identification with the mother because of the absence of an accessible father. The father failed to offer a motive for identification, namely, pleasure and joy in masculinity, resoluteness, and commitment to the welfare of his son. Strikingly absent was the most profound motive for the child to identify with the father: the love and respect the mother shows for him (A. Freud, 1965).

Clinical Study 2

Throughout childhood, Paul (preoedipal type I homosexual)[2] was dominated by a mother who was in complete charge of the family and responsible for all decisions. Her husband was passive and yielding, obviously afraid of his moody, irascible, and uncontrollable wife. The mother dominated the social and academic life of the patient and his brother, but concentrated mainly on Paul, the slightly younger of the two by two-and-a-half years. Until his entrance into analy-

---

[2]This patient's case history and the course of his successful psychoanalysis is reported in Socarides (1978a).

sis, every decision had first to be discussed with his mother and approved by her; no secrets were allowed.

Paul's childhood was marked by endless parental bickering, violent arguments, and, during his early years, physical assault. On at least two occasions the mother provoked her husband into a physical attack with a kitchen knife. She also threatened the patient with abandonment and divorcing his father if he did not comply with all of her requirements and desires. Paul could not handle his mother's aggression and soon began to identify with her, taunting his father at times, making fun of him, and siding with his mother on nearly all occasions. Paul learned that silence was his best recourse in protecting himself from his mother's vicious outbursts.

His mother constantly stimulated his aggression in early and late childhood by teasing, ridiculing, slapping, and clawing him. Whenever he tried to defend himself, she beat him to the ground, sitting or lying on top of him, scratching his arms and face, and hitting him in the stomach. Fighting back in self-defense only produced more physical damage.

He had difficulty eating during infancy and recalled that at three and four years of age he was often force-fed when he did not "clean up" his plate. On two or three occasions he vomited his food and was forced to "eat the vomit." Subsequently he vomited often on becoming even slightly upset.

Until he was sixteen years old, Paul's mother often slept in the same bed with him. He would fold his arms around her from the back and feel as if he were merging with her and her body's warmth. She frequently disrobed in front of him; at other times, half-dressed, she would walk around with her breasts exposed; in his late childhood and early adolescence, she constantly asked his opinion of the shape and size of her breasts and of her general physical attractiveness. She occasionally made fun of his penis, stating that he would never be able to function as a man with a woman in his later years. She criticized all his friends, especially girls, in an attempt to isolate him.

During Paul's adolescence, his mother constantly jeered at him for failing to match his brother academically. The brother successfully eluded the mother by staying in his room. The father sided with Paul's brother, and they both teased Paul for his attachment to the mother. Paul's brother and father spent a good deal of time together, often playing ball and attending athletic events. (The brother married in his early twenties, moved with his wife to a different city, and showed no signs of homosexuality.)

Paul achieved success in graduate school. He was somewhat feared by his colleagues for his angry, aggressive verbal attacks on those he felt were inferior to him or who tried in any way to take advantage of him. He took great delight in verbal onslaughts similar to his mother's and in revealing to people in authority their "falseness and weakness." His pleasure in this was a result of his identification with the aggressor (his mother) as well as his wish to heap abuse on his father for the latter's weakness and his failure to protect him as a child.

Paul entered psychoanalytic treatment at the age of twenty-seven to seek relief from the futility he felt was ahead of him were his homosexuality to continue. He complained that such a course did not lead anywhere and that his only friends were homosexuals. He was extremely unhappy and suffered intensely from his inability to desist from his homosexual practices. In a somewhat defiant way, he announced to his parents, shortly before entering treatment, that he was a homosexual, and requested their help. His father was alarmed, saying that he could not understand how his son could "live in a sewer." The mother apparently accepted his pronouncements, but felt that his homosexuality was "only a passing stage" and that he did not need treatment.

Paul was unable to disidentify from his mother during the preoedipal and oedipal years because he did not have a father to "go to." This produced both severe difficulties in separation and an excess of aggression. The father was unable to serve as a buffer against the mother's aggression toward the child and the child's aggression toward her. Paul dealt with this aggression by libidinization via the homosexual object, which represented both the maternal penis and the paternal body. By running to men and escaping the all-powerful mother, he sought refuge and salvation.

As Paul was helped to face the mother's ruthless, irresponsible, negative, and destructive behavior, he was able to

lift himself out of his unconscious masochistic sexual submission to her. Feeling threatened by his mother, he felt
threatened by all women. As a result of his treatment, he
gradually developed affectionate feelings for women.

During the course of treatment, Paul's father told him
that when Paul was two years old the father thought of
divorcing the mother, but didn't because of "us children. . . .
The fact that he could think of leaving us makes me feel
lonely now." Loneliness frequently led to massive anxiety,
which was then neutralized through libidinization in the
homosexual act.

Paul continued to relive occasions in his past when his
father "sided" with the mother. This represented a complete
capitulation to the hateful, destructive mother in order to
"save himself. . . . My father tells me that I should be a 'good
son to her.' He wants me to go all out and give myself to my
mother in order to protect *him*. Recently he took away from
me the promise that he was going to give me money for the
treatment." It was his belief that his mother was the only
potent force in his life and his father an essential incompetent. "In my homosexuality I think I'm giving in to her. I do
not take another woman, I take a man. . . . I remember how
she used to treat me, but it seems at least she loved me." His
despair at feeling unloved by his father, previously unconscious, was extreme.

As the analysis progressed, Paul felt increasingly liberated from both his destructive aggression toward his father
and his hatred of his mother.

> It's not a nice feeling to hate someone, but what was there is
> still there. She was a very sick woman and she still is, and this
> is what she did to me. I called my father after I felt these things
> last night, and I told him I was all right.

> When I spoke to him, however, he still seemed frightened. He
> suggested that I not come home as often as I did in the past
> because it upset my mother!

The full range of Paul's destructive aggression and murderous feelings toward men made their appearance in the
middle phases of the analysis. "I often have fantasies about

hitting a man, hurting him. I thought about the guy that I had sex with the other night, screwing him in his office, and sometimes it even changes from sex to pure aggression, just like jabbing him. And after I talk of these feelings I feel somewhat kindlier toward men."

His aggression toward men served multiple functions: it protected the breast of the mother by displacing aggression onto a substitute, the male with a penis; it punished the father for denying him his masculinity, for failing to protect him against the crushing mother; at the same time, having intercourse with men forced love and affection from father substitutes. His homosexual activities constituted a severe sadistic assault on men (his father) and were highly overdetermined. Anxiety, which always preceded homosexual arousal, was libidinized and neutralized through homosexual activities. Desire for homosexual relations occurred whenever he felt frustrated by life's disappointments and fearful of abandonment by his mother. The act quieted fears of loss of the mother and gratified sexual wishes toward both parents. He felt assured of their love in a substitutive way and warded off fears of castration by acquiring a potent and strong penis from the male partner.

Paul felt that his father threatened him with his mother in order to "get off the hook himself." For this reason he harbored profound feelings of bitterness and hatred toward his father. Protected by the confidence and trust in the analyst, he mustered enough strength through identification to consummate his first heterosexual experience, which he perceived as a triumph. He realized in therapy that his mother's dismissal of his homosexuality when she was first told about it was tantamount to sanctioning it. If he were interested only in men, he would never leave her for another woman.

In the ensuing months, Paul began to enjoy heterosexual relations more fully. He reported that the "bond between my mother and myself, that crappy bond was being broken. But it's like losing something when I tell you about my interest in women and when I begin to think of having sexual intercourse."

In the later phases of the analysis, Paul recalled a crucial memory, deeply repressed, of the beginnings of conscious

homosexual desire. The incident occurred at the age of seven
or eight years: "The children used to take a nap in the after-
noon in an afterschool group where *Mother left me,* and there
was something about a bigger boy. I wished to have him as a
substitute for my father and for a friend, and he would do
something in bed with me. The other boy was twelve years
old and he lay on top of me and I liked that. Before that I was
a sexless kind of kid" (emphasis added). This constituted an
organizing experience for the later development of homosexuality.

Paul could gradually remember that in the earliest years
of his life "my father loved me a lot and he loved me most,
and that's why my mother took it out on him." This reap-
praisal of the father–son relationship, his recognition that
his father had attempted, even if only for a short while, to
fight the mother's undue attention and domination, provided considerable relief from his hostile feelings toward his
father and led to a gradual turning toward the father once
again. He realized that his father did love him during an
early period of his life, that his father was not completely
helpless and weak, but eventually had to "sell out" to the
overwhelming, hateful mother. Yielding to the mother became a means of survival for both father and son.

Of crucial significance was Paul's identification with the
aggression of the mother. This further acted to isolate him
from his father:

> I began to make my father feel like a shit. He was a skunk and a
> shit, and I would hurt him and embarrass him and it would give
> me satisfaction and my mother satisfaction, too. If I couldn't
> fight with my mother, it seemed to me I could join with her. I
> would fight and hurt my father, and this would please her. I feel
> terrible and ashamed when I realize what I did.

Paul realized that sex with men arose from aggression,
whereas with women aggression did not create desire. He
began to comprehend that sexual intercourse with men was
really a repetition of the incident in childhood that he turned
into a childhood fantasy. It was not the erotic experience per
se that he sought in his homosexuality, but its reassuring
and reaffirming function. He recalled that, harassed, threat-

ened, and subdued by his mother and unprotected by his father, he would lie on his bed face down, violently move his body, and say, "Fuck you, father." He added:

> I had similar things happen to me with my mother, and when I was younger and angry with her I'd lie on the bed face down, and I'd get a genital feeling and I'd have to say, "Fuck you, too, shit-ass mother." These angry feelings always translated into sex, and finally I'd masturbate and take up some of the hate and then I could relax [erotization of aggression].

The substitution of men for the mother produced a quieting of hatred and was an essential factor in helping him retain his mental equilibrium.

A major insight was achieved in his discovery that, when angry with his mother, he developed homosexual desire:

> It is obvious that I do not have a father to stand between me and my mother, and the only way I can get one is through homosexuality, and the only way I can enjoy her is through homosexuality. The homosexuality has to do with my need for my father: wanting my father and hating my father and wanting my mother and hating my mother.

He noted that "the worst thing my mother could say to me and the worst things she could do which made me homosexual is when she told me, 'You're just like your father.' She would tear him down and then by saying this with a terrible smile on her face she makes me feel just awful." The homosexual act helped to restore Paul's self-esteem, but it only functioned as a temporary alleviating measure. Long-repressed incestuous desires of the oedipal period and feelings of destructive aggression toward the mother began to emerge into consciousness and to be assimilated:

> I know I wanted to have sexual intercourse with her for years. It brings tears to my eyes when I say this and I'm crying now. I'm loving her all over but I wish my mother had my father and my father her, and I could just let it go at that, the two of them.... I didn't feel I did anything wrong as a child, but I see now that in loving her I'm killing her and destroying her. The killing of her and below that is the intercourse with her. But I feel there is a

good reason to kill her, that is, to kill our relationship, to get her out of my life, and let my father have her. There is an expression, "Go in health and peace." If it could happen that way, my mother could have my father and my father her.

While many of the aspects of Paul's problems described here appear to represent an oedipal conflict, the conflict was superimposed on a more basic preoedipal fixation to the rapprochement phase. The nuclear fears were dependent on this phase-specific fixation and involved wishes to merge with the mother and fears of ego-dissolution if such merger were to take place. His object relations were from object to self; his partner represented the self.

In the later phases of the analysis, Paul began to perceive his father's good qualities, to enjoy them, and to love him.

I guess I really put him down in a way, as I don't think I could get anything from him, any support from him against my mother. I really didn't think he had a lot to offer in certain respects, but my mother put these ideas in my head, that he was weak. She can no longer do this, but she doesn't stop trying.... If I had to choose now between parents, who would be alive— and this may sound cruel—I'd rather it would be my father than the other way around because he really knew how to enjoy a lot of things. She knocked a lot out of him. For example, he loved music and art, loved going to the park and watching people play ball. She didn't like any of these things and always criticized him and said he only took me to free things, making him a cheapskate. In actuality, he tried to get for me those things he could offer. He tried to get me to enjoy them, even if he could not afford to take me to "paying things." He took me to concerts that didn't cost money, and museums.

In a follow-up interview years after the end of his psychoanalytic treatment, Paul attributed much of the success of his treatment, the removal of his homosexuality, his ability to enjoy heterosexual relations and love a woman, to the fact that he "reacted very strongly" to the analyst. He had to trust somebody and the analyst was the only person he could trust. He also felt a sense of accomplishment throughout the treatment, just being able to stop and think about himself in a more realistic way. He was profoundly affected by the tremendous encouragement he received from the analyst [father]. Throughout the treatment, except for short periods, Paul was confident that the analyst was on his side completely, "that no matter what happened, he was always there." In effect, a new object relationship had been achieved.

Summary

I have described one factor in the complex and multifactorial genesis of adult male homosexuality: the father's unwillingness or inability to function appropriately during crucial phases of his son's early development. The preoedipal homosexual has failed to achieve separation from his mother. He has been unable to disidentify from the mother and identify with the father. Although the mother plays a crucial part in the separation–individuation process, the father's role is also decisive.

Chapter 12
FETISHISM:
THE CASE OF CALVIN

Introduction

The fetishist is obliged to use a nonsexual object in preparation for or during the sexual act in order to obtain sexual
gratification. This process of libidinization is often directed
toward *parts of the body*, either of the subject or object,
which are threatened in an unconscious fantasy system; for
example, in the typical foot fetish. In others, further displacement introduces the additional element of defense in
disguise; for example, the clothes fetish. In others again, it is
the *mode of gratification*, rather than the objects endangered in the fantasy, that is libidinized (e.g., the inhalation
of the odor of feces or tobacco). The method of sexual release
may be either masturbation or some form of sexual intercourse.

Foot, shoe, and underwear fetishism are quite common as
objects used by fetishists while hair and fur are rather less
frequent. Rubber, leather goods, and articles with lacings or
ties, ropes or thorns, and shiny or odorous objects are also
used as fetishes. Very often the objects are closely related to
the skin, particularly to the odoriferous skin. There are probably many cases of minor fetishism which may involve
simply the fetish ritual. For example, the observation of the
female in a particular state of dress or undress, for example,
in high heels alone, preliminary to intercourse, but a neces-

sary precondition for arousal, usually escapes notice as a fetishistic perversion. Often, along with competent homosexual and heterosexual performance, fetishistic support may be necessary in the act itself. Fetishism in the female is rare. Women can also conceal a lack of orgastic response and thus avoid narcissistic injury. It may appear in women who have extremely strong masculine strivings and a strongly developed fantasy of possessing a penis.[1] However, forms of fetishism not obviously associated with genital functioning, for example, kleptomanias, rituals preparing for masturbation or intercourse, the use of lucky charms, and so on, infrequently serve a fetishistic function in females (Greenacre, 1953).

Rarely has the overt fetishistic act been traced back to the fourth or fifth year; it usually is described as appearing in late adolescence, occasionally in puberty. It is nearly always associated with other perversions, such as voyeurism, sadistic practices, homosexuality, and especially transvestism.

The fetish must be capable of symbolizing both the penis and the lack of a penis. Although it may have the quality of immateriality, this furnishes a kind of material incorporation through being breathed in without loss (Greenacre, 1953), for example, without diminution of its size or alteration of its shape. It must also be capable of remaining intact outside the body so it may at the same time be visually introjected and stabilize the sense of one's own body. The fetish must be *durable* in order to diminish the fear of annihilation impulses; *inanimate*, in order to be nonretaliative; *immobile*, to help counteract the anxiety of the sensations of changing size and shape of the penis and body. The fetish may have a double role: it may represent simultaneously the danger and protection against it. Intensely strong castration fears in the phallic period and more primitive body-disintegration anxieties are reactivated when the fetishist attempts intercourse, sees the penislessness of his partner, or feels or sees the disappearance of his own phallus into the vagina.

Although preoedipal factors such as oral and anal sadism

---

[1]Zavitzianos (1982) provides a convincing illustration for the existence of fetishism in women. "For women, the fetish represents the *paternal* phallus" (p. 424).

have been implicated in the genesis of fetishism, conclusive and detailed studies demonstrating the mutual relationship between oedipal and preoedipal conflicts have not been made with the exception of van der Leeuw's work (1958) and the present contribution. In 1960, in an earlier version of this material, I described the evolution of the fetish from its preoedipal precursor stages (Socarides, 1960).

Van der Leeuw (1958) demonstrated that the origin of a fetishistic *fantasy* was the conflict aroused by the wish for a child. Other theories have been proposed. Bak (1953), for example, considered the persistence of primary identification with the mother a crucial factor in fetishism. Greenacre (1953, 1955) was of the opinion that fetishism results from a disturbance in the development of the body–ego, with a consequent fear of disintegration of the body image; in many fetishists the need for primary identification was prolonged, a fact which indicated disturbances in preoedipal development. In the patient to be described, the disturbance in body–ego, the wish for a child and primary identification, together with body-disintegration anxiety were present and intimately related to each other. Through an identification with the mother who underwent Caesarian sections, the patient feared for his own bodily integrity.

Lampl-de Groot (1946), Jacobson (1950), and van der Leeuw (1958) have shown that the "specific experience in the pregenital or preoedipal phase is the realization that no real child can be made and that this fact must be accepted—a circumstance giving rise to rage, jealousy and helplessness" (van der Leeuw, p. 371). Kestenberg (1956a), from direct observational studies of the development of maternal feelings in both sexes during the preoedipal phase, concluded that the wish for a child is older than the wish for the penis, and the normal development in the male requires that he relinquish the wish of giving birth to a child. Kris (1939) and Jacobson, above, have demonstrated a connection between the wish for a child in this period and later creativity (or its inhibition).

Theoretical Considerations

Certain theoretical constructions must be set forth in order to further clarify the clinical material that is to follow. Following the birth of the child the biological oneness with the mother is replaced by a primitive identification with her; this may be manifested by copying her. "The mother is, however, not only active, but also almighty; she can do everything and possess every valuable attribute. In this phase the wish for a child already exists" (van der Leeuw, 1958, p. 334). Preoedipal fantasies serve as defenses against the emergence of oedipal material and vice versa. Hoffer (1954) has described such phenomena under the heading of defense organization. Castration anxiety, the direct result of the oedipal conflict, may be utilized also as a defense against anxieties of the preoedipal phase. Likewise, preoedipal drives have a defensive importance in warding off oedipal wishes and fears. There is always an interplay between the two. This is evident in the case material to be presented. For example, an individual with severe castration anxiety may regress to anal or oral stages—to a point previously determined by a fixation. In my patient, this fixation was in the preoedipal phase, in which the wish to become pregnant and bear a child like the mother was very strong. How to attain gratification of this wish was of paramount importance. The impossible was symbolically accomplished by means of the fetishistic perversion (a boxer-shorts fetish). It was also achieved through creative work begun in childhood (the making of puppets, writing skits, drawing, and later on through competent artistic productions). Thus, the normal channel for sublimation of the feminine wishes for a pregnancy helped to alleviate this conflict. The conflict between wish and the impossibility of its gratification was manifest in the anal or oral sphere, or in the fecal apparatus (defecation was equated with delivery). There appeared to be nothing genital in this wish for a child. By being like mother in every way, separateness and separation were undone. When the patient felt helpless in this respect he became violently angry at his mother.

The boy in this instance does not change either his love object or his sexual (genital) organ in the transition from preoedipal to oedipal phase. However, he must change his *attitude* toward it (her). He must proceed from the security of identification and oneness with the mother to active, competent separateness and male (phallic) striving. If this task proves too difficult, pathological defenses, especially an increased maintenance of the primary identification and archaic aggressiveness may result. These developments are of the greatest importance for the solution of conflicts appearing in the oedipal phase and in later life. In the oedipal phase, under the pressure of the castration fear, an additional type of identification with the mother in the form of *passive* feminine wishes for the father is likely to take place. However, beneath this feminine position in relation to the father lies the *original passive relation with the mother* (i.e., *an active feminine, preoedipal identification*). The latter in turn may express itself in very *primitive perverse fantasies*: the wish for female genitalia, the wish for a child.

It is obvious that the boy may wish to bear a child in either the negative oedipal phase or in the preoedipal phase. In the former, the wish connotes a passive, feminine object relationship toward the father; in the latter, it is experienced as an active achievement, bringing deep satisfaction and demonstrating that one is like mother and as powerful as she is. This became evident in the dream material to be cited. Dream 5 (see p. 307) is especially illustrative of this. During the emergence of preoedipal material the general behavior of patients, such as the one I shall describe, becomes more childish, and remembering is often replaced by acting out. Also, the father plays little if any part in that particular part of the analysis. Preoedipal material is often linked with particular traits, characteristic of object relations of that phase of development.

Aside from Greenacre's theoretical studies, van der Leeuw's case studies proved most helpful in the understanding of my patient's fetishistic perversion. Though his patients had experienced strong castration fear, van der Leeuw was ultimately more impressed by the intensity of their need to identify themselves with the woman. This identification seemed to represent "another form of identification" stemming from the preoedipal phase, namely, an identification with the almighty preoedipal mother. The reaction against the castration anxiety that drove van der Leeuw's patients into the negative oedipal phase revived the conflicts of the preoedipal phase, in his opinion. In my patient, feelings of helplessness, fear, and aggressive impulses had their origin in the revived preoedipal disturbance caused by the inability to give birth to a child. When faced with this conflict, my patient used the fetish or intense masochistic fantasies bordering on paranoia as part defense and part disguised gratification. The masochistic attitude was preferred to the injury caused by experiencing helplessness, depressive affect, and aggression. This was supplemented by an increase in his clinging to his primary active identification with the mother. The fetishistic perversion was a partial solution of his wish to bear a child, in that it alleviated anxiety, aggression, and guilt. The other part of the solution lay in the fact that he became a highly creative individual who was only rarely inhibited in his work.

The production of the underwear fetish is a remarkable testament to the activities of the cerebral cortex of man which is capable of profound symbolizations helping quell deep anxieties which threaten him. For example, the fetish (underwear/boxer-shorts fetish) had many functions:

1. It protected his entire body against change, delivering him from bodily disintegration anxiety.
2. It afforded him orgastic release.
3. It was a symbolic solution for his wish to have a child.
4. It assured him in his belief in the phallic mother.
5. It defended him against homosexual desires.
6. It warded off the activation of more primitive bodily destruction fears intimately connected with separation anxieties and his wish to have a child.
7. Clothing was a displacement from his own body; so that the clothing could be ripped rather than his own body or that of his mother.
8. The fetish represented not only the imagined penis of the mother but also the breasts, the swollen pregnant abdomen, and other parts of her body from which he did not wish to be separated.
9. In the case of the fetish, he recaptured the early object

relationship with his loved mother—the sameness and primary identification with her.

10. It helped terminate the savagery of fantasied attacks against the maternal body and breast, bringing sexual arousal and orgasm.

11. The fetish was a "stand-in" for the mother. When he felt he was losing contact with his mother he would become very unhappy and experience a sense of *loss of self*. The primary feminine identification with the mother and the excessive splitting off of parts of himself and their lack of formation into a cohesive self, and the anxiety attendant to this state of identity diffusion and threat of self disintegration was alleviated by the invocation of the fetish.

12. Since the fetish covered the penis, it became clear that the sight of the penis reminded him of impending mutilation. The fetish's durability symbolically protected him against the hostile impulses toward changes in form and shape of the female body.

13. It both gratified and protected him from his own wish to have a baby.

14. The fetish as revealed in the dreams showed a strong defensive function. It provided restitution for the desired destruction of the mother's body and helped continue the union with her in order to prevent the loss of her love.

Although my patient showed disturbances in self cohesion, his ego-developmental arrest was not characterized by a severe disruption in the gradual emergence of the autonomous self, or a consequent severe impairment in self-object differentiation. His fixation was in the rapproachement phase. The deficiencies in the self representation were not so severe that he developed a pathological grandiose self. Furthermore, internal conflict was present in comparison to those instances of fetishism in which there is such insufficient structuralization of the psychic apparatus that defenses are all in a primitive stage of development with splitting predominating over repression. Therefore, he may be classified as a preoedipal type I fetishist.

In the clinical material which follows, my aim is to show the contribution of the preoedipal phase conflicts to the development of this particular fetishistic perversion. In 1931 Freud, in his paper on "Female Sexuality," clearly foresaw the difficulties and controversies inherent in the study of clinical phenomena based on unresolved conflicts of the period of life which antedates the oedipal phase.

> Our insight into this early, pre-Oedipus phase . . . comes to us as a surprise, comparable in another field with the effect of the discovery of the Minoan–Mycenaean civilization behind that of Greece. Everything connected with this first mother-attachment has in analysis seemed to me so elusive, lost in a past so dim and shadowy, so hard to resuscitate, that it seemed as if it had undergone some specially inexorable repression [pp. 253–254].

Difficulties notwithstanding, Freud proceeded to evolve a remarkably accurate and verifiable theoretical structure of psychic events and behavior during that period for the female, touching only briefly on events occurring in the male. Subsequently, other observers have added materially to our knowledge of that period. Major contributions have been made by Brunswick (1928, 1929, 1940), Lampl-de Groot (1946), Jacobson (1950), Kestenberg (1956a), and van der Leeuw (1958). Brunswick's (1928) study of these phenomena appeared three years before Freud's. He referred to her 1929 paper, "The Analysis of a Case of Paranoia," wherein delusional jealousy in a female was traced to her preoedipal attachment to her sister.

This chapter presents clinical evidence from the psychoanalysis of a male underwear fetishist which supports the thesis that this form of fetishism may be linked with a nuclear conflict occurring in the preoedipal phase: the unresolved wish in the male to have a child. The authors mentioned above have shown that this particular childhood conflict may antedate the oedipal one. Childbearing is conceived as an achievement in power and competition with the mother, and represents being active like her. One of the most important tasks of the preoedipal phase in the male is to resolve this wish without a consequent disturbance in ego development. The wish and consequent fear of pregnancy in my patient (1) bore a direct relationship to the development of his fetishistic perversion; (2) led to a persistence of his identification with the preoedipal mother; and (3) through sublimation, was in part responsible for his creative activity from an early age. While the fetish served as a defense against his body-disintegration anxieties, it was also a solution for his wish to have a child. It is my belief that fetishism at its inception has no etiological connection with phallic or genital sexuality.

In tracing this patient's fetishistic perversion to its preoedipal roots, I show that the transition from his primary anxieties to a wish for a covering to protect the entire body against change arises from the wish for and dread of pregnancy, and thence leads to the development of a full-blown underwear fetish with its associated orgastic value.

Little attention will be given to the effects of castration fear and oedipal conflict, which have been comprehensively explored by Freud and others. Throughout this case study it will be observed that both oedipal and preoedipal conflicts coexist, and are in continual interplay with each other. The danger of castration was an accretion to the primary nuclear conflict, that of the preoedipal period, and the fetish constituted only a secondary line of defense against fears of genital mutilation.

Clinical Study

Developmental History

Calvin was an artistic, intelligent man in his late twenties. His mild, gentle manner and well-modulated speech gave way on many occasions to severe hostility and violent outbursts of speech, punctuated by attacks of stammering. As far back as he could remember, he had suffered from intense fears of separation from his mother, clinging to her and intensely resenting anyone who attracted her interest. His relatives often recounted that from his earliest infancy he hated anyone who took his mother away from him. During the second and third year of life he had severe temper tantrums, in which he would strike his mother. The latter, a successful architect, was often absent from the home for weeks at a time because of her work. On these occasions he was cared for by his grandmother, whom he disliked and resented. His father, a successful business executive, was cold and aloof from the child and usually saw him only for an hour during breakfast. For long periods in the analysis the patient referred to his father very rarely, and these references occurred only in responses to interpretations in which the analyst had introduced the father. The patient felt he really knew hardly anything about his father, nor was he ever particularly interested in him. All his thoughts and feelings were "tied up" with mother. From one-and-a-half to four years of age he would sing himself to sleep while rocking his head.[2] When forced to cease this activity, he fell prey to severe insomnia and multiple fears, especially of animals and of the dark. From his earliest infancy he treasured a teddy bear, screamed when it was absent from his side, and could not fall asleep without it (the transitional object). This attachment was unusually prolonged, lasting to his eighth year. [Dickes has carefully explored the significance of inanimate objects as precursors to fetishes (1963, 1978).] When the teddy bear was put into a traveling bag he became very anxious (age eight) because he thought it would be unable to breathe. He was intensely jealous of his sister and hostile toward her. She was three-and-a-half years younger. He had watched his mother's enlarging abdomen with fascinated interest, and during the analysis recaptured the closeness and warmth he had felt (going back to the age of two-and-a-half) when he would sit on his mother's lap and cling to her. When she put him down he nearly always experienced a feeling of depression and sadness. At three, he was told that at his birth his head had been too large and a Caesarean section had to be performed. One of his earliest memories was "a repeated image of somebody taking a knife and cutting mother open" (around the age of three to three-and-a-

---

[2]Mittelmann (1955) has shown that there may exist a close relationship between early motility disturbances and the later development of fetishism. Just as "rhythmic autoerotic activities may represent a self-centered, restitutive, consoling withdrawal from the frustration of the environment—an aspect which is common in fetishism," the use of the transitional object and later fetishism are ways to work off "complex reactions to disappointment" (p. 260).

half). From four to seven he would want to hear repeatedly and listen with rapt attention to stories of destruction by fire, houses being bombed, earthquakes splitting the land open with people being swallowed up, buildings collapsing, and so on. For hours he would draw such scenes before and after destruction (the symbolism in these drawings, which he had preserved was striking and obvious: e.g., the breast, vaginal opening, etc.). The *change* in the scene was the most important factor in his pleasurable excitement and fear. At five, his mother showed her curious and questioning son the Caesarean scar resulting from his birth. The intimacy involved in the telling and retelling of these experiences despite their fearfulness may well have constituted an organizing experience for the little boy, strengthening his tie to the mother, undoing threatened object loss, and enhancing object relatedness.

Throughout the oedipal period and into latency, puberty, and early adolescence he felt "apart and different" from his father. From this self-imposed isolation, however, he would emerge to pique him by minor infractions of discipline, and then skillfully withdraw to his books, hobbies, and mother. He secretly wished that his father would lose control of himself, "that he'd strike me, punch me, or hurt me just a little, then come to his senses, love me, be nice and tender to me, and ask me to forgive him." (This wish clearly reveals the masochistic feminine identification.) In early adolescence he avoided his father because of a growing sense of effeminacy, for which he feared disapproval. At six, he had often spied on his father while the latter was removing his trousers, but the patient felt that he had "not been interested" in seeing his father's penis, only the act of removing the trousers. It became clear that until the age of fifteen, he believed that the female gave birth to babies through the abdomen.

In summary, certain events contributed to producing a deficient body image: the sight of the pregnant mother's body while she was taking showers and the freedom with which she displayed her body to him throughout his infancy and early childhood; her vivid accounts of the Caesarean operation, the demonstration of scars on her body, and thus an early introduction to the knowledge of nonvaginal child-birth; the facts that he was told (at age five) that she had nearly died at his birth, and (at age seven) that she had delivered a dead child three years before he was born. After this last revelation he developed the obsessive thought (which lasted for approximately two years): "If father sticks his penis into mother, dead babies come out somehow." He represented his anxiety over such penetration by the father in numerous drawings during this period. They portrayed penetration by the paternal phallus, threatening to destroy the mother by impregnation.

Throughout the incidents described above, the patient clearly continued in the state of primary identification. The similarities between mother and son were striking to all her friends and were often mentioned by relatives. He moved his hands and body in the same manner, spoke with the same intonation, and always wanted to be close to her. He showed little interest in anyone else, including his sister and father, except for peeping into his father's room.

When he was seven his mother, carrying on the "education" of her son, which meant that all events and phenomena should be explained to him in detail, abetted, to be sure, by his now all-consuming interest and curiosity, described a circumcision which had "caused" the death of a boy in the neighborhood. This made him continually anxious for several months. Between six and eight the patient experienced a recurrent dream in which something was "around me, covering me up." Since the age of four he had insisted that his mother bind him in this way at least up to the waist before going to sleep. This binding of his body, and its later expression in a recurrent dream, was a precursor to the male underwear fetish which appeared later in life with its orgastic potential. "I would imagine what death was like, lying reposed in one spot perpetually, like in a coffin, covered, in a deadline state where I could not communicate with anyone, where I could not function, but I could still go on and on and never stop." Since childhood he had longed for a "surrounding material" to bind him, cover him, and protect him when he went to sleep. It provided the assurance that he would stay unchanged forever. He also began to fear that an attack would be made on his body during sleep if he were not completely covered. The transition from anxiety over bodily destruction to the use of a covering to ward it off had taken place. Later, this covering was to become a particular kind of clothing which provoked orgastic discharge: the male underwear fetish.

At eight, he became intensely interested in making, dressing, and manipulating puppets, which he imagined as being completely in his power. During adolescence he was writing and producing marionette shows for the entertainment of his family and friends.

> One early show that I repeated many times had to do with the birth of a baby and the baby coming out of the mother. I'd fix up the mother and father. The father and mother would decide to have a baby; the next scene, the baby coming; the third scene, some element of danger, perhaps something being destroyed or *changed*—some calamity that finally came out all right.

An explanation of this behavior is to be found in Freud's idea that:

> [I]n every field of psychical experience . . . an impression passively received evokes in children a tendency to an active response. They try to do themselves what has just been done to them. This is part of their task of mastering the outside world, and may even lead to their endeavouring to repeat impressions which they would have good reason to avoid because of their disagreeable content [Freud, 1931, p. 264].

Any show of "masculinity" on his mother's part, for example, being dressed in slacks, would exert a peculiarly depressing effect on him, whereas her femininity delighted him. Often he would lie languidly on her chaise longue, "feeling as she feels" and watching her dress and put on makeup. He openly envied her beauty, movements, manner of speech, and success in life. When she called his attention to his feminine attitude and asked him to be more masculine, he first became angry and then withdrawn. Mother should not give up her power to possess and experience everything, because her loss was his. Only late in the analysis did he recall that from five to six on he had fantasied that she had a hidden penis. If she appeared masculine, she was not a woman with a penis, but a man; all his excitement over her would subside.

In his early teens he went on with his creative activities, choosing the theater as his life's work. There he could dress actors, costume them, direct scenarios, and design sets. This tendency to sublimation is, of course, a well known phenomenon in fetishism (e.g., a scissors-hair fetishist may become a furrier).

At the age of nine he experienced strong erotic feelings at an Arabian Tales movie in which the heroine was violently stripped of her laces and silk and put into coarse clothing. At first he reported this as his earliest awareness of erotic sensations. However, later in the analysis, with the emergence of the pregnancy wish, he revealed that he had first used his underwear at five to bring about erection with the aid of the idea that his body was enlarging. He was thrilled and sexually excited by a musical play in which an all-male cast took the parts of women. Here was his dream come true—a woman with a hidden phallus. Beginning at ten, a fantasy of Douglas Fairbanks, the actor, having a silk shirt torn from his body, with the sudden exposure of the hairy chest, became a favorite method for producing sexual arousal. Because of his castration wish and fear he could not stand the sight of cuts, open wounds, or thoughts of operations. At twelve, a boy who had referred to him disparagingly as having a "melon head" wore shorts in his presence, whereupon he suddenly became so excited that he had an ejaculation. (His mother had told him that his head was too large to permit safe delivery; it was for this reason that she had to be "cut open" in order to give birth to him.) From the age of twelve on he was sexually aroused by the sight of male underwear which did not reveal the contour of the male genitalia. This was the beginning of the underwear fetish. The underdrawers had to be of the long variety, which did not permit the actual visualization of the genitalia or even their contour. Wearing the male undergarments himself, seeing other men wear them, experiencing the fantasy of their being worn by men, or on some occasions simply the sight of them in a store window produced sexual excitation and often ejaculation.

During his eleventh or twelfth year he first went to his father's room and wore the latter's underwear; this led to ejaculation. When the patient was thirteen his father died of a heart attack on a skiing trip. Just before this happened, the two had quarreled and the patient had walked off without apologizing. Subsequently he experienced a great deal of guilt. At thirteen he became embarrassed at the growth of pubic hair. He did not wish his testicles to enlarge, nor did he wish to grow up and become different from mother. At this age, when he walked into his mother's room, nude as usual, she told him to stop doing so because he was now "becoming a man." At this he felt humiliated, rejected, and in turn angry and depressed. When his father's underwear was given away, together with the rest of his clothes after he died, the patient felt frustrated. During this period he occasionally stole the shorts of an older male cousin and wore them. He began to admire older boys, and to have "occasional crushes" on them, especially those who appeared masculine, slender, and intelligent. There was never any overt homosexual contact.

At approximately fourteen the excitement over his sexual fantasies was intensified by a more overt pregnancy fantasy: the *change* in shape and size of the woman in the first three months of pregnancy induced a sudden sexual arousal and ejaculation. The figure of a man, previously slender and now showing a tendency to obesity, also began to stimulate him. The sight of a slightly overweight man emerging from water up to his waist would induce strong erection and orgasm (between the ages of fourteen and seventeen). In this instance, the water was a substitute for the fetish. The fantasy of a large, disembodied penis produced ejaculation; the "obesity" (pregnancy) is here displaced to the penis (fat penis-baby-breast).

His attitude toward his sister (except for the last six months in analysis) had always been one of contempt and hostility. In his early childhood he often frightened his mother by mock threats of violence toward the younger child. Once, in the presence of his terrified mother, who did not know the baby carriage was empty, he pushed it over a wall and into traffic. Between twelve and fourteen he continued to dominate his sister, frequently ridiculing her in the mother's presence. In fantasy he would pinch or tear at his mother's breasts. Whenever his mother paid undue attention to his sister, he would use any excuse to burst into rage and to accuse his mother of mistreating him. By reducing her to tears he punished her and forced love and attention from her.

The fetish was pressed into service whenever he felt depressed, lonely, and unloved, especially when he was separated from his mother or socially or professionally slighted. All of his sexually exciting fantasies were elaborations of his belief in the phallic mother (Bak, 1968). For example, a man beginning to gain weight was, in his unconscious, a woman with a penis (i.e., a male changing into a female). In addition, he was the pregnant phallic mother with whom the patient was identified. Any violence done to the body or to the clothes next to the body signified the distortion of the woman as a result of intercourse; that is, a woman with a penis inside her or ready to burst with the child. These sadomasochistic fantasies allowed him to experience the pleasurable-fearful excitement of sexual orgasm. After all, since it was only a fantasy heavily encrusted with substitutions and displacements (Sachs mechanism, 1923), it could easily be turned off. With increasing candor he ultimately declared, "The idea of doing something to myself that will hurt me but not kill me strikes a note. I want to experience a mild version of my body being ripped, so that I can get sexually excited—without it actually being ripped." This masochistic fantasy was a thin veil over his desires to become impregnated and bear a child.

As expected, the normal male or female figure produced no sexual feelings in him. If the penis became visible or if he touched his own penis, all excitement vanished. Because of his underlying feminine identification with his mother, the sight of the penis produced anxiety from three sources: (1) the danger of castration; (2) the danger of unconscious homosexual wishes; and (3) the activation of his more primitive bodily destruction fear, which was intimately connected with separation anxiety and wishes to have a child. In the early months of analysis, whenever he attempted to touch or hold his penis, he experienced the sensation that "it would fly off."

The stages in the evolution of the fetishistic object (the male undergarment) may be viewed as follows:

1. The use of the transitional object (the teddy bear) from six months to eight years signified his intense interest in remaining a child (Winnicott, 1953). From the earliest years of infancy he experienced a very marked degree of identification with and clinging to the mother.

2. From three to five years he was preoccupied with mother's delivering a child abdominally and traumatically. This preoccupation and the associated obsessive thoughts meant that it was his own delivery that he both wished for and dreaded.

3. From four to five years of age he needed to be bound tightly by a covering to protect his body against disintegration. Inasmuch as the tightness signified pregnancy, this was also gratifying.

4. Beginning at five years, he had an overt pregnancy wish, while, for the first time, the underwear appeared on the scene. The pregnancy wish was, however, at this point, the central issue, and the male shorts represented the surface of his body, now distended. Later the emphasis was *displaced* onto the clothing itself and more often than not the overt pregnancy fantasy was either (a) suppressed; (b) repressed; or (c) disguised through the idea of *change* and obesity. This is entirely in keeping with Hanns Sachs's important theory (1923) that the *mechanism* of perversion seems to be a "solution by division whereby one piece of infantile sexuality enters the service of repression and so carries over pregenital pleasure into the ego . . . allowing conscious expression to the perverse fantasy . . . whilst the rest undergoes repression" (Gillespie, 1956a, p. 397).

5. At nine, violence done to clothing (not necessarily underwear) produced erection and ejaculation. Here the pregnancy aspects are repressed and the interest in the lower parts of the body is displaced upward.

6. By twelve, the fully developed underwear fetish was

established. This is in accordance with Freud's view that only at puberty does the final form of the sexual organization take place (1905b). The patient now responded with sexual excitation to the sight of the male in undergarments (preferably one whose body begins to show slight overweight). A number of variations appeared. He was able to experience erotic sensations (a) by viewing himself in long shorts (he was always somewhat overweight); (b) by the fantasy of seeing shorts on another male; or (c) by seeing shorts in a store window.

7. From fourteen on, more overt pregnancy fantasies alternated with underwear fantasies: (a) the sight of a woman's body previously slender changing because of pregnancy; (b) the fantasy of the "fat" disembodied penis; (c) a "changing" man emerging from water.

As the analysis progressed, it became clear that the fetish did not simply represent the imagined penis of the mother, but also the breast, the swollen pregnant abdomen, and other parts of her body from which he did not wish to be separated. It represented himself in the impregnated state and also enclosed in his mother's womb. By reinstating situations in which the good breast was present and in which he had "gratified" the wish to bear a child, he reassured himself against his envy, rage, and destructive impulses toward the body of his mother. Thereby he recaptured the early object relationship with his loved mother (the sameness and primary identification). On the other hand, whenever he was frustrated, the good breast became a bad breast and he would savagely attack it with a mixture of relief and fear. Such attacks were likewise terminated by the use of the fetish, especially whenever he became alarmed by the savagery of his fantasied attacks. "I want to rip them with my hands and teeth because they are parts of her and that makes me angry. The breasts are old and cracked and it makes them easier to rip. My feeling is great anger; anger because mother is passive, serene, relaxed, content, and *filled up* [i.e., pregnant]." These aggressive fantasies produced relief, but it was only the fetish which brought true satisfaction of his unconscious wishes, sexual arousal, and orgasm.

Progress of the Analysis

After approximately a year-and-a-half of analysis the patient was able to hold his penis and on two occasions to masturbate manually. In this context he reported the following dream which revealed the major conflicts as viewed at that stage of the analysis:

Dream 1:

I am coming to see you, although not at this office, it is disguised. The whole atmosphere is changed, you have changed. I don't lie down on the couch immediately, I think there's someone else on the couch for a moment, don't know whether man or woman. You get up from your chair, and you are wearing a pair of gym shorts and one leg appears shorter than the other. Then you are leaning over the couch and that you are very improperly dressed comes to my mind. This disturbs me greatly. No, I don't think we do have a session. Suddenly to my right I'm aware that a girl I know is in an alcove with a potted palm partly concealing her. I think perhaps she can see me and I dart behind the potted palm. I don't want her to see me. You go over and talk to her. I leave the room and go down a short corridor and through a closet. Now, she won't see me. Then I go into a bathroom. I'm safe in here, and she won't come in here. Then, a knock on the door, and there's a man standing there. It's almost like she has become a man. Oh no, it's someone I know, a friend of mine who played Richard III (a man who had a limp and who always tried to show his superiority over me).

Then, another scene. This time I'm lying on the couch and I look at you and you're packing a lot of theatrical lighting equipment. You're very thin and emaciated and you say, "Fix that light." I say, "No, no." You say, "Yes, you can." Suddenly I see there is a gelatinlike capsule over the light and the light begins to look like a balloon which is getting larger and larger. I have a hatpin with a big pearl and I place the pin very carefully in the funnel, just the head of it and whoosh—the funnel closes up and it startles me. It goes down almost all the way, like air is in it (like a penis goes down). Then I'm not only conscious of you but of a female assistant present, and you say, "Not too bad." "No, but I hurt my finger." Then I take the pin, turn it around and the pearl goes in the balloon all the way down. You say, "See there, you did it, you see!"

Associations: The patient had found himself pleased by the compliments of a young buxom woman and had caught a glimpse of her breasts the day before. He promptly suppressed a beginning sexual excitement. If he ever truly accepted having a penis, he felt that there was danger of engaging in homosexual intercourse. The homosexual interest in and aggression toward the analyst were obvious, together with his wish to deny the presence of the analyst's penis through the use of the fetish (gym shorts). In his flight from the woman he endowed her with a penis and became uncertain whether he was male or female. The gelatinlike capsule enclosing the light also represented the covering (or fetish) which would protect both himself and the mother's breast (body, vagina) from destruction. Some months later he viewed this as representing his own body, now impregnated. At the end of the dream he again shifted roles (due to the split in the ego) by becoming the female assistant of the analyst.

The patient had intense fears of separation from his mother. This was due to his primary identification with her and his inability to successfully traverse separation–indiviuation phases, specifically the rapprochement subphase. The following statements demonstrate his lack of genital interest in her.

> All my life I just couldn't get along without my mother, she kept me going and still does. My most constant and strongest feeling is that I've got to be near her and have her personality around. Otherwise, I have no sense of direction or where I'm going. When I feel I'm losing contact with her, I become very unhappy with a sense of *loss of self.*

These remarks also reveal the extent to which his ego had been weakened by the excessive splitting-off of parts of himself through his identification with his mother.

In fantasy, he often found himself crawling through a tunnel which became smaller and smaller until he was suddenly unable to move, "way underground," feeling that he was about to be crushed. "I'll try and burst out of it. Bursting will produce destruction. It's like the bombing of the cities, the bursting of things, the earthquakes I used to be interested in." Here we may see (1) oral elements: the wish to be one with the mother, to be inside her, to eat her and be eaten by her; (2) the wish to be pregnant and the fear of his and his mother's bodily destruction and death. Freud (1931) felt that in the continuation of the preoedipal dependence on the mother we may have the "germ of later paranoia" in women. "This . . . is the surprising, yet regular, dread of being killed [devoured] by the mother" (p. 277) and is largely due to the projection of one's own hostile impulses toward the mother. It appears that a similar situation may exist for men; (3) anal elements: the tunnel signified the anal, abdominal explosive processes as part of the act of delivering a child. Since early childhood he had recurrently dreamed of bodily disintegration, heightened later, as he approached puberty and maturity, by the fear of tumescence in erection. This is a recurrent dream of late childhood:

Dream 2:

> I am shooting up in an elevator, high, high up and then the elevator is dropping at such a pace I will be killed. At other times there are no sides to the elevator and I'm terrified that I will fall out.

Whenever his intense masochistic wishes were at their height, he displayed tendencies toward paranoid behavior. For example, he became depressed and angry upon the slightest shift in feelings expressed toward him by anyone, especially the analyst. Frequently his dreams would consist of attacking or beating the analyst. He feared that a "little man" would jump out at him in the dark and attack his body. Whenever he was alone at home and occasionally on the street he would look over his shoulder to see whether he was being followed. Often he would awaken with hypnogogic hallucinations of a "presence" in the room, about to attack him. When he was unhappy and prevented from using the fetish successfully because of his physical surroundings, he would attempt to provoke quarrels with bartenders, waiters, bus passengers, or even professional colleagues in order to be attacked, shaken, or punched; he would drive people to desperate fury. At these times he would feel that his employers did not like him, misused him and abused his talents. These masochistic episodes occurred whenever he became aware of his helplessness. Instead of facing such feelings and the consequent aggression, he tried to escape in self-destructive behavior. In the same maneuver, he attempted a partial gratification of his passive feminine homosexual orientation to his father (oedipal elements).

The oedipal period became a *new* source of grave anxiety for the patient. The sight of the penisless woman enhanced his fear of bodily destruction. Consequently, as long as he could avoid this sight and confrontation with the anatomical differences between the sexes, he could ward off the activation of unconscious fears of his own bodily destruction and castration. This he proceeded to do through the use of the fully developed underwear fetish. The fetish protected him from the fear of bodily destruction, from the sight of his penis which reminded him of impending mutilation, and from his hostile impulses toward the female body. It both gratified and protected him from his own wish to have a baby, with the resultant frustration, envy, and rage at the mother. It also defended him from the unconscious homosexuality based on his feminine identification. As regards his homosexuality, the defense against this took a masochistic form which never reached the intensity of delusional masochism (paranoia) (Bak, 1946).

As regards his attitude toward castration, he displayed a classical splitting of the ego. While he obviously "knew" that a woman did not have a penis, he silently believed in the presence of a female phallus, which was covered up by the fetish. In the unconscious he could easily alternate between being male and female. His penis could be put on or taken off. Eissler (1958a) remarked that, unlike Freud, who considered denial of the absence of a penis the central issue in fetishism, he found that "the fetishist is ready to acknowledge that some human beings have no penis, but with the reservation that this condition is reversible" (p. 239). At other times he was a female awaiting the onslaught of the father's penis, with a mixture of pleasure and dread. This is manifest in the following dream:

Dream 3:

Somebody wearing a dress.[3] I think it's me, and I'm about to urinate. A man walks in and a terrible fear comes. He's going to do something horrible to my body—perhaps push knives into it. I'm absolutely terrified and yet excited by the idea.

By the mechanism of substitution a splitting of the object was effected.[4] In two dreams (Dreams 1 and 2) this split is clearly evident. The object, originally the mother, was split for the purpose of defending her against sadistic attacks. In order to protect her body the patient substituted for her an inanimate object worn next to his body surface. The sadism toward the mother was directed toward her genitals, abdomen, and breast; for these he substituted an object (the underwear) which he could not hurt or destroy and which would not frustrate him or retaliate. The object also prevented his own bodily destruction implicit in his wish for impregnation and delivery (see Dream 3). In the fetishistic act he not only acquired the breast, the mother's penis, but became the pregnant phallic woman. Reports (Payne, 1939; Gillespie, 1940; Bak, 1953), concerning clothes fetishes have in part stressed the above concept: the earliest love object must be protected not only because of fear of its loss and the consequent separation anxiety that would ensue, but also because one's own bodily integrity is endangered. The fear of bodily destruction may arise from both the nuclear conflict of the wish to have a child and from the intense primary identification with the mother.

---

[3] The significance of this patient's later transvestite tendencies will not be dealt with. However, it should be noted that aside from a short period of interest in wearing his mother's clothes (seven to nine years), and his sublimatory activities (e.g., making and dressing of puppets and his occupation), transvestism did not play a major part in the clinical picture. The relationship between fetishism and transvestism has been explored by other writers, notably Fenichel (1930c).

[4] Klein (1946) first defined the splitting of the object in fetishism by viewing the fetish as representing, on the one hand, the gratifying breast (heavily disguised through displacements and substitutions), and on the other, the still-dreaded genital or frustrating breast.

In the fetishistic fantasy both men and women were impregnated, the woman always being a phallic one. At first this was thought to be a manifestation of his passive, feminine, homosexual orientation to his father, a wish to be like mother in the flight from the oedipal conflict, in order to escape castration. The patient had apparently never achieved a satisfactory solution of his intense wish to have a child, nor had he ever forced himself to *change his attitude* with respect to the original love object, the preoedipal mother. These facts became increasingly apparent in the analysis and began to assume a more primary etiological significance. As he improved, however, the oedipal conflict and its resolution came into more prominence. Interpretations of oedipal material led to greater activity toward the female. The patient then recalled that between eight and ten years of age the fetish actually consisted of a *man* becoming pregnant:

> I would take men with good strong bodies and then I would somehow reverse the whole inside process within them and do over the insides of their bodies. I wanted them to become pregnant. I'd have them at the doctor's in these fantasies and they were diagnosed and notified that they would become fat. Where would the babies have come out? They would have to be cut open. It was a most exciting fantasy and a major source of sexual excitement to me. It was too perverse and unreal, however, so I never used it this way for long. A man getting fat is the same thing. It was the man's nonplussed humiliation at finding out that he was going to swell up like a woman that thrilled me, a doctor examining him or a group of men together, all having it happen at once to them. This has to do with the fetish, as the only clothing that they could continue to wear would be the underwear with an elastic band on it as they got fatter and fatter. [Historically, therefore, the pregnancy wish preceded the use of the fetish alone. Later he could use only the fetish or the fantasy of the changing pregnant phallic woman, having repressed his own wish to be impregnated.]

He then recalled a crucial memory:

> Before this period at approximately *five and six* I'd stuff pillows in front of myself with the underwear on to blow myself

up. Then I'd get an erection, but in those days I was afraid to bring on sexual excitement. . . . How did these men get pregnant you ask? I think they were having intercourse with *a girl* and something biologically went wrong. It wasn't a man having intercourse with men. The seed was placed in the wrong place. Seed is semen I guess. Maybe that's why I didn't ever want to have an ejaculation for years. *The seed would come out and be planted wrongly within me and I'd get pregnant.*

After he had begun to describe these fantasies, the patient became aware that while producing a large stool he felt an intense pleasurable excitement in the fantasy that he was delivering a baby through the anus. This material began to reveal his passive relationship to his father (the negative Oedipus complex). The *earlier* history of this fixation, with the residues of the original passive attachment to his mother, could also be clearly outlined. Was this indeed a true fixation at this stage or a regression to it? It seems likely that the former was the more correct analysis of this enigmatic situation. This passive man was never able to be truly active toward a woman until he had been in analysis. A further clue to the preoedipal nature of the nuclear conflict was his intense aggressiveness in object relationships; it was less libidinal and more ambivalent in character than in those who regress to preoedipal material. He preferred oral and anal gratifications, and behaved in an extremely infantile acting-out fashion when frustrated. [Lampl-de Groot (1946) has stressed similar differentiating points.] He once said:

This is what I believe. If mother dies a good part of me will die too. If she is ripped, I am ripped too. I am she, one and the same. She has babies cut out of her, I want to have babies cut out of me. She has intercourse with daddy, I want to, too, except now I want to have intercourse with men I guess who are like daddy. This is not possible—to have a baby—but I believe it, and this is why I am afraid of other women, why I am afraid to feel the desires that I know are there. If I have intercourse with a woman I'll blow up and I'll be cut open, all the things that happen to mother. I believe and don't believe these things can happen [denial mechanism], so I let myself go and enjoy the pleasures that won't bring terrible consequences for me. It's a very selfish attitude that I'm not concerned for the girl, it's concern for my own flesh. I don't think that I care much that a woman is cut open. She's going to hurt me before I hurt her. By having intercourse with me a woman can make me blow up; but how can she do that, she doesn't have a penis: I do. But she has a *hidden* one which will come down like a torpedo from a submarine as in my dreams, or a bomb from a plane, the bomb slowly coming down from a plane or a torpedo slowly coming out of a submarine. Yes, that's how women will have intercourse with me. [Significantly, it is the woman with the hidden penis by whom he wishes to be impregnated.] You know I can feel myself right at this moment; I can feel myself becoming the woman [i.e., split in ego] and I can see a penis, a real man's penis ready to go into my vagina. My vagina is in the front where the penis is, it's not between my legs. That's strange. Now there's a hole where the penis is. I know just as I describe this that I'm a man, that I can get an erection, that I can hold my penis *at the same time that I know the other.* The other day I began shifting roles constantly back and forth, back and forth. I could feel that I was a female and with a real determination I would then become the man again. When I touch a woman or put my arm around her I can become a man. When I become a female I don't always have a vagina. There is just *nothing* down there. It's forgotten about; it's *covered* up. I shift roles. By shifting to the female I want the man to love me, and then I can, however, be a man when I want to. And the feeling of not wanting to be alone comes into this. . . . I dislike kissing, I have an awful feeling about saliva. I don't want it to touch me, and I don't want to touch the opening of a woman's body. Don't let your mouth touch anybody else's mouth, it's dangerous. I had this way back as a child as far as I can remember [oral elements].

It's not so dangerous now as I can kiss a girl. But last night I felt it would go into me and do something to me. It was impure, it would make me diseased, I've got to wipe it away. It's sperm, I guess. I think this sperm could go into me and I'd become pregnant, then diseased, bloated, pregnant, and destroyed.

The patient responded to the progressive elucidation of the wish and fear to have a child with frustration and anger at the analyst. He would have preferred to talk of his homosexual wishes and the pleasure he would get from being loved by men, although upon questioning he could not picture any particular form of intercourse.

> You don't allow me to wallow in this satisfaction of having a man touch me and love me; you thwart me. I want to exult in the fact that I am a woman and can have a baby like mother but I don't want to admit it. And I don't want to have intercourse as a woman or with a woman as the female genital region will only remind me that I have to cut off my penis.

The following dream shows the nuclear fear: the wish for impregnation and its fateful consequences:

Dream 4:

> I'm on the street corner and I see a sign saying that someone's performing in a one-woman show, an actress friend of mine. It is amazing as this woman has just had a baby and she has gone home right after the delivery. What is the reason for her performing? I look at some pictures of her. Then I walk down the street to another building. I walk in and here's her husband. I ask, "Is she working?" "Yes, she went right back to work and didn't even wait a day." And then she comes from across the street into a building I'm in, and she looks awful as if all the blood is drained out of her and very weak, and she is in no condition to work. I ask her, "How come you went back to work so soon?" She says, "I had to." Oh, another part of the dream, I had forgotten. Something about a great mansion that I'm in. I don't know if it's my family's home or what and I go away from it for an afternoon and when I come back it's all burned up. A terrible fire, an awful feeling, "Is anything left in there that is mine?" On the outside I seem to have a lack of concern about this, but inside a sickening feeling that everything that is mine is burned up [oral elements].

Associations:

> If mother has a baby or I help produce a baby for a woman she's going to lose all the blood inside her and her health is going to be endangered. Everything is going to come out of her. She's going to be weak and defenseless. Also in the dream, the husband is totally unmoved. Oh yes, she's going back to work the

day after birth. She can do a one-woman show. One-woman
equals mother, I guess. *We* are one. This is a disguised version
of my home. The idea of being close to mother and the idea of
being separated. When I do get back it's burned up. Mother is
burned up [oral elements]. She'll be burned up because I'm not
as close as I used to be. I try to act casual: "Well, that's life." But
inside I'm going through terrible hellish feelings: I've lost her,
I've lost mother. I don't want to lose her, although I try to deny
that. I hold onto her as long as I can. That's why I only go so far
with my relationships with girls today. I'll *switch* roles and go
back to her and be like her. I make a relationship to a man and
look to him for a source of love, but then I go to mother. See, here
is someone who gives the appearance of a man, but I can't have
intercourse with mother as it's taboo [oedipal conflict]. I can't
love another woman because I'll lose her. And I have a series of
men who give me affection and then I've got it made. This is
crazy, but I do mean it. I had the experience last night. I saw
this man leaving the theater after the show with one of the
actresses. I'd like to deny that I felt this, but I had the overpowering feeling of hurt, "He doesn't want me," and a terrible
strong feeling of feeling this love and affection well up inside of
me and I wanted to release it on somebody and there was
nobody to release it on. It was an awful feeling of wanting to let
it loose. There was nobody, and I thought I was going to burst
inside. I thought, supposing there was a woman involved, how
fabulous it would be. The reason is that I want to give it to
mother, but no, I couldn't give that kind of love to mother
[oedipal elements]. I'd be so repulsed I would have to be another
human being. I still find myself being so tense about my
approach to girls. If I really give all my love to a woman and go
all the way, she'll eventually lose all that blood in her and it
would be *all my fault*. She'll be cut open, babies will pop out of
her.

The above dream clearly reveals the following elements:
(1) the wish to have a child like the mother; (2) the rage, envy,
and aggression toward the fortunate mother who can have
babies and be passive toward the father; (3) the oral and anal
nature of these wishes [the oral significance of fire in dreams
has been explored extensively by Arlow (1955)]; (4) the
attendant loss of the mother due to destructive feelings
toward her; (5) the coexistence of both the negative Oedipus
complex and the progressive tendency toward separating

from the mother with the beginning attainment of appropriate gender-defined self identity (vacillation between being a man and a woman). The dream also reveals the defensive function of the fetish. This defense consists of an attempt to make restitution for destruction of the mother's body and to continue the union with her in order to prevent the loss of her love and her death. By retaining his primary identification with his mother he is never separated from her. The orgastic satisfactions, which the mother must have enjoyed with the father, are experienced by the patient in a disguised form in his passive, feminine, homosexual, masochistic orientation toward him (oedipal elements). The disguise prevents the emergence of overt homosexuality.

Another dream reflects more clearly the preoedipal nature of the wish for a child and the pleasure, serenity, and freedom from anxiety derived from it. The fetish (snow) is a condensation of the wish for pregnancy. In addition, the fetish represents the enveloping mother's body. Not only is he like the mother in being capable of bearing a child, he is the child safe inside the mother's womb, but in danger from an intruder, namely, the paternal penis.

Dream 5:

I am alone. The atmosphere is strange. Deep, deep snow is everywhere. I sink down to my waist in it, but I am still able to walk easily. Everywhere there is whiteness—soft and still. Then suddenly along comes a train from behind me. It roars past. First comes the locomotive, black and huge. It belches forth black smoke. Though I am very close to the tracks and the train roars past me, I am not afraid of it. I *know* I am safe from it. The train passes on. I continue walking along in tne soft white snow. I am on the same curve in the track where the train passed. I hear another train. I turn around, and walk in the opposite direction. This train roars past me and my reactions are the same—the black, black huge locomotive belching black smoke, the sleepy gray cars. I am still safe. Though I know it is warm inside the cars, and cold outside, I do not care. *I am contented and peaceful and secure. Nothing can harm me.*

Associations: The patient recalled a movie in which he

had seen a train moving along the Hudson River. He always liked to be inside trains. The curve was the curve of his penis when it was erect. The white snow was the white body or the surface of the body; looking at his own body in the mirror with all its whiteness, especially the part that did not become sun-tanned. It was the whiteness of the underwear as opposed to the blackness of the penis. Being hip-deep in the snow was like touching a man's bandages in a previous dream and finding nothing there. It was like touching his underwear and finding no penis, but of course there is something there. As he contemplated the train moving along, he felt a sensation in his genitals—a beginning erection. The softness and whiteness seemed to him to connote going into his mother's body. This was being in the snow. He recalled an old double-entendre joke: "I was fifteen inches in the snow." Snow was, of course, the name of a girl. As regards the trains, the first train goes around the curve and then it is lost to view. As he turns in the opposite direction a second train comes toward him. This connoted the wish to have the man's penis inside him. The movement of the first train is "my penis coming out from me." Although the patient was out in the wilderness and alone in his dream, he did not feel alone. He felt comfortable and serene. As the second train with its luxury and security of the passengers sped past, it made him feel very warm. In the train men and women, husbands and wives, have intercourse with each other. "They are warm, they are in." Although he finds himself outside the train, he does not need anyone. He is covered up by the fetish (the snow), just as when he goes to bed he is serene, *protected*, and not cold. As he was leaving his apartment this morning, he had a great envy of people who are able to have intercourse—"preferably with women." He recalled a previous fantasy—that of a man emerging from the water—a favorite method of erotic arousal. The water was similar to the snow, just covering the lower abdomen. The water and the snow meant the fetish. The man emerging from the water was also becoming "fleshy"; he was becoming a woman. The emergence was the baby coming out, the delivery of the child. He suddenly recalled that he was told at the age of eight by his mother that he was conceived in the lower berth of a train.

Discussion

The core of my patient's difficulties lay in his fear of separation from the mother, a fear going back to the period of his earliest infancy. The early history of this patient's desperate clinging to his mother had often been discussed in his presence. The unfortunate preoedipal mother fixation led to a number of attendant complications, the most important among them being:

1. A lifelong primary feminine identification.

2. An unusually prolonged use of the transitional object (the teddy bear—a substitute for the baby).

3. The wish to bear a child like the mother. Kestenberg (1956a), directly observing children before the phallic phase, confirms the existence of this desire in boys as well as girls. Although actual memories of the wish to have a child could not be recovered before four or five years of age, the clinical material makes it highly likely that this wish developed out of the preoedipal fixation and not as a regressive phenomenon due to oedipal conflict.

4. The production of a fetishistic perversion whose foundation was to attempt a resolution of these primary problems, and secondarily to alleviate conflicts of the phallic period (e.g., fear of castration), which an already impaired ego had to master.

5. A great intensity of oral and anal aggressive drives and fantasies.

Preoedipal Type II Fetishists

In contrast to the preoedipal type I fetishist described above, who made a complete recovery from his psychosexual disorder in the course of a four-year psychoanalysis (see "Letter from a Grateful Patient" at the end of this chapter), *preoedipal type II fetishists*, that is, those fetishists with associated narcissistic personality disorder proper, pose a more guarded prognosis. Such fetishists have suffered a severe ego developmental arrest, the disruption in the emergence of an autonomous self, a more severe impairment of self–object differentiation, pathological narcissism and grandiosity, insufficient structuralization of the psychic apparatus, severe superego and ego defects, and defenses at a primitive stage of development with splitting predominating over repression. They are unable to function autonomously and require selfobjects to perform functions for them which individuals with better structured egos and superegos are able to do for themselves. As noted earlier, in chapter 9, my clinical research leads me to suggest an explanation for the striking clinical differences between these two types of patients; namely, the causative process involved in the formation of this particular form of perversion is dependent upon disturbances in the differentiating and practicing subphases of the separation–individuation process. These patients typically say they are unable to relate to others, complain that they do not exist, that they do not experience themselves in the world of social intercourse and personal relationships on a reciprocal basis whatsoever. They need others to complete them in order to make them feel alive and in reality. This earlier fixation leads to severe transference difficulties, as the patient is unable to maintain a representation of the good object, especially when frustrated by it. Transferences are of the primitive type, reflecting the state of the patient's internalized object relations. And while able to maintain reality testing, they are unable to maintain a representation of the good object when frustrated by it. They easily regress, may engage in psychoticlike transferences, have a great fear of the analysis, and splitting is predominant over repression as a defense mechanism.

In contrast to the warmth, vitality, and sustained object relations, even though they were from object to self in the preoedipal type I patient described, he was able to sustain, despite fluctuations of mood, fears, and the uncovering of repressed painful material, a therapeutic and working alliance with the therapist at almost all stages of his analysis. The preoedipal type II fetishist suffers from an inability to act, disturbances in the control of aggression, and severe threats to his self cohesion, with fragmentation anxiety. The threat of decompensation of their narcissistic pathology into the most severe or lowest level (Kernberg, 1980b), with episodes of intense aggressivity, paranoid ideation, and bursts of uncontrollable rage, suggest the presence of borderline pathology in some of these patients.

Bruce, a thirty-six-year-old executive, had a similar fetish as the clinical study described above. It consisted of a "jock strap" fetish in which he was aroused by the sight of this particular piece of underwear, whether on a man or in a shop window. He was completely unable to have any sexual relations with women, as was Calvin, and was plagued with the inability to complete actions. His only means of orgastic arousal and release was masturbation, the presence of the jock strap, and without any sexual partners. He complained that he did not feel alive, as if he did not exist; he was unable to act in his own enlightened best interest, he was completely lacking in confidence, was afraid to engage in public speaking, had marked feelings of inferiority alternating with convictions of grandiosity, and a sense of impending fragmentation when undertaking volitional action. His attendance at his sessions was spotty, and he occasionally felt the analyst was laughing at him or could read his mind. Bruce was afraid of his communications, and could not follow a plan of action in life although gainfully employed in an advertising business. He abruptly terminated therapy after six months of analytic work because of severe anxiety, an increase in paranoid distrust of the analyst, and what appeared to be a complete inability to follow the lead of the analyst in pursuing his free associations, dream material, and even the reporting of his daytime activities. He felt his communications might be revealed to others and that somehow he might "hurt" his mother through his psychological revelations. In addition, it became readily apparent to me that severely aggressive, destructive material had begun to emerge at the time of cessation of treatment.

The following verbatim material taken from two sessions reveals the pronounced difficulties in communication, feeling, and action which made him flee psychoanalytic treatment:

I better not say any more about my mother and father, like it's beating a dead horse; I feel like a betrayal feeling. I take a deep breath and try to believe I am me, a person—that I should have the ability to have my own thoughts and not worry about them and be an individual. Most of the time I feel I'm not. I try to be somebody else, *create* somebody else. It's like I don't want to stand up and speak my piece without panic, or that I cannot do

it. What is it that is scaring me, that stops me from doing this? Why is it that I'm not me? I am always amazed when somebody says nice things to me, or likes me. I find it hard to believe, but I revel in it for a while. I like the idea of being told, "You did a nice job"—praise, admiration, of close friendship or love. It astonishes me and it doesn't last. I find myself plodding along in aimless directions, not really connected, just moving along without a direction, without an enjoyment of life and living, without freedom. As if I'd rather be alone than not, wrapped up in my own little world. Then I try to think that that's such an awful way to approach life, as life is people, men and women. It is not something anyone should hide from or run away from. It's like a reconstruction I'm living under. But there's a feeling of wanting to burst out of it, take a big dash, to break through as I can do with music and singing. Or to become somebody else. Then I come back to me—I love to read, an avid reader, and I fancy myself as a writer, and I probably write quite well but I don't believe it. Sometimes at night, in the twilight, words flow and it's just a very eloquent feeling. It's the freedom, it's the free release feeling of emotion, and somehow the gates have lifted for the moment and the flow of words are good. I think of how I'd like to feel a few unrestrained feelings like that. . . .
I would like to be able to say this is me, really me. Other things are daytime fantasies. I might get the same feeling when trying to play the piano. But when I took piano lessons there was a restricted feeling. I don't credit myself with being able to do a lot of things, but I know I can somehow. I'm shaken by public speaking. It scares me. It must be I don't want to say—it's a lack of self-confidence, it's I don't believe I'm able. It's as if I'm forced to be the person I really am, and I'm afraid of that. I hide from being really me. If I face others, others might corroborate I'm *me* [splitting of the self].

Letter from a Grateful Patient

My underwear fetishist, Calvin, recovered completely from his perversion. It no longer had any influence over his life. He became heterosexual in that he was able to function sexually without the use of the fetish whatsoever and to cathect the opposite sex with affection and love. Eleven years after the end of his analysis, which lasted four years, during which there had been no communication, I received the following letter. It not only told me of his continued release from a devastating and inhibiting burden, but it revealed in its content and tone the status of his object relations, his capacity for love and affection, the neutralization of his once overriding aggression, the healthiness of his self-concept, and the firmness of his gender-defined self identity. This successful resolution brought rewards fully commensurate with the labors of both patient and psychoanalyst, for the work was hard, requiring both courage and endurance.

Dear Dr.,

You'll get the formal announcement of my marriage to Harriet early next week. But such missive only tells a slight part of the story—even though I know that that alone would make you very happy. For without question you are to a great extent responsible for this happy event. And no one understands that more fully than you (or me).

I've been on the verge of writing you so very often these past months. There were so many things to share with you of late. Nineteen-seventy was a rather incredible year for me. In April, my mother died after a brief illness. And by September, I was involved in the first really fulfilling relationship of my life— with Harriet. Along the way, there were certain delicious ironies to savor: most especially a production I directed in San Francisco last spring, where all the old stage-crew members greeted their "prodigal son returned" and the artistic director who hired me for the job was none other than K.—the same S.O.B. who fired me from that awful play he was directing back in '62, which brought a happy halt to my stage-managerial career (I've never been out of work since as a director).

The job at ——— (where K., among others, works) goes wonderfully. J. continues to be a marvellous stimulus in all areas. Yes, of course, he's a "father figure" to me (and others there, too) but it has been a wonderfully productive three years for me there. My initial traumas about my relations with the first batch of students (expressed to you) have resolved themselves very well. And I am privileged to work in an atmosphere that is essentially healthy and unneurotic in its many personnel.

As you gather, I still get to do outside assignments, the latest

being a new playwright's project at ———. Harriet and I will
have a belated honeymoon in Africa after that, and will come
back here come mid-August.

How can I adequately describe her to you? She's everything I
hoped to find in a woman and a wife. Very attractive, very
intelligent, involved in theater activities—and could you imagine me marrying a woman who wasn't at least sympatico to my
endeavors? She is also able to cope with my myriad varieties of
sillinesses in the most marvelous fashion. Over the past eight
or nine months of living together, we've experienced virtually
no problems, which in this day and age says a lot. She's two
years younger than me, and—like myself—has had her share of
growing-up problems. Her rather apt phrase a few months ago
to me was "We've both paid our dues, and now more than
deserve each other." I realize as I write this that I cannot
adequately express what she really means to me or I to her.
Let's just say she was worth the long wait, and I (We) are very
lucky in what I finally snagged.

Well, that about says it—in the kind of nutshell I never really
intended to write to you. Nor did I ever willfully intend to let our
paths go separate ways these last years. It just seemed to
happen. By that, I mean I seemed able to "cope" (an overused
word these days) with any and everything that came my way
personally and professionally—all of which is obviously due to
our sessions earlier. I never really believed I'd find just the right
One for me, and adjust to her so wonderfully. But I seem to have
done so. And I approach the ceremony tomorrow with little or
no trepidation about a great life with her to follow.

I hope I will hear from you when we're back in town in August
(or September, since I know that's *your* holiday time), for I do
regard you as one of the rare friends I have in this world, and
would love to function with you on that level alone, as a delight-
ful new experience.

Warmest regards,

C.

Fetishism in Women

Zavitzianos has shown in several papers that perversion
may exist in the female (1971, 1972, 1977, 1982). He has

described two cases of fetishism in women, one of exhibitionism, and one of transvestism and "homeovestism."

In all his case reports the female patient displayed a singular characteristic of female perverts, namely, the presence of an overwhelming, intense masculine identification, eschewing all things feminine, disdaining and repudiating the female genitals and secondary female bodily characteristics. [Fenichel's (1945) case of a female voyeur displayed similar characteristics.]

Zavitzianos states that fetishism does exist in women. However, it is used to deny the female genitals and represents the *father's* penis, not the mother's illusory penis. Fenichel also wrote that in women the fetish represents a penis which she wishes she possessed by virtue of identification with the father (1945).

In his 1982 paper, Zavitzianos reported on the appearance of childhood fetishism during the analysis of a young woman. This fetish was used for masturbation and it served to deny feelings of being castrated, which stemmed from the perception of her own genitals. The fetish was a vibrator bought long before the analysis on the advice of her gynecologist, who suggested that it might help to overcome her inability to experience sexual pleasure. She never thought of using the vibrator until after the analysis began, even though vibrators are often used by women to obtain sexual gratification. In his patient, however, the vibrator proved to be a classic fetish, in that it was the only way she could allow her genitals to be manipulated and achieve orgastic satisfaction. Her identification with her mother on a genital level was impaired. She was repelled by her own genitals and could not touch them. This avoidance helped maintain her denial of her female genitals, a complete disavowal of her entire genital anatomy. She had severe penis envy, refused to have intercourse with any man because she felt her genitals repelled her. She could never remember ever having masturbated, having sexual sensations in her genitals, or having experienced orgasm. Sexual arousal while asleep would immediately awaken her and sexual feelings immediately disappeared. If she ever touched her genitals in any way, she experienced pain. She was convinced that being a woman was a humiliation and defeat in every way. She stated, "If I cannot be a man, then I will have to create one. I want to be a man..." (Zavitzianos, 1982, p. 413). Her identification with her father helped protect her from her mother, whom she consciously idealized but unconsciously feared as dangerous and engulfing. However, her counteridentification with her father was not a satisfactory solution.

Zavitzianos's patient deeply wished to be a man, and realized she could never marry because of this. Her dream material revealed that she used the vibrator as a man's penis.

In addition to oedipal fantasies and fears, his patient, in my opinion, suffered from severe disturbances that had their origin in the separation–individuation phases. It is reported that she had fears of an engulfing mother and she was afraid that she would become "totally unantagonistic and impassive . . . totally dependent and regress to infancy" (p. 414). Despite her hatred and fear of men, she stayed with a male analyst because it protected her against her frightening unconscious desire "to be engulfed by a female." This material confirms my view that Zavitzianos's (1982) patient's difficulties was one of preoedipal origin and not due to structural conflict.

He proved conclusively that the vibrator was a fetish. In the words of this patient: "The vibrator is something more than my genitals . . . something moving . . . a penis. I have a feeling that the organ is missing . . . the fingers are close to the wound. But the vibrator tricks you because you do not know from where the orgasmic feeling will come" (p. 415). His patient's body was flying, emanating colors and magical powers in certain dream material. The image symbolized a phallic omnipotence "and indicated the existence of a body–phallus equation." In her associations to her dreams she compared herself to the vibrator, which also "emanates power." "With a vibrator you can deny your genitals and you have the feeling of something hard like a penis. When I have an orgasm, I feel the power of the protruding pubic bone which is raised, so it is a penis-to-penis business" (p. 417).

Zavitzianos's case is filled with allusions to a profoundly ambiguous gender-defined self identity, a state of emptiness and deadness and low self-esteem and depression which were relieved by fetishistic masturbation. "She would talk to the vibrator which she said represented a 'nameless and faceless person'" (p. 418). During orgasm, she felt "great" and "united" with that person, becoming "one with him" (1982, p. 418).

It is my impression that Zavitzianos's excellent case material could well be reinterpreted in the light of separation-individuation and preoedipal origin theories.[1] The disturbance in genital outline of the body, the separation anxiety, the fears of engulfment by the mother all seem to me to be the basic nuclear conflicts. Other oedipal conflicts including primal scene anxieties were secondary accretions to the deeper conflicts.

The fetish was:

> [I]ndispensable for sexual arousal and orgasm. Without the vibrator, sexual gratification was impossible. The fetish in this case allowed masturbation to take place. By replacing the hand it facilitated the denial of the female genitals and thus helped avoid painful feelings associated with the castration complex in women. The use of the vibrator helped restore self-esteem and encourage feelings of omnipotence. It also helped ward off anxiety due to fear of retaliation for the sadistic desire to destroy the object and safeguarded against self-destructive impulses to use her hand to destroy her genitals [p. 421].

The fetish also decreased the intensity of the guilt feelings related to masturbation. Lastly, Zavitzianos points out that fetishism in women may escape analytic notice because they unconsciously use the man's penis (as fetish) in what passes for normal sexual intercourse (1977, 1982).

Zavitzianos's clinical research in the area of female perversion led to a description of female exhibitionism (1971) and later to transvestism, and "homeovestism"; that is, fetishistic cross-dressing (1972). In his 1971 paper, he showed that a woman can expose her genitals, providing she *holds* a fetish, something that the male exhibitionist does not need to do.

---

[1]Zavitanos has recently expressed his concurrence with this view (personal correspondence, 1986).

Chapter 13
THE TELEPHONE PERVERSION: MEANING, CONTENT, AND FUNCTION

Introduction

The consensual use of the telephone for purposes of sexual arousal and orgastic release in a fantasied twosome is not an uncommon phenomenon. In addition to such telephoning, over 1½ million calls of an *intrusive sexual nature* are reported to the authorities every year (AT&T Report, Lexis Computer Service, 1984). Twenty percent of these were sexual, another 20 percent were sexual and obscene, and the remainder were reported as not only obscene and sexual but threatening and frightening.[2] While sexual arousal may normally be engaged in occasionally by consenting hetero-

[1] I wish to express my appreciation to the members of the Discussion Group, "Sexual Deviations: Theory and Therapy," American Psychoanalytic Association, May 1983, and especially to my cochairman, Dr. Vamik Volkan, for their valuable contributions during the group study of this perversion. The ideas expressed in this paper, however, are solely those of the author.
[2] Since the writing of this paper, Almansi (1985) has published an excellent analytic study on the wide range of telephoning, compulsive telephoning, and perverse telephoning with special emphasis on their social implications. This rich paper emphasizes the multiplicity of psychic motivations, the role of aggression, and the disturbance in object relations in these patients.

sexual pairs through verbalization of shared sexual experiences and fantasies, the obligatory, exclusive use of the telephone for sexual arousal by and with an anonymous person is part and parcel of a complex sexual perversion. Through the use of sexual or obscene words, the object is seduced into becoming an accomplice to a pornographic act, thereby heightening sexual excitement. Inducing the object to describe sexual feelings, organs, and acts over the telephone (and at a safe distance), a subject attempts to arouse sexual feelings in himself and often in the object, whose sexual feelings he shares vicariously. Threatening, aggressive, and sadistic elements elicit pain and terror in the victim and, when combined with sexual description, promote mounting sexual tension in the victimizer leading to erection and ejaculation as the sole means of achieving sexual satisfaction.

Transitory episodes of perverse telephoning are often reported during the psychoanalysis of patients suffering from homosexuality, sadomasochism, or transvestism. These, as well as the well-structured telephone perversion,[3] have received scant psychoanalytic scrutiny, with several exceptions. Weich's presentation (in press) contains the most complete description of such a patient with an emphasis on the concept of "language as fetish." Silverman (1982) described the use of the telephone in a nine-year-old boy during anxiety states. Shengold (1982) described a "telephone masturbation" in a patient who was compelled to use the telephone with complacent, susceptible women whom he *knew*, engaging them in titillating and suggestive conversation rather than sexual or obscene monologue or dialogue, without manipulation of the penis or attempt to produce orgasm. His patient's aim was to diminish anxiety, and if an erection occurred it was followed by spontaneous detumes-

---

[3]These are the relatively pronounced cases in which the perverse development is clear and definite. Because the perverse acts are usually the only avenue for the attainment of sexual gratification and are obligatory for the alleviation of intense anxieties, and because the intensity of the need for this gratification is relatively pronounced, I refer to such cases as "well-structured perversions."

cence. The motivation for this kind of telephoning was the "need to distance [both] frightening anal excitement and the impulse to anal masturbation" (p. 462). In contrast to the obligatory telephone sexual pervert who makes no actual sexual contact with the object, he would do his best to add them to his "list of degraded women." Harris (1957) described disturbances in vocal expression secondary to anxiety in certain individuals when they attempt to telephone or while engaged in telephone conversations. Wagenheim (1983) made a unique contribution in his psychoanalytic study of an obligatory, sadistic telephone pervert.

The purpose of this chapter is to build upon the valuable contributions of these authors, as well as several earlier ones (Freud, Bergler, Bunker, and R. Fliess), in order to weld into a coherent whole the multiple determinants of this perversion, as well as to describe the function it serves and to cite the major psychic mechanisms responsible for it. [4] Comprehension of this perversion requires careful analysis of the various components which have led to its ultimate design: (1) the obscene words; (2) the voice; (3) the symbol of the telephone and the act of telephoning; and (4) the contribution of sadistic aggression. The major psychic mechanism by which sexual excitement is ultimately achieved is auditory introjection.

The Function of Obscene Words

Freud was the first to subject obscene words to psychoanalytic investigation in *Jokes and Their Relation to the Unconscious* (1905a). He commented that obscenity was

---

[4] Limitations of space do not allow me to discuss the etiology of the well-structured telephone perversion, which I consider to arise out of a common core disturbance in the preoedipal phase of development similar to that I have found in other perversions (Socarides, 1979a). These difficulties include failure to traverse the separation–individuation phase (a preoedipal fixation) which results in the persistence of the original primary feminine identification with the mother, with consequent disturbance in gender-defined self identity, a disturbance in ego functions including pathological internalized object relations, and an object relations class of conflict (anxiety and guilt in association with insufficient self–object differentiation) (Dorpat, 1976).

primarily directed toward women: it was an attempt to seduce them through a powerful accentuation of sexual facts in the medium of conversation. Sexual talk is directed toward persons by whom one is sexually excited, to make them aware of the speaker's intentions, thus promoting sexual arousal in them. He noted the importance of aggression in the use of obscene words: he who laughs at an obscene story laughs as though he were an onlooker at a sexual aggression. The obscene anecdote is like undressing a person of the opposite sex toward whom it is addressed, and aims to force the listener into an exhibition of the organ described. The gratification experienced in voyeurism and exhibitionism may be achieved indirectly through the imagery connected with obscene words or by an obscene situation. One "views" the object or is "seen" by it. If the listener hears obscene words unwillingly, aggression is added to the exhibitionistic–voyeuristic component. He concluded that this form of sexuality is closely related to the excretory process in its total content.

Bergler (1936) enlarged on both Freud's and Ferenczi's (1911) seminal contributions in his statement that obscene words have an unusual power:

> [T]he power to force upon the listener a regressive-hallucinatory stimulation of a memory picture ... memories [which] harbor a number of auditory and written images with erotic [and coprophilic] content which are distinguished from other word pictures by their exaggerated, regressive propensities. In the act of hearing or seeing an obscene word, this propensity for uncovering a memory is stimulated [p. 228].

Jones (1920) described the perversion of coprophemia, the audible articulation of obscene words (not on the telephone) to female passersby, as being practiced largely by mild exhibitionists and voyeurs who, instead of actually exposing themselves or engaging in sexual peeping, are satisfied with just using words. The act of speech was psychologically the full equivalent of the deed.[5]

---

[5] In contrast, coprolalia is the automatic, obsessional expression of such words in order to promote sexual excitement, often during actual sexual intercourse.

It is well known that in some impotent men the speaking of obscene words is a prerequisite to sexual arousal. Bergler (1936) reminds us that in the unconscious, flatus and words are identical and obscene words are, psychologically speaking, "oral flatus." These patients may be potent only with prostitutes whom they devalue, and impotent with "respectable girls" who would not speak obscene words. Words are therefore an "agreeable oral–anal equivalent," and when a woman speaks obscene words it protects a man from castration, relieves him of guilt, and makes the woman responsible for her own sexual excitement. When a male asks a woman partner to relate her sexual experiences with other men in the most realistic manner possible in order for him to achieve erection and ejaculation, the male has almost always identified with the woman (mother) in the sexual act.

That obscene language may have a "fetishistic function" was first noted by Bunker (1934) and fully described by Weich (in press). Weich's patient's obligatory perverse symptoms, removed by psychoanalysis, proved to be overdetermined at oral, anal, urethral, and phallic-oedipal levels. At various times telephone calling unconsciously represented breast milk, feces, urine, and semen. The utterances he delivered to women on the telephone unconsciously took on a more "urethral-phallic" meaning, and the woman's words (once he had induced her to speak obscene language similar to his own) served to reassure him unconsciously that women had a phallus, that is, a "speech phallus," were not dangerous, and helped him to deny castration anxiety. These telephone conversations were a means of exhibiting his own powerful "speech phallus" while hiding behind the telephone in order to divest himself of feelings of inadequacy and fears of sexual impotence. The use of the telephone derived from both oedipal and preoedipal conflict, and was also associated at an oedipal level with sadistic primal scene memories.

The Contribution of the Voice

In addition to the voice's ability to produce sexual arousal and induce fearful excitement, two facts regarding the human voice are noteworthy: its quality, especially its pitch, and the sex of the individual speaking (Bunker, 1934). It is a "sensitive reflector of emotional states" whose "modulation and modification are an involuntary expression of emotional nuances—of which . . . the subject may be more or less aware" (p. 391). There is a correlation between maleness of sex and maleness of voice, psychologically at an unconscious level; alterations in the voice may signify castration anxiety. He concluded that in some male patients the female voice is unconsciously equated with the female phallus (which penetrates one at a distance through the medium of the telephone). Accordingly, the voice may be considered to be "a fetish of a somewhat unusual order" (p. 392).

Harris (1957) observed in his patients that vocal expression may be severely disturbed as a result of castration fears. The voice may be perceived as a cutting instrument or something to be cut; opera singers say that when their voices are good it is like "a throbbing phallus plunging into the ear of every woman in the hall" (p. 343). He observed that when a patient is euphoric he has no trouble using the telephone (i.e., verbalizing), but uses it with great reluctance when he feels castrated or fears he will be "cut off." In some individuals, in contrast to feeling castrated, telephone conversations are often highly erotic experiences, causing them to have erections as they talk, after the tension of initially making the telephone call has passed. Some patients, when they become potent, lose their telephone anxiety, while others with fears of the opposite sex are unable to use their voices. They fear, furthermore, what they are going to *hear* at the other end of the line. Some patients alter their voices and sound "like women" while on the telephone, similar to the homosexual patient (B) I shall describe and Shengold's patient (1982).

The Symbol of the Telephone and the Unconscious Meaning of the Act of Telephoning

Our most comprehensive understanding of the unconscious meaning of the use of the telephone in anxiety states derives from a psychoanalytic study by Silverman (1982). His patient was not a telephone sexual pervert but a nine-year-old boy who suffered intense anxiety when faced with his father undergoing surgery close to his genitals. The patient was no longer able to master anxiety through play and verbal expression alone, and made symbolic use of the telephone for its alleviation. Limitations of space permit only a highlighting of Silverman's conclusions: (1) the telephone may be used to facilitate the development of self and object representations, and the attainment of ego mastery; (2) in telephoning, an individual gets close but not too close to the object, joins with and separates from it, and secures oral needs; (3) in the handling of the telephone (penis, testicles, maternal phallus, and bisexual genital symbol), one may engage in a substitute form of masturbation. Utilizing Mahler's concept of separation–individuation, Silverman revealed how separation anxiety is worked out by the use of the telephone. "By calling people, he could establish affectionate, sensual, and aggressive contact with them, at a safe distance, on multiple developmental levels . . . and then return to being separate" (p. 608). The telephone stood for a means of regulating "closeness and distance," repeating the rapprochement-phase struggle with the mother. In establishing contact through repetitive telephone calls, he could "drive away the libidinal object" and at the same time reinforce "the sense of object constancy"; he could work through and master his excited but terrifying wish to submit to the strength and power of the preoedipal "phallic mother" (p. 609). As a bisexual genital symbol, the telephone could be used to attempt penetration into the "private spaces of desirable, mysterious, forbidden girls and women" (p. 609), a common finding in those who engage in perverse telephoning.[6]

---

[6] In connection with the maintenance of a sexual tie with the maternal object and/or the homosexual object, R. Fliess (1973) observed that in telephoning, one person initiates the contact and "invades" while the other receives, but the roles are readily reversible because each partner has both a passive receiving prosthesis and an active projecting one. These two people, according to Fliess, stand for mother and child, especially if there has been "sexual activity in childhood between a mother and child" and "compulsive telephoning serves . . . the maintenance of an identification with her" (p. 305).

The Contribution of Sadistic Aggression

While all intrusive and unsolicited sexual telephoning may be considered aggressive in nature, the erotic content of these verbalizations is often used to disguise their sexually sadistic qualities. Overtly sadistic, obligatory telephone perverts rarely come for psychoanalysis and, when referred by the courts for psychiatric evaluation, are rarely seen by psychoanalytic practitioners. Wagenheim (1976, personal communication; 1984)[7] had the good fortune to study psychoanalytically, for an extended period, an exclusive telephone pervert who had made literally thousands of calls over a decade to unknown women for orgastic satisfaction. The discussion group before whom this material was presented originally can only speculate that this patient in all probability suffered from a primary feminine identification with the mother. Other suggested findings were: an inability to make a counteridentification with an ambivalent, hostile, and abdicating father; a disturbance in gender-defined self identity; early and severe deprivation; narcissistic injuries prior to the age of three; and an overproduction of primary and secondary aggression. Along with a direct expression of severe destructive, sadistic aggression which was not neutralized by libido, there were exhibitionistic and voyeuristic elements.

At first he would engage a woman in quiet conversation in a modulated voice, then suddenly announce the abduction of the male member of the family and that his life depended on the woman's compliance. He demanded that his victim describe her own body or, if a daughter was present, her body in intimate detail, then masturbate and describe her erotic sensations while he himself masturbated. Every detail of erotic feeling and action was to be expressed (pornographic factor). On at least one occasion, he asked a woman to cut the hair off her head or genital region and masturbate. Many women, frightened by his threats, complied, and the patient, one may assume, experienced erection and ejaculation,

---

[7] I am indebted to H. H. Wagenheim for his kind permission to use this material.

although he claimed amnesia for both calling and sexual arousal.

Explanation of this man's symptomatology may be found in the following considerations: the patient's dream material disclosed (1) an unconscious feminine identification with the mother; (2) fears of oral deprivation;[8] (3) severe aggression relieved by the perversion, displaced and directed against the bodies of other women. Through the use of the telephone he attempted to maintain object relations, forestall engulfment anxiety were he to approach women too closely and directly, undid separation from the mother while remaining "close to her" through substitution of other females. While he rid himself of identification with a woman (through acting as a man on the telephone), it is likely that he simultaneously identified with her sexual responses.[9] The function of his erotic experience was to help maintain, stabilize, and reinforce his self cohesion against the threat of personal fragmentation, signaled by attacks of anxiety. Wagenheim concluded that his patient was functioning at a "borderline level" and, in my view, the telephone functioned to maintain object ties at a variable distance, providing separation without loss and contact without fusion.

Perverse Telephoning in
Homosexual Patients

Perverse telephoning is an additional route for sexual arousal and orgastic release in some homosexuals under special circumstances, both internal and external; for example, when the sexual object is unavailable for various reasons. Homosexual perverse telephoning occurs in those homosexuals who consciously wish to maintain their con-

---

[8] He frequently dreamed of being uncared for, being deprived or "bypassed"; for example, "I am in an unemployment office, it was like a nurses' station but I couldn't get their attention or get help. I am being bypassed by the female help. I feel angry and I wake up!"

[9] Conclusions as to the meaning and function of this patient's behavior must be viewed as tentative and speculative (except for the severe aggressive impulses) according to Wagenheim, for his patient was fearfully awaiting criminal prosecution, claimed amnesia/dissociation for these episodes, and therefore could not describe his motivational state during them.

scious gender-defined self identity in accordance with anatomy but unconsciously wish to be penetrated as women (in contrast to homosexuals who both consciously and unconsciously wish to achieve their appropriate masculinity). Gratification is achieved through the female (voice) phallus. These individuals greatly fear homosexual contact.

Patient A., a twenty-five-year-old male homosexual physicist, relied almost exclusively on telephoning male hustlers for orgastic release following his initial contact with a homosexual that left him anxious and frightened. He would inquire as to their looks and services, the size of their penis, the sexual acts they would perform on him or allow to be performed on them, all the while masturbating to ejaculation and hanging up promptly when orgasm occurred. He continued this practice for approximately five months, but ultimately reverted to more satisfying homosexual relations for a protracted period of time. Telephoning was a substitute for and defense against fantasies of destructive anal penetration by powerful men were he to engage in actual homosexual relations.

Patient B., a twenty-two-year-old male homosexual, was abandoned by a rich, powerful father at one year of age following a stormy divorce and flight with his mother to a foreign country. He suffered from a strong unconscious primary identification with an uncaring and rejecting mother who continually disparaged the father and, in an attempt to destroy any identification with him, cruelly suggested that he might not be the patient's father after all. Throughout childhood and into adolescence he had terrifying nightmares of being overwhelmed, smothered by a large mass that would come closer and closer and threaten to absorb or destroy him (fear of maternal engulfment). The telephone perversion began shortly after puberty while living with his mother who insisted that he sleep in an apartment next door to hers so that he would not "interrupt her sleep." Whenever he felt lonely, depressed, hopeless, and helpless, he would call men at garages, gymnasiums, and so on—places where he knew that men would be "tough and masculine." Using a feminine voice, he would induce them to describe sexual acts they would perform on him as a woman. Finally, by advertising himself in magazines as a young adolescent who was interested in meeting a man for sexual purposes and massage, he produced a constant stream of telephone calls to himself on a special number that he answered in a female voice. He thereby avoided the possibility of rebuff, was assured of being sought after and admired, and eliminated the aggressive and intrusive nature of his own sexual calls.

In his actual homosexual activities, Patient B. searched for a powerful homosexual male, a man who would "protect" him, and from whom he could extract love, not like his lost father whom he professed to hate and have no interest in whatever. Through identification, the homosexual partner would provide him with a sense of masculine identity as a means of salvation from the engulfing mother from whom he could not separate. At puberty, he frequently masturbated while looking at an enlarged photograph of his father. He wished to be a man, but his deep hatred for and unconscious guilt toward his father, together with the tie to the mother, prevented a successful counteridentification with the male. Perverse telephone calling was his major source of sexual satisfaction. He infrequently allowed himself to be picked up by older, elegant, and prosperous-looking men and went to their apartments where he enacted the role of the little boy in relation to an all-powerful, good father. He would only engage in mutual masturbation and preferred to see his partner having anal intercourse with a third man, as he identified with the one who was being anally penetrated (a woman). Telephoning was a means of overcoming separation anxiety through acting the role of the mother, eliminating feelings of loneliness and depression. He could express his wish to be treated like a woman only at a distance or through utilizing another man to play the female role. Up to the age of seventeen, he desperately wished to become heterosexual and nearly suicided when he was offered no help in this direction. His telephoning in the female role was an attempted solution, a compromise between his wish/dread of becoming a woman with its implied merger with the mother and his wish to maintain his masculinity through occasional homosexual acts whose purpose was to achieve emotional closeness with the loved/hated father.

Discussion

The function of heterosexual perverse telephoning is to achieve masculinity and self-object differentiation through eliciting and hearing the verbal/emotional and sexual responses to sexual/obscene/aggressive words at a distance. Verbalization is equivalent to exhibiting one's sexual organs and in complementary fashion to viewing those described by the object. The introjection of the female's response is achieved through the auditoriperceptive apparatus. The object's sexual response and the description of female sexual organs and reactions provide the subject with a sense of masculinity, as they reassure him of the anatomical differences between the sexes. Telephoning reassures against and lessens castration fear, diminishes separation anxiety, and promotes and simultaneously disavows the identification with a powerful mother. It neutralizes fear of her while unconsciously and at an oedipal level gratifying the infantile wish for sexual closeness to her. The psychosexual *motivation* for the act is orgastic desire: "If I depict myself as a man [verbally] and the woman reacts, then I am a man, and I do not desire men [denial of homosexuality] and I am not a female [defense against feminine identification]." The sexual object choice is a person of the opposite sex, less often of the same sex. All the telephone perverts described in the psychoanalytic literature and in my clinical experience have been male.

Homosexual perverse telephoning occurs in those homosexuals who struggle against their homosexual object choice, have paranoidlike fears and distrust of men, and fear anal penetration as bodily damage. In telephoning, they are experiencing an underground version of their femininity or may dramatize themselves as females in a transitory fashion. They attempt to keep an optimal distance from and/or closeness to the mother, all the while avoiding engulfment. The fear of the maternal body, the fear of homosexuality, and in many instances the severity of their aggression lead these individuals to avoid both homosexual and heterosexual intercourse. The telephone pervert avoids superego guilt as no actual intercourse has taken place. "I only spoke about my penis, my sexual and/or aggressive destructive wish and listened to those expressions from others; I did not use it or actually destroy anyone."

Despite the telephone's bisexual symbolic significance, it does not function as a fetish; rather it facilitates the sexual aim by virtue of its capacity to transmit and receive verbal messages (words) of a sexual nature through the vocal and auditory apparatus respectively, producing contact with the object, although at a distance. It may be compared to the hairbrush that is used by the spanker in relation to the spankee in beating fantasies and beating perversions (see chapter 16).

Words themselves, both spoken and heard, play the central role in this perversion. They have both a warding-off function and a compensatory function. As regards the former, they lessen castration fears of both oedipal and preoedipal phases, allowing the patient to assert his masculinity and/or femininity, all the while keeping his penis. They nullify fear of loss of the object and separation anxiety by allowing the individual to engage in a relationship, often of an intense and sadistic nature, over the telephone. Words relieve anxiety generated by the overproduction of primary and secondary aggression through the discharge of coprophilic and sadomasochistic impulses onto a substitute for the mother. In acting the part of the masculine penetrating figure, the pervert, through the use of the "voice phallus," reassures himself against merger with the mother while vicariously enjoying her "voice phallus" which penetrates his ear. In agreement with Bunker and Weich, words serve a *fetishistic function*. Through auditory introjection, the "phallus of the individual" is reinstated in a manner similar to that which occurs in other instances of fetishism so well described by Greenacre (1953) in which "the need to preserve the mother's phallus and to deny the anatomical differences between the sexes" is effected through "visual, olfactory and actual introjection" (p. 30).

In its *compensatory* function, the telephone perversion helps overcome loneliness and depression through enforced contact with another individual. It buttresses and consolidates the self representation in those with insufficient self--

object differentiation. It provides a need-tension gratification via the sensoriperceptive apparatus through auditory intro-jection of the voice and words of the partner.[10]

As in other perversions, the perverse acts are an attempt to master traumatic internal problems through control of actual external objects by concocting what Khan has termed "active ego-directed, experimental play-action object rela-tions" (1965, p. 409) in which the "technique of intimacy" plays a major role. Pathological internalized object relations which had led to despair and hopelessness are mitigated and the absence of healthy self-esteem in relation to internal parental figures is ameliorated through creating a "pseudo-object relationship" (Khan, 1965) and the production of imaginary mutual pleasure.

Perverse telephoning is similar to *showing* in exhibition-ism or *viewing* in voyeurism, a rudimentary mode of com-munication with an external object which serves multiple functions, including fetishistic ones. In this chapter I have explored both "word-sending" and "word-receiving" aspects of this perversion, described warding-off and compensatory functions, and suggested that auditory introjection is the major mechanism facilitating sexual arousal and release.

---

[10]These dynamic considerations prompt me to suggest that it would be more appropriate to designate this perversion as "word fetishism" rather than "telephone perversion." Weich (in press) had expressed a similar view in his use of the phrase "language fetishism" to describe certain aspects of this perversion.

Chapter 14

TRANSSEXUALISM:
THE CASE OF VICTOR-VALERIE

Introduction

Transsexualism may be defined as a psychiatric syndrome characterized by: (1) an intense, insistent, and overriding wish or desire for sexual transformation into a person of the opposite sex, a transformation to be effected through direct (surgical) alteration of the external and internal sexual apparatus and secondary sex characteristics of the body, and indirectly through the administration of endocrinological preparations; (2) a conviction that one is "basically" a person of the opposite sex. This idea is intense, insistent, and can be semidelusional or delusional, or may reflect an underlying psychosis; if not, it is always based on the failure to make the appropriate male or female gender-defined self identity in accordance with anatomy; (3) concomitant behavior imitative of the opposite sex (e.g., alteration in dress, interests, attitudes, choice of sexual object, and so on). This is a desperate attempt to strengthen the wished-for transformation; (4) the insistent search for surgical transformation even to the point of self-inflicted mutilative acts. The *wish* to change sex may be found in the following individuals: (a) neurotics who fear their masculine or feminine role may dream of changing sex. This dream may seek conscious expression; (b) homosexuals who cannot deal with their biological anatomical role in life may have a conscious and/or unconscious wish to change sex; (c) transvestites who are not content merely to wear the clothing of the opposite sex and enact this part may have the conscious or unconscious wish to solidify playacting through anatomical change. In the transvestite, the employment of the new sexual organs may not be a primary interest; simply "to be" a person of the opposite sex is sufficient; (d) in schizophrenics the wish is an attempt to find some relief from deep and terrifying unconscious mental conflicts. Homosexuals and transvestites who are also schizophrenic frequently have this wish. In such cases, surgical procedures may be attempted by the individuals themselves, especially during acute psychotic periods; for example, amputation of the penis by a schizophrenic while in a delusional state; (e) in hermaphrodites or intersexed individuals in whom there has been a failure of embryological development and the individual shows external anatomical defects (e.g., faulty development of the penis, faulty breast development, imperforate vagina, etc.), the wish may or may not be consistent with their true but hidden anatomical gender. These individuals, however, are a rare minority among those seeking a change of sex. Only in cases of true hermaphroditism or pseudohermaphroditism should surgery or hormonal treatment be directed toward the corrective measures in accordance with anatomical findings.

The clinical picture of the transsexual is of an anatomically normal male or female, quite often young, who feels that a strange change is taking place or an alteration of sex is occurring within him or her. Such an individual frequently says that he felt something "unnatural" within himself and that he was occupying the body of the wrong sex. These patients believe that this change should be expedited by surgical or endocrinological treatment. They fervently desire that an operation be performed to produce the alteration so that the body coincides with their emotional state. Some extreme cases will insist that they have often experienced menstrual bleeding through their urethra, anus, or even nose, but examination shows a normal physique and there are no signs of any such metamorphoses. Closer examination reveals that these individuals are either transvestites, homosexuals, or individuals who, by suppression or through repression, are struggling against intense homosexual wishes. Homosexuality and transvestism seem to be intimately related to the wish for a change of sex (transsexualism).

In a strict sense, transsexualism may prove not to be a separate and distinct clinical entity, a special sexual perversion in its own right, in the way that homosexuality, transvestism, fetishism, and so on represent clinically definable sexual deviations. The criteria mentioned above—wish or desire, conviction, imitative behavior, and insistent search— do not represent specific unconscious mechanisms which are then converted into a manifest perversion. They represent secondary elaborations on a preexisting disorder; for example, homosexuality or transvestitism. The function of male transsexualism is to achieve "femininity" through recasting; that is, through radical surgical and plastic procedures and endocrinological manipulation designed to remove all traces of true anatomical gender and to promote reenactment of a synthetic and assumed feminine role in the general environment and in the sexual act. Thereby one escapes visible homosexuality, undergoes the dreaded castration (riddance phenomenon), vicariously identifies with the powerful mother, neutralizes fear of her, and consciously enjoys the infantile wish for intercourse with the father (the negative Oedipus complex realized); escapes paranoidlike fear of aggression from hostile, stronger men who would damage one in homosexual relations; eliminates destructive impulses toward the self and object; enhances narcissistic pleasure and grandiosity; and reinforces feelings of power over other men.

The function of female transsexualism is to achieve masculinity and diminish similar and corresponding anxieties in parallel ways.

The psychosexual motivation of the transsexual, beyond orgastic desire, is his wish to maintain an optimal distance from and/or closeness to the mother without fear of engulfment, and the conscious yearning for a femininity and to enact it with anatomical reinforcements; there is a wish to displace the mother in sexual relations with the father. The sexual object choice (aim) is a person of the same sex prior to elective recasting.

The wide variety of clinical pictures these individuals present is explainable when one considers the psychiatric syndrome cited above may derive from an oedipal, preoedipal, or schizophrenic level. Thus, transsexualism may be classified as oedipal transsexualism, preoedipal type I and II transsexualism, and schizotranssexualism.

Transsexualism is evident in the homosexual who, in attempting to resolve his deep emotional conflicts, fastens upon the idea of changing sex through the mechanism of denial. He therefore abhors everything masculine about himself and develops an overwhelming desire to be a woman. It is well known that most homosexuals are content to keep their external genitalia intact. The sexual activities of the transsexual serve to deny the knowledge and resultant guilt that one is suffering from homosexuality. Significantly, in the delusional system of paranoid schizophrenics, the idea that one has been transformed into a person of the opposite sex is quite prevalent. In this way one may freely engage in homosexual activities (Freud, 1911). Most transvestites are content to remain simply that, individuals who cross-dress. The function of male transvestism is to achieve "femininity" through cross-dressing, while *retaining* the penis. This is the crucial difference between transsexualism and transvestism. Cross-dressing reassures against and lessens castration fear and fears of loss of the mother. The transvestite envies the mother and sisters, wants to be powerful like the mother, wants to have babies, and changes his *external* appearance by wearing feminine apparel while retaining the phallus (Fenichel, 1930c; Ostow, 1953). Some transvestites (see cases described in chapter 15), under extreme conditions of "feeling persecuted" by the police for their cross-dressing and unable to cease cross-dressing while at work or in other social functions, or experiencing severe depressions which can only be relieved through cross-dressing, will elect to undergo transsexual surgery as an attempted "solution" to their distress. Transsexuals and the advocates of transsexual surgery believe that some of these individuals suffer from biological or imprinting disturbances (Stoller, 1975a) in which the soma is male but the psyche is female. Such patients believe they are suffering from a *physical* defect whose correction they pursue with great insistence. Proponents of transsexual surgery put this in its extreme form: "A feminine brain in a masculine body," or vice versa. In this connection, Freud's statement in response to the confusion and misunderstanding that greeted his theory of bisexuality is particularly apt: "there is neither need nor justification for replacing the psychological problem by the anatomical. . . ." (1905b, p. 142). The male transsexual patient, whether transvestite or homosexual, suffers from an extreme form of primary feminine identification, abhors everything masculine about himself, and engages in the behavior imitative of the opposite sex. In a sense, he feels "there is a tumor between my legs, the tumor is my scrotum and my penis," and he wishes for the ablation of these organs. Although the penis is the major target for surgery, these patients are chronically dissatisfied with other aspects of their bodies: their nose, legs, larynx, facial structure, and so on. They search for "perfect femininity."

As regards the need for perfection, Volkan (1982, unpublished) noted that the surgical procedure "does not remove the mental representation of the penis" or what it meant to the patient. The patient continues his quest for ultimate perfection with more surgery in the genital area and surgical feminization of the Adam's apple, the legs, and so on. Volkan further found that: (1) The patient who demands such surgery has within him a type of defense constellation seen in persons with borderline personality organization. (2) The search for perfection undertaken by a transsexual of either sex is due to a need to be free of any contamination by aggression: the search for perfection defends against anxieties based in conflicted internalized object relations. (3) The male transsexual seeks union with his "all-good self representation" and his "all-good" mother representation in order to make himself into a perfect woman. At the same time he dreads merging with the "all-bad" object representation, which he keeps along with his own "all-bad" self representation, primitively split. Such splitting occurs at the level at which self and object images or other representations are differentiated, except in respect to sexually unlike body parts. However, the basic surgical change does not put an end to the search, and unless he or she undergoes a change in psychological structure, the transsexual seeks perfection and keeps arranging for more surgery. (4) The patient's main aim is to be rid of unwanted aggression, and for that reason Volkan proposed the term *aggression reassignment surgery* (instead of sex reassignment) for the procedures involved. Person and Ovesey (1974a,b) suggest that transsexualism may be classified as follows: *primary transsexualism* which arises from a core disturbance of a nonconflictual nature similar to that of Stoller's concept of "imprinting," and a *secondary transsexualism* arising from transvestism or homosexuality. In contrast, I view transsexualism as due to a persistence of a severe primary feminine identification with the mother arising from earliest years of life and conflictual in nature.

It behooves us to heed Rado's (1949) advice:

> Since the sexes are evolutionary products of reproductive differentiation, the anatomy of the reproductive apparatus as a whole is the only criterion by which we can tell who is what. In the human species, the male reproductive apparatus and the female reproductive apparatus are mutually exclusive despite the fact that they develop from a common embryonic origin. Hence, a human being is either a male or a female, or, due to a failure of differentiation, a sex-defective. It is common knowledge that these malformed individuals are possessed by the desire to be of but one sex [p. 209].

Clinical Study

My patient, Victor–Valerie, a prototype of the transsexual patient, was neither an intersex nor a hypogonadal individual. He was a gifted young biology research student of twenty, who lived only for the day when he would have his "operation." He agreed to undergo psychoanalysis, with the provision that his parents would reconsider their opposition to surgery.

Victor, whose feminine pseudonym was Valerie, appeared at our first appointment as a rather attractive man, looking somewhat younger than his age, erect in bearing. He spoke softly and courteously and with no particular distinction. He was pale, slender, of average height, and his body movements were feline and graceful.

Three months into treatment he informed me that he had regularly been receiving hormone injections during the analysis, contrary to our original agreement. At the end of six months he forced his parents to acknowledge defeat and, with his father's reluctant concurrence, withdrew from treatment.

Victor's first attempts to feminize himself, by wearing women's clothes and makeup in private, began at the age of nineteen, when a homosexual affair with a teacher ended because the teacher would not accept his feminine behavior. There was, however, unconscious interest in sex transformation before that time. He had begun to feel that his homosexual affairs were different from those of other homosexuals because he was "really a woman"; he tentatively decided to reinforce this belief by anatomical change. A "revelation" during an LSD experience confirmed to him that he was, indeed, "a female caught in a male body." He thereupon started electrolysis and hormone therapy, ingesting double the prescribed dosage whenever he could manage to obtain additional supplies.

Five months before entering analysis with me, he attempted a self-vasectomy, without anesthesia.

> I tried to cut my scrotum open. I shaved the scrotal sac with a razor blade and I started to cut the scrotum. The first cut was not painful as the blade was very sharp, but then it started to sting. I stopped. I feel I have a tumor between my legs. The tumor is my scrotum and my penis. Cutting the vas deferens would stop the sperm from forming and cause the testicles to atrophy.

He had been in psychotherapy at varying intervals since the age of fourteen due to homosexuality and severe depression, and had twice attempted suicide during late adolescence. He was expelled from college at the height of an LSD experimentation that had produced uncontrollable crying spells and "bottomless" depressions.

Victor was the youngest of three siblings, with a brother

seven years older and a sister five years older. An upper middle-class family, they enjoyed considerable financial status through the father's outstanding business talents.

Victor was born and brought up in a suburban area of a large southwestern city. By the age of four he was aware of his father's frequent and severe depressive states and recalls that his mother would leave him with the father in an effort to alleviate the latter's depression. He would get into bed with the father, cuddle him, and feel "great love" for him.

Severe oral conflicts were expressed in his rejection of solid foods, beginning at two or three and lasting until eight or nine. This symptom has recurred periodically when he was extremely anxious.

> I used to chew meat and not swallow it. I'd spit it up and put it on the plate. And I drank cans and cans of Nutriment, cold drinks, not hot drinks. I was never breast-fed. I feel somehow that I was deprived early. I would eat no solids whatsoever and I could not stand milk products. My mother would force me to swallow solid foods, chew them up, lumps of cold meat, sometimes in a restaurant. I couldn't swallow one. I have no comprehension of chewing and swallowing. That's weird. It's difficult for me to even do it now. I sometimes have to subsist on liquid foods for days or months. Now and then I get a craving to chew. Even now, however, there is a long period of abstinence from chewing. If I do eat meat now, I eat it raw.

He suffered from an intense oral fixation, which was shown by this inability to eat solid foods, a craving for liquids, and the "weird" feeling that he had almost no comprehension of the act of swallowing. He craved oral satisfaction but his fear of solid food, which symbolized the solid, impure, dangerous, destructive, poisonous maternal body, caused him to avoid it. Throughout the first three years of life he could not bear to be separated from his mother, clinging to her body.

By the age of five, his mother, who already complained about his feminine traits, would call him a "sissy" and make fun of his girlishness. Homosexual experiences with his brother began at age seven and lasted for a period of seven years. They regularly involved hugging, kissing, and anal intercourse, in which Victor played the passive role. During this period of life:

> [E]verything seemed to be in a dream. . . . I can't understand this hazy period. It lasted until I was about twelve. In the sixth grade it was quite strong. In prepuberty I kind of woke up. I was nothing up to that time. It seems to me I have never matured sexually but I did eventually. I became aware of my mind. Everything moved, however, from seven to twelve, as if I were in a dream, depersonalization. I couldn't tell a dream from reality. I can't tell whether a particular memory is true or not. It seems like I took a bath with a girl and defecated in the water, but I can't tell whether I dreamed this or whether it was real. [This was shown to represent a screen memory of castration.] By the age of thirteen, I knew there was something really different with me, that I was not like everyone else.

Throughout childhood he was "bored except for books." He felt that his sister had nothing to do with his family but he liked her best and he wanted to be just like her. "She once told me, when I was six, that I was the best girl friend she ever had." This was a displacement to the sister of a primary feminine identification with his mother.

Speaking of his parents, Victor said: "When my father is in a bad mood I simply smile at him now, although it would have upset me terribly in the past." The mother was reared in an orphanage, and the patient dwelt on this fact.

> She must have been terribly deprived. She had no sex explained to her as a child, and she has always felt that men only wanted sex from women. She told me this at an early age. She married my father at sixteen. To her, sex is not a thing to be given, just to be taken. If my father wanted sex, it was like a rape to her. "He took," my mother said, "Oh, it's really nothing, sex is really nothing, it's not a big thing at all and should not be."

He felt his father was very sadistic; his mother had once told him so.

> He slapped her around terribly. She was going to divorce him before I was born and she started to work in the hope that she

could become economically secure, but he had already impregnated her. She really hated him, and it was important to keep
her pregnant in order to keep her with him, even though their
lives were miserable. My father often told my mother that he
owed her nothing, just food and a roof over her head [the patient
murmured sadly] he told me the same thing.

Before Victor was born the mother attempted suicide by
taking sleeping pills and the father would not visit her in the
hospital. Victor feels that the father was made to take the
mother back "because the family threatened to stop talking
to him if he would not." He had been told his mother wanted
a baby girl before he was born and was afraid she might
have a boy. "She resigned herself to my being a boy and
that's all."

At age nine he revealed to his father that he and his
brother were engaging in kissing and hugging but did not
tell him the full extent of their sexual practices. "My father
said it was inconsequential. Had he said it was terrible, I
would have told him about the anal intercourse."

Fearful fantasies about the father's death began at age
eleven.

If my father dies when I'm twenty-one, I'll get money, but I'm
very afraid of his dying. One time when my father gasped over
some water I ran downstairs frightened that he was dying.
Another time when he awoke with an upset stomach, again I
was frightened that he would die. I remember playing baseball
and I let go of the bat and hit his genitals and he fell over. I
burst into tears and ran away and I never played baseball
again.

At thirteen he told his father he was homosexual. His
father said not to worry about it, that he would outgrow it.
Around that time the brother married and the patient felt
sexually jealous. A year or so later, when the brother's pregnant wife was in labor, Victor was again "seduced" into anal
intercourse by the brother, a sexual substitute for the father.

"Since I was fourteen, I have always been sexually
attracted to my father. Up to two or three years ago I'd
always have the fantasy that I was married to him. I don't

like that thought and I don't think I could live with his nonintellectual personality."

After confiding the incestuous homosexuality to his father, Victor began to flaunt his homosexuality to his brother and his enjoyment of anal intercourse. The brother panicked and turned against him. "My father hates him for seducing me, but I'm good to my brother, although I can't comprehend his being my brother. I do not hate him for these things, I don't understand why. My father made him leave the house when he found out."

In the presence of the mother the patient was always passive and yielding, except in the matter of his plans for sexual transformation. In the analytic sessions she was reviled: "My mother is two-faced, nauseating. She seems overly concerned with me, but now she's a shell, too, and she's dying. She's never satisfied with anything now, but ceaselessly strives to become socially superior with her country clubs."

At the age of thirteen, the patient developed moderately severe symptoms of duodenal ulcer and mucous colitis. Signs of the colitis began at the age of seven, simultaneously with his homosexual activities, and represented a defense against anal penetration and constituted a discharge of aggression. Colitis attacks continued to be intermittent and quite severe.

During the course of therapy the patient revealed that, at the age of seventeen, he wished to become pregnant and have a baby. He was engaged in a great deal of anal intercourse and would have sensations of fullness in the anus which persisted beyond the intercourse. "When men ejaculated into me I wanted very strongly to have a child by them." The wish to have a child is often a major unconscious theme in sexual perversion and arises from the primary feminine identification (van der Leeuw, 1958; Socarides, 1968b). Victor first attempted homosexuality to strengthen his weakened masculine identity by incorporating the male partner and his penis (A. Freud, 1949b; Socarides, 1968b, 1978a), but homosexuality was unacceptable to him. The intensity of feminine identification pushed him on to try to refute anatomy, at first by external masquerade through transvestism, but the transvestism did not suffice to resolve

his conflicts. Finally he demanded the removal of his external genitalia.

Although capable of excellent performance at work, Victor's tenuous hold on reality is illustrated by certain phenomena which occurred upon attempting to go to sleep.

> I start floating really fast, then I start sleeping, and then I can't
> open my eyes and I see faces as if I'm going to slip . . . I see these
> illusions, like my mind is not attached to my optic nerve, things
> flying past me. I see people, I see scenes. Then things move out
> of the way, and then figures around me which don't say any-
> thing in the beginning. I start to spin for I have to escape these
> faces and these figures. I think I hate them.

He had been plagued by a recurrent and horrifying fantasy for the past ten years:

> I see a man in a telephone booth with a large penis. It is
> growing and it fills up the booth and it starts spreading around
> him and he can't open the door. The man is stuck there. It's
> growing and it curves and it takes more space, like adding more
> rope. It looks like it's going to asphyxiate or kill him or strangle
> him.

The penis is a dangerous, growing object which will
asphyxiate or kill or destroy him. It represents both the
overwhelming maternal body and breast, his attempted
merging with the breast and the body of the mother, and the
threat of personal annihilation implicit in this. It is also the
father's tremendous phallus as seen by the infant which can
asphyxiate the child through penetration or oral incorporation. The telephone booth symbolizes his attempt to find
safety within the maternal body, but this enclosure into
which he puts himself through regression becomes an inescapable trap and threat to his survival. The analysis of this
fantasy revealed a crucial conflict: he dares not become a
female (merge and join with the mother), nor does he dare to
become a male (engage in homosexual activities) in which
case he will be killed by the penis itself, the father.

His desire for sexual transformation is nevertheless
necessary to defend him against paranoid fears of aggression.

I will sacrifice everything to change. If you have a vagina you can control people. You can control them sexually. The idea fascinates me. I think I'm scared of anal intercourse. I could do it with a vagina and I would not be harmed physiologically, but I already have been harmed through anal intercourse with men. I remember the first time my brother did it to me. He said he'd stay home to see that nothing happened to me afterwards. But I got a colitis attack after my first intercourse with him. My nervous rectum is due to having anal intercourse.

His primary feminine identification and his wish to replace the mother in sexual relations with the father were gratified in a substitutive way not only in homosexual relations but in the creation of a substitute father—the Plaster of Paris Man. Around the age of fourteen he would masturbate with pictures of his father in his mind. To heighten the fulfillment and satisfaction he devised a mannequin and preserved it until he was eighteen.

When I got hold of this plaster of Paris mannequin I was perfectly happy. I'd take my father's robe and put it around him. I loved my father's hands and I made a plaster of Paris cast of them and attached them to the sleeves of the bathrobe and would tie the hands around my body. It's a lost passion. I had one finger of the plaster hands lifted and I immersed it in paraffin so it would be softer and fleshlike.

I had gigantic pillows for his body and I would put this complete plaster of Paris man in bed with me. I liked to lay him beside me and have his arms around me and his hands on my penis or the lifted finger inside my anus. Sometimes I would use a sausage for this purpose while the plaster of Paris man was embracing me. One day I had hung him up in the closet and the maid opened the closet and she was terrified. I had put a hook on him and hung him on the back of the closet door.

Two dreams vividly portray his conflicts. The first represents his fear and dread of the surgery which consciously he so ardently desires:

A gigantic building, empty, built of white stucco but kind of old. There were no stairs, three levels. I was on the third floor and had two big doors open onto the third floor with no steps. I think

I'm being chased or I'm afraid, and then I remember jumping down. I was embarrassed for people to see me, only half of my legs were shaven. From my knees down, hair was present. Also on my face, it was like I hadn't shaved for six months. I was shocked when I kept getting views of my unshaven legs, of what they looked like to others. In this dream I'm also an observer. I only see what Victor sees, however. I see one half, similar to when I used to dream as Valerie. When I look into the mirror now I see Valerie's eyes, the rest is me. It's me looking at somebody else. It was like a big architect's studio. It was like the whole building was covered except for the doors. If you opened the doors there'd be nothing inside and you couldn't see anything. I think I have a fear of death because I don't think, somehow, in the end, I may live through this. Maybe it's a vagina I'm looking at. Could be because there are mahogany doors and my nipples are now like the color of those doors. There is a draping around, a kind of draping which one finds in an operation. I was thinking of the operation yesterday and I started shivering. The transsexual doctor tells me how calm people are having the operation and I remembered that and then I stopped shivering.

In this operation dream one discerns the intense anxiety over the creation of a vagina: a frightening, empty place where his penis used to be; the fear of death in surgery; the fear of psychotic disintegration upon being given an anesthetic with its alteration of consciousness and spatial relationships; the split between the unconscious image of self (e.g., only Valerie's eyes remain, and his actual male anatomical self which has disappeared). The patient is obviously terrified of the surgery which he so adamantly insists upon.

Another dream represents the patient's identification with his sister, who will die as he will die from the operation:

A party in New York, many people crowded into the place and checking their coats. I was helping him, mostly greeting the people, most of them his friends. He gave up since there were so many people. I then received a telephone call and it was from my father in Los Angeles. My brother came and gave me the message and I followed him into a quieter part of the house. He sat on the bed and told me to "take it easy" as I answered the phone. It was my father and he said the party in New York was for me—to help me accept some tragic news: my sister, Jane, is dying. She will probably linger on for a few weeks but she is definitely going. Many faces pass before me, each offering condolences. My aunt took it like saying, "Well, that's life" sort of way and I started screaming and crying and I couldn't stop. My father whispered, "I may even give you your change." I answered, "Don't promise such things at a time like this, you'll only change your mind later on." I woke up and continued crying for about fifteen minutes. I then made something to eat, something Jane had shown me years ago, and I went back to sleep.

In his unconscious he sees his father as wanting him to have the surgery and he himself harbors the wish to supplant the mother in his father's affections. The father promises that he will permit him to "change" sex so that they may have sexual intercourse. The patient is ambivalent about this and cries in desperation and despair. This dream is a projection of his own elimination of his rival, the mother, represented by the sister. The basic motivation for sexual transformation is herein revealed: in replacing the mother he is fulfilling his primary feminine identification (becoming the mother) and attaining the father's love.

Shortly after leaving treatment with me, the patient was seen by Dr. Harold Rosen of Baltimore, who conducted a hypnotic session with him as part of a psychiatric consultation to determine the advisability of transsexual surgery. Dr. Rosen knew nothing of my views at that time and had not yet received any report of the therapy from me. His independent investigation is quoted in part below.

While this patient was talking about his place of work, stating that he had already told his boss that he was going to live completely like a woman, get a job as a woman, he was hypnotized, bypassing his conscious awareness of this. Immediately upon hypnotic induction he started to breathe more deeply, started raising his left hand, and kept it partly turned with the index finger pointed toward the ceiling and then rose from the chair and started to walk toward the couch. Only by the second step did he develop *flexibilitas cerea*. Movements were so slow as to take him almost ten minutes to reach the couch. He raised his right leg in order, it seemed to me, to swing partly around and sit down or lie down but then retained the partly raised position remaining catatonic during the next fifteen to twenty minutes. He was mute. A suggestion was then given him: he could, he was told, if it did not provoke too much anxiety, tell me what he was thinking or picturing much the same way that a television newscaster discusses the pictures flashed on the television screen.

The suggestion was effective. He spoke very slowly—but he spoke. He was thinking of the operation he had had two years ago. (As he continued it turned out that he had progressed three years in the *future*.) He had taken six months to have his facial hair electrolyzed, to get a complete wardrobe, to give up his present job and get another job as a woman, to move, to take the name of Valerie instead of Victor, to black out his complete previous life, and to become established completely as a—he did not use the word *woman*—"girl." He had not let anyone know where he was living or where he was working. For an additional six months had lived completely as a woman. He then—this therefore was after a year—had had the operation here at Hopkins, and had gone back as a woman, to New York to his job hoping to meet someone who would marry him so he could become a housewife and raise an (adopted) family. Instead he was jeered at and despised, and called a "lesbian" or a "dike" just as he had been called this before he had undergone the surgery.

But worse still, his father had employed a detective, had located him, had forced himself upon him, and had begun having (heterosexual) relations with him against his will. There was no way he could stop his father. But he had struggled so much when his father's penis got into his vagina that he had damaged it—his father's organ—and made it atrophy (his phrase was *wither off*), which is what he wanted to do anyhow every time he heard that his father had been having relations with his mother three times a week throughout their marriage. But his father somehow managed to regrow a penis, a bigger one than before, and for the last year three times a week he would be having anal intercourse with this boy in just about the same way as between the ages of seven and fourteen his brother had had anal intercourse with him.

This was all apparently background material. To repeat: he had projected himself into the future three years after getting the surgery he is now requesting. What he had been thinking and planning (during the catatonic period in my office) was to kill his father. He would get some drug and sprinkle it on his food, but not quite enough to put him completely to sleep, so that when he is half-asleep or so he could still get him sexually aroused to the point of having a big erection—but because of the drug his father would be much too sleepy to have the strength to do anything about it—he would cut it off. His first thought was that of pushing it down his father's throat so that his father would choke to death with it. But what he was doing instead was to picture sewing it on himself and changing his vagina back into male organs. How long would he have to stop taking estrogen and instead be taking testosterone to be able to use it? Should he start using it on his brother and work up to his father or should he start using it on his father without practicing on his brother?

After the hypnotic trance, Rosen adds,

The patient discussed the fact that up to the present he had not been able to feel that he is either a male or a female. He is anatomically a male now taking estrogen but tells people he is a female on testosterone. Does this mean he cannot tell which way he is heading toward establishing a male or a female identity?

The hypnotic session reveals that beneath what has been referred to by others as simple neurosis, monosymptomatic delusion, encapsulated delusion, or perversion due to a "biological force" (Stoller, 1967b, 1968b), lies a full-blown paranoid schizophrenic psychosis with catatonic elements. The catatonic position while in the hypnotic trance with uplifted finger was a remarkable replication of the plaster of Paris man (his father, himself) from whom he wished to acquire love and masculinity in late adolescence. The insoluble dilemma of the transsexual: on the one hand, he wishes to be a woman replacing his mother and becoming the mother which would bring about his being raped by the father and a vengeful retaliation on his part against the father and brother; on the other hand, the wish to be a man induces great guilt as it is tantamount to castrating and murdering the father. In homosexuality there is a wish to be like the father; therefore the father's destruction is his own self-destruction. Consequently both positions—female and male— are unbearable.

His fears of aggression against him by others are clearly a projection of his own aggression. Contamination of the father's food will weaken him and make him vulnerable to castration. This is undoubtedly the origin of his food avoidances.

Behind his conscious wish to remove his penis surgically and therefore permanently, lies another wish: to change his body for a while and then change it back again. Having "withered" the penis of the father through intercourse (weakened him) he then appropriated the regrown erect and enormous paternal penis, thereby capturing his long-lost masculinity. The method by which this would be accomplished is by the sexual transformation procedure; that is, by getting rid of his own penis he entices the father to intercourse. The intercourse leads to the disarming of his father by acquiring the father's penis. He has the father in his power. In this position he has acquired the father's penis and now magically can become a man. The transsexual procedure working one way, in the unconscious of the patient, can certainly work in the opposite direction. Through the omnipotence of his thought he not only can be turned into a woman but he can be turned back into a man: not it is to be hoped the false, dead, plaster of Paris man, the father who did not love him except in effigy.

Further Contributions on the Psychopathology of Transsexualism

There has been a paucity of psychoanalytic reports available for study on this important disorder, with the exception of work by Stoller (1964, 1966, 1967a, 1968a, 1968b, 1975c), Greenson (1966), Newman and Stoller (1968), Socarides (1969a, 1970a), Werner and Lahn (1970), Weitzman, Shamoian, and Golosow (1970), Volkan (1974), Person and Ovesey (1974a,b), Volkan and Berents (1976), Limentani (1979),

Meyer (1980), and Lothstein (1983). Since the publication of this dramatic case history (Socarides, 1970a), several other reports in the psychoanalytic and psychiatric literature further document the observations of the deep psychopathology in transsexualism. [1]

Stoller and Newman (1971) report the case of a thirty-year-old transsexual, ten years postoperative, whose early childhood history was essentially that of similar cases of male transsexualism. For example, as a child he wanted to grow up to become a woman, dressed in feminine clothes as much as possible, played with dolls, always taking the female role, and avoided the company of boys. The patient lived as a woman for ten years after surgery. He said that as far back as he could remember he had wanted to be a girl, thought he would be a girl when he "grew up," and dressed and acted like a girl whenever possible in childhood.

The baby was recognized at birth to be a biologically normal male and the proper assignment was made unequivocally and accepted by the parents. Nevertheless, there was an excessive closeness between mother and infant. The father was psychologically and physically absent.

The patient was seen by Stoller for psychotherapy with complaints of boredom and anxiety ten years after reassignment. Although "she" had long since succeeded in passing as a woman, this did not resolve the problems of the "routine miseries" of her life, a life that was dull and not "glamorous." After the genitalia were removed and an artificial vagina constructed, she reported great pleasure and orgasm in intercourse with men. It seemed possible that this later boredom during sexual relations was:

> [P]artly the result of an inhibition due to her feeling that she had somehow retained a part of her body, a part of her old male self, and that this part was almost physically resisting the ... limitless sense of penetration and relaxation that she would otherwise be able to reach during intercourse [p. 23].

---

[1] Successful resolution of the transsexual wish to be a person of the opposite sex in male children aged four-and-a-half and five has been reported by Loeb and Shane (1982) and McDevitt (1985) respectively.

Newman and Stoller concluded that "awareness of having
once been and of still being a male, despite sex reassignment
surgery, interfered with the transsexual's complete integration as a woman." The patient could not lose the knowledge
that she had once been a male. This sense of maleness was
embedded within her, interfering with her total acceptance
of herself as a female, even with hormones, surgery, passing as
a woman, transformation is not successful, because awareness of having been and at a deeper level of still being a male
cannot be extirpated.

In 1970 Weitzman, Shamoian, and Golosow had the
opportunity to carefully study an adult male-to-female transsexual. Their case material was derived from the study of a
patient during a four-month hospitalization and observation and an eighteen-month follow-up. In this instance, the
patient entered the hospital because of the postoperative
development of a rectovaginal fistula.

The patient was a thirty-three-year-old male who had a
history of homosexual episodes in midadolescence and of
"bisexuality" in his early twenties, in which he progressively assumed the feminine role. The patient's parents'
marriage was a bitter one, filled with chronic violent arguments. The mother had hoped for a girl. There was a constant and excessive physical contact between the mother
and child which the patient described as "a monkey clinging
to its mother." The father usually did not interfere with this
"close relationship" but on occasions would become enraged
at the mother's permissiveness.

The mother, an "embittered woman," sabotaged all of the
patient's efforts at separation from her and thereby completely frustrated a developing sense of masculinity. He
became an effeminized boy, perpetuating early forms of
identification with his mother, and was unable to effect the
normal identification with his father.

In the midteens the patient engaged in mutual masturbation with another boy but ceased this activity after a year's
time due to fear of being labeled a homosexual. In his
twenties the patient consulted an "authority" in the field of
transsexual surgery, and was started on hormone therapy.
Psychiatric treatment was briefly suggested but summarily

refused. Six months later, a sex-reassignment operation was performed, consisting of penectomy, castration, creation of an artificial vaginal pouch, and mammoplasty. There was much ambivalence before having the operation; however, postoperatively, a rectovaginal fistula developed which required four operations, the last a colostomy.

The patient's feelings about the operation were mixed. Although at times she became enraged at the surgeons and resented her status as a "castrated male," she still would not have wanted to return to her former state.

> I resented the continuous pressure of sex, I had too many erections in one day. . . . My penis got the better of me, I wanted a freedom from it . . . I really wanted to be a neuter . . . I used to whip myself, to achieve, to prove success to my parents . . . but I failed as a man. Now I am a woman . . . I copped out. I can relax now. . . . Now that my penis is gone, my drive is gone, I really don't want to do anything, just sit on the beach and draw in the sand [p. 297].

The patient was discharged after four months and was seen as an outpatient on several occasions by one of the authors. She did not seek a job for several months but managed to "charm" several institutions and individuals into providing for her. Since then she has worked and maintained a moderate social life, although she has become increasingly grandiose as regards her "beauty" and artistic abilities. She has had sexual intercourse with men on a number of occasions, claims she has a "feminine type" of orgasm, but feels she is neither masculine nor feminine, but simply "neuter."

Weitzman et al. conclude that the earliest developmental periods of the patient were basically flawed. Excessive mother–child physical contact produced a symbiotic phase that was too strong, too long, and crippling. The crucial factor in the transsexual condition in this patient was a "regressive diffusion of the patient's always fragile gender identity into these primitive 'as if' parts and fusions of self and object modes of infantile identification" (p. 301). A further factor was related to the patient's aggression which was always marked but generally contained by massive denial. "In the ego fragmentation, this overwhelming aggression is released . . . the operative procedure . . . fulfills the fantasy of partial destruction of both the hated self and the hated internalized object" (p. 302).

Levey (1973–1974) reported a study of a presurgical case of male transsexualism in which the desire to effect sexual transformation was equated with the killing of the self and rebirth through the magic of endocrinological techniques and surgical procedures.

Psychotic psychopathology in transsexual patients has been reported in recent psychoanalytic literature. For example, MacVicar (1978) lucidly described the function of a borderline schizophrenic patient's transsexual wish: (1) it helped him to deal with his feeling of helplessness and panic, especially when his parents were away. Wearing women's underclothing allowed him to be away from them without deep anxiety. When his defenses were functioning effectively, so that he was kept in intrapsychic balance, wishes for sex change were diminished; (2) desires to become a woman:

> [W]ere another method of stabilizing the patient's relationship with the needed object, a method to which he resorted if he felt in extreme danger of losing the object . . . a function much like a delusion, helping the patient reintegrate from the initial panic of a psychosis. The feelings of disintegration, which occurred after a threatened or actual loss of the mother, were considerably abated by the transsexual wish [pp. 360–361].

In a published discussion of MacVicar's paper (Socarides, 1978b), I commented that the perverse actions of schizophrenics with self-object dedifferentiations show significant difference from those of others who have better object relations and ego functions. In schizotranssexualism, the psychotic has lost his internal object representations and strives to create new objects. There is a lack of adequate separation of self and object. The schizophrenic process itself has apparently undone repression, destroyed object relations, and laid bare the pregenital phases and primitive ego states. The patient attempts to make relationships to external objects through transsexualism, defending himself against imminent destruction and incorporation by the mother by becoming her.

Her patient attempted to "form" a perversion, alternately and ambivalently succeeding for varying periods of time. His perversion was only partially realized, but it contained elements which all perversions have in common; that is, a compromise between the simultaneous identification with the phallic and penisless mother; a wish to obtain an optimal distance from and closeness to the mother without fear of self dissolution and engulfment; faulty development of object representation, and lack of adequate separation of self and object.

The well-structured perversion of transsexualism (i.e., its preoedipal form), emerges out of a severe form of "feminine" homosexuality or transvestism. Transitory solutions of conflict via homosexuality or transvestism, which we very frequently hear of in the history of these patients, have not been able to maintain the mental equilibrium. Finally, large quantities of primary and secondary aggression cannot be neutralized except through the transsexual defense (Volkan, 1974, 1979) and the transsexual wish becomes increasingly imperative. In the preoedipal type of transsexualism (type I), the fixation is located in the later stages of the separation-individuation phase, in all probability in the rapprochement subphase. In schizotranssexualism, the fixation lies in the symbiotic period. From the foregoing it is readily apparent that along with Mahler (1975a), I do not believe that there is a form of "true" or "primary transsexualism" arising as a consequence of an "excessively blissful mother–infant symbiosis" (Stoller, 1975a, p. 237), the result of a process similar to imprinting and nonconflictual in nature.

In this connection, Mahler concludes:

> From my own rather limited experience, it is difficult for me to believe that transsexuality ever takes place in the baby's earliest stages without severe trauma or conflict, and particularly without some *contribution* in that direction being made by the baby's constitutional predisposition. It is essentially characteristic of every average or normal boy or

girl that what Dr. Stoller calls "excessively blissful mother–infant symbiosis" does not exist after the fifth month. This is because, purely maturationally, it is automatically dissipated during the developmental process by the ego's inner resources; that is to say, symbiosis does not continue to be blissful for the infant beyond the fourth or fifth month— whether or not the mother or the father wants it to remain so! . . . The mechanisms by which to achieve what Greenson (1968) has so felicitously called "disidentification from the mother" are operative, sometimes even against formidable environmental odds [1975a, pp. 245–246].

Dr. MacVicar correctly notes that surgery should not be attempted in patients with a psychotic core. Sad to relate, however, many patients of this type demand and receive surgery, as the underlying schizophrenic process may not be readily discernible, or be overlooked. The tendency to disregard such covert psychopathology is aided and abetted by the erroneous view that transsexualism involves no psychopathology and by the patients' tailoring their life histories to conform with published reports (both in the lay and professional publications) of life histories of apparently "normal" transsexuals.

In a case reported by Childs (1977), a twenty-three-year-old male-to-female transsexual developed an acute psychotic reaction three days after surgery. The history of his transsexualism was a typical one: early denial of the penis, separation anxiety regarding the mother, an apparent symbiotic relationship to her, and a feeling of being "imprisoned in a male body with a female mind." This patient had been approved for operation by a Medical Center committee two years before surgery was performed. While he had a history of periodic depressions, he was diagnosed as "nonpsychotic." Three days postoperatively, he developed hallucinations and wish-fulfilling delusions, severe panic, and most prominently an overwhelming, insistent need for continuous contact with anyone in his vicinity. He was "constantly touching and attempting to cling to everyone in the ward, stating that touching and being held was the only way 'she' could feel secure" (p. 41). She clutched whomever was present and did not break contact with anyone. She was actively delusional, believed people were tuning in on her thoughts, were talking about her. Her symptoms represented a delusional omnipotent symbiotic fusion with the need-satisfying object. In an "objectless state" she could not tolerate the loss of anyone. Ultimately she constructed a bridge between the nonobject and herself through finding a narcissistic self representation in another patient, by beautifying her through applying cosmetics and bodily care. Gradually a sense of reality began to make its return against a massive confusion, despair, panic, and overt psychotic symptomatology.

Applying psychoanalytic theory and clinical observation to these events, I believe, sheds considerable light on the meaning of the patient's psychotic reactions to surgery. The transsexual surgery had produced a totally fused identification with the mother, a further loss of whatever poorly defined and chaotic object relationships this patient had before surgery. Following it, he was unable to create new objects except through the use of a transitional one: another patient.

This striking event constitutes the well-known schizophrenic delusion of *transitivism*, in which there is a loss of ego boundaries. It represents a regression of ego development toward the undifferentiated phase in which there is no dear distinction between one's own body and that of the object, and no clear separation of ego functions belonging to the self or to the object (Bak, 1971). The panic that ensues is due to a sense that the unity, uniqueness, and separateness of the self has become lost. The patient experiences the terrifying conviction that his thoughts are known to everyone, that he may be thinking the thoughts of others, that the emotions of all the world are going through him, that he has been robbed of skills that he once possessed, or that they have been exchanged with others, and that his gestures may belong to someone else. The loss of object representations and their relation to objects takes place, therefore, on a symbiotic level of self–non-self undifferentiation.

Lothstein (1983) had the good fortune to conduct intensive long-term psychotherapy with fifty-three transsexual female patients over an eight-year period in a gender-disphoria clinic. His findings constituted a remarkable validation of my own psychoanalytic findings. He concluded: (1) there is a common pattern to female transsexual pathology; (2) the female transsexual is born into a family riddled with gender pathology; (3) the parents obstruct femininity in their daughter throughout childhood and adolescence and especially in the preoedipal period, disrupting the development of the little girl's femininity (separate from that of the mother) so that a separate and cohesive female self does not develop; (4) the mother during the rapprochement phase is unable to link empathically with the daughter and "offer" her a sense of femaleness. These factors, according to Lothstein, produce profound developmental arrest, gender-identity pathology, abandonment depression, and impaired ego functioning and primitive and pathological defense systems with splitting into "good–bad" self-images.

Finally, I wish to emphasize that the clinical and theoretical concepts that explain the perversions in general apply as well to transsexualism; namely, that the mechanism for the relief of unconscious conflict in perversions exists at any level of libidinal fixation and ego development, from the most primitive to the more highly developed levels of organization. Their underlying unconscious motivational drives are distinctly different, depending on the level from which they arise. Thus, a specific form of a particular perversion may have its origin in oedipal sources, preoedipal fixations, or schizophrenic processes. The same phenomenology has different structures in different transsexual individuals. Therefore, we may classify transsexualism as oedipal transsexualism, preoedipal transsexualism, and schizotranssexualism (the coexistence of transsexualism and schizophrenia). Dr. MacVicar's clinical example falls into the last category. Many schizotranssexuals, upon superficial examination, do not appear to have an active and/or covert psychotic process, as they may not present the secondary symptoms of schizophrenia (e.g., delusions, hallucinations, ideas of reference, etc.). It is often only after surgery that psychotic symptoms appear in a florid manner. In all likelihood, the *well-structured transsexual's symptom* is of preoedipal origin and does not arise from a schizophrenic process. From a study of over 500 patients requesting transsexual surgery at Johns Hopkins Hospital, Meyer (1980) arrived at a similar conclusion: "The syndrome of transsexualism is determined preoedipally" (p. 407). In this paper he presented an extremely valuable and succinct discussion of nonconflictual versus conflict/defense theories as to causation, expressed his belief in the latter and opined that the various forms of transsexualism suggest a "connected series" of clinical states. This "connected series" is also explainable in terms of my classification system (e.g., schizotranssexualism, preoedipal transsexualism, type I and type II). It is my belief that "oedipal transsexualism" is not a true form of the condition but is simply "transsexual behavior."

Concluding Remarks

Mechanistic, behavior-oriented social engineering approaches to sexual health, together with changes in the broader culture and environment, and in some instances an unfriendliness to the individual approach of psychoanalysis, have led many sex researchers to embrace surgery as a curative technique for transsexualism. From the foregoing, however, it is readily apparent that transsexualism is a psychological condition of serious import and consequence for both patient and physician. The tendency to engage in radical and mutilative surgery for its alleviation can only be approached with the greatest caution, if at all. While much remains to be learned about transsexualism, its etiology, and the psychic mechanisms responsible for its development, and while the study of "failed transsexual experiments" is illuminating, surgery appears to carry too great a risk to the patient's health and future well-being.

Chapter 15
TRANSVESTITISM:
THE CASE OF ALFRED

Introduction

The sexually significant wearing of clothes of the opposite sex was first called transvestitism by Magnus Hirschfeld (1910) and was later renamed "cross-dressing" by Havelock Ellis (1936). It is a sexual perversion almost exclusively practiced by men. Transvestitism arises from the basic preoedipal nuclear conflict from which all sexual perverts suffer secondary to a failure to traverse the separation–individuation phases, with a resultant disturbance in gender-defined self identity. Transvestitism reassures against and lessens castration fears, and keeps in repression deeper anxieties of merging and fusion with the mother and fears of engulfment by her. The aim is to attain and maintain an *optimal* distance and/or closeness to the mother by identifying with her. In these cases, there is a yearning for femininity, an envy of mothers and sisters, a wish to be powerful like the mother (in keeping with a continuation of the primary feminine identification), a desire to have babies, and, most of all, to appear externally as a woman through the wearing of feminine apparel while retaining the penis.

In male transvestitism, the sexual object choice may be a person of the same or opposite sex. Occasionally there is apparently no sexual object, but the sexual aim is of the greatest importance; namely, a blissful identification and reunion with the mother without orgastic desire for a person of either sex. Such an individual may become resentful if another male mistakes his cross-dressing as an invitation and makes sexual advances to him.

In extreme cases, a transvestite may, after dressing himself elaborately in female clothing complete to the last item of mimicry, for example, perfume, jewelry, wig, makeup, and producing a perfect illusion of femininity, will finish a tragic bout of playacting by committing suicide. Allen (1969) has reported cases in which such men dressed as women were found in confined places (e.g., garbage cans) and died of suffocation. The position of the body was such, according to Allen, that it could only have been achieved by voluntary effort and planning. The patient had merged with the mother in the state of complete perfection and blissful reunion with the phallic woman.

Transvestitism can take several forms: from those who simply dress in female clothes to those who actively engage in overt homosexuality while dressed as a female to those who engage in heterosexual relations wearing feminine apparel. A repeated observation is that some individuals before puberty pass through a brief transitory phase of transvestism before developing a well-structured homosexual or fetishistic perversion.

Beneath heterosexual transvestite sexual relations lies unconscious homosexual desire. Homosexuality is greatly feared and deplored and responded to with severe anxiety. It is well known that some homosexuals forego feminine clothing, and some long for it. This depends on the degree of identification with and "psychosomatic molding" to the mother (Socarides, 1968b). Pleasure in narcissistic self-display is easily seen as a conspicuous feature in homosexual transvestites with a severe feminine identification; for example, "the wearing of elaborate silk underwear, frills and laces, silk stockings, cosmetics . . . all give scope to a narcissistic element which is forbidden to the male (Allen, 1969, p. 246).

Some transvestites do not seek sexual satisfaction with either male or female. Instead, there is definite excitement in the wearing of female clothes, a feeling of bliss, happiness, wholeness, a freedom from anxiety, and an elimination of depression.

Transvestitism may take three forms: heterosexual, homosexual, and solitary transvestitism. It is never a manifestation of heterosexuality, even if the patient engages in sexual relations with an opposite-sex partner. He always suffers from a primary feminine identification with the mother. When faced with threats and dangers, castration, loss of self representation, fears of engulfment, fragmentation, and separation anxiety, he presses into service the use of feminine clothing in order to reinforce and buttress a failing self representation, a feminine one. In milder preoedipal type I or oedipal transvestitism, heterosexual intercourse may be attempted successfully on certain occasions when the individual is in a state of narcissistic compensation and there are few threats to his self-esteem and self cohesion. The ego deficits and disturbances in gender-defined self identity of the transvestite must first be buttressed or reinforced through the wearing of clothes of the opposite sex before sexual relations with either the opposite sex or the same sex can be achieved. This ensures orgastic release and preserves the integrity of his self representation, that of the phallic mother.

In addition to the basic preoedipal anxieties, the transvestite, similar to all perverts, is endeavoring to control anxiety by denying castration, and insofar as he succeeds in maintaining this illusion, there is no such thing as the lack of a penis. For, as Fenichel (1930c) succinctly states, "The homosexual has no regard for any human being who lacks the penis, the fetishist denies that such beings exist, while the exhibitionist, the scoptophiliac, and the transvestite try incessantly to refute the fact" (p. 180).

Major Psychoanalytic Contributions

A high point in the psychoanalytic literature on transvestitism was reached in 1953 with the English publication of Fenichel's 1930 paper, "The Psychology of Transvestitism" (1930c). In this paper, an extension and elaboration of an earlier paper in German (1930a), Fenichel dealt extensively with the symptomatology and meaning of transvestism as well as fetishism. Fenichel concluded:

1. What the transvestite has in common with the fetishist is the overestimation of the importance of feminine clothes and the female body, while he shares with the passive homosexual the feminine psychic attitude. The crucial point of difference lies in his specific sexual wish to assume the dress of the opposite sex.

2. The transvestite has been unable to give up the belief in the phallic nature of women, and, in addition, has identified himself with a woman with a penis. The crucial difference in transvestitism is that while other perverts identify with the mother and with the phallic woman, the transvestite *wears* her clothing.

3. In the act of transvestitism, both object love and identification are present.

4. The act has a twofold consequence: (a) object–erotic (fetishistic), and (b) narcissistic (homosexual). Instead of coitus with the mother or a substitute, Fenichel noted, the patient enters into *fetishistic relations* with female clothes, which he brings into as close contact as he can with his own person, and particularly with his genital organs. Fenichel considered the sexual relationship between the transvestite and his partner as typically "sadistic" (1930c). Fenichel noted that the penis has a twofold representation: (a) in his own genitals actually present under the woman's clothing, and (b) in the garment which is a symbolic substitute for the penis. He commented that female fetishists are extremely rare, and that female transvestites seem to be simply women who covet the penis out of a desire to possess it. Having identified themselves with men, they eschew their feminine identity.

Fenichel (1945) noted that the difference between male and female transvestitism was that the man "while playing a woman, actually has the possibility of demonstrating to himself that the penis is not lost by the game, whereas the girl is not in a position to reassure herself in the same manner; she can only pretend" (p. 345). He concluded that transvestitism in women is a displacement of the envy of the penis to an envy of masculine appearance. "Male transvestitism has a more serious character; female transvestism has a 'pretending' character" (p. 345).

Rarely does one have the opportunity to study cases of transvestism in *statu nascendi* or from direct observational studies. Eleven years after the publication in 1953 of Fenichel's 1930 paper (1930c), Sperling published her "Analysis of a Boy with Transvestite Tendencies: A Contribution to the Genesis and Dynamics of Transvestitism" (1964). Her treatment of a prelatency boy provided valuable information as to the circumstances under which transvestite behavior develops. Her contact with the child was first through the mother who had come into analysis with her for depression when the child was six months old. Consequently, the development of transvestite behavior could be followed from its very beginning. The child was less than five years of age when he began analysis with Sperling, and his rich dream and fantasy material was obtained with unusual freshness and clarity, together with a follow-up into the adolescent period. An outstanding feature of the analysis was the discovery that the mother needed to view herself and her child as being of both sexes. Sperling concluded that the equation of penis and breast, and the emphasis on the breasts, were special modes of dealing with castration anxiety, holding up promise of gain rather than danger of loss by the young patient. The identification with the phallic mother proved to be a basic mechanism in transvestite behavior. The preoedipal father was seen as a man with breasts. The fantasy of being a girl (his transvestite behavior) occurred because of the child's reaction to the trauma of the primal scene, in Sperling's opinion. By the time the boy terminated analysis at the age of nine, he had completely given up his transvestite behavior and not only acted but felt like a "real boy." In my own formal discussion of Sperling's paper at the American Psychoanalytic Association (Socarides, 1961, unpublished), I noted the theoretical advances of Sperling's conclusions, and suggested that, whereas the first symptom of cross-dressing began when the patient was three years of age, shortly after an aunt had given birth to a baby girl and was staying with the baby at the patient's home for several weeks, antecedants to this condition seem to have existed at two years of age, and perhaps even at age one-and-a-half. Sperling had mentioned in her case presentation another case of transvestism (Friend, Schiddel, Klein, and Dunaif, 1954), which actually began at one-and-a-half years of age. It was my feeling that the condition arose from a fixation derived from preoedipal-phase conflict rather than a regression to it due to oedipal conflict and castration fear. The oedipal problem and castration fear were probably only a secondary line of defense against deeper fears. Conflicts from both periods coexisted and in all probability were genetically interrelated. I suggested that the patient suffered from a *lifelong* primary female identification with his mother (sister). Out of this female identification the transvestite behavior began in the preoedipal period and emerged fully formed in the oedipal period. Sperling correctly noted her patient suffered from the knowledge that girl babies do not have a penis but that this was not the origin of his disorder. She then related her conceptualization of the genesis of his condition, citing the following: envy of the mother; a fear that he might be replaced by the baby; envy of girls' and womens' breasts; envy of the vagina; envy of all mother's and sister's possessions (the patient stole from his mother and sister but not from his father); a need to "have everything, want to be everyone, want to be the baby, and want to have babies" (Socarides, 1961). I felt that the most important of these envies from which the others derived was the envy of the mother's ability to have a child. A number of investigators, notably Brunswick (1929), Lampl-de Groot (1946), Jacobson (1950), Kestenberg (1956a), and van der Leeuw (1958), directly observing children in the prephallic period, confirmed the existence of this desire in boys as well as girls. Childbearing was conceived as an achievement in power and competition with the mother, and represents being active like her (see chapter 12, for an illustration of how the same conflict may lead to fetishism). One of the most important tasks of the preoedipal phase in the male is to resolve this wish without a consequent disturbance in ego development. Sperling's patient was reassured by dressing in the mother's clothes that he too was female. The wearing

of the sister's nightgown and slapping himself on the buttocks represented a violent conception of childbirth. The
transvestite wishes to keep his primary identification with
the phallic mother and what he fears is separation from her.

Chareton and Galef (1965) reported the development of
transvestism in a three-year-old child who was treated for
two years by one of the authors. The concomitant analysis of
both mother and child illustrated the crucial importance of
the mother's influence on the development of transvestitism.
The observation that transvestite behavior began before the
age of three proved the importance of preoedipal factors,
although castration anxiety of the oedipal phase was intensified by the mother's seductiveness, fluctuating attitudes of
laxity and severity, and a tendency to dominate and belittle.
Greenacre (1968) stresses the role of such belittlement and
lack of respect for the father in the home environment of
those who later become perverts. Some of the features of this
young boy's personality were: a persistent identification
with the mother, an effeminate manner, ingratiating ways,
teasing behavior, seductiveness mixed with "bossiness,"
and authoritarian attitudes. The child was also concerned
with the loss of love, and had an inordinate demand for
candies, gifts, and favors—a preoccupation with oral supplies which, if not fulfilled, led to anger and depression.
There were fantasies of incorporation, concern about mouth
and teeth, unconscious fears that he might be orally engulfed by the mother. The role of the father was blurred and
vacillating. His passive and withdrawn behavior frustrated
the mother's need for him, and caused her to turn increasingly to the child for satisfaction. She therefore kept him
close and did not allow him to undergo successful separation–
individuation. The father was unable to provide an adequate
masculine figure to allow for the promotion of masculine
identity and disidentification from the mother, in my opinion. The transvestitism represented defenses at two levels,
according to the authors: (1) an attempt to retain the frightening, powerful, and subtly rejecting mother by identifying
with her, and (2) a wish for the mother to gratify his unfulfilled oral needs, all the while avoiding the risk of incorporation by her. At the end of therapy there was an intense

regression in the face of separation from the analyst. In my opinion this led to a hallucinatory experience in which the patient fantasied a small person within himself, a projection of both being within the mother (undoing separation) and delivering a child himself. In this case, both oedipal and preoedipal factors were highly discernible in the genesis of transvestitism but the genesis of the perversion lay in the preoedipal phase.

From the study of a wide range of clinical types of male transvestitism, Rubinstein (1964) provided a phenomenological classification of this perversion. His rich clinical material appears to me to fall into four major types, with some overlapping.

Type 1

This type of patient is often a highly intelligent man in his thirties who changes into female clothes as soon as he comes home from work, and usually wears female underwear. In the evening, he frequently goes out alone dressed as a woman, wearing a wig and rather heavy makeup. He denies any intention to attract men through his attire, and is surprised that he attracts any attention. His feminine masquerade is somewhat grotesque, however, and may invite laughter, scorn, and humiliation. He denies any interest in homosexual activities or fantasies past or present. When accosted and kissed by a man who believes he really is a woman, he is shaken by his unexpected pleasure. In my opinion, his latent homosexuality remains completely unconscious. Such patients, Rubinstein finds, have desired to be women all their lives. Transvestitism starts at an early age, perhaps eight or earlier. In many of these histories there are early surgical traumas provoking castration anxiety. Transsexual wishes may appear at puberty. These patients often deny that they possess their own male genitals and suppress masturbation during adolescence. They experience severe distress if they are unable to secure and wear female garments for any length of time. The wearing of female clothes, which brings a sense of pleasure and relief from tension, is the only form of sexual outlet. Many of these individuals maintain a militant antihomosexual stance. They have been lucidly described by Ovesey and Person (1976). (In my opinion, this activity, which is mistakenly not considered "sexual" in itself by the patient, is interspersed with nocturnal emissions, same-sex contact in dreams, rare but occasional masturbation, and a rare homosexual contact as a result of an "accidental" seduction by another man.) Such dressing has often been encouraged by parents, according to Rubinstein. Very often, frustrations at school are handled by dressing as a girl as soon as the person returns home. Such individuals only begin to masturbate if the transvestite practices are seriously interfered with (e.g., in army service), and are restricted to times when there is an inability to change into female clothes. Often there are no transvestite-type fantasies, but simply purely automatic relief of tension is supplied through the wearing of female undergarments, without erection or orgasm in some cases. Rubinstein conjectures that this type is due to the patient's wish to identify himself with the mother and be an "innocent young girl or sexless child" (p. 181) who can enjoy the love of both parents "without conflict, anxiety, or guilt" (p. 181).

Type 2

Rubinstein's type 2 consists of transvestites who openly proclaim they are female, flaunt their cross-dressing, and pronounce that their female mind is trapped in a male body or vice versa. They openly adopt feminine mannerisms, speak in a high voice, but are caricatures of femininity. They are characterized by a total conscious acceptance of femininity, proclaim that ever since they can remember they wanted to be girls, were attracted by female garments, and/or enjoyed putting on their sister's clothes or mother's undergarments. The mother or sister has often aided and abetted their transvestitism since early childhood and the little boy grew to eschew everything masculine. In some cases, homosexual inclinations can be found, including homosexual acts for a brief period of time. According to Rubinstein, patients of this type may paradoxically experience their entire body as a phallus when dressed as a woman; for example, the female clothing surrounding the whole body represents the vagina, and through "the symbolic equation 'girl = phallus' (Fenichel, 1930c) . . . like the extreme fetishists who confine themselves to sexual acts with an inanimate fetish, the *pure* transvestite also escapes anxiety and guilt over sadistic impulses directed against a living love object" (Rubinstein, 1964, p. 182).

Type 3

This is an individual whose history reveals he has been fully potent in heterosexual intercourse with prostitutes or casual partners. He may marry, but then have to resort to fetishistic and transvestite buttressing for full enjoyment. Beneath his masculine attire he is compelled to wear female underwear. During intercourse with a woman he is penetrated anally with a dildo or some other object while remaining half-dressed as a woman. The need for such acts occurs typically when there is a sudden drop in self-esteem producing threats to self-cohesion (see the case of Alfred in this chapter). Since his earliest years, masturbation has been practiced while in partial female dress with a pretense of being a girl. Many of these patients may have intermittent periods in which they can function heterosexually without the use of women's clothing. The history of the transvestite described by Fenichel (1930a) contains the same sequence.

Although these patients engage in an active transvestite heterosexual intercourse, they do not consciously or wholly wish to be women. They may have feminine daydreams of being dressed as a girl and dancing as a movie star, and so on, but they are anxious to exert an aggressive maculinity in actuality, a defense against a passive wish to be loved like an infant. They often involve themselves in physical and verbal fights, and have explosive stammering as a symptom on some occasions. They fear a loss of control over sadistic impulses during intercourse (Rubinstein, 1964).

Type 4

The fourth type may be considered a "normal type" (Rubinstein, 1964, p. 184) in that they have all the "appearance of normality" until their confidence in masculinity is shaken by some disturbance in their relationship with a heterosexual partner (e.g., infidelity). They often respond with narcissistic withdrawal or with paranoid reactions. With resumed interest in the outside world, they turn to a "feminine kind of exhibitionism in adopting colorful clothing that stood in complete contrast to previous quasi-military bearing" (p. 184). They often have become involved with phallic castrating women, but they are disappointed with their partners and withdraw from heterosexual relations, regressing to masturbation fantasies while wearing women's clothes. In these fantasies they dream of seducing a powerful man. Occasional homosexual relations while dressed in women's clothes are reacted to with disgust after the act. Their transvestite behavior is a defensive position against largely unacceptable homosexual desires.

In their early history there has often been a "pubertal transvestitism" (p. 185). The child may be making himself:

> [I]ndependent of the as yet inaccessible sexual partner by a half-conscious, half-unconscious double act, in which he can pretend to be a boy as well as a girl, alternatively or simultaneously. His masturbation whilst wearing underwear, dresses, or raincoats belonging in the first place to his mother or sisters, ... which represent a fetishistic substitute for an incestuous relation [pp. 185–186].

In Rubinstein's opinion this form of fetishism and transvestitism may be "outgrown," but "it is very difficult to arrive at a reliable prediction" (p. 186).

Rubinstein's contribution informs us of the variegated clinical pictures and forms of this disorder, and Jucovy (1979) has presented an excellent review of several of the various forms of transvestism, their dynamic structure, and preoedipal origins. What is necessary, however, is to view these types in terms of (1) the level of developmental arrest or fixation of the patients themselves; (2) the status of object relations and the pathology of the internalized object relations; (3) the degree of self–object differentiation; and (4) the type of conflict which exists in each form.

Male Transvestitism: Clinical Studies

Heterosexual Transvestitism: The Case of Alfred

Alfred, a thirty-nine-year-old, highly successful professional man, had practiced a transvestite perversion since the age of thirteen when he first began to wear women's clothes. Although able to perform sexually on some occasions without the use of women's underclothes, he usually found them an absolute necessity for achieving orgasm. Whenever he was unable to secure women's clothing for sexual relations he experienced anxiety, depression, and feelings of emptiness. He wore the underclothing especially when angry, upset, or feeling "picked on" by associates or superiors, when he was lonely or bored, and on occasions inserted "feminine articles" such as diaphragms and vaginal douche syringes into his anus in order to reduce severe states of tension. This patient is referred to in two previous chapters. In chapter 7 I utilize his case history to show how the pervert dramatizes the repeatedly unsuccessful attempt by the ego, both in the past and in the present, to achieve mastery of libidinal and aggressive impulses and of their archaically cathected objects. Such an ego, when faced with the task of object cathexis, and in the absence of suitable substitute objects and satisfactions, and in the context of threats of further impoverishment, resorts to manifest dream formation of perverse content. In chapter 6 I describe how his developmentally arrested ego sought out perverse activities in an erotized flight from feelings of helplessness, deadness, grief, and depression. Through acting out of perverse fantasy an intrapsychic crisis is averted; passivity, guilt, and anxiety are reversed by an erotized flight to reality and toward an external object with the denial of the sensation of a depression, heaviness and sadness by specifically opposite sensations.

Alfred sought revenge and restitution for the suffering he experienced during his early years: a tonsillectomy at age two; frequent enemas administered by a "kooky," chronically depressed mother who never touched him except when she bottle-fed him (he was told); a weak, passive, and compliant father who abdicated his responsibility as a father in protecting him from his mother; feelings of personal physical ugliness ("big lips, short stature, too much hair"). He seldom was handled by his mother, forced to eat, given enemas, and screamed continuously in the first three years of life. Too-early toilet training was instituted that caused him to cry in despair. He suffered from a "negative affective predisposition" (Mahler, 1966b) as far back as he could remember. "She never hugged or held me." Alfred further suffered from tantrums which made him unmanageable in his mother's eyes, and at four he was sent away to a home for "difficult boys" for six months. This remained a terrifyingly upsetting incident throughout his life. His cries were filled with loneliness and rage. He could not bear to be separated from his mother at any time up to the age of ten, could not go to school, and cried when "mother wouldn't listen to me."

Despite these early difficulties, my patient achieved a high position in the academic world and became a prominent leader in his chosen profession. Despite his enviable achievements, Alfred suffered from severe narcissistic vulnerability with overwhelming feelings of inferiority. While he gave people the impression of being a successful, powerful, and well-functioning individual, inwardly he experienced himself as having a "ratlike complex, wandering around like a rat in a maze, not knowing what to do next, agitated, bewildered, unhappy, frightened, closed-in, unable to get out." Simultaneously, he felt he was able to "ensnare people," give them the illusion that he was a successful and powerful man. This "deception" put him in greater danger because everyone would make demands on him, that he make the "perfect speech," the perfect suggestion, and so on. He considered himself "defective," incapable of making up his mind, a chronic "exaggerator." "I'll say four instead of three, like three is nothing, insignificant, and four is more reality. The lie is more reality to me than three." Such exaggeration was a defense against depression.

In danger of his deficiencies being revealed, Alfred would feel that he was "nothing." "I'm hopeless, I'm hopeless about life. Everything is performance. Get through college, give a talk, give a speech, perform well. There is nobody to love me, and I'll always be unhappy." Whenever he spoke of his IQ, which he felt was extremely low but couldn't possibly be so, he sensed that he would be rejected by the analyst. This feeling of inadequacy permeated his work, and he felt ugly. "Like I had to take the flute up in order to be popular, but the flute then ruined my lips and made me look ugly. I once had a lot of hair on the top of my head and it looked ugly. There was too much of it. But now I am becoming bald." He spent much of his time attempting to attract women with whom he would then have sexual intercourse. He felt he had a right to demand love from women because he was so deprived as a child, and women had no right to retaliate when he did not provide them with security and loyalty.

Along with his feeling of inferiority and feelings of being found out, he feared that others would punish him for his failure. They would discover not only his physical ugliness, but they would find out that he was "empty" and unable to produce anything of value. "I have to conquer everyone or else they might hurt me. I especially fear being in a controversial position and I don't want to be. I'm afraid of what others might think of me. They might think I'm wrong or crazy."

When he was lonely, his need for women became almost insatiable. "I need to have someone almost every night." And his pain was eased when he fantasied how a woman might make love to him, whether she would lie on top of him. He would be curious as to what she would do that would be "different" in order to find a new form of "intimacy." He fantasied about how a woman would take a douche, and would like to watch her doing it and share in the intimacy of the act.

Several fantasies produced overwhelming excitement. A major fantasy was that of finding a fountain syringe which he could place over his genitals. "I remember last year I found a suction pump, a long tube, which I put over my penis. I felt I wanted to see if I could get an erection by filling myself up with the fountain syringe through my anus." The syringe was placed in his genitals and experienced as if it were inserted into his fantasied female genitals. He would place a pair of pantyhose over his head and leave his hands free so that he could rub his body with one hand and the female clothes with the other. A bra placed on his thighs would "ease the hunger" in him and fill him up. Being filled up had its counterpart in being "sucked dry." The wish to be filled up and the dread of being empty (devoid of oral supplies and nurturance) were exemplified in a disturbing childhood fantasy continuing into adulthood of having tubes inserted into his arms, legs, and breasts, and material sucked out from him. In later life he fantasied this being done to women. In such fantasies he was both the woman who is producing the milk or fluid which is nurturing him, and the one who is sucked dry, passively enduring this entire experience in order to achieve restoration. In the fountain syringe fantasy the smell of the nozzle:

> [E]xcites me, a feminine smell, like something has been in a woman and now it's close to me. It's identical with my penis . . . now I'm thinking of rubbing it against my penis, the lower side of my penis, and I get excited. The smell, it's like a male thing devoid of its maleness—it's feminized, stripped of its maleness. Thinking it's male but in my fantasies it's female, like the tube that puts jelly into a female, birth-control purposes. I think my problem is I miss my girl friend. I was looking for these things in her bag last night.

The fountain syringe is a substitute for the penis and provides phallic reinforcement (in the sense of a fetish) in the context of partial merger with the mother.

Alfred could not tolerate the idea that he might have homosexual wishes. This produced terror as well as feelings of being empty. Convinced that he had nothing to give anyone, he despaired of the future. On the couch and in dreams he experienced the sensation of "dropping down into a bottomless canyon" which represented fears of engulfment and fragmentation of his self representation. As he experienced these emotions, he had an intense hunger for women's clothes which temporarily restored himself and helped him to recover body-ego boundaries. Subsequent to a session in which this material emerged, he dreamed of having a mascara box in his hand, a small round box which he thought might be a diaphragm box. "I think I put it into my mouth and bit it. I think I shall use it in the future to make myself up with." Fear of fragmentation and loss of self cohesion sought resolution through partial identification with the mother in the use of feminine articles.

In the midphases of the analysis his use of the word *manly* made him "choke up" and become almost hysterical on the couch. In recalling the victory that he had had at a meeting on a previous day, he didn't dare appear too triumphant. "I feel *manly* about putting my fingers in a vagina, then in turn my penis. I want to love a woman. I don't want to wear women's clothes anymore. I want to be a man. I'm very upset now. Why am I so emotional about this? I am sad that I am not a *man*."

Frequent feelings of deprivation and emptiness are exemplified in the following dream, punctuated by déjà-vu feelings.

> Two people are driving, me and somebody else, through a New England town like my own hometown. But it was like bombed out. I say that when they get their new windows up this will be an attractive town. I now have a déjà-vu feeling. The other person in the car says this must be a good place to be. I don't know how I could have stayed and eaten. I feel sad and lonely now.

His associations led to early memories of depersonalization when he looked out the window of the "home" where he was sent as a child, waiting for his mother who only visited after long intervals. The bombing-out reflected his rage, aggression, his fear of loss of the mother, his deprivation, his sense of emptiness. Frustrated in his early incorporative needs ("I am unable to eat") he remained empty, unfulfilled, a state which could only be relieved through incorporation and merger with the mother. Alfred resented performing any acts which would significantly enhance others but not himself. For example, on a trip to City Hall to pick up a marriage license for a friend he felt very upset, inferior, and "paranoid." These feelings stemmed from the conviction that others might criticize him for being incompetent and consider him to be an "idiot."

On "bad" weekends he would have to wear women's clothes frequently. Such a weekend was occasioned by his girl friend being "mad" at him for his disclosing to a friend that he had an affair with her. In the ensuing feelings of being rejected, Alfred put on women's clothing and masturbated while using a powerful vibrator in his anus. He compulsively had to buy four pairs of women's underpants, pajamas, a brassiere, and a garter belt. He "almost panicked" at the thought that a woman would demand immediate payment of a loan she had made to him (fear of being sucked dry).

Alfred suffered from intermittent bouts of boredom. Analysis of his chronic boredom revealed its close connection with his sense of emptiness and his attitude of passive expectation that the external world should supply him with satisfaction. It was an affective state of longing, an inability to express exactly what was longed for, and a concomitant distortion in the sense of time. "The transvestitism has to do with boredom," he explained. "The clothing is also a way of passing time, of getting over boredom. The buying is an end in itself, and the wearing is another end. Sometimes they are the same end. They reduce my feeling of inertia."

He felt that people would disappear from his life and/or not like him. In this connection, he dreamed of people who were shaped and baked in clay so that they would not leave him and could not be destroyed.

Until they are baked and hardened they are dangerous. They are like the Golem. Maybe when they are dead they are no longer dangerous. I have to conquer everyone or else they might hurt me. I am controversial in my position and I don't want to be. I'm afraid of what others think of me and they might think I'm wrong or crazy. I don't want women dead, although I did feel this way once about a woman.

Faced with threats to his self cohesion, he dreamed of driving with his ex-wife along a country road, going to a hotel.

She's driving and I ask her to pull into a temporary parking

space over some boards, and now I have a déjà-vu feeling. I ask
her to stop, but she continues backing up and the car falls into a
crevasse. I've gotten out just by partially opening the door. The
car is horizontal twenty feet below the parking spot. I'm very
upset.

The patient's associations were of falling "into the woman"
during sexual intercourse, of being engulfed, losing himself,
falling a long distance and being unable to right himself. He
often thought of himself as an "empty dirigible" that might
fall upside down without anyone controlling it and that he
would become "lost in space" (loss of ego boundaries, sense
of personal dissolution). Further associations were of emptiness and a need to be recognized. "No one will pay attention
to me or know me." Such dreams were frequently followed by
fantasies of the fountain syringe and its use with a woman in
sexual intercourse. His associations, filled with pain and
suffering, were as follows:

How really empty I am, the rottenness of me. When my mother
called today I couldn't care less what she thought. I couldn't get
love from my mother or father, and I feel a terrible emptiness. I
always have déjà-vu feelings when I experience these fears,
looking at women, waiting at the institution for mother to come
back. Hungry, waiting for mother, being in a nothing state.
Screaming, trying to get there. Mother put me in the hospital,
angry. I don't want to get angry at the crib. Thinking of X. and
the silence, the silence of other women. It's all in relation to
feelings of early loneliness and I feel so sad.

Such feelings were punctuated with sadistic thoughts toward
women:

There is such a euphoria, a happiness when a woman came to
see me the other day, but the old dream of being attached to one
gives me a shuddery feeling. It's scary and wonderful when it's
happening to me. But I have a sadistic smile on my face when I
have a lot of women around. Maybe the sadistic smile is
against you. I have all the women and perhaps you do not. Is it
possible that I have all this stuff that you don't have? Why the
sadistic part? Maybe it's toward me, too. Maybe it's the knowledge that I need this in order to pass the time. It is a source of

great discomfort, that I need all these women to pass the time. It is something I am both proud and afraid of.

Manifest dreams of perverse practices helped to shore up a threatened and imperilled self representation secondary to severe feelings of depression and loss of self (Socarides, 1980b). He explained:

> I feel lost in space, the way I feel before I have to put on some female clothes. I feel like an empty dirigible. What touches me is the falling. Some sort of exalted feeling that I have sustained artificially, but now I am empty. [The becoming empty or the] fear of becoming empty, also the falling, is the key to my problem. What happens if I fall being upside down, loss of control, not being in control, lost in space? You never hit the bottom without relatedness, that is, if you have relatedness.

Alfred complained of guilt, "a deep guilt, almost my total being" both as a consequence of his sadistic feelings toward his parents for childhood deprivation and toward all women, and guilt associated with attempts at separation and self-object differentiation so typical of those who have not successfully traversed separation–individuation phases (Dorpat, 1976; Socarides, 1978a; Modell, 1965). "Maybe I have to feel guilty in order to feel real. I was sent away to the hospital because my mother couldn't handle me. I was an unmanageable child, perhaps a bad one. I think I was simply an object, or used as one. My mother said she only held me when she gave me a bottle. She was always sleepy."

He suffered from a sense of transience (Freud, 1916) due to his incapacity to successfully mourn and renounce lost love objects because he had never experienced fulfillment from them due to his poor object relations with them. Object relations were from object to self (mother). "Something is going to spoil everything, that I would do something to foul it up. Whatever I do is going to end." What he wants is "mother's love," a sense of self identity. He then dreamed of having tubes stuck in his body again, which while disgusting and upsetting, was sexually arousing. Sexual arousal then led to masturbation with the use of women's clothes, and a sense of temporary restoration of self cohesion and elimination of his empty depression.

Transvestite acts took place only with women or in solitude. Beneath his desire for women were lesser unconscious wishes to reinforce masculine identity through homosexuality, wishes which were feared and repudiated. Homosexual wishes were unacceptable to the ego because of a variety of fears associated with them; for example, narcissistic humiliation, fears of attack by more powerful men, and an inability to accept a partial female identity vis-à-vis a male sexual partner. His object relations were from object to self, his feminine self, the mother, rather than a person representing a lost masculinity which he yearned for. The transformation of homosexual desire into the more acceptable female object choice is succinctly illustrated in the following brief dream:

> I come into the [male] doctor's office and I say to the doctor, "Maybe you can examine me so that I don't need my crutches." [He had recently broken his leg.] Then I'm being examined by a woman doctor in several stages. She has a finger in my anus. "I came to examine your sphincter tone," she says. I'm shocked. I feel it's sort of preposterous, more surprised, but it's also highly sexual.

The resolution of anxiety arising from fears of merging and partial acceptance of female identity in heterosexual transvestitism can only be met by dressing as a woman in a heterosexual context. In homosexual transvestites, dressing as a female with penetration by a male tends to stabilize pathological, internalized object relations, all the while consolidating masculine gender-defined self identity through incorporation of the male partner's masculinity and penis and simultaneously preserving the tie with the mother. One may conclude that the gender of the sexual object choice in male transvestitism is dependent in large measure on the degree of both the unconscious and conscious acceptance of the continuation of the primary feminine identification (see chapter 3). In homosexual transvestitism such acceptance is more intense and complete.

In summary, transvestitism was employed by my patient when faced with fears of engulfment (fears of merging and anxieties related to threatened loss of self cohesion, separation and fragmentation anxieties) with the preoedipal mother due to a lack of sufficient self–object differentiation in the preoedipal phase with a concomitant inability to successfully traverse the separation-individuation phase, especially the practicing and rapprochement subphases. The patient suffered from a disturbance in gender-defined self identity. Early traumatic experiences, including a lack of appropriate empathy from either parent, led to a continuation of the primary feminine identification with the mother and a defect in his genital schematization (Roiphe and Galenson, 1981). Faced with threats of loss of the object and loss of the object's love, and his own inability to successfully cathect a love object, he was prone to separation anxiety and threats of ego dissolution and engulfment. His *déjà-vu* experiences represented a perceptual experience of returning to the mother through a hypercathexis of the primal love object. Threatened with imminent danger of merger with the object, a totally fused identification with the mother, and its implicit threat of further loss of object relations, the patient constructed a bridge back to a sense of reality through cross-dressing, thereby experiencing maternal closeness in identification with the mother without the dangers of complete merging. In the perversion he experienced in a transitory fashion the illusion of possessing both male and female genitalia, felt "filled up" (in contrast to emptied) through fantasy and masturbatory practices with pumps, syringes, and diaphragms, thereby nullifying his lifelong sense of emptiness. The acute sensations of wearing women's clothes and inhaling their smell promoted a partial merger with the mother, undoing loss, pain, humiliation, feelings of helplessness and hopelessness, and produced a temporary feeling of being alive and existing as a cohesive self. The contrast of being empty, alone, unloved, and the sense of providing mothering for himself dramatized his ability to overcome feelings of being destroyed, lost in space, dissolved, and nonexistent. Furthermore, the experience of orgasm at the height of such cross-dressing restored a sense of conviction of having a real, bounded, and cohesive self (Eissler, 1958b; Lichtenstein, 1977; Socarides, 1978b; Stolorow and Lachmann, 1980).

Homosexual Transvestite: The Case of Larry

Larry, a twenty-five-year-old homosexual transvestite, began to wear his mother's clothes at age eight. He was significantly different from Alfred in that he had openly expressed and consciously desired homosexual relations. He had made an early identification with a highly idealized female member of his family, an aunt, a much sought-after and wealthy movie star whose beauty, glamorous life, and romances filled the tabloids of the American press during his adolescent years. Brought up in this atmosphere of the entire family's adulation for the aunt, his fantasies consisted of imagining he was the aunt in various dress, apparel, and romantic situations with her leading men. I shall not recount here Larry's history or early development except to simply state that he had a profound disturbance in his gender-defined self identity with a resultant deficient sense of masculinity, and experienced severe separation anxiety in relation to his mother. There was early and severe damage to healthy self-esteem. Being brought up in an atmosphere of narcissistic pursuits promoted a search for ideal feminine beauty within himself.

Lone transvestitism continued into boarding school, but these perverse fantasies soon led to actual sexual relations with men without wearing women's clothes. This was in contrast to the fantasy of being a woman, being appreciated, admired, touched, and masturbated by young men, which no longer satisfied him. On occasion he would resort to the fantasy of his aunt and her heterosexual lovemaking in which he played her part, all the while dressed in fantasy or in reality in her clothes. Larry's homosexual practices had become overt, and shortly after beginning a long-term homosexual relationship the transvestite behavior was rarely utilized in fantasy in the context of homosexual relations in order to heighten arousal and reinforce sexual excitement.

Homosexual Transvestite: The Case of Norman

Norman,[1] a pleasant young man in his early twenties, neatly

---

[1] I am indebted to Drs. P. Loeffler and R. Shaw, formerly of the Albert Einstein College of Medicine, Department of Psychiatry, for permission to publish this case history.

and conservatively dressed, candid in manner, walked with long strides and sat with legs outstretched in typical masculine fashion. He was bright, and spoke slowly and articulately. He began treatment at the psychiatric outpatient department because of a desire to be a woman, a desire that he had held as far back as he could remember, as well as because of the recent breakup of his marriage. He wanted to "act feminine," live his life in accordance with his "true feelings and desires." These feelings had fluctuated in intensity, and when they were most severe he felt he really was a "woman forced to live in a man's body." At those times he wished to undergo transsexual surgery and actually "become" a woman. When this urge possessed him, he felt depressed, "just as a woman who is forced to dress like a man, support a family, and suppress her natural sexual desires would feel, constantly frustrated in the ability to get surgery." He loathed everything masculine during these periods, and was preoccupied by thoughts of wanting to be loved by a man as a woman. Simultaneously, however, he felt transsexual surgery might prove to be a "permanent and terrible mistake." When desires for sexual transformation were less intense, he wished to be cured of his feelings of wanting to be a woman and dressing as a woman, but was frightened that his desires would return and overwhelm him.

For three years before his marriage he felt relatively free of problems and believed he could become engaged. Six months after his marriage he began to feel increasingly troubled. When his wife discovered mascara on his eyelashes he broke down and told her of his problem. He then consulted a transsexual surgery "expert" who told him he could be helped by the surgery.

After the separation from his wife, he lived in his own apartment and was able to "go home" in privacy, dressed in women's clothes. He stated, "I like the feeling of constriction in feminine clothes"; that is, bulky rings, bracelets, chokers, narrow long sleeves, narrow pants, and so on. However, he soon tired of these, but they remained a "thrilling change of pace" which he found satisfying when he looked at himself in the mirror wearing these garments. At these times he became sexually excited and would often masturbate while he fantasied himself having intercourse as a woman with a man. His compulsion to act out this masturbation fantasy lessened considerably with his coming into treatment. The tension that he felt while married had disappeared, but he was becoming increasingly dissatisfied with masturbation and began to feel that he needed a regular "sexual relation with a man."

Norman was the middle of three sons in a chronically disturbed, arguing family in which the father assumed a weaker role than the mother. The father was violent, hostile, abusive, and cruel to Norman, often beating him with a stick. He remembered thinking at about five years of age that women were "the lucky ones," the ones who "got all the breaks and had everything desirable." At age six he stole a female cousin's bracelet and desperately wanted to touch a schoolgirl's dress. At this time he became unpopular with boys who began to call him "sissy." Mother often forced him to do the housework when he was tired, scrubbing floors, doing dishes, and other "feminine tasks." She said to him once, "If I had three daughters I'd have help. So why shouldn't you help me?" When his mother complained of "exhaustion," he pitched in and did the work for her. His mother often dressed him in female clothing, saying this was a way to save money. In kindergarten, when he came home, instead of taking a nap he would try on his mother's jewelry. Somehow he knew that she wouldn't mind. Between ten and twelve he would get up early on weekends in order to try on his mother's dresses. A recurrent fantasy was that he was a small baby or child and his parents would force him into wearing women's clothes so by the time he reached his teens he would grow up "naturally" into becoming a girl, that is, be "initiated" into becoming a female (Jucovy, 1979).

His mother frequently walked around nude from the waist up in his early and late childhood. "It was sloppy but I wasn't aroused by it." In the early years of grammar school he stuttered and stammered, "but often only in my head." He was often made to kiss and make up with his mother even though he was enraged at her, the mother insisting upon this practice.

At the age of twelve, when his brothers left home, he was moved into a room where there was an extra closet full of old clothes belonging to his mother. He would get up early in the morning, try them on, get erections, but did not masturbate as he was a "good Catholic." He became notably unpopular in school and was called a "happy homo" by his classmates because of his apparent femininity.

The father was described as a failure, "a Willy Loman, without a sense of humor," who often lost his temper, would shout and give orders, and belittle people, including Norman. The father took insignificant jobs, often working at night, and was rarely seen by the patient. A favorite mode of punishment was to hit the patient on the buttocks with a hairbrush. When he was discovered cross-dressing by the father, he left home at the age of twenty-one. He described his mother as a "base woman interested in herself, who was unable to take an interest in other people."

After graduating from high school, the patient attended college for one year. This year was made "terrible" as he was continually plagued by the thought of becoming a woman, was unable to study, and failed. Following this, he attended college at night, but transvestite thoughts were so intense that they interfered with both work and efforts to study. An excessive "respect" for authority led him to give in to anybody older than himself. Norman then masturbated for the first time at age twenty-one as he seemed for the first time to acknowledge that he had a penis.

He married a woman six years older than he who made a deep impression upon him by giving him a surprise birthday party at a place where they both worked. He had never been the recipient of such an act of kindness before. When he told his wife of his transvestitism she became extremely critical, authoritarian, and abusive, and sexual relations, which were never satisfactory, became worse. She wanted sex more frequently than he did, and he was only able to reach a climax during intercourse with the fantasy of being a woman and/or wearing women's clothes. Fantasy alone, however, often failed to produce ejaculation. With the end of his marriage, he initiated a homosexual contact in a bar, his first and only such homosexual experience up to the time of entering therapy. Fellatio was performed on him, but he was unable to have an orgasm, he believed, because he did not wear women's clothes. His fantasies during therapy were those of being completely dominated sexually as a woman by a man and forced to perform fellatio on him. In this fantasy he is dressed as a woman and becomes excited, but he later becomes depressed because being a woman means that he is "masochistic" and is responding solely to a man's "whims and pleasures." Another fantasy is that a man is performing fellatio on him. The most exciting part of this fantasy is the idea that he has found a man, someone he can trust (the good father), who will allow him to perform fellatio upon him while he is *dressed as a woman.* During therapy he was actively engaged in attempting to find a homosexual partner who would meet his needs. What he feared the most was not so much his desires, but the ridicule he would suffer if it was found out that he was a transvestite. While he desired to be a woman he was ashamed of this desire since he regarded women as occupying a second-class position, "weaker and less intelligent."

Applying a psychoanalytic classification, this patient would be classified as a preoedipal type I homosexual transvestite who had to dress as a woman while having sexual relations with a man to achieve orgastic pleasure. He was unable to traverse separation–individuation phases and remained in primary feminine identification with the mother. The mother's reinforcing of his feminine identity and the abdication of the father promoted his conviction of being a woman. Environmental factors (e.g., encouragement of cross-dressing by the mother, being mother's helper in household chores, and so on), appeared to have played an important role in leading him to transvestitism rather than homosexuality, and may well have constituted organizing experiences in the direction of the former. Transvestite masturbation made him feel secure, at one with the mother, protected from the father, loved and preferred over all the siblings. The presence of a harsh father for whom the mother had no respect made it impossible for him to make a counteridentification with the father in order to assume normal masculine, gender-defined self identity. He wished to find men as a substitute for the father in order to secure their love, men that he could trust, in whom he could place confidence, and in so doing, be the passive recipient of their benevolence. He needed to consciously maintain the idea of the female phallus, represented by the seminude mother covered by clothing below the waist but with exposed breasts. This latter symbolized the penis of the female, displaced upward.

Female Transvestitism

The function of female transvestitism is to achieve "masculinity" through cross-dressing. As in the male, it reassures against and lessens castration fear. The psychosexual motivation is both orgastic desire and a yearning for masculinity. In wearing masculine apparel, the female experiences a heightening of pleasure in vicarious masculine identification while in possession of an imaginary phallus. The sexual object choice or aim is a person of the same sex. Occasionally no sexual object is sought, and the sexual aim is to achieve a feeling of power in masculine identification.

As described earlier (chapters 2 and 3), the boy must disidentify with the mother, make a counteridentification with the father in order to achieve his appropriate gender-defined self identity. The female does not have such a double task, but must find her own unique identity separate from the harmful, depriving, destructive, and hated feminine figure of her mother. In female homosexuality she may find this in a resonance form of identification (de Saussure, 1929) with a homosexual partner, finding her lost femininity in the body of the same sex. She is thereby attempting to find an acceptable female gender-defined self identity. In female transvestitism she seeks the same goals with the proviso that she recast herself as a male. Female transvestitism is a rare condition, since a preliminary requirement for its existence is the strong belief, rarely semidelusional or delusional in quality, that she actually possess a penis with which she can approach women. This playacting cannot be sustained very long against the reality of the absence of the penis and the inability to penetrate with the illusory phallus, especially when sexual relations are actually attempted.

Developmentally, in female transvestitism the little girl persists in a conviction that she herself is a boy and later on a man, and may even "hallucinate" an imaginary penis. A typical history is of a young girl who vehemently wishes to be a boy, prefers to cut her hair short, wears masculine clothing from early or midchildhood. She prefers tomboy games that continue well into adolescence and from puberty on wishes to have love affairs with girls her own age, taking only the active role. She desires her partners to be very feminine, and stimulates them manually. Because of the denial of her femininity and the wish for a penis, she adamantly rejects attempts to touch her genitals or of their even being seen by other girls. She may develop tender feelings for her partner, and becomes depressed if the partner is attracted to boys (Rubinstein, 1964, p. 186).

Dynamically, she wishes to find the lost father, to identify with him in order to acquire love from the good mother, and be loved in turn. The young girl she loves may represent a child, and she may often assume the role of the active, preoedipal mother. Rejection at the hands of another woman may lead to episodes of kleptomania, the money or the article becoming a symbol of the contents of the mother's body and/or the penis.

Identification with the male (father and/or brother) may be so intense that the patient may insist on transsexual surgery. In such instances there is contempt for women beneath an apparent "love" for them. While these patients view themselves as men, seek homosexual relations with women, they often find power and strength, pleasure and relaxation, relief of anxiety and depression through simply dressing as a man. Some of these "male lesbians" (Rubinstein, 1964, p. 191) wish that they did not have breasts at all, but long to be given the breast by another woman.

Clinical Studies

Reports of case histories of female transvestites are extremely rare. Gutheil (1930) and Stoller (1982) have reported a total of three such patients. In all three cases I conclude that a strong masculine identification has been superimposed upon an unacceptable primary feminine identification in an attempt to eradicate the identification with the depriving mother. This "masculinity" is augmented by masculine clothing and other masculine paraphernalia. Gutheil's patient was a middle-European woman who said that simply putting on men's clothing gave her pleasure and on occasion just putting on a suit would initiate an orgasm. Her first orgasm occurred when she wore her brother's suit when she was approximately fifteen years old. Upon looking at herself in the mirror and discovering that she remarkably resembled her father, she became sexually excited and had her first orgasm. She found it unpleasant to walk in public in female clothing and in her fantasy life she saw herself as the father of a family caring for a wife and children. She could only masturbate successfully by not touching the genitals directly. She would lie on her abdomen and move her pelvis against the bedclothes as if she were a male having relations with a female. Depressions would be alleviated by taking off her dress and wearing men's clothes. Beginning at thirteen or fourteen, she actively began to engage in homosexual relations, preferring mutual cunnilingus.

Stoller (1982) has reported two case studies of female transvestitism. The first, known to him only through a lengthy correspondence, was a woman who would frequently wear a fake mustache and don male clothes. The cross-dressing experience was described as "short of orgastic" (p. 103). She felt excited in walking down the street in men's clothes and she experienced sexual pleasure in exhibiting herself as a male. The practice itself was satisfactory (solitary female transvestitism). At other times she would either have sexual relations with a man (heterosexual female transvestitism) or with a woman (homosexual female transvestitism). "Dressed as a man, I've sucked my partner's penis. I felt myself, during the experience, to be a 'gay male'" (p. 103).

Stoller's second case was that of a thrice-divorced American woman in her forties (Stoller, 1975b). This patient for a brief time "hallucinated" that she possessed a penis. When she put on blue denim Levis, she felt "much more than just masculine." She would feel an intense excitement, impossible to repress:

[S]trengthened, assertive, confident, totally unafraid. The sexual excitement I feel when wearing Levis is a more pronounced, stronger, and much more pleasant sensation that what is available at other times. When the Levis touch my skin I become intensely sensitive and I hold them very tight. It's like nothing else in my sensuality, or other sexual contacts. I don't mean that I have sexual intercourse with my Levis. I just become very aroused by them, and it goes beyond arousal when I choose—that still isn't exactly right—when I put my feet into them it's as if someone were caressing my skin; as I pull them over my ankles, legs, and thighs, they do caress my skin. I feel a surge of something like strength or power along with sexual desire. When I put on the Levis, I strut; I feel I can take what I want sexually. When putting on the Levis I feel very excited immediately. I feel the texture, the roughness of the material, as I pull them over my feet, over the calves of my legs, into my thighs, and somewhere inside as well as in my clitoris. It's a marvelous sensation but becomes close to painful if I'm unable to relieve the sexual tension. My sexual fantasies, when wearing the Levis, always involve a female [Stoller, 1982, pp. 105-106].

Chapter 16

PSYCHOANALYSIS OF A MASOCHISTIC (SPANKING) PERVERSION: THE CASE OF DR. X.

Introduction

In 1919, in "A Child Is Being Beaten," Freud enlarged upon the part played by sexuality in normal and pathological mental life introduced in the "Three Essays on the Theory of Sexuality" (1905b), choosing as his subject beating fantasies and actual beating practices. He noted that such practices are commonly found in obsessional neurotics, hysterics, in those "who would not have been classified at all by coarse clinical diagnosis" (p. 182), and conjectured that they are prevalent in the childhood and adult life of "many who do not come to analysis for manifest illness" (p. 179). Beating fantasies may be utilized in a variety of ways: during masturbation, as an accompaniment to heterosexual/homosexual intercourse, practiced for a short period in life, or for a lifetime. They may be replaced by reaction formation, undergo repression, or be transformed by sublimation (pp. 181–182). When they persist into maturity and are obligatory for sexual satisfaction, they may be considered a sexual perversion. As perversions, such fantasies and acts change in relation to the author of the fantasy, the object, its content, and its significance (Freud, 1919, p. 181). His "contribution to the origin of sexual perversion" (the subtitle of his 1919 paper) was admittedly a tentative and provisional one. As an explanation, he proposed that a "prematurely developed component of the sexual instinct" fastened upon an event which "offered an occasion for fixation." This event was "accidental" and often "commonplace and unexciting" to other people. He was unable to delineate why this event offered a particular occasion for fixation or the reason for the "premature development" of the patient's instinct. While he alluded to possible preoedipal features, he remained with the explanation that this perversion occurs secondary to oedipal conflict, castration, fear, and bisexuality, and bore a relationship to Adler's theory of masculine protest, although he did not define this connection (pp. 200–204).

Freud's *clinical* conclusions derived from the study of six cases, four female and two male, were less tentative: "*in both cases (male and female) the beating fantasy has its origin in an incestuous attachment to the father*" (1919, p. 198). In boys there is an inverted attitude in which the father is taken as the object of love due to a negative oedipal position. The boy changes the figure and sex of the person beating him by putting his mother in the place of the father, but retains his own figure, with the result that the person beating and the person being beaten are of opposite sexes. Essentially similar clinical conclusions were derived from psychoanalytic studies by Eidelberg (1954), Kris (1956), Rubinfine (1965), Kris Study Group (1957), Loewenstein (1957), Hunt (1973), and Ferber (1975).

In formulating his *theoretical* views as to etiology, Freud cautioned: "The present state of our knowledge would allow us to make our way so far and no further towards the comprehension of beating fantasies. . . . There remains an uneasy suspicion that this is not the final solution to the problem" (1919, p. 183). [1] Several analyst–authors during the

---

[1] In fact, Freud predicted that:
    [A]nalytic work deserves to be recognized . . . only when it has succeeded in removing the amnesia which conceals from the adult his knowledge of his childhood from its beginning (that is, from

next half-century confirmed Freud's clinical findings[2] and described additional clinical phenomena that appeared to have their origin in a period antedating the oedipal phase, namely, the preoedipal phase of development. In this connection, Bergler (1938) noted that oral sadism in boys plays a major role in the development of beating fantasies. The aggression in boys was first of all directed against the threat of the preoedipal mother, and then secondarily, under the pressure of guilt feelings, toward the self. He concluded that the buttocks could be equated with the female breasts, and the beatings represented a necessary narcissistic attempt at restoration. Interest was then transferred subsequently in the oedipal phase from the mother to the father. Eidelberg (1954) was the first to emphasize that "narcissistic mortification" was avoided through the perversion, the subject denying through his perverse acts that he was helpless, could not control his actions or emotions and the external object. The beating fantasy was an attempt to deny the feeling of being alone, abandoned, and unable to control others, and was, in his opinion, due to a preoedipal disturbance. Niederland (1958a) made a unique contribution when he detected that the auditory phenomena associated with spanking received by one of his patients constituted a primary auditory experience; that is, an experience that was once threatening to the child's ego, deriving from the earliest years of life. The patient was afraid of his father's voice, and

---

about the second to the fifth year). . . . Anyone who neglects childhood analysis is bound to fall into the most disastrous errors. . . . It is in the years of childhood between the ages of two and four or five that the congenital libidinal factors are first awakened by actual experiences and become attached to certain complexes. The beating-fantasies which are now under discussion show themselves only towards the end of this period or after its termination. So it may quite well be that they have an earlier history, that they go through a process of development, that they represent an end-product and not an initial manifestation [1919, pp. 183–184].

[2] Briefly returning to this problem in "The Economic Problem of Masochism" (1924a), Freud suggested that the wish to be beaten (spanked) also signified the desire not only to be castrated and copulated with, but to give birth to a baby. These feminine sexual wishes toward the father Freud continued to see, however, as relating to the oedipal phase of development and not to a preoedipal fixation causative of the perversion itself.

the crude, violent sounds in his spanking or beating were less a threat (a substitute, in a sense) than the actual threats to the infant, but were now experienced as body blows of a much lesser nature. The function of the spanking perversion was to ward off the destructive influence of such experiences by actively creating them in a symbolic way. These noises could also be organized as primal scene beatings. Ferber (1975), while emphasizing the importance of Freud's contribution (i.e., the passive sexual attitude, the negative Oedipus complex), strongly suggested a possible preoedipal origin as the most important factor in this perversion. He concluded that "the relation of the preoedipal mother [was] of equal significance, and desires for fusion in some form or other, and a sado-masochistic attachment to the mother [was] conspicuous" (p. 221). Ruffler's (1956) unique and detailed report of the psychoanalysis of an overt spanking perversion, its therapy and alleviation, described over three decades ago the preoedipal nature of this condition. He was unable, however, to present a schematized theoretical explanation for his findings, ascribing its causation to "secret guilt" secondary to an inhibition of "stepping out of the feminine sphere" and a "pregenital fixation on the mother" (p. 228). He observed that the patient *entered* the oedipal stage while in a "tense dependence on a maternal world." This dependence was strengthened by "the fact that the father failed to a large extent to stand for a positive formative figure; the female element was predominant in the patient's environment" (p. 228). Ruffler had made, in effect, clear-cut and accurate distinctions decades in advance of a theoretical understanding of the phenomena described and the theoretical concepts which would explain them; for example, concepts of primary feminine identification, separation–individuation phases (Mahler, 1967; Mahler, Pine, and Bergman, 1975), the pathology of internalized object relations, self–object differentiation, object relations class of conflict, disidentification with the mother and counteridentification with the father, pathological narcissism, and so on.

Clinical Study

This case material, only the second detailed description of the analysis of a spanking perversion in the psychoanalytic literature, illustrates what the writer feels were the central conflicts that had to be uncovered and understood by both patient and analyst for the ultimate removal of his perverse symptomatology. Predictably, varied and profound clinical and theoretical questions emerged in the preparation of this case study which could not be pursued in detail because they were not immediately relevant to spanking perversions; for example, the occurrence of rapprochement crises during the course of the therapy documenting the separation anxiety experienced in relation to his mother (and other women); the role of sublimation in perversion and character formation; the presence of oedipal conflicts superimposed on more basic preoedipal conflicts; the role of aggression, and so on.

My patient, Dr. X., was a fifty-five-year-old academician who had suffered from a beating (spanking) fantasy since the age of five or six, and an overt spanking perversion from the age of thirty-three. During the past decade there had been an intensification of his need to carry out his perverse acts, especially with a prostitute upon whom he had become increasingly dependent, even to the point where he felt he might be "falling in love" with her and might have to leave his family. One year earlier, depressed and masochistic, filled with shame and remorse, he had nearly confessed this liaison to his wife and left his family.

He introduced his wife into spanking him shortly before their marriage, and although she gratified his wishes on numerous occasions over the years, she had become bored and disinterested and recently reacted to her participation with considerable anger and even disgust. This element of their sexual life was always kept secret, practiced only when their two adolescent daughters were out of the house, because of the noise produced by the spanking. The female apparel required for its performance had to be kept hidden in a secret cupboard in their bedroom.

In addition to spanking, Dr. X. had engaged in a mild form of transvestitism[3] throughout his entire adult life, wearing the undergarments of women: underpants and

---

[3]The transvestite elements in this patient will only be briefly alluded to, as they did not occupy a central position in his sexual life, except when they were part and parcel of the spanking perversion.

occasional brassieres. These promoted a sense of solace, comfort, mild sexual arousal, and pleasure without the desire for orgastic release. On some occasions he masturbated wearing these clothes, with fantasies of being spanked or beaten on the buttocks, while rubbing his penis against the bedclothes.

The emergence of his overt well-structured perversion began approximately twenty-two years before, following the sudden death of a beloved sister one year older than he in an automobile accident, and the birth of two children approximately two and four years after his marriage. At the time of his entering therapy, spanking was the sole means of producing orgastic release. In both fantasy and act he dressed in young girls' clothes, or female lingerie whose bottom could be lifted or let down, thereby exposing his buttocks for a beating. He became Linda, a girl "who never wore a bra, was never younger than fifteen years of age, and was about to get married." His sexual partner was a "Lady Gainsborough-type woman," an aristocrat, a member of the upper social classes, a "snob," the mother to whom Linda said bad or naughty words such as curse words. When Linda continued to say "naughty things," a spanking was then administered before a mirror so that the patient could view the slipper or hairbrush with which he was being spanked, his female clothing up to his abdomen, and his buttocks, which became increasingly warm, red, and ultimately painful. (On rare occasions he fantasied being the spanker.) As he lay over the lap of his partner during the spanking, he did not attempt to touch his penis, nor did he wish to do so as he approached and reached orgasm. If the ejaculation was "complete," he felt considerable relief of anxiety, tension, or depression, emotions that he experienced preliminary to the act.

He suffered from a fear of rejection or rebuff from colleagues or friends, a fear of being disapproved of or being pushed aside despite his considerable popularity among colleagues and students. Contemplating retirement in the foreseeable future made him "wonder" if he could "go on" without the warmth and friendly exchange with favored male students. This concern represented, as revealed in the analysis, a threatened loss of a sublimatory activity, designed

to keep in repression and simultaneously gratify unconscious homosexual wishes.

He was the youngest of three children, a brother two-and-
a-half years older was "more handsome, taller, and acceptable," and a loving, warm sister older by one year. He
believed that his father preferred his brother and looked
down on him for his lack of interest in sports, and for his
"gentility." His father often sardonically quipped, "I have
two boys, and one of them is a girl." He felt closely tied to his
mother, and in his early years up to the age of six, could not
tolerate her absence from the house. By puberty, his feelings
had changed. She was a "dumpy, complaining woman"
whom he never wanted to "see naked, as her body repelled
me." She never made his father happy, as he could have
done. He was both attached to and ashamed of her. He
idolized his sister, with whom he often played, confided in,
and went to for comfort and "love" whenever he felt
unhappy, despised, ugly, small, or ineffective. He recalls
that by five years of age "I was a very pathetic and depressed
child. I could crawl into a hole in the ground, and I was afraid
of the dark." "I was born too short, penis too short, and I
deplored the fact that I was not of royal origin" (narcissistic
elements). He had only one desire during early childhood: to
be "good" and to achieve "distinction." Sensitive to any
criticism, he vowed to do everything to avoid being "coarse
and common"; "I sought the purity of the mind . . . I had no
desire to be one of the other boys, and I had no desire to be
sexual" (narcissistic features).

From the ages of four to eleven, he and his sister often
played in the attic, wearing mother's underclothes, and were
"girls together." He was unable to look at his own penis and
felt at five that "sex must be repulsive." In addition to cross-
dressing from three to five years of age, he began to play
"spanking games" with his sister and a neighborhood girl
friend who had introduced them to the game. "I first desired
to get spanked as I wet my pants, I recall." In these encounters he felt a sense of "physical and emotional closeness," a
sense of pleasure and well-being, in contrast to his usual
state of helplessness and hopelessness (organizing affective
experience). The sister's girl friend once disclosed that she

saw his sister spanked by her mother and, in identification with the sister, he felt both humiliated and excited. "I was envious of her seeing somebody else humiliated. The idea of my sister seeing me also excited me [i.e., the humiliation of it], and I wanted to see other people spanked from the earliest periods of my life." He began to believe that people did not have sex, actual sex, in adult life, but engaged in "spankings, even as adults." This disavowal helped keep in repression knowledge of sexual intercourse, the existence of the genitalia, and their function.

At two to three years of age, he saw his brother's penis and also his sister's genitals, as they all slept in the same room together. "Something was simply not there" when he looked at his sister. "I was furthermore disturbed by seeing the breasts of my mother, they looked scary and conspicuous. She had two, I had only one [feminine identification, penis–breast equation].... Everything in front—pubic hair and breasts, seemed to have repelled me." (In his perversion he positions himself in relation to his partner so that "everything in front" was omitted. Viewing himself as he is being spanked, he sees the arm with the hairbrush, but not the breasts of the woman, her face, her pubic hair, her vagina, or his own penis.) Breasts and buttocks were equated as both were "smooth, without hair." In recounting his fear of the pubic hair he noted: "The loss of something, or something not being there, is what upsets me" (castration anxiety). Since his earliest years there was a striking disavowal of anatomical differences between the sexes. "I have an image of people without sexual organs. I had this thought even again today, everything covered, everything covered up rigid and smooth."

He expressed a lack of knowledge of how babies were born until his late teens. "Somehow something could be cut off mother." He noted that whatever caused his perversion seemed to have caused a complete lack of interest in sex. "One could have said I was born in a cake of ice or from a cake of ice. I didn't know whether that was true or not. Everything that happened to me was to forestall my knowledge of the body of a woman."

At age thirteen, a male shop teacher suggested that he

must have a big penis and that he must like to play with it. "I was afraid of what he meant. I was fat, and I also felt at that time I wanted to be a girl."

The "high morality" in his family environment was a determinant to his choice of perversion. To "have sex without sex" was his aim. Whenever he thought of having real sex it made him "sick to my stomach." A discussion of Masters and Johnson in his early twenties led to a feeling of revulsion, and at age seventeen, a talk about sex and prostitution made him "nearly faint."

Any interest in masturbation was suppressed after age nine, when his father strongly warned against its dangers. He could not engage in normal heterosexual intercourse with penetration until his marriage, and then only when aroused by spanking in fantasy or in reality. Sexual relations up to the age of thirty consisted of rubbing his penis against the thighs of a woman without touching his penis and without viewing the genitalia of either himself or of his partner. Over the years he developed "crushes" on young women, but whenever he felt rejected he experienced separation anxiety, threats of personal disintegration and ego dissolution.

He married the daughter of a prominent writer who showed considerable interest in and appreciation of his work. He was able on several occasions to have sexual intercourse with penetration with her after he had induced her to engage in spanking him. Repeating this pattern resulted in the birth of two children.

Course of the Analysis

In the earliest phases of the analysis, considerable material emerged that depicted his fears of castration, fears of engulfment, and fears of merging with the preoedipal mother.

Dream:

> I was in a subway going downtown to an editorial meeting of a journal I am editor of. The next stop was 42nd Street. I asked, "Where does this subway go?" I didn't want to go to that street so I got off. I walked along Ninth Avenue, saw butcher shops on

both sides of the street. Saw giant hooks with pieces of meat. On top there was an entire enormous mutton or lamb, a leg of lamb, and below I don't know what.

The dream filled him with depression and anxiety. He recalled that his prostitute girl friend was singing in a night-club somewhere in that area, and he had gone down there the day before, and unfortunately got his pockets picked in the street. The lamb was an enormous leg of lamb—"butcher shop, castration shop, castration anxiety, hooks, pain." The thigh was the thigh of a great woman, and the lamb is the "lamb of God." He recalled that he frequently saw giant women in his dreams, or dreamed of holes and falling into them. The "large lamb" was a substitute for the convexity and concavity of the vagina. He avoids falling into the vagina. The big thighs are the thighs of women; while she is big, he is small, a child.

Dr. X. was not consciously aware of any homosexual fears or desires. Within several months after the beginning of analysis, dreams of homosexual conflict began to appear. The first was of homosexual desire in relation to the development of dependency cravings in the positive transference, and the second of homosexual fear and dread.

Dream:

There are two men sitting in adjacent chairs with a chaise longue between the two. They would lean quite far back and they were adjacent, contiguous, and neckties that each wore were interwoven with each other. How, I don't know. They went from one tie to another and the ties merged.

Associations: This dream might be a homosexual dream, he commented, but he had never been aware of any homosexual interest. But to whom was he tied? The thought frightened him. Is it the analyst? Is it his father? It was an unconscious form of bondage, in a sense, two men lying down together, the stripes uniting them, perhaps the beginning of the analysis. He was shocked to have such a dream but could not pursue the matter further. He vehemently reiterated that he had no interest in homosexuality, and never has had. The chaise longue may have been a bed, perhaps the analytic couch. The men could lean far back and their two neckties interwove with each other like two penises.

The strength of the transference had activated his infantile wish and need to merge with the powerful father/analyst. He was never loved by his father nor his brother, by no one, and he "needed to be loved." Several weeks later, he dreamed of his actual manifest spanking perversion, interrupted by a fear of homosexual attack. He is being taken over the knee of a young woman in the park, and when he looks above him, on a ridge he sees several men with tall fedora hats. They seem to be threatening him while watching him. He interrupts the spanking and runs away. The men on the ridge with their peculiar-looking hats are clearly large penises. (He diagrams for me the shape of these figures and the symbolism becomes much more apparent.) They are ready to penetrate him as his buttocks are exposed. The perversion itself cannot suffice to hold in repression the deeper unconscious wishes and dreads (i.e., his homosexual ones). [4]

The manifest content of the "Linda" game, which kept in repression more basic drives and conflicts, could be decoded into its latent meaning. Linda was a substitute for the patient, a boy. The Lady Gainsborough woman was a narcissistic substitute for the mother, and beneath that a substitute for the man, a powerful father. Instead of being penetrated by the father's phallus, he is spanked in a painful and humiliating manner by the narcissistic image of his wished-for mother. [5] His longing for the father's love, punishment, and humiliation is also a narcissistic one as he wishes to create a perfect image of himself as good, virtuous,

---

[4] In chapter 7, I describe the meaning of frequent and explicit sexual dreams of the perversion itself in those with a well-structured perversion. They signify the pervert's attempt to control anxiety and to stabilize a sense of self against threats of disintegration.

[5] In a recent American Psychoanalytic Association Panel on the contribution made by masochism to narcissistic disorders, pain and humiliation were cited as providing direct sensory experience for the purpose of consolidating a sense of self (Panel, 1979b).

lovable, handsome like his brother, and to put himself into a cohesive and essentially permanent psychic structure. He is attempting to overcome the bad image of himself—unattractive, untalented, fat, unwanted, ugly, and female like his mother, by creating an opposing type of identification, that of the aristocratic noblewoman.

A year later he dreamed of homosexual desire for his father. Perhaps he could achieve heterosexuality only if he first submitted to the father, gained his love, approval, and admiration. In the dream to be cited he is "not good enough." He does not wish to submit to having a sexual relationship with his father; that is, to pay him $100,000 with its sexual implications of circles and a penis, and cannot submit masochistically ("your daughter is not a slave"). His father chooses the brother to go off and "eat with" (have sex with).

Dream:

> I was in love with a girl. She doesn't look like my wife nor like my prostitute. I wanted to marry her and my father said, "You have to make a speech." And if the speech did not please him I'd have to pay him $100,000 in order to marry her. The speech was widely acclaimed and applauded, but my father came up to me and said, "It was not good enough. Pay me $100,000." I said, "Your daughter is not a piece of baggage or a slave, therefore I shall not give you the payment." He then saw a tall man with a mustache and walked away from me, past the other speakers on the platform, with my brother. I asked him where he was going. He said so-and-so asked him to go over and eat with him.

His associations consisted of his feeling of failure and his lifelong inability to impress his father. He was not deserving of his love (sex) as the speech was "not red hot." In other words, he was not sufficiently enticing to his father. He became aware that in the dream he was not upset because of losing the girl, but upset by not being loved by his father (i.e., having sex with him).

He now recalled having suppressed and repressed sexual desires of a homosexual nature at one point in his life. He suddenly remembered a "strong attraction" he felt toward a young man (resembling the tall man with the mustache of the previous dream) when he was in the Army at the age of twenty-five. This was indeed a "revelation," as homosexuality was more repellent to him than any other sexual activity. This was the only time he had homosexual impulses that he was now able to admit to himself. It was in London, and the desire lasted for a few days. He reflected at the time, "Maybe this man would have settled for a spanking." He was not effeminate in any manner, and that attracted him to the patient. "We became friendly, and I thought it would be nice to speak to him. Suppose I went to bed with him; I wouldn't know what to do. I wouldn't be able to do anything." The disavowal of genital functioning left him truly in an enigmatic position. Was the spanking perversion an attempt to escape from homosexuality? He noted in the next session that after his session he knew the analyst was correct.

> I saw somebody's ass in my fantasy and I was putting my penis in it. Somehow I was conscious of the penis–anus relationship, and then spanking suddenly came into my mind, in a sense to wash it away. I believe I have a lot of guilt about homosexuality. I gave up wanting the love of my father and tried to replace this with my relationship to my father-in-law. I now realize that this was one of the reasons I married my wife. He was so fond of me, a man of international reputation, he appreciated everything I did [narcissistic enhancement].

During this session he had fantasies of the body of a penis, an erection, a "pleasant sight, a huge penis. I can even see the vein. It is similar to when I get an erection at times during the spanking. If I could only have this in real life without the spanking, that is, the erection and the big penis. Even though I can't do it yet with a woman, I'm going to get there. That is my only solution."

He now remembered that he had had a dream the night before of a "naked bottom." The rest was clothed, or at least partially clothed. The message in the picture was, "Are you going to put me to bed after this? That is, after the spanking." Contemplating this led to a feeling of "wild excitement." Clearly, being put to bed meant sexual relations and sleep. It was the excitation of penetrating the anus of another man, perhaps his father or his brother, which produced the "wild excitement," fear, and revulsion, and led to his attempted escape through the spanking perversion.

In a subsequent session the homosexual theme was increasingly obvious in his dream of seduction by a man.

> I was walking along the street and an old man stopped me. He had several letters and he showed me the envelopes, and he was handsome. They were addressed to him, an Anglo-Saxon name. We walked along, and there is a six-year-old girl nearby. He walks along and becomes less and less innocent, and he's going to make love to the little girl [a younger Linda], and I wonder whether to call a policeman [superego element]. I did, and I said to him, "I'm sorry, but I'm a British officer," and he dropped the letter.

Associations: He was about to depart for England for a conference the next day, and had a fantasy of finding a young, blond prostitute in Britain with whom to conduct a spanking session. He was now getting rid of his strong attachment to the prostitute in the city. As they walked along, the man said to him, "I have a compartment and I want a girl to go in there." Perhaps he was the girl. "What things do you do, or what terrible things can we do to each other?" He identified with the girl, but in this instance *he* was being propositioned to have sex with the man. It seemed to him that he might be winning out over the perversion, as he did call the policeman, both to save himself and the girl. But he might now wish to have sexual relations with a man. Calling the policeman, and his statement that he was a British officer (i.e., a man), was reassuring.

Before the analysis, whenever he thought of real sex it made him sick to his stomach, but this had been gradually changing. The patient was able on several occasions to lie against his wife while naked and without spanking. He reported that there was no doubt that he truly loved her. He was suffering from an irritation of his penis, but he was able to speak of it, something he could not have done before, and sought the services of a dermatologist. He began to masturbate for the first time while holding his penis, and at the suggestion of the analyst masturbated successfully while viewing himself and his penis in the mirror. Repeated episodes of masturbation with pleasure reinforced his self representation and consolidated genital schematization. As the analysis progressed, he quipped that a miracle was happening on 78th Street, where the analyst's office was located. He and his wife "got quite involved" one night. She fondled his penis and he allowed her to do so. He became erect without spanking and without dressing up as Linda. She remarked teasingly, "If you don't give me an erection, I'll spank you!" This excited him further, she manipulated his penis, and he became sufficiently erect to penetrate the vagina for approximately five minutes. She commented, "You're getting tired of this thing [meaning the perversion] for a long time now." "We both 'came.' I don't know what it was that made me move this way, for it was right. It just seemed to grow."

The gradual lessening of the need for spanking was tied to a loosening of the need to repress homosexual feelings. This produced a loosening of repression of all sexuality so that heterosexual performance began to be entertained and attempted with considerable pleasure and success. All the while the patient was able to experience and accept into consciousness homosexual impulses and their meaning; that is, desire for the father's love. The "Linda game" was understood as hiding a homosexual wish and dread for the father secondary to an early primary feminine identification with the mother and an inability to make a counteridentification with the father. Spanking itself, with its built-in disavowal and denial of sexual anatomical differences, denial of penis, vagina, and sexual intercourse, kept in repression the entire sexuality of the patient. The sexual drive was now liberated to pursue new sexual objects (i.e., heterosexual ones), and homosexual object choice was not sanctioned by his superego nor did it offer a solution to his conflicts. By virtue of the transference relationship, a new object relationship with the therapist was being formed, with a gradual buttressing and solidification of a previously fragile self representation. The patient's sense of self cohesion and self-esteem had undergone further stabilization within the transference.

The onset of the full-scale perversion, from fantasy to overt acts, was precipitated by anxieties relating to fragmentation, separation, loss of the object, and loss of love of the object. He had attempted to recreate the closeness and relationship to his sister and wife through the "Linda game." Sibling rivalry was exacerbated by the birth of his children, and his fear that he would lose out (be pushed aside) by their birth.

His early family environment played a direct role in the formation of the perversion. An

[A]tmosphere of self-designed, self-imposed taboos made a pervert out of me. My mother and sister were as normal as Queen Victoria and Queen Elizabeth. What brought this on me? It was extreme moralism, a puritanical sense, a wish to be perfect. Why didn't I want to look at my penis? One time I fell in love in grammar school with a girl, even as a child. I wanted to be with her, but the idea of sex was repulsive to me even at the age of five.

The wish to be spanked was at its inception devoid of sexual or erotic connotations. Its function was to provide him with a sense of connectness, being grounded, being alive, and being loved. The only real love he expected in childhood and adolescence was what he received from his sister, supplied in the spanking games. "I don't remember when I was even embraced. I didn't know love existed except for my sister. My father was not given to admiration, nor was my mother, and I don't remember any demonstrativeness at home. If I ever did something wrong, I'd go to her for comfort." Positive feelings of warmth and affection and of being "cared for" were experienced in the transference.

A dream in the last year of his analysis depicted the dilemma of childhood that he now confronted and was conquering. "A woman is accused of raping her father, seducing her mother. She was arrested and retained me as her attorney. Our defense was not raping or screwing, neither one of them, but that she was showing them how to have sexual intercourse. She was a big, tall blonde, not like anyone I know, apparently."

Associations: A woman cannot rape her father, the vision of the two bodies lying next to each other, not contiguous, presumably the father and the woman, but the woman is clothed. She said, "I was teaching them sexual intercourse." "If the girl is me, it would be a wish to be a tall, blond man, an ideal image of myself. The defense is, 'It's okay to have sex.' That has been my problem." In this dream the patient has chosen to defend the charge against the accused. It had to do with the nature of intercourse, and he argued the normality of intercourse.

It means the defense of myself, it was the defense against my seeing my parents naked. It seems escape from rape, too [these remarks would seem to indicate a witnessing of the primal scene, although this material was not forthcoming in the analysis]. . . . *In the spanking I changed myself into a little girl . . . and I escaped the homosexual experience with my father and the heterosexual experience with my mother.* I become a girl, but I have no way of getting female organs. I cannot make a vagina either so I have to have intercourse without erection of my penis. And that answers the entire perversion. Not having a vagina, not being able to stick anything up the vagina to react with ejaculation. I have to escape by another position. *Spanking* puts me into that position. The movement of legs and thighs bring me closer to her, so close that she is completely naked. She's spanking my buttocks, and my penis is lying against her bare thigh. It certainly is for moral people.

The patient escaped both heterosexuality and homosexuality via the perversion, but could not acquire female organs and could not accept his own penis. In the spanking position he achieved morality, closeness, narcissistic enhancement, escaped homosexuality and heterosexuality.

The patient reported that he was "getting tired of Linda." She still wouldn't go away yet, but her behavior in fantasy was changing and indicated progress. Linda has been beating mother, but is now "screwing mother" instead of simply being spanked. It's a new change, he stated. "It's like this. The lady spanks me, Linda, and gets ready for bed. I'm in Linda's nightclothes. I lie next to her, but then I turn and penetrate her and say, 'Who are you?' She says, 'Who do you want, your mother?'" This change of the dominatrix into the mother, the change from a simple spanking activity to that of sexual intercourse, revealed the progressive interest in penetrating the vagina. Linda herself (the patient) still remained female, however.

Before analysis he thought of sex as something one engaged in to get it over with, analogous to constipation. "You love the urgency, you can't do it right away for obvious reasons. Sex didn't make me happy. It's a relief of pain rather than an act of pleasure. In the same way, if you have sex you get rid of pain and desire." Whenever he saw a woman on the street or on the subway, he had in the past an almost immediate desire to spank her. The earlier reaction was now transformed into the desire to have intercourse with her. In the later phases of the analysis he not only could masturbate[6] by himself, but also have intercourse with his wife. Linda was practically gone; he no longer needed the services of his prostitute. Significantly, he had been able to tolerate and understand his wish for sexual penetration by the father and his wish to get close to men. He wanted affection, but not sex with him. His intense attachment to, and at times disappointment with, several of his male students over the years could now be seen as sublimations of his sexual feelings toward men.

In keeping with the analytic treatment of all sexual perversions, I did not interdict any type of sexual activity on the part of the patient. Perverse activities were seen as necessary for the maintenance of self cohesion, self–object differentiation, and were a source of narcissistic gratification and restoration against threats to self cohesion. He was encouraged, when he had achieved sufficient insight and a sufficient degree of gender-defined self identity and self–object differentiation, to begin actual heterosexual relations with penetration. The diminished need for the perversion to func-

---

[6] Laufer and Laufer (1984) have convincingly described the crucial importance of masturbation in "enabling an adolescent boy to establish the primacy of genitality," changing the "image of his body to include his mature genitals as functioning organs" (p. 37). This maturational accomplishment had never been achieved by my patient prior to his analysis.

tion in establishing such object relations or to buttress his failing self representations led to a gradual atrophy of desire for perverse practices. The decoding and interpretation of his perverse practices into their hidden sexual and nonsexual meanings, and the diminishing narcissistic gains [7] provided by the perverse practices opened up avenues for sexual satisfaction previously closed to him. With the creation of a self separate from that of his mother and the establishment of appropriate gender-defined self identity (in identification with the male analyst), the possibility of satisfactory sexual performance began to become a real possibility. The perversion had both a restorative function and a warding-off function. It helped to eliminate preoedipal and oedipal castration anxieties, threats of object loss, threats of engulfment, fragmentation, and threats of anal penetration by the father, and reinforced a threatened self representation.

In the fourth year of analysis he finished some ongoing work on the Roman philosophers, but found it difficult to go on with work on Pascal, which he had also undertaken. He enigmatically stated, "Somehow I have a premonition of death which has been with me for some months. It may have to do with the fact that I can't get back to the Pascal, the work I planned to start. It may have to do with my muscle

---

[7] An identification with the French philosopher, Jean-Jacques Rousseau, who suffered from a similar need to be beaten and spanked, had for years provided him with a secret sense of specialness and narcissistic enhancement frequently alluded to, often in the form of a resistance to change in the early phases of the analysis. Psychoanalytic studies of Rousseau by Kligerman (1951, 1981; Panel, 1979b) reveal some striking similarities to my patient. Rousseau had sublimated his attachment to his mother by an intense interest in (Mother) nature, an idealization of the solitary man, and the essential purity and goodness of men when uncorrupted by other men (1951). He became aware of his perverse pleasure of being spanked at the age of ten when he was spanked for some minor infraction by Mlle. Lambersier, a mother-surrogate with whom he had boarded after his father had to leave Geneva. At about the same time, he was subjected to pleasure and humiliation by a domineering girl his own age. Rousseau claimed that these were the only times that he actually gratified his fantasy, but "it played a central role in his imagination for the duration of his life in his sexual activity as well as in his characterological difficulties" (Panel, 1979b, p. 223). Similar themes were prominent in my patient's literary contributions.

pains, as I don't feel well. I do want to live a clean life now, a clean man, as it were, what I came for in the first place."

He began to complain, "I think I'm finished, or I'm dying. Somehow, someday I won't wake up. I have no energy left. I'm tired of the pain. Where is my energy?"

My patient's presentiment of being physically ill proved to be correct. An inveterate pipe-smoker, he began to be troubled by difficulty in swallowing. He complained of feeling weaker in climbing the stairs to my office with his bulging briefcase, was somewhat out of breath, and began to lose weight. Physical examination revealed the present of an esophageal mass that proved to be malignant. The final stages of his analysis had to be interrupted as the patient had several operations, first for the attempted removal of an invasive tumor in the chest, and a second palliative procedure. I visited him several times in the hospital before his death a few months later, during which time he expressed his gratitude for the psychological freedom he had attained by the removal of his perversion, the thrill of engaging in heterosexual intercourse, something he felt was forever beyond his grasp, and together we shared the sad, heroic, and at times even humorous twists that he injected into this extreme and tragic turn of events.

Discussion

The clinical material I have presented provides further corroboration of Freud's clinical observations that in spanking and beating fantasies "the beating fantasy has its origin in an incestuous attachment to the father," but that such fantasies have an "earlier history" (than the oedipal phase) and that they "represent an end-product and not an initial manifestation" (1919, pp. 83–84). It affirms Freud's view that a "final solution to the problem" was impossible (circa 1919). Advances in our knowledge would be contingent upon new theoretical constructs and clinical studies, especially of the earliest years of life.[8] It differs from Freud in that the at-

---

[8]My theoretical explanation as to the etiology of this condition relies heavily on the application of theoretical constructs (the contribution of

tachment to the father does not derive from a negative oedipal position secondary to oedipal castration fears, but represents a wholesale flight to the male (father) for salvation from the engulfing female. The unconscious wish for the father cannot be accepted consciously and is replaced through the Sachs mechanism by a spanking perversion. It is not the erotic infantile experience per se which is sought for in the perversion: it is the *reassuring and reaffirming* function of the experience which is reanimated and preserved (Socarides, 1978a; Stolorow and Lachmann, 1980). Oedipal conflicts that may exist are an accretion to the primary and basic preoedipal nuclear conflict: the wish and dread of maternal engulfment due to a failure to successfully traverse separation–individuation phases.

Despite his high level of intellectual achievement, my patient suffered from a developmental arrest and showed unmistakeable signs of preoedipal fixation. A number of such indicators of psychic pathology found in those with preoedipal fixations were present; for example, a lifelong persistence of the original primary feminine identification with the mother; as a consequence, a sense of deficiency in one's masculine identity (a pervasive feeling of femininity or deficient sense of masculinity); a deficiency in body–ego boundaries with fears of bodily disintegration and disturbance in body–ego formation; a fear of engulfment with its threat of personal annihilation and loss of self; perverse acts, whose effects could be likened to the opium alkaloids in their magical restorative powers (reinstating the body–ego and sense of self against threats of disruption); a deep sense of inferiority, worthlessness because of severe narcissistic injuries in childhood; severe anxiety, tension, and depression which appeared whenever interruption of perverse acts was attempted.

The status of my patient's object relations was impaired

---

numerous psychoanalysts throughout a 30- to 40-year period) in the area of ego psychology (including self psychology), new theories of narcissism, the pathology of internalized object relations, infant observational studies, and our evolving knowledge in the area of preoedipal development. It focuses on two central areas of emphasis: the stress on preoedipal causation, and my view that object relations pathology is more important that the vicissitudes of the drives in perversions.

and consisted of object to self. The dominatrix stood for his narcissistic self-image as a female. He pursued partners who were representatives of his own self (narcissistic) in relation to an active, phallic mother. He identified with the dominatrix, as well as with the person being beaten (Linda). Implicit in the performance of the perversion was the unconscious enactment of a mother–child role (breast–penis equation) and a father–child role in which he was loved by the father and penetrated by him sexually. Due to a fixation in the later phases of the separation–individuation process (the rapprochement subphase), he suffered from an object relations class of conflict: anxiety and guilt associated with the failure of development in the phase of self–object differentiation. The nuclear conflict consisted of a desire for and dread of merging with the mother in order to reinstate the primitive mother–child unity with associated separation anxiety.

There was a successful utilization of the Sachs mechanism, the mechanism of the repressive compromise—a solution by division whereby one piece of infantile sexuality was allowed into consciousness, and its enactment helped to promote a repression of a deeper, more dangerous conflict through displacement, substitution, and other defense measures. The perversion was ego-syntonic, and the symptom was acceptable to the superego due to the splitting of the superego. The unconscious part of the superego stemming from the excessive morality of the patient and his family sanctioned the perversion. It is possible in therapy to establish a conscious split in the superego and analyze that part of the superego that supported the perversion (the parental part), thereby strengthening the ego against its commands. In effect, heterosexual sex was immoral, while spanking was a highly moral act. One is reminded here of Glover's (1960) comment:

> In the unconscious of the sexual pervert, his renunciation of adult sexuality is a moral act. His regression to infantile sexuality, though by no means guilt-free, is the lesser of two evils. . . . The sexual pervert who flaunts his perversion or involves others in his practices is regarded not only as a delinquent, but as a peculiarly disgusting species of crimi-

nal. Yet in the sense of primitive unconscious morality, both the neurotic and the sexual pervert are more "moral minded" than the normal heterosexual adult [pp. 183–184].

Vital narcissistic functions were served by the perversion. It represented a primitively sexualized attempt to restore and maintain cohesiveness and stability of a threatened self representation. Beneath my patient's narcissistic, exhibitionistic wishes to be all-powerful, all-pure, flawless, and special, lay deep feelings of narcissistic vulnerability and inferiority. For many years his creative activities in the area of literature and philosophy were a partially successful sublimation of these wishes. Any circumstance, however, which showed up deficiencies, real or imagined, produced a sense of humiliation, threats of fragmentation and self dissolution. These were handled through the enactment of the beating fantasy. They helped maintain and stabilize his self representation through merger with the powerful object of his wishes, the Lady Gainsborough woman. Unconscious feelings of shame, humiliation, and narcissistic rage, feelings of being crushed by his father and mother in early childhood, were changed into their opposites when he controlled others. He attempted to restore his self representation through an alternating identification with the aristocratic, sadistic Lady Gainsborough woman, and the adolescent girl, Linda. The acute sensations of pain and humiliation were a way of acquiring a temporary feeling of being alive and existing as a cohesive self. The contrast of being beaten and the sense of doing the beating dramatized the very essence of his inability to be imperilled or destroyed. Furthermore, the experience of orgasm at the height of such beating restored a sense of conviction of having a real and bounded and cohesive self (Eissler, 1958a; Socarides, 1978a; Lichtenstein, 1977; Stolorow & Lachmann, 1980).

During the analysis, his self representation was increasingly strengthened in identification with the analyst, so that the need for perverse reinforcement lessened and ultimately disappeared. This was dependent on correctly analyzing the multiple substitutions, displacements, and reaction formation, so that he could experience the reality of their meaning. For example, spanking was equated with sexual penetration; pain and humiliation were sought-after sensory experiences for the purpose of consolidation of a sense of self (Panel, 1979b); sensations were displaced from the genitals to the buttocks to avoid the terror of engulfment by the maternal body. A striking finding in this otherwise sophisticated patient was the lifelong massive disavowal and avoidance of the knowledge of the anatomical differences between the sexes.

In accordance with my provisional classification of the sexual perversions (Socarides, 1975, 1978a), I classify this patient's disorder as a preoedipal type I masochistic (spanking) perversion. The degree of potential analyzable transference was good and there was sufficient self–object differentiation and internalization of object representations to work with. Although his ego functions were impaired, his reality testing was intact, if consciously and unconsciously ignored to serve the pleasure principle at times. Thinking was clear, but dominated by the pleasure principle. Self-concept alternated between an elevated self-esteem bordering on omnipotence and desire for perfection, and feelings of self-depreciation and need for narcissistic supplies and narcissistic restoration.

I propose that my patient, as well as other patients with a similar disorder and with signs of preoedipal fixation, suffer not from a vicissitude of instinct, a premature development of a component of the sexual instinct, but from an object relations conflict involving anxiety and guilt in relation to separation from the preoedipal mother. The "accidental" and "commonplace and unexciting events" which were decisive in the choice of his perversion were based on early preoedipal attachments both to mother and sister and the "accidental" intrusion into his life of a "spanking game" enjoyed by sister and her girl friend. This provided him with an "organizing experience," a sense of belonging, a feeling of well-being and intimacy, undoing separation and diminishing other fears, and providing a source of orgastic satisfaction in a later period without genital involvement and in the absence of guilt.

Chapter 17
VOYEURISM:
THE CASE OF MARTIN

Introduction

In the "Three Essays" Freud (1905b) observed that the partial instinct of pleasure in looking (scoptophilia) becomes a perversion of voyeurism when, instead of being preparatory to the sexual aim, it supplants it. The primitive nature of the mental processes leading to voyeurism was reflected in his comment that they "seemed as though they were harking back to early animal forms of life" (p. 198).

The scoptophilic instinct, a component of the sexual instinct, was one of a pair of opposites, the opposite of scoptophilia being exhibitionism. In normal adults, looking serves the purpose of inducing forepleasure; an object that is only seen remains at a distance and end-pleasure requires contact with the object. "In all events, the scoptophilic instinct, like other component instincts, is liable to repression and may give rise to fixation" (Fenichel, 1935, p. 376).

One looks at an object in order to share in its experience. Very often, however, sadistic impulses enter into the instinctual aim of looking and one wishes to destroy something by means of looking at it, or the act of looking itself may acquire the significance of a modified form of destruction. That a considerable part of scoptophilia succumbs to repression and sublimation in childhood was noted as early as 1913 by Abraham. Such sublimation may lead to (1) a desire for knowledge in a general sense; (2) investigative impulse; (3)

interest in the observation of nature; (4) pleasure in travel; (5) the artistic treatment of objects in the act of painting. Following Freud's (1905b) lead, Abraham noted that there was a "constitutional" intensification of the scoptophilic instinct in some individuals who later became perverts.

If there is a severe inhibition of sexual activity in childhood, looking can subsequently assume a more important role in the mental life of the individual. Instead of active sexual behavior there is a greater tendency to look on inactively at things from a distance. The stronger the scoptophilic instinct the greater the need for sublimation in order to prevent the development of neurotic disturbances and the more severe will these disturbances be if they take place (Abraham, 1913, pp. 170–171).

By 1927, Freud, in his paper on fetishism, correctly noted that voyeurism as well as fetishism was not the result of a simple acceptance of an infantile wish or component instinct, but was rather a complicated defense against infantile polymorphous perverse sexual wishes. In his "Instincts and Their Vicissitudes" Freud (1915) noted that the function of looking produces aesthetic end-pleasure; further gratification is attained through the desire to be looked at.

By 1954 it appeared obvious that looking, similar to other functions that derived from sense organs (e.g., hearing, smelling, touching, etc.) carried with it a gratification or discharge of narcissistic and object libido, producing narcissistic satisfaction or pleasure whether aggressive or sexual (Eidelberg, 1954). Scoptophilic perverts were, while watching, unconsciously identifying with the watched object, thereby experiencing an unconsciously exhibitionistic gratification. The scoptophilia constituted a denial of the original exhibitionistic wish and further gratified the demands of the unconscious ego and superego. There appeared to be more male than female scoptophilic perverts. Both scoptophilics and exhibitionists were interested in the satisfaction of their wishes only if such satisfaction was forbidden so that aggressive as well as sexual tendencies were gratified in the act (Eidelberg, 1954).

Eidelberg (1954) discovered (1) the unconscious identification with the watched object; (2) the denial of the original wish to exhibit oneself, thus ameliorating and side-stepping ego and superego conflict; and (3) a simultaneous gratification of both aggressive and sexual wishes.

Only a limited number of full-scale voyeuristic perversions have been reported in the psychoanalytic literature (Spielrein, 1923; Fenichel, 1935; Nierenberg, 1950; Muller-Eckhart, 1955; Bergler, 1957b; Rosen, 1964, 1979; Socarides, 1974b). A considerable number of papers have appeared as regards symbolism of the eye in scoptophilia (Freud, 1910b; Ferenczi, 1923; Hart, 1949; Roheim, 1952, Klein, 1946, 1954; Spitz, 1955; Kris, 1956; and Allen, 1967).

Infant Observational Studies

While much has been written on psychoanalytic theory which emphasizes the mouth and its importance as the primal focal point of the body image (Spitz, 1955, 1965), few contributions were made prior to 1960 as regards the significance of the eye and the importance of eye-to-eye contact during early infantile development. Little was known as to the development of body image in connection with eye function. If the eyes play a significant early role, this would be reflected in the emerging body concept of a young child. Shapiro and Stine (1965) suggested that the earliest body representations are derived from visual experiences while tactile experiences are only later "projected." Drawings studied by these authors support the argument that the "locus vitae" of the infant consists of an interaction between the mother's eyes and those of the infant. This serves as an important organizer of the infant's perceptual world, and in the earliest weeks of life there occurs a two-way process of communication—looking at and being looked at (Shapiro and Stine, 1965; Almansi, 1960). According to Robson (1967):

[I]n the normal course of events this process continues to operate in human relationships. The fulfillment of physical needs and the experiencing of pleasurable stimulation in nonvisual modes are equally significant in the development of attachment. Eye-to-eye contact is one component in the matrix of maternal and infant behaviors that comprise reciprocal interaction. Yet the nature of eye contact between the mother and the baby seems to cut across all interactional systems and conveys the intimacy or "distance" characteristic of their relationship as a whole [p. 18].

The clinical validity of these observations is borne out by the fact that disturbances in eye contact are very commonly present in children who have suffered anaclitic depression (Spitz, 1946; Kanner, 1949). In both autistic and anaclitically depressed children, total gaze aversion is the rule. Such types of visual avoidance-behavior are indicative of gross disturbances in the mother–infant relationship. Attempts to rectify previously established but disturbed face–eye contact are, furthermore, seen in schizoid patients who are attracted to certain types of faces and who fear "paranoid-looking eyes." It is well known that fussing or crying babies may be quieted by their caretakers through eye contact. Other babies become extremely upset if eye contact is forced upon them after having suffered an earlier deprivation of such contact.

Ahrens (1954) observed that around the fifth month responsiveness to eyes diminishes and the mouth begins to assume a more important role together with an increase in listening, smiling, and attention.

The crucial importance of vision and eye contact was reported by both Rheingold and Freedman. Rheingold (1961) suggested that "not visual but physical contact is the basis of human sociability," but that the "basic and primary activity of the infant's *visual* exploration of his environment" (p. 144). Freedman (1964) observed that vision not only plays the obvious role in perception of the outside world that we give to it, but, even more importantly, helps differentiate the self from the nonself. The infant's capacity to initiate physical contact in clinging develops toward the end of the first year of life, while eye contact develops even earlier. Eye-to-eye contact is one of the most intense and binding interactions of the infant *before* the third month (Rheingold, 1961).

Robson (1967) described the unique peculiarities of the visual mode which favored its "preeminence as a major vehicle of the interpsychic and interpersonal development" even during the first five months of life. "Of all the neo-natal reflexes, visual fixation and following are the only ones that do not drop out over time, but on the contrary, demonstrate increasing facility" (p. 13). Remarkably, by the end of the second month visual behavior is in the form that it will keep throughout life.

> Furthermore, following a fixation are among the first acts of the infant that are both intentional and subject to his control. Vision is the only modality which, by closure of the eyelids, gaze aversion, and pupillary constriction and dilation is constructed as an "on-off" system that can easily modulate or eliminate external sensory input, sometimes at will, within the first months of life. And finally, the appeal of the mother's eyes to the child (and of his eyes to her) is facilitated by their stimulus richness. In comparison with other areas of the body surface the eye has a remarkable array of interesting qualities such as the shininess of the globe, the fact that it is mobile, while at the same time fixed in space, the contrast which is the pupil-iris-cornea configuration, the capacity of the pupil to vary in diameter, and the differing effects of variations in the width of the palpebral fissure [pp. 13–14].

It appears that nonhuman mothers seem to need far less responsiveness from their offspring than human mothers. Eye-to-eye contact plays a minimal part in subhuman attachments, and when such behavior serves a social function it is, according to Andrew (1965) an indicator of fear, appeasement, or intention to attack. The usual pattern of intermittent gaze fixation between humans in contrast as reported by Hutt and Ounsted (1966) signifies a readiness to interact and that scant human social interaction is possible without it. Therefore, it can be said that there seems to be no reason to believe that smiling and eye contact in human babies differs in origin from the primarily defensive function they play in the animal world, except that there are further complex developments involving object relations that ensue in human infants (Ahrens, 1954; Szekely, 1954; Freedman, 1964). These complex functions are well illustrated in the voyeuristic behavior of my patient, Martin, described later in this chapter.

Clinically, the damaging consequences arising from

faulty mother–child visual interaction is readily observable in infants during the first three months of life. Some mothers frequently avoid eye-to-eye contact with the infant because this releases strongly destructive feelings. These mothers may not recognize their child in a highly intimate and personal way:

> Eye contact may be equivalent to oral and bodily contact sensations in feeding, producing good or bad feelings in the infant [Ahrens, 1954].

Isakower (1938), along with Lewin (1950), and Spitz (1955), and Almansi (1960), describes the connection that exists between the breasts and the visually perceived face, the fusion of breast and face.

Significantly, when a child is spoken to he ignores the mouth of the speaker and fixates on the eye. The mouth itself is not involved in listening or smiling responses until the fifth or sixth month, which emphasizes the importance of eye contacts. Disturbances in this earliest mode of communication in mother–child interaction leave an indelible mark not only on childhood but on adult functioning; disturbances of the capacity to love, to neutralize aggression, and to construct satisfactory object relations, and disturbances in normal healthy self-esteem are consequences. The perversion of voyeurism is a monument to the importance of the visual function in the first years of life. The voyeur wishes to look at the object but not be seen, to control through visual incorporation, all the while fearing the eyes of the object and remaining deprived of those emotional supplies that can be taken in through the eyes.

Major Psychoanalytic Contributions

Freud (1905b) first noted that scoptophilia contains sadistic impulses; the individual destroys by seeing or gains reassurance that the object is not yet destroyed. Looking, on the other hand, may be unconsciously conceived of as a substitute for destroying. "I did not destroy it; I merely looked at it" (Fenichel, 1945, p. 348).

The counterpart to scoptophilia is exhibitionism, and often, exhibitionistic *behavior* will coexist with it. According to Fenichel (1935),

> [S]adism initially develops from the instinctive greediness with which the incorporation aims of the pregenital impulses are prosecuted, representing a way of striving for instinctive aims rather than an original instinctual aim in itself. Another root of sadism is the negative instinctual aim of getting rid (splitting away) of painful stimuli. . . . All pregenital impulses in their aims of incorporation, seem to possess a certain destructive component [p. 381].

Fenichel's 1935 paper is a classic among those dealing with the eye and scoptophilia. Later (1945), he described the analysis of a case of a female voyeur, and noted that this clinical entity only occurs in extremely masculine women. Further early contributions to voyeurism were made by Ferenczi (1923), Hart (1949), Roheim (1952), and Rosen (1964).

The symbolic equation "to look" equals "to devour" is a form of sadistic incorporation. The eye or a glance may be a sadistic weapon and the eye may be used to symbolize the penis (Freud, 1900). It may also be oral in character and is not only actively sadistic, putting a spell on its victim, but also passively receptive as the person who looks is fascinated by what he sees. In witnessing parental intercourse "the child identifies himself with that which he sees and this identification had important consequences for his whole life . . . to devour the object looked at, to grow like it (be forced to imitate it), or, conversely, to force it to grow like oneself" (Fenichel, 1935, p. 378).

Clinical correlations to the early importance of the visual function were made by Spitz as early as 1955 in a paper entitled "The Primal Cavity: A Contribution to the Genesis of Perception and its Role for Psychoanalytic Theory." Spitz (1955) observed that during nursing the child looks at the mother's face, the internalization of which becomes an essential component of the child's total sensory and psychological development. Spitz (1946), Ahrens (1954), Almansi

(1979), and McDevitt (1975), all concluded that visual images are an essential component of the perceptual cluster which exists during the nursing situation. This leads to the perceptual equation of nipples equal mother's eyes. They concur that around the age of three months, when children are deprived of the mother's nipples their eyes deviate from the mother's face to the general direction of the breast. From these studies Almansi concluded: (1) the hypercathexis of the visual function brought about by infantile trauma strongly increases the possibility that a patient may need to keep an object within sight and to incorporate it visually. This may be a predisposing factor in the genesis of the perversion of voyeurism. (2) Severe traumata of viewing repeated primal scenes, a strong Oedipus complex, and mother's exhibitionism often lead to a sensitization of the visual function and its libidinization. Genital drives when they emerge, according to Almansi, then become a "tool" in the all-important defensive struggle against object loss. (3) Genital urges may subserve a patient's need to be close to the pregenital maternal object and thus, while an erotic act takes place, it is the *viewing* that is important (i.e., the function of the erotic act). (4) Object loss, therefore, not only produces the general activation of visual functioning, in essence a hypertrophy of it, but plays a major role in the pathogenesis of perverse symptomatology. The early onset of this trauma has a causal relationship to the strongly compulsive character of the perverse activity itself. Object loss is one element along with ego and superego factors, the disturbance in sexual identity, and vicissitudes of aggression, playing roles in the production of the perversion itself (Almansi, 1979). There may be instances, according to Almansi, in which object loss is not a central issue.

Almansi's contributions in the area of the theoretical and clinical investigation of voyeurism began in 1960 with his paper on the "Face–Breast Equation." He described three patients whose drive orientation was directed toward the breast and not the eyes. He connected the patient's voyeuristic interest to the fear of object loss, oral deprivation, and causal relation to (1) the birth of younger siblings and the experience of watching them being bathed and nursed, evoking powerful aggressive impulses; (2) the unconscious equation of mother's eyes equal nipples; (3) the mechanism of incorporation through the eyes (ocular introjection). These findings were preceded by an earlier case of voyeurism in 1958 in which he described a scoptophilic patient with a powerful oral fixation. When the man's wife was pregnant or his financial security was threatened, he experienced intense frustration, anger toward mother, and felt both the wish to attach himself to the breast and a fear of losing it. During these periods he experienced a hypnogogic hallucination which Almansi attributed to the traces of his mother's face as it appeared during nursing (1958, p. 602). This phenomenon was related to severe separation anxiety and "was connected with scoptophilic urges" (p. 602).

Continuing his research in scoptophilia, object loss and voyeurism, Almansi (1979) concluded that fear of object loss in real life is the important factor predisposing one to voyeurism. He felt that the increasing need to maintain visual contact with the object, to incorporate it visually, led to a *hypercathexis* of the visual function which was later *sexualized*. Although object loss was undoubtedly significant in his patient, "it is not necessarily a factor in all cases of perverse voyeurism" (1979, p. 601). His patient suffered from a severe scoptophilic perversion with intense fears of losing the object, and he cited the following factors in its causation.

Almansi's patient was a businessman in his midthirties whose principal symptom was peeping through windows for hours while masturbating; frequently telephoning women he did not know during which time he would try to be recognized by the woman as an acquaintance, engaging her in a complicated game in which she attempted to find out his presumed relationship to her and what sort of person he was. Almansi concluded that this behavior was a way of controlling her through a discussion of sexual intimacies. He was compulsively fascinated by pornography (similar to the case of Martin described in detail in this chapter), and wished to read about women with big breasts. His other symptoms were (1) fear of death; (2) hypochondriacal complaints of cancer of the stomach, rectum, and penis; (3) frequent bouts of eating and drinking too much (needs for oral incorporation); and (4) episodes of depression.

Several important causal themes could be delineated: (1)

a near fatal illness beginning after weaning at the age of eight months. This illness lasted until the patient was eighteen months of age. At this point, the father lost his job and the patient developed severe attacks of bloody diarrhea, crying fits, and fell into intermittent periods of semistupor. Photographs taken at this time showed a feeble, emaciated, famished, depressed child, screaming and angry, sometimes passive but always intently *watching* his parents and feeling lonely in their absence. The patient shivered when he looked at these photographs. (2) The patient witnessed the primal scene between the ages of two and three-and-a-half when he slept in his parents' bedroom behind a screen and was able to see them in a mirror. This history of "hidden seeing" is a familiar theme in voyeurism (as in the case of Martin), and allows the patient to participate in others' lives, including their sexual and intimate life involving elimination and excretory functions. Severely lonely, Almansi's patient identified with both parents during the act, frustrated that he was unable to participate. (3) There was intense fecal play and an uncontrolled discharge of urine at times. The latter may have been due to the primal scene stimulation and the feces may have been an object to which he could relate in the situation of threatened object loss (Tarachow, 1966; Bach and Schwartz, 1972).

Where the mother does not allow the child to separate, an interplay by mutual visual communication may heighten and increase scoptophilia and become the nurturing soil from which voyeuristic perversions arise. In this connection, Greenacre notes that visual acuity in some instances may be a substitute for the experience of being touched. Voyeurism is a substitute for the need to be touched and fondled, kissed or hugged. She noted that it is a "reaching out with one's eyes" (1971).

Mahler (1965) noted that symbiosis was optimal when the mother naturally allowed the young infant to face her, permitting and promoting eye contact, especially when nursing or bottle-feeding the infant, talking or singing to him.

The genetic relationship between object loss, scoptophilia, and voyeurism is underscored by Settlage (1971). In Settlage's case the patient was separated from an excellent nurse when he was three weeks old. This was followed by a period of three-and-a-half to four months during which the mother was completely unavailable as a libidinal object. Both of the events served as a stimulus for "precocious, visual, verbal and intellectual development" (p. 602). Settlage's findings, therefore, support the suggested connection between object loss and the genesis of voyeurism.

It has been well known that hypersensitivity to stimuli and intense early separation anxiety may be associated with precocious development of certain ego functions such as intellectual, perceptual, and linguistic ability (McDevitt, 1975, pp. 602–603). Greenacre (1971) emphasizes the threat that occurs to the child when someone is withdrawing from emotional closeness (object loss). A female patient of hers was endowed with a "remarkable alertness, an outreaching and watchful hold on reality" but tended to develop eye symptoms which had both scoptophilic and exhibitionistic significance when she felt such insecurity. In a similar vein Sours (1973) described a number of patients suffering from false myopia caused by spasm of the ciliary muscles, producing blurring or misty vision, and variations of visual acuity. These phenomena were precipitated by separation from the object, real, threatened, or fantasied, and were associated with sleepiness, depression, listlessness, hypnogogic hallucinations, and dreams related to the oral triad (Lewin, 1933).

In milder cases of scoptophilia and voyeurism the causative trauma seems to have been limited to seeing siblings fed by the mother with resultant envy but without severe threat to the stability of the earliest mother–child relationship. In such instances, trauma occurs at a much later date and the fear of object loss is not as central. Do all voyeuristic patients have a frustration of oral drives which are then displaced to a need for incorporation with the eyes, as suggested by Kris (1956)? In his case, the mother was depressed and could only relate to the patient through facial expression. Depression in the mother often produces in the child a tendency to searching looks that are needed for visual contact and reassurance. Kris concluded that if the natural symbiosis occurs with frequent eye contact during nursing and bottle-feeding, talking and singing, the child will not become a voyeur. The mother's inability to allow the child to traverse the separation–individuation phase leads to a hypertrophy of the visual function, an uncanny and persistent reaching out with the eyes (Greenacre, 1971). Perverse activities including voyeurism represent attempts to establish union with narcissistically invested lost objects through many means: oral, sensory, and visual, and through archaic forms of idenification.

In 1974 (Socarides, 1974b), I noted that the voyeur's failure to successfully negotiate separation–individuation phases of life is responsible for his inability to differentiate sharply between what he sees and what he is (confusion between the body of the mother and of the self). This inability to separate also leads to feelings of sadism, the wish and desire to incorporate the object, the converse fear of its loss, and the fear of engulfment by it. Fenichel (1935) described the analysis of a female voyeur with a profound fear of engulfment. This was a fear of being attached to or enclosed in the father's abdomen, a substitute for the mother's abdomen. According to Fenichel, the patient's "seeing represented destruction and oral introjection of the pregnant body and the penis" (p. 385). "To force one's way into the body through the eye, represented in her mind as complete a process of introjection as is implied to the general run of people by entering it through the mouth." Furthermore, the fact that "no sight could actually bring about the reassurance for which the patients are striving . . . acquires a more and more sadistic significance" (Fenichel, 1945, p. 387).

In 1964 I. Rosen cited the following findings from his psychoanalytic study of voyeurs: (1) a very disturbed family background characterized by subjection to intense stimulation of aggression of a sexual kind together with deprivation of understanding and affection; (2) resentfulness toward the mother which often was expressed in cruelty to animals; (3) a wish to gain attention from the mother and a need for admiration; (4) primal scene viewing at the age of four; (5) wishing to view women's toilets as a way of degrading them; (6) a feeling of being "left out of life" and a profound and intolerable loneliness with a concomitant wish to become like the mother all the while greatly fearing her. A "female identification" (disturbance in gender-defined self identity) and a fear of the orifices of the female body were the most common findings. In contrast to my own views, Rosen stressed the role of oedipal conflict and incestuous desires which, in my opinion, are superimposed on a basic preoedipal conflict and, when present, are an accretion to the deeper conflict. Oral and sadistic fantasies were never acted out in contrast to those reported by Socarides (1974b) and Williams (1964).

A summing-up and update of the research views of Almansi was presented before a Discussion Group of the American Psychoanalytic Association in 1983 (Almansi, 1983). Central to the development of perverse scoptophilic voyeurism, Almansi concluded, is the fear of object loss. This leads to the need to maintain visual contact with the object, promoting a desire to incorporate it visually and as a consequence the production of a hypercathexis of visual functioning. Hypercathexis of such functioning leads to sexualization of vision. In addition, there was always a fear of engulfment; a fear of fragmentation; the overcoming and/or neutralization of powerful destructive and aggressive tendencies through the perverse act. In the well-structured perversion, the roots of the disorder lay in the nursing situation. I noted in the group discussion that with the loss of the object there is a need to seize the object visually in order to discharge primitive tensions and anxieties. This is part of the erotic function of voyeurism. It is not the "attractiveness" of the object or the inherent pleasure of watching (the instinct derivative) that is regressively reanimated in the perversion, but rather it is the early *function* of the experience that it retained and regressively relied upon. I further noted from Almansi's description of his clinical material that by contrast self–object differentiation is promoted through perverse enactment with temporary "restoration" of appropriate gender-defined self identity through visualization of the castrated female. In addition, control over the external object is maintained so that dangers of engulfment or fragmentation will be relieved.

Almansi emphasized that visual postnatal experiences become ingrained in the complicated fabric of object relations and psychosexual development of these patients, which predisposes them to perverse development. Many of

his patients show a disposition to (1) eidetic imagery; (2)
hypnogogic phenomena; and (3) a tendency to "visual
mindedness" evoking "in a flash" certain infantile memories. Visual impressions tend to become fixated in memory
and become an essential stimulant for the "need to see." In
addition, there is a symbolic equation between the breast,
nipples, and eyes, perhaps related to their unsatisfactory
experiences at breast-feeding.

A Case of Voyeurism with Special Reference
to the Development of Sexual Sadism:
The Case of Martin

Introduction

In my patient, Martin, voyeurism served many intrapsychic
purposes. One of its main features was a defense against the
more damaging perversion of sexual sadism. Satisfaction of
voyeuristic impulses no longer sufficed on many occasions
to keep in equilibrium massive destructive, aggressive forces
which threatened to destroy both himself and the object. The
origin of his voyeurism lay in the earliest years of his life. In
my classification (see chapter 4) he would be considered to be
suffering from the well-structured perversion of voyeurism
of the preoedipal type II in the most severe range of narcissistic pathology, with borderline features and severe ego
deficits, somewhat short of schizoperversion.

Regression to a symbiotic omnipotent fusion and oneness
with the mother was defended against through the perverse
act. Reality testing was impaired but not absent, and
although he had no real empathy for others, he was capable
of some object relations, although he continually displayed a
distorted perception of people and their motives (paranoid
elements). There was splitting of good and bad self and
object representations, and he suffered from a chronic subjective feeling of emptiness and impoverished perception of
himself and others, together with a pathological grandiose
self which would brook no interference with his aims and
desires. Unable to achieve object constancy, he responded
with acts of voyeurism and sadism whenever the "good

object" frustrated him. There was a strong tendency to regressive fragmentation of the self cohesion from which he sought salvation in acts of voyeurism.

Pressed by his suffering and unable to secure the object for perverse enactment, overwhelming feelings of threats to his self cohesion led him to attempt to secure the object by force. His defenses were primitive and centered around splitting, and he attempted to control the world through coercion and intimidation. This patient was fixated in the practicing and differentiating subphases. In addition, there was a severe disturbance in gender-defined self identity with conscious and/or unconscious feelings of femininity which were terrifying to him because of their connotation of homosexuality. His self concept was severely distorted and bizarre, and he frequently imagined himself to be a wolf. He was unable to control and neutralize aggression, and his body-image was severely distorted with a fusion of male and female identities. The incapacity to control impulses whenever he felt extremely lonely, depressed, tense, rejected, frustrated, or unhappy, and when he could not use his voyeuristic perversion, made him prone to disintegration.

Overt borderline features were present: (1) generalized impulsivity; (2) lack of anxiety tolerance; (3) disposition to explosive or dissociated rage reactions; (4) paranoid distortions of the external world. He was continually enraged, blamed others, and showed dissociated aggressively invested part object relations (Kernberg, 1980a). A narcissistic patient in this range of pathology, according to Kernberg, may show strong, sadistically infiltrated polymorphous perverse fantasies and activities. Kernberg states that "when such primitive regression directly infiltrates the pathological grandiose self a particular ominous development occurs, 'characterological sadism' " (1980a, p. 30). Direct sadistic pleasure and aggression are linked with sexual drive derivatives. Kernberg (1984b) later termed this "malignant perversion." Such a "stable outlet of aggression unfortunately militates against structural intrapsychic change" (Kernberg, 1980a, p. 31). In contrast to such patients, I have found that there are voyeurs with lesser narcissistic pathology in which the grandiose self, similar to that described by Kernberg (1984b), not expressed through direct aggressive sexual discharge and the patient is protected by repressive mechanisms against underlying primitive object relations.

In Martin, aggression was poorly integrated into a primitive superego structure beneath which lay severe paranoidal fears. Martin suffered from archaic sadistic aggressive impulses which his ego had no intrapsychic means of controlling, except through libidinization of activity—acting out—which tended to bind and partially neutralize his aggression. When in psychic balance through voyeuristic behavior, he appeared charming, mellifluous in speech, and "sympathetic to others." However, this equilibrium was easily disturbed and he turned to aggressive, destructive actions. Since adolescence, deterioration had taken place in that more direct expression of aggressive sexual sadistic behavior began to occur. Identification with the aggressor provided additional relief; what he feared to passively endure he imposed on others. Anxiety derived from object loss, threats to self cohesion, and castration fear, as well as that which occasionally arose from his aggressive behavior against others led to self-destructive tendencies so that he was tempted at times to commit suicide. Both tendencies, homicide and suicide, were defended against by being externalized into the act of viewing.

Martin's superego was an archaic though influential one. Because of its primitivity it did not function as an internalized automatic restraining mechanism of conscience. It was dependent upon external objects for both permission and/or forgiveness. As noted by Fenichel (1945), the sadistic act not only means:

> "I kill to avoid being killed," but also "I punish to avoid being punished," or rather "I enforce forgiveness by violence"... "If I do something sexual, I have to be punished... I torture you until I force you, by the intensity of your suffering, to forgive me, to release me from the guilt feeling that blocks my pleasure, and thus, through and in your forgiveness, to give me sexual satisfaction" [Fenichel, 1945, p. 356].

The sadist, although pretending to be indifferent to his victim, thus may betray his profound dependence on him. By force he tries to make his victim love him; for him to remain powerless and in his control. "The love he seeks is a primitive one, having the significance of a narcissistic supply" (Fenichel, 1945, p. 356). In accordance with the Sachs mechanism (1923), the sadist keeps in consciousness and exaggerates a part of infantile sexuality in order to facilitate the repression of the more objectionable parts (i.e., looking).

In this connection, Klein (1946) opined that the origins of voyeurism and sexual sadism stem from the earliest months of life, the depressive and paranoid positions. Klein's hypothesis was confirmed and illustrated by Williams' (1964) study of sexual violence (rape) and sexual (lust) murders. "The mechanism of putting parts of the self into a victim and killing them in the victim is of the greatest importance... [as is] the feeling of being possessed by cruel, savage figures who have been taken into the self and seem to have taken possession of the self" (Williams, 1964, p. 355).

Such fears of engulfment and incorporation were implicit in Martin. It became evident that his fear of engulfment was associated with a split-off modified image of a dominating and manipulating mother who allowed him no personal freedom, success, or love. This unconscious representation of the patient's mother was indeed a split one: idealized and at the same time demonified. As he could with all women, he could at times talk to her pleasantly, go shopping with her entirely unaware of his deep hostility and hatred (splitting of the self and splitting of the object). At other times he would project his own fear, hatred, and aggression onto women and demonify them. His voyeuristic activities and later his attempts at rape were anxiety-ridden efforts to remedy an intolerable internal situation. They were a repetition of early fantasied attacks upon the mother, including her breasts, internal and external sexual organs, even upon the imagined fetus within her. Part of his motivation was due to envy of the mother as a female and part was revenge for deserting him and taking care of his father's needs. When depressive anxiety became unbearable, Martin felt persecuted by internalized objects. It made him enraged and led to voyeuristic acts, and when these failed, to sexually aggressive acts, almost to the point of sexual murder.

Clinical Study

Martin, a thirty-nine-year-old unmarried man, entered psychoanalytic therapy on the day he was released from prison,
having served a nine-year sentence for rape. Despite his long
incarceration, he agreed to live behind locked doors in a
private psychiatric hospital, escorted daily to my office for
treatment. One year prior to this imprisonment he had
served a three-month term as a consequence of his voyeurism. Four prior psychiatric hospitalizations, each lasting
from six to eight months, in which psychotherapy and in one
instance electroshock therapy had been administered, had
not led to improvement.

In our first session he revealed that he felt in imminent
danger of carrying out both voyeuristic and sexually aggressive acts and did not, therefore, object to the immediate
voluntary hospital admission that was made a condition of
beginning treatment. His general appearance suggested
that of a successful businessman, somewhat overweight,
glowering, but quite articulate. He alternated between a mild
depressive and grumbling dissatisfaction with everything
about him, and a hearty optimism tinged with sardonic
humor.

He complained of feeling "much worse" than when he
went to prison. The disdain and contempt he met from fellow
convicts as a sex offender and his enforced isolation, even
within the prison population, resulted in his having felt
bitter and depressed, enraged and defiant, filled with hate
for all mankind. Except for the last year, when he "fell in
love" with a "queenlike fairy" with whom there had been no
sexual contact, the imprisonment had been an enormously
painful period.

He had suffered deep depression, lasting from days to
weeks, with intermittent intense abdominal pain and concomitant overt, persecutory ideation. On the advice of the
prison physician he stopped masturbating but subsequently
developed a severe degree of anal pruritis, apparently a
somatic defense against anal penetration fantasies.

The last four years of prison were filled with "bad sadistic
thoughts." He found excitement and solace in a popular

novel, *The Collector* by John Fowles (Boston: Little, Brown, 1963), which he read and reread. "I don't know if I was identifying with the girl or the boy. That's the ideal setup, I thought. I'll kidnap a girl and do what I want with her. What am I going to do with her? Am I going to kill her? I don't think I will do that. I wouldn't want to kill her, but I might have to." A female social worker, whom he had once seen in the prison, became the object of his fantasies of kidnapping, sadism, and rape.

The patient had been breast-fed for three months and weaned with great difficulty. Breast-feeding was stopped abruptly at three months, with severe weight loss, colic, and incessant crying. At one year of age his only sibling, a sister, was born, with whom he shared a bedroom until adolescence, and whom he "peeked upon" as early as he could remember. Whenever separated from his mother he developed temper tantrums and was extremely demanding and clinging. From the ages of two to eight, the patient's father was ill in bed suffering from severe hypertension, from six to eight the father was hospitalized, and he died when Martin was eleven. Significantly, from the age of two to six he watched, hidden behind a screen, his mother's ministrations to an invalided father that included attending to his urinary and defecation problems, as the father was paralyzed. During these experiences he felt excited and alive and filled with morbid curiosity. This proved to be an organizing experience that was replicated in his spying on women's sexual privacy both in the bathroom and bedroom. He felt somehow his mother was responsible for his father's attacks of swearing and disruptive and abrasive behavior.

Apparently the father also suffered a schizophrenic break for two years when the patient was six to eight years old; with both "nervousness" and hypertension, the father had been chronically ill for the last five years of his life, bedridden from a stroke during the final year. The patient recalled watching in dread and fascination while his mother dressed and bathed her husband. The father was also a collector of pornography, which the patient discovered and endlessly perused in his latency period. This experience destroyed the normal quiescence of sexual interest characteristic of this phase and led to a hypertrophy of sexually perverse interest. Before illness had prevented it, the father used to take long walks at night. The patient felt that he patterned his own nocturnal strolling (although not the peeping) after this paternal habit. Immediately after the father's death, whenever his mother approached him he would go into violent rages, physically attacking her. He was soon sent away to boarding school.

He described his mother as a very "nervous person, endlessly demanding and manipulative." Despite her wealth, she withheld promised sums of money from him and always insisted, even when he was hospitalized, that he was being extravagant. She urged him from childhood to wear the cheapest clothing, purchased garments for him at bargain stores. She alternately gave and withheld, was pleasant and angry, frustrating and yielding, consistent only in her ambivalence toward him, forever punishing and rewarding, bribing and depriving. Throughout the treatment that he received at various hospitals and with various psychiatrists, she complained both to the patient and to the analysts about its cost and the "self-sacrifice" it imposed on her.

Significantly, from early childhood the patient recalled an intense fear of the dark, a fear that something would come out of the night, engulf and destroy him. (A similar fear was present in later years, although he would venture out in the dark to try to find "light" to which he would gravitate and by which he would be fascinated.) At about the age of twelve, while at boarding school, he remembered that:

> [A] homosexual grabbed me and jerked me off. I felt, "this is it, this is what I've been missing all my life." However, I used to have a lot against the idea of being a homosexual. I guess I still do. . . . My fear of the dark . . . I was very scared. I would never dare to go to the basement alone. I wasn't afraid of the dark *if I was outside*, but I was afraid of it if I were inside the house [the conditions of his voyeurism required that he be "outside the house," i.e., outside the mother]. I think my voyeurism started because I tried to share other people's lives because I had none of my own and was terribly lonely.

The patient recalled that he saw the primal scene on

various occasions while secreted inside the parental bedroom between the ages of five and eight (his first episode of
voyeurism).

The mother regarded him as a "bad boy" and would
continually tell him so. He frequently got into fights in going
to and coming from school, and was even allowed to leave
fifteen minutes early, before other children, in order to avoid
fights in the street. This signified, even at this age, a pronounced increase in aggression in this patient. His tendency
toward physical attacks against others continued even in
high school, but were considerably lessened when he began
to engage in voyeuristic acts in the third year of high school.
This caused him to be arrested for the first time for voyeurism at the age of fifteen. He was not allowed to return to
boarding school for his third year, because once again he
was detected "peeping."

"My mother would often burst into the bathroom while I
was bathing. She would pull down her pants and use the
toilet. She would also walk around the house naked. She had
scars on her buttocks which upset me greatly." He would
peek at his sister on occasion when they shared a bedroom
but there was no sexual contact with her. An aunt lived on
the upper floor in their home until he was thirteen, and he
would attempt to "burst into" her bedroom, trying to catch
her in the nude. From passively enduring invasion by his
mother, he had proceeded to active invasion. He recalled that
in midadolescence even the thought of someone peeping in
on him was frightening, as was the feeling that someone was
in the room whom he could not see. By fifteen, however, the
surreptitious flitting from one back window to another,
through alleys and fire-escapes, and the careful planning
required to really "case" a house made him feel at times that
he was "like the Phantom of the Opera," an elusive, lonely,
misshapen, and ugly figure, who found ways to hide for
years, prowling throughout the night in order to satisfy his
voyeuristic needs. He confided that in periods of great
danger he wished his canine teeth would grow so that he
could more easily frighten, and thereby control his victims.
At this point his voyeuristic activities were all that he lived
for or cared about. Only through voyeurism could he achieve

satisfaction, "share in the lives of others," overcome his loneliness, stop a frightening sense of fragmentation and loss of self, and achieve relaxation and gratification, easing anxiety and violent feelings within him.

The well-structured voyeuristic perversion apparently began at the age of fifteen, although at the age of ten he had an interest in looking at women who were undressing. He would secrete himself in a locker of the ladies' side of the swimming club at the beach, and often stay there all day. If noticed, he would simply run away and soon return. At fifteen, he hid in his aunt's room with a handkerchief tied over his nose and mouth for disguise, and approached her, intent upon touching her. The police were called, but the episode was dismissed as a childish prank. He engaged in voyeurism throughout high school, completed college with great difficulty because of the enormous amount of time spent in climbing fire-escapes, looking into windows, and hiding behind small buildings where he could look directly into bathrooms and bedrooms. By seventeen, the perversion became so intense that he would spend nearly every night, from sunset to sunrise, looking into windows. He was interested in seeing women not only in the nude, but on the toilet. His interest in the process of evacuation proved to be related to his fear of incorporation through the orifices of the female body.

He began to want to touch the woman he was watching. He had seen at least "a thousand women" undress during his nightly excursions over the years. On one occasion, while employed quite successfully as a market researcher, he was sentenced to a three-month jail term (previously mentioned), and was never again employed in a comparably desirable job, one appropriate to his intelligence and education.

"Nightfall is exciting. If I see a light in a house, I will go toward it. I interpret the light as someone having intercourse or someone undressing. If I look in and see an old lady, I am disgusted" (a reaction formation against the original love-hate object, the mother). Preliminary to his actual peeping, which was accompanied by masturbation and some exhibitionism, he felt that he underwent a "change," that he was not himself, that he was perhaps another person, that he was in a daze (splitting of the ego). In an overdetermined effort to master the powerful internal tensions which remained undischarged from only partial success in seeing a woman nude, he would feel compelled to return to the same window despite the danger of being apprehended. It was an absolute necessity that he have complete control over the object; that the object not frustrate him from his view before orgasm was achieved through masturbation.

During psychoanalytic therapy he both enjoyed and was frightened by the thought of strangling a woman, although he did not want to kill her. "I simply want her to be completely in my power, as if she is anesthetized." He felt part of his purpose in looking was to satisfy his "curiosity, to know everything about women, to feel as a woman feels, to know what it is to be like a woman," all the while remaining a man and exhibiting his phallic powers. His unconscious motivation was to deny that he was a female by viewing the anatomical differences between himself and women, and by the simultaneous reassurance of manipulation of his penis.

When he was depressed or angry at his mother, or disappointed by someone, or had experienced narcissistic slights or rebuffs, voyeuristic impulses would overwhelm him. Often he blamed his voyeurism on his deep sense of loneliness; he felt he was an "unapproachable person" who quickly "sees through" others and thereby antagonizes them. These feelings reflected his pathological grandiosity, his sense of isolation, and his tendency to engage in paranoid reactions.

During his psychoanalytic therapy, a "young and beautiful" woman was admitted as a patient to the ward. He stated that she was "out of contact," and he made sexual overtures to her that were passively received, telling her that he was the only one who understood her, and that he was there to "test her." "I found that this woman was powerless. I had a tremendous sense of excitement. The same sense when I am looking into windows, that she really didn't know what was going on, that's what is important, and that she is in my power and I control her." After electroshock therapy the woman's condition changed abruptly. "She was perfectly in touch and she completely ignored me. I got a very violent reaction then. I thought of grabbing her around the neck. The violent feeling begins when women are not in my power."

Martin was largely cooperative in therapy, despite his distrust and fear of the analyst, especially when reporting fantasies of violence against women. He was grateful for the opportunity for treatment, but was always pessimistic as to its outcome. In the transference he had very little appreciation of the analyst as a person, often attempting to manipulate him into the granting of special favors such as weekend passes away from the institution. He had no trust or confidence that his condition could be cured but was willing to cooperate in the search for causes of his disorder. His manner was always cool, sardonic, questioning, distrustful, although he readily produced dream material, fantasies, and engaged in free association. Previous unsuccessful psychiatric therapies also led him to believe that the outcome was severely in doubt. Treatment was terminated in the eleventh month because of an attempted rape of a recently discharged former patient of the institution. Hostility and defiance were hidden behind any apparent eagerness to cooperate, and he attempted to reverse the position of analyst and patient and show his superiority over the analyst by his comments. He began the analysis with an attitude of distrust that remained hidden at first, and then gradually made its complete appearance. He wished to make the analyst feel useless and incompetent. Furthermore, his narcissistic grandeur could not tolerate the superiority of anyone in authority and for long periods of time he devalued the analyst. Any attempt to analyze the narcissistic components of his condition led to aggressiveness toward the analyst. He felt he had to omnipotently control not only his victims, the hospital, and his mother, but also the analyst. He engaged frequently in intellectual thought and frequent idealizations of himself, his ability to understand literature, art, and so on. In essence, there was a powerful effort throughout his treatment to prevent any hint of dependency in the narcissistic transference and as a result he remained "isolated" in the analysis as he was in everyday life, except when engaging in his perversion. He attempted to keep external objects devalued and apart from him lest they impinge upon his pathological grandiosity.

The following account of the attack on the discharged patient that led to the abrupt termination of the analysis and his transfer to another institution upon the insistence of the hospital authorities was given to me over the telephone by his victim, Eva. It resembled the fantasied attacks on other women that he had described in treatment. After calling Eva to say he wanted to visit her in the apartment where she was living alone after her discharge from the hospital, he told the ward nurse that he still had an hour left on his pass, which was true, and that his uncle, his regular weekend escort, was waiting for him in the lobby although, as he knew, his uncle had already left. Eva reports:

Martin made advances to me as soon as he arrived. I said, "No dice." I was in the kitchen. He went into the bathroom and took the briefcase he had brought with him. Later I saw that the case contained a hunting knife, several handkerchiefs, and some nylon socks. We both went into the living room and he asked if I would put on a record. I turned my back and as I was leaning over the phonograph he put something around my neck. I began to see black. He loosened it for a second and then tightened it again. He asked me to open my mouth, then he stuffed a handkerchief into my mouth and kept it there. I was gagged. Then he pulled my arms around my back and tied them. When he first put the thing around my neck, he pulled the knife around and said if I moved he would use it. When I managed to push the handkerchief out of my mouth I told him I wouldn't scream. He said, "I'm going to fuck you." He made me lie on the floor face-down and then from the back cut off my clothes with the knife. He turned me over. He was bending over me and I started crying. I kept asking him to stop. I kept saying to him and asking him, "Do you know what you're doing?" I got the impression he didn't know what he was doing.

I told him he was going to drive me back into the hospital and that I had had electroshock treatment. "You're going to drive me back to the hospital," I said. He kept telling me to be quiet. Once he was undressed, he took my bra and *laid it over my eyes*, and said, "I don't want you watching me." [In his version of this episode the patient did not reveal this important detail:

that he had covered his victim's eyes because he did not wish to be seen. Not only did he not wish to be seen, but he feared he would lose control of her if she could see. Her eyes might prove to be stronger incorporative instruments than his own and threaten him with sadistic aggression and engulfment. It became clear why he must see from the dark to the light and why he wished his victims to be in his complete control, even anesthetized and unconscious. Vision means aggression and control. If seen, he would become aware that it was *he* who was committing these aggressive acts despite the partial splitting of the ego and thus guilt would intrude upon him.]

He spread my legs apart and he started orally stimulating me and kept this up. After five to ten minutes he moved on top and tried to kiss me. I turned my head away and asked him to stop. He knelt there. He couldn't enter me. He did not have an erection. The bra had fallen from my eyes. He finally removed it completely and he looked at me. And then he looked around and at the floor, as if he were beginning to snap out of it. There seemed to be some indecision and then he started to say he was sorry. He looked as if he didn't know what to do. He untied my hands and said he was very sorry. Then he said, "There is something I have to tell you." And he told me of his history of voyeurism, that his father died, and his mother remained. Once he ran his fingers over the knife, and he kept saying how he was still scared, and he said he was afraid I would call the police. He kept saying his life was in my hands. He said he was probably seeking punishment. He wiped the fingerprints off everything. I stood up and said, "I want to put on a robe." He said, "I guess you'd better get dressed." He then started to call you but you were out and he called the substitute doctor. He picked up the briefcase, made sure everything including the cut clothes was in it. He straightened everything in the apartment. The whole thing took approximately two hours. He said, "Can I hold you?" After five seconds I pulled away. I was hurt in my neck and couldn't swallow. When he left I called my doctor and called the police in five minutes. Martin called me about an hour later when the detectives were at my apartment and asked, "Are you all right?" like nothing had happened.

The patient was terrified by this incident and feared arrest. The following night he had two dreams:

Somehow I lost the woman I was with, who was in a car, and I ended up somehow in a freight car. There was a man with a gun who looked cadaverous like the old-time actor, Slim Summerville. When I told him I was not trespassing, but looking for my woman, he seemed to acquiesce. I was in the freight car when suddenly it began to move and it was dumped into a tremendous body of ice water. Somehow I got out of the freight car and started swimming underwater but then I got into a cubicle where there were other people. They were doomed like me. I began to talk to a few of them and tried to talk them into trying to get out. A nearby woman had heard me, was against us, and tried to call and report it to the authorities. I grabbed her around the neck to prevent it.

In the next dream I was in a car. The car was in a network of roads and highways, and it veered and got out of control. It was the woman's fault. Somehow I'm doing something to her. I made the woman take a certain road.

Being in the cubicle, enclosed in the freight train, and trapped under water reflected the fear of engulfment. The dreams also revealed his paranoid fear of men and his delusional conviction that women would only destroy him. He attacked women to protect himself. He did not trust them and feared that if they ever got out of control (the car) they would kill him. This was a projection of his own paranoidal anxieties and aggression onto women. He feared engulfment in icy water, unlovingness, unhappiness, being destroyed and encased in a medium from which there was no escape— the uterus or the body of the female.

The victim did not press charges and Martin was subsequently transferred to another hospital facility.

Discussion

The genesis of Martin's perversion of voyeurism can be seen to have similar etiology as those reported by other investigators: namely, an early threat of object loss secondary to difficulties in the first two years of life; for example, intestinal complaints, colic, difficulties in eating; an environment in which certain elementary needs of gazing, viewing, seeing, taking in visually of the good object were not present; an early hypercathexis of the visual function; early primal scene experiences; organizing traumata involving visual perceptions of the father's being paralyzed and ministered to by a nurse-mother whom the patient blamed for the father's incapacities and rages; a feeling of isolation which later led to the wish to view, to see, be part of, and to incorporate through the eyes in order to overcome intense feelings of loneliness and object loss. The early origin of these traumata occurring in the differentiating and practicing subphases of the separation–individuation phase led to a disturbance not only in self–object differentiation and fears of engulfment by the object, but to the predominance of primitive, archaic defense mechanisms in which splitting predominated and defenses were in archaic prestages of development. Projection and incorporation were predominant mechanisms rather than repression. The patient suffered from severe anxiety secondary to impending disruption of his self cohesion which could only be relieved through his perverse acts. His transferences were narcissistic (primitive), the self–object was frequently deflated or diminished and, as a result, a therapeutic alliance could barely be formed and change was highly improbable. The sexual orgasm helped restore the sense of having a bounded and cohesive self (Eissler, 1958a; Socarides, 1978a; Stolorow and Lachmann, 1980), warded off fears of merger, destruction, and engulfment by the female, and reinforced his masculine gender-defined self identity. The perverse activity was an attempt to halt regression and neutralize aggression through sexualization.

The voyeur and sadist suffer from the basic preoedipal nuclear fear found in all perversions: the fear of merging and fusing with the mother. This is accompanied by a predominance of archaic and primitive psychical mechanisms, especially projective and incorporative anxieties. The failure to separate from the mother causes a disturbance in gender-defined self identity and the patient develops an intense primary feminine identification which is unacceptable to him.

The function of voyeurism is to reinforce masculinity

through the visual reassurance of viewing the female body as distinct from his own. By viewing intercourse which takes place outside himself he can be sure that it is not perpetrated upon or within his body. The entire event is taking place external to himself. He wishes also to reassure himself by means of distancing that he is not being swallowed up or enveloped through the woman's orifices.

While viewing his victim from outside the window he masturbates. Often during his voyeuristic acts he exhibits his penis to her so that she will react with fright (exhibitionistic component). His voyeurism proves to be a defense against unconscious homosexual wishes that he finds too threatening and disturbing with their connotation of being damaged by men in anal intercourse. He is reassured against his primary female identification and his fear of castration.

The occurrence of the sexual event outside of himself prevents a deep fear from arising within him of being invaded by the body of the mother. Engulfment by the female can occur through the eye of the female (a substitute for her genital) through the mechanism of ocular introjection. Her eyes can penetrate into his eyes, enter his body, and become an internalized persecutory object which threatens to destroy the insides of his body, to tear them out, to rob and deplete him of strength and masculinity, to weaken and depress him, to divest him of well-being. These fears originated in childhood fears of his mother robbing him of everything he possessed. Frequently, as he closed his eyes and attempted to sleep, he would fantasize or dream of an enormous hawklike bird flying through the window and attacking him. He dared not close his eyes, to stop looking, as he could then be attacked and destroyed.

The voyeur wishes to retain the optimal distance from and/or closeness to women (mother) without fear of engulfment; he yearns for masculinity, he dramatizes his masculine strength through his voyeuristic activities. Voyeurism, an act of invading others' sexual privacy, can proceed from looking to touching, to seizing to assaulting and destroying (sexual sadism).

In sexual sadism there is a complex interplay between the

sadist and his "love object": (1) the object of the sadistic sexual assault should be powerless. (2) The object should then undergo suffering. (3) The suffering undergone by the object is imposed by the sadist so he can be relieved of his own suffering and pervasive guilt. For the moment he may be relieved of his burden of archaic guilt or at least it may be diminished through the mechanism of enforced sharing of guilt with another, the victim. (4) The victim can undergo suffering *for* the sadist due to the latter's fluidity of ego boundaries and partial identification with the victim. (5) The object is "forced" to "forgive" and "love" the sadist as a move of self-preservation in the context of the sadist's complete control. The sadist is dominated by his need for control. Should the victim ever reject him, protest, or seek redress, she has, in effect, canceled the "forgiveness," taken back the "love," and thereby demanded that the sadist face the dangerous guilt he tried all along to conceal from himself and deny. In such circumstances, the sadist experiences a "violent reaction" and a wish to restore his lost control over the victim and resume his sadistic acts. (6) The paramount desire of the sadist, that the woman be powerless, is in contrast to the usual desire of a male that he himself be powerful (potent). The woman's powerlessness is a precondition of the sadist's basic aim: to gain control of the fearful demonic mother.

As in the case of Martin, voyeurism may function as a defense against a wholesale expression of destructive and sadistic impulses arising from the fear of being destroyed, invaded, engulfed, inwardly (bodily) despoiled, and persecuted. In such instances, voyeurism and sadism are intimately connected, now one, then the other dominating the clinical picture, depending upon the balance of psychic forces.

Chapter 18
PEDOPHILIA:
THE CASE OF JENKINS

Introduction

Well-structured pedophiliac perversions, though not uncommon, have received scant psychoanalytic attention. Those who undergo psychoanalytic treatment greatly fear the possibility of disclosure of their identities and those in treatment are prone to premature interruption of their psychoanalysis. Fenichel (1945), in his *Psychoanalytic Theory of Neuroses*, devotes only two short paragraphs to this perversion, noting that "It is true that sometimes . . . superficial reasons may suffice for persons to be attracted by children. Children are weak and remain approachable when other objects are excluded through anxiety" (p. 333). He concluded that this "love" for children was based on a narcissistic object choice. This apparent neglect of the pedophile, in my opinion, was in fact a product of a lack of analytic material derived from analytic penetration into this disorder, for there are few psychoanalytic reports on this condition. Sudden, fleeting sexual impulses toward children occurring in the course of handling or observing a child are frequent, however, and are often reported during psychoanalytic therapy. Such fantasies or even enactments do not necessarily signify that the patient is suffering from a pedophiliac perversion. Considerable numbers of individuals may be engaging in pedophiliac *behavior*. The diagnosis of pedophilia can only be made after a rigorous study of the patient's sexual history and the developmental phases that they have traversed. The true pedophiliac is one who out of inner necessity must engage in sexual relations with a prepubertal child (before the development of secondary sex characteristics) in order to achieve sexual gratification and to obtain relief from unconscious conflicts. Often fleeting periodic pedophiliac fantasies are reported by patients with intense fears of the opposite sex, together with suppressed (rarely expressed) homosexual tendencies. In this group is the startling appearance of a pedophiliac perversion in the elderly or late middle-aged whose sexual patterns have been altered by multiple psychological and organic brain changes accompanying aging, trauma, or neoplasm. Often individuals, in the course of making a transition from certain psychotic states (often paranoid) to neurotic symptomatology (or in the opposite direction), pass through a transitional symptom phase of pedophilia or other perverse formations; for example, exhibitionism, voyeurism, homosexuality. This phenomenon was first described by Glover (1933). Rare acts of pedophilia, reacted to with anxiety, may appear in the manifest content of dreams of those who temporarily retreat from adult sexuality to a less threatening infantile sexual object choice. Some adults have engaged in brief and isolated sexual contact with prepubertal children in the context of a seductive, curious child and in a state of drug intoxication. Such pedophile behavior may represent a loosening of impulse control and regression secondary to frustration. As a rule, these acts are not stereotyped, nor are they the sole avenue for the individual's sexual gratification, and are transitory. The high incidence of sexual abuse of children during the 1980s makes one conjecture that there may be a "facultative" or "epidemic form" of (nonclinical) pedophilia similar to that which may be occurring in homosexuality. Such epidemic or facultative forms of sexual perverse pathology have been known to occur at times of social disequilibrium, and there is no "authoritative prohibition by society" (Freud, 1905b, p. 222) against sexual license. In a sense, they represent the enactment of an earlier historical belief in the adulation and primacy of instinctual discharge processes, rather than a belief in the value of the sexual object per se.

Karpman (1950) reported a case of pedophilia in which the patient's conflicts seemed to center around a fear of pubic hair in women. It constituted a traumatic experience in the patient's childhood that he avoided by substituting harmless girls of prepubertal age. He noted the importance of incorporative elements, being swallowed by the pubic hair, but the developmental aspects of the ego, its defense mechanisms, were not clarified. He reported a twenty-year cure with the enucleation of this traumatic episode.

Cassity (1927) reviewed the literature up to that time, including the contributions of Krafft-Ebing, Havelock Ellis, Magnan, Bleuler, Stekel, and Hadley, and presented four cases treated by himself. He underscored the following etiological factors: (1) the early loss of the breast (weaning trauma) provoking strong retaliative tendencies which were alleviated through forcing the love object to gratify oral cravings, and at the same time dominating and controlling them; and (2) the avoidance of castration anxiety by choosing a love object like oneself.

Freud (1905b), in the "Three Essays," stated that it is:

[O]nly exceptionally that children are the exclusive sexual object. They usually come to play that part when someone who is cowardly or who has become impotent adopts them as a substitute, or when an urgent instinct (one which will not allow of postponement) cannot at the moment get possession of any more appropriate object. Even hunger does not permit of such cheapening, i.e., variation in its object, as does the sexual instinct does [pp. 148–149].

Freud remarked that the sexual abuse of children is more frequent among those who are in intimate contact with them (e.g., schoolteachers, and so on), and put forth the suggestion that those in whom the practice is exclusive may well be "insane" (p. 149). Bernard Glueck, Jr. (1956), a psychoanalyst with extensive contact with homosexual pedophiles in prison environments, confirmed the high incidence of schizophrenia (76 percent out of thirty cases) already predicted by Freud).

There have been no detailed psychoanalytic case histories since my early paper "Meaning and Content of a Pedophiliac Perversion" (Socarides, 1959). My brief communication at that time concentrated on only one facet of the problem, mainly that the patient's pedophilia served as a defensive maneuver against introjective and projective anxieties of early childhood, helping to eliminate anxiety, guilt, and pain. In this chapter I present a detailed study and interpretation of my patient's psychopathology as viewed from the vantage point of our present-day theoretical and clinical advances.

Clinical Study

My patient was a preoedipal type II pedophile at the most extreme range of narcissistic pathology. He posed a guarded prognosis because of the severity of his internalized object relations pathology, insufficient and marked fragility of self organization (self cohesion) with tendencies toward fragmentation, severe narcissistic pathology, and ego deficits with an impairment of superego functioning. Defenses were in a primitive stage of development, with splitting predominating over repression. Overt borderline features were present, such as severe impulsivity, inability to tolerate anxiety, tendency toward explosive rage reactions, and paranoid distortion of reality. An early increase in primary and secondary aggression produced a hypertrophy of aggression which directly infiltrated his actions, threatening both object and self. Bouts of aggression could only be controlled through libidinization and had not been integrated into any existing superego structure. At times, however, he was capable of experiencing depression. He was well aware of the consequences of his pedophiliac acts to his victims and as a reparative move had made the care of children (those he did not seduce) his life work. Part–object relations, invested with aggression, were acted out and relieved in sexual relations with prepubertal male children. The severity of his intrapsychic pathology was clearly manifest by the frequency of his pedophiliac practices, two to three times a week, even under conditions which could have easily led to his apprehension by the authorities.

Jenkins was an intelligent man in his late twenties whose sexual life consisted of the seduction of prepubertal boys. Increasingly disturbing symptoms of anxiety, depression, and a fear of death, which he at first believed were unrelated to his perversion, led him to seek psychoanalytic help. He had recently been frightened by a near-arrest for his pedophilia. Soft-spoken and apparently mild-mannered, he was often intensely hostile and uncooperative, doing his best to discredit the analyst and frequently stating that the analyst must hate him for his pedophilia. His productions were often of a paranoid nature, and on a number of occasions he accused the analyst of having hypnotized him during the sessions without his knowledge. He felt he had a "vendetta against society." It owed him a debt, and the analyst was a protector of society. Why should he stop what he was doing, what had society ever done for him? Often he became jubilant upon reading in the newspapers of the personal destruction produced by floods, civil wars, and earthquakes.

He was the second oldest of a large number of children in a disturbed, quarreling, financially borderline family. He often went hungry and continuously felt mistreated, as far back as he could remember. His father was often cruel and vicious to his mother. He remembered his father's angry outbursts and his wishes that he could protect what he later felt was a "cold and heartless woman." When the patient was five years of age, he and the children above him in age were placed in an orphanage because of economic hardship on the pretext that the mother would return for them the next day. "I just waited and waited, the nights led to days, the days to weeks, the weeks to months and then to years." On occasional Sunday visits, he would beg his mother to allow his return to home, pledging that he would be no trouble to her. Since his placement in the orphanage he had felt that there was no love in the world. At the age of approximately seven or eight, he was terrified by a story of cannibalism among white mice, and often played in his imagination with the fantasy that the mother eats the young that cannot take care of themselves. He often had fantasies of all the children in his family returning to the mother's womb, suppressing this when the fantasy of a frightful tearing-apart of his mother began to intrude. At eight years, he complained of some transitory visual hallucinations of a cruel-looking,

Christlike figure approaching him. His brother, two years older, was often cruel to him, making him carry out delinquent activities, frightening him, and then holding him close to his body and kissing him. At about eleven years of age he ceased imploring his mother to take him home, but shortly thereafter developed fears of death, often attempting to approximate this condition by becoming immobile and holding his breath. However, he soon became terrified over his inability to maintain voluntary control over what he called his "experimental state of suspended animation." At the age of twelve, when told by his mother that she had wanted to "abort him," he felt "lucky and happy to be alive." Shortly thereafter, while attending a father–son dinner as a guest from the orphanage, he began to suffer from severe depression upon seeing a young boy engaged in an animated conversation with a loving father. Beginning in his twelfth year, he was seduced by various older boys, his older brother, and by a counselor in the orphanage, fellatio and mutual masturbation being practiced. He responded to the growth of pubic hair with disgust, shame, and a feeling that the appearance of pubic hair meant a step closer to death. Only adults had hair, and he wanted to remain a young boy. By fifteen, a sense of personal dissolution and fragmentation of his ego appeared. At those times he would gaze intently at himself in the mirror in order to help control a threatening loss of ego boundaries and self cohesion. This very often failed.

> Some sort of thought would run through my mind as I looked at my face. I'd look into my eyes, and then like my mind would start to leave me. Maybe it has to do with death. I had the overwhelming feeling I'd vanish, break apart, dissolve, be no more. I could only stop it by calling my brother's name over and over again and then my body was reconstituted.

During anxiety attacks, he felt torn apart, in danger of imminent self dissolution. His thoughts would lack purpose, words would become meaningless, actions goal-less. This intense anxiety would cease upon the carrying-out of sexual relations with a prepubertal boy.

Although the most striking trauma to this patient appears to have been his being sent to an orphanage at age five, the previous five years were filled with memories of a quarreling family and a violent father. His earliest memories were those of being uncared for, "not having enough to eat." His mother would always act as if she were "doing me a favor in giving me a piece of bread." The parents were frequently "fighting" and he, like the other children, was left to his own "devices." Between three and four he witnessed parental intercourse, but stated "it had no effect on me," except that he pitied his mother and felt that the father was somehow treating her badly. By age four, he frequently told his mother that she would never have to worry, that he would "take care of her." However, at five, the traumatic removal to the orphanage took place. His reaction was overwhelming loneliness and "coldness." He wanted his mother to come back, and he felt that she had deserted him. On the other hand, he began to feel that he was put into the orphanage "to live," or otherwise "I might die." "My parents rejected me." He frequently promised to be "good" on infrequent visits home if he were not returned to the orphanage. However, he was always returned to and stayed in the orphanage up to the age of seventeen. At six years of age, he was "pushed around" by the older boys and by his brother, was often bounced on their laps and considered "cute." He was alternately hopeful of returning to his mother, and despondent, depressed, and lonely when he was not. He felt tricked by the mother: "waiting and waiting, I never gave up hope until I was seven. I would beg my mother not to send me back."

At age six he had his first sexual experience. An older orphanage boy, age sixteen or seventeen, played with his genitals, and he felt "cold sensations around them. I didn't realize what was going on." This first seducer was the monitor in the print shop, where he would occasionally go to be comforted. At age eight, he apparently suffered a febrile illness and saw the "man on the wall," a Christlike figure that appeared to him later on. Also at age eight he was spanked by a headmistress of the orphanage in front of others, and felt humiliated, but learned "not to cry." He remembered at that time also that his father came to the orphanage one day, and had a memory of his walking away slowly, and felt abandoned. From nine to ten, "we would occasionally watch with other boys chickens having their necks cut off and dying in an agony pit at a local butcher-shop." At age eleven, when he stopped asking his mother to come back he simultaneously developed a period of depression that lasted until he was thirteen years old. At that time also, two boys in the orphanage died, one from a fall from one of the windows, and another from an illness. He himself looked cherubic, like a little girl, was popular and easygoing, and liked by almost everyone. It was also at that time that his mother told him that she had wanted to have him aborted, that she had only wanted one child, and that he was the second. He wrote long letters about death to a former counselor at the orphanage at the age of twelve.

> I went through a period as a child when everything bothered me, between eleven and thirteen, and I was so *depressed*. Somehow or other I managed to control a great deal of these feelings. Maybe through sex I found a kind of adjustment. I began to realize that there'd always be sex around. If I wanted to badly enough, I would entice and have sex with any kid I wanted to. Sometimes I think of having sex with a boy during the day. Sometimes I feel depressed. Other times there would surge through me a feeling of great strength and superconfidence, that I wouldn't have to have sex with boys and that I could conquer worlds. I would have the ability to do great things (grandiosity).

Narcissistic grandiose pathology was expressed in his dream life. A frequent recurring dream up to the age of twenty was as follows: "Standing in a group where there are many faces, not bodies. I'd be standing in their midst and somehow or other they were watching. They wanted to see if I will really fly or could really fly. I put my arms up like a swan and then I was swooping around."

He first experienced thoughts of death while lying in the dark with "maybe a hundred other children."

> One boy amongst all those other boys. I'd feel lonely. And then the thoughts would center about my person and then that

somewhere, way off in the future, I would die. Was it true? Animals sense that they're going to die—the elephant graveyard— these feelings and a funny chill would run through my body. A feeling of dangling without support. No person on earth could help me. Only God, if there is a God. First I thought this was way off in the future, thank God. I don't have to worry about death now. I'm still young. Later on I had that same experience in life when I was older. Death to me is an undesirable state of affairs. One must want to live. I thought what would death feel like to me so I put myself in a state of suspended animation, a mystical feeling of what death would feel like. I'd even hold my breath so I could see what it would feel like. I'd be perfectly still and then just try to think of myself as having no life within me, "ΔΣΝ ΣΗΙ ΖΟΣ." Flashes of hot and cold, of chills going through my body, of being as close to the feeling of death as possible. It would get stronger sometimes. I was afraid that I might get myself dead, a funny fluttering chill like waves of time going through my body. My mind was controlling my thoughts. . . . Now when I see a dead person I feel very sad. I almost identify with them. Almost as if I were in the coffin. I feel very bad. The thought that I might someday have that experience occupied my thinking a lot between ten and thir- teen. I later understood that there is some thymus gland in here [points to his neck] and that it has a relation to sex, as if my self were centered there. That's where I'd get that horrible feeling.

Analysis showed that his fear of death was a derivative symptom arising from the threat of ego-dissolution and fragmentation anxiety.

Several months after the analysis began, the patient revealed: "I have sex with kids so I won't die. It keeps me young, keeps me youthful. Having sex with women means that you are grown up already. Kids don't have sex with women, only grownups have sex with women. If I don't grow up, I don't die." By incorporating the child he staves off death. Furthermore, having sex with children is better than having sex with women because women are "filthy. They have menstruation, blood . . . blood on the sheets. Kids are cleaner than women and men. They are in one whole piece. I see a kid as being nice and clean, something about a woman that's dirty. And women are designed so ugly and men are so much more graceful. Men have beauty in their legs and arms." The anxiety about death was heightened by reading *A Tale of Two Cities* at the age of thirteen or fourteen. Despite his pedophiliac acts, he was unable to overcome his fear of death. "Last night the fear of death came to me. I thought I had conquered it. I don't think it's possible to conquer that sort of fear."

His first sexual experience with his brother, three years older, occurred between nine and ten. Following this, he slept with another older boy in the same bunk from twelve to thirteen with very little guilt. He began to kiss an older man who was one of the counselors in the orphanage, from twelve to fourteen. He was the first adult who "befriended me." At age thirteen, other boys began to laugh at his growing pubic hair and he felt shame and wished the hair would disappear, as he equated it with growing old. Up to the age of fifteen he was dominated by his brother, but shortly after that he became a leader, a "spellbinder," as he said, "a prince," president of the club, and leader of the boys' and girls' student activities. He was afraid of adults and decided that he would somehow through his grace, manner, and "charisma" be able to be everyone's best friend and leader. At age seventeen he left the orphanage, attended a local college on a scholarship, and shortly thereafter received a bachelor's degree. His career choice was in the area of child guidance.

The patient's abandonment at an early age was poignantly relived during the analysis, with temporary lessening of anxiety and aggression.

> I used to sit and wait until my mother came. However, every day while we were at the orphanage, we never gave up hope. We just waited and waited. We were tricked, my brother and myself. My mother said, "Just for a day." It led to days, the days to weeks, the weeks to years, and we would wait until she came. She came for a while every second week, then not until months would pass. I was so unhappy when I came there. When she showed up on a Sunday, she showed up with food, apples, pears, and this is what she left with us when she left. The woman who was in charge used to spank us if we wet the bed. I stopped quite fast. She was so cold, though, so cold. Such a lack of warmth. I started to accept being there in about a year, I think. I think I did. Even then, when she took us back for a

Sunday I begged Mother, I begged her [the patient cries, shivers, and cannot go on; he is racked with sobbing]. I became certain I had to keep going back till around seven. I don't know why she sent me there, why my mother did this. I'd tell her I'd be good, I wouldn't cause any trouble. I became more and more alarmed that Mother didn't come back when she said she would. I was sure she would come the next day after playing there for a day. Things were so cold and loveless. . . . One day, age nine or ten, I ran away from the place with my brother. My mother was in the park where I know she went sometimes. I saw her there with my baby sister in the carriage. She acted surprised to see us. We said we wanted to come home. First she was good-natured, gave us something to eat, said we would stay overnight. Then the next morning she got ready to send us back. For the longest time we would beg her to let us stay. She would say, "Yes, tomorrow, but go back now." We begged her up to nine or ten, my brother and I. After eleven I stopped. I never begged her to take me home again. I felt rejected, unwanted, deserted. I learned to face that, and I've never seen any love in this world since. Where is this love? Show me. I want to see it [the patient becomes extremely angry]. These kids that grow up at home with their parents, spoiled brats! That's all they are. . . . All these parents, too, and I have to tell them how to raise their kids [he laughs sardonically]. They think I have "insight."

A crucial event in the patient's intrapsychic life leading to narcissistic pathology took place when he ceased asking his parents to be allowed to return home. The external world had failed to provide him with any positive response and a change which involved both grandiosity and splitting with the development of a "hollow self" occurred. A formidable, convincing, charming "false self" emerged. He became a "friend" to others in the orphanage (and later to the children he seduced), a role aimed at lessening his despair, pain, and need for love. He was, in a sense, a person without a center, who appeared strong on the outside but who had given up all hope of love and identity. He now would begin to secure needs through sexualization and through incorporation of external objects (younger boys). He no longer felt he could "join anyone"; instead he must impress them, overpower them with his personality, and prey upon them ("like the praying mantis") to keep himself alive, supplied with love, defended against threats of disintegration and death. Heightened narcissism and imperiousness were prevalent, but he usually managed to keep them under control except for occasional aggressive outbursts. He related that a "spirit of humanity" no longer remained inside him and he attacked life and people in a mixture of vengeance and pain. Reparative measures against his aggressive incorporative tendencies evolved in his choice of career; that is, counselling children and their parents for child welfare agencies—in order to undo the damage he himself was perpetrating through his sexual abuse of children.

Although in the orphanage everything was "done for us," he was always hungry and never had enough to eat. While working his way through college, he often went three days without eating, "virtually in the midst of plenty."

> I was too proud to ask my mother for something to eat. That taught me a great lesson: "If I am not for myself, who will be for me?" I was like Scarlett O'Hara: I vowed to myself I'll never be hungry again. From then on I started to think more of myself, and I had some sort of argument with my mother. I was paying for my own room and board, and she never gave me anything to eat. And she felt I was never giving her enough, like we owed her everything and we didn't. She would withhold food sometimes, or she'd make me feel kind of guilty if we ate something. She made my father also feel that way by nagging him. If you would sit down at the table, she'd throw food at you. "You want it? Here . . . !" When *she* wanted to feed you, she did. Occasionally she would give me something to eat. Even the way she'd ask nicely upset me. "Go ahead—eat! I have something for you. Everything you want. Butter, rolls. . ." That bothered me. She got me mad. She knew she did. I was never really mean to my mother, however, I felt sorry for her, and it would hurt me more to know I had hurt her. If my mother became sick I'd get so worried it would upset me so much. She was a hypochondriac, and she would say things that would turn me inside out, and I knew I didn't have any love from her.

In this connection the patient recalled a frequent upsetting and guilt-producing fantasy:

This is an image that gives me a terrible feeling of *guilt* and self-hatred. It flashed through my mind in a split second while walking along the street the other day. I am standing slightly above my mother, representing superiority, I believe, in a very rigid, emotionless, and stoical fashion. I seem to be demanding something from her, perhaps money. She is rummaging through a black leather purse, crying. What I am demanding of her is definitely not in the purse. She knows it—and I know it. But she continues to look for it because of the way in which I am coldly demanding it of her. Her tears, as she looks for this thing, are her way of telling me that she hasn't got it. But I am completely unmoved by her crying [in the image]. Actually, I am really very touched by her sobs—I should grasp her in my arms, kiss her, and ask her not to cry because I don't really need this thing. I am *playing a role that is entirely foreign to my wishes* [splitting of the ego]. I am very firm and villainous toward her in my demands—as though she were a complete stranger to me.

This whole image fills me with a terrible sense of *guilt* that I am so brutal and unmoved by my mother's tears. I feel that I have been desperately unkind to my mother for demanding something of her which she could not give me, and I hate myself for it.

In this fantasy the patient revealed one of the few episodes of guilt to occur during the analysis. The mother did not have what he wished for—maternal love—and he felt hypocritical in his demands as he was receiving these supplies from the children he seduced. He was vengeful, demanding, and cruel to his mother, for the maternal introject was a hateful and destructive one both to himself (primitive superego functioning) and to the external world. His harshness toward her induced separation guilt.

The patient was frequently sexually abused by others before he was twelve. But at age twelve he himself seduced another boy. This was a significant passage from passivity to activity. At that time he would never allow anybody to insert his penis into his mouth, and he used to hate his brother for doing that. His first act of pedophilia in which he was the instigator occurred at the age of thirteen or fourteen on a day on which he was roaming through the "tremendous" halls of the orphan asylum.

I had a terrible feeling, a feeling which is painful to me, a
vacuum that I even now feel when I don't have a boy. It's hard
to describe that feeling, that no purpose, that nowhere to go,
that nothing to do. On that day I had that feeling. There was
this kid sitting on the window. That was the first time I actually
ever had sex with him. It was the same feeling that I have
coming back over and over again, a purposelessness of life and
with everything, and with nothing to do, a complete blank, a
vacuum. I was lost, no one to talk to, an awful feeling, a horror
feeling. I don't know what it was. And then I saw that kid.
Somehow or other, I seemed to know somebody else had "used"
the kid. He had sucked somebody off. Suddenly, when I saw the
kid there I felt different. I didn't have the hollow feeling any
more. I took him someplace and had sex with him. I knew every
nook and corner of the place. He was docile, a sexy kind of kid,
like I knew he wouldn't refuse me [the child was ten years old].

The patient stated that on that day he did not have a nickel
carfare and was being punished by being made to stay in the
orphanage and not going home over the weekend. "You see
what I mean when I say it was a prison . . . no home for
children . . . we were in prison."

This incident became an *organizing experience* that later
led to the full-scale pedophiliac perversion. At eighteen, he
was to experience a similar moving situation.

At eighteen, a very important thing happened. I was sharing
an apartment with my brother. I am an opera lover and I was
listening to *La Bohème* and the main theme had a tremendous
nostalgia: "Your tiny hand is frozen. . . ." She pretends she
can't find her key and his hand touches hers. He notices it's cold
and sings the aria, "Your tiny hand is frozen." The aria was on
and I was looking out of my window. I was sad and lonely,
looking into the courtyard. One of the doors of the courtyard
opened, and a little boy entered, dressed in a navy-blue suit with
old-fashioned knickerbockers. He was brown-complexioned
and I figured he was going to the street. Suddenly an impulse
came to run down, to look at this child. I knew just about where
the kid would be at this time. I looked in the store. He was about
eight or nine. I looked at him. Something was gripping me
inside. I kept looking at him, I felt like I was in love with him. I
wanted to pick him up and hug him in my arms. He seemed

untouchable and unattainable, beyond me ... and awe about it and yet just looking at him was not enough. Some sort of pain. It tore at me inside and it made me very unhappy ... I was very lonely and sad that day, and as I looked into the courtyard the music had a sad beauty to it. The tenor sobs and is pouring out his heart ... cold, lonely, and a face out in the courtyard. He suddenly had come in. *Like something happened inside.* I left the record and it kept playing. I had to take a look at him. I stood in a position so our eyes would meet. His tan face, black hair, soft skin, I just wanted to hug him, to kiss him, to hold him in my arms. I can't recall wanting my penis between his legs or any of those things. . . . He was carrying a quart of milk and there was something about his actions. He seemed like a very well-disciplined child. Like a good kid ... *I feel I only woke up then ... the renaissance of me.* I began to develop a philosophy: "If I am not for myself, who will be for me, and if not now, when?"

Shortly thereafter, the full-scale pedophiliac acts began to occur at regular intervals.

His pedophiliac urges were precipitated by:

A hollow feeling which tears me up and destroys me, incapacitates me by the fact that I can't do anything to stop it. Also I don't want to do anything else. Sometimes I might force myself to do some work, and I feign it. I run around like a chicken with its head cut off. It makes me feel restless, unwanted, and that there's nothing in me. I'm hollow. I'm glad it doesn't last more than a day, usually. It's frightening. I think I have death on my mind. There's no purpose to my thought, to my work, or anything I might do. There is no goal, no sense of achievement. Things pile up on my desk and I can't deal with work. Everything is meaningless, including words. I was talking to my secretary the other day and all I heard was words. I couldn't feel what was important to her. When I'm in that kind of mood people have a tendency, it seems to me, to talk to me more. There is no direction, no meaning to things, no goal, no purpose, things don't matter, as if all the goals I had are gone. I can stand it for perhaps a day or less. The happiest moments are when I see a boy. Do you know that? A feeling of power when I see the boy. I decide I'm going to have sex with him. The sex itself is just a sexual release, I feel very good above it all, powerful, *alive.* It's going to keep me living, and it's a challenge that keeps me occupied. It tries my wits and ability. . . . The feeling is I want him, I want to hold him in my arms, control him, dominate him, make him do my bidding, that I'm all-powerful.

At other times, instead of the hollow feeling he wakes up in the morning with a feeling of numbness over his entire body, a feeling that he may be disappearing, like "I'm losing myself, as if my body has a whiteness."

The perversion has a warding off function, canceling out threats to the ego, and threats of annihilation. It has a compensatory function in that it makes up for the deprivations of childhood, provides him with a sense of power and control, and buttresses and reinforces his fragile self representation. The child must be subservient to him and responsive in the sense that he allows himself to be used, so that the patient can feel alive emotionally. He merges with the boy, secures love from the good mother (the good breast), and in his sexual excitement overcomes the deadness of his internal world.

The Choice of Sexual Object

Jenkins suffered from a continuation of primary feminine identification with resultant disturbance in his sense of masculinity. He sought salvation from engulfment by the mother and relief from his unconscious femininity by incorporating masculinity from a male child. Unlike homosexuals who also seek masculinity from male partners, the sexual object choice had to be a male child who represented his ideal self, whose youthfulness protected him from annihilation (death anxiety). His choice of perversion grew out of the specific environmental traumas and organizing experiences of his childhood years.

Jenkins stated that when he had sex with a boy, usually for the first time, he ejaculated very quickly but it was difficult to ejaculate the second time. "I find that if I get some sort of feeling that I'm a part of the boy I can have an ejaculation." He merged with the boy in the sexual act. "I'm having sex with boys because I want to be a boy, a part of him, a blend. I could feel it more than I can say. I'm a part of him and he's a part of me."

In a crucial session he remarked that he was seeing a movie in which there was a very beautiful girl on the screen. As he was watching the picture and the beautiful shape of her breasts, he imagined himself touching her breasts, but it "wasn't my hand, it was his hand." "I got a vicarious thrill out of it." It was only through an intermediary—the boy— that he could touch the breast of the mother. The boy also was a substitute for the good maternal breast.

> The strong sensation of a breast in his hand. I could feel it. Also I can recall when I had difficulty in ejaculating with a kid. I imagine we are together, we are merged. I'm afraid of growing up, afraid of death, afraid of growing old. I must get comfort here on earth, and I'm afraid I'll die before I'll ever be happy.

As regards the boys themselves, he wanted the boys to love him; he didn't want to love them. He stated:

> It sounds narcissistic, doesn't it? But I can't give love to a boy. I feel I become a part of the boy through the sex act. I'm the boy because I treat him the way I would like to be treated. No, I don't think the boy enjoys it, goddamn it. If the boy enjoys it too much, I don't. It's important. If the boy starts making sex advances toward me I don't enjoy it. If he starts to enjoy it too much, I don't like that [the patient laughs loudly]. You know, it's almost like having sex with a corpse . . . no responses—all I seem to want to do is to use his body—to satisfy my desire.

The boy, like a transitional object, is used, abused, loved, and must remain impassive so as not to take over and "deprive" the patient.

He compared his pedophilia to the devouring activities of animals in the jungle. He became satiated and relieved of his aggression by devouring his victims. "I like the smooth surface of the young boy's body, I don't like hair on it or any pimples. I don't like to touch that, I can't stand it. It's like eating something, like candy. Often I would pretend I was eating people as a boy. I would give this one life and the other one death."

He had only disgust for the feminine body. A woman was a filthy, angular, distorted monstrosity. "Not in one piece like boys," as their breasts protrude. "An adolescent boy is more feminine than any woman. There is no hair on him, hair is ugly. Boys' bodies are V-shaped, while womens' are angular, like a bag of shit tied in the middle." They disgusted him. A woman had no genitals, only a dirty hole where menstrual blood could contaminate and kill him by penetrating the opening of his penis during intercourse. Rare attempts to carry out heterosexual relations would put him into a "cold sweat." Adult homosexual relations, on the other hand, he found uninteresting, boring, and fearful.

The boy was a part-object, not a whole object, as a whole object might harm him; as mentioned above a woman's blood might go into the opening of his penis, and he might get sick. It might coagulate and destroy him.

In another session he elaborated on the feeling that he could get anything he wanted from a boy, and that he had to control him. "I can't give or receive love, that's my main difficulty. But what I must feel is that I can do anything I want with him, not hurt him, though, just have them in my power, just my penis between their legs and I'd kiss them. It's a good feeling. My penis becomes anesthetized sometimes, though, and it's hard to have an ejaculation." (This control over the object is similarly seen in all preoedipal type II narcissistic patients; see the Case of Willard, chapter 9.)

The equation boy=breast became readily apparent through the analysis. He was always afraid of breasts, he did not know what to do with them. He had a strong wish to incorporate the maternal breast. This could only be attained through merging with the boy (breast), thereby making up for his deprivation. During the perverse act itself, he not only identified with the boy receiving love at the hands of the good mother, but he had in his possession the good mother (good breast) devoid of her frightening configurations. It was obvious that he identified himself with the boy as a defense against destructive wishes toward more fortunate children.

The perversion was carried out when the patient found himself in a deep crisis: he had to satisfy his love needs and eliminate aggressive impulses which threatened to destroy him. This was accomplished in the case of Jenkins by an incorporation of the good love object (the child, a *substitute* for the mother) within the self, thereby maintaining relationship to objects and preserving the self through a fused relationship. At this point, without the child as the love object he would develop severe dissolution anxiety. This introjection culminated in orgasm and his primitive needs found a pathway for discharge through the genitals. Viewed in another way, the anxiety associated with the need for mother and aggression toward her, at least temporarily, was successfully libidinized and overcome through projection and introjection. In the joining of the object and self, and in the control of the love object, he overcame his sense of emptiness and abandonment. He avoided further regression into a somatopsychic fusion with the mother and loss of self in a state of dedifferentiation (regression to the symbiotic phase and psychosis).

The child-victim chosen for the pedophiliac act was an ideal image of himself, and the object relationship was a narcissistic one—from grandiose self to self. He had to have a particular kind of personality, a "selfish, attractive, pampered, loved child." He could not tolerate fat, ugly, or stupid children. They had to be "selfish" (i.e., able to look out for their own well-being). He was even proud of the way some boys took his money and called them "smart kids"; in effect, complimenting himself.

Splitting of the Ego and Splitting of the Object

Splitting of the ego and splitting of the object is a commonly found phenomenon in preoedipal type II patients. Such splitting was unusually severe in this patient. In splitting, Jenkins underwent a "transformation" into two distinct personalities. This was discovered when the analyst asked the patient to call him at a particular time in the evening in order to be informed of the time for his next appointment. In the next session the patient revealed:

I called at 8:30 but couldn't make a complete transformation. I couldn't be "A" or "B." Ordinarily my transformation would take place at 7 P.M., right after the meeting at the place I work. I had to call you at 8:30, so I had to hold off. I felt it right in the pit of my stomach. I was nauseous. I had a sort of dull headache. I was in the street and I was full of anxiety, and I had to keep waiting around until 8:30. I think I'm two different personalities. I was planning to have sex with a boy that night, and I knew that the only way to get rid of my anxiety was to have sex with a boy, but to have sex with a boy it is necessary I complete a transformation to "B." I could only call you as "A," not as "B." "B" was trying; "A" has control over the transformation. I knew that all day at 7:00 I would go through it as I needed the sex, and right away. I thought perhaps you wanted me [projection mechanism] to call you as "A."

The patient was asked how this transformation takes place.

The transformation happened five minutes after my call to you as regards our appointment. There is no obligation and no responsibility when I make the change after the call. Before that I was angry at you.... In it I change. I change, I become an entirely different person, in looks, too. I think I get a strange expression on my face. "B" is the child, irresponsible and without anxiety. My anxiety increased in that "A" was in the way. "A" must be shut out completely. All my awareness and responsibility has to be shut off [splitting of the ego] and "B" is unaware of the anxiety of "A." After sex I go back to "A" and that is painful. My facial expression is blank when I am in "B." Suppose I should meet anybody I knew as "A" when I am in "B." Then I would feel a terrible anxiety, as I would look and act differently. In sex, kids only know me as "B," a different person, easy-going and good-natured.

In the splitting of the object the boy represented that part of the split with which he was identified and who, in inner reality, was the harmless good mother; the other part of the split was the dreaded, destructive, hateful, castrated mother who was unacceptable to him and whom he dreaded incorporating. The object, therefore, had to be idealized and could not produce anxiety and guilt. This split of both ego and object allowed him to carry out his activity without conflict by denying a portion of reality.

Course of the Psychoanalysis

Jenkins' psychopathology was severe in its obligatoriness and harmful both to the sexual object and himself. His assertion that he had never hurt a boy "physically" was a source of some "pride." As I have stated earlier (chapters 3 and 4), crucial to the outcome of treatment is not the presenting sexual pathology or the life history of the patient, nor the apparent bizarreness of the perversion, but the nature of the spontaneously developing transference. Jenkins had been unable to achieve sufficient self–object differentiation and internalization of object representations to be able to form a transference neurosis. Furthermore, he did not possess a reliable enough observing ego to permit transference neuroses or transference manifestations to be analyzed. His poor impulse control tended to be acted out in the transference and there was a preponderance of hostile, aggressive strivings. Superego reactions of shame and feeling contemptible were present, projected onto the analyst. He was unable to maintain a working alliance, except for short period of time. The therapist was reacted to negatively on many occasions, although the patient was able to admit, at times, the extent of his desolation in the transference. A paranoid distrust of the analyst and of everyone else, intense pleasure to cruel fantasies, the presence of a pathological grandiose self, deficiencies in ego functioning, an infiltration of aggression into almost all of his activities, the presence of severe ego deficits characteristic of preoedipal type II narcissistic perverse patients, all militated against a successful outcome.

Beneath an apparent charm and gentleness, he felt that all people were "cockroaches." "Man is a pimple. He is rotten and he is worthless. He has done nothing to change the world and he never will. Do you think man is considerate? You just take something away from him he needs and you get basic, crude animal instincts. Everything he does is for sex." He left many sessions angry and despairing, wanting nothing from anyone, including the analyst. At times he expressed shame at having been put in an orphanage, but did not feel shame for his perversion. He felt fond of the analyst when he saw him as teacher, guide, and mentor, and at those times tried to abstain from his perverse activities, without much success. He was quick to feel the analyst might be "making fun" of him, and on one occasion when the analyst did not answer his question as to whether he was "psychotic," he terminated treatment with an angry telegram as follows:

> The fact that you did not deny Mr. K.'s self-diagnosis of psychosis is taken as tantamount to approval of the diagnosis. If Mr. K.'s conclusion of psychosis was incorrect you would surely have stated your more accurate opinion. On the contrary, your more accurate opinion was stated by your silence to imply agreement with the conclusion of Mr. K. as psychotic.

> Now, the psychotic cannot be aided by psychoanalysis, especially of the classic type. It is therefore respectfully requested that you cancel all future appointments. (signed) Sincerely, A. and B.

A telephone call from the analyst suggesting the appointments be continued with the hope of further improvement was met in a positive manner and the patient returned to treatment because he felt the analyst "cared." For many sessions he reiterated, "I can't seem to love people, and yet I want people to love me. If I could accept people's anger I could get through to them to love me, but I would rather give them hate."

Knowledge of the unconscious meaning of his need for boys led him for brief periods to attempt cessation of his pedophilia.

> The analysis gives me some sort of strength today, but it gave me anxiety when I felt the drive to have sex with a boy . . . like kind of an insight into myself that it was wrong, not right, that I shouldn't do it. I didn't have to do it today. I don't have anything to take its place, however. It's a fulfillment. I somehow feel that if I do it, the anxiety will go away.

The idea that by understanding the mechanisms behind his perversion would gradually empower him to have some degree of control over his dangerous sexual activities if he so desired were often met with taunts and accusations of hypocrisy. "I'd sooner love dogs or cats than human beings. They are more certainly worthy of my love. I don't want to change because I don't want to change myself for society. That's why I don't want to stop." In response to his question as to whether the analyst thought he could stop his sexual practices, I commented that he had "no control" as he was dominated by unconscious forces over which he had, as yet, no control. His response to my comment (which was taken as "belittlement") was both grandiose and paranoid in nature. He spoke defiantly: "I know that I don't want to stop. It's not that I can't. You're daring me?" He was filled with hatred, loathing, and bitterness. Quieting down later in the session, he managed to say, "I don't want to stop right *now*. I like you. You're the only sensible person I've ever talked to. You talk sense and you make sense. You could make me stop. You could do it. I like you. I wouldn't stop for anyone else."

Despite some evidence of a growing positive transference (the presence of a "basic transference" [Greenacre, 1954]), the patient was frequently paranoid, mistrustful and accusatory toward the analyst, even imagining that he was being hypnotized without his knowledge during several sessions. His hatred for humanity, his despair, and his need for relief from threats of fragmentation and the necessity to ward off a break from reality were too intense for him to continue therapy. We terminated treatment after approximately one year. Psychoanalytic treatment, however, was not without value, for he learned to understand in part some of the unconscious meanings enacted in his perverse activities, the mechanisms responsible for his perversion, and was able to share his grief and fear, his rage and despair with an understanding human being.

Lastly, it is important to emphasize that while Jenkins suffered from the most severe degree of sexual pathology, a preoedipal type II pedophilia with associated narcissistic personality disorder at the extreme range of narcissistic pathology, I have encountered other pedophiles in my psychoanalytic work whose level of fixation is not at the differentiating and practicing subphases and who do not present ego problems of the magnitude encountered in this patient.

In such instances, enriched by the psychoanalytic insights that very often come only from the study of the most serious cases, we may expect a more favorable outcome.

Chapter 19
EXHIBITIONISM

Introduction

The exhibitionist is an individual who brings about erection and orgasm by the abrupt exposure and manipulation of his genitals in the presence of an unknown and preferably young female. The act occurs outside the context of mutual sexual desire between a male and a female and is obligatory for erection and ejaculation. The perversion is one of the most common sexual deviations, as one-third of all sexual offenders arrested in the United States are charged with exhibitionism. These statistics may be misleading, however, as the built-in requirement for this perversion is that it be practiced in public with a nonconsenting partner who often responds with fright, so that complaints to the police are frequent. The exhibitionist is compelled to exhibit his genitals by an irresistible urge which may suddenly come upon him, or which may arise slowly and involve considerable planning leading to its enactment. The urge is felt in such a way that the individual is unable to control his behavior. What is essential for the act to be successful, that is, to result in orgastic satisfaction or to make a flaccid penis erect, is that the victim be impressed or even frightened or at least taken by surprise. The exhibitionist does not then make an attempt to make further contact with his victim, but prefers to stay distant from her, all the while experiencing sexual arousal and/or orgasm with a relief from tension and depression. It should be noted that minor episodes of *exhibitionistic behavior* may occur in individuals who have only rarely exhibited themselves within the safety of their rooms to nearby neighbors while they masturbate. A common and disguised form of exhibitionistic behavior occurs between heterosexual couples when the male may suddenly appear in a room completely naked, exposing his genitals in a way to startle his heterosexual partner. One of my patients exposed only his buttocks at first, and then quickly showed the reverse side of his body, a counterpart, the noncastrated aspect of himself. His exhibitionistic behavior was not an obligatory performance for sexual satisfaction: it was engaged in for purposes of seduction, was a means of narcissistic reassurance and/or "creating excitement" within himself. Clinical examination of the life histories of patients who engage in exhibitionistic *behavior* reveals that they have satisfactorily traversed separation–individuation phases and reach the oedipal phase, as well as the fact that their indulgence in this variant form of sexual behavior is not stereotyped and obligatory. Exhibitionistic *behavior* in women does not constitute the well-structured perversion of exhibitionism. The showing of the genitals by women does not have the reassuring effect it has in men. It has a hostile motivation, a teasing spitefulness, or may be an attempt to aggressively attract the attentions of men for purposes of sexual intercourse.[1]

Freud's Observations

In the "Three Essays" (1905b), Freud remarked that exhibitionists, instead of showing their organs preparatory to the normal sexual aim, simply display them and thereby supplant the act itself. He concluded from the findings of "several analyses" that exhibitionists exhibit their own genitals in order to obtain a reciprocal view "of the genitals of the other person" (p. 157). In a 1920 footnote he added:

> Under analysis these perversions . . . and indeed most others . . . reveal a surprising variety of motives and determi-

---

[1]Zavitzianos (1971) has described exhibitionism in the female. Such women must hold a fetish (symbolizing the paternal phallus) while exhibiting their genitals, thereby achieving sexual satisfaction.

nants. The compulsion to exhibit, for instance, is also closely dependent on the castration complex. It is a means of constantly insisting upon the integrity of the subject's own (male) genitals and it reiterates the infantile satisfaction at the absence of a penis in women [p. 157, footnote].

In contrast, he added that:

[L]ittle girls do not resort to denial of this kind when they see that boys' genitals are formed differently from their own. They are ready to recognize them immediately and are overcome by envy for the penis—an envy culminating in the wish, which is so important in its consequences, to be boys themselves.... Both male and female children form a theory that women no less than men originally had a penis, but they have lost it by castration. The conviction which is finally reached by males that women have no penis ultimately leads them to an enduring low opinion of the other sex [1905b, p. 195].

Prior to his analysis of exhibitionism as a partial sexual instinct in The Interpretation of Dreams (1900), Freud made several general comments on exhibitionism as a remnant of infantile sexual activity.

It is only in our childhood that we are seen in inadequate clothing both by members of our family and by strangers—nurses, maidservants, and visitors: and it is only then that we feel no shame in our nakedness. We can observe how undressing has an almost intoxicating effect on many children, even in their later years, instead of making them feel ashamed. They laugh and jump about and slap themselves, while the mother, or whoever else may be there, reproves them and says, "Ugh, shocking! You mustn't ever do that!" Children frequently manifest the desire to exhibit. One can scarcely pass through a country village in our part of the world without meeting some child of two or three who lifts up his shorts in front of one—in one's honor, perhaps.... In the early history of neurotics an important part is played by exposure to children of the opposite sex: in paranoia, delusions of being observed while dressing and undressing are to be traced back to experiences of this kind: while among persons who have remained at the stage of perversion there is one class in which this infantile impulse has reached the pitch of a symptom—the class of "exhibitionist" [1905b, p. 245].

Freud noted that in the sexual life of children the instincts of scopophilia, exhibitionism, and cruelty are independent of the erotogenic zones.

These instincts do not enter into intimate relations with genital (sexual) life until later but are already to be observed in children as independent impulses, distinct in the first instance from erotogenic sexual activity. Small children are essentially without shame, and at some period in their earliest years show an unmistakable satisfaction in exposing their bodies, with special emphasis on their sexual parts. The counterpart of this supposedly perverse inclination, a curiosity to see other people's genitals, probably does not become manifest until somewhat later in childhood, when the obstacle set up by a sense of shame has already reached a certain degree of development. . . . When repression of these inclinations (voyeuristic and exhibitionistic) sets in, the desire to see other people's genitals whether of their own or the opposite sex persists as a tormenting compulsion, which in some cases of neurosis later affords the strongest motive force in the formation of symptoms [1905b, p. 192].

He commented that in the perversions of scoptophilia and exhibitionism it is the eye which "corresponds to an erotogenic zone" just as the skin, "has become differentiated into sense organs or modified into mucous membrane, and is thus the erotogenic zone *par excellence*" in sexual sadism (1905b, p. 169).

Freud's comments on the topic of exhibitionism were by no means as exhaustive as those on other perversions (e.g., homosexuality). They placed heavy emphasis on the role of infantile sexuality and the importance of castration anxiety in the formation of this perversion. Psychoanalytic contributions during the next eight decades were largely formulated in terms of both castration anxiety and the libido frame of reference alone; for example, Starcke (1920) and Fenichel (1930a).

In what follows, I shall cite several important contributions on the subject of exhibitionism which have increased our understanding of this perversion through the description of certain clinical findings in these patients. The tendency to place them almost solely within an instinctual framework and not a developmental schema, hindered an adequately scientific explanation of etiology, meaning, and content of this perversion. I shall first describe these clinical observations, reinterpret their meaning in many instances, and attempt to place them in the theoretical structure of my unitary theory. This in no way minimizes the significance and importance of the contributions to be discussed.

The Contribution of Christoffel

Christoffel (1956) had seen eleven exhibitionists in psychoanalytic psychotherapy and from his work arrived at certain conclusions which he felt were characteristic of male genital exhibitionism. He observed that exhibitionists often marry and have heterosexual lives along with their exhibitionism. They suffer from phobias, especially of the vagina (colpophobia) and of close places (claustrophobia). Exhibitionistic reactions were often precipitated by the state of their marriages which led to a public display of their whole sexual organs only to females, often of a tender age. He noted that they were compelled to be caught by the police, as they seldom took advantage of opportunities to escape (psychic masochism). The latency period seemed to be lacking in these patients. They suffered from a decrease in self-confidence, a deficit in their relations with teachers, educators, and those who "train them." The exhibitionist is usually childless and youthful, has a "momma complex." Many had suffered a "weaning trauma" secondary to a deprivation of maternal love and overall care. With the outbreak of male genital exhibitionism, Christoffel felt, the interest in acquiring the female breast to suck on was now displaced onto the exhibitionist's own genitals as a whole. "Thus the genitals, because of an intensified secondary narcissism and of the primary process in general, carried the unconscious meaning of the female breast" (p. 250).

He cited as one of the chief causes of the patients' difficulties their feminine character. In my theoretical conceptualization, this finding is explainable as a persistence of the primary feminine identification with the mother which I perceive to be a major defect in the developmental history of all perverts.

Furthermore, he noted an extreme degree of destructive aggression and frequent dreams of oral aggression and violence toward women. Voyeurism may or may not play a part, but in many instances (as I have also noted) voyeurism and exhibitionism alternate or occur together (see the case of Martin, chapter 18). Christoffel was of the belief that the reason they did not solicit sexual congress with a female was that they only needed female partners to "increase narcissism." "By retreat from object libido, the male exhibitionist arrived in his act at a feeling of hermaphroditic self-fulfillment, a sense of intoxication with his own power" (p. 262). The exhibitionist says, "It is not true that I want to have breasts. The truth is that I am proud of having a penis. It is not true that I am interested in watching women who undress. The truth is that I want to show them my penis." Christoffel noted that "it is not just the penis but the whole sexual region which is engaged in the exhibitionist's attitude to femininity and women" (p. 263). In essence, the matter may be summed up as "I am you, all of you, and—whether you swallow it or not, still more" (1956).

The Contribution of I. Rosen (1964)

From the detailed case study of a patient with "compulsive exhibitionism," Romm (1967) summarized the psychopathology of her patient as follows: (1) an intense fear of the father; (2) a turning toward the mother for love and security; (3) an inability to identify with the male parent; (4) an identification with the mother with the resultant fear that the patient himself would be a castrated individual like her; and (5) a constant need for reassurance that he possessed a penis.

Rosen (1964), working in a clinic setting (Portman Clinic, London), had the opportunity to make a psychoanalytic

study of the largest number of cases reported in the literature, observations on patients over a two-year period. Eighteen of these patients were treated in group therapy by
psychoanalysts in three separate groups, and six others
were treated in individual psychoanalytic psychotherapy on
a weekly outpatient basis. Although these sessions could
only be held on a once-per-week basis, they supplied important information. His conclusions specifically referred to
two aspects of these patients' difficulties: (1) character formation and its link with the Oedipus complex, including
early object relations; and (2) the exhibitionist's handling of
instinctual drives with particular reference to aggression,
narcissism, and the affect of depression. Most significantly,
he placed particular emphasis on the importance of early
preoedipal experiences for the later vicissitudes of phallic
levels of fixation.

Rosen classified exhibitionists into two main groups with
gradations in between. The first was the *simple or aggressive* type, in which the exhibitionistic act followed some
rather obvious social or sexual trauma, disappointment, or
was associated with severe mental or physical illness, aging,
or alcoholism (on close perusal of his report, these would
constitute, in my view, episodes of exhibitionistic behavior
and not the true well-structured perversion). The second was
one in which there was severe personality disturbance that
he called the "phobic impulse type." These individuals (1)
regularly exhibited their genitals; (2) were recidivists with
"impulsive aspects predominant"; (3) were often of an
"amoral cast or line . . . prone to other forms of character
disorders and actual perversion such as transvestitism and
voyeurism as well as the commission of crimes of stealing"
(p. 299). They frequently changed objects, jobs, interests, and
were orally fixated. They were also prone to hysterical and
obsessional symptoms. One of his patients reported recurrent fantasies that his genitals would be bitten off by sharks
in a swimming pool, in his bathwater, or in bed (evidence of
severe phallic castration anxiety expressed in phobic terms).
In another patient, obsessional symptoms were viewed as an
intensification of a reaction formation of tidiness, where the
patient picked up all the papers in the street prior to exposing
himself. The act of exposure was a defense against the anal

component of "dirtiness." Rosen was of the opinion that the phobic-compulsive group existed as a syndrome or entity separate from cases where exhibitionism occurred symptomatically, secondary to other specific causes. I am in agreement with his conclusion that "the phobic impulsive group" would be the "true perverts."

In the first group, precipitating events were "internal sexual excitement" arising spontaneously in adolescence by sexually stimulating sights. In the second group, a nonsexual tension had the symbolic meaning of a loss of security and/or castration. Depression due to the loss of status was a common precipitating event in the true perversion. In agreement with Freud, Rosen felt that passivity and castration anxiety were especially important causes, but these factors were part of a sequence of underlying bodily loss which started from birth, proceeded through weaning, loss of the feces, loss of the object (a theory which is consistent with my own theoretical formulations on the structure of perversion in general). A major theme of loss of love and low self-esteem ran through their early object relations. These patients were "greedy people, dependent on narcissistic supplies from outside. . . The exhibitionist regresses to the sadistic phase of childhood where any loss of object, self-esteem or threat of rejection results in a withdrawal of libido from the object or external reality, and a subsequent investment of this libido as secondary narcissism in the infant's own body via a specific organ, his penis" (p. 304). Rosen concluded that "although the organ involved is the genitals, the mechanism employed from an economic point of view is that set up by the oral-sadistic phase" (p. 306). It should be noted that while Rosen emphasizes preoedipal fixation, he simultaneously provides an alternative theoretical hypothesis that it is a regression from later stages to the anal-sadistic phase of childhood which is important in the genesis of these conditions, rather than a primary preoedipal nuclear fixation.

His findings that the exhibitionist is severely intolerant of depression and is unable to postpone impulses are in keeping with my own observations. Although he cites preoedipal factors, be believes that the exhibitionist regresses to the oral-sadistic phase of childhood when he meets the difficulties aroused by the Oedipus complex during the genital phase, when castration anxiety is at its height. He holds that fixations and components from the pregenital phase, oral and anal, influence both the castration and Oedipus complexes. In my opinion, however, the basic preoedipal nuclear origin of this perversion is in the preoedipal phase and arises from a disturbance in successfully traversing separation-individuation phases with resultant gender-defined self-identity confusion or disturbance, a dread of maternal engulfment, disturbances in self-object differentiation, together with anxiety and guilt associated with attempts to separation from and/or loss of the maternal object. Pursuing my own theoretical bent, I would explain Rosen's statement that "love is expressed in a preoedipal way [toward the mother] via a strong feminine identification" is due to a persistence of the primary feminine identification with the mother secondary to an inability to successfully traverse the separation-individuation phases. The feminine identification, is, therefore, not a regressive return to the mother but is a *primary* feminine identification, and not a consequence of oedipal phase conflict. Oedipal phase conflict may lead to a secondary feminine identification that may be superimposed on a more basic primary feminine identification, which may be easily confused with it. (In Chapter 12, Fetishism, I have carefully differentiated between the characteristics of the two forms of identification).

I am in agreement with Rosen that the exhibitionist is severely intolerant of depression and is unable to postpone impulses, but ascribe these features to an early negative affective state of hopelessness and helplessness due to insufficient maternal care and to an underlying ego deficit, respectively. I furthermore am in agreement with him on his comment that homosexual wishes and/or dread are commonplace in exhibitionists, and "the act of exposure to a woman is defense against a homosexual component" (p. 306). This should not be construed, however, to mean that the exhibitionist is a latent homosexual, as there are always unique determinants for the choice of perversion for the exhibitionist, making the exposure of the genital itself the only method of attaining sexual satisfaction, and cannot be replaced by either homosexuality, transvestitism, or any other perverse behavior, although impulses in these directions may be associated perverse phenomena.

Rosen's other clinical findings are further confirmation of my own observations that I explain in terms of failure to successfully traverse separation-individuation phases. For example, it is his opinion that the mother unconsciously gains satisfaction through the body and phallic experiences of the child and the early attachment to the mother and subsequent sense of deprivation often results in increased sadism. He has often found that the father of the exhibitionist is felt to be a threatening figure, an inadequate and unworthy model for identification.

Finally, Rosen's significant contribution in an important reminder that the psychoanalytic method of investigation, when applied to large numbers of patients with similar psychopathology, can yield crucial information, even when these patients are not in full-scale psychoanalytic therapy.

The Contribution of S. Stein (1968)

In 1968, Stein reported a case of exhibitionism in a twenty-year-old man of Italian extraction who was treated at the Mental Hygiene Clinic, Albert Einstein College of Medicine, from 1966 to 1968 with psychoanalytically-oriented psychotherapy on a twice-a-week basis, supervised by the author.[2] I cite this unpublished case history in detail as it beautifully depicts the typical life history of the exhibitionist; the early attachment to the mother, and the lack of a satisfactory male model in the father; the struggle to attain heterosexuality; the role of the depressive affect in precipitating exhibitionistic acts; the importance of sadistic elements; the ego's frantic, unsuccessful attempts to provide alternative solutions to unconscious conflict through homosexual, transvestite, and even transsexual fantasies.

---

[2] I am grateful to Dr. Stefan Stein of the New York Hospital, Westchester Division, Department of Psychiatry, Cornell Medical School, for the opportunity to use this case material.

Stein's patient was an attractive young man who had difficulty achieving a degree in architecture and had numerous sexual affairs with married women. He was unable to make a lasting relationship with any one of them. He was living at home with his parents, a sister younger by seven years, and a brother younger by twelve years. He shared a room with his brother and was unable to move from the household; attempts to do so produced separation anxiety and depressive symptomatology. He had a "compulsion" to exhibit himself to women while masturbating in front of his bedroom window. Occasionally, homosexual fantasies accompanied this masturbation that made him extremely anxious as he feared that he might be "a latent homosexual." He had difficulties concentrating and attaining any goals, and overindulged in marijuana. A socially active mother was "the boss" in the family, while the father paid little attention to the patient, gave him little affection, and was heavily in debt due to gambling. Throughout the treatment, it became obvious that the patient viewed his father as a damaged, castrated man, both spiritually and physically. The earliest memory (around three years of age) was of his father, who had developed osteomyelitis of the hip, being treated with surgical debridement at home. The image of his father was one of having his leg in traction in a large white cast, and walking with a limp. Another early memory consisted of his being in his crib awakening after a bad dream, crying out to his mother in terror that he was "turning into a woman."

The patient traced his urge to exhibit himself back to about the age of eleven, although it was not until he was twenty years of age that the full-scale perversion and its enactment dominated his life. Since that time, he had frequently exhibited himself from his room in his home to women in a nearby building. This occurred when he felt "frustrated," unable to do schoolwork, and, later, professional work. He preferred to be seen by attractive young women, whom he then avoided meeting. His aim was to elicit their intense interest and reaction, but if the woman continued to look at him, his reaction was to begin to "feel numb in his genitals." "It feels as if it isn't even there." In this connection, he related an early experience as follows: He was about ten or eleven years old and he noticed a woman in a window across the courtyard in another apartment. He took off his clothes and did not look at the window but felt that she might be looking at him while he attempted to insert his penis into the barrel of an old shotgun that had been given to him by his uncle (a reminder of his father's upstretched leg in a cast). During the next several months, he masturbated in a nearby lot, somewhat out of view of others, but still able to be seen. At age thirteen he was severely reprimanded by his father and his mother punished him by making him stay in his room for one month, except to go to school. This provided him with the opportunity, when he was sent to his room with the door locked, to take off all his clothes and sit in front of the window. He attracted the attention of a woman in the building across the street, felt considerable pleasure and excitement. His face became flushed ("my skin was burning") and he masturbated watching the woman watch him. He fantasied that she greatly desired him, at which point he masturbated to ejaculation. There was no exhibitionistic activity outside the confines of his room during childhood or adolescence.

At about ten or eleven years of age, he would masturbate while rubbing one of his mother's head scarves on his pubic region, but he did not recall any fantasies associated with this activity. He also recalled having put on his younger sister's undergarments (transvestite element) and becoming excited at the idea that they had been close to her genital area. At eighteen or twenty, he included this fetishistic component into his exhibitionism, masturbating while rubbing the sweaters of the women who worked in the same office as he did against his body, all the while exhibiting himself.

His wish for married women to become involved and to be aggressive in proposing sexual relations with him was to ward off superego guilt as a consequence of severe aggressive feelings toward them. At eight or nine he would draw pictures of women's genitals with pins sticking in them. While having intercourse with women during adulthood, his pleasure was greatly increased by the woman's experiencing pain and telling him about it. On some occasions, he had fantasies of wishing to be a woman because "women get it all the time"; they were more favored and more powerful.

In addition to his overt exhibitionism, the patient fantasied "orgies" of female homosexuals or both male and female homosexuals, during which he would take part in anal intercourse and fellatio in both active and passive roles. He had two homosexual experiences at age twelve and thirteen. Once he attempted anal intercourse as the active partner, but was "too naive" to have had a "real homosexual relationship." A few months later, he experienced mutual masturbation with a male friend who later became a "homosexual dancer." He also had wishes at times to have an operation in order to become a woman.

Of central importance in Stein's patient were the following: (1) a pronounced primary feminine identification with the mother; (2) the wish to become a woman; and (3) the fear that he might be turned into one. In addition, he had deep fears of engulfment by the maternal figure, a feeling that he would fall into the void of a woman's vagina (represented in dreams). His chief defensive measures against engulfment by the mother were exhibitionistic acts that assured him that he was neither castrated nor becoming a woman. These occurred in the context of feeling depressed, angry, "pushed aside," and helpless.

Stein was able, in the context of a positive transference, to have this patient separate from the mother and begin sexual relations with several girls without the use of transvestite fantasies. At first these acts were fatiguing and traumatic, filled with anxiety and with an inability to act in a socially easy and conventional way. As the treatment progressed, he began to make satisfactory relations with younger women, and began to understand the origin and nature of his symptomatology.

Stein's patient's disorder would be classified as a preoedipal type I exhibitionistic perversion, as he was a patient whose object relations were from object to self, since he identified with the female's response toward exhibiting his own penis. He also separated himself simultaneously from the female in this act, hypercathecting his own genital. In addition, his ego functions were relatively unimpaired. The perversion was usually practiced in the relative safety of his room and there was no serious disturbance in reality testing. There was a considerable degree of unconscious aggression toward the body of the women, a basic fear of engulfment by the maternal body if he approached too close to it. Exhibitionism provided the necessary distance from the object; the act of exhibitionism also provided a differentiating function, separating the self from the non-self, the hated and feared feminine self that he deplored but which he both desired and dreaded becoming.

The Contribution of M. Sperling (1947)

No review of the major psychoanalytic contributions on exhibitionism would be complete without a report of Melitta Sperling's (1947)[3] detailed and unique report of the psychoanalytic treatment of a patient who was in analysis for over two-and-a-half years on a five-times-a-week basis. Sperling's case history carefully documented the preoedipal basic nuclear conflict existing in an exhibitionistic patient, although the theoretical structure derived from research in separation-individuation, disturbances in gender-defined self-identity, problems of differentiating from the mother, pathology of internalized object relations and separation anxiety had not yet been formulated. Thus, clinical observation and conclusions had antedated the theoretical structure adequate to explain them.

Her patient was a twenty-nine-year-old single professional man referred to her by the courts, who frequently exhibited himself in subway stations and on the street. Because of the absence of such finely detailed reports, I shall relate her findings and conclusions in some detail. It was her belief that the relationship with the father in this patient was not very important, at least not as important as that with the mother. Her patient suffered from intense castration fear and unconscious homosexual submissiveness to his father. The deeper roots of his perversion, she correctly concluded, sprang from his early relationship and identification with the mother. In the course of analysis she noted a fact of central importance, namely, that it was the narcissism—the

---

[3] Awarded the Clinical Essay Prize, London Psychoanalytic Society and Institute, 1947.

"narcissistic resistance"—that when psychoanalyzed leads to these patients being able to be successfully treated like any other psychoneurotic. Much of her explanation of the mechanisms essential to the formation of genital exhibitionism were based on Freud's posthumously published paper (1940), "Splitting of the Ego in the Process of Defense." In this paper, he noted that a very traumatic experience that would have simply overwhelmed the child's ego may be handled by denial and displacement and splitting of the child's ego. She clearly recognized that the patient's exhibitionism was a reaction to frustration, a frustration in early childhood in which he had to watch one baby after another take its place at the mother's breast. This constituted the most unhappy theme of his life. He defended against this loss of the mother (mother's breast) by denial and through identification with her. By identifying himself with the nursing mother he protected himself against intolerable pain and depression, overcoming feelings of helplessness and hopelessness by teasing others in only showing his penis, "not giving it to them (like mother, who only showed her breast to him but gave them to other children)" (p. 44).

She made a connection between his extreme oral frustration and his tendency to engage in oral activities, such as sucking lollipops on the street while simultaneously experiencing a strange longing and a strong urge to exhibit himself. In the later parts of the analysis, he was able to relinquish his exhibitionism and to replace it with food, temporarily. Even his castration complex had an oral coloring, as it expressed his fear of being devoured, fears of vampires and dogs. When confronted with a frustrating experience affectively associated with his earlier traumatic experiences, the patient reacted compulsively with the symptoms of exhibitionism. He behaved as though he had to save himself from an impending catastrophe. When his sense of panic was accompanied by physical symptoms he could not stop himself from exhibiting his penis. Although he had strong latent homosexual tendencies, he never became a homosexual. She suggested that in his unconscious he believed women had a penis (the penis equals the breast) and as a result women were not a totally unacceptable sexual object. As a result, he was capable of heterosexual relations with them (a fragile heterosexual functioning is commonly found in exhibitionists). While castration fear was apparent in one layer of his unconscious, at a deeper layer was a fear of "losing his life" (being abandoned by mother, losing the mother). The irresistible nature of his urge to exhibit was due to ego weakness in the patient. Unable to tolerate frustrations, he tried to work them out by reassuring denials of being afraid, denial of castration by exhibiting his penis, denial of the earlier frustrations—the trauma of weaning, and the loss of the mother's breast. By exhibiting himself he announced, "I have a breast myself, you can see it, I am showing it to everybody" (p. 44). Sperling concluded that the root disturbance in the patient was a consequence of an oral fixation.

Concluding Comments

In this chapter I have reviewed and reinterpreted many of the findings of other analysts derived from the psychoanalytic study of exhibitionists and placed them within the schema of the unitary theory of sexual perversion in the male.

The exhibitionist suffers from a basic preoedipal nuclear conflict, in addition to a deep oral deprivation. There has been a failure to make an adequate intrapsychic separation from the mother and a consequent fear of merging and fusion with her, together with a predominance of primitive archaic mental mechanisms characteristic of the early phase of fixation, an increase in early aggression both primary and secondary, and a disturbance in genital schematization secondary to threatened or actual early object loss. As a result, he suffered from a persistence of his primary feminine identification, a disturbance in his gender-defined self-identity. Specific traumas leading to the choice of the exhibitionistic perversion related to oral deprivation and the breast-penis equation, together with a fear of merging with the mother and a loss of masculine identity.

Exhibitionism has the capacity to neutralize psychic conflict, to help the patient attain, for limited intervals, a pseudo-adequate equilibrium and pleasure-reward, often permitting him to function, however marginally and erratically, in other areas. Those in whom exhibitionism arises from earlier fixations, e.g., from the practicing and differentiating subphases of the separation-individuation process or from the symbiotic phase, show along with their perversion even more severe ego deficits than pictured in the case histories cited, e.g., profound inability to curb any perverse acting out and severe disturbances in object relations. Thus we will find a wide range of clinical forms of exhibitionism, from those that derive from very archaic, primitive levels to those that are a product of more highly differentiated ones. The clinical picture of exhibitionism does not necessarily correctly describe the particular mechanism responsible for it. Our further understanding of the types of exhibitionism (most of them described in the case material by the numerous authors cited in this chapter) may well lead us to conclude that the true perversion of exhibitionism is a preoedipal disorder and does not arise from oedipal conflict with a regression to earlier phases. Only in this way, only by viewing the perversion from this theoretical frame of reference, can we understand the varied and multiple symptomatology of the patient, the developmental arrest, the signs of ego deficits including disturbance in object relations, increase in primary and secondary aggression, tendencies to transvestitism, homosexuality, and other perversions. The exhibiting of one's genitals is a repressive compromise (Hanns Sachs mechanism) in which a portion of infantile sexuality may be allowed expression, be acceptable to the superego, and help keep in repression the deeper anxieties relating to oedipal conflicts and their consequent fixations.

The function of exhibitionism is to achieve "masculinity" through the visual reassurance and emotional reaction of others. "If I show myself to a woman and she reacts, then I am a man and do not need men [avoids homosexuality] and I am not a female [defense against primary feminine identification]." It reassures against and lessens castration fear of the oedipal phase. The psychosexual motivation is orgastic desire, a yearning for masculinity, and a dramatization of this desire. There is a need to deny one's feminine identification. Decoding the wish to exhibit one's genitals leads to the conclusion that in many instances the penis-breast equation is operative in the form of an unconscious statement: "I need no longer feel deprived of the maternal breast and oral needs, for I have the breast (penis)." These patients announce that they have the breast, will not give it to others, and will only "show it" to them. Oedipal and castration fears are accretions to the deeper preoedipal nuclear conflict, that is, a dream and/or wish for maternal re-engulfment.

Chapter 20
COPROPHILIA AND COPROPHAGIA

When we remember that every perversion represents an attempt to establish union with a narcissistically invested lost object through our senses, our mouth, and our perceptual apparatus (in an archaic form of identification [Greenacre, 1971]), the perverse symptoms of coprophilia, coprophagia, analingus, and coprophemia lose their strangeness and bizarreness. Coprophilia, the sexual pleasure in handling, seeing, smelling or otherwise perceiving excrement, is rarely encountered as a perversion by itself. It commonly occurs as part of a perverse symptom picture in voyeurs, transvestites, sadomasochists, and homosexuals with sadomasochistic inclinations. When present it may take the form of coprophagia, the actual or symbolic ingestion of feces. Fenichel (1945) noted:

> [T]he impulse of coprophagia, which certainly has an erogenous zone (representing an attempt to stimulate the erogenous zone of the mouth with the same pleasurable substance that previously stimulated the erogenous zone of the rectum) simultaneously represents an attempt to re-establish a threatened narcissistic equilibrium; that which has been eliminated must be re-introjected [pp. 349–355].

Unconscious coprophagic fantasies may lead to reaction

formations such as disgust at eating certain foods in which the substance ingested is disgusting and equated with excrement. Analingus, the desire to lick the anus of a partner, whether in homosexual or heterosexual pairs, implies coprophagic impulses and a strong desire for forced intimacy with a partner. Coprophemia, a perversion in its own right, consists of the utterance of obscene words related to feces as a stimulant to orgastic arousal (see chapter 13). Fenichel (1945) suggested that a "specific danger against genital wishes" exists in coprophiliacs, as they deny the danger of castration through stating that there is "no sex difference in anal functions" (p. 349) and therefore they can be engaged in. The symbolic equation penis=feces plays a role in those who watch women defecate (voyeurs) in order to view a "penis" (the scybalum) emerging from the female body. Ritualistic cleaning of the rectum by homosexuals is often presented defensively as a wish to be "clean" for one's partner, but is usually a reaction formation against coprophagia. For example, while Willard (chapter 9) took great pride in cleaning his rectum daily, ostensibly for that purpose, he was capable of defecating on the floor during periods of depression and leaving his fecal material in his room untouched for days. The fecal mass itself represented an object relationship, and tended to decrease feelings of loneliness.

Patients with intense oral-sadistic feelings for the mother and passive homosexual feelings for the father tend to develop sadomasochistic fantasies involving the oral ingestion of feces or urine of their partners, a substitute for the incorporation of the paternal phallus. For example, a twenty-nine-year-old homosexual college student at six years of age continually fantasied kissing the toes of both parents. By age eight, these fantasies changed to sucking the father's or some other man's toes as a substitute for the penis. However, the smell of the feet became increasingly important, and this later became connected with the idea that the feet were stepping on his face. By puberty the following fantasy developed:

Mother and I were captured by some sort of enemy, taken prisoner. I was tied down with her above me so that if she urinated or defecated it would be on my face. Sooner or later she would. She would not do it willingly, but she could not control it anymore and she would have to let go, and she would be trying to hold it back and it would be coming out little by little—so I say to her, not to hold back. She is only making it more uncomfortable, for soon it would come out. So then, with regrets and apologies, she would "let go."

Despite the patient's attempt at levity in recounting this material, his fantasy betrayed the sadism he attributed to his mother and his own masochism in the disguise of being "taken prisoner" so that the mother was "forced" to be cruel to him. There was a strong oral wish to be fed from her body, her breast, her fictive anal penis. He covertly attributed destructive feelings toward her. Her aim of demolishing his sense of self-esteem and masculinity had a basis in reality during the earliest years of life. Such fantasies led to grandiosity and megalomania, as he fantasied that he would be able to endure any light, demeanment, or cruelty inflicted by anyone.

Another patient, a twenty-five-year-old homosexual scientist, had fantasies of his "entire insides" being ripped out by homosexual lovers. This produced sexual arousal and orgastic release. A favorite fantasy that led to mounting sexual excitement was to have a foot planted on his skin, and that portion of the skin corresponding to the outline of the foot excised. He longed for analingus during homosexual relations.

A unique and comprehensive study on coprophagia and allied phenomena was provided by Tarachow (1966). One of his patients had obsessional thinking, periods of depression, and homosexual fantasies. He took pleasure in odors, in flatulence, in sweat, and in constipation, together with strong interest in and affection for his stool, which he could not bear to flush down the toilet. He would fondle and caress the stool in the bowl before reluctantly permitting it to be flushed away. Simultaneously he had peculiar sensations in his mouth and frequent fantasies and compulsive thoughts of eating his own excrement. After a bowel movement, he would have "an empty feeling" (a depression, it would seem) and have an overwhelming urge to consume his own feces. A second patient described by Tarachow was a non-psychotic transvestite who was addicted to dressing himself in tight women's clothes, including corsets and shoes, and would manufacture an artificial penis that he then inserted into his rectum. This had the meaning of a homosexual penetration of the rectum, but it also meant playing with his stool at his anal opening. This was all done while tightly encased in women's clothing. His greatest pleasure was in *almost* expelling the object from the anus and at the same time keeping it there indefinitely. Similar to my own patient cited above, "with strong regrets" it was finally expelled. He wanted to remain soiled and defecated into his transvestite clothing and slept while soiled.

In his important paper, Tarachow reviews the important question as to whether feces or fecal play constitute a real object relationship in these patients. He recalled that Abraham (1920) took the position that the stool was the forerunner of object relations and a close tie to the stool constituted a precursor of tenderness toward objects. In contrast, Spitz and Wolf (1949) regarded fecal play as a real object relationship, while Bychowski (1954) regarded the stool as a pseudo-object and the autoerotic play as constituting a withdrawal from dangerous reality. Arlow (1965) was of the opinion that the relationship with the stool constituted an object relationship, albeit a narcissistic one. The taking in of feces orally was an attempt to reestablish a threatened narcissistic equilibrium; that which has been eliminated must be reintrojected. Tarachow himself felt that coprophagia and other allied phenomena represent not true object relations or even transitional object relations but a narcissistic withdrawal, an attempt to maintain the narcissism and megalomania of infancy. These phenomena are closely tied to dependency and self-centeredness and as a result are frequently found in association with perversions. These patients wish to keep the illusion that the stool has not been lost and that they control the mother via an object (the stool) so that there is no need for external objects.

Bach and Schwartz (1972) cite evidence that coprophagia is largely a manifestation of narcissistic pleasure closely tied to impulses of sadomasochism, megalomania, and grandiosity. They state that "it is through the coprophagia that all objects become what they eat, reduced to an elementary denominator which can be manipulated for purposes of self-aggrandisement" (p. 469). "The narcissistic trauma [once endured] is transformed into a grandiose affirmation of the self and its omnipotence" (p. 470). They cite the case of de Sade as an example of an individual who engaged in sadomasochism, coprophagia, coprophilia, and narcissistic grandiosity. Sadistic fantasies functioned in de Sade as an attempt to prevent final dissolution of a delusional self and to prevent a yielding or submission equated with death (megalomanic factor).[1] Masochistic fantasies, on the other hand, are invoked as the ideal parental imago, and the function of these fantasies involve coprophilia, coprophagia, and so on. They are restitutional attempts to reanimate and cling to an idealized imago which has been denied and destroyed. The sexualization of both masochistic and sadistic fantasies, the former having to do with attempts to reconstitute a delusional idealized self-object; the latter an effort to create a delusional grandiose self, are sexualized in an attempt to deny the experiences of self-fragmentation, body disruption, and "death of the self" (p. 474). It is in connection with this last observation that one is then able to explain some of the grandiose, sadomasochistic acts which ultimately result in the death of the self or the death of the partner during sexual perverse sadomasochistic acts.

In my clinical experience, the function of coprophagia and coprophilia is to feed one's self, overcome loneliness, and make "new things" out of one's body. It is furthermore a retreat from a reality that has proven too dangerous. Since the stool equals the parent, the relationship of the patient to the stool constitutes an object relationship. Traumatic toilet training may bring about a renunciation of the infantile megalomania of childhood, predisposing the child to the development of a compensatory pathological grandiose self.

---

[1] Hitler's alleged perversion reported by Langer (1972) and Bromberg and Small (1983), which consisted of having women squat over his face and perform excretory acts to his mounting sexual excitement, may well be another case in point.

The child has suffered a double loss: a loss of the object (the parent) and the loss of a substance of the body. These losses produce feelings of deep inadequacy, and narcissistic impulses. The impulse for coprophagia constitutes an effort to reestablish narcissistic equilibrium.

Chapter 21

MULTIPLE PERVERSE FANTASIES, ALTERATIONS IN BODY–EGO EXPERIENCE AND PATHOLOGICAL PERCEPTIONS: THE CASE OF THE BARKING MAN

Introduction

Sexual perverse fantasies and acts serve to repress a pivotal nuclear complex: the urge to regress to a preoedipal fixation in which there is a desire for and dread of merging with the mother in order to reinstate the primitive mother–child unity. The patient I shall describe was unable to stabilize himself through the formation of a well-structured perversion, and was therefore constantly in danger of regressive experiences and fears of engulfment. The alternation and slipping from one perverse fantasy to another was vividly evident throughout the analysis. Regressive production was subliminally evident in the patient's daily activities and erupted dramatically into consciousness in the protective atmosphere of the psychoanalytic setting and under the influence of the transference relationship. The decision to pursue these manifestations despite their psychoticlike nature was rewarded by the patient's being relieved of his emotional burdens (his "stones," as he referred to them) whose weight was slowly crushing him. These consisted of the following: seeing curved forms in the air; the air being heavy and filled with oppressiveness; clouds emitting sounds, mumbling and rumbling; something "rotten" inside his abdomen; gasping sensations secondary to oppressive sensations in his chest; hissing sounds, grunts, groans, and gasps, and explosive barking sounds both of an involuntary and often voluntary nature; anal sensations ("something being pushed into me"); changes in size and weight of his hands and chest (becoming heavier and larger or lighter and smaller); fears of darkness descending; "an inability to feel my body, to get back to myself, a feeling of floating around in a black room where I might disappear"; a fear of the vagina; a fear of the "ape"; a dislike of people, "and I wish to be loved by the very people I don't like"; a severe sense of "overcriticalness" of himself; "my capacity to bear pain and suffering and little capacity to enjoy pleasure"; a conviction, bordering on a semidelusional belief, arising from strange bodily sensations and compulsive movements, that his body had somehow been "invaded by demons."

The persistence of an intense primary feminine identification with the mother led to a crucial conflict: the wish to be a woman, to have female genitals, to engage in sexual relations as a female, to deliver a baby. This preoedipal conflict produced the dangers of engulfment and loss of self (ego dissolution), while the danger of castration was powerfully intensified. The attempted solution in the face of these dreaded events lay in the formation of various perverse fantasies, which simultaneously warded off nuclear fear, defended against and gratified instinctual drives and primitive wishes.

Freedman (1968) has observed that "the hallmark of symbiotic representations are experiences of fusion in which the boundaries of the self are in an amorphous way fused with those of the object; and secondarily, the experiences of *envelopment* [emphasis added] in which the patient feels himself enclosed and contained within the object" (p. 2). According to Sprince (1964):

> The passive surrender to the love object may signify a return from object love proper to its forerunner in the emotional development of the infant—this is to say primary identification with the love object. This regressive step implies a threat to the intactness of the ego—a loss of personal characteristics which are merged with the characteristics of the love object. The individual fears this regression in terms of dissolution of the personality, loss of sanity . . . wish to merge with the object [p. 106].

For some perverts it is much easier to accept one particular aspect of infantile polymorphous sexuality than another. To allow this aspect of infantile sexuality into consciousness serves to keep in repression and also alleviates the deeper anxieties (Sachs, 1923). Philip could not consciously accept and enact his perverse impulses except in the most transitory way. He was therefore unable to create a mental equilibrium and to stabilize himself through the formation of a well-structured perversion. This increased his vulnerability to regressive episodes in which he experienced the engulfment phenomena, a loss of ego boundaries, and the tendency to loss of self in the earliest phases of separation. The earliest phases are not truly undifferentiated but are already manifesting important beginnings of structure formation (Hartmann, Kris, and Lowewnstein, 1946; Arlow and Brenner, 1964).

This patient's psychopathology arose from practicing and differentiating subphases of the separation-individuation process. He had extreme fears of merging and desires to merge with the preoedipal mother. He had frequently witnessed primal scenes. His psychopathology included: (1) fear of dissolution of the self representation; (2) fluidity of ego boundaries with impairment of body–ego; (3) introjective and projective anxieties; (4) fluctuating states of object relationships; (5) threatened loss of self cohesion; (6) fear and/or wish of merging with the maternal body; (7) preoedipal and oedipal castration fears; (8) a continuation of the primary feminine identification with the mother; and (9) archaic aggressiveness which was easily stimulated into violent, sadistic fantasies or masochistic acts.

These regressive episodes do not constitute an actual return to the oral and anal phases. They can best be conceptualized as "reactivations of earlier childhood regressive experiences which, because of the loss of maturational gain and secondary autonomy, represent a return to the helplessness and dependency of infancy" (Panel, 1977, p. 558). Such episodes, if left unanalyzed, allow fixations to endure. The content of his anxiety proved to be related to the preoedipal problems of self preservation and identity.

Throughout my patient's life history there was a continual interplay of the four major themes which dominated his life, now one, now the other gaining ascendancy in the clinical picture: (1) the powerful primary feminine identification; (2) the regressive episodes with their fear/wish of engulfment and ego dissolution; (3) pathological perceptions and altered body–ego experiences; and (4) perverse fantasies. (The stabilizing effect of perverse dreams, fantasies, and acts is fully explained in chapter 7.)

Clinical Study

Philip was the oldest of five siblings with three sisters and one brother, the youngest child being twelve years his junior. He was born and brought up in a middle-class Jewish family in a large urban community. A tall, intelligent, somewhat athletically built man, he presented an unusual clinical picture. In the second session, he complained that he felt the air above him in the consultation room very "heavy and round" and he could sometimes feel or see "curved forms," could even almost taste them, "a heavy, oppressive feeling all about." He had experienced these phenomena many times before, especially when he lay down or thought "certain things." They could be prolonged at will and often were pleasurable. Since the age of four, he had daydreamed that "clouds would emit sounds, a muffled rumbling, as if the world was enormous in my mind, as if my mind could become so large and the clouds and sounds fill it up completely." He would suddenly and inexplicably have to catch his breath with a high-pitched gasp. His productions were interrupted by grunts and groans and explosive, extremely loud barking sounds (a violent exhalation against a partially closed glottis), as well as voluntary and involuntary jerkings of his body. Upsetting sensations of deficits in body-ego erupted into consciousness. "At times my hands and chest feel enormous, but at other times they fell light and sometimes they feel so big." (These phenomena are discussed in separate sections of this chapter.)

The father, an importer, was frequently absent from the home for extended intervals. "Even when he was home, I got little attention from him except criticism for hanging around my mother and sister too much. I felt he knew my 'secret,' that I wanted to know everything about them and even that I felt like a girl, even wanted to be one, and I therefore avoided him." He was a chronic worrier, a reclusive man, and a "hypochondriac."

The mother chided Philip about his lack of interest in sports, his tendency to stay in his room and sketch, and his excessively soft-spoken, gentle, and overly polite manner. The latter was both a manifestation of his unconscious feminine identification and a reaction formation against severe aggressive outbursts against his mother. She was perceived by him as a powerful "giant" who dominated the home and alternatively behaved toward the father with bemused tolerance and outright hostility. Intermittently seductive and indulgent of Philip when he complied with her demands, she was often harsh and deprecating if he moved toward independence. Inviting other children to accompany him home from school, especially girls, met with her caustic opposition. In addition to teasing and provoking him during childhood, she would physically attack him, literally wrestling with him, beating him down and making him feel helpless and enraged. "I felt I couldn't exist if anything happened to her, like I would cease to exist." He was secretly envious, however, of her ability to control his father.

The mother apparently didn't "bother much" with the other children, devoting most of her attention to the patient "from the day I was born." When he went on a bus trip at school, at age eight, without first discussing it with her, he experienced a severe panic reaction (separation anxiety) mixed with feelings of loss, loneliness, pains in the chest, and feelings of confusion which necessitated his being brought home. He recalled that during his earliest years his favorite game was to "crawl" all over his mother.

> If I were only able to be like my father, it would be a touch with reality. I would thereby avoid being totally swallowed or engulfed by her. I feel that my mother really didn't want me to be a boy. I don't like to admit it. Almost like she selected me as I was the first to satisfy some whim of hers. I remember how she would dress me in her clothes before I started going to school, admiring me in her clothes. Also her saying that father was no good, that I would never leave her side. It's just that she picked me out to be her girl. That's pretty awful. I can remember now my perfectly defeated attitude. She never gave me any privacy and would walk into the bathroom while I was there.

A screen memory dating back to the age of three or four occupied his mind throughout adolescence:

> I was sort of watching, and I can recall my father standing there. He had on a white shirt. He opened his trousers and lifted up mother's skirt, and they were holding each other and kissing. I was embarrassed then, and I probably saw my mother's legs and she wasn't wearing bloomers. I was very, very frightened.

He was trying to repress a memory of engulfment by creating "associatively connected substitute" ideas offered to his memory. (Fenichel [1945] was the first to note that screen memories of parental intercourse find a parallel in the symptom formation of perversion.)

He had rejected his mother's breast from birth and felt that this was related somehow to his lifelong tendency to gag, even when brushing his teeth. Around two or three, his mother often would hide in a closet, suddenly open the door and scare him. "At the age of one, I am told, I became a very pugnacious, aggressive child." He recalled feelings of terror at age three when the family was at the seashore and his father carried him into the water against his protests.

Since the age of four, his penis "always seems to get in the way" (a complaint voiced by "transsexual" individuals). "I can remember, at the age of seven, taking a bath with my mother, looking at her and being very puzzled." His incessant drawing of nude men and women during late childhood represented a counterphobic reaction to his fear of viewing the "castrated" female. He was therefore trying to master traumatic "impression[s]" passively received with an "active response" (Freud, 1931, p. 264). "She knew I was doing it and she didn't stop me. The feeling was that it was very comforting. I felt serene and happy and also very excited."

By the age of seven or eight, thoughts of having female genitals and sexual activities between men and women preoccupied him. "In school I would clasp my hands and keep a finger in between them to simulate intercourse. I'd try to make the teacher know what I was doing so she would know I was very much aware of her." This did not signify an actual sexual interest in the teacher but represented a wish to be acknowledged by her as a "female." In his teens, still afraid of the water, he would repeatedly swim out dangerous distances "where it was difficult to swim back to shore" (a counterphobic reaction to the fear of engulfment and an attempted mastery of it).

The heaviest "stone" of all was the mounting dread and horror he experienced up to the age of eighteen as dusk approached and the darkness of night descended. He would hurry home from any engagement so that he could turn on the light and not be "caught in the dark." This fear of nightfall was his wish for and dread of engulfment by the maternal body.

This highly intelligent, creative man was unable to decide on and pursue a career. His disturbance in the work area was a result of his intense feminine identification with a consequent sexualization and aggressivization of all activities. Kris (1953) has shown that achievement, productive activity of the ego, can only come about when there has been adequate neutralization of aggressive and libidinal energies. Philip abandoned two college courses after a few months, abruptly terminated a promising start as an artist, wrote numerous short stories that he never offered to any publisher. At age nineteen, he seriously undertook the study of the violin, abruptly stopping after six months. He began to collect antique violins and to manufacture them by hand. The making of violins was an attempt to create the female genitalia; the inner chamber from which sound would emerge symbolized the insides of the maternal body.

He succinctly summarized his relationship to his environment as follows:

> I'm not for or against, it's more that I don't have to be part of the group—just as I won't say I'm a man or a woman. That's why I am so opposed to any radical idea counter to what's going on. The same things apply to jobs. It goes back to a fear of being swallowed, destroyed, losing my individuality. Also I sometimes feel I can do anything—sculpt, paint, compose, write, influence people [pathological grandiosity]—be I guess all-powerful, and at those times I feel like my mother. I guess from what we've been saying, my mother with a penis.

At eighteen, owing to his profound identification with his mother, he became depressed and "sick" for six weeks during the time of his mother's hospitalization and surgery.

When he was fourteen or fifteen, he played with the idea that he was "bisexual." "The idea was very intriguing. I would never be a fish out of water then." During his late teens and twenties he became greatly depressed over any homosexual feelings, although he never engaged in homosexual acts. Homosexual desires were interrupted by bouts of anger, desires to hurt or destroy a man as protection against homosexual impulses.

He had severe guilt feelings for many years, beginning at age five or six, because of intense destructive aggression toward his brother or sisters.

> I would have times when I would hit my brother or sister, and I'd be enraged at myself for losing control. The next thing I'd want to do is be punished for it, be punished severely and get that out of my system. I wanted it beaten out of me: this wild, dangerous, unmanageable thing. I had always to be watched, it seems. I guess it's like the little man inside me. This is myself—the wild little child.

He would bite and thrash and scratch, and be violent. "It didn't seem to be a part of me. I wouldn't accept that this is what I was. On one occasion at age six, I was guilty, so guilty that I remember I set fire to an apartment house but no one would believe me."

Fears of dissolution of his self representation pervaded him whenever the optimal distance from and closeness to his mother could not be maintained. At these times:

> I think I might be dead and there is no contact with my body. I can't feel my body, afraid I'm lost. I can't get back to myself. I'm separated from my body and it's a real crazy sort of thing. The sensation isn't frightening sometimes because it is very close to a sexual sensation. But I don't know whether I will be forced to remain like that forever. . . . Forced to be floating around like that, like I am in a black room floating for such a length of time that I can't find myself anymore. Like a little spot of my brain is my whole being, just wisping around [fears of ego dissolution and merging phenomena].

The last ten years before entering analysis were a "nightmare" of increasing pain and suffering and perverse fantasies from which he received little satisfaction but much despair. He became aware of increasing tendencies to seclusiveness and withdrawal from social contacts, occasional paranoidlike fears of sexual attacks by men. As perverse fantasies/acts were unacceptable to his conscious ego, especially those involving a homosexual object choice, and thus primarily of an aggressive destructive quality against the object (he was unable to neutralize the anxieties), he was subject to severe regressive experiences in which the very anxieties from which he sought salvation in the perversion were experienced in a new and more primitive form. These episodes were characterized by altered body–ego experiences and pathological perceptions in the visual, auditory, tactile, and somatic spheres. Pathological perceptions were experienced as reality and responded to accordingly. During analytic sessions, there were repetitive, involuntary contractions of various parts of his body, especially of the extremities, mouth, torso, and neck, interspersed with screaming, shrieking, hissing, gasping, and strange explosive barking noises. He felt compelled to utter obscene words and had the conviction that his tongue was being forced out of his mouth.[1] These phenomena reflected the conflict between succumbing to the devouring mother and sexual penetration by the father, and were, in part, an attempt to ward off these disastrous culminations.

The decision to seek analytic help was further promoted by his oncoming marriage to a woman who had just completed hers, and who was strongly urging him to seek help because of his inability to attain and/or maintain an erection. His engagement provoked severe anxiety, intensifying his primary feminine identification with his mother. Both desire and dread of heterosexual functioning augmented threats to the intactness of his ego, increased his fear of merging with the characteristics of the love object, increased his tendency toward regressive experiences perceived in terms of dissolution of his personality, loss of sanity, wish to merge with the object.

The three phenomena I am about to describe—the perverse fantasies, body-ego experiences, and pathological perceptions secondary to rapid regression—could occur singly or alternate with each other; now one, now the other dominating the clinical picture. For further clarity I present them under two headings.

Perverse Fantasies

The Wish To Be a Woman

The patient tried to resolve the desire and/or dread of merging with the preoedipal mother and/or becoming a woman in various ways. At one time, he used to believe that he could make himself into two people (the desire to be both sexes). This enabled him to see himself "as both man and woman."

---

[1]Some of these unusual and at times bizarre symptoms bore a resemblance in part to the symptomatology of Gilles de la Tourrette's syndrome, a symptom complex which is first manifest in childhood and is currently ascribed to organic brain pathology.

My fears were that I had made myself into a woman even when I was much, much younger, in my earliest years. *An outer coating of being a woman, and inside a little man,* because I couldn't trust myself to anyone. I've had a tremendous desire to get inside my mother, but it seemed I dreaded her, too. The only one I could trust was myself—I just couldn't trust her. All these people, mother and father, are all too dangerous. And this business about clouds—they represented being enveloped by my mother. It starts off with a small cloud around me, then a rumble, it is not controllable. Then my need to control comes on. Only if I can have mastery over myself can I escape being engulfed. For example, I gave up most foods when I was fifteen or sixteen. I shouldn't be controlled. I've tried to give up salt and other things.

At other times he could *be* a woman, but not *completely*, as opposed to being a man. As a woman:

I'd have to get laid. I guess I wanted to be naked in some ways. With Catherine, how much I wanted to be her little baby. And she always insisted upon calling upon me to be a man, and I couldn't do it. That's what led me into treatment. It's like I've been trying to operate with some sort of masculine idea that I don't have the vaguest idea about. So I'd have to go along each day. My bubble had to burst, you know, and it did in treatment. I am not a woman and I can't make myself into a woman. [Another possibility was to] do what I had done in the past, to *hide*. It was a very disillusioning feeling to find this out, because I felt for so many years I was doing something very special, like I was some sort of supernatural being. To be supernatural, but still down to earth, almost like a Christlike figure. Many times I have thought of this—to be like Christ—his physique and his softness, and his inner strength. He gave me the impression that he's just not cut from one cloth. He's tender, gentle, yet a very painful, womanish creature, and yet inner fire and strength of many, many men. While I never actually thought of myself as being Jesus Christ, I was like the image of Christ—a soft-hearted woman and a man inside.

This constituted an attempt at solution through a merger with an all-powerful, Godlike creature (pathological grandiosity).

Perverse Fantasy of Exhibitionism and Voyeurism

He reported a dream of exhibiting his penis:

> I am making love to my sister, Mary, on the floor. We are both nude. First a woman and then a man watch us from their apartment through the windows [voyeuristic element projected]. My penis is not in her vagina. I move it against the vaginal lips. I feel excited, and I want to have an orgasm. Mary tells me, "Not yet." Then she goes away, and the man and the woman are still looking at me. I sit up, exposing my penis, and let them look [exhibitionistic display to ward off paranoid feelings].

The patient's associations were of watching his parents standing up and "screwing" during his early childhood. Mary is his mother, and he cannot get pleasure that he wants from her. She rejects him as a man, or tells him he cannot become one this easily. With his penis exposed, however, he feels like a caged animal that people can look at, control, castrate, and do whatever they want to.

Another dream illustrates a *transsexual* wish: "I'm in a house. A detective is looking for me. Mother is not telling him where I am. I go out to a nightclub. I get a jacket and a red coat to put on, to somehow disguise myself. Then I find this detective has tortured my mother."

Associations:

> The detective is my father and the fact that they are together. My understanding of them—my father tortures my mother. Also I'm talking about my desire, I guess, my own desire. The nightclub—Harry and a friend and I went to see the man at the nightclub a number of nights ago. This man I went with is a bookie, with nightclubs on 65th Street. I will not go to a homosexual place, but I will go to somebody sweet, make another daddy for myself, like Harry. I went down also in an elevator in this dream. The experience of going down in an elevator I know, this to me is in a sense an attempt to *get into my mother*. I still use this as a symbol of my mother's womb. Also feeling *I'm disguising myself*: a sense of being in disguise, that this man must not be able to find me because I have taken something on

myself that is not of myself [transsexual wishes, being a woman]. It's more than just shifting—this has to do with really *changing myself*, because when I put this on, it's not just with the idea of taking it off in a day or two. This is going to be what I have and it is something very permanent. There is a certain amount of idea in it that is masochistic. These people place themselves in a situation which could be dangerous, but isn't. I find it very difficult to keep thinking about the subject, it makes me angry. I saw my parents last night.

Dream Material Illustrating Homosexual Wishes

Dream:

I'm in bed with you. I think I'm about twelve years old. I'm holding you and I am sucking your breast, and I am enjoying this. I feel wonderful and you say, "Will you stay longer?" I've got to go to work, I say, but I say okay. Then there's a sensation in my penis. After you have said to me to stay a little longer, a certain amount of anxiety comes up in me ... Then it is a funny sensation, like I've got to use it. Then I start thinking of my mother. Then, the first thing I know, I am still sucking at your breast and I'm trying to screw you through the rear. Then I awake, terribly frightened and very depressed.

Associations: The patient was depressed at the thought that he might have homosexual desires for the analyst:

Well, I don't really feel this way. I know what you mean by all this, dredging up all these feelings that we will unravel, feelings and desires. The feeling that I do like you is stronger than the fear—I can recognize the feeling for you is stronger than the fear I would want to screw you or be screwed by you, or have homosexual relations with you. This would happen if I were afraid of you. How much more reality there is in really liking you, and how stronger it is than fearing men and the wish to take something from them.

The breast–penis equation was quite evident. The patient sought the man's penis as a substitute for the breast. He could not approach a woman (mother) due to the fear of engulfment and merging. However, the breast became a penis again, and the patient protected himself by having both penis and breast at his disposal—an ambivalent position reflecting his whole life history of ambivalences. In his associations, the patient succeeded in achieving his appropriate gender-defined self identity for the moment by knowing and caring about the analyst and the analyst caring about him. He did not have to rob him of his penis (i.e., by seducing him and having intercourse with him). The man was a substitute for the mother, the penis for the maternal breast.

Although he had not engaged in actual homosexual intercourse, the patient had homosexual interests and fantasies in adolescence. During the analysis, he had dreams of anal penetration of male partners and of fellatio in which the penis and breast were interchangeable. His homosexual desire led to suppressed impulses of physically attacking men.

> The worst thing, though, the greatest fear of all, the feeling driving me crazy, is the feeling of being a homosexual. Something happens to my face, a certain softness, like a young girl's. Being a homosexual and being a woman, or being female, have something to do with each other; they slip from one to the other.

Sadomasochistic Wishes

The patient walked around after he left the session feeling quite well. Ultimately, however, he wanted to hurt himself "in the worst way." He went into a bar and he wanted to hurt the people in the bar, too. "I was actually afraid to get off the bar stool." The next woman he met he was going to make love to, force himself upon her. He had felt good and he tried to channel it, but he started to become depressed. There were no women around. The good feeling started leaving him and then:

> I lit a match and started to burn my hand. It would be satisfying to burn myself. It seemed to release much more. It told me something as regards masochistic desire, a desire to hurt myself. Also there was a real desire to punch a hole in my hand with a spike. At this point, I had lost that real buoyant feeling from the session. I had felt good walking down the avenue, but

now I wanted to feel intense pain, the idea of somebody punc-
turing me. It was almost as if that was going to *satisfy something within me.* From that, I then started to think of you. I
realized I hadn't been in such bad shape for a long time. I
thought I'd call you. The image was of calling you and being
like a little baby crying and whining. And I got into that
imaginary conversation with you, and it worked, and I felt
better.

Transsexual Wishes

When he left the session on Saturday he looked into the
mirror, and his face never looked so smooth or so young. But
later on he thought that he never looked so much like a
homosexual. This upset him. He felt young, and as if there
was no more hiding since the analysis started. Something
had happened to his face: a certain softness, like that of a
young girl. He looked young without being young. His feelings of being a woman (transsexual wishes and primary
feminine identification) reappeared many times in the
analysis.

> I had the sensation of being castrated for a long time after I left
> the session last time. I thought I'd probably have to go through
> that feeling right now. I didn't try to run away from it. It was
> something about breasts and face, and that perhaps both are
> the same. I was thinking something about my breast, and I had
> some anxiety. Okay, I feel castrated, I said. But what else am I
> going to feel? Am I going to feel something in my breast, in my
> face? I thought I would feel things in my chest. My face. I
> thought . . . that I would see something there. I thought I must
> have these feelings again. I knew I didn't have a cunt; I knew I
> had a cock—except the feeling was that I didn't have a cock, but
> a *big hole* inside of my thighs and the whole area was a hole. I
> thought, "This is the way a woman must feel." She's always so
> conscious of this area.

> In that framework of thinking it was much easier for me to
> accept it, accept everything. I wanted to see the analysis take
> its natural course. I know this is what a woman feels. Also I
> have the sensation that I have a cunt. I felt I must have felt this
> before. It was the sort of thing I used to be able to run from. I feel
> very strange right now in talking about it. I feel I can relax a

little more with this sensation than I ever could before. The last session it got me very angry and it made me very uncomfortable. But it is now as if I'm *accepting* the same thing. I wonder why I am not getting angry. When I got angry on the couch I told myself that's what I didn't want. Not like I *want it*. Before I was angry. Something about it, oh, oh, ugh, ugh [he gasps and groans and barks] like a different sensation. Also what makes me feel that really strange feeling is that it brought me very close to a feeling like a homosexual. Yes, this is one of the main ingredients of it: being a homosexual and being a woman, or being a female has something to do with each other, but they slip from one to the other. Also, would it show? Is someone likely to see it? These things were in my unconscious, I guess, and they are not now, they are *out now*. Yes, I can talk about it now. It seems so far out of the nature of possibility.

Following this session, the patient experienced considerable relief of tension and anxiety, as if he were beginning to be unburdened of one of his "stones."

On another occasion he reported:

I feel I am approaching a certain condition in which I am in possession of certain intuition that women have, that I know certain feelings of women, that I can very easily remain a woman permanently and it would feel right. Then I have ice-cold burning sensations. I think, "This is the way a woman feels"—so conscious of this area in the genitals. I know I don't have a vagina, I know I have a penis—except the feeling is that I don't have a penis but a big hole. I know this is what a woman feels. I am referring to a walking sensation that I have been having, that in me there is basically a sensation of a great deal of grace, a certain flow within my body, definitely female. I always felt a woman had more of the secrets of life than a man does [transsexual wishes].

The Wish To Become Pregnant

I'm so convinced at times that there is something inside my abdomen. It moves about. It is perhaps five inches long, a half-inch wide. It may be a penis or a baby, an embryo. It's like something rotten in there. Like I'm being invaded. Oh, oh, oh.

When these feelings were severe, he almost felt "persecuted" by them as there was no escape.

On other occasions, he felt he was being sucked into a vortex, a whirlpool, the mother's body, as if parts of his body were disintegrating (body-disintegration anxiety and loss of body-ego). He wished to be penetrated, to have a baby, and at the same time feared the loss of self. Simultaneously, he felt he was the baby who was being reborn (Glauber, 1956).

The following dream portrays some of these phenomena:

> It is daytime. I am on a wide street. I look into the kitchen of a restaurant. There are large garbage pails near the street, and the mixed smell of garbage and cooking coming from the kitchen. Looking in, I see many swinging doors, wooden work tables, and knives.

> When I get to the top I see an enormous area, like the crater of a volcano. I walk around the edge and then go down another side. I am now walking with my sister. At the bottom of the hill is a small pond. A path continues through the pond. Here my sister tells me that she is pregnant. I say that it is nice that she can talk about it for eventually this would come out. There does not seem to be more substance to her than there is to a breeze. I have the feeling that she might float away or disappear any moment.

In his associations, walking up a hill was a disguised way of showing himself that he had an erection, a penis. The arena and crater were like vaginas. His sister tells him she is going to have a baby and that's "okay"—but he is not speaking of his sister, he divulges, he is speaking of himself. Like he knew something was going to be found out, that he was pregnant; like something is going to be revealed. The whole point is that she will tell about it now, that this isn't something that can be hidden indefinitely.

A calm, peaceful aura pervaded some of the dream, a feeling he had at times in speaking with the analyst. The displacement of his own wishes or dreads upon his sister saved him from the intolerable anxiety of penetration, impregnation, and delivery.

Ideas of violence would occasionally assail him. This aggressiveness was a defense against his unconscious feminine wishes to be penetrated by the paternal phallus in the transference. "The ideas may start with loving feelings. Like I would incorporate you, like becoming part of my hands, hold you so tight that there is no room for you except within me." He had an impulse to embrace the analyst, and simultaneously an impulse to attack him. "Almost like it's the same thing. There's no clue to which is which. I can't tell them apart."

Masochistic Fantasies

Philip was beset by masochistic fantasies: "I have this almost terrible craving to be hurt. A real longing. If the hurt were bad enough my need and yearning to be a woman would be taken away." Simultaneously with this verbalization he experienced the sensation of a needle being stuck through his penis. His masochistic wishes defended him against being turned into a woman. They were a substitute for sexual relations in which he would be penetrated. Painful sensations helped to reassure him that he was not losing a part of himself and gratified him in a substitutive fashion.

He attempted to avoid facing his desire to be a woman, but there was no escape from this dreaded wish as he encountered it in free association.

I have a trick about this. During the day I try to live like in a vacuum. I find I still have the desire to watch people screw [voyeurism], and to exhibit myself [exhibitionism]. All this is to relieve the tension of having this happen to me. I can feel myself screaming so loud, like a pole is pushed up there, like my spine is a penis. My eye hurts, like it is too full in there. Even imagining your writing, it's like a penis. My right arm is starting to hurt now. I have such a feeling that I am going to have a horrible reaction to this session, and the desire to smash myself against the wall is enormous. I also saw a friend I used to know downstairs. It's like I believe he can sexually assault me [homosexual dread].

I can feel something building up in me, a slow anger, anger like somebody is chopping my penis off. A penis with a hole in it. It's chopped off, turning in, and it turns into a vagina and swishes into my body [transsexual wishes]. It's like it could really happen. Now this kind of a fantasy is very calming, as a matter of fact, and I am very pleased with it. I have the feeling I have figured out something. The pain in my eye just went away. It's strange, it's so mixed, like I don't believe it and I do.

Although possessed by relentless perverse fantasies for many years, Philip only rarely carried them out, and then only when they involved voyeuristic or exhibitionistic activities. In both voyeurism and exhibitionism he successfully removed himself from contact with the object. For example, when asked by his sister to come to a party with a girl friend, he felt unaccountably frightened, "as if turned to jelly." Two women to whom he felt close were too many to be with at the same time. He could not do his work, was unable to sleep, and developed mild feelings of persecution in the course of regressing to being a helpless (female) child. "I then had a wish to *expose* myself, and I wanted to *see* the sex act. That's when I want to run to the window to look at others. On three separate occasions last year I actually did it." By projecting the scenes of intercourse outside his body, he escaped bodily penetration by exhibiting his penis, affirming and bolstering his male gender-identity. In typically ambivalent fashion he swung from passivity to activity (exhibitionism and voyeurism). Activity, however, released the aggressive aspect of his perverse life and he became in fantasy the sexual sadistic murderer, which in turn was handled through words (coprophemia). Jones (1920) has reported on the perversion of coprophemia in which the "sexual act consists solely of uttering indecent words to women" (p. 258). It is a substitute for a sexual aggression. The thought of speech is psychologically the full equivalent of an actual deed. "To watch others screwing, to be very excited, and then to crush them, to destroy them, to hurt them between the head and shoulders. In the fantasy of exposing myself and afterwards, I also imagined I was using the foulest language imaginable" (coprolalia).

Regressive Episodes, Alterations in Body Ego, and Pathological Perceptions

Regressive episodes occurred during free association, during the course of associations to dream material or in the actual telling of a dream. These were followed by "good periods" in which he felt "high, better than I ever felt before, full of smiles, elated."

The first such episode occurred at approximately the fifth week of analysis. As he spoke, he began to utter strange sounds: "Oh, oh, ugh, ugh." He said, "I'm being touched and I don't know where. They are touching me. The doctor, the one that gave me the injections when I was so young." The patient screamed: "Just a few minutes ago I had the feeling that this has happened to me before, this convulsive thing that goes oh, oh, oh, oh (scream). I got an awful headache then." The patient's voice changed to an angry growl, and he uttered a scream like an angry animal. He snarled, "I put a bat into a vase and I saw it drown." He growled, "I can feel his hands touching me, his hands on my shoulders, so warm. Ugh, ugh, ugh." He made jerking movements of his extremities. "I won't let him come and put that needle into me." There was a violent movement as if pushing someone away. Within a few minutes after the beginning of this session, the patient, while sitting up, began to have feelings that his mouth was becoming smaller. The perioral region was becoming "frozen, numb," and he was hardly able to speak, as if he were becoming a child. He stated that he carried fantasies around with him, images that got into his life. "I find myself having fantasies in the daytime. I don't seem to deal with concrete things. I look at people and try to imagine how they'll look and how they'll act."

In another session in which regressive experiences occurred, he reported a dream about his girl friend. In the dream he was upside-down, and he started to kiss her vagina and she takes his penis into her mouth and "bites my penis and eats it." At this point in the recounting of his dream he emitted a loud yell, gagged, and made a violent movement of his head. He analyzed this dream as follows: He wished to get into the womb by performing cunnilingus, "and I'm going to lose my identity and masculinity if I do that, and I'm afraid." He now felt that his tongue was "stuck in place" behind his lips and he couldn't speak. Something was trying to force itself into his mouth and he had to close it. He felt very small, like a child, "like I'm losing myself." He screamed in order to regain himself: "Like I'm getting myself back to myself. It's like I'm split into an outer person and an inner person" (splitting of the ego).

He suddenly experienced a sensation that a needle was being stuck through his penis, and he cried out in pain and terror. He also felt paralysis over most of his abdomen. He was filled with aggressive, destructive feelings and kept thinking of "hitting." He had a fantasy of a hairy ball, like an eye inside it, and he kept dropping into a well, and then felt the pain in his penis return. He suddenly experienced the sensation that he was being thrown into a kind of vortex:

> Right now it's also like I'm playing inside the cunt, and right now I feel a certain mastery over the fantasy, like I'm playing inside there, like playing with the clitoris. And now I'm getting that terrible flushed feeling all over me, and I feel very violent, and I feel like cursing, cursing, and cursing. And then I feel the sensation that something is happening to my penis.

These experiences were reported with assorted gasps, barks, grunts, shudders, shakes, terror feelings, and spasmodic movements of the arms, torso, trunk, and legs. He shrieked loudly and used obscenities.

During the early phases of his analysis, he complained of some alteration in consciousness before he experienced these regressive episodes. He complained of being in "a sort of fog or stupor" the day before, as if he were in "a different world." "I couldn't relate myself to being in my room, to doing anything, to being in the world." He would sit as if in a "cocoon" and frequently sleep. He had fantasies of being diminished in size, but this led to a dilemma: how would he get in touch with the analyst if he were that small? Another fantasy was that of becoming "insane." By insanity he meant running away inside himself where he wouldn't want anything, "where I wouldn't have to eat or sleep or be in contact with anything. Not to be crazy, insane, but to be insane in that I do not relate myself to anything." Yet when he woke up that day before coming to the session, he felt fine, went to work, and did not feel particularly good or bad in contrast to his

usual feeling of being "quite dead." When he spoke of dying
or death during the session he developed "pains" in his body
and occasional twitches of his leg muscles. He had a fantasy
that morning that he'd walk up to a woman on the street, put
his hands around her throat, and she would slump to the
ground and cry.

> She would take pity on me and take me home, and I'd go to the
> corner and turn into some kind of *devil* of some kind. I'd tell her
> she was very foolish, because although I didn't go through with
> this thing this time doesn't mean that I wouldn't the next. It
> was not to destroy her. What I did was try to get her to put me
> away.

He suffered both from fantasies of himself becoming smaller
and of other people diminishing in size, even becoming tiny.

> When I'm three to four inches tall, I guess I won't have to face
> anything. It isn't that I want to face that I care about you—it
> has to do with the phallic mother I'm not facing. The only thing
> I have to face is envy. This is an old fantasy—just three to four
> inches tall. I've gone into it before. It's dangerous, though. But
> then I knew I could get in touch with you and it would not be
> dangerous. I will try to be part of the phallic mother and I don't
> have to separate from her. [The analyst asked which part.] The
> penis, when I would be small, too, I couldn't be screwed and I
> also couldn't kill anyone, I guess. I was afraid of the aggression
> in my killing or choking the woman. Why should I feel aggres-
> sion toward you?

In the following session, the patient regressed and his
fantasy life assumed a new vividness, although he continually remained in contact with the analyst and would readily
reply to his questions or comments. He felt lost and abandoned, as if he were getting smaller. There was a split-second
"when I lose the whole conception of reality. I think I'm
always in the state of trying to ward off abandonment and
anxiety. And if I'm unsuccessful, then I get thrown off, and
then I begin to get more and more scared as the anxiety
builds up." At this point, the patient developed various pains
throughout his body, his chest, and especially his genitals.
Floating sensations intervened and he emitted loud noises,

gasps and barks. He suddenly had an "image" before him— a fantasy of lying on a raft with a monster beside him whose mouth opened and he started going down the mouth. He rushed in and started to disappear. He jumped, both in fantasy and reality, from the couch, and almost fell off, as if running away from the monster at that moment. The fantasy was "real" to him, he later stated. He could not control it, but his tongue was being thrust forward by something inside him. It reminded him of some of the pictures of the medieval artists who painted people who had been invaded by monsters.

Associating to feelings of "invasion" led him to his fears of homosexuality. "An oversized man with an enormous penis, it might be ten stories high. Now I imagine the tip of the penis being rubbed around my ears and he is trying to get in my ear. Oh, oh, ugh, ugh (gasp, bark, yell)." He emitted a very loud scream. "That is like your voice would make me yell. I'm getting a terrible headache now."

> I have a feeling that something has been done to me, and I have to do something back. My stomach hurts, I have a headache. I'm beginning to get a cramp in my abdomen, like I used to get when I was a small boy—like something rotten in there. I have the feeling now like I'm being abused in some way. Now it's like after the act, like I've been invaded, ugh, ugh (growl). The whole idea of the penis: a thing like a love filter—ugh, ugh, ah. Just before the last reaction I started to have a fantasy of having my right arm cut off.

The patient snorted, snarled, and made a violent movement of the right side of his body. He had to sit up. He had a terrible pain, pointing to his right arm.

The Appendix contains a verbatim transcript of parts of two sessions preserved by tape recording, illustrating some of the unusual and striking phenomena referred to above. The sessions took place during the first three months of his analysis.

Course of Therapy

Within a few weeks after starting analysis, Philip began to experience hallucinatory phenomena with affective and motoric discharge together with body-ego disturbances. There was seldom any alteration of consciousness preceding, during, or after these experiences, although they were more likely to occur when he felt drowsy, contemplative, or distracted from external events, especially when lying on the couch and free associating. His voice changed and he emitted angry snarls and explosive utterances. He complained of changes in the size and shape of his mouth; convictions of oral, anal, aural, and ocular penetration; feelings of being very small or other people becoming smaller (micropsia fantasies); a feeling that he was split into two people, an outer woman and an *inner small man.*

The presence of the "little man" phenomenon was a further corroboration of separation-individuation theory when applied to perversions. It is due to the presence of an ego segment separate from the rest of the ego, and has been described by Kramer (1955), Niederland (1956, 1965), and Volkan (1976). By the end of the third year, according to Kramer (1955), it separates from the rest of the ego and passes through different stages of libidinal development, aspects of which attach themselves to "the little man." Its function is to make the mother equivalent available to the rest of the ego from which separation would never be required. This isolated segment, however, interferes with the development of a properly integrated ego and impairs the function of synthesis. It leads to a weak, helpless, impoverished, and limited ego even though the "little man" gives evidence of "possessing great power" (Kramer, 1955, p. 71), having come about as the end result of a succession of narcissistic injuries at every level of early development. These injuries have undermined the feeling of infantile omnipotence, and the "little man" accordingly has illusions of omnipotence but is unable to form true object relations "in the sense of investment of genital, or aim-inhibited energy in the object." According to Volkan (1976), the primary function of the "little man" is to deal with separation anxiety, but it is used subsequently as a defense against castration anxiety at a time "when the anal-phallic components are added" (p. 12). Furthermore, the "little man" acts like a "token triumph" over the threats of castration and is a safeguard against it. In Volkan's patient the "little man" phenomenon occurred as a feature of separateness from the mother "at a stage when the mother was not yet felt as an external object but was perceived as one with the child." The "little man . . . has as its primary aim the restoration of the lost early infantile omnipotence and its continuation and preservation" (Volkan, 1976, p. 23).

Before analysis, Philip would often think of "whirlpools" and he wanted to "go into the whirlpool."

> I accomplished this in the analysis. I never wanted anything quite so badly; this would be the safest time to do it . . . like I could take a chance on dying, since I was in treatment, like nothing terrible would happen to me, even if I died. Like I found the safest place in the world, right here with you. There was something so wrong, so crazy about this, but never more appealing or more right. Like I finally made up my mind. I was not doing it to expose my neurosis. I read something about this that kind of shocked me, sort of told me that this is so crazy to want to do that, like some sort of mastery over death. And also like it wouldn't matter if I died. The falling into that whirlpool, you would be here to see that I didn't suffer, and I would experience that dropping feeling with you here. You wouldn't let that go on. You are a sort of insurance. I have more real crazy ideas: the pool, the crater, my mother's womb—like they're all the same thing. Dying doesn't matter. You would know just what to do to save me. You would bring me out of it.

Significantly, this patient's first dream in analysis consisted of his standing beside a deep, black, unfathomable pool from which deep rumblings, groans, and painful sounds issued. At first alarmed, he became suddenly calm and serene when he noticed standing beside him a Greek warrior with unsheathed sword.

By the end of the first one-and-a-half years of analysis, the patient revealed what he considered to be the task of the therapy. He often thought of his love for a man, but he found that this was quite impossible. He would try to kill him if a man tried to love him.

> *I couldn't love a man—it would mean I would want to be*

screwed by my father. The problem is that I have never given up the position of being a child; like I'm acting like I'm still one or two years old. I've had these wishes to become a baby physically and mentally all my life. It's always been imaginary. I've developed physically only. *Then I try to bring myself back* to be a child solving the problem of love—the feeding, the being warm, being relieved of pain. It's always been involved with love and I've never solved it. But if I solved it I might go on to other things. Now to still try to do it today I think is ridiculous, and yet I feel I'm going to have to solve that problem.

The first step I have to do is to *take* the step. I'm not even up to the step of *separation from my mother.* I'm at the step *before,* which I never worked out. Like I'm trying to feel secure. I instinctively would try to go to my mother, and I couldn't do that, realistically. I should have done it when the separation took place, and I am trying to do it now. I think it has something to do with the breast. I know I didn't take the breast the first year. I was even difficult on the bottle and I refused to be breast-fed.

During his four-year analysis, his unconscious conflicts (e.g., wishes for engulfment, to become a baby, to be penetrated, to deliver a child, to be dead, to kill a woman, to be castrated, the sadomasochistic impulses, the wish to become a woman), were expressed in the analysis as symbolic perceptual experiences so that their unconscious meaning could be understood. He was left "purged," as if he had been exorcised. Nearing the end of analysis he stated:

The cock inside me used to eat me away. When I was younger, all these things, the rotten things inside me, gave me a feeling of sickness, a smell of rottenness about me. I could smell myself, or that there was like a demon inside me and I was possessed. What I have done is open up a part of me, zipping it open and letting something out in order to crush it. It is like a demon inside and I have been possessed. When I was having the reaction I knew it would come to this, that all this would finally happen, this getting it out in our sessions. And depressing as it is, it was inescapable. I have always been afraid that I would have some real convulsive reactions like these movements I make, outside the sessions. This happened sometimes after I left the session. It reminds me of something of childbirth, as if I were having a baby or as if I am being reborn. I feel almost a wailing or a moaning at times. It was like some evil spirit inside me, the evil which could take over. It has been ugly, violent, destructive, and powerful. It has been almost like the whole center of me, the whole center that was. All of me was built around it. Remember how I used to drink scalding hot coffee to kill a pain inside me, as it was eating me away and I was trying to kill it?

Pathological Perceptions and Their Relationship to Dreams

At various points in the analysis, I inquired as to *how* these remarkable phenomena took place, as I had progressively understood the "why" of their occurrence but not the "how." I commented that although he seemed to "lose reality" during these episodes, he remained in contact with me and always seemed to know where he was. He stated that he could "lose reality" in a second when he was on the couch and also when sitting in the chair, and when certain material emerged. He came back to reality simply by the analyst's "bringing me back" through his voice.

> It is also now my decision not to keep feeling this, while at one time I really wanted to feel this for a whole session. Another thing: I was able to get to it very quickly. These split seconds, I lost reality at that point. Why do I lose reality? At that moment the only reason I lose reality is because I don't want reality. I want the other thing. I was the fantasy of me being the woman; being loved and being screwed, and that's what I recognize now. I don't know how I could get to the feeling of it unless I do it this way. The feeling between my thighs and abdomen—something nice happening to me. It comes from something else, something pleasant.

What happened when he "left reality"? How does one get away from it?

> At the moment when I feel the cock, there is no longer reality. Because I want it so much. I try to create something I want. I have no regard for all the laws of nature. Like if I wanted to have more than two arms, I would have a fantasy.

Asked if he could produce the "reality" of having more than two arms, he replied:

> No, *because it doesn't have the meaning for me that I need.* I don't want to have two more arms. But I do want the penis. I couldn't stop it, the disembodied penis, before, but I can now, perhaps. I think I've had it all my life and I never knew what it was. *It was in symbols. Symbols make it more difficult to stop it.* It is more difficult to stop it as a bulb, say, an electric light bulb, or something like that. And this time I can see it was a penis [see verbatim transcript, Appendix, p. 565].

I asked whether he could always bring himself back from the loss of connection with reality, for on several occasions (three or four out of twenty-five sessions during which they appeared) he cried out in pain and despair that they would not "go away" and he felt powerless to prevent them.

> There was one time when it was most difficult, when we were dealing with the mystery, at the time at the very beginning of the analysis when things were happening to me. A dream, a devil, the faces I'm afraid of that we were loosening, like I was being flooded with pus and it was everywhere, and that was terribly frightening.

When he frequently awoke from a dream, he could either go back to the dream or go back to some other dream. This gave him the illusion of participating in "some kind of like.... Images in my mind—a feeling, like going to a movie—I can do that during the day, too. If I am hurt or very, very disturbed I can lie down and start 'dreaming.'"

He recalled that around the age of twenty-one, when he'd go to his studio:

> [I]t was characteristic of me to go into some sort of dream world because it was pleasurable. [How did he go into it?] It is easy to remember the dream elements of something I have dreamt and to believe that they are real. For example, if I remember in a dream someone attacking me, a dog, for example, I would just go back to it. If the dreams are two days old, it would be very difficult to "go back into it." *I can go back because I haven't really left the dream—I haven't really given it up.*

I asked if at these times he simply went back to sleep.

> No—you feel your way back. If a man is attacking you, part of it is *believing there really was a man there*, and feeling that way back is to remember that mood and just *crawl back into it* [a conscious volitional element was present]. Like you've been on a stage and you haven't really left the theater. You go back into it—into it, because it is not only the situation, it's the entire atmosphere. The whole scenery is not enough to control an additional dream, though. As I go back I'm practically aware that I'm dreaming—I'm not awake or asleep: a twilight state. Before I wake up, I'm not aware that I'm dreaming. After I'm awake I *decide* to go back. I am not really asleep or awake, because all this time I am aware that I have to get up and go to work. The "dream" would be composed like a regular dream. The only difference between these dreams and dreams we've analyzed is that the ones I've had at night are much better worked out, and these others are more fragmented.

I remarked that I thought it more likely that the "controlled dreams" (i.e., the ones at night) might be better than the "uncontrolled ones." He differed:

> No, it seems so natural. For example, if I have the feeling of anxiety today, previous to perhaps a visit to my parents, I become tired and anxious. Therefore you think of your family, you go into something, you see a room. It has the element of a dream in it or it is distorted.

I asked about the differences between his reactions in dreams, his experiences on the couch evoked by telling his dreams and associating to them, and other regressive experiences on the couch because the differences remained unclear to me. The experiences on the couch were the fears. They were unpleasurable but apparently then became pleasurable. Were not the dreams and the events on the couch the same? "No, but it is being convinced of the reality. In the dream I am participating. The things on the couch, like something is coming out of the blue. They start with anxiety and what my family has done to me. They are not dreams, they are dream pictures." In one session he felt he was being attacked and slowly strangled by a python. He was extremely frightened, screamed and thrashed about, gasped, barked, and snarled. I asked, "Were you 'dreaming' on the couch when you had this experience?" He said:

> No, I was just believing that this is reality. I accept the emotion as reality to start with. *It's that all the emotions that come to my mind have the semblance of reality.* It seems so natural—have the anxiety, then think of a python on the floor. Then I have a problem. How do I solve it? Then it gets out of hand as it gets closer to me. I want the python closer as this is love. I want to be eaten and I also want to be held. *There is contact with reality in this.*

> On that occasion, it happened in a fantasy of being in a subway car, as I recall, but I got into it too deeply. It's possible that I try to put myself against this subway car pole thinking I have a python in my hand or run screaming. Your voice then becomes a reality and it brings me back. There's no way of shutting you out. These are fantasies, I guess. Since I am controlling them, they are more likely to get out of hand. In a dream there are safety factors. In free association I allow myself to do things that I wouldn't do in a dream.

He was asked what he meant by safety factors. "I don't know. But I never woke up screaming the way I have here."

I wish to suggest that the phrase *dream-pictures* (after Silberer [1951], and my patient's view of them) describes these phenomena as they represent visual symbolic hallucinatory wish-fulfillments similar to those found in dreams, but they differ from hypnogogic states in that the individual in the former may be in a state of altered consciousness or fully awake. They differ from *conscious fantasies* in that they are not memories derived from external perceptions which are modified and rearranged to create an internal world. The function of such conscious fantasies is to supply a certain amount of gratification when actual reality is unable to function in this manner.

Discussion

In an earlier contribution (1980b), I suggested that the perverse fantasies and dreams constitute a prophylactic device against the enactment of a perversion and reduce tension states faced by an archaic ego during sleep or while awake. A patient, therefore, who struggles against his perversion and its enactment may experience not only emotional flooding in the form of fits of despair, crying, anxiety, and the fear that he is "going crazy," but may be subject to regressive reexperiencing of primitive archaic wishes and/or dreads relating to the earliest conflicts surrounding separation from the mother: wishes to be mother, to be inside her, to be eaten by her, even to experiencing the primal scene as a female. Well-structured perversions, on the other hand, through their heavy disguises and encrustations and pleasure-fulfilling functions, lead to ego-syntonicity and provide a way out. Alterations in body-ego and pathological perceptions are a further means (in addition to transitory multiple perverse fantasies) of expressing as well as defending against unacceptable yet fundamental wishes through perceptual experiences (Freud, 1900).

For example, a masochistic wish to be hurt was experienced as a needle stuck through his penis. The wish to be engulfed was experienced in many ways: dropping into a well, fear of darkness descending, feelings of floating and disappearing, being sucked into a whirlpool, being wrapped in a ball, and lying on a raft with a monster nearby which opens its mouth and swallows him. The wish to be turned into a woman was experienced as his penis disappearing, swishing into his body, accompanied by howls, grunts, barks, hisses, and violent movements of his body. The wish to become a baby was experienced as perioral region sensations of smallness, numbness, and a diminishment of his body size.

The wish to be penetrated (derived in part from the primal scene experiences) was experienced in perceptual terms as oral, anal, aural, ocular, and penis penetration with cramps, rage, tongue-protrusion, and coprolalia. Being eaten by the python—being swallowed, eaten, and/or drowned, signified being with the preoedipal mother.

The wish to deliver a child was experienced as sensation between his legs and expressed in violent movements of his pelvis. An internal object moving around inside him reflected his conviction of something "rotten" inside him which had to be purged. The wish to regress so as "not to relate to anyone" was experienced in several ways: a state of fog or stupor, being in a cocoon or asleep, being diminished in size to three or four inches, becoming "insane." Furthermore, in becoming a woman he became her clitoris or her phallus. This also protected him from dangerous, destructive, murderous aggression.

The wish to be dead was experienced as defensive twitches in parts of his body, reaction formations to the numbness and deadness he felt. The wish to choke or kill a woman was experienced as the wish to be "put away" so that he could not damage anyone, a reaction formation. The wish to be castrated was experienced as a perceptual experience of his right arm being cut off, with full affective and motoric discharge. The wish to hurt someone was often turned into its opposite and experienced as a concrete wish to hurt himself (sadism into masochism). The fear that there were demons inside him and his wish to give birth to a baby arose from his wish and/or dread of being penetrated by the father. This produced convulsive reactions as if giving birth to a baby (see Appendix). The feeling that a penis was inside him was experienced as evil spirits, demons, ugliness within himself, and led to a concomitant wish to destroy himself and thereby destroy demons inside him. (This was done before analysis by drinking scalding fluids.) The latter was further experienced as wailing and convulsive feelings, smells of rottenness, flesh rotting away, and penises being pushed out through his skin.

The fear of dissolving and being swallowed up was reacted to by barking, crying out, shouting, violent movements of his head, and grunting. The barking (a violent exhalation against a partially closed glottis) represented a reaction of rage against oral penetration. Primal scene experiences were conceived of as fears of dark water, cats' eyes, and fears of the ape. Feelings of being abandoned were experienced concretely as the desire to see others having intercourse (voyeurism) or to exhibit himself and masturbate, or throw himself out of the window. In addition, wanting himself to be "screwed" as a woman and sadomasochistically loved were reacted to by severe headaches and anal pain. The desire for anal penetration by the father was experienced concretely as anal sensations and a fear of the "ape" (the giant father).

The wish for the father's love was experienced as unconscious homosexual urges (shocking anal sensations of penetration since early childhood) which were unacceptable and dealt with by substituting conscious desires to suck at the breast of the mother (breast-penis equation).

My understanding as to the meaning of his feeling of being invaded by demons is corroborated by Freud's (1923a) explorations in this direction. In his analysis of a seventeenth-century demonological neurosis he cited the following as explanations for being possessed: (1) The adoption by males of a feminine attitude toward the father; (2) demons are bad and reprehensible wishes, derivatives of instinctual impulses that have been repudiated or repressed; (3) the phenomenon of being possessed (e.g., convulsive attacks, painful sensations and visions), are expressions of such internalizations; and (4) the feminine attitude toward the father culminates in a fantasy of bearing him a child.

A major characteristic in the regressive experiences of my patient was a threatened symbolic omnipotent fusion with the mother, a state of impending dedifferentiation, a psychotic refusion. The issue in his analysis revolved around merger versus autonomy, and pathological perceptions were used in the process of externalizing this internal danger. In a less structurally deficient patient (e.g., a *neurotic* phobic patient), such an internal danger may be transformed into an external one, the anxiety localized and restricted to a phobic situation. In perverse patients with a more structurally deficient psychic apparatus, the internal danger is often externalized into mild to severe, acute or chronic pathological perceptions and body-ego disturbances. M. Sperling (1959) observed that

> [V]isual perceptions fulfill this task in a hallucinatory way when the appropriate and more affective modes are *not yet developed* or where their use is *prohibited by the ego* opposed to these wishes [emphasis added]. In regression to

the oral level, all libidinal objects will be treated in the same way, namely with the aim of being taken in. On the oral level, the object is never given up, although it may disappear in reality, but becomes part of the self by the process of internalization [p. 306].

She provided examples in which:

[T]he pathological changes of perceptions, e.g., the phenomenon of objects coming closer or objects receding from view, can be regarded as regressive phenomena occurring in certain individuals at the time when there is a threat of massive regression. These pathological perceptions not only serve to fulfill specific instinctual needs, but at the same time, like symptom formation, have the important function of preventing the imminent break with reality by limiting it to the sphere of the specific pathological perceptions [pp. 306-307].

"Analysis revealed that the basic conflict of these patients was dramatically expressed in these episodic, hallucinatory experiences" (p. 307). Sperling's patient felt as if she were losing her mind, and although there was no change in size of the objects as with my own patient, objects were rapidly moving away from her and the room seemed to expand.

My patient was prone to experience sensations of a change in the organization and sense of unity of the body-ego, its size, configuration, and spatial orientation; that is, "altered body-ego experiences" (Woodbury, 1966, p. 273). Such disturbances had an effect both on object representations and self representations. Woodbury, in an extensive study of patients who experienced such body-ego disturbances and pathological perceptions (schizophrenics, perverts, borderline and acute psychotics), explained this phenomenon in terms of energy investment; for example, withdrawal of cathexis from the adult body-ego from self and object representations, producing a flooding of the primitive "visceral body-ego complex" (p. 294). While such altered body-ego experiences are often under considerable conscious control (as in my patient), they frequently appear as hypnogogic hallucinations. The Isakower (1938) phenomena, Lewin's (1958) dream screen, and so on, are examples of such events. Woodbury noted that the absence of successful object relations in perverse patients, the emotions of yearning, anger, rage and frustration called forth, often lead to perversion formation but may often fail to do so. His conclusions cast light on my own clinical material. He stated: (1) "Perversions, altered body-ego experiences, and primal scenes are frequently found together" (p. 278); (2) Altered body-ego experiences in perversions are attempts to obtain instinctual gratification through someone else's ego, suggesting an ego defect in such patients; (3) Pain is used to stimulate skin sensations and to cause the reinvestment of the body-ego boundaries; (4) A frequent finding is that there is a feeling that objects and people are actively inside of one; for example, the "little man" phenomenon (p. 287); (5) Such experiences may flood the tridimensional body-ego, producing symbolic representations while awake and "very primitive fantasies" (p. 294); (6) The tongue is both the oral cavity experiencer as well as a "filter or a shield" (p. 295), and an organ of speech, and the perception that is is undergoing a change in size, shape, position (tongue-protrusion) is an "important model for the feeling of change in the body-ego" (p. 295).

Woodbury explained his findings, made before theoretical constructs derived from Mahler's infant observational studies, in terms of shifting cathexis of instinctual energy. In contrast, I consider these phenomena to be regressive reenactments of a fear and dread of engulfment by the mother and wishes to be penetrated by the father. They derive from faulty self-object differentiation, a fixation in the differentiating, practicing, or late symbiotic subphases of the separation-individuation process. Such fixation leads to a profound gender-defined self identity confusion, a persistence of primary feminine identification, and a predominance of archaic and primitive psychic mechanisms.

Finally, I wish to conclude with two observations. The unusual, dramatic, and often bizarre symptomatology of patients such as Philip, the hallucinatorylike nature of his productions, may well lead the analyst to lay down his therapeutic arms in the face of such apparently overwhelming obstacles of a preoedipal nature. The resolution of this patient's psychopathology, accomplished through a relentless pursuit and perseverance on the part of both patient and analyst, informs us once again that what is decisive in the psychoanalytic treatment of perverse patients is not the patient's symptomatology per se or his life history, but the nature of the spontaneously developing transference and the willingness and ability of the patient to follow the lead of the analyst in a mutual endeavor of tracing and understanding the genesis of his condition (the therapeutic alliance). My second observation is concerned with the pathological perceptions and altered body-ego experiences which have received scant psychoanalytic attention. It is my hope that my experience with this remarkable patient will encourage others to pursue such investigations, for such pathological perceptions and body-ego experiences, despite their florid and dramatic manifestations, have arisen simply from abstract ideas, and while they express unacceptable impulses, they are largely a means to express fundamental wishes (Freud, 1900) whose understanding remains a fundamental task of all psychoanalytic inquiry.

Chapter 22
PSYCHOANALYTIC TECHNIQUE IN THE TREATMENT OF SEXUAL PERVERSIONS

In the history of psychoanalysis every advance in insight has been followed closely by an advance in technique; conversely, every technical rule has been considered valid only when rooted in a specific piece of analytic theory. Any doubt concerning the justification of a particular technique, therefore, had to be dealt with by inquiry into the theoretical assumptions which had given rise to it. While our standard technique equips us with the understanding of character analyses, the various forms of perversion, fetishism, homosexuality, etc., which we now consider accessible to treatment, seem to justify deviations of technique (Anna Freud, 1954, p. 381).

In what follows, I shall discuss my technical digressions against the backdrop of their theoretical background, which has already been presented. It is my belief that the deviations of technique I shall describe are justified on the basis of the deviations in the patient's ego structure and the preoedipal origin of these conditions. It is my belief that when perverse patients are treated in the manner to be described, that unconscious anxieties of the preoedipal period (as well as those anxieties of the oedipal period) become manifest and can be dealt with in a modified psychoanalytic therapy.

It is necessary that the analyst provide the patient from the outset with an opportunity to admit the extent of his desolation to the paternal figure in the transference. Unconscious material revealing aspects of himself that he abhors and wishes to change may not appear for a long time. Eventually, the patient realizes that he is the victim of childhood events and early intrapsychic conflicts that have produced an interference in normal sexual development and functioning. As a consequence, he is forced to utilize roundabout methods for sexual arousal and sexual gratification. The pathological form of sexuality for which he seeks our help is, however, only one manifestation of a complex deeper disorder affecting all areas of development and functioning. The patient may fear the reawakening of hopes for heterosexuality, long suppressed, and express disbelief that anything can be done to remedy matters. Kohut's (1971) admonition to those who would treat narcissistic personality disorders should be well heeded in the treatment of perverse individuals, that they be sympathetic in tone, manner, and voice. One proceeds with correct empathy for the patient's feelings, ever mindful of his need for gratification through perverse acts in order to insure the development of both a relationship and a successful outcome. The patient's anxiety tolerance depends on his ability to identify with the therapist, who can both accept the patient's anxieties, his vulnerabilities and depressions, and pathological sexuality, as well as be a container for them.

Since the prognosis often depends on the patient's determination to change, and the extent to which this determination can be awakened in analysis, it is important that no authoritative assertion of incurability has been made regarding perverse practices. I make it clear from the outset that I view the obligatory performance of perverse acts as a form of psychopathology, a disturbance in psychosexual functioning, a form of developmental pathology, and a consequence of preoedipal conflict. The essential task is the resolution of preoedipal conflicts in order to promote a process of developmental unfolding, in Spitz's words, "free from the anxieties, perils, threats of the original situation" and through the "transference relationship enable the patient to reestablish his object relations or form new object relations at the level at which is development was deficient" (1959, pp. 100–101). The removal of these conflicts and obstacles make it possible for the patient to progress along the road to heterosexual functioning as the need for perverse gratification becomes less obligatory. In time, it becomes neither tension-relieving, fear-reducing, nor a compensatory mechanism, and must then compete with newly established heterosexual functioning for pleasure and self-esteem. Thus, the treatment of all perverse patients is the treatment of the preoedipal developmental arrest, which is the *fons et origo* from which the perversion emerged.

Obligatory homosexuals must be exposed to the information that neither homosexual *nor* heterosexual object choice is constitutionally determined; that is, hereditary in origin, biologically determined, or due to chromosomal tagging. Both are learned behaviors, the perverse act constituting "abnormal learning" and the heterosexual act a normal form of sexual expression. It is vitally important that when the patient asks the analyst if *he* (the analyst) was somehow not "born that way" (i.e., heterosexual), the analyst inform the patient that heterosexuals were not "born that way" either. It is well known that even when a patient announces at the beginning of therapy that he does not wish his homosexual perversion to be changed and that he is undergoing analysis simply for the treatment of "ancillary" symptomatology, psychoanalysis may well remove perverse activities (A. Freud, 1954). In recent years, the "normalization" of exclusive homosexuality by nonanalytic psychiatric establishments has led some well-intentioned but uninformed practitioners to express the view that the homosexuality of a patient be preserved and not "tampered with" analytically, as it is not a form of psychopathology.

A similar view is expressed by those who ransack nonanalytic literature, novels, and ancient documents for proof of the "normality" of homosexuality. Others engage in scholarly studies of history (Liebert, 1986) and the writings of modern writers, or examine the sexual customs of aborigines and natives. Some assert that certain gifted and famous individuals appear devoid of psychopathology, although "homosexual," and others may confuse documented ritualized fellatio practiced between adult men and younger boys, and engaged in by entire native communities for certain periods of time with true obligatory homosexuality. Such studies, while of interest to the psychoanalyst for the cross-cultural information they supply as regards prevalence of sexual practices, have limited value when applied to our understanding of whether a piece of sexual behavior constitutes perversion or not.[1] Since these individuals were not and could not be subjected to psychoanalytic individual scrutiny, the conclusions put forth do not meet the basic criteria by which we can judge or evaluate the meaning of a particular piece of behavior. Only through psychoanalytic investigation can we answer the question as to whether certain sexual activities, when they depart from the standard male-female design, can be considered perversions. This basic principle (as noted in chapter 2) was supplied by Freud in 1916 when he stated, "Let us once more reach an agreement upon what is to be understood by the 'sense' of a psychical process. We mean nothing other by it than the intention it serves and its position in psychical continuity" (p. 40). Thus, whether or not sexual practices can be termed perversions or not can be determined only by the study of the conscious and/or unconscious motivations from which they arise.

This extreme view, held by some, that the "homosexual identity" of a patient should be "preserved," notably Isay (1985, 1986), destroys therapeutic effectiveness and eliminates the possibility of the removal of symptomatology. Such a position may have various sources: social-political

---

[1]Incidentally, Stoller and Herdt's (1982) cross-cultural findings were that Stone-Age New Guinean boys, removed from their mothers' influence (during the late preoedipal phase), which was pictured as damaging and draining at all levels, and subjected to ritualized fellatio with older men beginning at age seven, did not grow up to be obligatory homosexuals. Their fathers insisted upon masculine identification and preparation for life as warriors and hunters.

activism in an era of sexual permissiveness and liberation, including genuine concern but misguided efforts to remedy the plight of the homosexual who has suffered social disapproval for centuries for something over which he has no control; the ego-syntonic nature of homosexuality;[2] undue pessimism as to the value of psychoanalytic therapy for this disorder. To the clinician versed in the treatment of homosexuality, however, unfavorable outcome in therapy should lead psychoanalysts to more rigorous pursuit of their theoretical and clinical understanding of this condition, and the techniques most efficacious in its treatment, and not to pronouncing it a "nondisorder." All homosexual patients wish *more*, not less help from psychoanalysts. The growing tendency and even abhorrence in some quarters to viewing homosexuality as a clinical disorder and the criticism leveled against those who treat such patients have been compared to the vilification heaped on Freud for his initial discovery of infantile sexuality and its consequences for normal and pathological development (Fine, 1980). That such social/political activism, clinical naiveté, personal bias, or therapeutic pessimism could be decisive in removing homosexuality from the realm of psychiatric inquiry represents a scientific travesty comparable to that which occurs in human genetics through the substitution of Lamarckian theory in place of Mendelian genetics for social/political purposes in the Soviet Union. Those who take these positions often rationalize them by the statement that homosexual individuals are thereby spared the pain of treatment and what they assume to be its inevitable failure.

Some parents unwittingly and unconsciously encourage their children into perverse sexuality. Vicarious satisfactions of this kind arise from the parents' own faulty gender-

---

[2]Homosexuality (similar to other perversions) is, furthermore, unique in its capacity to use profound psychic conflicts and struggles to attain, for limited intervals, a pseudoadequate equilibrium and pleasure-reward (orgasm), often permitting the individual to function, however marginally and erratically. This neutralization of conflict allows the growth of certain ego-adaptive elements of the personality, and the homosexual may therefore have appeared not ill at all to others except for the obvious masquerade in his sexual life.

defined self identity. I often find a specific superego defect in perverse patients, a defect which is a duplication of a similar distortion in the parents' own personalities, along with a faulty and disturbed heterosexuality. That political and social activists' positions on a clinical disorder can lead to a compounding of ignorance is evident in the assertion by the individuals who wish to "normalize" homosexuality that analysts betray a basic principle of psychoanalytic therapy, namely, the concept of neutrality when they attempt to change one's "homosexual identity" (Isay, 1985). Those who espouse this view unfortunately misunderstand the concept of neutrality as used in psychoanalysis. This concept does not mean that the analyst is "neutral" as to whether the patient is helped in the removal of either phobia, obsession, or perversion; the analyst does care and the patient comes with the implicit understanding that the analyst wishes to help ease his suffering through the analysis of his preoedipal fixations, his object relations conflict, thereby eliminating perversion and opening the pathway to heterosexuality. Correctly used, the concept of neutrality means that the analyst must be neutral so that the patient can better allow affects of the past to be projected upon him; in other words, to promote the transference.

Exceptions to my position that perverse patients may be treated successfully and much of their suffering alleviated are found in situations similar to those described by others; for example, Kernberg (1984a) in the treatment of severe personality disorders. A poor outcome may be predicted in those patients who exhibit severe antisocial personality structure; are unwilling or unable to attend sessions; show severe disturbances in verbal communication with an inability to make connections in the analysis; produce little or no dream material throughout the analysis; have a severely defective superego so that they are unable to profit either from the therapeutic alliance or the positive transference; engage in chronic lying and withholding of information; or are severely drug-dependent. The worst prognosis in my perverse patients are those who are in the most severe range of narcissistic pathology (borderline cases), who demonstrate a severe splitting of the ego with projection more prominent than repression, and a tendency toward paranoid thinking of an insistent and intractable nature. They evidence psychosislike transference reactions with a chronic inclination to misunderstand others, and continually feel that the analyst is letting them down. Under conditions of severe stress and environmental frustration of their unrealistic goals, they may retreat to a "malignant part" of their pathological grandiose self (Rosenfeld, 1971), a haven for revenge which is to be visited upon imagined depriving powerful figures. These patients may remain in regression for extended periods of time, unaffected by interpretation and empathic responses.

Having defined the level of ego-developmental arrest, my overall strategy is to discover the location of the fixation point, delineate ego deficits and the type of object relations dominating the patient's life. I make it possible for the patient to retrace his steps to that part of development that was distorted by infantile or childhood traumas, conflicts, and deficiencies due to unmet needs and tensions. I eliminate compensatory, reparative moves in the maladaptive process that have distorted and inhibited functioning, and remove self-perpetuating defenses. With their removal, I encounter head-on preoedipal conflicts, especially reenactments of rapprochement–subphase conflict, separation and fragmentation anxieties, disturbances in self cohesion, and castration anxiety of both oedipal and preoedipal origin. No matter the form of the perversion, I routinely find anxieties relating to separation from the mother, which are then relived and abreacted to in the course of therapy. In all patients, a central task is the elucidation of the three great anxieties of the rapprochement subphase (Mahler, Pine & Bergman, 1975): fear of the loss of the object, fear of losing the object's love, and an undue sensitivity to approval and/or disapproval by the parents.

Any preoedipal developmental arrest must be treated with supportive measures until the patient can begin full analysis. A longer psychoanalytic treatment may be necessary in order to first break through the developmental arrest and the pathological character structure activated in the analysis. Defenses in these patients may be immature, in a prestage of development, a prestage of defense (Stolorow and Lachmann, 1978). In addition, appropriate self-object differentiation and integration have been interfered with. The need to engage in perverse activity is a manifestation of this arrest in development. It is a developmental necessity, at least for the time being, and not a resistance. In such cases, special techniques are necessary to promote the maturation of arrested ego functions. The aim of these techniques is to promote structuralization of ego functions sufficient for later exploration of the defensive aspects of the patient's psychopathology in terms of the instinctual conflicts they serve to ward off. Developmental imbalances can be reconstructed from memories and dreams in the transference and can be placed correctly in the specific developmental stages to which they belong. For example, self and object representations were vulnerable to regression in a homosexual patient who yearned for self-object dissolution and a mystical oneness and union with the saints (Jesus, St. Sebastian, Hindu mystics, and so on). Vulnerability to these regressions vitiated and blocked his progress. He needed archaic self-objects for self-esteem regulation and, as a result, a long period of symbioticlike idealizing transference had to be promoted. This helped him gain the feeling of an individual, idealized self (a real self), first based on identification with the analyst. This approach of permitting such idealizing transferences with borderline patients is not, however, without its perils; for in the borderline preoedipal type II narcissistic perverse patient there is a tendency to fusion with the object and a confusion between self and object, between analyst and patient. The subsequent "failure" of the object (analyst) to gratify the omnipotent and grandiose needs of the patient may be then responded to (if suitable interceptive interpretations are not made) with severe aggression, regression paranoid feelings, and psychosislike transference reactions.

In order to facilitate the structuralization of the psychic apparatus, the analyst must promote gradually differentiated and integrated self and object representations within the therapeutic relationship. During this period, the analyst restricts his interpretations to an empathic understanding of the patient's primitive arrested self and object representations, which the patient attempts to restore. This insures the continuation of the positive transference, whether or not these ego deficiencies arise from the predominance of *aggressive* conflicts themselves in the earliest years of life (Kernberg, 1975) or were due to a lack of empathic response from early caretakers (Kohut, 1971). Neutrality and consistent understanding of archaic states promote differentiations and integrations and contribute to the formation of the patient's new world of self and object representations. Once sufficient structuralization of the psychic apparatus has taken place, one may proceed with the analysis of transference manifestations of libidinal and aggressive conflicts.

Interpretive Stance

Transference

One can observe in the transference behavior and fantasies of perverse patients early forms of ego, id, and superego functioning. Regressions, however, are usually temporary, circumscribed, and these patients rebound from them. Success in treatment may well depend on the degree of transferential rapport which can be established (Panel, 1977).

Perversions require full-scale, thoroughgoing analysis of all phases of development, manifestations of arrested development in the transference, and the acting out of impulses (Panel, 1977). The considerations I have cited in an earlier work (1978a, pp. 425-453) regarding homosexual patients and their transferences apply equally to other perverse individuals.

Many of these patients suffer from mild to severe degrees of narcissistic pathology, depending on the level of fixation, whether at rapprochement, differentiating, or practicing subphases. They show considerable variations in ego strength and/or weakness, their therapeutic alliance is often tenuous, and they may distort the analyst's interpretations. Transference interpretations are often felt to be intrusive or too critical. In a state of "nonrelatedness," they experience themselves as living in a "cocoon," "plastic bubble," or "bell jar" (Volkan, 1976; Modell, 1978).

In early phases, the therapeutic approach is one in which the positive transference is strengthened, the focus being on analyzing the patient's distortion of current and past events and his acting-out behavior. I attempt to create a neutrality similar to that recommended in the treatment of borderline conditions: one that is experienced as implicitly protective and supplying a holding environment, in the sense of Winnicott (1965). As these patients experience a fusion between self and object and a disturbance in the adequate testing of reality, I prefer, during early and middle phases of treatment, to make genetic reconstruction of the patient's conflicts and examine these distortions in the extra-analytic transference, rather than engage in a concentrated analysis of them as they appear in the transference neurosis. I find the specific genetic reasons for the perversion are more easily understood and accepted in this context. In later phases, with an improvement in ego functions, including object relations, transference interpretations may be given as in the treatment of neuroses. These "rules" pertain as long as the transference remains positive. Transference revivals, especially those of hate and aggression toward feared and devouring parental figures, however, unless quickly eliminated through transference interpretation, become an important source of resistance. They indicate profound negative reactions to the therapy itself, and are an attempt to rationalize and justify the continuation of perverse activity. The repetition in the transference of erotic perverse libidinal needs toward the analyst are rare, but sometimes occur in the analysis of male homosexual patients with a male analyst. They usually signify a disruption in the therapeutic alliance and a conscious resistance to change. They once again simply express the *manifest content* of disguised wishes and dreads toward a "new homosexual object," the analyst. Interpretation of the meaning of homosexual encounters (e.g., the wish to seize, incorporate, conquer, and appropriate the masculinity of other men), tends to restore the therapeutic alliance and eliminates the need to act out through these impulses in the analysis. If they persist, they help keep in repression the deeper and more meaningful anxieties, whose uncovering is the central task of the analysis. In finding specific genetic reasons for the perversion, my aim is to revive once again the impact of these early events by abreacting them, providing insight into their meaning, and assimilating them in the context of the new object relationship.

Erotic transferences between male and female homosexual patients and female analysts have a different significance, however, as they express the uncovering of previously repressed love for the consciously feared and hated preoedipal mother. Erotic transferences are frequent between female homosexuals and male analysts and are useful analytically, as they represent the reawakening of earlier, strongly repressed and disavowed desires for the father's love, approval, and admiration. They are a harbinger of heterosexual feelings and are responded to with surprise by the patient. They tend to reactivate early convictions of inferiority and bitter accusations against the father/analyst for real or imagined slights or rejections, due to one's being a female. They also signify an emergence of superimposed oedipal conflict.

The fate of the transference rapport and ultimately the success of the treatment in narcissistic patients with the most severe degree of narcissistic pathology is directly related to the degree of success met with in (1) the systematic interpretation of the defensive functions of the grandiose self, and (2) the analysis and diminution of the tendency to devalue parental images and real parent figures, as they occurred in real life and in the transference. It is well known that these patients, similar to narcissistic personality disorders, may engage in total devaluation of the analyst for even minor reasons and rail with overwhelming aggression against the object (Kernberg, 1970). The optimal technique in these patients is that suggested by Kernberg (1970, 1975); for example, the systematic interpretation of both positive and negative transference aspects, rather than focusing exclusively on libidinal elements. The persistence of narcissistic transferences and the necessity that they be transformed into less primitive forms of object relations before real progress can be made, complicates the treatment of these patients and lengthens the analysis.

Extratransference Interpretations

Extratransference interpretations are particularly important in the treatment of perverse patients. It is well known
that repetition of real traumatic experiences occurs in extra-
transference situations as well as in the transference. They
are preparatory to transference interpretations and are valuable in their effect on the analytic process in general (Panel,
1984). For example, a pedophile's seduction of little children
during the analysis repeats his own aggressive sexual abuse
at the hands of an older brother and adults in an orphanage
to which he was sent in midchildhood. Focusing on this
event as a manifestation of acting out of the transference
alone and not concentrating on anxiety and need for gratification arising from past experiences but triggered by the
patient's current experiences, leads to isolating the analysis
and impedes the working through of his conflicts. This
approach, analyzing the precipitating life situation which,
like a trigger mechanism, activates the need for perverse
activity, lessens confusion in the minds of these patients.

In narcissistic or borderline perverse patients, focusing
mainly on transference analysis furthers their turning away
from their external life and makes it more difficult for them
to focus on their internal reactions to external problems. As
noted in a recent panel (1984), to restrict oneself to transference analysis in these patients may further the "consolidation of their narcissistic system," allowing reality testing to
remain tenuous and object relations severely impaired.
Some of these patients regularly announce that analysis has
become the most important thing in their lives, but unfortunately, it may be utilized for narcissistic purposes of "self-
enhancement" rather than self-discovery.

The Therapeutic Alliance

The bedrock of my therapeutic efforts rests on the establishment, consolidation, and maintenance of the therapeutic or
working alliance (Greenson, 1967; Greenacre, 1971; Dickes,
1975), the condition of "basic trust" (Greenacre, 1969) which
allows the patient to follow the lead of the analyst in search-

ing for the meaning, content, and genesis of his condition (see chapter 1).

These patients have failed to experience healthy ego functioning, have not achieved object constancy, and suffer from an inability to attain healthy object relations. The analytic situation offers them the opportunity for experiencing in depth "both the real and unreal ways in which they deal with the world" (Greenson, 1969). When I make interpretations to these patients, my aim is not only to remove their unconscious, anachronistic anxieties, but also to help them experience appropriate ego functions and new object relations. In this manner, structuralization of the mental apparatus takes place not only through interpretation and assimilation but by a positive recognition in dealing with the patient's effective levels of performance. To achieve this, there must be a "real" nontransference relationship, all the while keeping an appropriate psychological and physical distance. Communication is designed to increase the development of object relations and restore internal self representations. In those patients with severe object relations pathology (fusion between self and object) and in those with severe projective anxieties and tendencies to severe regressive episodes, the analysis proceeds for a long initial period in a face-to-face relationship. A unique indicator that a therapeutic alliance has been achieved is the patient's (especially the homosexual patient who has engaged in numerous face-saving rationalizations, including that of constitutional bisexuality to explain his need for men) beginning awareness that he is not simply responding to an instinctual need in his perverse activities, but he is dominated by a tension which he can neither understand nor control.

The Specific Tasks

In what follows, I describe four specific major tasks to be achieved for the successful psychoanalytic treatment of perverse patients: (1) separating and disidentifying from the preoedipal mother; (2) decoding the manifest perversion; (3) providing insight into the function of erotic experience in perverse acts; and (4) spoiling the perverse gratification. The delineation of these tasks fundamental for the treatment of perversions (and perhaps for some addictions, kleptomanias, and other forms of ego-syntonic pathology) in no way minimizes the importance of other tasks, either implicit with them or related to them; for example, promoting differentiation and integrated self and object representations; resolving castration anxiety of both preoedipal and oedipal phases; eliminating the "narcissistic resistance" to change; diminishing of unneutralized aggression, and so on.

Separating from the Preoedipal Mother

A primary task in the treatment of all perverts is to disclose and define to the patient the primary feminine identification with the mother that has led to the disturbance in his gender-defined self identity, the core of his disorder (see chapter 3). The ultimate purpose of this interpretation is to effect dis-identifying from her (promote intrapsychic separation from her) so that a developmental step, previously blocked, a counteridentification with the father (analyst) may now begin to take place. My aim is to aid the patient in successfully traversing separation–individuation phases, and assume an appropriate gender-defined self identity in accordance with anatomy. The consistent, disciplined, hopeful, and helpful attitude of the analyst toward the patient facilitates the identification with the analyst, a reopening of masculine identity in a new object relationship provided by the analysis and extra-analytic experiences.

The identification with the all-powerful, almighty preoedipal mother permeates every aspect of the pervert's life: he feels he cannot survive without her. Efforts to separate from her produce separation anxiety in evidence well before the age of three and persist unabated throughout life. Castration anxiety, when present, is the result of superimposed oedipal conflict, and is utilized as a defense against anxieties of the preoedipal phase. Similarly, preoedipal drives may have a defensive importance in warding off oedipal wishes and fears. Oedipal conflicts, however, are an accretion to the basic preoedipal nuclear conflict involving separation.

The patient is shown that the lifelong persistence of the original primary feminine identification has resulted in conscious–unconscious, pervasive feelings of femininity, or a deficient sense of masculinity. The patient is symbiotically attached to the mother, has fantasies of fusing with her (as elicited in dreams, fantasies, and in actual interaction with her), but is also intensely ambivalent toward her. A severe degree of masochistic vulnerability is manifest, especially in relation to the mother, to whose attitudes and behavior the patient is unduly sensitive. Early in therapy we encounter a deficit in body–ego boundaries accompanied by fears of bodily disintegration, unusual sensitivity to threats of bodily damage by external objects, explainable in part as a manifestation of castration anxiety, as well as threats of bodily damage involved with object loss. Aggressive impulses which threaten to destroy both the self and the object are also commonly found in this phase of treatment.

I demonstrate to the patient through dreams, transference, and extra-analytic transferences, and in my interpretation of his sexual enactments that his perverse practices preserve identification with the mother, albeit in a disguised form. He attempts to relieve anxiety, tension, depression, paranoidal feelings, and other intense archaic ego states by pressing into service perverse enactments. These make him feel secure, as he has thereby reinstated the previously disturbed optimal distance from and/or closeness to the mother.[3] These interpretations occupy much of the course of the early and middle phases of the analysis, as the patient endlessly engages in an obsessive repetition of this pattern of perverse enactments in order to relieve himself of intolerable anxieties, often made worse during this period of analytic investigation. While these acts represent flight from mother, it is made clear that these perverse practices are simultaneously an attempt to maintain contact with her and constitute a reassurance against loss of self through merger in a somatopsychic fusion with her. They provide affirmation of one's own individual existence through orgastic experiences (Eiss-

---

[3]The term *optimal distance and/or closeness* refers to a psychological state in which the patient feels secure against both the loss of the mother and the preoedipal needs she supplies, and his own wish/dread of reengulfment (see chapter 3).

ler, 1958b; Lichtenstein, 1977; Socarides, 1978a; Stolorow and Lachmann, 1980).

In essence, all perverse patients are reliving an object relations conflict (Dorpat, 1976) consisting of anxiety and guilt in association with the failure of self–object differentiation and separation from the mother. When we speak of separation we are of course referring to an *intrapsychic* event, independent of any physical separation. In all these patients, an intrapsychic conflict exists around both a wish for and a fear of "re-engulfment by the object" (Mahler, 1966a).

These patients experience *critical periods* during the course of therapy. Emboldened and strengthened through identification with the analyst, they attempt to effect separation from their pathological attachment to the mother. They are then catapulted into crises that have all the characteristics of rapprochement-phase crisis (Socarides, 1980a). As noted earlier (see chapter 3), some patients with established perverse practices may never approach these rapprochement crises with its dangers of regressive experiences, especially if they do not seriously attempt to interrupt their perverse practices. Others, deeply afraid and unprepared analytically to face this anxiety, may prematurely terminate psychoanalytic therapy in a period of resistance, and with many rationalizations for a premature interruption. Some of these will return to therapy for shorter or longer periods of time to relieve their suffering, only again to escape facing their deepest conflicts. The failure to successfully understand and resolve these conflicts and overcome these fixations is largely responsible for the inevitable later continuation of perverse practices.

Patients in rapprochement-phase crises experience incorporation anxieties, projective anxieties, fears of loss of self and loss of the object. In effect, they undergo a threatened dedifferentiation of psychic structure and of object relations. Gradually, repetition of such separations in which their own aims, objectives, thoughts, and feelings predominate over those of the mother, result in less threats of object loss and less personal disruption. They gradually overcome the fear of object loss and the fear of losing the object's love.

The undue sensitivity to approval and/or disapproval by the mother is attenuated and ultimately disappears.

These patients do not suffer irreversible loss or destruction of object relations or other functions as they attempt to separate. Although they may regress to earlier phases in which there was a threat of loss of ego boundaries between two physically separate individuals (i.e., the mother and the patient), they remain in contact with the analyst and are gradually desensitized to such experiences (see chapter 10). Such critical events should not be responded to with undue fear on the part of the analyst that the patient will suffer a break from reality, for these patients are able to maintain the transference relationship despite vivid reenactments of oral and anal fantasies and fears of engulfment. The successful reenactment of these regressive experiences, wishes, and dreads, in almost all instances results in a strengthening of the patient's ego, lessening the strength of isolated affective states which have continually threatened to erupt into consciousness in derivative forms throughout their lives [e.g., hypochondriasis, migraine attacks, anxiety attacks, masochistic fears, prolonged feelings of lethargy, physical incapacities, inability to act, splitting phenomena (e.g., a conviction that one has two faces, etc.)]. Losing the reassuring and anxiety-diminishing optimal distance from and/or closeness to the mother has been an event to be avoided at all costs. Perverse practices had been the only means of relief, designed precisely to forestall and prevent the realization of these powerful affective states, although at a great personal psychological cost. Interpretation of the function and content of these crisis states leads to a deeper understanding of the earlier predicament, which led to the disturbed gender-defined self identity, and consequent sexual practices.

To summarize what has already been stated: maturational achievements are unconsciously perceived and equated with intrapsychic separation and reacted to with anxiety and guilt of various degrees, which is then analyzed in a manner similar to that used with neurotic conflict. These anxieties relate to actual or fantasied threats, intimidations by the mother, and are placed in a genetic restructuring of the patient's childhood. Archaic conflicts and rapprochement crises ultimately lose their strength and disappear. The patient is then able, after the phobic avoidance of the vagina is analyzed and genital schematization fortified through the patient's acknowledgment of the ownership of his own penis and elimination of castration anxieties of both the preoedipal and oedipal periods, to begin to function heterosexually at first with and ultimately without perverse fantasies. Such therapeutic progress requires months of analytic work and mutual dedication to the task. Therapeutic results are, however, fully commensurate with the labor required. Most patients respond with newfound hope and exhilaration secondary to both their diminished dependence on perverse activities for alleviating anxiety, as well as a newfound capacity to attain orgastic satisfaction in a manner previously closed to them. A homosexual patient's euphoric announcement of such an accomplishment after one-and-a-half years of analysis was received by the analyst while on vacation in the form of a telegram utilizing the words of the first man to set foot on the moon: "Tranquillity Base here. The Eagle has landed."

Pathological object relations are corrected through the transference relationship and through the gradual formation of new object relations. My aim is to create emotional insight, an awareness of symptom behavior and the emotional processes which underlie it, through reexperiencing "forgotten" past experiences and their assimilation through interpretation and working through. My overall goal is to produce a gradual improvement in performance and functioning in all the major areas of the patient's life, leading to an increased self-confidence and pleasure in living, in effect, to improve the patient's overall psychological functioning.

Decoding the Manifest Perversion[4]

The perversion is an ego-syntonic formation, the end result of unconscious defense mechanisms accomplished through

----

[4]The earlier view that perversion was simply the "negative of neurosis" (Freud, 1905b) and the pervert accepted impulses which the neurotic tried to repress led to the general belief that the analyst had nothing to uncover or decipher as regards the hidden meaning of the perverse act itself.

the Sachs mechanism. This is a solution by division whereby one piece of infantile sexuality enters the service of repression, is helpful in promoting repression through displacement, substitution, and other defense mechanisms, and so carries over pregenital pleasure into the ego while the rest undergoes repression. The repression of the wish to penetrate the mother's body or the wish to suck and appropriate the mother's breast, for example, undergoes repression in homosexuality; instead of the mother's body it is the male body that is penetrated, and instead of the mother's breast it is the penis that is sought after. Homosexuality then becomes the choice of the lesser evil. This basic mechanism in the production of homosexuality in both males and females is revealed to the patient through the decoding of the manifest content into its unconscious, more frightening meaning in a manner similar to that of dream interpretation.

To elaborate further: the attachment to the mother, hatred toward the father, and punitive, aggressive, destructive drives toward the body of the mother in homosexual patients undergoes disguise so that the homosexual substitutes the partner's penis for the mother's breast. The female similarly substitutes the fictive penis of her female partner in place of the abhorrent maternal breast. This then takes the form of a masculine attitude on the part of the female partner and/or herself: the substitution and introduction of the finger and tongue in this contact, and the use of a penis-like device. Simultaneously, the female homosexual avoids her incestuous wishes toward the father. The breast–penis equation is a common finding in homosexuals.

That the manifest perversion is a heavy disguise for "something else" is vividly depicted in my analysis of a spanking perversion described in chapter 16 (Socarides, 1985). The "Lady Gainsborough woman" spanking the patient was revealed to be a substitute for the father and the spanking itself a substitute for anal penetration by the paternal phallus. That the manifest content is a disguise for latent content is strikingly evident in those perversions, often with sadomasochistic content, which take an unusual if not bizarre form. For example, a patient could only experience orgasm after he placed a bug on an unsuspecting female's shoulder, who then brushed it off and crushed in beneath her heel. Fantasies of the crushing of the bug during later masturbation produced orgasm in a case described by Stolorow and Grand (1973). A further example is that of a young man reported by Keeler (1960) who could only achieve sexual excitement and orgasm if he placed himself in a situation where one of his limbs was run over by an automobile driven by a young woman. The act was performed over a soft surface of earth so that he was not permanently maimed.

The object choice in these perversions is further dictated by certain need-satisfactions (narcissistic needs) to be met through one's sensoriperceptive apparatus. These need-satisfactions simultaneously gratify an archaic form of identification with the mother and represent an underground version of a union with narcissistically invested lost objects (Greenacre, 1968).

It is important to show the patient that all the above events occurred before the oedipal phase and have little to do with genital sexuality. Perverse formations constitute an "end-product" (Freud, 1919), are usually manifest before the age of five, and are subject to later modification as a result of specific organizing experiences (Socarides, 1985) before they reach their final form at puberty (Freud, 1905b). Self–object differentiation, need-tension, and preoedipal conflicts are all expressed in the ultimate form taken by the perversion.

Through decoding, the patient can perceive his disorder in its original form: the archaic longings and dreads, the primitive needs and fears which arose from his struggle to make a progression from mother–child unity to individuation. He can now perceive what he seeks to rediscover in his object choice and aims the primary reality of narcissistic relations with different images of the mother and later with the father. He becomes a woman through transvestism and transsexualism; keeps the mother close through a symbolic substitute (the fetish). The fetishist realizes that his need for a covering for his body (an underwear fetish, for example) represents a fear of bodily disintegration secondary to identification with the mother, a wish to have babies like her. The homosexual perceives that his fear of engulfment (due to a lack of separation from the mother and his wish and/or dread of fusing with her) forces him to seek salvation from her by running toward men. Ironically, he does not seek femininity in approaching men but is attempting to regain lost masculinity so cruelly denied him in the earliest years of childhood. Preoedipal type II narcissistic homosexuals realize in addition that they are warding off threats to self cohesion and fragmentation and desperately need to experience emotions through the responses of their selfobjects, their sexual partners. The voyeur perceives that he must "keep looking" because of his fear of engulfment by the female body and his fear of object loss. Through visual reassurance he is reassured that he is not female, nor is he merging with the mother. Through distancing he temporarily overcomes his fear of closeness to the destructive maternal body. The homosexual pedophile, in embracing and sexually possessing the body of a prepubertal child, is capturing through substitution the long-lost and wished-for symbiosis with the pure, nonmalevolent maternal breast of the hated and depriving mother.

We should not overlook a unique function of all perversions: each dramatically restores the sense of having a bounded and cohesive self through the production of orgasm. This reinforces an "incontrovertible truth" (Lichtenstein, 1977) of the reality of personal existence separate from the mother. Therefore, it has an "affirmative function" (Eissler, 1958b; Lichtenstein, 1977).

Ego-Syntonicity Versus Ego-Dystonicity
(see chapter 2)

In making perverse acts no longer pleasurable, we are converting the act from an ego-syntonic one to an ego-alien or ego-dystonic one. The term *ego-syntonic* has long been used in psychoanalysis to denote behavior which is compatible with the integrity of the self. This concept requires further clarification and refinement, especially as it is misused in the psychiatric nomenclature as signifying "acceptance" or "nonacceptance" by the individual of his own symptomatology dependent on his response to (external) societal approval and/or disapproval.

When one speaks of the ego-syntonicity of the perverse practices, it is evident that we are dealing with two components: conscious acceptance and unconscious acceptance. The degree of conscious acceptance of the perverse act varies with the person's reactions to societal pressure and consciously desired goals and aspirations. The conscious part of ego-syntonicity can be more readily modified than its unconscious component. Analysis of perverse patients reveals that ego-syntonic formations accepted by the patient are *already the end result of unconscious defense mechanisms in which the ego plays a decisive part*. In contrast, where superego or id plays a decisive role, the end result is often ego-alien symptoms. The splitting of the superego promotes ego-syntonicity; the superego is especially tolerant of this form of sexuality, as it may represent the unconscious acceptable aspect of sexuality derived from a parental superego. A split in the ego and a split in the object leads to an idealized object or activity, relatively free of anxiety or guilt. The splitting of the ego leads also to an ego relatively free of anxiety, which is available for purposes of [unconscious/conscious fantasied] incestuous relationships at the cost of renunciation of a normal one" (Socarides, 1978a, pp. 108–109). It is possible, as indicated in chapter 16, to establish a conscious split in the superego and analyze that part of the superego that supports the perversion (the parental part), thereby strengthening the ego against its commands.

Providing Insight into the Function of Erotic Experience

As the analysis progresses, it becomes increasingly evident that it is not the fixated erotic experience per se (the instinct-derivative—its polymorphous perverse derivative) that is regressively reanimated in the patient's perversion, but rather it is the *early function* of the erotic experience that has been retained and regressively relied upon (Socarides, 1979a; Stolorow and Lachmann, 1980). In this way, through eroticization, the patient attempts to maintain his structural cohesion, and implement the stability of threatened self and object representations.

The patient's erotic experiences are understood as providing two functions: (1) a warding-off function to forestall the dangers of castration, fragmentation, separation anxieties, and other threats; and (2) a compensatory function consisting of intrapsychic activities which help maintain and decrease threats to the self representation and object representations. Through eroticization, anxiety and depressive affects are also eliminated. Depression is turned into its opposite through a "manic defense," a flight to antidepressant activities, including sexuality.

Through acting out, the pervert further stabilizes his sense of self, reinforces object relations, overcomes destructive aggression and feelings of vulnerability, and brings pleasure to an internalized object. The symptom represents an overcoming of earlier severe intrapsychic crises by displacing and projecting the inner need and tension onto another person or object. It is an attempt to master a traumatic internal problem through controlling the actual external object by concocting what Khan has termed "active ego-directed, experimental play-action object relations" (1965, p. 409) in which the "technique of intimacy" plays a major role. Affective release into the external world diminishes internal threats provoked by destructive aggression. Pathological internalized object relations which have led to despair and hopelessness are mitigated. The perversion is experienced as a creative and reparative act. Similarly, the absence of healthy self-esteem in relation to internal parental figures is lessened through "creating a pseudo-object relationship and mutual pleasure," and reestablishes a "rudimentary mode of communication with the external object" (p. 408). Because no true object relation is achieved through the perverse act, and no internalization of the object takes place, there is no true ego enhancement and the perversion must be incessantly repeated, often with numerous partners. This acting out is facilitated by (1) deficiencies in the ego, due in part to a lack of neutralized energy which has impaired the ability to control immediate responses and instinctual discharges of aggression; (2) lack of internalization of superego function; and (3) a splitting of the ego, so that the perversion is sanctioned by the split-off part representing parental attitudes. "In a primitive manner, the acting out helps to maintain the cohesiveness of the ego and supplies it with the opportunity to initiate reparative moves toward a real object" (Socarides, 1980b, pp. 252–253).

Spoiling the Perverse Gratification

Perverse patients, unlike neurotic individuals, suffer from a widespread cessation or disturbances of both libidinal and ego development throughout the major phases prior to the oedipal period. Neurotics, in contrast, show points of fixation in the various psychosexual stages of development without an interruption of the broader development of character structure or a major cessation of ego development. There is a relative absence of *internal conflict* regarding their overt perverse practices in these patients, resulting in character structure characteristic of a phase chronologically earlier than the individual's age and always short of oedipal development. Furthermore, most preoedipal developmental arrests, as noted by Kolansky and Eisner (1974), are complicated by an additional factor: "an unconscious compliance between patient and parent, reinforcing each other's wishes for a continuation of direct instinctual gratification. . ." (p. 24). These patients experience anxiety in the early phases of treatment mostly secondary to *external conflicts*; that is, when gratifications or frustrations are interfered with by the environment.

As a consequence, in these patients we are confronted at the outset with a seemingly insurmountable major task: stimulating sufficient neurotic conflict which can then be analyzed. My intention is to bring about this conflictual situation. To this end, I have adopted Kolansky and Eisner's (1974) phrase, "spoiling the gratification of a preoedipal developmental arrest followed by analysis" to connote therapeutic activity which, although leading to discomfort and anxiety in relation to previously held ego-syntonic areas of immaturity, results in the conversion of an addiction or impulse neurosis or perversion into a condition similar to a neurosis. "Spoiling" is accomplished through the analytic comprehension of the defined psychopathology resulting from the failure to make the intrapsychic separation from the mother, educating the patient as to the nature of his specific vulnerabilities, and uncovering and decoding the hidden meaning and content of his perverse acts and underlying fantasy system. This is accomplished with tact, without injury to pride, as traumas to these individuals are so early and severe that narcissistic defenses are held onto tenaciously. It would be a narcissistic manifestation on the therapist's part to fail to acknowledge the difficulty or perhaps the impossibility in some instances of the patient ever giving up a specific need. On the other hand, one must keep in mind the *relativity* of the *need* for perverse gratifications. Such needs are determined by other needs, are not absolute or independent. They are dependent for their existence, intensity, and significance upon the total functioning of the individual. Kolansky and Eisner (1974), referring to such needs in impulse disorders and addictions, point out the differences and distinctions between the phrases "can not do" and "will not do" or "do not want to," and note that the analyst must question the "can not" before the "do not want to." The same can be said for the phrase "need for immediate gratification." Is it a "need" like breathing is a need or is it a "wish" for gratification such as a wish for candy? There is a back-and-forth movement as to the relative strength of "need for gratifications" at various points in treatment.

Lest I be misunderstood, I equate "spoiling" to uncovering conflict and comprehending the meaning of symbols. A fetish, for example, while necessary for sexual release and pleasure, may symbolize both the phallus and the body of the mother. It is used as a self-protective device against fears of bodily disintegration as well as castration. Uncovering its meaning leads to relief rather than frustration, as the patient is no longer a "slave" to the imperativeness of the fetish, nor is he driven by total reliance on its use as his only means of sexual arousal. Similarly, a homosexual's obligatory need to swallow another man's penis and semen is decreased when it is revealed to be a search for his own lost masculinity through incorporation of the masculinity and body of another male, who also feels similarly deficient. It is an attempt to find lost masculinity rather than a desire for femininity. This interpretation has a profound effect on most homosexuals, diminishing shame and guilt at an unconscious level, regular accompaniments, both conscious and unconscious, to homosexual practices. In such instances, "spoiling" leads not to frustration but to an increase in self-esteem, a release from importunate tensions and obligatory performances, as well as setting the stage for previously blocked new possibilities of sexual arousal and release.

The Rule of *Non Prohibere*

"Spoiling" perverse gratifications in order to stimulate neurotic conflict that can then be analyzed does not mean that a perverse patient remains without sexual pleasure during the analysis. Prohibitions against perverse activity should not be engaged in, as indicated by the rule of *non prohibere*. This rule, however, should not be misconstrued by the patient (and the analyst) as representing passive permission to persist in patterns of self-destructive, antisocial, perverse behavior, or an inadvertent permissiveness which may precipitate acting out of perverse impulses. It is not a policy of indifference on the part of the therapist which would tend, according to Arlow (1954), to perpetuate already established patterns of overt perverse behavior (Panel, 1954). The patient's increasing knowledge of the psychological conflicts responsible for his perversion and the analyst's position that the perversion is an end-product of deep intrapsychic trauma/need, reinforced by continuous analysis of the motivational forces leading to each individual perverse act, militate against such misunderstandings. This therapeutic approach not only reduces the patient's feelings of failure when perverse practices continue for lengthy periods of time, but lessens countertransference reactions during periods of severe acting out. For example, working through and reconstruction often leads the analyst to expect improvement and gradual diminution of perverse practices. Increased perverse activity at this point may then lead him to feel that his integrity is threatened by the patient's enactments. An exacerbation of perverse enactments, however, may well be a sign of progress since the need for perverse acts to sustain threatened self representations and ward off fears of engulfment is typically increased as ties to the mother are loosened and heterosexual impulses with their attendant dangers begin to emerge.

Once the perverse act is fully understood by the patient to be a symptom, that is, a compromise formation, a necessity in order to avoid more painful and damaging anxieties (a measure taken by the ego to ward off dangers at the same time compensating for them), he may more actively join the analyst in seeking to modify the enactment of his perverse needs. There may be, as noted earlier, a partial disbelief on the part of the patient that these activities may be modifiable; but ultimately the patient's belief in that possiblity becomes as strong as that of the analyst. Modification of perverse practices should be first suggested by the patient, analyzed fully before they are attempted, and undertaken only when a full knowledge of the underlying structure of the symptom is known and understood by both patient and analyst. Similar ideas have been set forth by Anna Freud (1954), Lorand (1956), and Panel (1976). The analysis of successful, short-lived attempts, followed by exacerbation of perverse symptomatology, yields especially valuable insights into the warding off and compensatory functions of perverse acts.

To elaborate this proposition further, activities on the part of the analyst, including those of protecting the patient against real dangers (except in those individuals whose activities are both dangerous and buttressed by semidelusional rationalizations) should not be engaged in. Let us take for example the case of a patient with a well-structured sadomasochistic (spanking) perversion, who finds himself in the hands of a prostitute who threatens to tell his wife of his perversion. It would be unwise to strongly urge him to reduce his activities with her, for she is his sole source of sexual release and relief from his importunate anxieties. Similarly, it would prove untherapeutic to *insist*, for different reasons, upon a pedophile's cessation of his enactments with prepubertal children by threatening him with termination of treatment if he does not cease his harmful and dangerous practices. These interdictions are met with anxiety and flight from therapy. Abrupt termination of treatment is well known during the analysis of transvestite patients when a premature interruption of dressing in women's clothing is undertaken by the patient himself, often without discussion in the analytic sessions. He develops intense anxiety due to an unrelenting fear of premature separation from the mother with a threatened loss of self cohesion. In those suffering from a preoedipal type II perversion, the need to engage in perverse activity is a manifestation of need for selfobjects to complete one; the perversion is a developmental necessity, at least for the time being. These patients respond with great sensitivity to even the slightest negative comments on their encounters, fearing both loss of self cohesion and experiencing narcissistic injury.

Homosexual Patients and Their Management

Prior to Socarides (1968b), the traditional rule of asking the patient to desist from any activity from which he derives pleasure and which is also self-damaging was almost invariably followed by psychoanalysts in their attempt to help the patient rid himself of his perversion. In Socarides (1978a), I enlarged on this topic, following the lead of Anna Freud (1968). This prohibition was based on the belief that there was little chance of successfully treating any disorder in which we allowed the gratifying aspects full scope. For years, psychoanalysts believed that homosexuals should be treated for the most part like phobics, the feared activity—heterosexual intercourse—being faced and undertaken, and activities involving phobic avoidance (homosexual intercourse) interdicted. The rationale for this procedure was also based on the idea of *producing* conflict, since the patient appeared to be at peace with his perversion. While such a tactic evoked fears of the female, of the vagina, fears of failure of performance, it did not elicit any insight into the basic nuclear conflict (i.e., anxiety and guilt in association with self–object differentiation and separation from the mother), nor did it lead to the discovery of this basic nuclear conflict. Anxiety secondary to prohibition and initiation of forced heterosexual relations was usually viewed as arising

from oedipal (structural) conflict rather than an object relations class of conflict. This approach, while of considerable
value in the treatment of phobics, can have disastrous consequences in the course of therapy for homosexuals. In this
connection, Anna Freud, in her "Problems of Technique in
Adult Analysis" (1954), was intrigued with the problem of
"prohibition" in the treatment of homosexuals at least a
decade before Socarides (1968b). She noted that in one of her
homosexual patients, an attempt to prohibit his homosexual
activity would move him to "outbreaks of hostility and anxiety," threatening the continuation and the effectiveness of
the analysis. To insist upon prohibition, she noted, would
have been a grave technical error. In another homosexual,
his own desire to desist from perverse activities following the
analysis of his unconscious motivation, led to anxiety but
also a decreased frequency in duration of homosexual episodes. In the second case, cutting down on homosexual practices (not prohibited by the analyst) played a beneficial role.
She concluded that identical symptomatology may be based
on somewhat different psychopathology, and it is the latter
not the former which decides how a case should be dealt with
technically (A. Freud, 1954). In the first patient, the outbreaks of homosexual practices served to reduce the anxiety
aroused by active, aggressive masculine urges, so that passive advances to male partners served as reassurance and
lessened anxiety. In the second case, it was possible for the
patient to reduce his perverse practices because of the transference: a new attachment, that to the analyst, had taken
place. The analyst was in the role of protecting the patient
"against dangerous, destructive impulses" (p. 390). "When
the analyst filled this role in the patient's imagination" (p.
390), the patient did without the perverse act. In a third
group, the perverse act may serve a completely different
purpose. For the patient fell into that group of men whose
homosexuality represented "the investment of other men
with the attributes of his own phallic masculinity" (p. 391).
He could not bear to be without these "ideal male figures and
pursued them unremittingly." By urging a patient of this
type to restrict his homosexual practices, as was done in the
past, one urges him to commit self-castration. What then

ensues is an immense resistance and hostility to the analyst if he insists upon imposing this restrictive edict. Interpretation of the patient's projection of masculinity has to come first and will enable him to assume his own phallic properties; he is then no longer dependent for his masculine identity on the homosexual partner; male partners begin to lose their importance and the patient will be better able to do without them (A. Freud, 1954).

To summarize: activity necessary for psychological survival which defends against both oedipal and preoedipal anxieties and object loss should not be interfered with without the full analysis of its unconscious meaning and structure. The lessening of perverse practices is first suggested by the patient, and analyzed fully before being attempted, as many patients prematurely attempt cessation of perverse activities which they often unconsciously deplore, for which they feel guilty and wish to be punished. If cutting down is motivated by the desire for expiation, it is always followed by an exacerbation of perverse practices and a temporary loss of confidence in the analysis which is then utilized as resistance.

Unfolding of Heterosexual Desire

The patient's relief from anxiety and the diminishing of the need for obligatory performance of perverse acts and postponement of such gratification from perverse practices, leads to a gradual and spontaneous interest in the possibility of heterosexual gratification. This may be first noted in the patient's dream life or take the form of tentative comments on attraction to the opposite sex, accompanied by a rise in self-esteem. During this period, the patient may engage in heterosexual fantasy as well as perverse fantasy (e.g., homosexual, fetishistic, and so on) with masturbation. At no time does he feel desperate, for on these occasions, when there is a reactivation of primitive fears, he can return to perverse practices for a prompt alleviation of anxiety and the subsequent analysis of the motivational forces responsible for his anxiety. To some patients, this budding heterosexual desire is reminiscent of an earlier blighted desire, which they vaguely recall occurred before they reached puberty, lasted a brief time, and then disappeared. In this connection, we are reminded of Freud's comment (1919):

> [W]e find often enough with these perverts that they too made an attempt at developing normal sexual activity, usually at the age of puberty; but their attempt had not enough force in it and was abandoned in the face of the first obstacles which inevitably arise, whereupon they fell back upon their infantile fixation once and for all [p. 192].

Desires to engage in heterosexual activity are usually preceded by an overall improvement in all areas of functioning: work, competition, and socialization. These desires and their associated conflicts over fears of the vagina, fears of sexual failure, find confirmation in the dream material. They are a reliable indicator of the emotional status of the patient and his improvement. Acknowledgment of the patient's belief that he is now able to engage in his first tentative approaches toward heterosexuality (a developmental achievement) both fortify determination and decrease anxiety in this new endeavor. In many of my patients who have achieved heterosexuality, their first heterosexual intercourse is conceived of as requiring the imaginary presence ("you were right over my shoulder, cheering me on") through identification. Further sexual relations no longer require the illusory presence of the analyst. Heterosexual relations with pleasure provide us with an additional and unexpected ally and further dissipate the inevitable sense of emptiness that is experienced with the renunciation of a pleasure, even a perverse one, unless it is supplanted by a new one. Many patients now engage in both perverse and heterosexual activities long before the complete atrophy of perverse activity. Although the attainment of pleasurable heterosexual intercourse is a major developmental step, it should not be misconstrued by either the patient or analyst as truly successful heterosexual *functioning*, for the latter is based not only on adequate heterosexual performance but the attainment of object love; for example, the ability to cathect an object of the opposite sex with libido. Furthermore, it is well known that, at various times in their lives and under specific circumstances, a small percentage of all perverts are capable of penetration of the vagina with the penis, but with very little or no pleasure. (In such men, their aim or object is a perverse one, despite ability to penetrate the vagina.)

Before heterosexual intercourse can be successful, the unconscious and/or conscious partial or complete conviction expressed by some patients that they do not possess a penis, or if they do, it is largely defective, too small, or of little use, must be thoroughly explored. Most perverse patients have long remained in conflict over masturbation, so that when it was attempted, it (1) occurred late in development in the late teens or twenties; (2) stopped short of orgasm; (3) was performed without manual stimulation or visualization of the erect organ; or (4) could only be successful (i.e., result in orgasm), through the utilization of the perverse fantasy. Manual masturbation with heterosexual fantasy helps promote genital schematization. Therefore, acknowledgment of their readiness for masturbatory practices with full visualization of their genital area helps promote genital schematization. A number of such patients had been exposed to actual severe castration threats for masturbatory acts in early childhood, and acknowledgment of their readiness is interpreted unconsciously as superego sanction of previously forbidden activity by new parental figures. Characteristically, when such patients attempt masturbation, they feel that their penis will "fly off" (see chapters 12 and 16) or become numb, insensitive, or completely anesthetic. Masturbation in an imaginary heterosexual twosome not only consolidates and repairs a defective body–ego, but promotes the individual's awareness of the differences between the sexes, a major factor in the attainment of appropriate gender-defined self identity. Successful manual masturbation contains a built-in acknowledgment of one's penis, an awareness of one's anatomical and physical structures, as well as an awareness of objects with different genitals. It represents the completion of a developmental phase never before reached in those with perversion. Greenson (1964) has described these phases in the attainment of gender-identity in simple and succinct language. Phase one: "I am me, John." Phase Two: "I am me, John, a boy with a penis." Phase

Three: "I am me, John, a boy with a penis, which means that I like to do sexual things to those different creatures, to girls" (p. 195).

This therapeutic technique is not only efficacious but is bolstered by strong theoretical argument. Bernstein (1973) and, more recently, Laufer and Laufer (1984) have convincingly described the crucial importance of masturbation in "enabling an adolescent boy to establish the primacy of genitality," changing the "image of his body to include his mature genitals as functioning organs" (p. 37). This maturational accomplishment has not been achieved by perverse patients prior to their analysis. There has been a lack of integration of the sexual body-image before adolescence, with the establishment of psychopathology before the end of adolescence. In an earlier paper, M. Laufer (1968) maintains that masturbation and masturbation fantasies play a crucial role in enabling the adolescent to achieve the primacy of genitality. He must "change the image of his body so that this image will include his mature genitals as functioning organs" (p. 114). Normal masturbation "serves a very important function in normal adolescence, namely, the function of helping the ego reorganize itself around the supremacy of genitality. . . ." In a similar vein, Anna Freud (1949) noted that:

> [The] child's struggle against masturbation is directed on the one hand against the content of the fantasy, which as a result may disappear from consciousness, on the other hand against the bodily act itself. . . . The inner prohibition may concern the use of the hands in stimulating the genitalia. . . . As a result, the masturbation fantasy is deprived of all bodily outlet, the libidinal and aggressive energy attached to it is completely blocked and dammed-up, and eventually is displaced with full force from the realm of sex life into the realm of ego-activities. Masturbation fantasies are then acted out in dealings with the external world, which become, thereby, sexualized, distorted and maladjusted [p. 203].

In attempting heterosexual functioning, the patient at first experiences anxiety connected with the loss of the mother. This is represented in dreams that she will become sick or die, or perhaps go insane (react with destructive aggression). The patient responds with separation guilt and separation anxiety. An interpretation to be made to the patient at this point is: the gradual assumption of heterosexual functioning and the establishment of his appropriate gender-defined self identity separates him from the mother and leads to dreams of her loss with guilt and fear. Ultimately, the achievement of an appropriate gender-defined self identity and functioning as a male will well compensate him for the renunciation of this lifelong infantile, debilitating connection.

Concluding Comments

In this chapter I have described my psychoanalytic method for the treatment of well-structured perversions, correlating advances in psychoanalytic theory with my extensive psychoanalytic clinical research. I have described my therapeutic stance regarding the transference, extra-analytic transferences, the therapeutic alliance, and have delineated four major tasks to be accomplished for the possible successful alleviation of these conditions. These therapeutic tasks are: separating from the mother; the decoding of the manifest perversion; the providing of insight into the function of erotic acts in perversions; and the spoiling of perverse gratification.

When psychoanalytic therapy is guided by these principles and goals, it is my contention that it acquits itself with distinction. We not only succeed in awakening a desire for new pleasure with the casting-off of old fears, inhibitions, and defensive processes, but also increase the patient's psychodynamic awareness of himself and the world about him in the protective setting of psychoanalytic treatment.

Finally, I wish to emphasize my belief that the pursuit of knowledge in the area of sexual perversion is representative of the highest aims of psychoanalysis as envisaged by Freud from the beginning of our science. Freud believed that man could not control his sexual impulses by suppressing them. These impulses, he said, would then arise, perilously deformed, out of the hidden recesses of the mind and give rise to "nervous unrest, disorder, and illness." In *Mental Healers* (1933), biographer Stephan Zweig pays homage to Freud's daring and pioneering courage, his scientific penetration into the psyche of those with whom this book is concerned, and whose suffering requires alleviation. Those who sought his help were "driven to frenzy" by the cruelty, unreason, and ignorance of a "civilized morality." Unworthy of scientific study, they were treated as "morally inferior" or regarded as suffering from a hereditary taint or branded by the legal code as criminals with a "blackmailer at their heels" and "prison in front of them."

> Freed from his illusions, Freud discovered that the impulsive energy of the libido, though condemned by moralists, was an indestructible part of the human organism, a force that could not be annulled so long as life and breath remain, and that the best way of dealing with it was to lift it into the conscious where its activities would be free from danger. The old method had aimed at covering it up. His aim was its revealment. Where others had cloaked it, he wanted to lay it bare. Where others had ignored it, he wanted to identify it. No one can bridle impulses without perceiving them clearly; no one can master demons unless he summons them from their lurking places and looks them boldly in the face . . . Freud insisted upon the disclosure of the repressed and the unconscious. In this way, he began to cure not only numberless individuals, but also a whole epoch that was morally sick, a cure that was to be effected by the removal of its repressed fundamental conflict from the realm of hypocrisy to the realm of science [pp. 261–262].

Appendix
VERBATIM TRANSCRIPT OF REGRESSIVE STATES WITH ALTERATION IN BODY-EGO EXPERIENCE AND PATHOLOGICAL PERCEPTIONS

Session I

Patient: When I did get up this morning I took a boiling hot shower; I just couldn't get it hot enough (grunt). It also made me think of when I lived with my parents (explosive bark), there were times when I'd go to sleep at night I'd use as many as six or seven blankets. Not that I was cold, but I wanted to feel all that pressure. I'd use so many blankets and I'd wake up in the morning (rise in voice) and I'd be exhausted. I'd still feel all that pressure and I just couldn't give up those blankets (explosive bark). That cunt is like an eye, and the little hole is like an eye (explosive bark) that I can get in so small (explosive bark) and yet if I hit it right (explosive bark) I'd be able to get inside of it (explosive bark). Also, this summer I became very afraid to dive (rise in voice). I was with Marion at the beach and it was from a platform, it wasn't far, about four to five feet from the water and I realized I was afraid to dive into the water. But I made myself dive in anyway (explosive bark). I was really frightened. The thing is like a whirlpool, it just keeps sucking at me (explosive bark). It's like a snake wrapping itself around me. It's like when I stand on it, it has no support and it sinks under me (screams, growls).

Dr. Socarides: What happened?

Patient: (Growls) The cunt closed around my neck (growls and snarls).

Dr. Socarides: Did you think it was going to kill you?

Patient: It almost swallowed me. I went into it feet first, and I kept slowly sinking into it, and it got around my neck and I felt myself sinking more. Oh, God! You know what's so terrible about it, it was so big, huge, it was so big (laugh). That's what made it seem so possible, it was so big (explosive bark) . . . it was so big (heavy breathing). Oh . . . that's why I believe it.

Dr. Socarides: That's why you believe it?

Patient: Yeah, because it was so big. And if there was a cunt that size, it would be possible. But that's ridiculous. That's impossible (explosive bark).

Dr. Socarides: It was so big maybe because you were so small?

Patient: (Snarls and grunts).

Dr. Socarides: What's that?

Patient: I keep seeing a baby being born (explosive bark). I see the head and the shoulders. It comes out of the cunt like he was a cock (explosive bark). Oh . . . it's just stuck there (grunts and snarls).

Dr. Socarides: Who's the baby?

Patient: I don't know.

Dr. Socarides: Brothers or sisters, or you, or what?

Patient: Just a baby, had no face. It's a gray-colored baby. Very pale. Pale like ashes. Ashes (explosive bark). The baby slips back (explosive bark). And its lips just fold over it (explosive bark). Like those man-eating flowers or quicksand. That's what it's like. Also before it forced my tongue out. Then it started to choke me (explosive bark). Feel like tongue was pushed all the way out. I see eggs coming in and going out of the cunt.

Dr. Socarides: What do you see?

Patient: Eggs.

Dr. Socarides: What do you mean, eggs?

Patient: Eggs!

Dr. Socarides: Ordinary eggs?

Patient: Yeah, from a chicken. Chicken eggs. I remember when I used to go to the butcher, the chicken market, and I used to see them pop open a chicken and take those eggs out (explosive bark). Some of the eggs didn't have shells on them, some did (explosive bark). Thinking of the lady sitting there and eating those eggs. She ate them raw right from the chicken. The cunt looked so big, like it could swallow anything. The mouth . . . the mouth. I don't know why that thing is so real, God! God! It's real! This woman is so enormous, that this is possible. All this reminds me of something. I used to think of a giant woman—a real giant woman. And I used to play around her cunt. Oh, she is a giant! And I'd play around her body. And I'd have to be very careful (explosive bark). I never thought of her swallowing me, just had to be careful so she shouldn't hurt me.

Dr. Socarides: You never thought of her following you, you said?

Patient: Swallowing me.

Dr. Socarides: Swallowing you.

Patient: Yeah. This woman was such a giant.

Dr. Socarides: What do you mean, you have to be careful?

Patient: Well, she could just move her legs and kill me.

Dr. Socarides: When did you have that fantasy?

Patient: You know, not so terribly long ago. Maybe a year or two. Yeah. It might be a year or two, it's not very long. As a matter of fact, I used to like that fantasy.

Dr. Socarides: You used to like it?

Patient: Yeah.

Dr. Socarides: What did you like about that fantasy?

Patient: I don't know; it was sort of dangerous and I liked it, and I guess I liked the body very much. I (mumble) this body . . .

Dr. Socarides: What?

Patient: I liked this body of the giant. I always used to find myself by her cunt. I'd never go inside. Just like to play on it, it was nice, it was soft, warm. It was also dangerous. I never thought of her swallowing me with her cunt.

Dr. Socarides: Why could it be dangerous then?

Patient: Once she was so big, she could move, could just touch her cunt and she could just squash me. She'd scratch herself and kill me.

Dr. Socarides: You were very small?

Patient: Oh, I was just a fraction of the size of her. I was . . .

Dr. Socarides: Just how big was she in your fantasy?

Patient: Well, I was only as big as her cunt. No bigger than that, so the proportions would be me to somebody about two inches tall or three inches tall. A real giant.

Dr. Socarides: Were you actually the same size as you are now and she was bigger, or were you diminished?

Patient: No, I was the same size.

Dr. Socarides: The same size as you are now?

Patient: Yeah.

Dr. Socarides: She was a real giant?

Patient: She was the real giant. I was the same . . .

Dr. Socarides: Did you ever have any fantasies like that as a little boy?

Patient: I can't think of any. I know I've known about giants for a long time.

Dr. Socarides: Had you forgotten this? Had you this thought?

Patient: You mean, I didn't tell you about it?

Dr. Socarides: Yeah.

Patient: Well, I recall now that I've had it as recently as about a year or two ago.

Dr. Socarides: Then you had it before, too?

Patient: I can't remember about it, I can't remember that. I just know that I had it about a year or two ago. And I don't recall that it was a continuation of any other fantasy. But I have thought of large women. As a matter of fact, when I think back to since I was three, my mother appears like some sort of giant to me. I mean, I remember her, I don't remember looking straight at her, I had to be looking this way at her. My memories of her are never the same as if I was to look at her today; I mean the perspective is completely different. And that is the way I remember her. And if each year that I remember her the way I look at her is just different, until my eyes reach hers and today I don't look up, I don't look straight at her, I look down. I guess my perspective is again different. There's a memory of my mother or father then, was always that of looking way up, way up. And it's true about my mother and my father, had some sort of a giant aspect. Even when they were lying down there was something like my eyes couldn't take all of them in at once. And I've been gagging since yesterday, something horrible (explosive bark). It's all I can do to keep myself in the dry heaves. I've been taking antigag pills and sucking licorice, anything to keep that feeling away. For instance, when my father would take me to the water when I was about three, there was that feeling of a giant there. That's where I would feel so helpless and I would fight and thrash, but I couldn't get out of his arms. He just held me there and walked into the water with me. I'd just scream and scream and I'd beat him and kick, I didn't want to go into the water.

Dr. Socarides: What does that mean?

Patient: The water?

Dr. Socarides: Um. What do you think it means?

Patient: Today . . . Well, let's see. Then I thought it meant that I was going to drown. I mean, I couldn't swim. He would take me into the water over my head and I was completely dependent upon him. I didn't want that. I was completely helpless, when he got me out into the water. I think that's what it means, that I was afraid of being that helpless, being . . .

Dr. Socarides: If you were that helpless then what might happen?

Patient: If I were that helpless, I could be killed.

Dr. Socarides: How?

Patient: How? I could sink to the bottom of that water and be drowned.

Dr. Socarides: Do you think it was the water or what the water means?

Patient: The water? The water is that soft substance that I could sink into like the quicksand, like the cunt, I suppose. Yeah . . . God, I would do anything, and I don't understand why he carried me into the water. I could play around the edge, but he carried me into that water time after time. And I guess he felt that was how I'd lose my fear of it (laughs). Oh, God! But that's what I was terrified of. That he might lose his grip on me and that I might be sucked into the water and killed, drowned. Sucked down to the bottom.

Dr. Socarides: You see, it wasn't just water you were afraid of. The things that the water meant to you.

Patient: Well, water over my head would mean to me that there was no bottom there. Would just keep going down and down, I suppose. And I'd never get back (explosive bark). Water meant something else? Oh, I'm just thinking of that dream, you know, where I had that fight in the water, with that mulatto? All these tied-up helpless things. Remember that one? What is there no control?

Dr. Socarides: That's why you've always been search-ing for control.

Patient: Yeah.

Dr. Socarides: Huh?

Patient: Yeah.

Dr. Socarides: That's right.

Patient: Say like once I could swim I wasn't afraid of the water. And I learned to swim when I was fairly young, but I had to do it myself. It was very important that I shouldn't be afraid of the water (explosive bark).

Dr. Socarides: All right.

Session 2

Patient: (Dream). And I could actually see the lips part-ing there and I was just fascinated by it. And the doorbell rang and Marion got up out of bed to answer the doorbell and she told me it was just some people canvasing. Got back to bed, started looking at her again. Then I heard that some-body had walked into the room and I went out into the living room (explosive bark) and there was this woman or girl there and there was something wrong about her. She either looked like she was drunk or a little crazy. And I realized that only Marion would be able to help her, so I called Marion and Marion made like she was a doctor, like she was an analyst, and Marion told me to go into the other room and wait for her and Marion would take care of this girl. And so, I went into the room by myself, closed the door and I tried to switch on the lights and the lights didn't go on. I became very, very afraid; here I was in the dark. And the funny thing was here in my dream I did that same thing that I'm trying to do on the outside: I tried to reason with myself not to be afraid, I tried to make myself understand what it is I'm really afraid of, and I started to try to fix the bulb so that I could have light on and be comfortable. And (explosive bark) and then (explosive bark) I found it was a very funny bulb I was working with. Almost makes me think of a penis right now (explosive bark). Then there were a lot of people who came into the room that seemed to be friends of Marion and myself, and I found that we were entertaining them, but I was still just in my robe. And then Marion came in with this girl and (explosive bark) then we all decided to go on a bus ride and it seemed that there were an awful lot of us, we filled up the bus. And Marion told me to drive and I said I didn't want to drive the bus. So someone else in the middle of the bus, drove the bus from the middle, and then we were walking in the street, the whole group of us and there was some women by a building. They were pulling the building down, parts of the building, and (explosive bark) I looked at them and said, These are crazy women. And one of the women who pulled part of the building down, and hit one of the people in our party, and I turned around to these women (explosive bark) who were pulling the building down and I yelled at them at the top of my voice, "Bastards!" (explosive bark) and that was the dream. But I was so angry at those (explosive bark) women for pulling it down (explosive bark). And (explosive bark) the dream I had last night, God . . . I'm angry now. The dream I had last night had a ship (explosive bark). Marion and I went on a ship, and this was a small ship, it was right next to some very large ships—my throat is beginning to hurt, my neck (explosive bark)—and the ship wasn't finished yet. And I was inside the hull of the ship and I can see where it hadn't been finished (explosive bark). There was a mixture of old, rotten wood (explosive bark) and wood that hadn't been planed yet. And there were big holes in a lot of the beams for, oh, other pieces of wood to fit into. And there was a chaperone along (explosive bark) and then the boat, this smaller boat, pulled away from the very large boat and I had this feeling that we were losing (explosive bark), that we were leaving (explosive bark), that we were (explosive bark) like we were a part of that bigger ship (explosive bark).

Dr. Socarides: It's on the word *losing* that you make these noises?

Patient: Yeah, it's hard for me to talk about that. It's like (explosive bark) (scream and anger) it's almost like being castrated.

Dr. Socarides: Like losing something?

Patient: Yeah, that's the dream (explosive bark), like it belonged next to that ship. Oh . . . God! This first dream (very loud explosive bark) . . . (scream, agony).

Dr. Socarides: What happened now?

Patient: In that first dream, I forgot to tell you that that girl turns into a boy (explosive bark) towards the end of the dream. She was a girl and turned into a boy, the one that Marion helped. That's you (scream, breathing hard). I'm so cold (explosive bark). Yes, I thought about this, I thought about that (explosive bark). Between my legs, I feel so moist. Yes, I thought of that. It's almost like (explosive bark) I . . . I . . . I want to become a man with Marion (explosive bark). That's what it makes me think of. That I'm trying so hard (explosive bark).

Dr. Socarides: You're trying so hard to be a man?

Patient: Yeah.

Dr. Socarides: And really you're a woman, or you can be made into a woman?

Patient: No, I don't think . . .

Dr. Socarides: Well, what?

Patient: The fact that all this contact with Marion is like I'm trying to tell you that being with her is making me more like a man.

Dr. Socarides: Being with her is making you more like a man?

Patient: Yeah. It's like I'm telling you that because it's (explosive bark) . . .

Dr. Socarides: It's what?

Patient: I was going to say it's almost like it cuts me so keenly each time I see when I make love to her that it's because I'm afraid, it bothers me so much (explosive bark). Like yesterday, we were sitting and talking and then she happened to lift her foot up and put it on the hassock and I looked between her legs, and immediately I got so frightened, and then I became so affectionate and I became very angry (explosive bark). I was disturbed and then I became disturbed with myself. And that part about the bus, it's like she tells me to be a man, to drive, the shape of the bus is like a penis, and I wouldn't do it (explosive bark).

Dr. Socarides: She says for you to take the penis, is that what you mean? Drive the penis or what?

Patient: Yeah, drive it.

Dr. Socarides: Be a man?

Patient: Yeah, and I wouldn't take it. I wouldn't do it. Those women knocking the things down, I can't figure out what that is. Those parts of the building, they were like decorations. You know, all the gingerbread you sometimes find on buildings, scraping that off. I don't know who those women were. They were having a wonderful time. I don't know whether it was Marion by my side who complained about (explosive bark), then I just turned around and I screamed at them, "Bastards!" I keep thinking of this eye in the middle of the cunt. It shoots for the bullseye (explosive bark). You know, the last time when I told you I wasn't afraid of death, I didn't mean that (explosive bark). Because you remember this part when I told you about when I thought I was dead I became very afraid?

Dr. Socarides: Umhum.

Patient: Yeah, I think I'm also afraid of death. Because there was a situation where it was pleasant and I thought I was dead and was frightened of it. I don't want to be dead no how.

Dr. Socarides: You want to be capable of controlling it. You want to be capable of controlling the sensation of death, that's why you would make those experiments. Hum? To be stronger than death? You put yourself in and out of it.

Patient: Yes, I used to have these daydreams about not dying. As a matter of fact, it took me many, many years before I would believe that it was possible for me to die, and I don't know if I even still believe it, but for the longest time I would never believe it possible, for me to die. And anything that I could run across, any stories or myths with longevity in it, it would always fascinate me. Anything you know, something of the Shangri-La about it. Anything of that nature, any way of prolonging or controlling, and I would never be very interested in the myths of heaven or hell, it was always something else I was interested in. But those things never had any appeal to me. Always this business of being able to keep going all the time, never dying. Or this business of, I don't know what the proper word is, uh, trans . . .

Dr. Socarides: Transmigration?

Patient: Yeah, transmigration. And I would also play with that idea, but I would always be looking for where I came from. And it's very easy for me to play with the fantasy of where I'm going to, I can never—always felt this would be some sort of contact, but I always—and I spent an awful lot of time looking for it, I know it's crazy, but I would look for things like that. Try to find myself in some people who were dead, to relate myself to. All the dead people I have ever read about, all the people who have ever lived and try to make some sort of contact. Yeah, I would say that I am afraid of death. I guess it's for the same reason, this note that I will not be able to handle it (explosive bark). And I, for the life of me, can't figure out if that isn't what I'm afraid of, what is there about it that I'm afraid of. Oh . . . What there is about it. I don't seem to have any background, either a real background as to something horrible in death, or a fantasy background. There is no material there I can say, well, what it is, I can't say that I'm afraid of fire and brimstone or that I look forward to a heaven where there is milk and honey. It's something else, something else I don't like, like in that— Let's go back to the time when I was having these nice sensations, but I thought I might be dead, and there was no contact with my body. I felt this was very frightening. It was nice and yet I was afraid I was dead. Yet I imagine that being dead and feeling that good, it can't be bad.

Dr. Socarides: What was bad about that sensation?

Patient: It frightened me, there was nothing bad about it, it was a real nice sensation.

Dr. Socarides: Where no one had contact with your body?

Patient: Yeah, it was very good.

Dr. Socarides: Well, what was frightening about it?

Patient: I thought I was dead. That's what frightened me, there was no contact with my body. I couldn't feel my body. Afraid I was lost.

Dr. Socarides;   That was anxiety.

Patient: Oh, God, yes. I thought I was lost.

Dr. Socarides: Were you lost?

Patient: Was I couldn't get back to myself. I was afraid I'd lost my body, like I was separated from my body, and it was a real crazy sort of thing. The sensation wasn't frightening because, oh, it was very close to a sexual sensation. It was very good, it was very nice. But I had—you see part of it was a control—if I knew that at that point I just wanted to stop, just cut it off and I could be right where I was, that would be okay, but I didn't know. And that's what frightened me. I didn't know whether I would be forced to remain like that forever, or whether I'd be able to get back. How could I even know at that time? And it frightened me enough that I would never try it again because I still didn't know, even though (explosive bark) . . .

Dr. Socarides: What do you mean, I would be forced to be that way?

Patient: Well, to be just floating around like that. I, well, it was like I was in a black room floating, like floating in the water for such a length of time that I couldn't feel myself anymore. It was just like a little spot of my brain was my whole being, I was just wisping around. Was really very, very comfortable, feeling very, very good. It was like I would never get back and never see, or talk to, or hear all the things I wanted. It was like I was giving up life, like I was making a choice between living with all the things that it meant, and that death, even though what I thought was death there was nice, I still didn't want to make the break. I wasn't going to choose between those two, and what frightened me was that I thought I had made the choice and that I couldn't undo it. I didn't want to, I didn't want to die then. This sounds so crazy to me as I'm talking about it . . . But the earaches, still that doesn't seem like enough to me, there isn't enough of it. Not enough. Because you know as far back as I can think, I always had the feeling that my spirit was broken very, very early . . . Very early. And I've always had the feeling that it was broken by something. I never put my finger on it, and that there are four things that I told you about, they're not enough. It has to be something really awful. And I feel right now like I want a real powerful case to believe in, in other words, I want to see such an accumulation of evidence right now, that I can believe that this is why I wanted to go back. Even though there was enough to show me that I was trying to go back or that I kept trying to go back, or I kept thinking about going back, all that other evidence is hidden from me as to why. Why I want to go back. Just when I figure myself three or four, I always find myself so timid, so timid, so fearful of everything. Like I find myself late here the past few days, sounds and noises just are driving me crazy. I'm like a horse that's always shying away from things.

Dr. Socarides: What about your dreams? Perhaps your dreams tell us more information about getting back inside, and hints about . . .

Patient: To getting back inside.

Dr. Socarides: Yes.

Patient: I think the ship does.

Dr. Socarides: The ship, yes.

Patient: The ship does. You mean if it tells me why I want to get back?

Dr. Socarides: It might give a hint indirectly.

Patient: Well, if inside that ship that I'm very coarse and crude and undone, and especially those beams with the holes going through, it's the cock and the cunt. So that I have seen a lot of that, I've had to see a lot of that. I couldn't do it just seeing it once or twice. I've had to be exposed to it an awful lot. But somehow it's not enough.

Bibliographical Notes

CHAPTER 1 GENERAL CONSIDERATIONS IN THE PSYCHOANALYTIC TREATMENT OF SEXUAL PERSIONS was adapted from a paper presented at the 19th Emil A. Gutheil Memorial Conference of the Association for the Advancement of Psychotherapy, New York City, November, 1978. It was first published under the title "Some Problems Encountered in the Psychoanalytic Treatment of Overt Male Homosexuality" in the *American Journal of Psychotherapy*, Vol. 33, No. 4:506–520 (1979). Published with permission of American Journal of Psychotherapy, Inc.

CHAPTER 2 DEFINING PERVERSIONS is published here for the first time.

CHAPTER 3 A UNITARY THEORY OF SEXUAL PERVERSION was first presented at the American Psychoanalytic Association, December, 1967 in preliminary form. It was first published in revised form in *On Sexuality: Psychoanalytic Observations* (1979), edited by T. B. Karasu and C. W. Socarides. New York: International Universities Press, pp. 161–188. The version in this book has been adapted, expanded, and revised. Published with permission of International Universities Press.

CHAPTER 4 PSYCHOANALYTIC CLASSIFICATION OF SEXUAL PERVERSION. Some of the ideas in this chapter were first presented before the American Psychoanalytic Association, December 1977 in a paper entitled "Considerations on the Psychoanalytic Treatment of Overt Homosexuality: Part IV: A Provisional Classification and Differentiating Criteria of the Homosexualities." A revised version of the "Classification of Homosexuality" is to be found in my 1978 book, *Homosexuality*, New York: Jason Aronson, pp. 89–103.

CHAPTER 5 AGGRESSION IN PERVERSION. A section of this chapter entitled "Violence and Its Relation to Acts of Sexual Perversion" was a contribution to the fifth Bertram D. Lewin Memorial Symposium on "Psychoanalytic Perspectives on Hostility and Violence," sponsored by the Philadelphia Psychoanalytic Institute and the Philadelphia Psychoanalytic Society. Nov. 5, 1977.

CHAPTER 6 DEPRESSION IN PERVERSION was adapted from a paper presented at the American Psychoanalytic Association, December 21, 1984 entitled "Depression in Perversion: With Special Reference to the Function of Erotic Experience in Sexual Perversion." It was first published in *Depressive States and Their Treatment* (1985), edited by V. D. Volkan. New York: Jason Aronson, pp. 317–334.

CHAPTER 7 PERVERSE SYMPTOMS AND THE MANIFEST DREAM OF PERVERSION was presented at the December 1979 meeting of the American Psychoanalytic Association and first published in *The Dream in Clinical Practice* (1980), edited by J. M. Natterson. New York: Jason Aronson, pp. 237–256. Published with permission of Jason Aronson, Inc.

CHAPTER 8 THEORETICAL CONSIDERATIONS ON FEMALE HOMOSEXUALITY Section I: Historical Development of Theoretical and Clinical Aspects of Female Homosexuality was adapted from two papers: a Panel Report of the American Psychoanalytic Association entitled "Theoretical and Clinical Aspects of Overt Female Homosexuality," C. W. Socarides, reporter. *Journal of the American Psychoanalytic Association*, 10:579–592; and "The Historical Development of Theoretical and Clinical Concepts of Overt Female Homosexuality" (Socarides, 1963). *Journal of the American Psychoanalytic Association*, 11:386–414. Published with the permission of the editor of the Journal of the American Psychoanalytic Association and International Universities Press, Inc. Section II: Female Homosexuality: Current Conceptualizations is published here for the first time.

CHAPTER 9 PREOEDIPAL TYPE II HOMOSEXUAL PATIENT WITH ASSOCIATED NARCISSISTIC PERSONALITY DISORDER: THE CASE OF WILLARD is an expanded and adapted version of "Considerations on the Psychoanalytic Treatment of Overt Male Homosexuality: Part V: Homosexual Patient with Associated Narcissistic Personality Disorder Proper," presented before the American Psychoanalytic Association, December 22, 1984.

CHAPTER 10 THE RAPPROCHEMENT SUBPHASE CRISIS IN A PREOEDIPAL TYPE II NARCISSISTIC HOMOSEXUAL is an adapted and revised version of "Homosexuality and the Rapprochement Subphase Crisis," published in *Rapprochement: The Critical Subphase of Separation-Individuation* (1980), edited by R. F. Lax, S. Bach, and J. A. Burland. New York: Jason Aronson, pp. 331–352. Published with permission of Jason Aronson, Inc.

CHAPTER 11 ABDICATING FATHERS, HOMOSEXUAL SONS: TWO CLINICAL EXAMPLES was adapted from "Abdicating Fathers, Homosexual Sons: Psychoanalytic Observations on the Contribution of the Father to the Development of Male Homosexuality" in *Father and Child: Developmental and Clinical Perspectives* (1982), edited by S. H. Cath, A. R. Gurwith, and J.M. Ross. Boston: Little, Brown & Company, pp. 509–521. Published with permission of Little, Brown & Company.

CHAPTER 12 FETISHISM: THE CASE OF CALVIN is a revised and expanded version of "The Development of a Fetishistic Perversion: The Contribution of Preoedipal Phase Conflict." *Journal of the American Psychoanalytic Association*, 8:281–311 (1960). Published with permission of International Universities Press and the Journal of the American Psychoanalytic Association, Inc.

CHAPTER 13 THE TELEPHONE PERVERSION: MEANING, CONTENT, AND FUNCTION Published here for the first time. Some of the concepts expressed in this chapter were stimulated through discussion with members of the Discussion Group: Sexual Deviations: Theory and Therapy (May, 1983), American Psychoanalytic Association, Inc.

CHAPTER 14 TRANSSEXUALISM: THE CASE OF VICTOR-VALERIE was adapted from "A Psychoanalytic Study of the Desire for Sexual Transformation (Transsexualism): The Plaster of Paris Man." *International Journal of Psycho-Analysis*, 51: 341–349 (1970). Published with permission of the *International Journal of Psycho-Analysis*.

CHAPTER 15 TRANSVESTITISM: THE CASE OF ALFRED is published here for the first time. I acknowledge my indebtedness to Drs. Peter Loeffler and Rhona Shaw, formerly of the Department of Psychiatry, Albert Einstein College of Medicine for permission to adapt for publication the case history of a homosexual transvestite.

CHAPTER 16 PSYCHOANALYSIS OF A MASOCHISTIC (SPANKING) PERVERSION: THE CASE OF DR. X is an adapted and expanded version of a paper presented before the American Psychoanalytic Association entitled "Psychoanalysis of a Masochistic (Spanking) Perversion," December 21, 1985. It is published here for the first time.

CHAPTER 17 VOYEURISM: THE CASE OF MARTIN has its origins in a 1974 paper entitled "The Demonified Mother: A Study of Voyeurism and Sexual Sadism." *International Review of Psychoanalysis*, 1:187–195. Permission for publication of the revised clinical material granted by *International Review of Psychoanalysis*.

CHAPTER 18 PEDOPHILIA: THE CASE OF JENKINS originated from a short clinical communication "Meaning and Content of a Pedophiliac Perversion," published in the *Journal of the American Psychoanalytic Association*, 7:84–94 (1959). Permission to publish a revised and much expanded clinical and theoretical proposition granted by International Universities Press and the Journal of the American Psychoanalytic Association, Inc.

CHAPTER 19 EXHIBITIONISM is published here for the first time.

CHAPTER 20 COPROPHILIA AND COPROPHAGIA is published here for the first time.

CHAPTER 21 MULTIPLE PERVERSE FANTASIES, ALTERATIONS IN BODY-EGO EXPERIENCE AND PATHOLOGICAL PERCEPTIONS: THE CASE OF THE BARKING MAN was presented in an abbreviated form before the Western New England Psychoanalytic Society, Yale University, New Haven, January 1970; the Southern California Psychoanalytic Society, Los Angeles, March, 1970; and the American Psychoanalytic Association, San Francisco, May, 1970; and published under the title of "Sexual Perversion and the Fear of Engulfment." *International Journal of Psycho-Analytic Psychotherapy*, 2:432–448 (1973). The fascinating and bewildering symptomatology of this patient, reported in greater detail in this version, could only be comprehended after a decade of reflection and return to the careful psychoanalytic notes I took at the time of his treatment. Appendix includes several verbatim psychoanalytic sessions.

CHAPTER 22 PSYCHOANALYTIC TECHNIQUE IN THE TREATMENT OF PERVERSE PATIENTS is published here for the first time.

References

Abelin, E. L. (1971), The role of the father in the separation-individuation process. In: *Separation-Individuation: Essays in Honor of Margaret S. Mahler,* ed. S. B. McDevitt & C. F. Settlage. New York: International Universities Press, pp. 229–253.

_____ (1975), Some further observations and comments on the earliest role of the father. *Internat. J. Psycho-Anal.,* 16:293–302.

Abraham, K. (1913), Restrictions and transformations of scoptophilia in psychoneurotics: With remarks on analogous phenomena in folk psychology. *Selected Papers of Karl Abraham, M.D.* London: Hogarth Press, 1948, pp. 169–234.

_____ (1920), The narcissistic evaluation of excretory processes in dreams and neurosis. In: *Selected Papers on Psychoanalysis.* London: Hogarth Press, 1942, pp. 318–322.

Ahrens, R. (1954), Beitrag zur entwicklung des physiognomie und minikerkenneos. *Z. Exp. Engew. Psychol.,* 2:412–454.

Alexander, F. (1956), A note to the theory of perversions. In: *Perversions: Psychodynamics and Therapy,* ed. S. Lorand & M. Balint. New York: Random House, pp. 3–15.

Allen, C. (1969), *A Textbook of Psychosexual Disorders, 2nd Ed.* London: Oxford University Press.

Allen, D. W. (1967), Exhibitionistic and voyeuristic conflicts in learning and functioning. *Psychoanal. Quart.,* 36:546–570.

Almansi, R. J. (1958), A hypnogogic phenomenon. *Psychoanal. Quart.,* 27:539–546.

_____ (1960), The face-breast equation. *J. Amer. Psychoanal. Assn.,* 8:43–70.

_____ (1979), Scopophilia and object loss. *Psychoanal. Quart.,* 47:601–619.

_____ (1983), Research and clinical psychoanalytic findings in voyeurism. Presented at Discussion Group: The Sexual Deviations: Theory and Therapy. American Psychoanalytic Association, April 28, 1983.

———— (1985), On telephoning, compulsive telephoning and perverse telephoning: Psychoanalytic and social aspects. *Psychoanal. St. Soc.*, 11:218–235.

American Psychiatric Association (1968), *Diagnostic and Statistical Manual of Mental Disorders, 2nd ed., DSM2.* Washington, D.C.: American Psychiatric Association, p. 44.

Andrew, R. S. (1965), The origins of facial expression. *Sci. Amer.*, 213:88–94.

Arlow, J. A. (1955), Notes on oral symbolism. *Psychoanal. Quart.*, 24:63–74.

———— (1961), Ego psychology and the study of mythology. *J. Amer. Psychoanal. Assn.*, 9:371–393.

———— (1963), Conflict, regression and symptom formation. *Internat. J. Psycho-Anal.*, 44:12–22.

———— (1965), Personal communications and formal discussion at the reading of "Coprophagia and allied phenomena" by S. Tarachow, April 30, 1965. *J. Amer. Psychoanal. Assn.*, 14:685–699.

———— (1986), Discussion of paper by J. McDougall and M. Glasser. Panel on identification in the perversions. *Internat. J. Psycho-Anal.*, 67:245–250.

———— Brenner, C. (1964), *Psychoanalytic Concepts and the Structural Theory.* New York: International Universities Press.

Bach, S. (1977), On the narcissistic state of consciousness. *Internat. J. Psycho-Anal.*, 58:209–233.

———— Schwartz, L. (1972), A dream of deSade: Psychoanalytic reflections on narcissistic trauma. Decompensation and the reconstitution of illusion of self. *J. Amer. Psychoanal. Assn.*, 20:451–475.

Bacon, C. L. (1956), A developmental theory of female homosexuality. In: *Perversions: Psychodynamics and Therapy*, ed. S. Lorand & M. Balint. New York: Random House, pp. 131–160.

Bak, R. C. (1946), Masochism in paranoia. *Psychoanal. Quart.*, 15:285.

———— (1953), Fetishism. *J. Amer. Psychoanal. Assn.*, 1:285–298.

———— (1956), Aggression and perversion. In: *Perversions: Psychodynamics and Therapy*, ed. S. Lorand & M. Balint. New York: Random House, pp. 231–240.

———— (1968), The phallic woman: The ubiquitous fantasy in perversions. In: *The Psychoanalytic Study of the Child*, 23:15–36. New York: International Universities Press.

———— (1971), Object relationships in schizophrenia and perversion. *Internat. J. Psycho-Anal.*, 52:235–242.

Barahal, H. S. (1953), Female transvestitism and homosexuality. *Psychiat. Quart.*, 27:390–438.

Beach, F. A. (1942), Central nervous mechanisms involved in the reproductive behavior of vertebrates. *Psychol. Bull.*, 39:200.

———— (1947), A review of physiological and psychological studies of sexual behavior in mammals. *Physiol. Rev.*, 27:240.

Benedek, T. (1952), *Psychosexual Functions in Women.* New York: Ronald Press.

Bergler, E. (1936), Obscene words. *Psychoanal. Quart.*, 5:226–248.

———— (1938), Preliminary phase of masculine beating fantasies. *Psychoanal. Quart.*, 7:514–536.

———— (1944), Eight prerequisites for psychoanalytic treatment of homosexuality. *Psychoanal. Rev.*, 31:253–286.

———— (1951), *Counterfeit Sex.* New York: Grune & Stratton.

———— (1957a), Fear of heights. *Psychoanal. Rev.*, 44:447–451.

———— (1957b), Voyeurism. *Archs. Crim. Psychodyn.*, 2:211–225.

Bernstein, I. (1973), Integrative aspects of masturbation (abstract). *Bull. Phila. Assn.*, 23:274–278.

Bibring, E. (1953), The mechanisms of depression. In: *Affective Disorders*, ed. P. Greenacre. New York: International Universities Press.

Bieber, I., Dain, H. J., Dince, P. R., Drellich, M. G., Grand, H. G., Gundlach, R. H., Kremer, M. W., Rifkin, A. H., Wilbur, C. B., & Bieber, T. B. (1962), *Homosexuality.* New York: Basic Books.

Blum, H. P. (1977), The prototype of preoedipal reconstruction. *J. Amer. Psychoanal. Assn.*, 25:757–786.

Boehm, F. (1926), Homosexuality and the Oedipus complex. *Internat. J. Psycho-Anal.*, 12:66–79.

———— (1933), Uber zwei typen von mannlichen homosexuellen. *Internat. J. Psycho-Anal.*, 19:499–506.

Bonaparte, M. (1953), *Female Sexuality.* New York: International Universities Press.

Brierley, M. (1932), Some problems of integration in women. *Internat. J. Psycho-Anal.*, 13:433–448.

———— (1935), Specific determinants in feminine development. *Internat. J. Psycho-Anal.*, 17:163–180.

Brill, A. A. (1934), Homoerotism and paranoia. *Amer. J. Psychiat.*, 13:957–974.

Bromberg, N. & Small, V. V. (1983), *Hitler's Psychopathology.* New York: International Universities Press.

Brunswick, R. M. (1928), A supplement to Freud's "History of an infantile neurosis." *Internat. J. Psycho-Anal.*, 9:439–476.

———— (1929), The analysis of a case of paranoia. *J. Nerv. Ment. Dis.*, 70:1–22, 155–178.

———— (1940), The preoedipal phase of libido development. *Psychoanal. Quart.*, 9:293–319.

Bunker, H. A. (1934), The voice as (female) phallus. *Psychoanal. Quart.*, 3:391–429.

Bychowski, G. (1954), Discussion: Problems of Infantile Neurosis. *The Psychoanalytic Study of the Child*, 9:66–88. New York: International Universities Press.

—— (1956a), The ego and the introjects. *Psychoanal. Quart.*, 25:11–36.

—— (1956b), Homosexuality and psychosis. In: *Perversions: Psychodynamics and Therapy*, ed. S. Lorand & M. Balint. New York: Random House, pp. 97–130.

Cassity, J. H. (1927), Psychological considerations of pedophilia. *Psychoanal. Rev.*, 14:189–209.

Chareton, F. D. & Galef, H. (1965), A case of transvestitism in a six-year-old boy. *J. Hillside Hosp.*, 4/3:160–177.

Childs, A. (1977), Acute symbiotic psychosis in a postoperative transsexual. *Arch. Sex. Behav.*, 6:37–44.

Christoffel, H. (1956), Male genital exhibitionism. In: *Perversions: Psychodynamics and Therapy*, ed. S. Lorand & M. Balint. New York: Random House, pp. 243–265.

de M'Uzan, M. (1973), A case of masochistic perversion and an outline of a theory. *Internat. J. Psycho-Anal.*, 54:455–467.

deSade, M. (1791), *Justine ou les Malheures de la Virtu*: Hollande. Ches les Libraires Associes (Paris). 2 volumes.

de Saussure, R. (1929), Homosexual fixations in neurotic women. In: *Homosexuality* (1978), C. W. Socarides. New York: Jason Aronson, pp. 547–601.

Deutsch, H. (1923), *Psychoanalyse der Weiblichen Sexualfunktionen.* Vienna: Internationaler Psychoanalytischer Verlag.

—— (1932a), Female sexuality (also homosexuality in women). *Internat. J. Psycho-Anal.*, 14:34–56.

—— (1932b), On female homosexuality. *Psychoanal. Quart.*, 1:484–510.

—— (1933), Motherhood and sexuality. *Psychoanal. Quart.*, 2:476–488.

Dickes, R. (1963), Fetishistic behavior, a contribution to its complex development and significance. *J. Amer. Psychoanal. Assn.*, 11:303–330.

—— (1975), Technical considerations on the therapeutic and working alliance. *Internat. J. Psychoanal. Psychother.*, 4:1–24.

—— (1978), Parents, transitional objects, and childhood fetishes. In: *Between Reality and Fantasy: Transitional Objects and Phenomena*, ed. S. A. Brodnick, L. Barkin, & W. Muensterberger. New York: Jason Aronson, pp. 305–321.

Dorpat, T. L. (1976), Structural conflict and object relations conflict. *J. Amer. Psychoanal. Assn.*, 24:855–875.

Edgcumbe, R. & Burgner, M. (1975), The phallic-narcissistic phase: The differentiation between preoedipal and oedipal aspects of development. *The Psychoanalytic Study of the Child*, 30:161–180. New Haven: Yale University Press.

Eidelberg, L. (1954), *A Comparative Pathology of Neurosis*. New York: International Universities Press.

Eissler, K. R. (1958a), Notes on problems of technique in the psychoanalytic treatment of adolescence; With some remarks on perversions. *The Psychoanalytic Study of the Child*, 13:223–254. New York: International Universities Press.

_____ (1958b), Remarks on some variations in psychoanalytic technique. *Internat. J. Psycho-Anal.*, 39:222–229.

Ellis, H. (1936), *Studies in the Psychology of Sex*, Vols. 1 & 2. New York: Random House.

Erikson, E. H. (1950), Growth and crisis of the healthy personality. In: *Identity and the Life Cycle*. New York: International Universities Press, 1959, pp. 50–100.

Fain, M. (1954), Contribution a l'etude du voyeurisme. *Rev. Franc. Psychoanal.*, 18:177–192.

Fairbairn, W. (1954), *An Object Relations Theory of Personality*. New York: Basic Books.

Fast, I. (1984), *Gender Identity: A Differentiation Model*. Hillsdale, NJ: Lawrence Erlbaum.

Fenichel, O. (1930a), Die symbolische gleichung madchen phallus. *Int. Z. Psa.*, 16:21–34.

_____ (1930b), The pregenital antecedents of the Oedipus complex. In: *Collected Papers*, vol 1. New York: Norton, 1953, pp. 181–204.

_____ (1930c). The psychology of transvestitism. In: *Collected Papers*, vol. 1. New York: W. W. Norton, 1953, pp. 167–180.

_____ (1934), Further light on the preoedipal phase in girls. In: *Collected Papers*, vol. 1. New York: W. W. Norton, 1953, pp. 241–289.

_____ (1935), The scoptophilic instinct and identification. In: *Collected Papers*, vol. 1. New York: W. W. Norton, 1953, pp. 373–397.

_____ (1945), *The Psychoanalytic Theory of Neurosis*. New York: W. W. Norton.

Ferber, L. (1975), Beating fantasies. In: *Masturbation From Infancy to Senescence*, ed. I. M. Marcus & J. J. Francis. New York: International Universities Press, pp. 205–222.

Ferenczi, S. (1909), More about homosexuality. In: *Final Contributions to the Problems and Methods of Psychoanalysis*. New

York: Basic Books, 1955, pp. 168–174.

———— (1911), Obscene words. In: *Sex in Psychoanalysis: Contributions to Psychoanalysis*. New York: Robert Brunner, 1950, pp. 132–154.

———— (1914), The nosology of female homosexuality (homoerotism). In: *Contributions to Psychoanalysis: Contributions to Psychoanalysis*. New York: Robert Brunner, 1950, pp. 296–318.

———— (1923), On the symbolism of the head of Medusa. In: *Further Contributions to the Theory and Technique of Psychoanalysis*, 2nd ed. London: Hogarth Press, 1950, p. 360.

Fine, R. (1980), Presidential introduction. The First Sigmund Freud Memorial Lectureship Award. New York Center for Psychoanalytic Training. New York City (unpublished).

Fleming, R. N. (1983), Presentation of "A case of voyeurism" at Discussion Group: "Sexual Deviations: Theory and Therapy." American Psychoanalytic Association, December 1983.

Fliess, R., Ed. (1950), *The Psychoanalytic Reader*. New York: International Universities Press.

———— (1973), *Symbol, Dream, and Psychosis*. New York: International Universities Press.

Frank, G. (1966), *The Boston Strangler*. New York: New American Library.

Freedman, D. G. (1964), Smiling in blind infants and the issue of innate versus acquired. *J. Child Psychol. & Psychiat.*, 5:171–184.

Freedman, N. (1968), Varieties of symbiotic manifestations. In: *Work in Progress*. New York: Institute for Psychoanalytic Training and Research, pp. 1–10.

Freud, A. (1949a), Certain types and stages of social maladjustment. In: *The Writings of Anna Freud*, Vol. 4:75–94. New York: International Universities Press, 1949.

———— (1949b), Some clinical remarks concerning the treatment of cases of male homosexuality. Summary of presentation at International Psychoanalytic Congress, Zurich, 1949. *Internat. J. Psycho-Anal.*, 30:195.

———— (1951), Homosexuality. *Bull. Amer. Psychoanal. Assn.*, 7:117–118.

———— (1954), Problems of technique in adult analysis. In: *The Writings of Anna Freud*, Vol. 4. New York: International Universities Press, 1968, pp. 377–406.

———— (1965), Normality and pathology in childhood. In: *The Writings of Anna Freud*, Vol. 6. New York: International Universities Press, 1965, pp. 1–247.

———— (1968), *The Writings of Anna Freud*, Vol. 5. New York: International Universities Press, 1969, pp. 384–390.

_____ (1971), A discussion with Rene Spitz. In: *The Writings of Anna Freud*, Vol. 7. New York: International Universities Press, 1971, pp. 22–38.

Freud, S. (1887-1902), *The Origins of Psychoanalysis*. New York: Basic Books, 1954.

_____ (1900), The Interpretation of Dreams. *Standard Edition*, 4 & 5. London: Hogarth Press, 1933.

_____ (1905a), Jokes and Their Relation to the Unconscious. *Standard Edition*, 8. London: Hogarth Press, 1960.

_____ (1905b), Three essays on the theory of sexuality. *Standard Edition*, 7:125-145. London: Hogarth Press, 1953.

_____ (1909), Some general remarks on hysterical attacks. *Standard Edition*, 9:227-234. London: Hogarth Press, 1959.

_____ (1910a), Leonardo da Vinci and a memory of his childhood. *Standard Edition*, 11:59-137. London: Hogarth Press, 1957.

_____ (1910b), The psychoanalytic view of psychogenic disturbance of vision. *Standard Edition*, 11:209-219. London: Hogarth Press, 1957.

_____ (1911), Psycho-analytic notes on an auto-biographical account of a case of paranoia (dementia paranoides). *Standard Edition*, 12:2-80. London: Hogarth Press, 1958.

_____ (1914), On narcissism: An introduction. *Standard Edition*, 14:67-105. London: Hogarth Press, 1957.

_____ (1915), Instincts and their vicissitudes. *Standard Edition*, 14:117-140. London: Hogarth Press, 1959.

_____ (1915-1916), Introductory Lectures on Psychoanalysis. *Standard Edition*, 15. London: Hogarth Press, 1963.

_____ (1916), On transience. *Standard Edition*, 14:305-307. London: Hogarth Press, 1957.

_____ (1917), *A General Introduction to Psychoanalysis*. New York: Garden City Pub. Co., 1943.

_____ (1919), A child is being beaten. *Standard Edition*, 17:175-204. London: Hogarth Press, 1955.

_____ (1920a), Beyond the pleasure principle. *Standard Edition*, 18:3-64. London: Hogarth Press, 1955.

_____ (1920b), *General Introductory Lectures*. New York: Garden City Pub. Co., 1943.

_____ (1920c), Psychogenesis of a case of homosexuality in a woman. *Standard Edition*, 18:145-175. London: Hogarth Press, 1955.

_____ (1922a), Group psychology and the analysis of the ego. *Standard Edition*, 18:67-145. London: Hogarth Press, 1955.

_____ (1922b), Some neurotic mechanisms in jealousy, paranoia, and homosexuality. *Standard Edition*, 18:221-235. London: Hogarth Press, 1955.

_____ (1923), A 17th-century demonological neurosis. *Standard Edition*, 19:19–100. London: Hogarth Press, 1961.

_____ (1923a), The infantile genital organization: An interpolation into the theory of sexuality. *Standard Edition*, 19:141–147. London: Hogarth Press, 1961.

_____ (1923b), Two encyclopedia articles. *Standard Edition*, 18:235–263. London: Hogarth Press, 1955.

_____ (1924a), The economic problems of masochism. *Standard Edition*, 19:157–170. London: Hogarth Press, 1961.

_____ (1924b), The passing of the Oedipus complex. *Collected Papers*, 2:269–277. London: Hogarth Press, 1946.

_____ (1925a), Some additional notes on dream interpretation as a whole. *Standard Edition*, 19:125–178. London: Hogarth Press, 1961.

_____ (1925b), Some psychical consequences of the anatomical distinction between the sexes. *Standard Edition*, 19:243–261. London: Hogarth Press, 1961.

_____ (1926), Inhibitions, Symptoms and anxiety. *Standard Edition*, 20:77–175. London: Hogarth Press, 1959.

_____ (1927), Fetishism. In: *Collected Papers*, 5:198–204. London: Hogarth Press, 1950.

_____ (1931), Female sexuality. *Standard Edition*, 21:223–247. London: Hogarth Press, 1961.

_____ (1932), The psychology of women. In: *New Introductory Lectures on Psychoanalysis*. New York: W. W. Norton, 1933, pp. 153–186.

_____ (1937), Constructions in analysis. *Standard Edition*, 23:255–270. London: Hogarth Press, 1964.

_____ (1938), An outline of psychoanalysis. *Standard Edition*, 23:141–207. London: Hogarth Press, 1964.

_____ (1938a), Splitting of the ego in the defensive process. In: *Collected Papers*, 5:372–375. London: Hogarth Press, 1950.

Friend, M. R., Schiddel, L., Klein, B. & Dunaif, S. (1954), Observations on the development of transvestitism in boys. *Amer. J. Orthopsychiat.*, 24:563–569.

_____ (1974), Emergence of genital awareness during the second year of life. In: *Sex Differences in Behavior*, ed. R. C. Friedman, R. M. Richart, & R. L. Vande Wiele. New York: John Wiley & Sons, 1974, pp. 223–231.

Galenson, E. & Roiphe, H. (1973), Object loss and early sexual development. *Psychoanal. Quart.*, 22:73–90.

_____ (1979), The development of sexual identity: Discoveries and implications. In: *Sexuality: Psychoanalytic Observations*, ed. T. B. Karasu & C. W. Socarides. New York: International Universities Press, pp. 1–17.

———— Vogel, S., Blau, S., & Roiphe, H. (1975), Disturbances in sexual identity beginning at 18 months of age. *Internat. Rev. Psycho-Anal.*, 2:389-397.

Gedo, J. E. & Goldberg, A. (1973), *Models of the Mind.* Chicago and London: University of Chicago Press.

Gillespie, W. H. (1940), A contribution to the study of fetishism. *Internat. J. Psycho-Anal.*, 21:401-415.

———— (1952), Notes on the analysis of sexual perversions. *Internat. J. Psycho-Anal.*, 33:397-402.

———— (1956a), The general theory of sexual perversion. *Internat. J. Psycho-Anal.*, 37:396-403.

———— (1956b), The structure and etiology of perversion. In: *Perversions: Psychodynamics and Therapy*, ed. S. Lorand & M. Balint. New York: Random House, pp. 28-42.

Glauber, I. P. (1956), The re-birth motif in homosexuality and teleological significance. *Internat. J. Psycho-Anal.*, 37:416-421.

Gley, E. (1884), Les aberrations de l'instinct sexuel. *Rev. Philosophique*, 17:66 (143n).

Glover, E. (1933), The relation of perversion formation to the development of reality sense. *Internat. J. Psycho-Anal.*, 14:486-504.

———— (1939), *Psychoanalysis.* London: Staples Press.

———— (1960), *The Roots of Crime: Selected Papers on Psychoanalysis*, Vol. 2. New York: International Universities Press.

———— (1964), Aggression and sado-masochism. In: *The pathology and Treatment of Sexual Deviation*, ed. I. Rosen. London: Oxford University Press, pp. 146-162.

Glueck, B. C., Jr. (1956), Psychodynamic patterns in the homosexual sex offender. *Amer. J. Psychiat.*, 112:584-590.

Goldberg, A. (1975), A fresh look at perverse behavior. *Internat. J. Psycho-Anal.*, 56:335-342.

———— (1977), Some countertransference phenomena in the analysis of perversions. In: *The Annual of Psychoanalysis*, 5:105-119. New York: International Universities Press.

Greenacre, P. (1953), Certain relationships between fetishism and the faulty development of the body image. In: *Emotional Growth: Psychoanalytic Studies of the Gifted and a Great Variety of Other Individuals*, Vol. 1. New York: International Universities Press, 1971, pp. 9-31.

———— (1954), The role of transference: Practical considerations in relation to psychoanalytic therapy. In: *Emotional Growth: Psychoanalytic Studies of the Gifted and a Great Variety of Other Individuals*, Vol. 2. New York: International Universities Press, 1971, pp. 627-641.

———— (1955), Further considerations regarding fetishism. *The Psychoanalytic Study of the Child*, 10:187-194. New York:

International Universities Press.

———— (1960), Further notes on fetishism. *The Psychoanalytic Study of the Child*, 15:191-208. New York: International Universities Press.

———— (1967), The influence of infantile trauma on genetic patterns. In: *Emotional Growth: Psychoanalytic Studies of the Gifted and a Great Variety of Other Individuals*, Vol. 1. New York: International Universities Press, 1971, pp. 260-299.

———— (1968), Perversions: General considerations regarding their genetic and dynamic background. In: *Emotional Growth: Psychoanalytic Studies of the Gifted and a Great Variety of Other Individuals*, Vol. 1. New York: International Universities Press, 1971, pp. 300-314.

———— (1969), The fetish and the transitional object. In: *Emotional Growth: Psychoanalytic Studies of the Gifted and a Great Variety of Other Individuals*, Vol. 1. New York: International Universities Press, 1971, pp. 315-334.

———— (1971), Notes on the influence and contribution of ego psychology to the practice of psychoanalysis. In: *Separation - Individuation: Essays in Honor of Margaret S. Mahler*, eds. J. B. McDevitt & C. F. Settlage. New York: International Universities Press, pp. 171-200.

Greenman, G. W. (1963), Visual behavior of newborn infants. In: *Modern Perspectives in Child Development*, eds. A. Solnit & S. Provence. New York: International Universities Press, pp. 71-79.

Greenson, R. R. (1964), On homosexuality and gender identity. In: *Explorations in Psychoanalysis*. New York: International Universities Press, 1978, pp. 191-198.

———— (1966), A transvestite boy and a hypothesis. *Internat. J. Psycho-Anal.*, 47:396-403.

———— (1967), *The Technique and Practice of Psychoanalysis*, Vol. 1. New York: International Universities Press.

———— (1968), Dis-identifying from mother: Its special importance for the boy. In: *Explorations in Psychoanalysis*. New York: International Universities Press, 1978, pp. 305-312.

———— (1969), The non-transference relationship in the psychoanalytic situation. In: *Explorations in Psychoanalysis*. New York: International Universities Press, 1978, pp. 359-387.

Groddeck, G. (1923), *The Book of the It*. New York: International Universities Press, 1976.

Gutheil, E. (1930), Analysis of a case of transvestitism. In: *Sexual Aberrations*, ed. W. Stekel. New York: Liverright, pp. 281-318.

Handelsman, L. (1965), The effects of early object relationships on sexual development: Autistic and symbiotic modes of adaptation. *The Psychoanalytic Study of the Child*, 20:367–383. New York: International Universities Press.

Harris, H. I. (1957), Telephone anxiety. *J. Amer. Psychoanal. Assn.*, 5:342–347.

Hart, H. H. (1949), The eye in symbol and symptom. *Psychoanal. Rev.*, 36:1–21.

Hartmann, H., Kris, E., & Loewenstein, R. M. (1946), Comments on the formation of psychic structure. In: *Papers on Psychoanalytic Psychology*. New York: International Universities Press, 1964, pp. 27–65.

Henry, G. W. (1934), Psychogenic and constitutional factors in homosexuality. *Psychiat. Quart.*, 8:243–264.

Herman, G. (1903), "Genesis" das gesetz der Zeugung, Bd. 5, *Libido und Mania*. Leipzig, 143n.

Hirschfeld, M. (1910), *Die Transvestiten*. Berlin: Pulvermacher.

Hoffer, W. (1954), Defense process and defense organization: Their place in psychoanalytic technique. *Internat. J. Psycho-Anal.*, 35:194–198.

Hollander, M. H., Brown, W., & Robash, H. B. (1977), Genital exhibitionism in women. *Amer. J. Psychiat.*, 134:4:436–438.

Horney, K. (1925), The flight from womanhood. *Internat. J. Psycho-Anal.*, 7:324–339.

Horowitz, L. (1985), Divergent views on the treatment of borderline patients. *Bull. Menn. Clinic*, 49:525–546.

Hunt, W. (1973), Beating fantasies and daydreams revisited. Presentation of a case. *J. Amer. Psychoanal. Assn.*, 21:817–832.

Hutt, C. & Ounsted, C. (1966), The biological significance of gaze aversion with particular reference to the syndrome of infantile autism. *Behav. Sci.*, 11:346–356.

Isakower, O. (1938), A contribution to the patho-psychology of phenomena associated with falling asleep. *Internat. J. Psycho-Anal.*, 19:331–345.

Isay, R. A.,(1985), On the analytic therapy of homosexual men. *The Psychoanalytic Study of the Child*, 40:235–254. New York: International Universities Press.

———— (1986). Homosexuality in homosexuals and heterosexuals: Some distinctions and implications for treatment. In: *The Psychology of men: New Psychoanalytic Perspectives*, ed.: G. I. Fogel, F. M. Lane, & R. S. Liebert. New York: Basic Books, pp. 277–299.

Jacobson, E. (1946), The effect of disappointment on ego and superego function in normal and depressive development. *Psychoanal. Rev.*, 33:255–262.

———— (1950), Development of the wish for a child in boys. *The*

Psychoanalytic Study of the Child, 5:139-152. New York: International Universities Press.

—— (1964), *The Self and the Object World*. New York: International Universities Press.

Jones, E. (1912), *Papers on Psychoanalysis*, 5th ed. London: Balliere, Tindall & Cox, 1948.

—— (1920), A linguistic factor in English characterology. *Internat. J. Psycho-Anal.*, 1:256-261.

—— (1927), Early development of female homosexuality. *Internat. J. Psycho-Anal.*, 8:459-472.

Joseph, E. D., reporter (1965), Beating fantasies: Regressive ego phenomena in psychoanalysis. In: *Kris Study Group*, Monograph 1. New York: International Universities Press, pp. 68-103.

Jucovy, M. E. (1979), Initiation fantasies and transvestitism. *J. Amer. Psychoanal. Assn.*, 24:525-546.

Kanner, L. (1949), Problems of nosology and psychodynamics of early infantile autism. *Amer. J. Orthopsychiat.*, 19:416-426.

Karpman, B. (1950), A case of pedophilia (legally rape) cured by psychoanalysis. *Psychoanal. Rev.*, 37:235-276.

Katan, M. (1960), Dreams and psychosis. *Internat. J. Psycho-Anal.*, 41:341-451.

Keeler, M. H. (1960), An unusual perversion: The desire to be injured by an automobile operated by a woman. *Amer. J. Psychiat.*, 11:1032.

Kernberg, O. F. (1970), Factors in the psychoanalytic treatment of narcissistic personalities. *J. Amer. Psychoanal. Assn.*, 18:51-85.

—— (1974), Barriers to falling and remaining in love. *J. Amer. Psychoanal. Assn.*, 22:486-591.

—— (1975), *Borderline Conditions and Pathological Narcissism*. New York: Jason Aronson.

—— (1976), *Object Relations Theory and Clinical Psychoanalysis*. New York: Jason Aronson.

—— (1980a), Contemporary psychoanalytic theories of narcissism. Presented at The American Psychoanalytic Association, December 1980.

—— (1980b), *Internal World and External Reality: Object Relations Theory Applied*. New York: Jason Aronson.

—— (1980c), Mahler's developmental theory: A correlation. In: *Internal World and External Reality: Object Relations Theory Applied*. New York: Jason Aronson, pp. 105-121.

—— (1984a), *Severe Personality Disorders: Psychotherapeutic Strategies*. New Haven: Yale University Press.

—— (1984b), Malignant narcissism and its relationship to perversion. The Sandor Rado Lecture, June 4, 1984. *Bull. Assn. Psychoanal. Med.*, 24:38–43. P. R. Moskit, reporter.

———— (1986), A conceptual model of male perversion. In: *The Psychology of Men*, ed. G. Fogel, F. M. Lane & R. S. Liebert. New York: Basic Books, pp. 152–180.

Kestenberg, J. S. (1956a), On the development of maternal feelings in early childhood. *The Psychoanalytic Study of the Child*, 11:257–291. New York: International Universities Press.

———— (1956b), Vicissitudes of female sexuality. *J. Amer. Psychoanal. Assn.*, 4:453–476.

Khan, M. M. R. (1965), Intimacy, complicity and mutuality in perversions. In: *Alienation in Perversions*. New York: International Universities Press, 1979, pp. 18–30.

———— (1979), *Alienation in Perversions*. New York: International Universities Press.

Klaif, F. S. & Davis, C. A. (1960), Homosexuality and paranoid schizophrenia. *Amer. J. Psychiat.*, 116:12.

Klein, H. R. & Horowitz, W. A. (1949), Psychosexual factors in the paranoid phenomena. *Amer. J. Psychiat.*, 105:697–701.

Klein, M. (1946), Notes on some schizoid mechanisms. *Internat. J. Psycho-Anal.*, 27:99–110.

———— (1954), *The Psycho-Analysis of Children*. London: Hogarth Press.

———— Heimann, P., Isaacs, S., & Riviere, S. (1952), Notes on some schizoid mechanisms. In: *Developments in Psychoanalysis*. London: Hogarth Press, pp. 292–321.

Kligerman, C. (1951), The character of Jean-Jacques Rousseau. *Psychoanal. Quart.*, 20:237–252.

———— (1981), Jean-Jacques Rousseau: The artist as parent. *The Annual of Psychoanalysis*, 9:225–236.

Knapp, R. H. (1953), The ear, listening and hearing. *J. Amer. Psychoanal. Assn.*, 1:672–689.

Kohut, H. (1971), *The Analysis of the Self: A Systematic Approach to the Psychoanalytic Treatment of Narcissistic Personality Disorders*. New York: International Universities Press.

———— (1977), *The Restoration of the Self*. New York: International Universities Press.

Kolansky, H. & Eisner, H. (1974), The psychoanalytic concept of the preoedipal developmental arrest. Paper presented at The American Psychoanalytic Association, December 1974.

Krafft-Ebing, R. (1893), *Psychopathia Sexualis*, 8th ed. Stuttgart.

Kramer, P. (1955), On discovering one's identity. *The Psychoanalytic Study of the Child*, 10:47–74. New York: International Universities Press.

Kris, E. (1939), On inspiration. In: *Psychoanalytic Explorations in Art*. New York: International Universities Press, 1952, pp. 291–302.

––––– (1953), Psychoanalysis and the study of creative imagination. *Bull. NY Acad. Med.*, 29:334–351.

––––– (1955), Neutralization and sublimation. *The Psychoanalytic Study of the Child*, 10:30–46. New York: International Universities Press.

––––– (1956), The recovery of childhood memories in psychoanalysis. *The Psychoanalytic Study of the Child*, 2:54–88. New York: International Universities Press.

Kris Study Group Report (1957), *Beating Fantasies: Regressive Ego Phenomena in Psychoanalysis,* ed., E. D. Joseph. New York: International Universities Press.

Kubie, L. (1978), Distinction between normality and neurosis. In: *Symbol and Neurosis: Selected Papers of L. S. Kubie*, ed. H. J. Schlesinger. New York: International Universities Press, pp. 115–127.

Lachmann, F. & Stolorow, R. D. (1980), The developmental significance of affective states: Implications for psychoanalytic treatment. *The Annual of Psychoanalysis*. New York: International Universities Press, pp. 215–229.

Lampl-de Groot, J. (1933), Problems of femininity. *Psychoanal. Quart.*, 2:489–518.

––––– (1946), The preoedipal phase in the development of the male child. *The Psychoanalytic Study of the Child*, 2:75–112. New York: International Universities Press.

Langer, W. C. (1972), *The Mind of Adolf Hitler: A Secret Wartime Report*. New York: Basic Books.

Laufer, M. (1968), The body image, the function of masturbation, and adolescence: Problems of the ownership of the body. *The Psychoanalytic Study of the Child*, 23:114–187. New York: International Universities Press.

––––– Laufer, M. E. (1984), *Adolescence and Developmental Breakdown: A Psychoanalytic View*. New Haven: Yale University Press.

Le Coultre, R. (1956), Elimination of guilt as a function of perversions. In: *Perversions: Psychodynamics and Therapy*, eds. S. Lorand & M. Balint. New York: Random House, pp. 42–55.

Levey, S. G. (1973–74), A case of transsexualism. Case presentation in supervisory session with the author. Department of Psychiatry, Albert Einstein College of Medicine, New York (unpublished).

Lewin, B. D. (1933), The body as phallus. In: *Selected Writings of*

Bertrand D. Lewin, ed. J. A. Arlow. New York: The Psychoanalytic Quarterly, pp. 28–47.

———— (1950), *The Psychoanalysis of Elation.* New York: W. W. Norton.

———— (1952), Phobic symptoms and dream interpretation. *Psychoanal. Quart.*, 21:295–322.

———— (1955), Clinical hints from dream studies. *Bull. Menn. Clinic*, 19:78–85.

———— (1958), *Dreams and the Uses of Regression.* New York: International Universities Press.

Lichtenstein, H. (1961), Identity and sexuality. *J. Amer. Psychoanal. Assn.*, 9:179–260.

———— (1977), *The Dilemma of Human Identity.* New York: Jason Aronson.

Liebert, R. S. (1986), History of male homosexuality from ancient Greece through the renaissance: Implications for psychoanalytic theory. In: *The Psychology of Men. New Psychoanalytic Perspectives*, eds. G. I. Fogel, F. M. Lane, & R. S. Liebert. New York. Basic Books, pp. 181–210.

Limentani, A. (1979), The significance of transsexualism in relation to some basic psychoanalytic concepts. *Internat. Rev. Psychoanal.*, 6:139–153.

Loeb, L. & Shane, M. (1982), The resolution of a transsexual wish in a 5-year-old boy. *J. Amer. Psychoanal. Assn.*, 30:419–433.

Loewenstein, R. (1957), The psychoanalytic theory of masochism. *J. Amer. Psychoanal. Assn.*, 5:197–235.

Lorand, S. (1956), The therapy of perversions. In: *Perversions: Psychodynamics and Therapy*, ed. S. Lorand & M. Balint. New York: Random House, pp. 290–307.

Lorenz, K. (1953), *Man Meets Dog.* Baltimore, Md.: Penguin Books.

Lothstein, L. M. (1983), *Female-to-Male Transsexualism: Historical, Clinical and Theoretical Issues.* Boston: Rutledge and Kegan Paul.

MacVicar, K. (1978), A transsexual wish in a psychotic character. *Internat. J. Psychoanal. Psychother.*, 7:354–365.

Mahler, M. S. (1961), On sadness and grief in infancy and childhood: Loss and restoration of the symbiotic love object. In: *The Selected Papers of Margaret S. Mahler*, Vol. 1. New York: Jason Aronson, 1979, pp. 261–279.

———— (1965), On the significance of the normal separation-individuation phase: With reference to research in symbiotic child psychosis. In: *Drives, Affects, Behavior*, Vol. 2, ed. M. Schur. New York: International Universities Press, pp. 161–169.

_____ (1966a), Developments of symbiosis, symbiotic psychosis and the nature of separation anxiety. *Internat. J. Psycho-Anal.*, 46:559-560.

_____ (1966b), Notes on the development of basic moods: The depressive affect. In: *The Selected Papers of Margaret S. Mahler*, Vol. 3. New York: Jason Aronson, 1979, pp. 59-75.

_____ (1967), On human symbiosis and the vicissitudes of individuation. *J. Amer. Psychoanal. Assn.*, 15:740-764.

_____ (1968), *On Human Symbiosis and the Vicissitudes of Individuation*, Vol. 1. New York: International Universities Press.

_____ (1971), A study of the separation-individuation process and its possible application to borderline phenomena in the psychoanalytic situation. *The Psychoanalytic Study of the Child*, 26:403-424. New York: International Universities Press.

_____ (1972a), The rapprochement subphase of the separation-individuation process. In: *The Selected Papers of Margaret S. Mahler*, Vol. 2. New York: Jason Aronson, 1979, pp. 131-149.

_____ (1972b), On the first three subphases of the separation-individuation process. In: *The Selected Papers of Margaret S. Mahler*, Vol. 2. New York: Jason Aronson, 1979, pp. 119-131.

_____ (1973), Personal communication to the author.

_____ (1975a), Discussion of "Healthy parental influences on the earliest development of masculinity in baby boys" by R. J. Stoller. Margaret S. Mahler Symposium, Philadelphia. *Psychoanal. Forum*, 5:244-247.

_____ (1975b), Discussion of "Early development and the deja vu" by B. L. Pacella. *J. Amer. Psychoanal. Assn.*, 23:322-326.

_____ (1975c), The epigenesis of separation anxiety, basic mood and primitive identity. In: *The Psychological Birth of the Human Infant*. New York: Basic Books, pp. 210-220.

_____ Furer, M. (1966), Development of symbiosis, symbiotic psychosis and the nature of separation anxiety. *Internat. J. Psycho-Anal.*, 47:559-560.

_____ Gosliner, B. J. (1955), On symbiotic child psychosis: Genetic, dynamic and restitutive aspects. *The Psychoanalytic Study of the Child*, 10:195-212. New York: International Universities Press.

_____ Kaplan, L. (1977), Developmental aspects in the assessment of narcissism and so-called borderline personalities. In: *The Selected Papers of Margaret S. Mahler*, Vol. 2. New York: Jason Aronson, 1979, pp. 195-210.

_____ Pine, F., & Bergman, A. (1975), *The Psychological Birth of the Human Infant*. New York: Basic Books.

McDevitt, J. B. (1975), Separation individuation and object constancy. *J. Amer. Psychoanal. Assn.*, 23:713-742.

────── (1985), Preoedipal determinants of an infantile gender disorder. Paper presented at the International Symposium on Separation-Individuation, Paris, France, November 3, 1985, and at the New York Psychoanalytic Institute, February 25, 1985.

────── Settlage, C. F., eds. (1971), *Separation-Individuation: Essays in Honor of Margaret S. Mahler.* New York: International Universities Press.

McDougall, J. (1970), Homosexuality in women. In: *Female Sexuality: New Psychoanalytic Views*, ed. J. Chasseguet-Smirgel, C.-J. Luquet-Parat, B. Gruneberger, J. McDougall, M. Torok, & C. David. Ann Arbor: Michigan University Press, pp. 171–212.

────── (1972), The primal scene in sexual perversions. *Internat. J. Psycho-Anal.*, 53:371–384.

Meyer, J. K. (1980), The theory of gender identity disorders. *J. Amer. Psychoanal. Assn.*, 30:381–418.

Mittelmann, B. (1955), Motor patterns and genital behavior: Fetishism. *The Psychoanalytic Study of the Child*, 10:241–263. New York: International Universities Press.

Modell, A. H. (1965), On having the right to a life: An aspect of the superego's development. *Internat. J. Psycho-Anal.*, 46:323–331.

────── (1968), *Object Love and Reality.* New York: International Universities Press.

────── (1978), The conceptualization of the therapeutic action of psychoanalysis: The action of the holding environment. *Bull. Menn. Clin.*, 42:493–504.

Moore, B. E. & Rubinfine, D. L., reporters (1969), The mechanisms of denial. In: *Kris Study Group*, Monograph 3:3–57. New York: International Universities Press.

Muensterberger, W. (1956), Perversion, cultural norm and normality. In: *Perversions: Psychodynamics and Therapy*, eds. S. Lorand & M. Balint. New York: Random House, pp. 16–27.

Muller-Eckhardt, H. (1955), Analyse eines Jugendlichen voyeurs. *Prax. Kinderpsycho*, 4:285–289.

Nacht, S. (1948), Clinical manifestations of aggression and their role in psychoanalytic treatment. *Internat. J. Psycho-Anal.*, 29:201–223.

────── Diatkine, R. & Favreau, J. (1956), The Ego and Perverse Relationships. *Internat. J. Psycho-Anal.*, 37:404–413.

Newman, L. E. & Stoller, R. J. (1968), Gender identity disturbances in intersexed patients. *Amer. J. Psychiat.*, 124:1262–1266.

Niederland, W. G. (1956), Clinical observations on the "Little man" phenomenon. *The Psychoanalytic Study of the Child*, 11:381–395. New York: International Universities Press.

────── (1958a), Early auditory experiences, beating fantasies and primal scene. *The Psychoanalytic Study of the Child*, 13:471–504. New York: International Universities Press.

———— (1958b), Linguistic observations on beating fantasies. *J. Hillside Hosp.*, 7:478–480.

———— (1965), Narcissistic ego impairment in patients with early physical malformations. *The Psychoanalytic Study of the Child*, 20:518–535. New York: International Universities Press.

Nierenberg, H. H. (1950), A case of voyeurism. *Samiksa*, 4:140–166.

Noble, D. (1951), The study of dreams in schizophrenia and allied states. *Amer. J. Psychiat.*, 107:612–616.

Nunberg, J. (1938), Homosexuality, magic and aggression. *Internat. J. Psycho-Anal.*, 19:1–16.

———— (1947), Circumcision and problems of bisexuality. *Internat. J. Psycho-Anal.*, 28:145–179.

Olsen, J. (1974), *The Man with the Candy: The Story of the Houston Mass Murders*. New York: Simon & Schuster.

Ornstein, P. H. (1978), Introduction. In: *The Search for the Self*, Vol. 1. New York: International Universities Press, pp. 1–106.

Ostow, M. (1953), Transvestitism. *J. American Med. Assn.*, 152:1553.

———— Blos, P., Furst, S., Gero, G., Kanzer, M., Silverman, D., Sterba, R., Valenstein, A., Arlow, J. A., Loomis, E., & Rappaport, E., Eds. (1974), *Sexual Deviation: Psychoanalytic Insights*. New York: Quadrangle/New York Times.

Ovesey, L. & Person, E. (1976), Transvestitism: A disorder of the self. *Internat. J. Psychoanal. Psychother.*, 5:219–235.

Pacella, B. L. (1975), Early development and the deja vu. *J. Amer. Psychoanal. Assn.*, 23:300–317.

Palombo, S. R. (1978), The adaptive function of dreams. *Psychoanal. and Contemp. Thought*, 1:443–447.

———— (1985), The primary process: A reconceptualization. *Psychoanal. Inq.*, 5:404–437.

Panel (1952), Psychodynamics and treatment of perversions. J. Arlow, reporter. *Bull. Amer. Psychoanal. Assn.*, 8:315–327.

———— (1954), Perversions: Theoretical and therapeutic aspects. J. Arlow, reporter. *J. Amer. Psychoanal. Assn.*, 2:336–345.

———— (1957), Preoedipal factors in neurosogenesis. V. Rosen, reporter. *J. Amer. Psychoanal. Assn.*, 5:146–157.

———— (1960a), An examination of nosology according to psychoanalytic concepts. N. Ross, reporter. *J. Amer. Psychoanal. Assn.*, 8:535–551.

———— (1960b), Theoretical and clinical aspects of overt male homosexuality. C. W. Socarides, reporter. *J. Amer. Psychoanal. Assn.*, 8:552–556. Paper presentation: The treatment of overt male homosexuality by I. Clyne.

—— (1960c), Theoretical and clinical aspects of overt male homosexuality. C. W. Socarides, reporter. *J. Amer. Psychoanal. Assn.*, 8:552–556. Paper presentation: On the choice of sexual object in homosexuality by O. Fleischmann.

—— (1961), Frigidity in women. B. E. Moore, reporter. *J. Amer. Psychoanal. Assn.*, 9:571–584.

—— (1962), Theoretical and clinical aspects of overt female homosexuality. C. W. Socarides, reporter. *J. Amer. Psychoanal. Assn.*, 10:579–592.

—— (1962), Severe regressive states during analysis. E. M. Weinshel, reporter. *J. Amer. Psychoanal. Assn.*, 14:538–568.

—— (1969), Dreams and psychosis. J. Frosch, reporter. *J. Amer. Psychoanal. Assn.*, 17:206–221.

—— (1973), Technique and prognosis in the treatment of narcissistic personality disorders. L. Schwartz, reporter. *J. Amer. Psychoanal. Assn.*, 21:617–632.

—— (1976), Introductory comments by G. Wiedemann. The psychoanalytic treatment of male homosexuality. E. C. Payne, reporter. *J. Amer. Psychoanal. Assn.*, 25:183–199.

—— (1977), The psychoanalytic treatment of male homosexuality. E. C. Payne, reporter. *J. Amer. Psychoanal. Assn.*, 25:183–201.

—— (1978), The role of the father in the preoedipal years. R. C. Prall, reporter. *J. Amer. Psychoanal. Assn.*, 26:143–163.

—— (1979), The infantile neurosis in child and adult analysis. J. S. Malkin, reporter. Paper presentation: A crucial developmental distinction: Prestructural selfobject and oedipal object. *J. Amer. Psychoanal. Assn.*, 27:643–654.

—— (1979b), The masochistic-narcissistic character. N. Fischer, reporter. *J. Amer. Psychoanal. Assoc.*, 29:675–677.

—— (1981), Masochism: Current concepts. N. Fischer, reporter. *J. Amer. Psychoanal. Assn.*, 29:673–688.

—— (1984), The value of extra-transference interpretations. E. Halpert, reporter. *J. Amer. Psychoanal. Assn.*, 32:137–147.

Parens, H. (1973), Aggression: A reconsideration. *J. Amer. Psychoanal. Assoc.*, 21:34–60.

—— (1977), Aggressive psychoanalysis. In: *International Encyclopedia of Psychiatry, Psychology, Psychoanalysis, and Neurology*, ed. B. J. Wolman. New York: Aesculapius Publishers, pp. 334–339.

—— (1979), *The Development of Aggression in Early Childhood*. New York: Jason Aronson.

Payne, S. (1939), Some observations on the ego development of the fetishist. *Internat. J. Psycho-Anal.*, 20:161–170.

Person, E. & Ovesey, L. (1974a), The transsexual syndrome in males, I: Primary transsexualism. *Amer. J. Psychother.*, 28:4-20.

———— (1974b), The transsexual syndrome in males, II: Secondary transsexualism. *Amer. J. Psychother.*, 28:174-193.

Pulver, S. E. (1978), On dreams. *J. Amer. Psychoanal. Assn.*, 26:673-683.

Rado, S. (1933), The fear of castration in women. *Psychoanal. Quart.*, 2:425-475.

———— (1949), An adaptational view of sexual behavior. In: *The Psychoanalysis of Behavior: Collected Papers of Sandor Rado*, Vol. 1, rev. ed. New York: Grune & Stratton, 1956, pp. 186-213.

———— (1955), Evolutionary basis of sexual adaptation. In: *Psychoanalysis and Behavior: The Collected Papers of Sandor Rado*. New York: Grune & Stratton, 1956, pp. 312-323.

Rangell, L. (1965), Some comments on psychoanalytic nosology: With recommendations for improvement. In: *Drives, Affects, Behavior*, Vol. 2, ed. M. Schur. New York: International Universities Press, pp. 128-157.

Rheingold, H. L. (1961), The effect of environmental stimulation upon social and exploratory behavior in the human infant. In: *Determinants of Infant Behavior*, Vol. 1, ed. B. M. Foss. New York: John Wiley, pp. 143-177.

Richardson, G. A. & Moore, R. A. (1963), On the manifest dream in schizophrenia. *J. Amer. Psychoanal. Assn.*, 11:281-302.

Robinson, M. (1979), A screen memory in a child analysis. *The Psychoanalytic Study of the Child*, 33:307-327. New Haven: Yale University Press.

Robson, K. S. (1967), The role of eye to eye contact in maternal infant attachment. *J. Child Psychol. & Psychiat.*, 8:13-25.

Roheim, G. (1952), The evil eye. *Amer. Imago*, 9:351-363.

Roiphe, H. (1968), On an early genital phase. *The Psychoanalytic Study of the Child*, 23:348-365. New York: International Universities Press.

———— Galenson, E. (1972), Early genital activity and the castration complex. *Psychoanal. Quart.*, 41:334-347.

———— ———— (1981), *Infantile Origins of Sexual Identity*. New York: International Universities Press.

Romm, M. E. (1967), Compulsion factors in exhibitionism. In: *Psychotherapy of Perversions*, ed. H. M. Ruitenbeek. New York: Citadel Press, pp. 285-298.

Rosen, I. (1964), Exhibitionism, scopophilia and voyeurism. In: *The Pathology and Treatment of Sexual Deviation*, ed. I. Rosen. London: Oxford University Press, pp. 293-350.

_____ (1979), The general psychoanalytic theory of perversion: a critical and clinical review. In: *Sexual Deviation.* Oxford/-New York/Toronto: Oxford University Press, pp. 29–64.

Rosenfeld, H. A. (1949), Remarks on the relation of male homosexuality to paranoia, paranoid anxiety and narcissism. *Internat. J. Psycho-Anal.,* 30:36–47.

_____ (1971), A clinical approach to the psychoanalytic theory of the life and death instincts: An investigation into the aggressive aspects of narcissism. *Internat. J. Psycho-Anal.,* 52:169–178.

Ross, J. M. (1975), The development of paternal identity: A critical review of the literature on nurturance and generativity in boys and men. *J. Amer. Psychoanal. Assn.,* 23:783–817.

_____ (1979), Paternal identity: The equation of fatherhood and manhood. In: *On Sexuality: Psychoanalytic Observations,* ed. T. B. Karasu & C. W. Socarides. New York: International Universities Press, pp. 73–97.

Rubinfine, D. (1965), On beating fantasies. *Internat. J. Psycho-Anal.,* 46:315–322.

Rubinstein, L. H. (1964), The role of identification in homosexuality and transvestitism in men and women. In: *The Pathology and Treatment of Sexual Deviation,* ed. I. Rosen. London: Oxford University Press, pp. 163–194.

Ruffler, G. (1956), The analysis of a sado-masochist. In: *Perversions: Psychodynamics and Therapy,* ed. S. Lorand & M. Balint. New York: Random House, pp. 209–240.

Sachs, H. (1923), On the genesis of sexual perversions. In: *Homosexuality,* C. W. Socarides. New York: Jason Aronson, 1978, pp. 531–546.

Sadger, I. (1926), A contribution to the understanding of sado-masochism. *Internat. J. Psycho-Anal.,* 7:484–491.

Sandler, J. (1960), On the concept of the superego. *The Psychoanalytic Study of the Child,* 15:128–162. New York: International Universities Press.

Settlage, C. F. (1971), On the libidinal aspects of early psychic development and the genesis of infantile neurosis. In: *Separation-Individuation: Essays in Honor of Margaret S. Mahler,* ed. J. B. McDevitt & C. F. Settlage. New York: International Universities Press, pp. 131–154.

_____ (1977), The psychoanalytic understanding of narcissistic and borderline personality disorders: Advances in developmental theory. *J. Amer. Psychoanal. Assn.,* 25:805–834.

Shapiro, T. & Stine, J. (1965), Drawings of three-year-old children. *The Psychoanalytic Study of the Child,* 20:298–309. New York: International Universities Press.

Shengold, L. (1980), The symbol of telephoning. *J. Amer. Psycho-anal. Assn.*, 30:461–470.

Shengold, L. (1982), The symbol of telephoning. *Amer. J. Psycho-anal.*, 30:461–470.

Siegel, E. (1988), *Female Homosexuality: Choice without Volition.* New Jersey: Analytic Press, in press.

Silberer, H. (1951), Report of a method of eliciting and observing certain symbolic hallucination-phenomena. In: *Organization and Pathology of Thought*, ed. D. Rappaport. New York: Columbia University Press, pp. 195–233.

Silverman, M. L. (1982), A nine-year-old's use of the telephone: Symbolism in *Statu Nascendi. Psychoanal. Quart.*, 51:598–611.

Socarides, C. W. (1959), Meaning and content of a pedophiliac perversion. *J. Amer. Psychoanal. Assn.*, 7:84–94.

—— (1960), The development of a fetishistic perversion: The contribution of preoedipal phase conflict. *J. Amer. Psycho-anal. Assn.*, 8:281–311.

—— (1961), Discussion of "The analysis of a transvestite boy" by M. Sperling. Paper presentation at The American Psychoanalytic Association, December, 1961.

—— (1963), The historical development of theoretical and clinical concepts of overt female homosexuality. *J. Amer. Psychoanal. Assn.*, 11:386–414.

—— (1965), Female homosexuality. In: *Sexual Behavior and the Law*, ed. R. Slovenko. Springfield, Ill.: Charles C Thomas, pp. 462–477.

—— (1968a), A provisional theory of etiology in male homosexuality: A case of preoedipal origin. *Internat. J. Psycho-Anal.*, 49:27–37.

—— (1968b), *The Overt Homosexual.* New York: Jason Aronson, 1974.

—— (1969a), The desire for sexual transformation: A psychiatric evaluation of "transsexualism." *Amer. J. Psychiat.*, 125:1419–1425.

—— (1969b), The psychoanalytic therapy of a male homosexual. *Psychoanal. Quart.*, 38:173–190.

—— (1970a), A psychoanalytic study of the desire for sexual transformation ("Transsexualism"): The plaster-of-Paris man. *Internat. J. Psycho-Anal. Psychother.*, 51:341–349.

—— (1970b), Homosexuality and medicine. *J. Amer. Med. Assn.*, 2:432–448.

—— (1973), Sexual perversion and the fear of engulfment. *Internat. J. Psycho-Anal. Psychother.*, 2:432–448.

—— (1974a), Homosexuality. In: *The American Handbook of*

Psychiatry, Vol. 3, 2nd ed., ed. S. Arieti. New York: Basic Books, pp. 291–315.

_____ (1974b), The demonified mother: A study of voyeurism and sexual sadism. *Internat. Rev. Psycho-Anal.*, 1:187–195.

_____ (1975), Discussion of "Healthy parental influences on the earliest development of masculinity in baby boys" by R. J. Stoller. *Psychoanal. Forum*, 5:241–243.

_____ (1976a), Considerations on the treatment of overt male homosexuality; Part III: The analysis of regressive phenomena. Paper presentation at The American Psychoanalytic Association, December 1976.

_____ (1976b), Transference considerations in the psychoanalysis of adult male homosexuality. Paper presentation at The American Psychoanalytic Association, Panel: The Psychoanalytic Treatment of Male Homosexuality, May, 1976.

_____ (1977), Considerations on the treatment of overt male homosexuality; Part IV: A provisional classification and differentiating criteria of the homosexualities. In: *Homosexuality*, New York: Jason Aronson, 1978, pp. 426–497.

_____ (1978a), *Homosexuality*. New York: Jason Aronson.

_____ (1978b), Transsexualism and psychosis: A discussion of "The transsexual wish in a psychotic character." *Internat. J. Psycho-Anal. Psychother.*, 7:373–383.

_____ (1979a), A unitary theory of sexual perversions. In: *On Sexuality: Psychoanalytic Observations*, ed. T. B. Karasu & C. W. Socarides. New York: International Universities Press, pp. 161–188.

_____ (1979b), Some problems encountered in the psychoanalytic treatment of overt male homosexuality. *Amer. J. Psychother.*, 33:506–520.

_____ (1980a), Homosexuality and the rapprochement subphase crisis. In: *Rapprochement: The Critical Subphase of Separation-Individuation*, ed. R. F. Lax, S. Bach & J. A. Burland. New York: Jason Aronson, pp. 331–352.

_____ (1980b), Perverse symptoms and the manifest dream of perversion. In: *The Dream in Clinical Practice*, ed. J. M. Natterson. New York: Jason Aronson, pp. 237–259.

_____ (1982a), Considerations on the psychoanalytic treatment of male homosexuality; Part V: The preoedipal homosexual with associated narcissistic personality disorder (unpublished).

_____ (1982b), Abdicating fathers, homosexual sons: Psychoanalytic observations on the contribution of the father to the development of male homosexuality. In: *Father and Child: Developmental and Clinical Perspectives*, ed. S. H. Cath, A. R.

Gurwith & J. M. Ross. Boston: Little Brown, 1982, pp. 509–521.

―――― (1982c), Why Sirhan killed Kennedy: Psychoanalytic speculations on an assassination. *Psychoanal. Inq.*, 2:133–152.

―――― (1985), Depression in perversion: With special reference to the function of erotic experience in sexual perversion. In: *Depressive States and Their Treatment*, ed. V. V. Volkan. New York: Jason Aronson, pp. 317–334.

Socarides, D. D. & Stolorow, R. D. (1985), Affects and selfobjects. *The Annual of Psychoanalysis*, 12/13:105–119.

Solnit, A. J. (1966), Some adaptive functions of aggressive behavior. In: *Psychoanalysis—A General Psychology*, ed. R. M. Loewenstein, L. M. Newman, M. Schur & A. J. Solnit. New York: International Universities Press, pp. 169–189.

―――― (1972), Aggression: A view of theory building in psychoanalysis. *J. Amer. Psychoanal. Assn.*, 20:435–450.

Sours, J. A. (1973), On psychogenic false myopia: A clinical essay on object separation, loss and aggression. Paper presentation at Emory University Psychoanalytic Clinic, Atlanta, Ga.

Sperling, M. (1947), The analysis of an exhibitionist. *Internat. J. Psycho-Anal.*, 28:32–45.

―――― (1959), Some regressive phenomena involving the perceptual sphere: The phenomena of objects coming closer and of objects receding from view. *Internat. J. Psycho-Anal.*, 40:304–307.

―――― (1964), The analysis of a boy with transvestite tendencies: A contribution to the genesis and dynamics of transvestitism. *The Psychoanalytic Study of the Child*, 19:470–473. New York: International Universities Press.

Sperling, O. (1956), Psychodynamics of group perversions. *Psychoanal. Quart.*, 25:56–65.

Spielrein, S. (1923), Ein Zoschauertypus (A Voyeur Type), *Internat. Z. Psychoanal.*, 9:210–211.

Spitz, R. A. (1946), Anaclitic depression—An inquiry into the genesis of psychiatric conditions in early childhood, II. *The Psychoanalytic Study of the Child*, 2:313–342. New York: International Universities Press.

―――― (1955), The primal cavity. A contribution to the genesis of perception and its role for psychoanalytic theory. *The Psychoanalytic Study of the Child*, 10:215–240. New York: International Universities Press.

―――― (1959), *A General Field Theory of Ego Formation*. New York: International Universities Press.

―――― (1965), *The First Year of Life*. New York: International Universities Press.

——— Wolf, K. M. (1949), Autoerotism: Some empirical findings and hypotheses on three of its manifestations in the first year of life. *The Psychoanalytic Study of the Child*, 3/4:85–120. New York: International Universities Press.

Spitzer, R. R. (1974), The homosexual decision—A background paper. *Psychiat. News*, Jan. 16:11–12.

Sprince, M. P. (1964), A contribution to the study of homosexuality in adolescence. *J. Child Psychol. & Psychiat.*, 5:103–117.

Starcke, A. (1920), The reversal of the libido sign in delusions of persecution. *Internat. J. Psycho-Anal.*, 1:231–234.

Stein, S. (1968), A case of exhibitionism. Unpublished presentation to the author.

Stewart, W. (1967), Comments on the manifest content of certain types of unusual dreams. *Psychoanal. Quart.*, 36:329–341.

Stoller, R. J. (1964), A contribution to the study of gender identity. *Internat. J. Psycho-Anal.*, 45:220–226.

——— (1966), The mother's contribution to infantile transvestite behavior. *Internat. J. Psycho-Anal.*, 47:384–395.

——— (1967a), Etiological factors in male transsexualism. *Trans. NY Acad. of Sciences*, 29:431–434.

——— (1967b), Gender identity and a biological force. *Psychoanal. Forum*, 2:318–338.

——— (1968a), A further contribution to the study of gender identity. *Internat. J. Psycho-Anal.*, 49:364–368.

——— (1968b), *Sex and Gender*. New York: Science House.

——— (1975a), Healthy parental influences on the earliest development of masculinity in baby boys. *Psychoanal. Forum*, 5:234–240.

——— (1975b), *Perversion: The Erotic Form of Hatred*. New York: Pantheon Books.

——— (1975c), Fathers of transsexual children. *J. Amer. Psychoanal. Assn.*, 27:837–866.

——— (1982), Transvestitism in women. *Arch. Sexual Behav.*, 2:99–115.

——— Herdt, G. H. (1982), The development of masculinity: A cross-cultural contribution. *J. Amer. Psychoanal. Assn.*, 30:29–59.

——— Newman, L. E. (1971), The bisexual identity of transsexuals: Two case examples. *Arch. Sexual Behav.*, 1:17–28.

Stolorow, R. D. (1975), The narcissistic function of masochism (and sadism). *Internat. J. Psycho-Anal.*, 56:441–448.

——— (1977), Psychosexuality and the representational world. *Internat. J. Psycho-Anal.*, 60:39–46.

——— Atwood, G. E. & Ross, J. M. (1978), The representational world in psychoanalytic therapy. *Internat. Rev. Psycho-Anal.*, 5:247–256.

_____ Grand, H. T. (1973), A partial analysis of a perversion involving bugs. *Internat. J. Psycho-Anal.*, 54:349–350.

_____ Lachmann, F. M. (1978), The developmental prestages of defenses: Diagnostic and therapeutic implications. *Psychoanal. Quart.*, 47:73–102.

_____ _____ (1980), *Psychoanalysis and Developmental Arrests: Theory and Treatment.* New York: Jason Aronson.

Szekely, L. (1954), Biological remarks on fears originating in early childhood. *Internat. J. Psycho-Anal.*, 35:55–67.

Tarachow, S. (1966), Coprophagia and allied phenomena. *J. Amer. Psychoanal. Assn.*, 14:685–699.

Thomas, D. (1976), *The Marquis de Sade.* Boston: New York Graphic Society.

Tolpin, M. (1979), Remarks on pathogenesis and symptom formation in disorders of the self. In: *The Course of Life*, ed. S. Greenspan & G. Pollock. Washington, D.C.: U.S. Government Printing Office.

_____ Kohut, H. (1979), The disorders of the self: The psychopathology of the first years of life. In: *The Course of Life*, ed. S. Greenspan & G. Pollock. Washington, D.C.: U.S. Government Printing Office.

Trilling, L. (1968), The Kinsey report. In: *The Liberal Imagination.* New York: Charles Scribner's, 1976, pp. 242–252.

Van der Leeuw, P. J. (1958), The preoedipal phase of the male. *The Psychoanalytic Study of the Child*, 13:352–374. New York: International Universities Press.

Van Ophuijsen, J. H. W. (1920), On the origin of the feeling of persecution. *Int. J. Psycho-Anal.*, 1:205–230.

Van Ophuijsen, J. H. W. (1929), The sexual aim of sadism as manifested in acts of violence. *Internat. J. Psycho-Anal.*, 10:139–144.

Volkan, V. (1974), Transsexuals: A different understanding. In: *Marital and Sexual Counseling in Medical Practice*, ed. D. W. Abse, E. Nash & L. Louden. New York: Harper & Row, pp. 383–404.

_____ (1976), *Primitive Internalized Object Relations: A Clinical Study of Schizophrenic, Borderline and Narcissistic Patients.* New York: International Universities Press.

_____ (1979), Transsexualism: As examined from the viewpoint of internalized object relations. In: *On Sexuality: Psychoanalytic Observations*, ed. T. B. Karasu & C. W. Socarides. New York: Jason Aronson, pp. 189–222.

———— (1980), Narcissistic personality organization and "reparative leadership." *Internat. J. Group Psychother.*, 30:131–152.

———— (1982), The transsexual search for perfection and "aggression reassignment" surgery. Paper presentation at Discussion Group: "Psychoanalytic Considerations About Patients with Organic Illness or Major Physical Handicaps." The American Psychoanalytic Association, Dec. 16, 1982.

———— Berents, S. (1976), Psychiatric aspects of surgical treatment for problems of sexual identification (transsexualism). In: *Modern Perspectives in the Psychiatric Aspects of Surgery*, ed. J. G. Howells. New York: Brunner/Mazel, pp. 447–467.

Waelder, R. (1960), *Basic theory of psychoanalysis*. New York: International Universities Press.

Wagenheim, H. H. (1984), A telephone perversion. Presentation at Discussion Group: "Sexual Deviations: Theory and Therapy." The American Psychoanalytic Association, May 1984.

Weich, M. (in press), Language fetishism. *Psychoanal. Quart.*

Weitzman, E., Shamoian, C. A. & Golosow, N. (1970), Identity diffusion and the transsexual resolution. *J. Nervous and Mental Disease*, 151:295–302.

Werner, M. W. & Lahn, M. (1970), A case of female transsexualism. *Psychiat. Quart.*, 44 (supplement):476–487.

Wiedemann, G. H. (1962), Survey of psychoanalytic literature on overt male homosexuality. *J. Amer. Psychoanal. Assn.*, 10:386–409.

Williams, A. H. (1964), The psychopathology and treatment of sexual murderers. In: *The Pathology and Treatment of Sexual Deviation*, ed. I. Rosen. London: Oxford University Press, pp. 351–377.

———— (1965), Rape-murder. In: *Sexual Behavior and the Law*, ed. R. Slovenko. Springfield, IL: Charles C Thomas, pp. 563–577.

Winnicott, D. W. (1935), The manic defense. In: *Collected Papers: Through Pediatrics to Psychoanalysis*. New York: Basic Books, 1958, pp. 129–144.

———— (1953), Transitional objects and transitional phenomena. *Internat. J. Psycho-Anal.*, 34:89–97.

———— (1965), *The Maturational Process and the Facilitating Environment*. New York: International Universities Press.

Winterstein, A. (1956), On the oral basis of a case of male homosexuality. *Internat. J. Psycho-Anal.*, 37:258–302.

Woodbury, M. (1966), Altered body ego experiences. *J. Amer. Psychoanal. Assn.*, 14:273–303.

Zavitzianos, G. (1971), Fetishism and exhibitionism in the female and their relationship to psychopathy and kleptomania. *Internat. J. Psycho-Anal.*, 52:297–305.

_____ (1972), Homeovestism: Perverse forms of behavior involving wearing clothes of the same sex. *Internat. J. Psycho-Anal.*,
53:471–477.

_____ (1977), The object in fetishism, homeovestism and transvestitism. *Internat. J. Psycho-Anal.*, 58:487–495.

_____ (1982), The perversion of fetishism in women. *Psychoanal.
Quart.*, 51:405–425.

Zweig, S. (1933), *Mental Healers*. London: Cassell Press.

AUTHOR INDEX

615

SUBJECT INDEX